CONSTANT TURMOIL

CONSTANT TURMOIL

The Politics of Industrial Life in
Nineteenth-Century
New England

MARY H. BLEWETT

UNIVERSITY OF MASSACHUSETTS PRESS

AMHERST

Copyright © 2000 by
University of Massachusetts Press
All rights reserved
Printed in the United States of America
LC 99-047848
ISBN 1-55849-239-9 (cloth)

Designed by Dennis Anderson
Set in New Baskerville by Graphic Composition Inc., Athens, Georgia
Printed and bound by Sheridan Books

Library of Congress Cataloging-in-Publication Data
Blewett, Mary H.
Constant turmoil : the politics of industrial life in nineteenth-century New England /
Mary H. Blewett.
p. cm.
Includes bibliographical references and index.
ISBN 1-55849-239-9 (alk. paper)
1. Textile industry—New England—History.   2. New England—Economic conditions.
I. Title.

HD9857.N36 B58 2000
338.4'7677'0097409034—dc21
99-047848

British Library Cataloguing in Publication data are available.

To my husband, Peter,
who first attracted my attention to
English manhood

CONTENTS

Illustrations

Defalcators S. Angier Chace, George T. Hathaway, Charles P. Stickney, and Walter Paine III

John Summerfield Brayton

Following Page 324

David Anthony Brayton and the Durfee Mills, c. 1870

The Labor Riot at Fall River, 1875

Village of Lonsdale, Rhode Island, 1888

George Gunton

Robert Howard

M. C. D. Borden, 1895

The Fall River Iron Works, 1895

"Matt" Borden starting the Corliss Engine, 1895

Andrew G. Pierce Sr. of New Bedford

New York Journal's "The Great American Cotton Industry," 1898

New York World's vision of the New Bedford strike, 1898

Mrs. Harriet Pickering, activist New Bedford weaver, 1898

CONSTANT TURMOIL

Prologue

Unlikely Acquaintances

EVERYONE IN Fall River, Massachusetts, knew it was January, but it felt like April. A prolonged thaw in early 1906 had melted the snow and driven the ice and cold fogs out into Mount Hope Bay, the northern tip of Narragansett Bay. A weak sun warmed the city, and mild winds drew people from their kitchens and parlors into the streets and parks. The air was full of talk about the future of the weavers' union.

One afternoon, the familiar tottering figure of weaver Thomas Evans appeared in the main city park and mounted the bandstand as he had done so often to criticize the direction of labor politics. Evans was an immigrant from Bolton, Lancashire, one of the centers of English working-class agitation. Born in 1826, he was the son of Annie Blackwell and John Evans, a handloom weaver.[1] Bolton had established a reputation as early as 1818 for open-air meetings, mass demonstrations, and the intimidation of strikebreakers or "knobsticks," practices which immigrants such as Evans had brought with them.[2] Arriving in Fall River before the Civil War, he had been a Chartist supporter of universal manhood suffrage and the ten-hour day.[3] Evans became involved in the labor protest led by Lancashire immigrant weavers that periodically convulsed the city after the Civil War. He often signed his numerous and at times controversial letters to the editors of local newspapers as "Labor Agitator." He continued to weave until old age and shaking hands forced him from the mills. A sympathetic citizen had arranged for Evans to be housed in the Home for Aged Men, but he had found that life too confining. In and out of the poorhouse and estranged from his wife, Bridget, a devout Catholic, Evans preferred the freedom of the streets even if it meant an attic room and little food. He appeared to thrive on this life.

1

On that January afternoon in 1906 as Thomas Evans spoke from the bandstand to the crowd milling about and enjoying the unusual weather, a Republican president who called himself a "trust-buster" occupied the White House. Progressive reforms had begun to reshape municipal, state, and federal government. After the loss of a lengthy and significant strike in 1904–1905, the weavers in Fall River were debating whether they should again abandon their independent union and rejoin the American Federation of Labor headed by Samuel Gompers, a man on easy speaking terms with President Theodore Roosevelt and the heads of giant corporations. To Evans, the likely outcome of this debate represented a betrayal of his political heritage as a Lancashire weaver. The weavers' union, he believed, must not cooperate with the immorality of capitalist tyranny. He said so loudly to the people strolling in the park. As he warmed to the subject, he became visibly agitated attempting to gain attention, but the crowd in 1906 remembered little of the Lancashire heritage of vigorous protest so dear to Evans. To some, he sounded simply crazy. Policemen arrived, listened for a while, and arrested him. They took Evans to nearby Taunton State Asylum, where he was committed on January 11 with others from the area, one of them a young man with a compulsion to rearrange the crucifix on the altar of his parish church.[4] He did not last long confined in this place where his advocacy of moral reconciliation and class harmony under Christian Socialism became part of the incoherent babble.[5] After two weeks he died on January 25 of a ruptured heart and was buried in a pauper's grave in Taunton, Massachusetts.[6] On January 30, 1906, the weavers' union voted to rejoin the AFL.

Jonathan Thayer Lincoln, the scion of a prominent Yankee Fall River textile machinery manufacturing family, recorded his memories of the last days of Thomas Evans. Born in 1869, Jonathan had learned as a boy and young man about the tumultuous decades when Lancashire weavers and mule spinners had shaken Fall River with their strikes. After graduating from Harvard in 1892, he worked for his father at the Kilburn, Lincoln Company and sat on the board of directors of many mills in Fall River, becoming acquainted with labor problems. He later became fascinated with the ideas of British radicals William Morris and John Ruskin and came to know the leading local agitators whom he described as mostly sons of English Chartists.[7] He particularly admired Thomas Evans and a group of Lancashire men who had formed the Coffee Tavern, a temperance restaurant where they debated political, economic, and social questions.

After Evans' death, Lincoln transcribed part of a poorly spelled manuscript of his philosophy of Christian Socialism for a book on Fall River. The original manuscript, titled "A Common Sense Sermon on the Labor Question" and signed by "Justice of the Peace and Old Labor Agitator," was lost. Part of Lincoln's transcription reads:

> Common sense tells me there can be no political question which is not also a religious question; and all real progress must be by honest legislation; such legislation, however, will not come about until the intelligent and industrial manhood of this country brushes aside their bigotry and prejudice, and learns with Tolstoy that we cannot be saved separately; we must be saved collectively.[8]

Evans had often been a severe critic of labor politics in Fall River and the rise of conservative trade union leaders who distanced themselves from the ordinary worker.

> Statesmen do not lead public opinion, they follow it. Reforms have to germinate and develop among the people themselves. . . . The great question before the country to-day, the labor question, can never be settled by salary-grabbing politicians. We must be Christians first and partisans afterwards. . . . I have suffered for daring to oppose many movements which had the support of sectional unions. We have heard a great deal about what trades-unions have done, but few leaders can be found with manhood and moral courage to name the cruel wrongs to thousands of helpless and defenseless fellow men and women perpetrated by the selfishness of labor leaders looking for political honors.[9]

His involvement in nineteenth-century labor politics shaped Evans' vision of a moral, manly leadership of the working class, oblivious to any personal gain and essential for genuine reform.

In 1906, the same year that Evans died, Jonathan Lincoln organized the Lincoln Manufacturing Company, not another mill for print cloth, the dominant Fall River fabric in the nineteenth century, but one for diversified products: fine cotton goods and mixed silk and cotton textiles.[10] While writing his book, he was invited as a "practical" mill man to speak on the labor question at the Amos Tuck School of Finance at Dartmouth College. Lincoln's lectures were printed in *The Atlantic Monthly* and other progressive magazines. The Houghton Mifflin Company of Boston collected and published them as *The City of the Dinner Pail* in 1909.[11] Lincoln stayed on at Dartmouth to earn a master's degree in economics in 1911. A year later, Houghton Mifflin also brought out, *The Factory,* his analysis of the industrial revolution with a striking sympathy for the working class, for English Chartism, and for socialism. The book contained this challenge to American employers: "The Captain of Industry, in order to obtain the loyalty of the toilers, must not only demand but deserve it; he too must be loyal to the great cause he serves—the eternal cause of human freedom."[12]

Lincoln's associates among the Fall River manufacturers called him "a dangerous fellow, disloyal to his class."[13] In 1903 he married Louise Sears Cobb of West Newton, Massachusetts, who supported labor unions and worked for child labor legislation and better sanitary facilities in factories.

Even as a member of the prominent Sears family of Boston, she was not entirely welcome in Fall River.[14] Local society women openly ridiculed "with silvery tinkles of laughter" her interest in restrooms for working-women, but Louise Lincoln remained elusively attractive to their men. Her daughter remembered that "Guerlain's L'Heure Bleu [her perfume] mixed with her body chemistry in a way that made men sniff and dream. . . . She had sex appeal dressed up with full *human* life—it did something to her face."[15]

Jonathan Lincoln's views reflected those of his father, Leontine, who had always supported local educational and library reform in Fall River and chaired the trustees of both the B. M. C. Durfee High School in 1887 and the Bradford Durfee Textile School in 1903. For twenty-five years he headed the Massachusetts State Board of Charities. The Kilburn, Lincoln textile machinery factory had the shortest hours and highest wages in the state.[16] His granddaughter Victoria Lincoln wrote that "He was wholly remote from Fall River society" and was "a Victorian saint and gentleman." Leontine Lincoln had known Andrew J. Borden, the father of Lizzie Borden, and considered him "a boor." When the famous murders occurred in 1892, his reaction was: "Oh, dear, poor girl, no wonder!"[17]

As the Fall River mills declined in the early twentieth century, Jonathan Lincoln overcame a drinking problem triggered by depression over family tragedies and unwanted responsibilities inherited at Kilburn, Lincoln. After enduring these for years, he eagerly left the city with his family in the early 1930s for Cambridge, Massachusetts, to teach at the Harvard Business School.[18] To his students, Lincoln spoke, as Thomas Evans might have, about the relations between workers and employers.

> The man who works for you is a human being endowed with the same inalienable rights of life, liberty and the pursuit of happiness as yourself; . . . He is the same compost of dust and spirit as yourself. . . . Remember the laboring man has as much heart and mind and spirit. . . . [19]

Coming across a thirty-year-old unpublished essay, "Labor and Life," Lincoln, somewhat amused at his pretensions as a young writer, still liked what he had written.[20] He never forgot the vision of a moral economy influenced by his contacts with Lancashire men like Evans. Labor was not a commodity. It represented nothing less than the lives of men as fellow human beings. Economics and ethics could not be separated. Lincoln must have known that Thomas Evans would have approved.

Constant Turmoil is an analysis of the political dynamics in nineteenth-century New England industrial life, a setting in which, however improbable, these two men, the son of a handloom weaver from Lancashire and the son of a Fall River manufacturer, met, shared similar values, and, in doing so, transcended their social and class boundaries.

HERBERT GUTMAN AND CLASS, CULTURE, AND POWER

During a series of fierce battles with his academic critics in the mid-1970s, social historian Herbert Gutman warned in a moment of uncharacteristic despair against the fragmentation of social history research into narrower and narrower categories of human experience. Historians who sliced up the field into examinations of every diverse facet of existence would, he argued, make it impossible to capture the experiences of "an Irish born Catholic female Fall River Massachusetts textile worker and union organizer involved in the disorderly 1875 strike. . . ."[21] I intend to rescue that woman from such a fate through a combined analysis of class, culture, and power. The evidence in this study demands large, overlapping conceptual arenas to connect class development and cultural resources with partisan politics as well as with the exercise of corporate power in extra-legal, non-electoral activities, such as workplaces and markets.[22] The multiple meanings of human identity also require a more inclusive use of the category of power to capture the tensions over changing relationships of gender, ethnicity, race, family, sexuality, religion, and generations, issues that remain central to the history of class and culture. Only then can the multiple but connected experiences of that Irish workingwoman be appreciated and evaluated.

This is a story of nineteenth-century industrial development and the politics of industrial life. Textile capitalists in southeastern New England, especially the owners of huge mills built in post–Civil War Fall River, Massachusetts, resolved to dominate the domestic print cloth industry. The chronic instability that flowed from their decisions to control the market, to use or ignore the political system, and to force submission from their predominately immigrant workforce created constant turmoil throughout the region. I will use the intersection of class, culture, and power to capture the workings of the last New England textile empire as well as the cultural and political resistance which native-born and immigrant workers, male and female, organized to oppose this system.

The influence of Edward P. Thompson's *The Making of the English Working Class* (1963) shifted the study of American labor history away from unions and labor economics toward the interconnections between class formation and cultural experience in working-class communities and workplaces. Gutman and other labor and social historians in the Thompsonian tradition seek to link partisan politics with the many, varied aspects of social and cultural identity.[23] Defending the capacity of social history based on Thompson's class and culture analysis to include the political world, the historian Geoff Eley envisions a "working-class public sphere" as a locus of political expression.[24] His vision, however, excludes the dynamics of power between the private and the public spheres of activity as

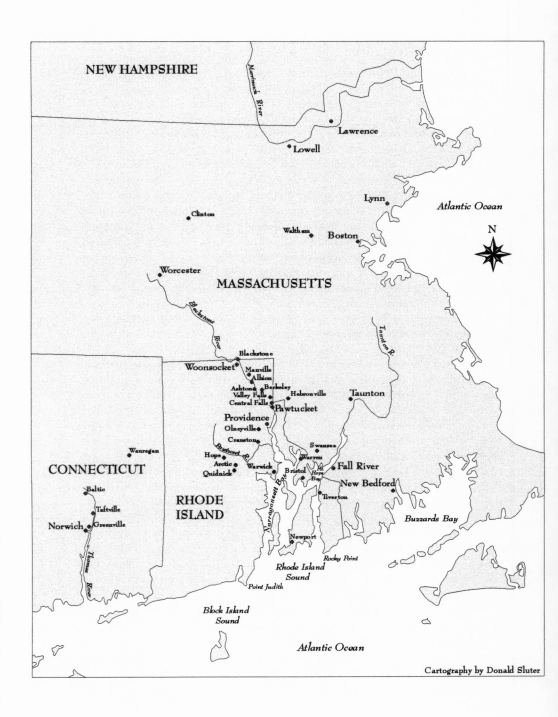

NEW HAMPSHIRE

Merrimack River

● Lawrence

● Lowell

● Lynn

Atlantic Ocean

N

● Clinton

Waltham ● ● Boston

Worcester ●

MASSACHUSETTS

Blackstone River

Taunton R.

Blackstone ●

Woonsocket ●

Manville ●
Albion ●

Ashton ● Berkeley ●
Valley Falls ● Hebronville ●
Central Falls ●

Pawtucket ●

Taunton ●

Providence ●

Olneyville ●

Cranston ●

Swansea ●

Pawtuxet River

Warren ●

Hope ●

Arctic ●

Quidnick ●

Warwick ●

Bristol ●

Mt Hope Bay

Fall River ●

Wauregan ●

New Bedford ●

CONNECTICUT

Tiverton ●

RHODE
ISLAND

Narragansett Bay

Baltic ●

Taftville ●

Norwich ● ● Greenville

Thames River

Buzzards Bay

Newport ●

Rocky Point ●

*Rhode Island
Sound*

Point Judith ●

*Block Island
Sound*

Atlantic Ocean

Cartography by Donald Sluter

well as the social and cultural life embedded in both. A broader, more flexible definition of the political as power can prove more inclusive. Gutman's emphasis on "the themes of class and community, power and authority" allows for the examination of politics at differing levels of experience.[25]

The analysis in my study draws on Gutman's approach but differs in important ways. I pursue his research on the mass of workers generally uninvolved in partisan politics and labor unions, and the evolving system of class exploitation they experienced. As David Roediger argues, Gutman maintained "a focus on power and [class] exploitation even as he moved toward a culturally-based history," and I also share his interest in the transatlantic movement of laboring people, their cultures, and their class activism, including the "growl" of immigrant leaders in Paterson, New Jersey.[26] Like Gutman, I rely on rich evidence from the nineteenth-century press but find the federal census manuscripts unexpectedly opaque on job categories and thus divisions among the workforce.[27] I use labor strife to disclose social, cultural, and economic relationships and the distribution of power in communities. But the ability of New England textile capitalism to organize its economic and political interests regionally means that Gutman's focus on single communities severely limits an understanding of broader-based networks of both corporate power and working-class politics. Regional analysis of industrial organization and the diverse workforce can reveal these other dimensions of power. Gutman argues that small centers of industrial production permitted more social cohesion among classes. But heavy-handed paternalism by local elites backed by outside investors in many Rhode Island and Connecticut mill villages created divisive tensions and sustained tyrannical policies. A regional focus can examine various centers of industrial production and compare their uses of class power.

In this study, the center of cultural and political life rests less on the family and religion, as Gutman argues, and more on the protest heritages, workplace realities, and labor politics of those native-born and immigrant workers caught up in this regional industry. As does Gutman, I emphasize the contingencies, not the eventualities, in changing class relations, cultural legacies, and labor politics.[28] The meanings of gender, race, and ethnicity are constructed and embedded within the overlapping spheres of class, culture, and power. This triple framework can place social and cultural identity in context and reveal why those meanings change in complex ways. Gutman's work on the connections between race and class in the nineteenth century is extended here to include conflicts among diverse immigrant workers, expressed through imposed racial categories and nativist language and encouraged by capitalist managers.[29] These conflicts among various groups of workers produced alternating moments of both cultural resistance and adaptation, of political solidarity and fragmentation.

Gutman's work, like Thompson's, does not focus on working-class gender relations in the workplace or in the family. *Constant Turmoil* examines the changing meanings of manhood and womanhood throughout the prolonged struggles of this period. Regiments of seasoned English factory hands from textile centers in Lancashire and Yorkshire, including Irish-born operatives trained in England, brought to New England a well-established culture of plebian or popular radicalism. These immigrants and their politics of protest add a different layer to Gutman's vision of waves of preindustrial immigrants from peasant cultures who provided major, long-term opposition to American industry and urban life. Prior to his death in 1985, Gutman began a study of the second generation of immigrant workers and the development of the American working class in the late nineteenth century.[30] Among these are those English immigrant textile workers, leaders of the native-born and other immigrants, who found New England's factory discipline and amoral values obnoxious but familiar. Drawing on their culture of protest, immigrants from Lancashire and Yorkshire contested the power of New England textile capitalists for decades. Finally, in concert with Gutman's efforts, this work attempts to assess to what extent and under what circumstances working-class culture either denies or reinforces the attempts of corporate power to gain authority. The arenas of corporate power and partisan politics collided with class and culture. The results of these contests defined industrial life.

Historian Iver Bernstein eloquently calls for broadening the boundaries of political life in an age of industrial transformation to consider the multiple aspects and meanings of political activity.[31] In New England, contests over formal and informal power occurred among elite families as well as within the textile workforce of men, women, and children with varying levels of skills and backgrounds, native-born and immigrant. The political culture of working-class women in industrial communities, within labor organizations, and during political agitation for state regulation augments Paula Baker's analysis of nineteenth-century middle-class women and politics.[32] Conflicts over power often produced divisive disagreements over the meanings of political heritages, gender relations, economic ideologies, and strategies for labor politics. Many native-born men, committed to American republicanism and evangelical religion, regarded the nineteenth-century political economy as threatening to a Christian republic. Corporate managers and their middle-class supporters embraced the legal construct of freedom of contract and the natural laws of supply and demand as essential to economic progress. Debates over the shaping of the Massachusetts ten-hour law involved cherished English immigrant traditions of popular radicalism, standards of manly and womanly behavior, styles of labor protest, and the rejection of the fundamental immorality of New England textile capitalism. The gendering of ten-hour legislation in the 1870s resolved issues about the proper legal relationship between adult white men and the state. All this was contested, but only those issues and events that expose working-class culture and labor politics in reaction to industrial power and political control form the backbone of this study. A systematic analysis of southeastern New England partisan politics must wait for another historian.

Politics, defined in this study as a flexible concept of power, thus includes the social and cultural aspects of class relations and family life and the meanings of class, gender, race, sexuality, emotion, and ethnicity.[33] The story unfolds when, where, and how cultural and class heritages asserted their power or were stymied and altered during moments of strife. It illustrates how economic might, backed by wealth, capitalist ideology, and political power, faced, undermined, or transformed the cultural and political legacies of industrial workers. A particular set of managerial policies created the Fall River system of production that was different from the familiar nineteenth-century models of Rhode Island, Lowell, and Philadelphia. Corporate power in southeastern New England proved ruthless but, when unable to stamp out class, cultural, and political opposition, forged ties with small numbers of skilled male workers, dividing working-class activism. Vulnerability, temptation, bad judgment, charged emotion, the "fortuitous," and necessary adaptation characterized the experiences of both textile capitalists and the workforce.[34] I will investigate human agency and responsibility; managerial and technological changes; the clash of political and cultural legacies; changing images and meanings of working-class gender, family relations, ethnic and racial identity; and the variations of class power. All these elements contributed to the building of the Fall River system.

SOCIAL HISTORY AND POLITICAL AND BUSINESS HISTORIANS

Sensing a profound crisis over their standing in the discipline and in contemporary political culture, political historians call for the use of social history methods to study politics.[35] In a 1997 essay, "The Future of Political History," Steven Gillon surveys these efforts to integrate social and political history. In contrast with Gutman and Eley, Gillon regards social history and its multiple interests as inherently fragmented and divisive, suggesting that an expanded definition of political history offers the best grounds for attempts at meaningful synthesis. He cites Thomas Bender's concept of public culture as a possible new framework for political history to integrate a "wide range of manifestations of power," including the state as an institution, and the ways that power is distributed in society.[36] But missing from this view is exactly what excites social historians when they write about politics: the private realm, social and cultural identities, community dynamics, and the contested meanings of class politics and political power.[37] Gillon omits poststructuralist theory, one of the most disputed methodologies of social history, and its interest in how historical meanings and power are constructed and reconstructed. If political historians seek to integrate social history into their work, but avoid discourse analysis while continuing to rely primarily on an empirical analysis of the state and structural realignments of political parties organized around "the vote," they will miss an opportunity to probe how political concepts are constructed and how they change.

Political historians and social historians disagree about the nature and origins of power and how it operates in society.[38] Political historians analyze the workings of power through party politics and electoral contests, governmental decisions at all levels, lobbying activities, policy making, the passage of legislation, and the enforcement of law, testing their interpretations with quantitative analysis of elections and realignments and of the structures and ideologies of partisan politics.[39] Social historians regard politics more broadly as reflections of ongoing conflicts over power in all aspects of society and culture. These conflicts occur in various arenas: a workplace, a community, a region, or a society. Politics involves the beliefs and activities of various groups drawn together by cultural and economic experiences, often in conflict with groups of differing experiences. The resulting class and ideological struggles operate both inside and outside formal political organizations and policy-making institutions. Perhaps the greatest gap between political and social historians is the primacy social historians attach to economic power and the significance of class in shaping political life.[40] Social historians also pay attention to the ways in which meanings are constructed and reconstructed in society and how these changing meanings reflect the distribution of economic power as a vital factor in understanding how political power is formed and used. My intent is to demonstrate this.

Richard Oestreicher's effort in 1988 to combine the most perceptive insights from the new Thompsonian labor history and the new political history concludes that political systems remain fundamentally "systems of power . . . with dramatically unequal power struggle[s]. . . . Power [or the lack of it], not reason," he reminds historians, shapes "values, opinions, and behavior."[41] Political mobilization in the late nineteenth century varied, he argues, according to region, historical context, contingencies, and specific historical actors. The term *politics* used in this study embraces significant conflicts over power in southeastern New England, primarily in Massachusetts, Rhode Island, and eastern Connecticut.[42] These include electoral contests and legislative struggles over municipal, state, and federal policies, such as the provision of fire protection in Fall River, the passage of ten-hour laws in Massachusetts and Rhode Island, protective tariffs for the textile industry, the nationalist fervor of the Spanish-American War, and a proposed federal regulation of the working day. Politics also covers many other kinds of economic, social, and cultural conflicts over power. Attempts by corporations, backed by elite, wealthy families in southeastern New England, to dominate the domestic cloth market used managerial policies and new technologies in the industrial centers and mill villages, while trying first to destroy, and then to control the labor organizations of a largely British immigrant workforce. The interactions between corporate power and working-class culture remain the focus of political analysis.

Since 1990, business historians have also considered including issues of political power, human agency, and culture to widen their traditional approaches which emphasize corporate structure and the process of economic development. New business historians seek to incorporate various schools of analysis in social and cultural history and search for a dynamic of change that includes a frank confrontation with the implications of concentrated economic power in a democratic society.[43] Louis Galambos, a pioneer in the new business history, welcomes such investigations, especially of rationalization as a key economic process. Still, he regards cultural experience as lagging behind economic and political changes, rather than as a powerful resource, an independent variable, a potential ground for conflict, or a stubborn opponent to economic and political transition. Unlike Galambos, another new business historian, Kenneth Lipartito, regards culture as central, powerful, and persistent in business corporations, but his view of culture remains primarily restricted to the firm and its managers, the traditional bastion of business history.[44] Underscoring the benefits of cultural analysis to business history, he argues that "all human actors must always and everywhere filter their perceptions and hence their actions, through a set of cultural constructs."[45] This position, however, excludes the class, behavioral, customary, political, and historic bases of culture in the larger society. Social and cultural historians would be more encouraged if cultural constructs are expanded beyond the corporation.[46] Meanwhile, feminist social historians urge business historians to examine the changing meanings of gender, the diversity of race, and how the comparative study of several firms can disclose changes in broader cultural values.[47] The development and workings of the mature Fall River system in southeastern New England, for example, provoked and sustained a complex regional industrial culture.

Gender Analysis, Manhood, and Masculinity

The analysis of gender, rising out of the field of women's history, has within the last decade embraced the historically changing meanings of manhood and masculinity. The concept of gender means culturally produced, historically appropriate masculine and feminine behaviors which are worked out in political controversies, expressed in representative language and symbols, and become established for a time as the fundamental "natures" of men and women. I welcome recent efforts to reconcile methodological and political splits between women's history and gender studies.[48] Gender as a changing social construction has always been fundamental to feminist work, which must include the experiences, relationships, and discourses of both men and women to capture the politics inherent in social and cultural worlds. Historians have often attributed patriarchal masculinity and the working-class family wage to sweeping social and economic changes, rather than the result of intense, specific contests, such as those in New England labor politics, between classes and sexes.[49]

Sociologist Michael Kimmel identifies shifting cultural models of American manhood. Although acutely aware of the multiple meanings inherent in manhood and masculinity, Kimmel nonetheless drops from his 1997 overview, *Manhood in America: A Cultural History,* the crucial, changing relationships between manhood and womanhood. Instead, he analyzes persistent cultural standards, present in contemporary society, against which American men have measured their masculinity, including "self-control, exclusion, and escape."[50] These unchanging cultural standards can be read as essentialist and ahistorical. Furthermore, his view of nineteenth-century working-class white men as racist, sexist, and xenophobic ignores male workers with other views. Gail Bederman's *Manliness and Civilization: A Cultural History of Gender and Race in the United States, 1880–1917* examines a crucial historic shift from nineteenth-century manhood as an ideal of behaviors, beliefs, and duties to twentieth-century masculinity as a test of physical virility measured in contests against other races.[51] The analysis in *Constant Turmoil* confirms the historicism of Bederman's arguments and endorses sociologist Ava Baron's agenda for future gender analysis.[52] It emphasizes the historically contingent, changing character of manhood and womanhood, considers other aspects of identity such as class, race, ethnicity, sexuality, and age, identifies power relations between men and women, and places the analysis within the context of economic and social changes. My study offers additional evidence on the agency of women in defining working-class manhood and on specific conflicts among workingmen and middle-class reformers over activist women and expressions of female sexuality.

Michael Roper and John Tosh agree that manhood and masculinity not only change meaning historically but that these changes cannot be understood except in relation to others: women, other classes and races, the nation, the young, homosexuals, and the circumstances and ideologies of patriarchal power.[53] Tosh argues that both nineteenth-century elites and working-class groups established and maintained male hierarchies with their own masculine codes, backed by wealth and power for capitalists and by skill and control of labor politics for workingmen. Each cherished code or heritage became contested in the public arena of economic and political conflict. Tosh, drawing on the work of sociologist

R. W. Connell, reminds historians that "hegemonic" or culturally domineering masculinity not only carries great ideological weight in society
and culture but also makes "crippling distinctions" between men and
women, classes, and nationalities. These distinctions must be maintained
"by force, as well as validated through cultural means."[54] Resistance to
such class power and its cultural apparatus produced constant turmoil in
the nineteenth-century New England textile industry.

Historian Theodore Koditschek assesses the relationship between class
and gender, based on recent studies of workingwomen in British industry
in the nineteenth century.[55] Koditschek accepts the centrality of gender
to class relations but does so in a manner that merges both categories of
analysis. For him, class is inherently gendered and gender is inherently
classed. This confluence of class and gender, in my view, loses the critical
edge of gender analysis and will likely privilege class analysis. Indeed, as
Koditschek integrates both categories, he reveals a vision of eighteenth-,
nineteenth-, and twentieth-century working-class history as a series of
changing but totally domineering capitalist patriarchies. He thus dismisses meaningful conflicts, contingencies, or alternatives, accepting a
dismal determinism. Joan Gadol Kelly and Laurel Thatcher Ulrich offer
more promising paradigms to encompass gender, class, and community
relations. Kelly's overlapping dual spheres of gender and class experience
and Ulrich's homely image of blue and white threads, representing gender roles in the community, intersecting through the weave of checked
fabric, avoid Koditschek's conflation of gender and class.

IMMIGRANTS, LABOR POLITICS, AND CORPORATE POLITICAL CULTURE

The complex experiences of nineteenth-century immigrants from Lancashire and Yorkshire, England, and Quebec Province, Canada, to southeastern New England textile centers has been either unappreciated by
labor historians or viewed simplistically by ethnic historians. Hardly "invisible immigrants," both English-born and Irish-born industrial workers reshaped nineteenth-century New England labor politics, based on their
working-class culture of popular radicalism.[56] The fundamental historical
concept of French Canadian working-class life in New England, *la survivance,* the struggle for basic economic and cultural survival in an alien
world, requires more from historians than adherence to a cultural piety.
Discourse analysis of the gender politics embedded in *la survivance* and
new evidence on labor militancy among Quebec immigrants in late nineteenth-century New England textile centers challenge the customary survival paradigm. James Barrett calls for studies of "the widespread contacts
and interactions" among diverse immigrant workers to understand their
"gradual acculturation" and "the transformation of immigrant worker

consciousness."[57] Like Gutman, he argues that the process proved uneven, shaped and reshaped by new waves of immigration which offered
distinct alternatives to capitalist values. Textile workers from Britain and
Quebec, relying on their differing cultural and political resources, proved
crucial to nineteenth-century labor politics. They provided oppositional
definitions of justice, community, and morality that challenged corporate
power in New England textile mills.

Many nineteenth-century textile workers from England would have
agreed with historian Michael Merrill's assessment of the rule of power in
economic relations. Disputing the misuse by economic and social historians of the terms *market economy* and *capitalism*, he insists that

> Capitalism . . . is not just an economic system based on market exchange,
> private property, wage labor, and sophisticated financial instruments. . . .
> Capitalism, more precisely, is a market economy ruled in the interests of
> capitalists.[58]

Industrial development by capitalists becomes the amassing of power,
wealth, and control by one privileged group at the expense of less privileged groups. Much of that self-interested rule by southeastern New England textile managers involved their power to define and control the
availability and meaning of information and knowledge about the industry. They invented and used specific industrial language to promote and
protect a particular market ideology, to create repressive work rules, and
to exaggerate competitive crises, frequently in defiance of accepted industrial practices. They attempted to rule their increasingly volatile market
through sheer productive capacity, indifferent to the rise of modern, efficient, and "rational" corporate policies. Self-defined fears of competitors
lurking in the region justified both wage cuts and the glutting of an increasingly unstable market with cheap goods. Their control over production data, reports of profits and losses, conditions of employment, and
ultimately the cloth market itself meant that vital information was denied
to others, including the state. Mill owners thus interpreted politically and
culturally through self-serving pronouncements all the power they possessed and used against organized class resistance and state regulation.

Over the last several decades and despite the envy of others, social and
labor historians have been battered, yet buoyed, by the challenges of new
forms of analysis: gender, ethnic, racial, cultural, linguistic, and spatial.[59]
Critics call for a return to fundamental issues of power and authority, to
more narrative, and to political analysis linked with state and national
developments. Others demand further explorations of human agency in
class relations or as poststructuralists dismiss an emphasis on class experience and empirical data as a theoretical dead end.[60] Historian Marc
Steinberg argues that discourse analysis and Thompson's cultural Marxism share common ground, both viewing moral and political language as

a site of class battles over power.[61] Indeed, English immigrant workers in southeastern New England appropriated the language of authority or the "dominant discourse" of their opponents, recasting it into cultural and political weapons for their struggles. Both the die-hard resisters and the more acquiescent used the language of the Fall River system for their own purposes. In doing so, many searched for justice, respect, fairness, and morality, rather than merely more beef and beer or the AFL's pure and simple unionism.

Current debates over the ways historians use poststructuralist theory to construct meaning from often scanty or obscure evidence involve the relative merits of linguistic or discourse analysis of texts versus empirical data, sometimes dismissed as "raw facts." These disputes raise fundamental questions about how historians think they know what they know. Eleni Varikas appreciatively but critically assesses the pitfalls of linguistic analysis and cultural Marxism, both of which, she argues, may decline into ahistorical determinism. Astutely combining the theoretical categories of empiricism and discourse analysis, she insists that historians examine the political dynamics that surround documents or texts to better understand and explain them.[62] But no historian can understand with certainty, either through discourse analysis or reconstructions of empirical data, what working-class people or any other group actually thought and felt or how and why they behaved in the past. My primary interest is to recover whatever evidence may still exist on the circumstances of nineteenth-century industrial life and to understand both the various meanings it may convey to the historian and the ways it might have reflected meanings ascribed by those who lived in the past. I use discourse analysis for some key texts and ideologies, but my main interest lies in understanding the meaning and context of the empirical to provide a persuasive and inclusive explanation of the complexities of historical experience.

Linguistic analysis, however powerful in illuminating meanings in existing texts, must also confront inescapable voids in the historic record. One key source in this study, the Fall River *Labor Journal,* edited by English immigrants in the 1870s, has disappeared. The only surviving copies from September 26 and October 3, 1874, open a very brief but rich perspective, creating a tormenting vision of what I might have understood about the culture and politics of working-class immigrant life. This loss is a void, not a silence; an empty suitcase cannot be unpacked. Furthermore, the destruction or the suppression of historical documents is often a reflection of powerful class interest.[63] It is too beguiling to imagine that the correct theoretical approach might provide a means to understand what has only been partially preserved.

The structure of my book offers the reader a mix of narrative and analysis based on empirical evidence and discourse analysis. The narrative, based on a chronological pattern, seeks to illuminate human agency and textured experiences.[64] Each chapter will situate its story and argument around one or more major, often classic, interpretive studies of nineteenth-century industrial life. I will indicate in what ways my analysis alters or supports those works. The narrative will unfold the social and political dynamics of nineteenth-century industrial life in all its dimensions of class, culture, and power. This approach may apply primarily and most appropriately to this particular nineteenth-century regional industry. Eileen Boris offers another model in her 1994 analysis of the politics of industrial homework.[65] Using an inherently flexible definition of politics, Boris considers the tenement, the factory, the labor movement, the state, and the courts. Her study centers on the discourses about and the changing meanings of motherhood, working-class masculinity, the family wage, and gender relations in the family and at work. In reaction to the labor politics among those homeworkers, skilled white men in AFL unions adopted a policy of exclusion in the late nineteenth century.

Similarly, the bumpy course of New England industrial politics contributed to the rise of conservative, exclusionary policies in the emergent national AFL. Long-term battles over the political meanings of mutualism and the validity of popular radicalism as the ground of working-class power in capitalist America ultimately fostered exclusion, racism, and gender inequality in trade unionism. English popular radicalism represented another more inclusionary vision and strategy for all textile workers, regardless of skill, sex, religion, or nationality, plus a determined commitment to resist corporate injustice, whatever the consequences, backed by the faith that resistance itself—win, lose or draw—demonstrated working-class power. But all this was subdued. The radical political heritage that British textile operatives, such as Thomas Evans, brought from Lancashire and Yorkshire to New England in successive waves throughout the nineteenth century gradually became suppressed by the rise of trade unionism. This occurred during a prolonged series of struggles in southeastern New England communities, revealing a perceptibly lived dynamic of class, culture, and power.

Contests with corporate power undermined the faith of many native-born and naturalized male citizens in the promises of republicanism, political reform, and state regulation. Failure in strikes and partisan politics ultimately pitted skilled workingmen against workingwomen and newcomers from Quebec, both of whom became targets for conservative trade unionists. After a prolonged struggle, the ideology of the exclusive trade union and the family wage for skilled white men assumed dominance. The powerful mule spinners' unions of New England, controlled by English and Irish immigrants, became leaders in the new AFL. They increasingly distanced themselves from amalgamations with other operatives, lent themselves to the ascendant power of textile capitalism at the turn of the century, and embraced American partisan politics.

By the early twentieth century, the heritage of English popular radicalism, embodied by Thomas Evans and his friends, had been forgotten by
most, a road not taken. Still, Evans' belief in the vital necessity of morality,
justice, and ethics in industrial life did not die with him in 1906. Those
like him, who rejected American capitalist values, advocated inclusive
amalgamations for textile workers in the Northeast, and believed in and—
when they could—voted for socialism, provide a nineteenth-century foundation for early twentieth-century labor radicalism in New England.[66] In
addition, successive waves of new immigrants with radical traditions of
their own from Italy, Belgium, Portugal, and Eastern Europe joined with
American socialists. English immigrant operatives in Lawrence, Massachusetts, organized a branch of the Industrial Workers of the World in 1905,
while in New Bedford IWW supporters went out on strike in 1910 and
1912.[67] All these activities kept alive the dream of Thomas Evans. But that
is another story of the politics of industrial life.

1

THE FALL RIVER PATRIMONY
Those Legendary Bordens, 1799–1865

IN 1900, an embittered S. Angier Chace died in his opulent mansion on Rock Street, overlooking Mt. Hope Bay in Fall River. Among the papers of the disgraced Fall River industrialist lay a rare personal reminiscence and appreciation of the local industry's founder, Holder Borden.[1] Chace had gone to jail in 1879 for embezzling corporate assets for reasons that he convinced himself Holder Borden would have understood.[2] Borden's obituary, published on September 16, 1837, in the Fall River *Monitor,* had concentrated on his wealth and benevolence. Other nineteenth-century writers would later embellish this portrait of Fall River's most formidable early nineteenth-century entrepreneur who died at age thirty-eight.[3] His legend included heroic acts of domination and initiative. To those existing accounts, Chace's reminiscences provided additional laudatory stories about Borden, a relative by marriage whom he very much admired. Fall River industry and all it came to represent begins with the achievements of Holder Borden. The Borden family and its allies in the community built a system of production that came to dominate the post–Civil War textile market through unparalleled capacity.

The life of Holder Borden and the subsequent activities of his uncles, Richard and Jefferson Borden, became major contributions to the cultural, economic, ideological, and political patrimony that the first generation of Fall River industrial capitalists left to their sons, nephews, male cousins, and kin by blood and marriage. This is a story about ingenious and daring ventures acted out by men consumed by the pursuit of industrial power in nineteenth-century New England. The Bordens, their families, and their relatives among the Durfees and Braytons of Fall River shaped a community and a social order with their economic wealth and political power based on an elaborate network of kin and influence. Their achievements, aspirations, and cultural style also helped define their view of manhood and womanhood, the measure of being a Borden of Fall River.

Trained as farmers, traders, clerks, ship carpenters, and cashiers, the Bordens and Durfees learned the elements of textile manufacturing, railroading, and steamboat operations from other early entrepreneurs and from manufacturers influenced by developments in Rhode Island. But the Fall River developers were "new men" or "men on the make," as the wealthy, socially prominent Boston Associates who organized textile manufacturing in Lowell and Lawrence, Massachusetts, definitely were not.[4] The Bordens and their associates meant to establish themselves through control of wealth and power as leaders in textile production, first in their own town, taking on local competitors, and later in the region of southeastern New England. Since there was no local, traditional elite as in Boston, New Bedford, or Providence, they also shaped Fall River society. In contrast to the Boston Associates or the New Bedford and Providence Quakers, they possessed no inherent sense of restrictions on their economic and social goals and tastes.[5] In addition, the private and the public spheres of human emotions, gender relations, and family dynamics in Fall River revealed the influence wielded by a few female members who inherited, developed, and controlled industrial property. All these became part of the Borden legacy of economic and political achievement and served as a source of social and ideological capital that established their growing power in the region by the Civil War.

IN A MONUMENTAL book published in 1991, Charles Sellers sums up the impact of early market expansion and industrial growth on the American republic. *The Market Revolution: Jacksonian America, 1815–1846* is a grand synthesis by an eminent historian. Sellers assesses how early nineteenth-century economic change influenced politics, religion, culture, society, family relations, and a host of other regional and national issues.[6] While he recognizes the achievements of the Boston Associates in building the Massachusetts textile industry in the 1820s, the Bordens and Fall River did not yet deserve recognition.

Historians criticize Sellers' work, however, as viewing the economic changes of the market revolution as overly determined: that is, irresistible, even inexorable, in terms of its economic momentum and overpowering in the changes it brought to American society and the threats it posed to democratic institutions.[7] "Rather than a series of decisions made by specific capitalists to position themselves for profit," Sellers endows the market revolution with "surging energy, calculating [but impersonal] egotism, ... and proliferating dynamism."[8] In his account, the potency of market forces remains detached from human agency. The patrimony of

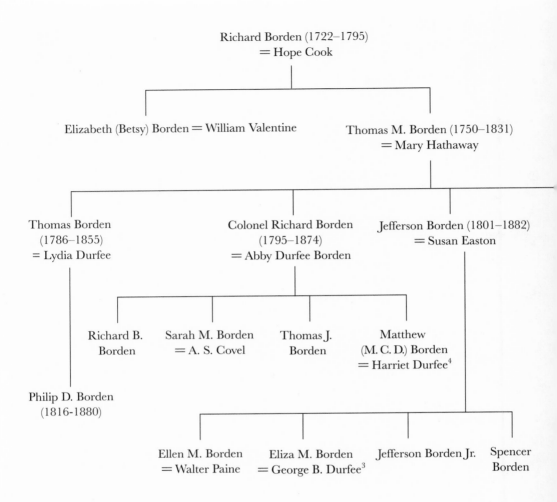

Richard Borden (1722–1795)
= Hope Cook

Elizabeth (Betsy) Borden = William Valentine

Thomas M. Borden (1750–1831)
= Mary Hathaway

Thomas Borden
(1786–1855)
= Lydia Durfee

Colonel Richard Borden
(1795–1874)
= Abby Durfee Borden

Jefferson Borden (1801–1882)
= Susan Easton

Richard B.
Borden

Sarah M. Borden
= A. S. Covel

Thomas J.
Borden

Matthew
(M. C. D.) Borden
= Harriet Durfee[4]

Philip D. Borden
(1816-1880)

Ellen M. Borden
= Walter Paine

Eliza M. Borden
= George B. Durfee[3]

Jefferson Borden Jr.

Spencer
Borden

[1] Joseph Durfee's first marriage was to Sylvia Borden, second marriage to Minerva Chace Durfee, sister of S. Angier Chace.

[2] Maria Chace Durfee, sister of S. Angier Chace, was second wife of Matthew Durfee

[3] George B. Durfee married Eliza M. Borden

[4] Harriet Durfee married M. C. D Borden

[5] Holder Borden Durfee married Sylvia Borden Chace Durfee

[6] Matthew Durfee's first marriage was to Fidelia Borden, second marriage to Maria Chace Durfee

KEY MEMBERS OF THE BORDEN, DURFEE, AND BRAYTON FAMILIES

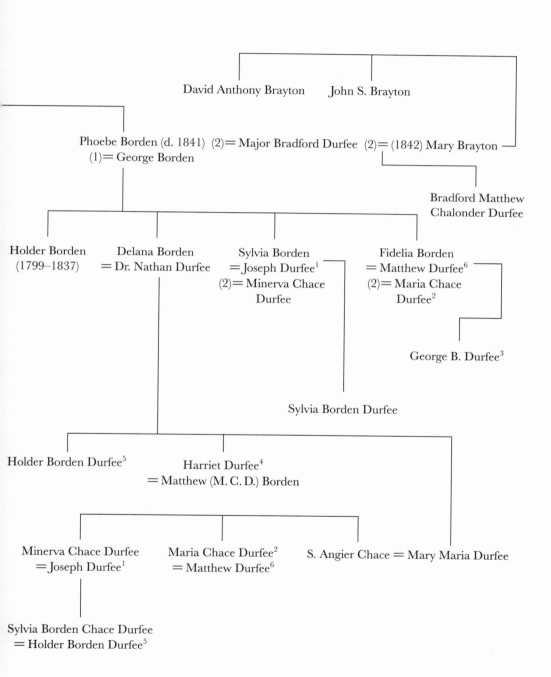

David Anthony Brayton   John S. Brayton

Phoebe Borden (d. 1841) (2)= Major Bradford Durfee (2)= (1842) Mary Brayton
(1)= George Borden

Bradford Matthew
Chalonder Durfee

Holder Borden   Delana Borden   Sylvia Borden   Fidelia Borden
(1799–1837)   = Dr. Nathan Durfee   = Joseph Durfee[1]   = Matthew Durfee[6]
                       (2)= Minerva Chace   (2)= Maria Chace
                             Durfee   Durfee[2]

George B. Durfee[3]

Sylvia Borden Durfee

Holder Borden Durfee[5]   Harriet Durfee[4]
                    = Matthew (M. C. D.) Borden

Minerva Chace Durfee   Maria Chace Durfee[2]   S. Angier Chace = Mary Maria Durfee
= Joseph Durfee[1]   = Matthew Durfee[6]

Sylvia Borden Chace Durfee
= Holder Borden Durfee[5]

the Borden families explored here, however, makes concrete the complex mix of personal calculations, family connections, social conflicts, and unswerving ambitions that drove early industrial endeavors. Human energy and emotion contributed to the growing belief among these families in their own legends and their destiny to rule in their town, in the region of southeastern New England, and in the national market for print cloth. In 1846, the year in which Sellers ends his book, the families of Fall River were not yet of even regional importance. Their activities, driven by the early nineteenth-century market revolution, were just beginning to develop. After the Civil War, applying their own vision of the market, the Bordens and their kin would achieve national importance.

HOLDER BORDEN was born in 1799, the first child of two cousins, George and Phoebe, descended from a Rhode Island family of Bordens. They lived on a farm in rural Freetown, Massachusetts, divided off for thirty years after 1804 as the town of Troy, later changed to Fall River in 1834.[9] Situated on Mt. Hope Bay at the northeastern end of Narragansett Bay off Rhode Island Sound, Freetown in 1803 had eighteen dwellings, nine occupied by Bordens. Mariners, such as Holder's father, George, sailed sloops carrying agricultural produce to nearby points of exchange. George Borden died in 1806, leaving his wife Phoebe with Holder nearly eight, three younger daughters, and a little land. Phoebe belonged to a local Borden family of thirteen children, headed by her father, Thomas M., and her mother, Mary Hathaway Borden, and including her two brothers, Richard and Jefferson, who would later join their nephew Holder Borden in his business ventures. After consulting her many relatives, the widow Borden sold the farm and built a house on a lot she owned in the village center where she opened a tavern and boardinghouse.

Holder's boyhood chores shifted from washing pigs in the farm pond to tending horses and running errands for the travelers between Newport, Rhode Island, and Boston, while his mother and sisters fed the boarders and did their laundry. Packet boats and daily stagecoaches to Providence also brought customers. With no time for school, the boy was taught to read, write, and cipher by his mother. The tavern became a popular wayside stop and a thriving business, providing Holder with plenty of chances to learn. A twenty-one-year old unemployed ship carpenter, Bradford Durfee, whose mother and grandmother were Rhode Island Bordens, made himself useful around the busy tavern and in 1809 married thirty-year-old Phoebe, his second cousin. Holder, described as "always puny" but nonetheless the little man of the family, was only eleven years his junior. The vital, black-haired Bradford Durfee, "a brawny, handsome" man, became family head. He took over the proprietorship of the tavern, renamed it the Mansion House, and fathered two daughters.[10] He also organized a small ship-building yard with Phoebe's brother, Richard. Holder

Borden's relationship with his stepfather appeared amicable, but the youth, deeply challenged, became intensely competitive and eager to improve the family position on his own.

The more attractive commercial targets of Newport and Providence protected the residents of tiny Troy from British raids during the War of 1812. Nonetheless, the young men of the town joined local units of the state militia and arranged for their own elections as "Major" and "Colonel," although none was ever called into active service. These local military titles stuck. The Mansion House became known as Major Bradford Durfee's house. Holder Borden's uncle Richard was always called Colonel Borden. Holder took no interest in these honorific ranks; he remained the militia company's clerk.[11] Later associated with wealth and power in the community, these titles added an aura of military prowess and manly patriotism to the leaders of Fall River's economic development.

THE BEGINNINGS OF THE FALL RIVER MILLS

Holder Borden did not build or run the first cotton manufactories in Fall River, but as a young man, he watched the activities of those who did. David Anthony, his cousin Dexter Wheeler, and Abram Bowen, mechanics from nearby towns who boarded at the Mansion House, organized the Fall River Manufactory in 1813, the first cotton-spinning operation.[12] Anthony, then twenty-seven years old, had worked for four years at Samuel Slater's Mill in Pawtucket, Rhode Island.[13] The new company bought Borden farmland along the Quequechan stream, a very narrow, spring-fed river that had slowly cut its way through granite ledge and ponded below a "Great Falls" of 68 feet before it ran out the course of its 130-foot drop into Mt. Hope Bay.[14] The granite ledge provided solid foundations for mills built next to the water power of the stream. The ledge also supplied granite blocks cut by local labor to construct the mills giving a special look to Fall River operations, in contrast with the red brick mills of Middlesex County. The stockholders included Wheeler, Anthony, and Bowen as well as members of the Borden family and their cousins, the Durfees. When the mill began operations in October 1813, thirteen of its thirty-three employees were Bordens.[15]

Anticipating an end to the British blockade of southern cotton during the War of 1812, agent David Anthony planned a picker house to clean raw cotton, a water-powered spinning mill to produce yarn, and a company store to provide goods in payment to outwork weavers. At the turn of the century, mechanics and overseers from Slater's mill at Pawtucket, the origin of the American textile industry in 1791, had spread the processes of water-powered spinning and handloom weaving throughout the rural villages of Rhode Island, southern Massachusetts, and eastern Connecticut, wherever there were suitable rivers or streams.[16] After the 1815

Treaty of Ghent reopened the flow of raw cotton to spinning mills, Holder Borden at age seventeen was named clerk of Anthony's company store. But the end of tensions also brought competition from English textiles that depressed New England production until tariff protection came to the rescue in 1816. At first, Anthony and his investors were very nervous. Anxiety over shaky investments and uncertain profits was general in spinning mills throughout New England.[17]

Nonetheless, a group led by Oliver Chace from neighboring Swansea, Massachusetts, incorporated the Troy Cotton and Woolen Company in 1814. Chace's mill was situated on land with mill privileges near the Great Falls held by widow Amey Briggs Borden, a descendent of John Borden, who in 1714 had owned the "stream," the land, and all the water privileges.[18] Chace acquired New Bedford backers who owned large farms in Troy and hired experienced machinists from the Waltham, Massachusetts, mills run by the Boston Associates.[19] In 1821 Samuel Rodman, a Quaker from New Bedford—which had no suitable water power—used profits from commercial and whaling operations to form the Pocasset Company, developing its water privileges at the Great Falls and building small mills to lease. Rodman was a colorful figure who still dressed in Revolutionary era knee britches, silk stockings, buckled shoes, and a long waistcoat, but he avidly encouraged the development of textile production.[20] These young companies formed a village called Fall River within the town of Troy, with 1,594 residents by 1820, boasting a regular packet service to Providence and daily stages to Boston to avoid the long dangerous voyage around Cape Cod. Manufacturing interests soon swallowed Troy, and in 1834 the town accepted the name of the village.

These operations adopted the Rhode Island system of cotton manufacturing, begun at Slater's mill and supported by crafts and metal trade firms, such as the Wilkinson Brothers of Pawtucket along the Blackstone River. The firm of Almy and Brown of Providence which backed Slater developed their own manufacturing interests at the Blackstone Company in Providence. Spinning mills used child labor under close supervision to tend the throstle frames and then put out the yarn to be woven into cloth by families in the surrounding countryside. Both yarn and cloth were marketed on consignment, and it was not unusual to barter them for grain or lumber.[21] After 1820 capital from New Bedford and especially from Providence stimulated Troy's steady but slow mill development.[22]

Meanwhile, in northern Massachusetts the Boston Associates invested in the much more rapid development of fully integrated and mechanized cotton mills at Waltham and Lowell equipped with water-powered looms.[23] The Waltham and Lowell system, in contrast with the Rhode Island system, provided both integrated production and paternalistic boardinghouses for women factory workers. By the end of the decade, Lowell had become the big success story, boasting ten of the largest corporations in the United States, capitalized between six hundred thousand and a million dollars.[24] The economic and political power of Boston investors created a model of mass production copied by many mills in northern New England.

In Troy during these early years, Holder Borden associated himself with the Providence investors, the Troy mill owners, and the Wilkinson Brothers of Pawtucket. In 1821 these key investors—Holder Borden's relatives in Troy, the Wilkinson Brothers of Pawtucket, and Borden family connections in Providence—organized the Fall River Iron Works Corporation, which later developed cotton manufacturing and calico printing. According to local legend, Holder Borden was the driving spirit behind this endeavor. The major capital came from a Providence "Gentleman," Joseph Butler, a friend of Providence merchant William Valentine who also bought Iron Works shares in 1821.[25] Valentine had married Elizabeth Borden of Freetown, sister of Thomas M. Borden. The Valentines would later develop intimate social and financial connections with Jefferson Borden. The complex genealogy, large families, and multiple marriages of the Bordens and Durfees produced Jefferson born in 1801, an uncle to Holder, born two years earlier in 1799. The Bordens' connections with Providence families provided important financial support, essential training, and marketing outlets before the Civil War.

The incorporation meetings for the Iron Works in 1821 convened at Major Durfee's tavern. Abraham Wilkinson, acting for the company, purchased from Thomas M. Borden, the father of Richard, Jefferson, and Phoebe and the grandfather of Holder, his remaining farmland and water privileges, located below the Great Falls and leading down to the bay. The thirty-two stock certificates representing twenty-four thousand dollars in capital assets were divided into eight lots of four shares each distributed to Abraham and Isaac Wilkinson, William Valentine, Joseph Butler, Holder Borden, Colonel Richard Borden, Major Bradford Durfee, and David Anthony. In contrast, the Boston Associates' venture at Waltham in 1813 had capital assets of four hundred thousand dollars, while the Merrimack Manufacturing Company also organized in 1821 had six hundred thousand dollars in assets, twenty-five times larger.[26] The Iron Works bought metal molds from the Wilkinson Machine shop in Pawtucket for an iron-rolling operation that would make barrel hoops for New Bedford whale oil casks, nails and spikes to be marketed out of Providence and New York, and machine castings for local use. In 1825 the Iron Works shareholders decided to build and lease a cotton mill, the Annawan, with Major Durfee as agent.[27]

In 1822 David Anthony, who married Mary Borden, a daughter of Thomas M. Borden, sold his Iron Works shares to his nephew Holder Borden. Caught in a financial crisis in 1829, the Wilkinsons also sold their shares to him.[28] The Borden-Durfee-Valentine-Butler interests now controlled the Iron Works. Two years after Holder Borden's death in 1837, Jefferson Borden and Major Durfee became the trustees for the nine hundred thousand-dollar Valentine estate which included Iron Works shares.[29] Integral to the formation and development of the Iron Works project were these entangled ties of wealth and kinship that came to characterize manufacturing and finance in nineteenth-century Fall River. Economic ideology, business policy, and corporate structure would connect with the culture of family, kinship, gender, and class. Such blurred lines between the private and the public realms were not peculiar to Fall River. The Wilkinson brothers were related by marriage to Samuel Slater. The Boston Associates also featured intermarriages and interlocking directorates, and the Browns, Ives, and Goddards of Providence formed another close-knit group of financial and family interests.[30] Close family relationships in textile companies, or "cousinhoods," were also common in the English cotton manufacturing center of Lancashire.[31] But the promotion of heroic legends about one man, such as Holder Borden, was specific to Fall River and probably had helped to secure Rhode Island investment.

Meanwhile, the New Bedford investors in the Pocasset Company continued to develop the Great Falls area. Their first mill, rebuilt after a fire in 1821, housed a machine shop run by Oliver Hawes, an experienced mechanic who had built power looms in the Waltham shops run by Paul Moody. Hawes was also well trained in the Slater-Wilkinson tradition of manufacturing spinning frames. In 1824 the Pocasset Company built a second mill, half of which was leased to Samuel Rodman's son-in-law, Andrew Robeson, who began a small calico-printing operation, later called the Fall River Print Works. In 1830 the Pocasset Company constructed the largest mill building in town, the Massasoit, to lease portions to other small manufacturers. By 1830 access to the water power in the village of Fall River was divided in two: the Upper Falls owned by the New Bedford-backed Pocasset-Troy group and the Lower Falls controlled by the Providence-backed Iron Works group.[32] The Bordens remembered a time when they had owned it all. Even though the New Bedford investors competed keenly with the Iron Works promoters in developing local waterpower, the two groups cooperated to organize a commercial bank in 1825 with Holder Borden as a director. In 1828 the Fall River Bank, a savings bank, was founded with David Anthony as president.[33] They also supported the building of a stone dam by the Watuppa Reservoir Company to pond more water and pay any flowage damages to upstream landowners. Because the Pocasset Company did business in Tiverton, Rhode Island, the Watuppa Reservoir required acts of incorporation from both state legislatures, a political annoyance resolved legally by an interstate land swap in 1862.

Still, the activities on the Quequechan stream were hardly noticeable compared to the much more rapid growth of the cotton mills of Waltham and Lowell. In 1826 Troy had only ten small factories, six of them spinning cotton, some with power looms, and a total workforce of thirteen hundred, including many outwork weavers. The two thousand village residents patronized four churches, one bank, the tavern, three stores, three physicians, and two attorneys. A mechanics' society held meetings. Interest in a regular steamboat line to other ports was growing, but sloops such as the *Argonaut,* owned by Captain Thomas Borden, brother of Richard, Jefferson, and Phoebe, still carried nails and hoops produced by the Iron Works to New York and Hudson River Valley markets.[34] The wonderful developments in the Merrimack Valley that later drew European notables, such as Charles Dickens, totally overshadowed Troy's activities.

THE RISE OF HOLDER BORDEN

The years between 1827 and 1834 were a time of consolidation and cautious consideration of future development for many—but not for Holder Borden. Borden watched and envied the success of Andrew Robeson's calico-printing works, supplied with cloth from the mills in the Pocasset.[35] Characteristic of the owners of many New England mills, Robeson had no experience in the cloth printing trade; his father was a Pennsylvania flour miller. But Robeson added his connections with the Pocasset group to his own driving energy and physical powers which he liked to demonstrate by piling three full barrels of flour, one on top of the other, to the amazement of spectators.[36] He imported English and Scottish engravers and printers, using block printing at first and introducing English engraved copper rollers by 1832.[37] The print works prospered so much that it had to purchase half of its cloth outside of the village. In 1830 management forbade all visitors for fear of imitators and organized its own bank, the Fall River Union Bank. By 1832 Robeson's Fall River Print Works joined the Merrimack Manufacturing Company and the Hamilton Company in Lowell and the Taunton Manufacturing Company, just north of Fall River, as one of the three successful calico-printing operations in Massachusetts.[38] Robeson's success inspired a local rival.

Holder Borden's interests in calico-printing represented only one item on his crowded agenda of enterprise. He spent much of his time before 1830 in Pawtucket and Providence, working for the Wilkinson Brothers mill in Valley Falls, Rhode Island, and for the Iron Works and their Annawan mill. Jefferson Borden took over Holder's place in 1819 as the clerk of the Fall River Manufactory's company store and later assumed his position representing the Iron Works in Providence.[39] Holder's big chance came in 1825, when the wealthy manufacturers Nicholas Brown and Moses Brown Ives of Providence, who had observed his work at Valley Falls, offered him the agent's position at their Blackstone Manufacturing Company in Providence. While in their employment, Borden bought raw cotton with company funds; in fact, some said he bought so much that he had cornered the market. When Brown and Ives found out that Borden had acted without their authorization in such a risky speculation, they confronted him. His response became part of his personal lore:

> Very well, gentlemen. I supposed I was placed here to act on my own judgment. . . . Now as the purchase has been made if you will trust me for the amount of money I have used for this cotton I will assume this purchase for myself, leave the cotton in your store-house and charge the company for the cotton as it is wanted for use at the market price when used.[40]

They agreed. What the Blackstone did not use was sold off and yielded sixty thousand dollars for Borden, in addition to paying off Brown and Ives. Borden used some of his proceeds to buy shares in the Pocasset Company's Massasoit Mill.

The year 1825 also represented the emotional depths of Holder Borden's personal life. He had for some time been engaged to one of his mother's cousins, Hannah Valentine, a daughter of William Valentine and Elizabeth Borden Valentine, whom he had met in Providence.[41] She was reputed to be even prettier than her attractive sister Elizabeth, both of whom had blond curls. Their marriage was planned for the spring of 1826. In the summer of 1825, Elizabeth paid a visit to her relatives in Troy and was stricken by a virulent form of scarlet fever, a strep infection that led to pneumonia. Hannah rushed to be at her side, but also fell ill. Both died in September. The effect of Hannah's death isolated Holder from any society except his immediate family. He poured his grief and energy into work. Within six months his three well-dowered sisters married first cousins of Major Durfee.[42] Then he built them large houses. He presented his mother with a splendid pair of Saratoga grays for her carriage, which drew so much attention around the town, it was said, that his female relatives became embarrassed. The horses served long after Borden's death, a reminder to the town of his wealth and tastes. Major Durfee enjoyed tavern life and had enlarged the property, but he was persuaded (probably by Holder) in 1828 to give up the business and convert the new building into a large private residence. Durfee then devoted himself to constructing mill buildings and wharves. The death at fifteen of the only surviving child of Phoebe and the Major darkened family life.

Holder Borden divided his time between his interests in Fall River village and others developing in Providence. He had persuaded the Iron Works shareholders in 1828 to buy a steamboat built in Castine, Maine, to run between their wharf and Providence, but, as a fancier of fast horses, he drove a small sulky between Fall River and Providence. Following the lead of Almy and Brown, Borden marketed goods through wholesale or commission houses in Philadelphia and, after the opening of the Erie

Canal, through prospering New York City.[43] Sometime after 1825 he developed an annoying itch in his throat that persisted and probably was the
reason it was said he spoke little. When he did speak, it was always to the
point with growing irritation at long-winded or impractical discussions. In
an effort to alleviate his discomfort, he grew a long beard for protective
warmth when other men went clean-shaven. Nicotine became another
soothing anodyne. He smoked cigars "at all hours of the day or night."[44]
This too became part of his legend. Concealing his physical and emotional afflictions, Borden worked prodigiously. He seemed constantly on
the road between Fall River and Providence, dashing from one business
activity to another, keeping fresh horses at relay points in outlying villages.
For the Providence trip, he boarded a lively pacer at the halfway point,
Slade's Ferry on the Taunton River, where he also stored a supply of cigars, especially rolled to a length that would last the rest of his journey.
He rejected enough inferior cigars to provide his innkeeper and stable-
man with their own smoking materials. He completed this distance of
eighteen miles from the ferry to Providence in one hour.[45] Farmers said
he went by like a streak of lightening, while young boys sometimes gathered on the road to watch for him. The glowing point of those long cigars,
like a tiny meteor in the night, marked his dashes between the two towns.

His greatest coups came in 1835 after Borden leased the entire Massasoit Mill from the Pocasset Company for Brown and Ives and equipped it,
imitating the scale of the Lowell mills, with nine thousand spindles, an
amazingly bold act for the town. He was also running his own very profitable calico-printing works. Described as "congenitally independent," Borden had begun a print works in 1832 in an abandoned mill operation in
Tiverton, Rhode Island, and cleared profits of thirty thousand dollars in
one year.[46] This persuaded most of the Iron Works shareholders in 1834
(despite the unexplained opposition of Major Durfee) to back him in
building what Holder ambitiously called the American Print Works. Working in so many capacities severely drained his stamina. He served as agent
for the Blackstone mill of Brown and Ives in Fall River and for the Iron
Works' Annawan, both mills then headquartered in Providence; as agent
of his own print works, the American, and as treasurer of the Fall River
Manufactory, partly controlled by the Iron Works. He was also a bank director and a prominent shareholder in the Iron Works and the Troy mill.
His successes contrasted sharply with the high incidence of bankruptcy
and failure in small Rhode Island mills between 1815 and 1860.[47]

Holder Borden became so compulsively involved in the process of calico printing that one day, when his color mixer became sick, he himself
mixed up a highly successful shade that became quite popular. He replaced the gears in the power-delivery system with leather belting, a common solution in the industry to maximize efficiency. By his "force and example," Borden set the future course of Fall River textile manufacturing:

staple coarse cloth made for printing.[48] Robeson's Fall River Print works
went bankrupt in 1848, long after Borden's death, but the company had
specialized in the complicated process of indigo blue prints and little else.
In contrast, Holder Borden and the American Print Works had developed
a larger vision of a more varied market for its products.

Borden became so busy and self-consumed that Brown and Ives sold
him their shares in the Massasoit and moved their mill operations to
Lonsdale, Rhode Island, where they not only obtained better control over
the water power but could disassociate themselves from the unpredictable Holder.[49] Borden then organized the firm of Borden and Bowen to
handle his Providence affairs. At one point during the drought years of
1834–36, he tried unsuccessfully to hire away the agent of the Troy mill
located at the Upper Falls in order to get a steadier supply of water. He got
it anyway. Borden persuaded the Iron Works and American Print Works
shareholders to reinvest the profits, not distribute them. He put a million
and a half dollars into the print works alone to maintain quality and provide the most efficient and effective industrial processes.[50] Holder Borden
meant to shape the regional market for print cloth, not just dominate
local production, and drummed his policies into his handpicked successor, Jefferson Borden. Historian Robert Lamb has commented: "All this
activity was [the] breath of life to him. He seems to have been unable to
get his fill of it, until it finally killed him."[51]

His increasing weakness left him unable to rise from his bed during
the financial panic between February and September 1837.[52] Still, Borden gave orders from his sickbed. With his uncle Richard paralyzed with
anxiety, Holder summoned to his bedside his nephew Philip D. Borden,
the bookkeeper of the print works, and directed him to take his horse
and carriage, drive through a threatening storm to Providence for the
mail, and fetch Holder's Providence partner. If he could, he would have
done it himself. "[Philip] answered promptly, knowing that Holder always
wanted a decided and unwavering answer, 'Yes sir.'"

> As soon as he had crossed Slade's Ferry there came up a terrific storm. It
> was dark as midnight. He could see nothing, neither the road nor the
> stone walls beside it. He put up the boot of the carriage around him, gath-
> ered up the reins and started. He saw nothing until he arrived at the
> bridge in Providence. The horse knew the way and whither he was going.
> He turned every corner in the road more safely than the driver could have
> guided him if he had seen the way and more speedily than he would have
> dared to drive on sight.

Philip returned the next morning with the mail and the partner. According to the legend,

> Soon after this ride the crisis of the panic was passed, the credit of Fall
> River was triumphantly sustained and the business under the financial
> care and management of Colonel Richard and Holder Borden . . . was

placed upon a foundation so stable that great prosperity attended it for many years. . . . [53]

Apparently Holder had dispatched his partner to New York where, pledging all his property as security, he borrowed enough (perhaps from a commission house) to sustain the local bank.

Borden's debilitating illness must have been a terrible agony for him, as his condition worsened in 1837. He refused to write a will and died intestate.[54] The enterprising young man resisted his fate to the end. His material legacy was impressive. Holder Borden's estate was estimated at three hundred fifty thousand dollars; he was the richest man in town. He had "loaned new vitality to old undertakings."[55] He had strengthened the hold of the Iron Works on the Troy and Fall River mills, established a print works that later bested the Fall River Print Works, consolidated the Bordens' financial access to Providence and New York banks and marketing firms, and inspired the organization of the Bay State Steamboat Company out of which grew the famous Fall River Line between Newport and New York City.

And, some wondered, what if he had lived? One of his associates who worked for the Wilkinson brothers in Valley Falls believed that Holder Borden possessed "the largest business capacity I have ever seen in a young man." His buildings went up like magic. People said that he was as hard on himself as he was on man and beast, consuming himself with his work. The *Providence Journal* mourned him as one of its own leading citizens. In a significant and acute appraisal long after Holder's death, S. Angier Chace described him as active and energetic, courteous and refined, manly and exemplary. He emphasized Holder's Puritan background as a bloodline of men with "a vision penetrating beyond the present moment" and as "men who had gained control over their passions. . . . He appeared to have arrived at manhood almost without any boyhood or youth."[56] Indeed his father's death in 1806 had left him without any choice, while his stepfather acted as a goad. His business prowess, determined energy, and intense emotional repression defined his manhood. Without a wife or children, he poured all his passions into business. His anguished private life invigorated his public enterprise. Other testimonies insisted that when he died he had only just begun to establish a model of daring enterprise and strong kinship control of investments to which his uncles, Richard and Jefferson, had to aspire and build upon to deserve the name Borden. Under their leadership, the Iron Works "waxed" fat.[57] The "old heroic spirit . . . did not quail."[58]

SLOWLY GROWING COMPETITION

Whatever Fall River's opinion of Holder Borden's abilities as an entrepreneur, the great textile interests of Rhode Island held by Brown and Ives and the rising Sprague family of the A. and W. Sprague Company, keen competitors with each other, seemed much less impressed.[59] Samuel Rodman, a Pocasset Mill founder, never mentioned Borden in the diaries he kept between 1821 and 1859 in spite of his frequent travels to Fall River, staying at the Mansion House and conducting business for the Pocasset. In 1827 he expressed admiration for the Iron Works' Annawan mill.[60] To Rodman and Andrew Robeson of the Fall River Print Works, Holder Borden may have been an annoying competitor but hardly legendary. Still in 1846 when Joseph Grinnell and Thomas Bennett Jr. organized the Wamsutta Mills in New Bedford, they decided to make fine sheeting rather than compete with Fall River's print cloth.[61] This decision was something of a tribute.

In 1837 when Borden died, Lowell had eight major mills and a workforce of seventy-eight hundred; by 1840 with a population of twenty thousand, it was the second largest city in Massachusetts.[62] When Scottish immigrant James Montgomery, the superintendent of the York factories at Saco, Maine, reported on the development of American cotton mills for British interests in 1836 and 1837, he was most impressed by Lowell, then Paterson, New Jersey. His tour of Rhode Island and Connecticut mill villages convinced him of their promise, but Fall River's development seemed very slight. As a trained British mill man, Montgomery bemoaned the lack of "competent persons" in charge of the otherwise potentially threatening competition from new American factories.[63] What counted was the number of spindles, capital, and the value of cloth. In 1837 Bristol County ranked third in all categories to Middlesex and Worcester Counties.[64]

The Borden-Durfee families and their supporters in Fall River not only promoted the Holder Borden legend, but also created others. After Holder's death in 1837, Major Durfee assumed control of his estate as family trustee, while Richard and Jefferson Borden divided the manufacturing responsibilities. Richard took on the problem of transporting and marketing the cloth that Jefferson was having produced in the American Print Works. Richard Borden was born in Freetown in 1795 and lived on the family farm while attending the town school.[65] As a young man, he ran a grist mill. He and his brother Jefferson would often take a sloop to the large fertile islands in Narragansett Bay, picking up grain for their mill and returning it as flour or provisions. They willingly marketed any surplus flour in the coastal Rhode Island towns of Warren, Bristol, and Providence, returning home with groceries and raw cotton. His farm and maritime work gave Richard great physical strength, handy for his sawmill and ship-building yard. When the Iron Works was organized in 1821, he was named treasurer and then agent in 1843 when Major Durfee died. Colonel Borden supported all of Holder's ventures: the Iron Works, the Watuppa Reservoir, the banks, the Annawan, the shares in the Troy and Fall River mills, and the creation of the American Print Works. He used this accumulated power for over fifty years.

Richard Borden's greatest achievement was the development of a transportation system of steamboats and railroads between Boston and New York, via Fall River.[66] The Iron Works began to run a regular steamboat to Providence in 1827. The first steamer, the *Hancock,* was succeeded by three others, the last the *Richard Borden.* When he noticed the success of small steamboat lines launched from Stonington and Norwich, Connecticut, to New York, Colonel Borden organized the Bay State Steamboat Company in 1849 which owned a series of steamers, including the *Empire State.* By 1854 the largest of all, the *Metropolis,* carried passengers along the Connecticut coast to New York City and back via Fall River, either to catch the train to Boston or go on to the developing summer colony at Newport. This was the origin of the Fall River Line, later acquired for a time by New Yorker speculators Jim Fisk and Jay Gould, which after the Civil War drove out all other serious competition on Long Island Sound.

Establishing an overland connection to Boston from Fall River to avoid the perilous Cape Cod route proved Colonel Borden's greatest challenge. Busy Massachusetts railroad developers failed to share his conviction that the only logical southern terminus was Fall River. He was determined to use all of the Borden-Durfee power and money to get it. The Iron Works group vied with the New Bedford investors in Fall River to establish their own railways, but neither had enough money to go it alone.[67] In 1844 Borden worked out a plan to design and build the Fall River Branch Railroad Company that would connect—in a meandering way, so as not to offend the shipping interests at Assonet, Massachusetts, on the Taunton River used by Fall River businesses—both New Bedford and Fall River with the Old Colony Railroad line to Boston. The Iron Works and the Fall River Print Works cooperated to support this plan, and the road, designed initially for passenger service, opened in late 1846.[68] To create a feeder for the Fall River railroad, Borden began to build a line to Cape Cod from Middleboro, just east of Taunton. The Old Colony Railroad grew alarmed at this provocative competition and agreed to buy out the Fall River road in 1854. In 1860, when the Old Colony tried to make Newport the terminus of a steamship line to New York City, Colonel Borden projected another railroad to compete with the Old Colony's route to Boston. This financial duel ended with the Old Colony buying out the Bay State company in 1864 and agreeing after several years to return the steamboat terminus to Fall River. Borden's plans were backed by his access to the city's banks, the financial assets of the Iron Works, and its Providence connections.

Richard Borden's railroad schemes also convinced him to purchase a cheaper source of coal for the Iron Works. Until the acquisition of mines at Frostburg, Maryland, in 1849 by the Iron Works, expensive bituminous coal was shipped from Pictou, Nova Scotia. He also promoted the building of a private gasworks for the town, which became a city in 1854. In this, Fall River was behind Lowell but ahead of Providence and New Bedford.[69]

Bored with his term in the Massachusetts state Senate in 1854 as a waste
of precious time, Borden preferred to immerse himself in other ventures:
the Providence Tool Company, the Bay State Steamboat firm, the Cape
Cod Railroad, and the Old Colony Railroad.

The wealthy Bordens—and the Durfees to whom they were connected
by many marriages—shaped an elite society. Phoebe Borden's daughter
Delana (Holder's older sister) had married Dr. Nathan Durfee, a cousin
of Major Durfee, Phoebe's second husband. Dr. Durfee dropped his medical practice to live on his investments, funded by the Holder Borden estate, and on his nearly one thousand acres of real estate, while dabbling
in whaling and flour milling. As the only college-educated man in town
for years, he was known as an arrogant bore who never moved beyond
his experiences at Brown and Harvard.[70] Nevertheless, as a Borden ally
he was a community leader and served several times during the early 1840s
as a Whig in the state legislature. Durfee's daughter Mary Maria later
married S. Angier Chace.

Colonel Richard Borden became the model of a staunch Whig and
a supporter of temperance. He demonstrated his moral character as a
nineteenth-century Christian man of property by personally conducting
the Sabbath school in the Central Congregational Church's mission to
the poor. Borden also contributed to the local Children's Home and acted
as a corporate member of the American Board of Commissioners of Foreign Missions.[71] By 1860 model Christian gentleman Richard Borden possessed one of the largest estates in Fall River, estimated at three hundred
and seventy-five thousand dollars, and a commanding position in the
city's social circles. To supply a feminine counterpart to his Christian manhood, Abby W. Durfee Borden, the Colonel's wife, served as the head of
the ladies' sewing circle at the Central Congregational Church. It was she
who at a ladies' prayer meeting for foreign missions in 1849 had instituted
the local Sunday school for the "heathen about us [needing] to be saved.[72]
During the Civil War, Abby Durfee Borden headed the city's relief activities to support local soldiers.[73] After the war Colonel Borden donated land
and a monument for the burial of Fall River's fallen men. In gratitude,
the local Grand Army of the Republic post was named after him. He lived
to see the large Richard Borden Mill erected in 1873. When he died in
1874, his obituary described him effusively as "fragrant with all the best
qualities of our New England life."[74] Combined with the pious, patriotic,
and home-loving activities of a devoted father and husband, his manly
legacy included his outright defiance of the Old Colony Railroad and its
backers and the successful domination of transportation on Long Island
Sound. Power and piety reinforced his image of enterprising manhood.

Richard and Abby Borden's sons would play important roles in sustaining Fall River's growing preeminence. The most active were Thomas
J. Borden, Richard Borden, and Matthew Chalonder Durfee or, as he in-

sisted (probably to distinguish himself from a sickly, effete cousin), M. C. D. Borden. Jefferson Borden and his wife produced no such worthy male heirs; Jefferson Jr. and Spencer served the family interests without distinction. One of their daughters married Walter D. Paine III, an able young man more than willing to take orders and serve family interests. Another daughter, Eliza, married her cousin George B. Durfee. He was the son of Fidelia Borden Durfee, youngest sister of Holder Borden, who had married Matthew Durfee, a cousin of Major Durfee. When Jefferson Borden married off a daughter, he gave each new son-in-law a cool hundred thousand dollars in gold.[75] The idea of course was that the money stayed in the family.

EXPANDING CLOTH MANUFACTURING AND PRINTING

While Colonel Richard Borden handled his responsibilities for the family enterprises, Jefferson Borden exceeded even his nephew Holder in the estimation of those who counted the most: the Providence investors. He did so by expanding the American Print Works and organizing mills to supply it with print cloth.[76] Jefferson was born in 1801 in Freetown, twelfth of the thirteen children of Thomas M. Borden. Like Richard, he worked on the farm and helped with the sloop, but like Holder he left at sixteen to clerk in a provision store, first in Troy and later in Providence. In 1821 he became clerk of the Iron Works and a year later its Providence representative. Jefferson Borden became known for his ability to develop markets for the Iron Works products. He remained in Providence for fifteen years, a close friend of the Valentines, his relatives by marriage and original investors in the Iron Works, but returned home when Holder died in 1837. For the next thirty-nine years he managed the American Print Works. In 1839 he became one of the major trustees of the Valentine estate worth two hundred thousand dollars, which he put to good use in expanding manufacturing capacity.[77]

Meanwhile, Major Durfee, a large shareholder in the American Print Works, made sure that the Fall River mills possessed advanced technology. In 1838 he took his young nephew William C. Davol to England to observe the self-acting mule spinning machine, designed to improve the productivity of the spinning process. The spinning mule, in contrast to the throstle frame usually run by female spinners, was operated by skilled men and their helpers and produced various kinds of the finest yarns. Durfee saw the self-acting mule as a way to cut manufacturing costs. Davol, a skilled mechanic, spent several months in Manchester making machine drawings. The first machine he tried to import to America, however, was still subject to strict controls on mechanical exports and had to be smuggled out of England, repeating Samuel Slater's industrial espionage with the Arkwright water-powered spinning frame. It arrived in 1840 cut into thousands of pieces, packed as plate glass.[78] The first mule was set up in the Annawan mill, named the Tippicanoe in honor of the military prowess of prominent Whig William Henry Harrison.[79] Major Durfee subsequently bought the American rights to the English Sharp and Roberts mule, which Davol improved in the Iron Works machine shop. Durfee then helped organize the firm of Hawes, Marvel, and Davol to build mules, carding machines, drawing frames, and other textile machinery for the Fall River mills.[80]

Durfee and Davol also visited the Lancashire town of Bolton to see the mill reputed to be the model of the English cotton trade. In 1846 Jefferson Borden had a new Fall River mill—the Metacomet—built according to those specifications, using cast iron posts and girders for the first time in American textile mills. He equipped it as much as possible with American-made machinery, powered by steam and water. The mill produced 28 inch-wide print cloth to feed into the printing machines at the American Print Works. The Metacomet's construction costs were paid off by the profits from one year's operation of the Print Works.[81] Jefferson Borden then built a market in cheap printed cloth to replace costly dress goods, reaching for all classes of consumers through the appeal of a constant change in styles and designs. Observing what he believed to be the caprices of popular female tastes, he produced novelties for one season only and always changed for the next. They became known in the dry goods trade as "American Prints."[82] Jefferson Borden's son-in-law George Borden Durfee was sent to New York to learn how to merchandise print cloth in the selling firm of Low, Harriman.[83] After the Civil War, Colonel Richard Borden's son, M. C. D. Borden, took over this responsibility. Connections with a New York selling house meant access to capital as well as markets.

Interested in expanding its printing capacity, the Iron Works shareholders acquired in 1854 the old Globe mills in Tiverton, Rhode Island, the site of Holder Borden's first printing business. At twenty-two years of age, Thomas J. Borden, the oldest son of the Colonel, was put in charge. The site of the old print mill, however, lay on land with conflicting claims based on colonial land grants to Roger Williams in 1643 and a charter granted to Massachusetts Bay Colony by Charles II in 1663. The question of which state governed this land involved a few square miles of very valuable property by the 1850s. The northern half of Tiverton had formed a new town, Fall River, Rhode Island, with the encouragement of the Iron Works interests. After failing for years to settle the issue, Massachusetts and Rhode Island appealed to the Supreme Court. During 1860 court-appointed surveying engineers studied the problem.[84] The result was a decision in 1861 that shifted state borders, amounting to a swap of land between the two states. Endorsed in 1862 by their legislatures, the compromise served both Providence and Fall River investors. Republican Governor William Sprague of Rhode Island, a prominent textile manufacturer in Cranston, encouraged the deal.[85] Rhode Island got Massachusetts land in Rehoboth near the mill village of Pawtucket, and Massachusetts—the city of Fall River, that is—acquired Tiverton, an additional eleven square miles, thirty-six hundred people, and two million dollars in taxable property, including the old Globe Print Works.[86] The Supreme Court issued the decision in February 1861 effective on April 10, while national tensions mounted over Lincoln's presidency and the Fort Sumter crisis.[87] Colonel Borden, a prominent Massachusetts Republican, cast a ballot for Abraham Lincoln in 1864 as a member of the Electoral College. The Bordens and their connections in Massachusetts, Rhode Island, and Washington, D.C., had helped them redraw state lines for their own family purposes. All had gone remarkably well.

THE TIRELESS JEFFERSON BORDEN

Jefferson Borden developed his own legend based on his dogged commitment to build and, when necessary, rebuild and improve the properties of the Iron Works. A "great fire" on July 2, 1843 destroyed the Pocasset mills and most of the town. Major Durfee collapsed and died trying desperately to save the Iron Works' property. The blame was placed on "Sabbath-breaking boys" who could not wait for the Glorious Fourth and fired off a small cannon in a carpenter's shop, setting it ablaze.[88] It was a hot windy day in a very dry season, and much of the town was built of wood. Volunteer firemen were equipped with hand-operated pumps but there was no water. A bucket brigade of citizens could do little, although a shift of wind saved some of the residential section.

With Major Durfee's death, Richard Borden became the agent of the Iron Works and Jefferson Borden became the sole trustee of the Valentine estate. With his brother's backing, Jefferson acquired and rebuilt the Pocasset in six months and improved the Iron Works rolling mill using company assets. His actions were quick and decisive. Later during the financial panic in 1857, although confined to his bed in a curious repetition of Holder Borden's situation during the panic of 1837, Jefferson Borden saved the Iron Works' financial assets by judicious borrowing. The Providence investors again were impressed.[89]

The introduction of steam power to textile production became essential during Jefferson Borden's years of expansion. By 1850 all the likely water power sites along the Quequechan River had been developed. Two years earlier, George Corliss of Providence had greatly increased the fuel efficiency of his steam engine. It became widely adopted and magnificently celebrated as a marvel of American technological ingenuity and a symbol of the new industrial age. The Iron Works shareholders had observed Samuel Slater introduce steam power into Providence mills, while on their own wharves coal was already piled up to make nails and other iron products. The Works had experimented in 1843 with early proto-types of steam engines in the Massasoit Steam Mill built in the Pocasset complex. Jefferson Borden waited no longer. By 1852 a second steam mill, the Linen Mill, was in operation near the waterfront. The Union Mill organized in 1859 by stockholders of the Iron Works located the new mill conspicuously above the Troy Dam that fed the water turbines down-stream. S. Angier Chace and David Anthony ran this small mill with a Cor-liss steam engine, for they too embraced the future. By 1875, Fall River industry used only eleven water wheels and turbines with a capacity of just over a thousand horsepower, while eighty-one steam engines generated nearly thirty thousand horsepower.[90] Meanwhile the mills of northern New England still depended as late as 1880 on water-powered turbines fed by rivers in Massachusetts, New Hampshire, and Maine.[91] But in loca-tions with limited or without any water power, steam would make falling water unnecessary to making cloth. Along the Atlantic coastline where coal could easily and cheaply be imported, steam took over. Mills in New Bedford, Fall River, Providence, Newburyport, Salem, Portsmouth, New Hampshire, and even rural Taftville, near seaboard Norwich, Connecti-cut, made cloth with machinery driven by steam engines.

The requirements of thirty-one million yards of print cloth for the three Fall River printing mills—the American, Robeson's Fall River Print Works, and the old Globe, renamed the Bay State Print Works—greatly exceeded the local output of eighteen million yards. With the printing machines idled, the Bordens needed more cotton mills. In 1857, the Iron Works were in position to enlarge the Troy, making Thomas J. Borden the agent. By 1862 the Troy had a capacity of nine million yards of print cloth a year. The American Linen Company was converted from linen cloth to print cloth in 1858 and expanded with Jefferson Borden's son-in-law, Wal-ter Paine, as treasurer. It became the largest mill in Fall River until the period of tremendous growth after the Civil War. Jefferson Borden orga-nized the Metacomet Bank in 1854, the largest bank in Massachusetts outside of Boston. The bank's capital of four hundred thousand dollars was raised the first year, mostly from either familiar or familial stockhold-ers in the Iron Works.[92]

By the 1850s, the general attitudes of the Bordens toward their work-force resembled their views on mill buildings and technology. They had rejected the paternalism that had marked the early years of the Boston Associates. Developing after the market revolution had established the acceptance of industry in America, their goals of control and dominance encouraged indifference toward moral guidance, religious values, or pro-tective institutions. These things appeared simply irrelevant or obstacles to market dominance. A remark, attributed in 1868 by an outraged for-mer Lawrence agent to a Fall River mill owner in 1855, provides a telling example of Borden attitudes. The miscreant was either Jefferson or Richard Borden.

> As for myself, I regard my work-people just as I regard my machinery. So long as they can do my work for what I choose to pay them, I keep them, getting out of them all that I can. What they do or how they fare outside my walls I don't know, nor do I consider it my business to know. They must look out for themselves as I do for myself. When my machines get old and useless, I reject them and get new, and these people are part of my machinery.[93]

None of the Bordens or Durfees or their successors applied ethical principles to their industrial pursuits.

The growth of the Iron Works properties and its related activities quadrupled its capital by 1848 and enabled it to launch new ventures and meet disasters. Robert Lamb credited to the Bordens a "natural entrepreneurial ability" and the "instinct to monopolize their control of the means of transportation, communications, credit, and later even merchandising . . . if they could do it."[94] Yet natural ability or instinct or, in a similar vein, the "fragrant" New England heritage of Yankee cultural and economic values attributed to the deceased Colonel Borden remain dubious explanations. The Bordens and the Durfees as well as their rivals in New Bedford and Rhode Island were in pursuit of power, control, and wealth in the market revolution that was profoundly altering American society.[95]

THE DURFEE AND BRAYTON FAMILIES

By the 1850s the Bordens began to face new local competition from allies among the Durfee and the Brayton families. It was no time to alter their attitudes or change their vision. Holder Borden's estate supported the resident Durfee cousins in Tiverton until Major Durfee's death in 1843. These assets pooled by kinship ties had been used to build banks and textile mills to produce print cloth, but not for competitive printing operations. In 1843 S. Angier Chace's sister Minerva became the second wife of Joseph Durfee who had married Sylvia, Holder Borden's middle sister. When Joseph and Minerva Chace Durfee died, her brother, S. Angier Chace became the guardian of his young niece Sylvia Borden Durfee, whose estate, including Iron Works shares, was worth fifty-three thousand dollars in 1854. Having thus obtained a seat on the board of directors of the Iron Works, Chace began insisting upon cash, rather than a distribution of dividends in stock shares, a company tradition.[96] With the encouragement of Sylvia Durfee's uncle, Dr. Durfee, Chace began to invest her estate in the Steam Flour Mill on the waterfront and in two local banks: the Five Cents Savings Bank and the Wamsutta commercial bank. Through these banks he was developing connections with local merchants, small manufacturers, and residents like the Brayton family, perhaps resentful of local Borden dominance and eager to make print cloth and money.

Meanwhile John Summerfield Brayton, the brother of Mary Brayton Durfee (Major Durfee's second wife), became the official administrator of the Major's estate, fat with Iron Works shares. "The estate dropped into his [John Brayton's] lap represented the second largest accumulation of private capital in town."[97] Born in 1826 in nearby Swansea, educated at Brown University, and trained as a lawyer at Harvard, Brayton organized and became president of the First National Bank in Fall River in 1864, just a few months before his nephew could inherit.[98] He also founded and became president of the B. M. C. Durfee Trust Company which backed the 1866 organization of the Durfee Mills, the first in a large number of Brayton family holdings in Fall River. Brayton dropped his law practice to manage the family investments.[99] Together S. Angier Chace and John S. Brayton organized two new print cloth mills in Fall River in 1865, the Granite Mill and Mill #2 for the Union. The race for local dominance had begun and would continue after the Civil War.

FALL RIVER'S BENEVOLENT AND ENTERPRISING LADIES

The competition among Fall River families shaped the social and occasionally the economic activities of their female members. The women of the Durfee and Brayton families, including Holder Borden's mother and sisters, joined the Ladies' Benevolent Society of the First Congregational Church, organized in 1816 by five members of the two families. The church did not thrive until the ministry of the Reverend Orin Fowler in 1831, when membership swelled to nearly five hundred. The Anti-Slavery Society of Fall River had its supporters among some elite families, and the church contained a special pew in a side gallery for "colored" people. Fowler gave up his pulpit for politics, representing the congressional district in 1850 and opposing the Fugitive Slave Act.

The Female Benevolent Society of Troy organized in 1831 with Phoebe Borden Durfee, her daughters Delana and Fidelia, and Hannah Durfee, the sister of Major Durfee, as charter members.[100] Most were middle-class, strictly Calvinist daughters or wives of merchants, lawyers, or large farmers. Several were schoolteachers. The women of the Durfee and Brayton families became prominent; most Bordens were not. Competition among families sometimes divided the social world of these enterprising capitalists. Benevolent society members raised money for training ministers, embellishing the church, distributing caps to boys, and making garments suitable for the poor. They preferred, however, to do fancy needlework to sell at fairs. Their activities were all carried out within the carefully prescribed limits for middle-class women of church and home.

For a few, inheritance or control of substantial estates enlarged their world beyond these strict proprieties.

Undistributed profits and the control of companies and new undertakings by kinship networks among shareholders created interlocking directorates in Fall River backed by marriages, births, and inheritances. Female relatives helped to forge those links by blood and wedlock. Unlike the women of the Boston Associates families, Fall River wives and widows attended the shareholders' meetings, held in the comfort of family homes where female influence might be exercised.[101] When widowed, the Borden-Durfee women usually administered their own estates, relying heavily, like Phoebe Borden, on the advice of their male relatives until they remarried and their new husbands assumed control. Most, but not all, were persuaded to go along with the objectives of the Borden-Durfee men.

At least two women backed rival and annoyingly competitive economic ventures. Amey Briggs Borden, reportedly possessing "sterling traits of character and superior business qualifications," had agreed in 1813 to sell her land and water rights at the Great Falls to New Bedford investors who proceeded to build the Troy mill and the Pocasset Company. The widowed mother of five children, she made the investors promise to employ her oldest son, Nathaniel Briggs Borden, who later bought real estate with his inheritance and represented Bristol County's Ninth Congressional District in the late 1830s and early 1840s. He prospered through his mother's defiant connection with outsiders.

A more impressive example of an independent female was Mary Brayton Durfee Young. Mary Brayton was the daughter of a country storekeeper and the niece of early mill owner David Anthony, Holder Borden's uncle. She attended a state normal school and clerked at her father's store during the summers between 1834 and 1841 when she was not teaching school in Fall River.[102] In 1837 she joined the local female antislavery society. After Phoebe Borden Durfee died at sixty in 1840, she caught the eye of Major Durfee but refused his first offer of marriage. After a lonely trip to England in 1841 to inspect developments in textile machinery, Major Durfee tried again, and Mary accepted. As a new bride in 1842 she lived in the Mansion House on Main Street. In June 1843 Mary Brayton Durfee gave birth to Bradford Matthew Chaloner Durfee. One month later the "great fire" of 1843 made her a widow. She was twenty-nine years old.[103]

The fire that killed Major Durfee also destroyed most of the town, including the only copy of his will. Mary Brayton Durfee decided to contest the legality of her dead husband's trusteeship of Holder Borden's estate which provided generous legacies to the dead Major's wards, the Durfee cousins. Why should her infant son's inheritance subsidize the surviving in-laws? Although Major Durfee's lawyer, John Ford, the new editor of the Whig *Monitor*, testified to the will's contents, the probate court gave the entire Durfee and Borden estates to Mary Brayton Durfee and her son. At once she was rich, and the Durfees (who may have questioned the wisdom of the 1842 marriage) lost their allowances. She threw her influence and wealth as the executor of her son's inheritance, including his father's Iron Works shares, behind new banks and mills organized by her brothers, John S. Brayton and David Anthony Brayton.[104] She and her two brothers organized the Durfee Mill in 1866, intending to make huge quantities of print cloth. John Brayton devoted all his energies to the management of the large estate of his sister and nephew.[105] This post–Civil War development, along with the investment of other interests in competing print cloth mills, would threaten the commanding position that the Borden and Durfee-controlled Iron Works enjoyed in Fall River's economy.

In addition to her widow's one-third, Mary Brayton Durfee paid herself handsomely to administer her son's share of the estate, helped her siblings, and lived well.[106] She was listed in a survey published in 1851 as one of Fall River's richest "men," richer than either Jefferson or Richard Borden or Nathan Durfee. Her son, young "Matt," was named "the richest boy."[107] Her aggressive spirit of competitiveness and her business activities were carefully balanced by a feminine devotion to her son and domestic pursuits. She stayed on in Major Durfee's fine house on Main Street and competed avidly with her neighbors, winning first prizes at the county fairs for the fruits, vegetables, and flowers raised in her extensive gardens. In 1851 when her son was eight, she married Jeremiah S. Young, a Congregational minister from Andover, Massachusetts. He retired from the ministry and became involved in mill investments in Lawrence, while the couple lived both in Andover and Boston. When Young died in 1861, Mary Brayton Young returned to the mansion on Main Street and devoted herself to the education and health of her eighteen-year-old son.

Bradford M. C. Durfee was never robust, unlike his parents. Tutored at home, "Matt" enrolled at twenty as a freshman at Yale College in 1863 but was not well enough to complete more than one year. When he turned twenty-one in 1864 and claimed his inheritance, he donated the Durfee Dormitory, renamed Durfee Memorial Hall after his death, to Yale, established a professorship in history at the college, and made several relatives (probably Durfees) financially independent.[108] John S. Brayton had been his legal guardian since 1860 and quickly acquired power of attorney in 1865. Matt Durfee then spent several years in Europe, obtaining all of his income through his uncle. Well aware that his inheritance was being exploited, Durfee's relationship with his uncle quickly became embittered. From Interlaken, Switzerland, in July 1865, he confronted "Mr. Brayton" with his complaints.

> You who owe everything that you have in this world, the house that your
> sons [were] brought up in, your education and your present support, from

the estate, that I as the only child represent, seem to Care [sic] very little about informing me, about my own business, not even to write once a month, and in fact–never write except when you want more money [from the trust] placed at your disposal.[109]

When he returned, young Matt began to spend his inheritance freely. He bought a yacht, joined the New York Yacht club, and hired a crew. He sailed off to the West Indies to escape the dreary winters in Fall River and his equally dreary duties on the boards of mills and banks. He appeared quiet and courteous, but possessed "inflexible determination."[110]

Durfee made several more trips to Europe, attending the Paris Exposition in 1867 as an official representative of Massachusetts. He remained a frail and cooperative son, while his mother and her brothers continued to invest his money during the frenetic post–Civil War years of industrial growth. Several summers before he died at twenty-nine in 1872, the young "millionaire" from Fall River with money to burn showed off in the resort center of Newport. He drove a span of handsome black horses through the streets, their feet shod in felt to silence their hoofbeats, but their necks garlanded by jingling bells. His death caused by a stroke or "brain seizure" sent his mother into seclusion for a time.[111] Without him to provide for personally, she put all of her investments in the hands of her brother John and withdrew into the Brayton family social circle, emerging occasionally to perform good works.[112]

THE BORDEN LEGACIES

Dogged, energetic efforts by Holder, Richard, and Jefferson Borden to protect and expand the family investments they owned virtually in common inspired the storied activities of the male founders who had built Fall River's industrial might. Amey Briggs Borden and Mary Brayton Durfee Young controlled part of this power and wealth, going their own ways on behalf of their children. These emotionally driven, family-interested decisions can hardly be said to reflect Charles Sellers' spirit of an impersonal market revolution motivated by its own vitality or even simply enterprising individualism.[113] Indeed the Bordens "regarded these related companies [and banks] just as if they were their [own family] company store."[114] The Durfees, Mary B. Young, and the Braytons helped themselves to the inheritances of their wards and relatives, to young Matt's growing disdain. These combined efforts represented their own version of Borden capitalist enterprise, founded on village kinship and family relations.

During the pre–Civil War years the Bordens developed a grand vision of gaining monopoly control in the local production and marketing of print cloth. On behalf of their sons and with the support of brothers, two enterprising women with capital assets sustained the general direction of local industrial ventures. This was the Fall River patrimony of achievement handed on to the sons, sons-in-law, nephews, and male cousins who would manage the post–Civil War industry. The challenge was always to embrace the patrimony and strive to better it. To measure up, they had to shape and dominate the workplace and the workforce as well as the market.

2

GENDER POLITICS AND LABOR REFORM IN THE PROTEST HERITAGES OF ANTEBELLUM NEW ENGLAND

IN 1817, as the first cotton mills appeared in Troy, fourteen-year-old Hannah Borden, a cousin to Thomas Borden's children, including Jefferson, Richard, and Phoebe, coaxed and pestered her father until he allowed her to run a power loom in David Anthony's Fall River Manufactory.[1] She had been taking yarn from local spinning mills and weaving at home on her mother's handloom, used for both household needs and outwork. At eight, Hannah wove her first yard of cloth. She operated the enormous oak-frame loom with foot treadles that raised the harnesses holding the warp, creating a shed of yarn through which she threw a shuttle wound with weft. The work was demanding and time consuming. As her curiosity grew about a water-powered loom, she teased until her father, a shareholder in the mill, spoke to Anthony about a job. He assigned her the village's third power loom made in the Slater shops at Pawtucket. She earned $2.50 for a six-day week. Work began at five in the morning and lasted with meal breaks until half past seven at night. She found the primitive mechanism balky and the warp threads that provided the basic structure for the cloth badly prepared and often simply rotten.[2]

Hannah Borden was not a typical operative in the early Troy mills. She wove custom cloth orders on only one loom, receiving extra pay, although not in cash. Anthony's mill store kept the accounts, paying the operatives only in goods. When Hannah found herself overdrawn on her account, actually in debt to the mill, she asked the clerks, one of whom was Holder Borden, to show her the books. They all refused. Undeterred, she asked

45

Anthony himself. He ordered the clerks to show her the account, where she discovered charges for rum and suspenders.[3] After that she examined the books every month, while the clerks grumbled that no other operative had this privilege. She always said that if other folks would allow themselves to be cheated, she wouldn't. She was the daughter of a prominent Borden. After a year or so of increasing dissatisfaction with the quality of goods at the mill store, she went to Anthony and asked for cash wages. This time he became indignant: "Why if I give it to you all the rest of 'em will want money and I can't stand that. It would ruin me."[4] The mill store provided a steady source of backup profits for early, risky textile operations. Hannah replied in that case she would quit, but Anthony relented, gave her ten dollars, and swore her to silence. She worked as a weaver for two more years until 1820. Hannah Borden alone received cash wages.

The disputed issue of the payment of wages in store goods, not cash money, was one of the early signs of unrest among the workers in the new cotton mills. The men and women of eastern Massachusetts working in the developing system of outwork production in boots and shoes shared this grievance. Textile factories, shoemaking operations, and the various construction trades that built the new towns, the textile mills, and the central shoe shops became the seedbeds for the development of New England labor politics in the early nineteenth century. Most of these workers shared similar social, religious, and economic backgrounds: rural upbringings, Protestant religion, artisan training, and the republican heritage of the American Revolution to which they believed they were entitled heirs.

But there were also many divisions: among cities, towns, rural mill villages, and farms, among skilled trades, low-paid outwork, work performed in mechanized, centralized production, or artisanal jobs done in the shop or at home. These divisions added to differences experienced by men and women workers, native and immigrant, white and nonwhite, operative and mechanic, and among the various ideologies and programs offered by religious and temperance societies, utopian communities, and labor reformers. The similarities and differences shaped a rich and hardy but politically fractured and contentious pre–Civil War heritage of labor reform. Fall River became a crossroad of some of that activity. The industrial development brought to the mill village by the Bordens, Durfees, and Braytons, and by the Rodmans and Robesons, activated local labor protest which reached out into a region swept by profound economic and social change.

IN HIS CLASSIC 1924 study, reissued in 1964 and 1990, *The Industrial Worker 1840–1860: The Reaction of American Industrial Society to the Advance of the Industrial Revolution,* Norman Ware challenged the common belief among historians and the public that the explosive issue of slavery and the coming of the Civil War totally dominated these two decades. Basing his book on extensive research in the pre–Civil War labor press, he argues that in the Northeast—New England, New York, and Pennsylvania—the more important issue was the reaction of the American working class, men and women, to the increasing power of industrial capitalism.[5] As generations of historians have since argued, the antagonistic relations of capital and labor began with the development of the market economy and the early capitalization of the textile industry, continued through the Civil War, and became the primary issue during the postwar era. Ware's book endures as the origin of these arguments. This generally explains what happened in southeastern New England.

Ware separates working-class activities during the decade of the 1840s from those in the 1850s. He labels the labor movement in the 1840s "defensive," rather than "aggressive" as in the 1850s. Defensive labor activists, like the mechanics in the construction trades who sought a ten-hour day, were unwilling to accept the changes brought by industrial development, fearing a dangerous loss of status and independence.[6] Fall River and Boston mechanics and Lynn shoemakers organized in the 1840s, insisting that their white American manhood—embedded in their skills and their rights as freeborn citizens and Protestant believers in the republic—were in peril. The male and female factory workers of Waltham, Pawtucket, Lowell, and Fall River entered the new industrial system but, beginning in the 1830s and 1840s, sought ways to confront it aggressively, in Ware's terms, to reduce hours and raise wages. Certainly Lowell textile operative and labor reformer Sarah G. Bagley, a vigorous supporter of an 1848 Fall River strike (see chapter 3, below) believed that antagonism between labor and capital was inevitable. As powerful as Ware's analysis is, no phenomenon as complex as the industrial growth in the Northeast at this time lends itself to such a simple pattern of defensive and aggressive decades as Ware notes at the end of his work.[7] Fall River's experience with labor protest followed a different path, dividing mechanics and artisans from textile operatives in far more complex ways than defensive and aggressive postures.

Economic Change and the Growing Workforce

The workforce in the early nineteenth-century mill village of Fall River grew slowly. In 1820, the town of Troy had 1,594 residents and two cotton manufactories that employed 850, including numerous outwork weavers, such as Hannah Borden's mother. Seven years later in 1827, the village population increased by about five hundred, with seven hundred laboring in small shops: six cotton factories, two cloth printing mills, and in the Providence Furnace Company and the Iron Works, puddling, making nails, and rolling iron.[8] The cotton factories employed mostly women and children under sixteen. The two print shops required skilled, immigrant English and Scottish block printers and later engravers.[9] In 1827, forty-two of the total seven hundred employed in the village were recorded as "foreigners": English, Scottish, and Irish immigrants. Of these, twenty-eight or 67 percent worked in the print shops as block printers.[10] The population of Troy in 1827 equaled the entire workforce in the renamed town of Fall River by 1837, but the nearby thriving seaport of New Bedford was larger.[11] When a group of leading citizens, including Holder Borden and Major Bradford Durfee, greeted Whig leader Henry Clay in 1833, they described Troy without modesty as the "second manufacturing village" in the state.[12] Lowell with several mills averaging six thousand spindles, was still a town but hardly a village.

In 1837 the Massachusetts economic census listed ten small textile mills in Fall River, averaging 3,100 spindles, half the Lowell average, and employing 357 males and 648 females of unrecorded ages. As in the 1820s and 1830s, they were paid off in goods at the company store, while some lived in small mill-owned tenements. A woolen mill owned by J. and J. Eddy had a workforce of spinners and weavers: sixty-five men and fifty-five women with an unspecified number of child workers. Another 350 men made stoves, hats, nails, and hoops, worked as block printers, as mariners on whaling ships, or made textile machinery. Most were native-born Yankees. By 1840 Fall River had doubled its population to seven thousand. The numbers of spindles and looms rose, requiring a workforce of about 1,800, in addition to the 250 men employed in the Iron Works and ninety in the new Hawes, Marvel, and Davol machinery company and related businesses. In contrast, the Lowell machine shops in 1840 employed from five hundred to twelve hundred men, depending on seasonal demand.[13] The nine mills employed thousands of textile workers. Fall River despite its growth remained a comparatively small village.

A workforce of men, women, and children labored in the early Fall River mills. Hard work, long hours, and severe physical punishment of mill children, as young as eight years old, was routine at work and in school. Benjamin Pearce's memories of his harsh experiences as a young mill boy, beginning in 1827 after his father's death, at first surprised, then angered, and later hardened him. He earned fifty cents (fourteen hours a day) for an eighty-four-hour week in a woolen mill. As weariness overtook him during his first day on the job, his supervisor, a Durfee, woke him with a "stunning blow with the flat of his hand on the ear. . . ." Each morning as he passed through the mill's countinghouse, he faced serious trouble if even a minute late. While young Pearce was in the mill, one fourteen-year-old female operative died of "overwork," according to the assessment of several local physicians. Girls and boys alike received the same harsh treatment. Parents accepted as necessary to learning the whippings and the blistering of children's hands by their schoolteachers. Sometimes as at work, their children resisted. In 1824 Pearce's teacher, a gin-soaked sadist, found himself at the mercy of his angry pupils when they discovered him publicly drunk, unconscious, and helpless.[14] Such revenge was unusual.

Pearce endured the torment in the mills for five years until he was thirteen, frequently receiving beatings with a knotted leather belt. On one occasion his supervisor hit him in the eye with a piece of wood. Benjamin was comforted by his mother at night but awakened before five each morning. Not all young mill hands submitted passively to severe punishment for trivial mistakes. One boy hid out under an opening in the mill floor over a swiftly running stream to the embarrassment of his frantic overseer who believed that he had drowned. Another fitted his jacket with a strip of leather studded with tacks facing outward. As his supervisor began to beat him on the back, the hidden tacks forced the man to withdraw his bleeding hand. The youngster had the satisfaction of seeing his boss wearing a bandage for several days.[15] Mill owner David Anthony treated his own sons, Jim and Fred, much the same way. During the long week he worked them hard without any pay, along with the rest of the "help" or operatives, then insisted on the strictest observance of the Sabbath. His sons were confined to the church or house all day. When the more defiant son asked his father for a day off, the answer was no. Fred then "went down into the wheel pit [of the mill] and cast a large spike into the gearing. . . ."[16] Repairs took several days. Fred got a beating as well as a vacation. Both boys frequently ran away from their father's mill to Boston, and Jim once shipped out aboard a merchantman to China, returning after a few months. Unlike his treatment of Hannah Borden, the daughter of a local investor, Anthony's training of his sons gave them no quarter of any kind.

Most mill women endured harsh language, insults, sexual harassment, long hours, and low wages. They often complained that they had to eat their meals in such a hurry that, in the words of one, "It hurts me." Some were in such fear of missing the factory bell that they could not sleep and rose in the middle of the night. Children cried out in their sleep in fear of missing the 5:00 A.M. deadline. One female operative complained that the overseer's language was "exceedingly profane. . . . It makes me tremble. . . . We live all the time in fear of their abuse." Another said, "I bear it [the abuse] as well as I can. . . . I know we ought to . . . [rise up against it], but there is no union among us."[17] High turnover rates or poverty made organized resistance difficult. The first occurred among Fall River's skilled male operatives.

As members of an early New England association, the mule spinners in the Annawan Mill went on strike in 1832 and tried to prevent the factory from replacing them, but many disappeared from the village as the strike collapsed.[18] Block printers who struck the Robeson works in 1840 over the introduction of engraving machinery lost their jobs.[19] Some stayed on in Fall River to keep shop, learn another trade, or read law, like block printer Louis Lapham, later an ardent labor reformer.[20] Lapham, born in 1810 in Burrillville, Rhode Island, had married young, desperately needed work, and taught mill children for Andrew Robeson, while he studied law.[21] The only successful—but quite surprising—strike occurred during the winter of 1832 when the overseers at the J. & J. Eddy satinet woolen mill joined the operatives in refusing to work an extra half hour a day to fill a large order. Facing financial loss and astonished at the uprising of their own overseers, the Eddys relented. This was the first successful strike in Fall River.[22]

FOUL MURDER AND SEXUAL PROPRIETY

The 1832 murder in nearby Tiverton, Rhode Island, of a Fall River millhand, Sarah Maria Cornell, an enthusiastic but troubled follower of the Methodist church, caused a great sensation.[23] The event revealed growing tensions over class, sexuality, and evangelical religion in the village. The trial of Ephraim Avery, an evangelical Methodist minister, for Cornell's murder by strangulation disclosed evidence of her concealed pregnancy, previous sexual activity and venereal disease, and her reputation as a wanderer from job to job in the textile mills of Massachusetts. These revelations stirred up the widespread fears in early nineteenth-century New England about the consequences of industrial employment to the morality of females, living away from home and family. They recalled the images of degraded, immoral English textile workers in Manchester, England, publicized by early textile developers in paternalistic Waltham and Lowell. The excited disorder of evangelical camp meetings contrasted badly with the regulated discipline of the small mills in Fall River village. Public opinion assumed that Cornell's minister had impregnated her during one such meeting and then murdered her. There were no other suspects.[24]

Cornell's murder and Avery's trial in 1833 intensified the public's belief that women textile workers were morally suspect, safest under the strict rules of company-owned boardinghouses and their mills. Perhaps fearing a loss of female operatives, the town in 1834 changed its name from Troy to Fall River after the trial. The local manufacturers, Congregationalists, Baptists, and Quakers, were forced to defend the unsavory Cornell as a hapless female victim, badly in need of their protection against a predatory Methodist clergyman. Cornell's image, produced in an 1833 engraving for a sensational New York pamphlet on the case, emphasized her partially exposed buxom figure, curly hair, and attractive features as she gazed immodestly at the artist.[25] Her employers described Cornell's sexual exploits as regrettably unfeminine, while Avery, despite his moral profession, was vilified as an aggressive seducer. He was acquitted, but the trial ruined his ministry.

Fall River manufacturers hired Catherine Read Arnold Williams, a forty-six-year-old divorced resident of Providence, to defend Cornell in print. Williams denounced her tragic death, while commending the wholesome factory system in Fall River village. Her sympathy for the lot of women left alone in the world and her genteel abhorrence of evangelicals and camp meetings dominated her account, *Fall River, An Authentic Narrative,* quickly published in Providence in 1833.[26] According to the preface, the book was intended as a warning to young women, not of the dangers of factory work as conducted in the Fall River mills, but of moving from town to town and relying on evangelical ministers, far from the advice and comfort of friends and family. In an appended observation, she lamented the injury done by the notoriety of the case to "that class of young women whose lot in life has compelled her [*sic*] to labour in a manufactory." Her defense of Cornell produced "a great hue and cry" as an injury to religion, but Williams argued that Christians who failed to recognize "the difference between true and false religion" did so at society's peril. At the end of her account, she wrote these lines about her martyred factory girl:

> The waves still wash the peaceful shores around
> where the poor wanderer a grave has found.[27]

The manufacturers' campaign to blame popular religion and aggressive male lust for Cornell's death, supported by Catherine Arnold's praise for the moral order of the factory system, convinced Fall River's mechanics to distance their reform activities from local textile operatives. Abused, overworked children and women, who might be replicas of the notorious Sarah Cornell, were not fit allies for the Christian freemen in the ten-hour day campaign that dominated labor politics in the 1840s. Manly artisans would have nothing to do with wandering females or factory drudges. To some New England women, however, the death of Cornell was an indictment of the dangers women faced in a rapidly changing society where even a clergyman might prove suspect. The rope that had killed her had been tied into a clove hitch, a knot that required two hands pulling in opposite directions. Suicides did not use this method, but strong male hands could kill a feebly resisting female. Immediately after the incident, an eighty-year-old Rhode Island woman wrote a widely read poetic condemnation, "Avery's Knot," adding the infamy to Rhode Island folklore.

> Young virgins all a warning take
>   Remember Avery's knot
> Enough to make your heart ache
>   Don't let it be forgot, . . .
> Hang him, hang him on a tree
>   Tie around him Avery's knot
> Forever let him hanged be
>   And never be forgot.[28]

Polarization of gender definitions arising from the Cornell murder, with men seen either as predatory, heartless sexual aggressors, or as kindly, paternalistic factory owners and with factory women as defenseless, sometimes morally dubious victims, helped divide female operatives and male artisans in labor politics. No coalition emerged to capture the activism stirring within the textile workforce. In the 1820s and early 1830s, "turnouts" or strikes among female textile workers occurred in Waltham, Pawtucket, and Lowell, while the building trades in Boston grew restless and Quincy quarry workers began to complain openly.[29] Temperance movements led by reforming ministers and generally supported by manufacturing interests attracted part of the workforce in the 1830s and 1840s, while evangelical religious societies flourished. Fall River mechanics and some clergymen who supported the ten-hour day seemed particularly stirred by evangelical religiosity and temperance reform.[30] But there were other powerful voices pushing for labor and political reform.

EARLY ADVOCATES OF COOPERATION AND CONFRONTATION

During the years of early labor protest in New England—deeply divided by occupation, community, race, and gender, while generally caught up in religion and temperance activities—one mechanic, Seth Luther of Rhode Island, had a wider, more compelling vision.[31] Born in 1795, Luther was a carpenter who had worked in small local textile mills. What he witnessed in those textile mills propelled him into labor reform. His father's service in the Continental Army during the Revolution and the reactionary nature of Rhode Island government inspired his radical thought and politics. Historian Gary Kulik argues that a concept of the "public good" or "moral economy" shaped the values of Rhode Island dissenters, perhaps including Luther's father, against infringements on preindustrial rights.[32] In addition, the artisans and women weavers of Pawtucket, Rhode Island, joined together in 1824 to strike successfully against a wage cut.[33] Seth Luther emerged from this dissenting political culture. He also possessed deep religious convictions, emphasizing human sinfulness and the need for immediate, harsh retribution. Rhode Island was the strongest anti-Federalist state, the last to ratify the Constitution, and an arena of "class disparities and class cleavages."[34] Luther's radicalism was a response to the inequities of power in his native state, confirmed as a national pattern during his travels to the West and the South in the 1820s where he witnessed the injustices of the government's policy toward Indian tribes and the developing system of slavery. Rhode Island became for him just another arena of privileged white humanity's appetite for oppression.

When Luther returned to New England, he joined the movement to limit the working day for mechanics and artisans to ten hours and became a popular orator in labor politics, well known for his "Address to the Workingmen of New England," printed in three editions in 1832. Described as "tall and lanky" with the ungainliness and "tobacco-stained lips" of a frontiersman, he wrote the address in anger after the defeat of a Boston ship carpenters' strike in early 1832.[35] This document deplored "the state of education and . . . the condition of the producing classes in Europe and America . . . and the safety of our Republic." He spoke to audiences in Boston, Charlestown, Cambridgeport, Waltham, and Dorchester; in Portland and Saco, Maine; and in Dover, New Hampshire. Others in New York and Philadelphia eagerly read his words in print.[36]

The title page of his 1832 address exposed distinguished politicians, such as Henry Clay and John Quincy Adams, as in the service of organized "avarice." The text contained excerpts from speeches in the House of Commons and New England newspapers, and he hoped for translated versions in France and Germany in whose radical politics he took a keen interest. Luther possessed a unique vision of uniting New England's native-born and immigrant people, white male textile workers and mechanics, and connecting them with the wider world of nineteenth-century European industrialization. Both textile centers and commercial towns heard him denounce with scoffing sarcasm the "SPLENDID EXAMPLE of England" as a model for the future of America. He quoted English poet Oliver Goldsmith:

> 'Tis yours to judge how wide the limits stand
> Between a splendid and a happy land.[37]

Luther seemed well acquainted with the miserable working conditions of English textile workers and their struggles with the mill owners. His knowledge came from contacts with numerous immigrant workers in Massachusetts and Rhode Island. Many Americans believed him to be British.

Luther's Whig critics claimed that he opposed the "American system" of Henry Clay. He stated boldly his own republican version of an American system "where education and intelligence is generally diffused, and the enjoyment of *life* and *liberty* [is] secured to all." What, he wondered, would General Washington think of "the American System" and its British "Splendid Example"? "We are the Majority," he closed his speech, often to thunderous applause, thanking God that "the world is not lost." He praised the labor press and pointed out the enemy: monopolists and tyrants who attempt to deprive freemen of their rights. In America, as in England's "Splendid Example," the "Higher Orders" intended to rule the "Lower Orders." His last sentence insisted that the "Declaration of Independence asserts that 'ALL MEN ARE CREATED EQUAL,'" on both sides of the Atlantic.

Luther's interest as a mechanic in American and British textile workers, especially his exposure of chilling stories of the mistreatment of mill children and female operatives in Rhode Island mills, marked him as unusual in New England labor politics. His vision connected English textile workers and their wrongs with those of white American workers, for whom the same fate seemed inevitable. For Luther, the extorting system was not only local and regional, but also crossnational, crosscontinental, perhaps even universal. His understanding of the dimensions of the endangered position of the working class in the United States was unique. Historian Louis Hartz argues, "No American thinker in the whole early American labor movement was so acutely conscious . . . of the world-wide implication" of their labor politics.[38]

Luther criticized pro-manufacturing religious institutions, shouting to his audiences: "Ye cannot serve God and mammon!"[39] This resounding phrase would be familiar to dissenting, chapel-going textile workers from Lancashire and Yorkshire as well as New England natives. He became a writer for Boston's labor reform paper, *New England Artisan,* helped build the Boston Trades' Union, and founded the Children's Friends Society in 1836 to support education.[40] But in the 1830s, New England workers were not organizing effectively. Many textile workers refused to abandon the distinctions pointed out by pro-manufacturing interests between free American workers and English industrial slaves or between white freemen and enslaved blacks. For New England working-class men and women, the connotations of slavery, race, and nationality remained divisive political issues.

ANTISLAVERY POLITICS AND LABOR REFORM

One possible solution to advancing labor reform in New England was a political coalition with antislavery critics of textile manufacturing. A group of Rhode Island Quakers and their sympathizers in New Bedford and Fall River introduced abolitionist politics in the 1830s into the growing industrial region. The key link in this developing chain of antislavery activity was the Buffum, Chace, and Lovell families, men and women who became Garrisonian abolitionists in the 1830s. The most politically active was abolitionist lecturer Arnold Buffum. His daughter Sarah would later marry Nathaniel B. Borden in 1843, thus greatly enhancing his political standing as a Conscience Whig.[41] Sarah's sister Elizabeth married Samuel B. Chace of Fall River. When Elizabeth Buffum first arrived in town in 1825, she and her other sister Lucy, who married a Baptist minister, helped organize the Fall River Female Anti-Slavery Society including plenty of Chaces, Buffums, and Lovells but excluding all black members. The former block printer and lawyer, Louis Lapham, became another friend of the antislavery movement. Strong opposition to antislavery agitation in a rising center of cotton manufacturing convinced the Chaces to move to Valley Falls where in 1839 they took over a cotton mill. They may have been Garrisonian abolitionists, but slave labor continued to produce the raw material for their small mill.

Their experiences of religious persecution as children sensitized the sisters, Elizabeth Buffum Chace and Lucy Buffum Lovell, to the requirements of both pious men and women to fight for religious and social justice. In that, they generally agreed with Seth Luther, a man they never met and whose political reform activities in Rhode Island they probably opposed. Similarly the trial of Sarah Cornell would have distressed and offended them. Their notions of both moral manhood and womanhood included public commitment and personal strength in the face of intimidation and danger. All this constituted, as Chace wrote, "noble self-sacrificing manhood and womanhood. . . ."[42] Elizabeth Chace also remembered the deference paid by Quaker women to the male head of the family, as private patriarchy lurked behind the public face of egalitarian antislavery activism. The Chaces hid fugitive slaves from New England ports, such as New Bedford, on their family farm in Valley Falls, and on such occasions the windows and doors were kept tightly locked. The fugitives were traveling from Fall River safe houses, such as that of Nathaniel and Sarah Buffum Borden. The Chace family also frequently housed antislavery lecturers such as William Lloyd Garrison, Wendell Phillips, Abby Kelley, and Lucy Stone. After 1850, they defied the Fugitive Slave Act, teaching their children its penalties and preparing them for their parents' possible arrest and conviction. Moral right was the duty and responsibility of both sexes, young and old. After the Civil War, Elizabeth Buffum Chace continued to oppose racial segregation in Rhode Island public schools and civic organizations and supported woman suffrage. Still, this wife and sister of Rhode Island cotton manufacturers remembered that her parents and grandparents had never had sympathy for the poor or unemployed and did not believe in charity as a rule, blaming the unfortunate for their condition. Chace never mentions in her reminiscences either ten-hour politics in Rhode Island or the Dorr Rebellion in the 1840s. The fight of the Buffums, Chaces, Lovells, and Bordens against slavery was limited by the class values they all shared.[43] Seth Luther's reform politics and the ten-hour movement for textile operatives would find few allies among them.

The most prominent figure in early nineteenth-century Fall River politics was Conscience Whig Nathaniel B. Borden, the son of Amey Briggs Borden. Never a textile manufacturer, he dealt in real estate, leasing mills to others and losing heavily in the 1843 fire. When he became a man of property, his political interests and party affiliation shifted. As a National Republican and later a Whig, he opposed the secret societies of the elite Masons, holding antimasonic meetings in his own home at the height of public agitation over the issue.[44] In the early 1830s he backed President Andrew Jackson's policies against re-chartering the U.S. Bank and was elected as a Democrat and Antimason to Congress in 1834 and in 1836. Backing away from Martin Van Buren's wing of Jackson's Democratic party, he was defeated as a National Republican in 1838 and became a

Conscience Whig.[45] Borden came to believe that slavery endangered the republic as much as his other nemesis: free trade. He lent his office building in 1834 to house the formation of the local antislavery society. The father of his third wife, Sarah Gould Buffum, was the first president of the Massachusetts Anti-Slavery Society. While in Congress, Borden eagerly backed the fight of John Quincy Adams against the gag rule, restricting antislavery petitions. After his defeat in 1838 he served one more term in Congress in 1840 as an antislavery Whig who abhorred President John Tyler's views on a weaker tariff and on the extension of slavery in the West. He vigorously denounced the Jacksonian Democracy as anti-American just before the 1841 elections, but the town of Fall River still went narrowly Democratic. After his years of service in Congress, Borden confined himself to an occasional term in the Massachusetts senate and house in the 1840s and 1850s. His support for free trade and local industry overrode any reformist sympathies.

PARTISAN POLITICS AND WORKINGMEN'S VOTES

As the workforce in Fall River grew, so did its political activity. The local Workingmen's Party ardently supported Jackson in the 1828 campaign, but without any real influence, they soon rejected both major parties as "mad factionalists" and "greedy partisans."[46] In 1832, a convention of "Farmers, Mechanics and other Workingmen of Troy" assembled to nominate candidates to the state legislature, but none was elected.[47] After a local Whig victory in 1840, the Fall River *Monitor,* edited by John Ford, tried to attract the rising mechanics' movement for a ten-hour day away from the Democrats and to the Whigs. In 1841 an Association of Industry composed of various workingmen, operatives, and mechanics, headed by mechanics Philip Smith and H. N. Gunn published a dignified appeal: "To the Employers of Fall River."[48]

An analysis of this declaration of principles reveals much about the masculinist ideology of early mechanics' politics, including their republicanism and their rejection of class distinctions. They declared, "We are brethren. Our interests, then, must be identical, when properly understood." Mutual economic interest and American patriotism tied manufacturers to workingmen and youth. "All men love their country." Overlong working days threatened the cherished republic with the "twin demons" of "ignorance and vice." Adopting the ten-hour day would provide time for intellectual, religious, and moral reflection by workingmen, activities crucial to the maintenance of republican institutions and manly citizenship. Mechanics' associations would provide lyceums for the mental improvement of white men of all ages. Children under fifteen would attend school for three months a year. Twelve-year-old female operatives trudging through snow at dawn needed the protection provided by the paternal instincts in all men. The association aimed at mutual advancement, man by man, regardless of class. "Without capital, our labor would probably yield a less return; without labor, your capital would not have existence." But, something in this new industrial system had gone seriously wrong and required reform.

Another strand in the Association of Industry's ideology was an emerging nativist imagery, just as the numbers of British immigrants rose in the textile mills.[49] The condition of American society and industry was contrasted with the "abundant and melancholy proof" from English manufacturing, the "Tales of darkness . . . fiery and destructive circle[s] of over-grown stocks, glutted markets, stagnant trade, commercial failures, shut up factories, and a starving population. . . ." Such conditions would be wrong for America and its "virtuous and intelligent people." The declaration ended by inviting a committee of employers to meet with delegates from the association to reduce hours and to enforce the school laws. Although they waited for months, their appeal met only "profound silence."[50] This initial refusal to speak with any delegations of workers became a consistent policy of Fall River mill owners.

The Whigs in Fall River eagerly seized upon the nativist strand in the mechanics' arguments to draw them into their party based on mutual interests in tariff protection. The leaders of the Association of Industry, Gunn and Smith, appeared at a Taunton convention of Whigs in March 1842 on behalf of the "Encouragement and Protection of Home Industry." For the Whigs, the key issue to unite workingmen and employers became the protection of wages through higher tariffs. The ten-hour day had been forgotten. Again and again until the fall elections, the editor of the *Monitor* assaulted "the contemptible pittance" of European labor and the "Locofoco" (Jacksonian) tariff policy of "free trade." Insulting editorials called the Democrats "*Tories*" and simply "locos." European workers were labeled serfs, paupers, and vassals. Colonel Richard Borden, writing under the name "B," insisted that even the coarsest goods would be driven from the domestic market with the slightest tariff revision or what was damned over and over in the *Monitor* as "free trade."[51] On the eve of the 1842 elections, Nathaniel Borden made a final appeal on behalf of the Whigs to the mechanics and laborers of Fall River and Bristol County. Writing in the *Monitor* as "N," he summed up the nativist politics that the local Whigs were embracing. The Democrats, he argued, had become the unprincipled, "anti-American" instruments of English interests, "the tools of the British Capitalist." Vote Democratic and Fall River's mechanics and operatives alike would be reduced to "the miserable" status of English workers.[52] The appeal failed. In 1842 the Fall River Democrats won by a small majority, electing three Locos to the state House. Bristol County went Democratic, and the Ninth Congressional district sent a Democrat to Washington. Former governor and Democrat Marcus Morton, loathed

by Whig editor Ford, won his second term as governor by one vote cast
by a maverick Whig member of the state House of Representatives.[53] Most
mechanics rejected the Whig tariff and nativist appeals and still voted
Democratic in the 1840s.

ARMED REBELLION IN RHODE ISLAND

Rhode Island's "Dorr Rebellion" in 1842 paralleled the political struggle
over the tariff and the workingmen's vote in Massachusetts. Dissidents organized the People's Party and endorsed white manhood suffrage—a
cause championed in the early 1840s by Democrats in Massachusetts and
New York—and called for the abolition of imprisonment for debt, and
suspension of militia duty for those without the property qualification to
vote.[54] They wrote a new state constitution to abolish Rhode Island's
colonial charter (the only one left in the nation) as the legal basis of government and moved to set up an alternative, reformist state government.
At first the editor of the *Monitor* embraced the changes occurring just over
Fall River's town border and rejected "the old rotten [colonial] charter"
in favor of a government with liberally extended suffrage. Bowing to prominent local antislavery Whig opinion, he pointedly proposed extending the
vote, "not excepting the colored population."[55] But as the rebellion
against the established Rhode Island government spread, held its constitutional convention, and elected Thomas Dorr as governor, the old, established Rhode Island government simply refused to be replaced.

When the Dorrites, including Seth Luther, armed themselves against
arrest, editor Ford in Fall River forgot the "rotten charter" and sounded
the alarm.[56] Peace and order in neighboring Rhode Island were being
disturbed. Even worse, the Democrats would undoubtedly back the Dorrites and their reforms to appeal for the votes of disgruntled workingmen.
The *Monitor* transformed the Dorrites from democratic reformers into
lustful traitors, "the *worst men,* acting under the *worst passions.*" Even in
their homes, wives and daughters were in peril from midnight assault by
impassioned Dorrites, who were equated with the scum and dregs of the
notoriously criminal Five Point section of New York City.[57] He expected
Fall River mechanics with manly, moral values to recoil in horror, but the
Dorrite cause for extended suffrage had many Massachusetts sympathizers. When Dorr was arrested in 1842, convicted of treason in August 1844,
and sentenced to life in solitary confinement, some Fall River workingmen assembled to protest his treatment and commend him as a patriot.[58]

When the Dorr rebellion broke out in Rhode Island, Seth Luther was
there, representing the Providence branch of the New England Association of Farmers, Mechanics and Other Workingmen. He had supported
manhood suffrage without property qualifications in addition to many
other working-class reforms. In 1822 the Rhode Island legislature had

made race an electoral qualification, disenfranchising all black men but taxing their property. In the early 1830s a coalition between working-class white and black men, especially in Providence, to undo all voting restrictions seemed a possibility.[59] Luther joined a group pledged to the language of universal suffrage. In *An Address on the Right of Free Suffrage in 1833*, he had compared the condition of Rhode Island's disenfranchised men with slaves, with Polish rebels against Czarist Russia, and English vassals fighting for Magna Carta.[60] While the Rhode Island reformers supported male equality and universal suffrage, no one in the 1830s, including Luther, specifically mentioned race with the exception of a denunciation of slavery. Race would become a major divisive issue in the Dorrite movement.

The future of black suffrage in Rhode Island remained unresolved. Abolitionist Thomas Dorr, the leader of the 1842 rebellion against the old charter, reportedly believed in racial equality. Many advocates of Rhode Island suffrage reform, including Luther, cited the example of Massachusetts law under which free blacks could vote.[61] Others advocated the New York model of universal manhood suffrage for whites and property qualifications for black men. But the Suffrage Association of Rhode Island, formed in 1840, advocated universal white male suffrage in its constitution, even though it encouraged men of all races to participate. Furthermore, many middle-class members of the association distrusted Luther and his radicalism, regarding him as a dangerous eccentric. Indeed he had adopted a phrase from his 1833 address as his motto: "Peaceably if we can, forcibly if we must."[62] Luther had not forgotten his father's Revolutionary legacy, but his reform agenda for white workers turned many middle-class and manufacturing interests in Rhode Island against the Dorrites and universal suffrage.[63]

By early 1841, Dorrite reformers, including Luther, had accepted a white-only clause in the Peoples' Party Constitution.[64] In 1842, abolitionist lecturer Abby Kelly was snowballed by members of the Suffrage Association when she tried to speak in Providence.[65] Swept along by events, Luther, armed with two pistols and a sword, fought in the streets to defend the Dorrite state constitution and to protect Governor Dorr from arrest, while Providence blacks alienated from the People's Party over the suffrage issue formed a home guard to defend the old state charter. Seth Luther was convicted of high treason along with other Dorrites and jailed. Once the old charter remained in place, the state government responded shrewdly to this dangerous situation by enfranchising all native-born men, white and black, but retaining a property qualification of $134 in real estate for the foreign-born—a blow to the fast-growing Irish community.[66] Thereafter in the 1840s, black men in Providence voted the Whig ticket, joining those opposed to Luther's demands for working-class reform and the ten-hour day. Voting Whig did nothing, however, to end widespread segregation in the Providence public schools.[67] Racial divisions and nativism seriously damaged the extension of manhood suffrage and ten-hour reform. Racism and nativism had won over republicanism and labor reform.

TEN HOURS AND NEW ENGLAND MECHANICS

Responding to local politics and the market revolution, *The Mechanic* of Fall River printed its first issue in early 1844. This labor newspaper was directed at "every one," but especially at the "Mechanic, Laborer or a Professional man if he is in favor of the cause of Humanity." The editor, Thomas Almy, had served an apprenticeship with a Providence printer, arriving in Fall River in 1840. He warned his readers: "We expect to meet with opposition . . . , but let the opposition be manly, open and candid." The newspaper's cause was "Human Equality" and the strenuous and fearless defense of "the interests of Labor" against the undue "potency of capital."[68] Almy defined this crisis of manly potency as the oppression of degraded white American craftsmen, resulting from uncontrollable economic change. The rising numbers of immigrant Irish, drawn to Fall River after the 1843 fire by construction jobs, faced open hostility from nativist Yankee workers.[69] Their mechanics' ideology, based primarily on protecting native-born men, would separate mechanics from all immigrants and from textile operatives, male and female. The pre–Civil War drive for the ten-hour day suffered from these divisive issues of nationality and gender. But the *Mechanic* pictured American society in 1844 as divided between capitalists and producers. Two hundred and fifty local mechanics, carpenters and masons, rebuilding the town after the devastating fire, organized to demand a limit of ten hours per day for all skilled workingmen in Fall River. Textile operatives were ignored, but the mechanics themselves were seriously divided. Most declared themselves ten-hour men. They called others "all day men," regarding them with contempt as virtual slaves of the employers, a derisive, racist concept that challenged their status as manly, white citizens.[70] Despite these taunts, needy Irish immigrants and rural workers were eager to work a longer day.

Construction bosses in Fall River recruited workers from other neighboring states, such as Maine, to fill the jobs of ten-hour holdouts. Rural carpenters and masons with farms in nearby Swansea were accustomed to walk miles to their jobs, arriving at sunup and working until sunset, then walking home, arriving about midnight. The next day they farmed, then set out again on foot.[71] The growth of Providence, Fall River, and Boston drew them as well as Irish-born manual laborers. Regardless, the *Mechanic* and the Fall River Mechanics' Association made ten hours the test of the fundamental rights of the majority of white American male citizens. Enterprising interests, which opposed ten hours for mechanics, endangered republican rights through tyrannical class politics by assuming "that the few, with the assistance of wealth, should govern the many." As Almy put it:

> When we behold rapid accumulations of wealth in unhappy contrast with successive reductions of wages, and long hours of labor, with increasing rents and other increasing expenses of the consequently impoverished laboring classes, . . . we feel that it is high time that . . . ameliorating reform take place. [Without reform] there is a great and growing disparity of conditions which is truly lamentable and adverse to the prime aim of our political and social system.[72]

Appeals in the *Mechanic* to other skilled workers in surrounding communities to stay away from Fall River in 1844 and not undermine the local ten-hour contest meant that the mechanics were on strike, although they avoided the term. With the British Parliament debating a law that would limit textile factory workers to a ten-hour day, it was galling to Almy that "even England" should be ahead of "this land of the free" in its thinking on ten hours.[73] The ten-hour mechanics were defining their manhood as courageous republicans, distinct from lesser men such as "all-day" workers and male factory operatives who acted like slaves and were associated with female factory workers. Mechanics defined the ten-hour movement to reflect their artisan skills, manhood, native birth, and political status, but this exclusive policy could mobilize only limited political support.

The use of American freemen's rights to justify the shaping of working conditions in their own community rested on memories of their grandfathers fighting the British at Concord, Lexington, and Bunker Hill. But by the 1840s, the heirs of this revolutionary political legacy began to question the appropriate degree of resistance. After the Dorr disaster, mechanics in 1843 and 1844 swore to use no force or intimidation and not to interfere with the rights of others. Forsaking the spirited activities of their forebears, they decided not to confront their employers aggressively or actually fight for their rights, although the articles, letters, and editorials in the *Mechanic* were full of verbal hostilities, ridiculing satires, and harsh denunciations of their "oppressors."[74] By the 1840s, the meaning of a valiant freeman had changed; the growing economic and political power of manufacturing interests proved too intimidating. Still, a similar republican or "equal rights" ideology encouraged the labor activism of the male artisan shoemakers of eastern Massachusetts who supported the Lynn labor reform paper, *The Awl,* in the early 1840s.[75] Lynn artisans became allies with the ten-hour mechanics in statewide labor politics.

Women workers in textile factories or laboring at home as outworkers for the developing shoe industry in eastern Massachusetts embraced but redefined republicanism and artisan rights. In the early 1830s, women shoebinders in Essex County applied artisan political ideas to their own grievances. They organized protests and, like Almy, expressed moral outrage at their low wages and the overweening power of capital. Women shoe workers did not claim equality with men, "the stronger sex," but they sought to extend their public activities and exercise their claim to "inalienable [political] rights" of "peaceably assembling to consult upon the common good."[76] Like female textile operatives, they believed that they shared in equal rights won by their ancestors in the American Revolution. The violation of Christian values by immoral market competition reinforced their activities.[76] Women textile workers, as historian Thomas Dublin argues, had no craft or artisan tradition to draw upon, but, as "daughters of freemen," they conducted strikes, made speeches, wrote articles, and organized ten-hour petition drives.[77] Their activities combined artisan culture, gender experience, religion, and politics. As the shoe-binders claimed and refashioned the political culture of artisans for the language of their activism, so the women textile workers created a rhetoric of protest out of the religious and political culture they brought with them from rural New England to the factories. The mechanics' ten-hour movement would fail to respond to these women activists.

In *Ten Hours' Labor,* Teresa Murphy argues that labor protest among female textile workers in Massachusetts was more empowered by their use of Protestant religious ideology and moral reform as critiques of market capitalism than by a male-oriented assertion of republican political heritages. Workingwomen, only virtually represented politically, could more readily participate in the public arena as moral activists and in reform politics when these were transformed into a religious cause. Without women's religious activism, Murphy argues, the ten-hour movement would have remained the domain of men: skilled, white, and oblivious to the interests of female operatives. The use of religious language and Biblically inspired attacks on textile capitalism helped activists operatives wield the ten-hour petition as a political weapon against opponents. But despite the use of piety and religious rhetoric by workingwomen, religious institutions and reform politics remained highly patriarchal. Female preachers could find only roving ministries, raising additional questions about the morality of evangelical camp meetings. Labor reformer and textile operative Sarah G. Bagley of Lowell possessed a broader vision of women's rights and a well thought-out political and economic critique of industrial capitalism. She organized a regional association of female factory operatives for labor reform, but religious motives did not appear to be *more* significant to her activities than political and class analysis.[78] But Murphy, unlike other scholars examining the connections between religion and labor reform, insists that battles over moral authority in growing factory towns involved tensions over gender relations between men and women, reaching into family life as well as the workplace and the church. Female factory workers and the wives of artisans and mechanics became objects of patriarchal reaction, defined as vessels of domestic virtue and best confined to the household and out of politics. The gendering of the ten-hour movement produced images of resistant skilled white mechanics who protected useful but subordinated female activists and domesticated women.

WHIGS, MECHANICS, EVANGELICALS, AND TEN-HOUR POLITICS

Fall River mechanics also used religious language and imagery to develop a critique of industrial capitalism and to push for ten hours, and so did the manufacturers to oppose ten hours. Whig Nathaniel Borden defended the local textile mills in 1844 against criticism from the *Mechanic's* editors and their outspoken clerical allies, such as pro-ten-hour Baptist clergyman, Asa Bronson, revealing class divisions between the manufacturing interests and the mechanics' ten-hour movement. As a prominent local politician, Borden attended a Fall River Mechanics' Association meeting to hear the Reverend Bronson speak on the issue of ten hours, which in Borden's view, had left Fall River "considerably divided."[79] Borden denied that fewer hours of labor would lead to moral improvement, citing the corruptions of New York City as an example of more leisure time for workingmen. He linked strenuous industry and the development of manly Christian virtue. But more important, he insisted that the ten-hour issue was fundamentally an economic issue, not a moral or religious one. If mechanics worked the same hours as in other industrial centers, Fall River's advantage of lower costs and its resulting prosperity would vanish. Furthermore, he warned, if Fall River's mechanics got ten hours, the textile operatives would demand the same, allowing competitors to undercut the local textile business. Borden, in contrast with Thomas Almy and the ten-hour mechanics, saw the general workforce as inherently interconnected. "[I]f Fall River succeeds and prospers, as a manufacturing place, she must produce her manufactures as cheap as they are produced elsewhere."[80] Borden elevated industrial competition to the status of natural law, turning it into a hallowed ancestral heritage. "The cheapness of the production is the governing principle. . . . "; we must maintain "the system as practiced by our fathers." Because natural, time honored economic laws regulated production, all must obey or else all would fail. This argument—using supply and demand and the threat of Fall River's competitors as a justification for every wage cut, changes in working conditions, or any other policies that the mill owners chose—became their staple response to worker protest throughout the nineteenth century.

Rev. Asa Bronson responded vigorously to Borden's arguments. Ten hours and the world of work were indeed issues for religion and morality. "We must," he wrote, "meet the question now before us like *men, patriots,* and *christians.*"[81] To view industrial competition as a supreme law was "idolatry." For Bronson, God's laws commanded men to take care of their families' morality, religious duties, and health. He regarded patriarchy as essential to a Christian republic. The skilled white Protestant freeman became the symbol of moral reform, but Bronson also pointedly *included* textile operatives in the ten-hour movement, setting Borden and the whole Fall River industry unalterably opposed to such talk. Most mechanics and artisans would have agreed. The local pro–ten-hour clergymen developed their own definition of American manhood. Bronson admitted that the current maxim that "money makes the man" had become widely accepted. The equation of success and the work ethic with manhood which led to the unjust oppression of the laborer, therefore, required the elevation of the down-trodden mechanic to his rightful place in society. But the ten-hour clergy of Fall River faced opposition from more conservative ministers.[82] Bronson thus rejoiced at the potential moral influence of a "ladies' auxiliary" formed by the wives of mechanics, much like one in Lynn in the early 1840s. He warned the mechanics' association to reject "*kick ups and turn outs* or *any thing* that looks like *mobocratic violence.*" Seek your rights, he insisted, in "a calm and respectful, but *decided and manly* tone, assert them; they will be heard and the cause will triumph. Let them show themselves as *men.*"[83] Reform-minded clergy reinforced both the manly rhetoric and the moderate tactics of the association, but by the autumn of 1844 ten-hour reform stalled. Pro-labor clergy in Fall River like Bronson were helpful to ten-hour reformers but in a strictly limited way. They were exceedingly useful as allies in local politics, but they did not speak directly for the mechanics or for the operatives. Instead, they acted primarily to reassure the town's middle class, the boss mechanics, and the wavering skilled male workers that the ten-hour movement was both moderate and moral. Furthermore, in late 1844, Bronson left Fall River and his divided Baptist congregation, which included Jefferson Borden, for another pulpit.

Historians Jama Lazerow and William R. Sutton challenge the dismissal by many labor historians of the significance of religion and religious rhetoric as central to antebellum working-class culture and labor reform.[84] Like Murphy, who also uses Fall River as a case study, Lazerow criticizes the privileging of workingmen's republican ideas over the values of Protestant evangelicalism. But unlike Murphy, Lazerow and Sutton ignore gender analysis and focus on white male artisans. In my view, the evidence on Fall River fails to demonstrate that evangelical religion or the support of pro-labor clergymen was more important to working-class labor reform than the issues of politics, class, skill, race or gender.[85] Both manufacturers and workers quoted the Bible with ease on behalf of their interests, including that model Christian gentleman, Colonel Richard Borden, who spoke eloquently against the ten-hour day. Religion and religious expression remained central to antebellum working-class culture, even if religious movements failed to empower reform politics any more than had pre–Civil War artisan republicanism. Nonetheless, this religious heritage as a critique of industrial capitalism had the potential to link American labor reformers with the increasing numbers of British working-class immigrants from Lancashire and Yorkshire, many of them chapel-going religious dissenters, who had already dismissed industrial capitalism as anti-Christian and amoral. After Seth Luther emerged from prison, he would find allies among them in 1846.

DILEMMAS FOR THE MECHANICS' MOVEMENT

Eighty percent of the 250 carpenters, masons, and mechanics in Fall River vowed in 1844 to work only ten hours. Almy quickly appealed to skilled workers in other communities "as men of honor" and "as christians" to stay away from Fall River and instead help to spread the ten-hour doctrine from Maine to Georgia. He also ridiculed antislavery politicians, such as Nathaniel Borden, for ignoring the "white" slaves and drudges in the town's factories.[86] A letter from "Ten-Hour Man" in May 1844, stated boldly the mechanics' definition of real American men.

> The time has come when we must come up to the work manfully and make a strong and long effort to knock the shackles from the hard hand of the laborer, riveted by unfeeling aristocracy. The inalienable rights of him, who is the power and glory of our nation, will be respected and revered equaly [sic] with the capitalist.[87]

Advocating strength, courage, power, glory, and republicanism while using phrases about "strong and long effort," knocking shackles off the hands of [white] workers, and defending inalienable republican rights against offensive aristocrats sum up the mechanics' exclusive ideal of early nineteenth-century manhood. There were even a few ready to act forcibly, advocating the taking up of arms to conquer or die, as did their revolutionary forefathers.[88] Seth Luther had done so in Rhode Island. This decidedly minority view that threatened violence and class strife alarmed Almy and quickly vanished from the pages of the *Mechanic*.

Almy and his supporters faced a nasty dilemma over limiting true American manhood to the supporters of the ten-hour movement. Were the fifty or so mechanics in Fall River who worked longer than ten hours less than real men? What were the liabilities in sneering at "all-day" men? If the ten-hour mechanics had already lost their inalienable rights to capitalist oppression, what means were manful, moral, and forceful enough to regain them? After agitating "legally, firmly, and fearlessly; temperately, prudently, wisely and perseveringly," what if they were ignored?[89] In the mid-1840s, this incessant use of the terms *manhood* and *manfully*, and the admonitions to be a republican Christian man for ten hours turned into an ideological obsession and a political snare, not a solution or a strategy for labor reform.

How to achieve reform remained a vexing question for Fall River mechanics. Long before 1844, economic power had shifted into the hands of the local wealthy capitalists. Gaining ten hours through united, local action seemed the best way to alter the imbalance and restore equal rights. The mechanics of New York City, Philadelphia, and New Bedford had already achieved a ten-hour day. The employers in Fall River had to be made to respect religion and morality everywhere: in the counting-houses, at building sites, and, once achieved for mechanics, perhaps even in the textile factories. Workingmen must have time to think about their situation in the new economic system. How would they achieve ten hours and change that system? And to what? The Massachusetts ten-hour movement in the 1840s never resolved this issue.[90]

THE NEW ENGLAND WORKINGMEN'S ASSOCIATION

During the summer of 1844, the arrival of "all day" men from Maine, recruited and escorted to the town by a local Quaker minister, Jacob Viney, seriously challenged the ten-hour movement. Something had to be done. Almy had severely criticized incidents in which the tools and tool chests of Maine workers ended up in the harbor, but now he personally led a delegation of sixteen to the house where Viney boarded. He was about to leave for Maine to get more men. They went directly to confront him after a meeting of the local mechanics' association, arriving a little after 9:00 P.M. Two men approached the boardinghouse, but Samuel Shove, the son of the boardinghouse keeper, refused to admit them. Almy insisted that he "called us mean, good-for-nothing scoundrels" and that they left after five minutes.[91] John Ford of the *Monitor* leapt on the situation, printing a letter signed by "A Mechanic" picturing the visit as a night of terror by cowards who had unmanned themselves by attacking a helpless woman.[92] A "mob" led by Almy had surrounded the house of widow Elizabeth Shove late at night, insulted and abused the family, refused to disperse, mocked, hissed, disrupted the peace, and outraged the "decencies" of society. This incident, along with the destruction of property and insults hurled at "all day" men, revealed the repulsive, unmanly character of the leaders of the mechanics' association. Sensing an opportunity to destroy the ten-hour movement in Fall River, editor Ford let himself go, calling Almy "an ass without brains" and "a scoundrel devoid of every honest and manly principle." "I despise," he concluded, in defense of the supposedly cowering Widow Shove, "a mean and cowardly spirit in every man." The association could only advance with a more "judicious, prudent and manly course."[93] After the uproar, there were no more street meetings, tool breakages, or confrontations. Almy realized that Ford's charges of unmanly and repugnant behavior injured public support for the ten-hour cause and damaged the movement. Reformers were being denounced in public, caught in their own rhetorical and ideological trap.

In response to their deteriorating situation, the mechanics' association sent a circular during the summer of 1844 throughout New England calling for a regional convention to discuss the ten-hour movement. Almy believed that, "we are fast approximating toward the disagreeable, servile and degrading state of the English laborer." The ten-hour movement, he stated, was based on God's design and the great principle of the Declaration of Independence, that all men are created free and equal on "*the common ground of EQUALITY, MAN WITH MAN.*"[94] Almy's desperate call for a statewide convention, however, shifted the ten-hour fight away from the construction sites of Fall River and into the complex and unpredictable labor reform politics of Boston, Lynn, and Lowell.

Differences emerged at once. The Mechanics, Operatives and Laborers of Lowell responded very quickly, "as a strong man awaketh out of sleep, full of vigor and manliness."[95] The members welcomed the convention call as a means to unite the workingmen of Fall River, Lynn, Boston, and New York. But in contrast to Lowell's united coalition of mechanics and factory operatives, Almy was advising the Fall River textile workers to organize a separate delegation to the convention.[96] The Lowell Association proposed a Boston meeting in early August to champion ten hours, universal white male suffrage, religious toleration, free schools, an end to piecework in the mills, and, most important, to invite female textile operatives into the new association. Millworker Sarah Bagley began to organize the Lowell Female Labor Reform Association to represent workingwomen and their grievances throughout the New England textile industry. Manly workers in the Fall River Mechanics' Association would face the prospect of sharing the public platform with activist female factory operatives. Women without a craft tradition or accepted public role, without the vote or access to apprenticeships—all conditions linked to respectable manhood—might have political goals or unknown reputations that could complicate, divide, and defeat labor reform. Similar political problems faced antislavery and temperance women. In these movements, activist females seemed to undermine unity and action.

The Mutual Benefit Society of Lynn Cordwainers welcomed the convention appeal, writing "as your brother craftsmen in the *Awl.*"[97] But their grievances differed somewhat from the ten-hour demands of mechanics and millworkers. They wanted to protect apprenticeships and obtain cash wages instead of store credits, regarding both as central to their ability as artisans to earn a "competency," a term that meant both family security and independence in old age. Their confidence in the righteousness of their cause was total. They were "American freemen," the descendants of their "patriot sires." Well organized, they wanted a meeting as quickly as possible, perhaps in Lynn. The Boston mechanics supported the idea of a convention and suggested a date in September that coincided with the Mechanics' Fair held at Fanueil Hall, described in the *Boston Laborer* as the cradle of liberty, "where our fathers were *waked up, . . .* [and] can never *rock to sleep* the sons."[98] All the construction trades in Boston had first to be brought into one strong association. As for textile operatives or unskilled laborers, they must—as in Fall River—organize themselves. But the obstacles to combining even the Boston trades into one united group prompted second thoughts. The editor of the *Boston Laborer* asked: Were the mechanics ready for such a convention, would there be time to spread the word, would the representation of Massachusetts mechanics be complete?[99]

Each community and each system of production had its own difficult problems. Lynn shoemakers worked by the job lot, not by the hour, as the Reverend S. C. Hewitt discovered during his travels as an agent for the Fall River Mechanics' Association. Almy had hired Hewitt to probe the potential for labor reform in the region and supported delaying the convention until September.[100] Meanwhile the *Mechanic* opened its columns to advocates of Associationism, the followers of the utopian ideas of Charles Fourier, for whom ten hours was a minor concern, and to advocates of national land reform and worker cooperatives.[101] As Hewitt scoured the region for reform sentiment, D. S. Pierce, also representing the Fall River Mechanics' Association, went to Portland to address the Maine Mechanics' Association on ten hours. He was rudely rebuffed. Ten hours was a "Massachusetts question," not for men Downeast, who voted not to send any delegates and criticized the convention circular's "excited passions."[102] The likelihood of organizing as a region seemed more and more in question. Local politics distracted mechanics in Vermont, and in New Hampshire only Manchester had a mechanics' association. The millworkers in Connecticut villages were discontented but unorganized, and in Rhode Island, any talk of ten hours turned the advocate into a despised Dorrite, especially in Providence. In late September the *Boston Laborer* worried that "no course of action has, as yet, been pointed out for the convention to pursue." Furthermore, only Massachusetts planned to send delegates, some representing only one craft and from "a very small part of the State." In what way, asked the despairing editor, can harmony and unity among employer and worker be restored in the face of the "general scramble after glittering dust . . . ?[103] The convention had already been postponed until October.

On the eve of the first New England Workingmen's Association convention, Almy, like the editors of the *Boston Laborer,* became genuinely perplexed. Where, he asked, is the plan of action? Who will be the leaders? Shall we join the National Reform Association against the sale of public lands to speculators? Or shall we adopt the ideas of Charles Fourier of which we know little?[104] The Boston activists also worried about doing something. "This is no boy's play. . . ."[105] We must act like men but how? If we do nothing, the Boston editors worried, we will have cruelly destroyed our own efforts. This sense of critical urgency to decide and act in a convention hastily organized—that nonetheless had to propose *something*—left the door wide open to articulate advocates of Fourierism, supporters of land reform, and the spectacular speech-making of both Mike Walsh of New York City and of George Ripley of the Brook Farm cooperative in West Roxbury, Massachusetts.

Two hundred delegates from many Massachusetts towns and villages, but mostly mechanics and artisans from Lowell, Lynn, and Fall River, met at Faneuil Hall on October 16 to pass virtually every resolution that was proposed, indicating that no definite solution or strategy had been adopted.[106] Nonetheless, the convention endorsed ten hours, and resolved to petition the legislature. Producer cooperatives, free education, land reform, and a permanent organization of labor reformers were encouraged. Associationism was to be examined, while the delegates scheduled another convention in March at Lowell. But the tedious formalities of convention protocol and election of officers during the morning hours delayed the passage of resolutions until the afternoon and evening sessions while the working-class delegations began to leave.[107] An eloquent convention address, reported in the *Mechanic,* repeated the well-known political charges against an unjust economic system. "Money has become power" [and] "labor [has become] a commodity to be bought and sold in the market." When man "must sell his commodity—his labor—his manhood—to another," he becomes "a helpless victim." Workingmen must be elevated through unity of action, frequent meetings, and a permanent organization. "At present," it was admitted, "we are divided, isolated and opposed . . . , but the undaunted zeal of the fathers once more reanimates the sons. . . ." A "bloodless victory" was expected with the recognition of the workingman "as EARTH'S TRUE NOBLEMAN."[108] Almy praised the convention's work, printed the speeches, and watched as his debts mounted.

STIRRINGS AMONG THE FALL RIVER TEXTILE OPERATIVES

In early September, the textile operatives of Fall River revived the old Association of Industry and renamed it the Fall River Workingmen's Reform Association. Significantly, it included female operatives. One reform-minded, if oblivious, clergyman called on them to "work together . . . as one man."[109] Meanwhile, the leaders of the Fall River group, including H. N. Gunn, admitted: "we had almost forgotten we are men—with rights and duties as men; and citizens. . . ." The public rhetoric of ten-hour reform in Fall River remained stubbornly masculine, despite growing female involvement. Almy urged these operatives to unite to fight overwork and wage cuts, but as the approaching autumn shortened each day's light, the textile workers seized an issue that might arouse genuine middle-class support. Mill owners had already begun to light their factories with oil lamps and candles against the winter's approaching dark, both in the morning and at night, a policy that occasionally caused small mill fires. This "lighting up" in the morning required operatives, young and old, to drag themselves out of bed before 5:00 A.M. and trudge without breakfast through the dark, muddy, snowy, and often bitterly cold streets. Light up only at night, the operatives in Lowell and Fall River asked, "for humanity's sake."[110] Almy claimed that in Chicopee Falls, Massachusetts, united action had persuaded the mill owners not to light up in the morning, allowing their operatives to begin work after breakfast.[111]

The *Mechanic*'s support for the organization of factory operatives was tardy and quickly became openly contemptuous. Almy published articles, based on male fantasies about morally degraded female workers and full of denunciations of factory work as contemptible white slavery, the grounds for the ruin of female workers. These letters regularly appeared in the issues between November 1844 and April 1845 when the *Mechanic* ceased publication. In contrast to superior mechanics' daughters and wives, factory girls were depicted in these articles as unfit for marriage or household work, uneducated, ignorant, and unable to raise children. "A thorough factory girl is a wasteful, tawdry, slatternly person," who would cut bread and pie for supper without washing her dirty hands and who preferred her dress oily to keep off the rain. As a group they were "but sluts."[112] Both factory oppression and "too close familiarity with males" injured their gentle female natures. They lost their femininity, developed "loud coarse voices," and became "too *bold*." Expressions of moral but dependent womanhood in the 1840s were far harsher but just as exclusive as those of the artisan shoemakers of Lynn. As historian Jeanne Boydston argues, the hidden nature of women's housework in the early nineteenth century provided an ideological context in which mechanics' wives could be idealized, while factory girls might be scorned as loud, greasy slatterns.[113]

The writers "N. N." and later "Howard" claimed considerable experience in the mills and characterized factory work in New England as wage slavery "far viler than slavery." Both claimed that southern slaves were treated better under the law than northern workers, both at work and during old age. "N. N." castigated male factory workers as political slaves, forced to vote for their employer's candidate. "Assert and defend your rights as free men, or as men that by right ought to be free."[114] Elevating white male workers remained the ten-hour mechanics' central interest, while factory slaves and female operatives became objects of contempt.

Despite some outcries of indignation and letters of protest, "N. N." continued his harsh attacks.[115] Factory operatives failed to perform their religious duties properly, he argued, sleeping through church meetings. As parents, they had no time for morning prayers or table blessings, and they allowed their children to break the Sabbath for playtime. Factory children ended up ruined and immoral. The factory system also corrupted the mill owners' families. "They [the sons] . . . believe that they are born to be supported, to live in splendor, and to rule . . ." [T]his is "anti-republican."[116] In early 1845, "Howard" took over from "N. N." in the *Mechanic* and continued to blast the factory system. He had worked in a mill for four years, felt his physical strength ebbing, and left, but he too complained that "ignorance, immorality and vice go hand in hand" with factory work. Less scornful of millworkers and more aware of the employer's power, he explained that fathers had to send their children to work if they wanted to keep their own jobs. Considerably more optimistic about the possibility of change, he believed that ". . . had the population . . . *time* and *power,* . . . they would unite as English workers had done, to reform the system."[117]

The editorial policy of the *Mechanic* shifted its main interest away from the ten-hour campaign after the inconclusive October mechanics' convention. Almy found that land reform, meant to draw off surplus city workers and raise wages, was more in step with his own developing acceptance of the marketplace ideology of supply and demand and the realities of regional economic competition. He urged New England workingmen to give both land reform and Associationism "candid and earnest consideration" as the way to reorganize society and protect the "primary rights of man."[118] But the editors continued to advocate the merits of the ten-hour system. Almy's shift proved divisive. Benjamin Chace, the coeditor of the *Mechanic,* immediately and strongly disagreed with Almy's drift toward utopian solutions and insisted that ten hours remained the most significant reform for workingmen. Editorial disputes and rising debts began to undermine the *Mechanic.*[119]

To Almy, the greatest danger lay in the inaction of Fall River's mechanics as the 1845 spring building season approached. In 1842 they had signed and sent to the legislature the first petition for ten hours, but the Lowell movement with its female members was far more active.[120] Lagging attendance hampered both the local mechanics' association and the Workingmen's Reform Association. Almy's response was to blame the workingmen themselves for apathy: "if they will not relieve themselves from their burdens, they must bear them."[121] By mid-January, Almy grew even more concerned that his efforts were failing: "WORKINGMEN, IF EVER REDEEMED, MUST REDEEM THEMSELVES." Fears divide us, cause disaffection, and create disunion,

> Yet we advise no rash and retaliating measures. Outbreaks of passion and violence can never raise you up one step. . . . Demand your time [ten hours] with a man-like behavior and perseverance, accumulate wealth if you can, associate to control your own business and to share the profits.[122]

These sentiments came close to embracing the ideology of the new industrial order. Without reflection on the consequences, Almy was equating Christian manliness with the laws of industrial capitalism. Meanwhile, the *Boston Laborer* had suspended publication in late 1844.[123]

By February Almy was so discouraged with the Workingmen's Association that he urged them either to disband or unite with the mechanics.[124] Everyone looked toward the next building season. Harsh words against those who abandoned the ten-hour system turned the manly rhetoric of American mechanics into vituperative attacks on the hesitant or the slacker.[125] Almy grew more outspokenly critical in his editorials.

> Who is a man but he who resists wrong? Who is a man but he who maintains the right, though with the patriots of the revolution, he may have to pledge his life, his fortune and sacred honor? . . . Never let it be said that the mechanics of Fall River, have treacherously and cowardly yielded up their rights."[126]

Criticism of the anti-ten-hour employers vanished from the *Mechanic*'s pages. Nothing but the "disunion or avarice" of the local carpenters, masons, and manual laborers, he argued, can prevent the adoption of the ten-hour system. Yet after this crushing denunciation, he offered a compromise to the employers: eleven hours in the summer and nine in the winter. Almy's opinion of the prospects of the coming season were shared with many others as rumors circulated of "all day" men from Boston streaming into Fall River. A letter from "D," a ten-hour man, was merciless in his condemnation of those willing to work longer.

> You commenced vigorously, resolutely, manfully . . . [to] have your rights restored. . . . Now your interest is growing cold while your enemies will seek to break the cause in the coming season. Do you repent supporting the ten-hour cause? If so, go like men and make your confessions. . . . Tell them [the employers] and all others you were very wrong, and return again "like a dog to his vomit." You sell yourself for "a mess of pottage."[127]

The derision of those who, as lesser men, gave in to economic pressures coincided with the decline of the mechanics' ten-hour movement. The rhetoric that once inspired freemen to action could turn reformers into cynics and vilifiers of their own divided class.

The New England Workingmen's Association convened in Lowell on March 18, 1845. Fall River sent delegates, but as in October this convention, although formally admitting the Lowell Female Labor Reform Association, could not find a coherent strategy. The convention embraced utopian and countless other reform proposals, including "cheaper access to lawyers."[128] Few local workers bothered to attend a Fall River convention in September 1845, although Mary Reed broke the silence of the Fall River factory girls by briefly addressing the meeting in the interests of ten hours.[129] The association had already fallen under the influence of middle-class abolitionists, land reformers, and communitarians, who like Almy, blamed the workingmen for their plight.[130] Between 1845 and 1848 the labor reform movement would be taken over by middle-class reformers, but ten hours remained the major goal of Sarah Bagley and other articulate women millworkers in the New England Labor Reform League.[131]

Almy had a surprise announcement in the April 1, 1845, issue, his last. Increasingly drawn to conservative views, he reported the formation of a new, quite different, association: the Bristol County Charitable Mechanics' Association which would include employers. This association intended to open a library and build a hall for the education of workingmen. In the *Mechanic*'s last issue, he recommended to his subscribers the newest paper in town, the *Fall River Weekly News* which he would edit with John C. Milne, also a member of the new charitable association. Almy and Milne began publishing the *News* as a Democratic alternative to the *Monitor*, appealing to workingmen to stay away from the Whigs. But as the Civil War approached, the *News* embraced the rising Republican Party.[132] Meanwhile one of the key opponents of ten hours, Conscience Whig Nathaniel Borden, contributed to the emerging Republican organization. In 1851 as a state senator during a general political revolt in Massachusetts over the Fugitive Slave Act of 1850, he abandoned the official Whig candidate for the U.S. Senate to cast a crucial vote electing antislavery advocate Charles Sumner. His constituents, he insisted, had demanded it.[133] The election of Sumner split the Whig party in the state, destroying it. Borden had defied the conservatives in his party on the slavery issue and remained popular enough to be elected the second mayor of the city of Fall River in 1856. Pro-manufacturing political interests captured the antislavery issue, while labor reformers had consistently used racist rhetoric to distinguish free white men from slaves.

THE HERITAGE OF THE MECHANICS MOVEMENT

In the 1840s, neither the Fall River mechanics nor Thomas Almy acknowledged any inevitable hostile relations between capital and labor. As white, native-born freemen, they expected a share in the benefits from industrial development. They possessed a political and ideological heritage from their forefathers based on the values of republican manliness, apprentice-trained skill, whiteness, and Protestant religion. They tried to organize regionally to extend their influence while articulating an ideology of republican manhood to justify the pursuit of their rights. In this they failed. Their definition of a mechanic's manhood excluded too many other male workers of different skills and nationalities and in other industries. Their hostility toward textile operatives, especially workingmen, exposed the narrowness of their organizational and political vision. For these mechanics, their own homebound wives and daughters represented respectable womanhood, unlikely among female textile operatives with whom they would form no political alliance for reform.[134] They could not forget the character of Sarah Maria Cornell and the imagery of those dirty factory sluts.

Norman Ware in *The Industrial Worker, 1840–1860,* divides the strikes during the 1840s and 1850s into offensive and defensive. The evidence on Fall River suggests that during these two decades community, occupational, gender, racial, ideological, and skill differences, not aggressive or defensive stances, were more important characteristics of labor protest and ten-hour politics. New England workers created two persistent strands of labor protest in the 1840s: one by native-born, skilled, white, male mechanics and artisans and the second a coalition of white, native-born, male and female factory operatives. The terms *mechanic* and *operative, male* and *female* indicated vast differences in status and politics. Yet Ware's conclusion that this period ended "practically in nothingness" is not justified.[135] Even in his own terms, the Lowell textile strikes in the 1830s and 1840s were aggressive. He does not include in his argument the aggressive textile strikes in Fall River in 1848 or in 1850–51.[136] According to Ware, even the great New England shoeworkers' strike in 1860 was primarily defensive for many workers and "utterly lost." This complex strike, however, represented a turning away from the labor politics of white male artisans and mechanics toward a confrontation with the new factory world.[137] The labor protest of workingwomen as shoebinders in the 1830s, as textile operatives in the late 1840s, and stitchers in shoe factories in 1860, pointed toward the future of labor conflict in New England.

Ware argues that the year 1845 represented the high point of the pre–Civil War labor movement. But in Fall River both workingmen's associations, composed of mechanics and textile operatives, had already collapsed. The *Mechanic,* Lynn's *Awl,* and the *Boston Laborer* had ceased publication by early 1845. Disintegration and decline in Fall River and in Lynn did not, however, continue into the 1850s. The mechanization and centralization of shoemaking, especially for women workers, and new sources of aggressive labor reform followed. Ware may have oversimplified his categories, but his emphasis on the significance of conflict between labor and capital in the pre–Civil War decades remains without challenge. His pathbreaking book, emphasizing both the political and religious opposition of working people to industrial capitalism, continues to inspire additional research and writing.

Seth Luther's views on the potential for reform if white male mechanics and male and female operatives united on religious and political grounds represented the most radical, promising inheritance from these years of Yankee protest, despite the racism inherent in his Dorrite politics. Luther's conception of equal rights and social respect included all white industrial workers in the American republic and those in Europe. His insistence that industrial life and politics must involve questions of morality, religion, and economic justice constituted a valuable protest heritage, as British textile workers with similar values immigrated to New England in the 1840s and 1850s.

3

BRITISH IMMIGRANT TEXTILE WORKERS AND THEIR CLASS CONSCIOUS LEGACIES, 1820–1865

AFTER THE defeat of the Dorr rebellion, Seth Luther spent some time in Rhode Island jails. Unable to bear the confinement, he set his cell on fire in Newport and tried to escape but was recaptured, then released in 1843.[1] Although a broken man, both physically and emotionally, he went to Manchester, New Hampshire, in 1846 to support a ten-hour rally organized by English immigrant John C. Cluer, a former weaver, temperance advocate, and radical reformer.[2] With Seth Luther at his side during these ten-hour meetings, Scottish-born Chartist John Cluer, who had fought in England for the ten-hour day and universal manhood suffrage, represented the transfer of English political legacies and agitation to New England textile centers. After he returned to Massachusetts, Luther collapsed and was committed to another prison: the East Cambridge lunatic asylum.[3]

Skilled British immigrants proved essential to the early development of the American textile industry. When parliamentary legislation in 1825 lifted a ban against the emigration of skilled workers and artisans, mill agents hired British immigrants as machinists, mule spinners, dyers, and cloth printers who had learned the block method in Manchester, the major textile city in Lancashire. Immigrant calico printers filled "English Row" in Lowell.[4] As experts in indigo dyeing, these men helped run Andrew Robeson's printing works in Fall River. Beginning in 1837, William Martland, a block printer from Burnley, Lancashire, worked for decades at the American Print Works.[5] Male and female handloom weavers from England and Scotland produced fancy checked, plaid, and twill cloth. Nearly every mill had some skilled British help, and many aspired to become small manufacturers or at least overseers. English immigrant Samuel Slater, who had broken the pre-1825 English blockade on mechanics, and his protégé, Yankee Paul Moody, contributed priceless mechanical abilities for technical improvements. Without them, there would have been no Pawtucket, Waltham, or Lowell mills.[6]

Although many British immigrants guarded the secrets of their trades, native-born workers, despite their suspicion of English textile workers, would learn from them both advanced techniques at work and new protest tactics in strikes. Lancashire workers also immigrated to the textile industry of Philadelphia in the 1820s and 1830s where they contributed their skills and experiences of radical politics to local labor protest.[7] When British textile manufacturer James Montgomery visited the New England mills in the 1830s to offer managerial and technical advice, he carefully warned the agents "not [to be] overbearing and tyrannical" or "too distant and haughty" when dealing with their immigrant workers.[8] He was warning American capitalists that the traditions of Lancashire and Yorkshire popular radicalism were mass-based and ran deep.

By the 1850s, immigrant labor from England, Scotland, and Ireland dominated the workforce in New England textile factories. New Bedford's Wamsutta Mill, incorporated in 1846, employed many English workers.[9] Lancashire cotton operatives in Fall River and New Bedford "abounded as nowhere else" and far more than any other immigrant group. Some later rose to supervisory positions.[10] Rhode Island mills filled up with them. Their subsequent labor activity contributed to new levels of class consciousness and new styles of protest among New England textile workers beginning in the late 1840s and early 1850s and continuing throughout the nineteenth century. This contradicted the destiny that the Borden and Durfee families believed belonged to them: domination of their sector of the textile market through investment, innovation, and firm control of the workforce.

CHARLOTTE ERICKSON's work on nineteenth-century British emigration represents a lifetime of toil among carefully selected primary sources of private letters and diaries, passenger lists, English and American population censuses, and county histories in both countries. In *Invisible Immigrants: The Adaptation of English and Scottish Immigrants in 19th-Century America* (1972) and *Leaving England: Essays on British Emigration in the Nineteenth Century* (1994), she recovers the detailed experiences of relatively few immigrants on farms and in small businesses, largely in rural American society.[11] Erickson chose to avoid issues of class consciousness or labor conflict in either nation. She rejects class analysis explicitly: "I have tried to develop a history from below free from the preoccupations with the making of the working class and the congealing of class consciousness."[12] In spite of her repeated warnings that her chosen few were not representative, her work on these immigrants has assumed great weight among historians, as has Roland Berthoff's *British Immigrants in Industrial America, 1790–1950*. Based on Berthoff and Erickson's work, British immigrants became defined as culturally invisible and politically conservative people who adjusted easily to American society.[13]

Erickson's choices of primary sources made it impossible for her to trace major groups of British immigrants to industrial cities such as Fall River. Passenger lists and private letters underrepresented women and overrepresented male immigrants with the money or desire to buy land and farms. She commonly equates artisans with industrial workers. Erickson's use of New England county histories—books paid for and scrutinized by the native-born upper middleclass—is helpful as a source for only the most successful immigrants. Erickson's studies provide little information on how working-class immigrants from Lancashire and Yorkshire or any other region behaved or thought in the United States or how they might have influenced politics and culture in their new homes.

Roland Berthoff's earlier work follows immigrants into American industrial cities but deals with no particular industry, city, or region in depth. His survey covers textiles, mining, metalworking, building, quarrying, papermaking, and potteries. The skilled British workers in these industries, without language or cultural difficulties, assimilated quickly into nineteenth-century American society. Berthoff regards Fall River activists as exceptions to the conservative nature of most British immigrants. This chapter begins an exploration of the complex experience and politics of working-class immigration from Old England to New England textile mills throughout the nineteenth century. Based on their legacies of organization and protest, many Yorkshire and Lancashire immigrant operatives in New England were neither invisible nor conservative.

Popular Radicalism and Gender Politics in Lancashire

British workers brought with them, depending on the timing of their nineteenth-century immigration, varied experiences of political activism and labor protest. These included bread riots, strikes, mass demonstrations, and in the early 1830s and 1840s, working-class demands for increased political representation, the ten-hour day, annual Parliaments, secret ballots, and universal manhood suffrage: later the keystones of the Chartist movement.[14] Long before the Chartist movement got under way, the impact of early mechanization on hand spinning and weaving and the use of steam engines in Lancashire inspired collective resistance, machine breaking, arson, and other less violent but well-organized opposition to the shift of craft work into steam-powered factories.[15] Earlier, the displacement in the late eighteenth century of household spinning done by women on distaffs, wheels, and small jennies (spinning frames with multiple spindles) by larger mechanisms run by water power in mills created open and covert resistance. Both men and women outworkers destroyed machinery and held back materials as protest against low wages.[16] The British political and economic establishment in Lancashire often reacted to early nineteenth-century strikes, mass demonstrations, and Chartist agitation with repression.

No act of repression proved more bloody and lethal than the Peterloo Massacre of August 1819. Eleven peaceful demonstrators, weavers and spinners, nine men and two women, were killed and scores of others injured by local troops in St. Peter's Field near Manchester. Contemporary illustrations of the gathering crowd emphasized its mass and "dreadful" potential. Conservatives equated popular radicalism with the hated Jacobinism of the French Revolution, its symbolic red cap of liberty, and haunting calls for liberty, fraternity, and equality.[17] Historian James Epstein's study of this language, ritual, and symbol in radical protest between 1790 and 1850 also analyzes the symbolic involvement of women textile workers from Lancashire in these radical, public politics and the spread of this female activity to Yorkshire and beyond. English conservatives ridiculed and condemned the sexuality of female working-class activists in radical politics although, according to Epstein, the demeanor, dress, and activities of these respectable women were carefully controlled. The Tory cartoonist George Cruikshank lampooned female radicals in 1819 as wanton mothers of dwarfed children and as females with bulging bosoms and bare thighs overshadowing one emasculated man dressed in skirts.[18] Radicalism, according to this image, unleashed female sexuality and upset gender relations in the family. As in New England, most men of all classes came to oppose the prospect of uncontrolled female intrusion into the manly realm of political activism.

Another cartoon by George Cruikshank, printed in December 1819, illustrates how to English conservatives, the symbolic cap of liberty represented not only radicalism but also the sexual threat implicit in demands for political reform. Titled "Death or Liberty," a reference to the imagined threats of republicanism associated with Jacobinism, the drawing depicts a collapsing, almost prostrate female Britannia with an ineffectual sword, "The Law," in her strong right arm, her back against the rock, "Religion." A skeletal male figure of Death, representing radical reform by wearing the cap of liberty and masked with the calm face of a moderate reformer, clutches Britannia's left breast. The figure's penis is an iron arrow from which hangs an hourglass, its sand running low. A cruel rape is imminent. Howling radical skeletons in chains stand by ready to join in. In the distance the British lion of manhood hastens to the rescue. The shocking possibilities displayed in this image—the likely consequences of British men's failure to defend the nation from radicalism—revealed the primitive sexual tensions that Cruikshank believed all Tory men should feel in the face of mass demonstrations organized by the working classes and their sympathizers, as in Manchester in 1819. Sexual tensions were especially provoked when some of those threatening demonstrators were female. These Cruikshank cartoons suggest that British honor and virtue had been saved at Peterloo, even if women were victims.[19] English conservatives derided female political activity as the equivalent of sexual perversion.

Historian Catherine Hall chooses two participants in the mass meeting that turned into Peterloo, weaver Samuel Bamford and his wife Jemima, as reflecting prototypical sexual divisions within the early nineteenth-century English working-class family at work and in radical politics.[20] Their gender roles made their experiences on that day quite different, but Hall notes the "discord" that persisted among some women, despite the almost universal agreement among male activists and later the Chartists that women should be controlled by, and subordinated within, the patriarchal family. Tensions rose over the egalitarian gender ideology of Owenite socialists and the mobilization of women to support radical causes, some of whom voted in public meetings, indicating a measure of female interest in political equality. Jemima Bamford told her husband that she was determined to attend the Manchester meetings, with or without his explicit permission, which he gave her anyway. When he was jailed, she took over his handloom and became a textile worker, supporting her child.[21] The ideology of the hierarchical domestic circle dependent on the male breadwinner and the tensions resulting from conflicts over gender politics became part of the heritage of Lancashire working people.

Anna Clark's *The Struggle for the Breeches: Gender and the Making of the British Working Class* emphasizes the significance of gender relations in the organization of early nineteenth-century radical reactions against industrial capitalism. She argues that the textile workers of Lancashire, not the London artisans, provided the vanguard for English class formation based on the inclusive organization of family and work life in cloth production. The misogynistic and persistently violent gender antagonism between radicals and artisans and their families in London limited and subordinated women in radical politics and the Chartist movement. Women later involved in Chartist agitation were marginalized politically and forced to accept a domestic ideal imposed on the movement by middle-class reformers and radicals tied to London artisans.[22] These struggles between men and women reflected conflicts over power and access to power and were thus fundamentally political. The legacies of class consciousness and gender relations among Lancashire workers would become important to New England labor politics.

The Lancashire heritage also included a traditional social order sym-

bolized, in the words of historian Lawrence Stone, by the "hat" of deference—the opposite of the cap of liberty—doffed to one's betters to ward
off the "whip" of hierarchical authority.[23] Even as the rise of textile industrialists and a propertied middle class challenged the remnants of this
traditional society with a new political economy based on market calculations, mid-nineteenth century Lancashire society, especially at the local
level, retained elements of the old social order of "ascribed status, lineage,
traditional sources of wealth, patronage, deference and vertical ties of interest linking rich and poor. . . ."[24] Historian Theodore Koditschek's analysis of the worsted wool center of Bradford demonstrates a local commitment to community values by early nineteenth-century working-class
activists, largely skilled male woolcombers, that defended the traditional
values of a moral economy against than the new market ideology.[25] Lancashire traditions also cherished the ideal of a moral economy as a measure
of mutual obligations and social justice in the community.[26] Thus English
immigrants transferred to New England a skepticism toward amoral supposedly "natural" economic laws, such as supply and demand, controlling
marketplace activities.

Responding to heightened class tensions after Peterloo, the Reform
Bill of 1832 granted more parliamentary representation for growing industrial districts such as Lancashire, but no further reform legislation followed. This ineffective effort at conciliation led to renewed demands for
political change organized by the Chartists.[27] The political uprising that
advocated the People's Charter, a list of radical reforms emphasizing universal manhood suffrage, alarmed the supporters of established politics
and institutions in England. The repression of Chartism in the early 1840s
meant that its leaders were jailed or hounded from politics. Many immigrated to the United States and headed for Fall River, New Bedford, and
Lawrence.[28]

Working-class immigrants who fled repressive English policies were
also drawn to the United States by demands for their skills, the promise
of the vote, and ease of acquiring free land, avoiding the leases common
in overcrowded and land-poor England.[29] Although the English working
class did not have a written republican heritage, such as the Declaration
of Independence, the Bill of Rights, or manhood suffrage, as immigrants
they generally agreed with many angry American workers that textile capitalists in the United States were tyrannical, un-Christian, unjust, and
amoral.[30] They readily joined in and helped reshape the labor politics of
pre–Civil War strikes and union organization in New England. They
brought with them the traditions of the hiss, haloo, and British salute of
"Hip, Hip, Hurray" to use in derision against strikebreaking "knobsticks."
They also brought a political culture of labor protest, including union
organization, strike activity, consumer cooperatives, and friendly societies.

Protest Legacies of Lancashire Spinners and Weavers

British immigrants prior to the Civil War brought specific organizational forms and strategies of labor politics as well as a general legacy of popular radicalism to the New England textile industry. Sexual divisions of labor and class politics that subordinated women formed part of that legacy. Spinners in Lancashire in the 1830s and 1840s joined "short-time" or ten-hour reformers to keep women out of mule spinning. They defined working-class manhood and respectability through the authority of adult mule spinners to supervise their helpers, called piecers and minders, in English spinning factories. The spinners successfully prevented women from operating the self-acting mule in Lancashire but not in Scotland. Manhood was also associated with the ideal of the family wage, one large enough for the male "breadwinner" to support his wife and children and keep them out of the mills, while female respectability meant devoted domesticity and social and sexual propriety.[31] Some spinners used their daughters in the 1830s as piecers to contribute to family income, but unlike their brothers, these young women had no chance to become mule spinners. If it was a question of employing their children to sustain the family economy, some mule spinners did not object to females around their machines.[32] Manhood linked to skilled work and degrees of authority had practical limits. Still, English mule spinners defined working-class male respectability through skill, workplace authority, and the family wage, while the ideal of female respectability became domesticity and moral propriety.[33]

Negotiations between union men and their Lancashire employers at midcentury, during what historians call the mid-Victorian compromise, involved a gender component that also defined manhood as rational, sober, and conciliatory. "Master" and "hand" appeared mutually respectful. English male workers shed their brutish public images, formulated by their opponents during the early days of violent reactions, demonstrations, and Chartist agitation. They began in the 1840s and 1850s to cultivate the behaviors and attitudes of conscientious, self-educated, and serious men who ran consumer cooperatives like small businesses. These complex behaviors helped secure the respectability of working-class men also regarded as responsible breadwinners.[34] Most important, however, by the 1850s mule spinners had begun to negotiate wages and working conditions as union men with their employers. This moderate course, aptly termed by historian Deborah Valenze a "fitful dialogue," continued as long as the business cycle did not produce mass unemployment and provoke strikes. Then moderation turned into confrontation as in the hard-fought strike in Preston, Lancashire, during 1853–54.[35]

In the early nineteenth century, handloom weavers in England had opposed the employment of women and children in factories, regarding them as cheap labor, easily coerced. In this they failed. Before and after the legal establishment of the ten-hour working day in 1847, both sexes commonly tended steam-driven power looms in Lancashire.[36] Consequently, English mule spinners and weavers developed different kinds of organizations and strategies to defend their interests. Spinners recruited young men and boys to the trade, chosen to assist operations as piecers and minders. Under the direction of the spinner, they watched for and tied up broken ends as the huge, wheeled mechanism was driven back and forth on its rails, twisting out the yarn to specifications, graded by numbers rising from coarse to fine. Young male piecers and minders put up with low wages in exchange for the chance to become mule spinners. As spinning machines grew larger and heavier, they required physical strength beyond the capacities of most women who could still operate lighter mule frames. This system also required supervisory authority regarded as inappropriate for women. Many Lancashire spinners brought to New England in the pre–Civil War years their experience in the effective organization of small numbers of carefully trained and closely supervised, skilled male workers which empowered their unions. After this was accomplished in key textile centers, they would seek a strong regional organization.

In contrast, the weavers' organization in Lancashire accepted both men and women who had worked together in the handloom weaver's cottages and later in the steam-powered factories for equal piece rates. But equal piece rates did not mean equal wages.[37] Male weavers commonly ran more looms on better paid work, but women weavers still earned the highest wages available to most females in textile work. The overriding goal of all weavers was the establishment of a standard list of piece rates that determined wages in the Lancashire cotton goods industry. The structure of the work and the employment of both men and women in weaving meant that a regional standard of wages was far more important than the sex or skill composition of their unions. In Bradford, Yorkshire, however, male woolcombers, like the mule spinners, formed a key element in trade unionism, friendly societies, cooperatives, and Chartist politics that distanced female powerloom weavers in factories from their organizational activities.[38] These different experiences and policies would shape the activities of British immigrant textile workers in nineteenth-century New England mills. Thus Lancashire working people brought with them conceptions of the proper relationship between men and women in the family, in the mills, and in labor politics, policies that would be tested in post–Civil War New England during this period of rapid change, economic depression, and popular struggle. The meaning of working-class republican manhood in antebellum New England was already being contested between the ideology and politics of the mechanics' movement and the textile workers' political agitation for ten hours in factories.

British Activists in New England Labor Politics

Chartist John C. Cluer, born in Glasgow, Scotland, in 1806, had become such a "forceful" and disruptive presence in English labor politics that he left in 1839 for New York City.[39] He spoke as a former weaver and fellow-worker to audiences in Manchester, New Hampshire, and Lowell, Massachusetts. Throwing himself into the ten-hour movement of the 1840s, he became as popular a public speaker as the ten-hour agitator Mike Walsh of New York. Once, using his knowledge of the industry and posing as an English textile manufacturer, Cluer gained entrance into the mills of Fitchburg, Massachusetts, attracting at least twenty female workers to a meeting on labor reform. Textile workers showed few signs of believing the charges of drunkenness, immorality, or criminality thrown at Cluer by the anti-ten-hour editor of the *Lowell Courier,* William Schouler. Invited to a Lowell meeting in 1845, he addressed a large and friendly audience. One activist woman, who worked in the Lowell mills during the late 1830s and early 1840s, remembered that although she often fell asleep at ordinary lectures after work, "I was never too tired, however, to listen to . . . the friends of Labor Reform, such as . . . John C. Cluer or Mike Walsh."[40]

Cluer's great moment came in Manchester, New Hampshire, during the winter of 1845–46 when he seized the leadership of the ten-hour movement. He proposed "to mobilize operatives throughout the region" to hold discussions with their employers about a ten-hour day—an unlikely prospect. Then Cluer advised a vigorous petition campaign to the legislature, like English ten-hour reformers were then pressing on Parliament, to be followed if unsuccessful by a mass demonstration on the Fourth of July, the American commemoration of republican resistance to tyranny. His audience of Manchester men and women textile workers vigorously endorsed his bold proposals. Cluer thereby combined "Old World patterns" of resistance and tied them, with Seth Luther at his side, to New England republicanism and labor reform.[41] The divisions and failures of the ten-hour mechanics' movement in New England made new sources of inspiration, strategy, and style vitally welcome.

There was no demonstration on the Fourth in 1846, but in 1847 the Lowell mills cut the working day by forty-five minutes. The New Hampshire legislature passed a ten-hour law, but one full of loopholes. Still, both manufacturers and politicians had at least taken some notice of Cluer and his ten-hour supporters. Meanwhile, in 1847 Parliament adopted a ten-hour day for textile workers. In 1848, when immigrant weaver John Norris led a weavers' strike in Fall River, he too, like Luther and Cluer, would blend elements of English and American labor protest. British immigrants and New England workers in Fall River joined together to oppose unjust treatment in 1848. And in 1850 they did it again.[42]

THE FALL RIVER STRIKE OF 1848

On February 24, 1848, John Norris, Michael Clark, and Thomas Nelson were indicted by a Fall River grand jury for creating "riot" and "terror" on February 7 in connection with a weavers' strike.[43] The weavers and other operatives, including the mule spinners, overcame their differences to create a coalition born of discontent and unrest. Native-born Yankees and foreign-born workers from England combined as workingmen and workingwomen to oppose a surprise wage cut and introduce English protest customs and tactics into the streets of Fall River. The events of the strike and the results of the jury trial point to patterns that would persist in regional labor politics for the rest of the nineteenth century. Likewise, when the mill owners decided to crush this uprising and eliminate its leaders, they too established a policy followed consistently thereafter.

At the grand jury proceedings, open to the press and the public, the prosecutor vividly described the case against the three men. Profits had fallen and wages were reduced; "Great alarm and terror had existed for days in the community." A public meeting largely of male and female weavers had been held and, according to the prosecution, "a narrow view taken." The weavers decided to try to prevent those lawfully employed in the Troy and Metacomet mills from working, shutting down operations. In a final dramatic flourish, "he, the counsel, had witnessed them attacking an orphan."[44] All this, he insisted, constituted riot. The defense lawyer, Louis Lapham, the former block printer and a ten-hour man, argued that there was nothing in the laws of the Commonwealth that prohibited the weavers' activities and that they were protected by the Bill of Rights. Therefore, there had been no riot. His statement received "hearty applause" which the judge immediately silenced.

John Norris, a recent immigrant from England, "where [he later admitted] he had incurred the displeasure of the manufacturers," had arrived in Fall River a few months before the strike erupted.[45] A wage cut between 5 and 17 percent had been announced without warning for weavers and many other categories of workers including mule spinners. Overseer Stephen Davol at the Troy mill testified that for the last twenty-five years no advance notice had ever been given for wage reductions. The overseer at the Metacomet mill stated that he had announced the cut on "the night [of January 29 when] I got my orders," to take effect on February 1.[46] No trouble was expected, but native-born and English immigrant weavers felt differently.

According to Norris, the town filled with angry textile workers holding meetings in Mechanics' Hall. He was invited to join them and offered to provide some leadership based on his experience in the "Old country," but he immediately faced the anger of the Yankee operatives at the increasing competition from experienced British immigrants. Nativist ten-

sions between the two groups threatened to undermine the strike. At one
meeting, Norris was told that:

> the Old country people were the cause of the reduction of wages; that
> they had come to take the bread from the mouths of the Natives. One
> Native girl said that they were never exposed to such unjust proceedings
> before the emigration of the Old country people, and that if the Old coun-
> try people would do their duty, the Yankees would do theirs.[47]

Duty meant a turn-out or strike, the provocative word that the ten-hour
mechanics in the early 1840s had never used.

Norris later said that he had tried to conciliate the situation by requesting a meeting with the manufacturers to learn the reason for the
wage cut. If they refused, the operatives should refuse to work and persuade as many as possible to do the same. He recalled that Colonel Richard Borden, the president of the Troy mill, had told him that unless he
stopped his agitation, he would become "*a marked man*" and would be refused employment or blacklisted throughout New England.[48] This routine
threat was frequently carried out against labor activists in the textile industry throughout the nineteenth century.

Nothing further happened until February 7, 1848. During a morning
meeting with Norris presiding, the strikers agreed to go to the Borden-
owned Troy and Metacomet mills and, as the operatives came out at noon,
confront them and follow them home. The natives would handle the
native-born workers; the English, the English; the Irish, the Irish; and the
Scots, the Scottish.[49] There were nearly fifteen hundred operatives in Fall
River, about 5 percent mule spinners.[50] Eyewitnesses at the meeting later
testified that Norris had continued drawing on his experience in "old England." "There they got their rights, [stood] up to their rights."[51] The
meaning of these rights differed profoundly from those sought by the Fall
River mechanics in the 1840s. Norris was referring to the rights of industrial workers, not the republican patrimony of Yankee free-born sons.

As he began to get worked up, remembering the old days, Norris drew
on his English experiences. For those women who remained at work, "we
must go with them from the mill and if they continued to work their green
veils would be torn from their faces. . . ." A great sensation swept the room
at this allusion to male interference with female operatives especially from
English immigrants. The allusion to "green veils" had a specific, cultural
meaning for the British; in popular slang, "green" suggested a sexual lib-
ertine or even a harlot.[52] Norris hastily added, "not [torn] by our own
hands, but by the [wage] reduction."[53] He then moved on to state that he
had known "manufacturers reduced from wealth to poverty in England
by turn-outs" and advised the strikers to give those who continued to work
"three British cheers" in derision: Hip, Hip, Hurray! Call any English
strikebreakers "knobsticks," he advised, a term quickly applied to all who

refused to join in.[54] Norris was telling the operatives that they had some potential collective power in the situation and how to use it.

A crowd of several hundred went to the Troy mill. At first, the strikers let the mill owners know they were there by kicking at the door of the Troy countinghouse and knocking on the windows. This was unheard of; the feared sanctuary of the countinghouse had been violated. An overseer at the Troy came out and told them to go about their business. One female striker (probably a woman named Bridget Mullin) who was dancing her defiance in front of the door replied that "she wouldn't go about her business."[55] A few women strikers later testified that they told this "very bold young woman" to stop at once. They strongly disapproved of this and other aggressive female behavior such as snowballing strikebreakers.[56] Tensions later became apparent between native-born and immigrant female operatives. Nevertheless, many of the activists, even among those who threw snowballs at the non-striking workers, were workingwomen. Many came forward to testify for the defense. The most rebellious was Bridget Mullin, although she was not charged.

Norris, who was standing in front of the Troy carrying a walking stick, quickly began to lose control of the situation. Scottish immigrant David Wilson, a striking weaver at the Metacomet, admitted under cross-examination at the grand jury proceedings on February 24 that he believed Norris "was going to do all he could to force us out of work."[57] Other prosecution witnesses identified Norris and Michael Clark as the leaders. Despite the morning protests, many of the Troy workers returned to work after dinner. Then Norris, flourishing his cane, led the crowd to the Annawan Mill.

The prosecution at the grand jury proceedings chose its witnesses well: young Yankee women new to town who had worked only briefly in the mills, including a timid wife clinging to her husband. Twenty minutes before noon on February 7, operative Ann Bell had come out through the Troy countinghouse door. She testified to the grand jury that "they said I was one of them. I did not know any of them." As an American, she felt no connection with striking immigrants. When she failed to respond to the invitation to join in, she was pelted with freshly fallen snow until she reached her boardinghouse but returned to work after dinner. She admitted that she was "some afraid when they followed me."[58] Others who left at noon were yelled at, snowballed by young women and boys, and also followed home. Mill personnel escorted several workingwomen. Isabelle Morey's shawl was taken from her and stamped upon in the snow. "Somewhat frightened," she had a nervous headache after work. Morey had been at work in Fall River for less than a year. Maria Stockworth from Salem, Massachusetts, recalled that she was pushed off the sidewalk and snowballed. "I was so afraid I could not see. . . . Had I known that they would have done so, I should not have come; I was a stranger to the place and people." Lydia Knopp, who had worked at the Metacomet for about a year, testified that she was so afraid that she asked her husband to accompany her to and from the mill.[59] Their testimony of fear and confusion particularly influenced the grand jury, confirming the image created by the Cornell murder in 1832 of the factory girl, alone, insecure, and in great need of protection from all kinds of danger. The mills would try to provide this protection, especially against the antics of striking foreigners.

The defense conducted by Lapham produced some hardier, more experienced female witnesses as well as male operatives who were familiar both with Fall River and with the indicted Michael Clark who had worked there for over ten years. They repeatedly testified that Norris and Clark had not counseled violence nor engaged in throwing snowballs. Norris' cane, which he needed to help him walk, had been used in helpful ways to discourage snowballing youths, to open a way for the workers to depart and reenter the mills, and to summon the crowd to move on. They explained Clark's shaking his hat in the faces of the overseers as a signal to the strikers to give the British cheers and to encourage derisive yelling at the operatives. Ellen Ennis, an unmarried twenty-eight-year old English immigrant with nine years of experience in the Fall River mills, defended Norris's behavior as peaceable and as an attempt to protect the nonstriking women. A number of young female operatives at the Metacomet reinforced this testimony. But, under cross-examination, operative Flora Bennett determinedly admitted, "We come for our rights. Yes, to get the wages put back."[60] All three men were indicted, and the trial was set for mid-March.

In support of the defense, editor Thomas Almy argued in the *News* that the British cheer was piece of "merriment." As a hit at locally prominent Whigs, he insisted that everyone had the right to hurrah in public, even if it was for "*log cider* and *hard cabins,*" a reference to the 1840 presidential campaign slogans of log cabin–born and hard cider–drinking Whig William Henry Harrison. Solid citizens and newspaper editors in Fall River had, furthermore, derided their Democratic opponents as "locos." Cheering, Almy argued, was not a riotous act, and Norris could not be held responsible for the acts of others.[61]

Through his connections among the block printers, attorney Lapham produced an alibi for Thomas Nelson from a former block printer and boardinghouse keeper. Nelson was acquitted. The outcome of the trial in mid-March turned on the legal definition of *riot*. Timothy G. Coffin, a more experienced lawyer, replaced Lapham and summed up the case for the defense. There had been no repetitions of "disgraceful" English scenes in Fall River.[62] The meeting that proceeded the congregation at the mills on February 7 had been entirely lawful and peaceful. What is a riot? he asked. An assembly of persons who on their own authority behave in a tumultuous manner, committing unlawful acts and carrying dangerous weapons to attempt to terrorize the community. Being afraid, he pointed out, was not necessarily the same as being terrorized.

The prosecution zeroed in on just those fears inspired by strange doings in the streets near the mills and by Norris' and Clark's role in promoting them. A tumultuous crowd had assembled on their own authority to prevent the operatives by violence and threats from going to work. "All this was done to the terror of the people. Actual violence is not necessary to terrorize." The prosecution's female witnesses had so testified. Norris was to be held responsible for all the "evil consequences" that resulted from his speech at the February 7 meeting, regardless of his intentions. The result was an "infatuated rabble led on by demagogues." Fall River citizens, the prosecution went on, feared violence. Those fears confirmed the charge of riot.[63]

In his charge to the jury, the judge went further. He insisted that striking operatives had the right to meet and combine but possessed no right to obstruct other operatives from leaving and going to work. Their attempts at forcible obstruction constituted riot. These activities had been encouraged by Norris' speech—and thus his speech had inspired riot. The terrified operatives had asked for and received protection. Whatever Norris' intentions, "still he was answerable for any disturbance" that followed. This jury, the judge continued, must decide why Norris had used his cane and "what he meant, and not . . . what he said." Endorsing a legal concept of conspiracy to riot and collective guilt for which the leaders of the strikers were held responsible, the judge insisted that "the act of each bound all." The jury found Norris and Clark guilty, and both were jailed. Many of the participants in the strike who testified for the defense left town, fearing the blacklist.[64]

Initially, Almy's editorials in the *News* had supported the striking operatives in 1848 and their leaders. He pleaded for the public to understand factory conditions and the "trying position" of the workers. He championed equal rights and equal justice for "the whole human brotherhood." But he also admitted that in moments of excitement, "when men are hurried," improper means may be adopted. The obstruction of working people, the British cheer, the threatening crowd, and the snowballing were all wrong: "morally wrong" and "injurious to their interests."[65] Still, the ten-hour mechanics in the 1840s had been careful to keep their cause moral and peaceable, and their efforts had failed. Almy continued to question the wisdom and even the ability of skilled workingmen or textile operatives to act as successful adversaries to capitalists in a strike. In addition, the contest in 1848 seemed to pit natives against foreigners, stirring up antagonistic feelings on both sides.[66] Almy believed that none of this advanced the interests of American workingmen. The convictions and the sentencing of Norris and Clark did not move the editors of the *News* even to comment.[67]

In contrast, Sarah Bagley in the April 7, 1848, issue of *The Voice of Industry* agreed heartily with the letter sent to her from the jailed John Norris. She insisted that his conviction had not been a government prosecution but a "Corporation prosecution." "This infamous prosecution," she wrote, "of innocent and well-intentioned men . . . prostitutes the law to purposes of selfish oppression. It demonstrated the oppressive and dangerous power of combined capital, in hostile competition with labor."[68] Bagley saw no reason that American workers should not join with immigrants or use British tactics. But after championing Norris' cause, the *Voice* ceased publication in 1848, and Bagley literally disappeared from the textile industry and from the ten-hour movement in New England.[69]

Lancashire Lessons Again in Fall River

Undeterred by the failed 1848 strike, on November 25, 1850, all sixty-eight of the Fall River mule spinners, some native-born but most immigrants, stopped work. They decided to ignore the legally required ten days' notice (a law not applicable to the mill agents when they fired operatives) and instead left after just five days. The haughty editor of the *Providence Journal* observed that the wage reduction that had led to the walkout was the result of inalterable market conditions: the high cost of raw cotton and the lack of demand for printed cloth. The men, facing the oncoming winter, should and would go back to work.[70]

The mule spinners in Fall River, however, had their own compelling reasons not to return to the mills. Their complaints during this strike not only challenged the overseers' manliness but also the mill owners' calculations of costs and profits. In addition, the unusual length of the strike, the arguments of the spinners, the cooperation of native and immigrant, and the later participation of organized weavers and carders signaled a new phase in New England labor protest of more effective organization and a new militancy. Indeed, the strike was hailed in a letter to the *New York Tribune,* signed "A Workingman" just returned from Fall River, as not only an issue of regional but also of national importance for working people.[71]

The Fall River mule spinners had watched as their counterparts at the Wamsutta mill in New Bedford were given notice of a similar wage reduction earlier in 1850. When they refused to accept the pay cut, the Wamsutta's agent systematically replaced them with new men. "We suspected," wrote "A Spinner" to the *Fall River News* on December 5, 1850, "that we should be treated the same way. . . ." The mule spinners and the managers in both cities were facing each other openly and collectively, adversarial behavior which signaled a developing class-consciousness among the native and immigrant mule spinners in New England. "A Spinner" wrote bitterly of "numerous petty tyrannies and unjust actions" by the overseers in the Fall River mills. He indignantly denounced the "character" of the overseers, questioning their manhood on the grounds of their tyrannical behavior at the behest of their employers. To the spinners, an overseer who merely carried out the orders of his superintendent, either for money or out of fear, without any individual sense of just treatment, was servile. The willful abuse of power in the mills contradicted the operatives' sense of justice and their view of manly behavior. As an embarrassment to the solid front of the Borden and Durfee-run mills, the New Bedford-backed Robeson print works, the Bordens' old rival, did not cut wages and continued to operate during the strike at a profit.[72] The strikers seemed vindicated about market conditions.

The December 5 letter from "A Spinner" also revealed that some mule spinners had been compelled to clean their mules on "the Sabbath day" at a "certain mill" and "under curious circumstances." A violation of the Sabbath by the mill owners represented a fine chance for operatives to charge that the Fall River factory system was anti-Christian. Rather than specify the mill or the circumstances, the writer quoted the contemptuous words of Lord Byron:

> Oh man, thou feeble tenant of an hour,
> Debased by Slavery or corrupt by power,
> Thy love is lust. Thy friendship all a cheat;
> Thy smile hypocrisy, thy words deceit.
> Who knows thee best must recoil in disgust,
> Degraded mass of animated dust.[73]

In his letter, the "Spinner" referred to his employers at the mill as "the masters," a word marking him as an English immigrant.[74] No white American male in pre–Civil War New England would voluntarily use the word *master*, although many spoke derisively of the condition of wage slavery or white slavery and complained about their overseers as slave drivers.[75] For an American freeborn white worker to use that term to address an overseer, agent, or boss would place a white man on a level with black slaves, thus violating republican manhood. In addition, Massachusetts artisans and textile workers recoiled against the "disparity of power," as the historian Christopher Tomlins puts it, when the discourse of master and servant became embedded in the pre–Civil War legal concept of free contract.[76] Employers could thereby punish operatives who left work without giving notice by withholding wages. Furthermore, used informally, collectively, and extralegally, mill owners could draw up and circulate "blacklists" of offenders. The common use of "dishonorable" discharges as disciplinary measures impugned female moral respectability.

In England, however, *master* was a commonplace word for employer among Lancashire textile workers, based on industrial culture, indicating the expectation of mutual obligations between the master and the male operatives. *Master* was an integral part of the deferential language and behavior in union negotiations worked out in mid-Victorian labor relations. Furthermore, the New England term *help*, used to designate operatives, offended English workers. To them, this association with domestic service or menial labor seemed insulting and demeaning. They preferred the term *hand*, which had artisanal connotations.[77] In the strike of 1848, coalitions of textile workers in antebellum New England faced troublesome cultural contradictions involving race, status, and language in addition to tensions and organizational problems. Still, various understandings of working-class rights and distinctive rhetorics based on different cultural experiences became blended during the process of class strife. Gestures and acts, such as defiant dances, British cheers, and Yankee snowballs, were forming a new culture of protest.

The conduct and words of the mill owners provided sufficient cause for united outrage. When several mule spinners, learning of the wage cut, approached the treasurer of the Metacomet mill, Colonel Borden, he made his position clear.

> Pointing to the sides of the granite mill, he said: "I saw that mill built stone by stone; I saw the pickers, the carding engine, the spinning-mules and the looms put into it, one after the other, and I would see every machine and stone crumble and fall to the floor again before I accede to your wishes.[78]

Indeed, when the Bordens and other nineteenth-century Fall River mill owners meant to fight, they pledged all their resources.

The "Spinner" had written his letter on behalf of both native and immigrant workers, but pointed out the special liabilities of the wage reduction to the English. "A great many of the spinners are from England," he explained. Unused to the bitter winters of New England, they had already purchased coal, staples, and warm clothing. If the reduction had been announced last spring or even during the summer, the immigrants would have had alternatives: to go to another town or even return to Lancashire. "A Spinner" charged that the wage reduction had been timed to keep them in Fall River throughout the winter to work at reduced wages or suffer "a very great loss."[79] This was a damning charge because it indicated a conspiracy by the mills to injure and coerce the men and their families.

In another letter, printed in both the *News* and the *Monitor* on January 30, 1851, the spinners' organization boldly questioned the employers' figures on their profits and the costs of production. No other group of textile workers had dared challenge the mills over the accuracy of quoted prices of raw cotton or profit margins in the cloth market. Admitting that their own figures, indicating more profits than the mills cited, might be faulty, they asked the superintendents to compare calculations by opening their books to public scrutiny. When English manufacturers had done so, they argued, a reconciliation between employers and workingmen usually followed.

This request to open the mill accounts was a far more potent act than pounding on the door of the countinghouse during the strike of 1848. The employers absolutely refused to comment, while their sympathizers used the local press on February 20 to dismiss the spinners' cost and profit figures. One writer insisted that the operatives "could not decide for their employers; they cannot appreciate their situation, and do not know their interests and duty.[80] This tight-lipped policy of disclosing nothing to the public or even to the few shareholders who were not family members became the managerial strategy of the Bordens and the Durfees until the late 1870s, even after financial reverses forced them to raise capital by selling public shares. Shareholders who attended board meetings might try to ask the directors a question, but they were always met with a swift motion for adjournment. These tactics became well known, and another indication of the desire of Fall River mill owners for total control of their enterprises.

During the 1850–51 strike, the mule spinners' raised two issues, the first, technical, and the second, political, that underlay their refusal to accept the 10 percent wage reduction.[81] The agents claimed that the Hawes, Marvel, and Davol Company was supplying the mills with self-acting mules so efficient that one spinner could do the work without the assistance of even one piecer, an apprentice spinner. The mule spinner was to do the work of two with only the help of a young boy.[82] Instead of the piecers used in Lancashire on self-acting mules, American textile agents had created the job of "back boy," allowing the spinner to choose his helper from his own family but undermining the authority of the mule spinners as supervisors of other adult males. The youngster scrambled about and under the mule, tying together or piecing up broken ends of yarn. Back boys between eight and twelve years of age and, during the post–Civil War period, little girls became common in New England mule-spinning operations. So did accidents to factory children.[83] This reorganization of spinning operations undercut the mule spinners' claim that spinning was fit work only for strong, experienced men, based on customary practices in the mule spinning rooms. In addition, New England mills posted each spinner's rate of production, while in Lancashire, these figures remained private, not used to provoke increased productivity.

The technical capacity of the improved self-acting mule, supporters of the mill owners proclaimed, allowed spinners to earn 10 to 15 percent more than the average New England mill for the same number of hours and days worked.[84] This became a consistent reaction of the mill owners throughout the nineteenth century. At higher speeds on improved machinery, the "help" could spin more yarn. Who, after, all should reap the benefit? Not the spinners, but the capitalists who sacrificed and paid for the new machinery. Furthermore, the wage cut was reasonable, given the uncertain state of the cloth market. Those foolish townspeople, they argued, who were contributing to the spinners' relief fund were supporting the Yankee sin of idleness. "An honest man, if he rightly understood the matter, would rather work his hands off than submit to such degradation."[85] Striking spinners were thus cast as unmanly loafers as well as supervisors of mere boys.

The mule spinners' organization rejected this reasoning, protesting that they were not earning more than other spinners, citing cases in Massachusetts, New Hampshire, and Rhode Island. The data they used indicated a regional information network operating in New Hampshire, Rhode Island, and northern Massachusetts.[86] A key issue, in addition to the wage reduction and the help of only a back boy to piece up broken yarns, was the increase in the speed of the new machinery. "An Operative" wrote that indeed more wages were *earned* and more yarn spun by the spinner, but less *money* was paid to him, as piece rates fell. "O, my God! What a life is ours. It is emphatically, 'drive, drive, drive,' from early morning till night."[87] And, the writer admitted, the overseers were similarly pushed. The mills could not claim they paid higher wages when a man was doing the work of two but getting the pay of one. As historian Isaac Cohen argues, craft control was being undermined.[88] The only way to retrieve it after 1851 was to return to Lancashire, which many did both before and after the Civil War.

The political issue raised in early January by the striking spinners centered on the unequal power relationships between the operatives and their employers and their deeply felt anger at acts of injustice. The spinners' public statements undercut the ideology of New England mechanics in the 1840s who accepted the mutual interests of worker and employer. The hands were openly hostile, the strikers argued, and the manufacturers deserved their hatred because of the mistreatment. The mill owners and their overseers were charged with "severity, haughtiness, inhumanity, and contempt," provoking the men's "worst passions." Unlike the rhetoric of 1848, if there was trouble in the streets, the mills would be responsible. In fact, it was argued, the arrogant employer feared his workers exactly because he knew they were not treated as men should be. As one spinner wrote,

> Remembrances of personal haughtiness towards men, every way his equals, perhaps, except in wealth; of an ill concealed scorn, of a consistent endeavor to obtain the largest amount of toil for the smallest amount of money; of an almost perfect indifference to the social and intellectual condition of his hirelings . . . , these abuses of power were more than sufficient to produce fear in the countinghouse.[89]

This open show of hostility and contempt by the mule spinners for the mill owners and overseers challenged the general acceptance by middle-class New Englanders that economic development would involve general advancement for employers and their workmen. The hatred inspired by ill treatment touched both English and American textile workers and brought them closer. Skilled immigrant spinners knew they were essential to mill operations, while open contempt and mistreatment backed by power and wealth undermined hope among native-born American workers that their employers might share their belief in republican equality.

The spinners' ideological stance in 1851 was: "Right against Might." The manufacturers insisted on submission to their terms, and their tactics included the use of bribes, threats, evictions, and dismissals, even for those sympathetic mule spinners in New Bedford who had donated to the Fall River strike fund. The strikers reassured the New Bedford spinners that "our effort shall prove to the country . . . that we are what our Maker intended us, —MEN—not slaves or machines, to be used as others may dictate . . . :

> Self abasement paves the way
> To villain's bonds and despot's sway."[90]

No man was a mere piece of machinery. To the contrary, skilled and experienced adult white males operated complex machines that produced the textile mills' profits.

The meaning of manliness as it developed in the early 1850s differed from the ideas of the ten-hour mechanics of the 1840s and the 1848 strikers. Skilled white men, native-born or immigrant, encouraged by their religious and political convictions, demanded decent treatment and fair wages. A broad coalition of native Yankees and Lancashire immigrant mule spinners, English and Irish-born with contacts in other textile centers, conducted the 1850–51 strike. Unafraid to let it be known that they despised their employers, they publicly exposed both the greed of the mills for profit and the contempt of the owners for honest workingmen. No longer a sacred but intimidating center of early industrial growth, the countinghouse had become the home of un-Christian despots and "fawning sycophants."[91]

And this was not all. The work stoppage of the mule spinners had halted the entire operation of the mills. Carders who prepared the cotton for spinning had no work, and the weavers had no yarn. Both faced even deeper wage cuts, 24 percent to the spinners' 10 percent, and went out on strike as the spinners did, numbering thirteen hundred, the entire workforce of the town's seven cotton mills. In January 1851, weavers and carders formed an organization and tried to raise a strike fund.[92] They held their meetings at the Free Will Baptist Church provided by the sympathetic Reverend Nathaniel Hewson. This association of religion with actual strike action in the early 1850s went far beyond the endorsement of the pro-ten-hour clergy of the 1840s. Men and women weavers and carders attended the strike meetings. One female weaver made the trip with a delegation of male strikers to New York City to raise money.[93] Other self-supporting women workers agreed to board out in rural farm homes either for nothing or in exchange for housework in order to sustain the strike.[94] Throughout 1851, following the lead of the spinners, the striking weavers, many also English immigrants, publicly rejected the manufacturers' arguments about costs and profits. In a letter to the *News* on February 20, 1851, a weaver argued that the mills could well afford to pay the old prices and that periodic reductions were part of a calculated plan to reduce labor costs without cause. Furthermore, the employers were simply too arrogant to change their minds. They could pay if they chose to, but would not, "believing that it is a humiliation to comply with a request from their workpeople." The weavers had been paid more and treated better in Lancashire and, like the spinners, they had some pointed advice to the mill owners on how to manage costs. Let there be fewer cupolas on the mill roofs and fewer spans of horses for their carriages.

Arguments inspired by Lancashire experience dominated the weavers' public letters, which insisted that "well-conducted" strikes were not injurious but useful to defend the interests of workers. Submission to wage reduction after reduction would prove much worse. A strike in "other" European countries, they argued, always led to investigation in the press, whereas "Here an employer shrinks from [this] . . . , maintaining the right to act as he thinks proper without being accountable to any one."[95] The weavers thus blended a potent ideological mix of the Yankee working-class belief in producerism, or the creation of all wealth by the laboring classes, with Lancashire traditions of the need for defiance and denunciation of masters who worshipped mammon. They also condemned Southern slavery as comparable to European feudalism, even though like most white Americans, they regarded African slaves as fundamentally more ignorant and helpless than white workers. Furthermore, the weavers had began to raise strike funds from nearby towns in Massachusetts and mill villages in Rhode Island. The regional patterns of late nineteenth-century labor protest were emerging in pre–Civil War Fall River.

Also like the spinners, the weavers let their contempt and disgust show. The overseers should learn to "respect their help, and treat them as men and as women" instead of behaving with "sullenness and conceit . . . [as if] they were above questioning."[96] The Fall River weavers were beginning to associate specific notions of respectable working-class womanliness— unlike the Fall River mill owners' earlier images of dependent, vulnerable Yankee mill girls—with respect for manliness. This rhetoric recalled the testimony of the female witnesses for the defense in the 1848 trials that convicted Norris and Clark and also reached further back to the beliefs of the Lowell Female Labor Reform Association activists in the dignity of workingwomen.[97]

Unwilling to depend on the town's two newspapers to print their full views, in March the weavers put together the *Trades Union and Fall River*

Weavers' Journal with Irish-born, Lancashire-trained carder Thomas Webb as the editor.[98] The weavers' strike held out until June, while the mule spinners all decided to return to work in April. The weavers thanked the people of Fall River, New Bedford, Providence, New York City, and Boston for their support and contributions.[99] Their resolutions at the final meeting insisted that weavers should go anywhere else rather than work at the wage reduction and should discourage all others from accepting jobs in Fall River. Many families and individuals found work in other cotton centers, such as Biddeford, Maine.[100] This dispersion of the strikers left labor politics in Fall River in confusion.

The defeat of the strikes in 1848 and 1850–51 meant that textile workers in the Fall River mills remained formally unorganized, but they continued to support labor protest and ten-hour reform. Immigrant spinners in Fall River contributed funds to the 1853–54 Preston strike in England that disrupted a period of conciliation and compromise in Lancashire.[101] They hoped some day to create a series of New England mule spinners' unions to prevent strikebreaking and blacklisting. When the financial collapse of 1857 hit, many unemployed workers were humbly forced to accept relief, such as it was, from the city. Those who stayed in Fall River remembered, formed underground networks of discontent, and continued to feel the bitterness of past and present injustices. The politics of nativism became the greatest enemy to this growing sense of cross-cultural class unity.

CHOLERA AND NATIVIST POLITICS

Just as the town of Fall River became a city in 1854, an outbreak of cholera swept the nation, hitting the Northeast hardest during late summer, especially in immigrant neighborhoods. The rising popularity of the anti-immigrant and anti-Catholic Know-Nothing Party in Massachusetts coincided with this epidemic.[102] Cholera linked with foreigners contributed directly to the 1854 victory of the Know-Nothings in Fall River. As the citizens of Fall River struggled against contagion and death, the Irish immigrant community came to be increasingly regarded as a deadly threat. The initial reporting in the *News* on the cholera outbreak in New York City focused on its incidence among the poor, ignorant, and intemperate working-class immigrant population. Some of the presumed victims were later discovered with stomachs full of cabbage and half-chewed potatoes, the staples of the Irish diet. Among the stricken middle class, opium or morphine controlled the early symptoms of debilitating diarrhea, while the poor relied on traditional doses of brandy or rum. Medical opinion favored total bed rest and relieving the maddening thirst from continuous diarrhea with pellets of ice, remedies not available to working-class people.[103]

As local illness and deaths increased, the editor of the *News* invented the term "rum cholera" to explain the many deaths that supposedly re-sulted from one night-long wake of heavy drinking over the corpse of an Irish cholera victim. Ill-advised eating, alcoholic "jollifications" on a Saturday night, and the neglect of over-worked mill children led to quick deaths, too quick even for the described course of the disease. Thefts of property and acts of ignorance and malice were deplored as common-place among the victims' relatives and friends. The great majority of the dead in Fall River were Irish. The disease seemed, to Almy, confined to "that class" of unfeeling and intemperate people where it reportedly origi-nated. By September 7, only three "Americans" had succumbed, but the contagion spread through the city's water supply.[104] A Citizens' Commit-tee assembled and, "to a man," resolved with the support of Mayor James Buffinton to try to halt the spread of the disease by destroying under or-der of the Board of Heath all liquor owned in the city. But before the vigilantes had time to descend on the Irish community, Sarah Buffum Borden, the wife of the Honorable Nathaniel Briggs Borden, and her daughter died of cholera, despite the best medical care and hardly a suspi-cion of rum imbibing. Their deaths and others among the respectable middle class halted the immediate danger of violence to the suffering immigrant neighborhoods. By the end of the epidemic, over 150 resi-dents of the city had died. The last was an Irish immigrant woman in mid-October as the electoral campaign warmed up.

The American Party, known widely as the Know-Nothings, swept the elections of 1854 in Massachusetts. Few politicians, whatever their parti-san stripe, survived unless the K. N. label appeared next to their name on the ballot. Mayor Buffinton went to Congress as a Know-Nothing, while the entire Fall River delegation to the Massachusetts legislature plus the successful top state officials overwhelmingly supported the nativist party. The disgusted Dr. Nathan Durfee, a Cotton Whig, cast a single vote for himself for governor.[105] Industrial centers such as Lowell, Waltham, Law-rence, Lynn, New Bedford, and Taunton voted heavily for Know-Nothings, putting Henry J. Gardner of Boston into the governor's office. In Rhode Island, the new party became equally popular. "The result," wrote the *News* editor, "has astonished almost every one."[106] The victorious party had no platform or legislative agenda except a vague commitment to the interests of Americans above all others. Simple distancing of the native-born from foreigners proved politically sufficient.

Historian Ronald Formisano has found the party's success hard to ex-plain. He suggests that the issues of the secret electoral ballot or ten-hour reform may have played a major role.[107] While in late 1853 most Massa-chusetts textile factories and machine shops had adopted an eleven-hour day, the operatives and ten-hour reformers in Massachusetts and Rhode Island continued to agitate for a ten-hour law.[108] Blacklisted carder-turned-shopkeeper Thomas Webb represented the operatives of Fall River at labor reform conventions. The failure of the Know-Nothing-controlled state government to pass a ten-hour law, a statute that some argued would actually have encouraged the mills to replace native-born workers with immigrants, might have divided textile workers along national lines. This nativist division, historian David Montgomery argues, proved fatal for labor reform in the 1850s.[109] How ten-hour advocates voted in 1854 is not clear, but native-born workers may have seen hope in political change. The nativist party victory in Massachusetts shattered both the Whigs and the Free Soil Party statewide and dug deeply into Fall River politics until 1860.

The Know-Nothings won Massachusetts again in 1855.[110] By 1856, growing numbers of Fall River Republicans cooperated with them to nominate a "Citizens Union Ticket" for the state House of Representatives with two American Party candidates and two Republicans. The ticket won. Congressman Buffinton adopted similar tactics and carried both Fall River and Taunton heavily, as did Know-Nothing Governor Gardner. Still clinging to a coalition with former Whigs in the process of becoming Republicans, Gardner was defeated in 1857 by the "American Republican" candidate for governor, Nathaniel P. Banks, who carried the city of Fall River and gained a majority in the Massachusetts Senate and House. Fall River Republicans running for election, however, continued to play coalition politics with the local American Party that year, waiting until 1858 to absorb the remnants of the Know-Nothings into "another brilliant victory for the American Republicans. . . ."[111] In that election, city councilors, state senators, and state representatives ran as American Republicans and won. Clearly the American Party, far from being a popular craze, had solid support in the late 1850s.

Finally Governor Banks, campaigning in 1859 against Democrat Benjamin F. Butler of Lowell, dropped the "American" from the Republican banner and won. In Fall River the activities of the Know-Nothings split the party so badly that the senate seat from Bristol County District West went to an obscure Republican candidate from tiny Rehoboth on the Rhode Island border. In 1860 Republicans Abraham Lincoln and gubernatorial candidate John A. Andrew swamped both the Democrats and the American Party. Significantly, however, the die-hard, former governor Gardner tried to stay alive by running for the state senate in Fall River's district, but was soundly beaten in the city by a local Republican lawyer.[112] In the 1850s, Fall River's Republican Party with close ties to manufacturing interests came into being hand-in-glove with nativist sentiment.

NATIVISM ENTRENCHED AND THE RENEWAL OF LABOR POLITICS

As the impetus for nativist politics eased, the mule spinners in Fall River began in 1858 to resurrect their organization.[113] A group of Irish-born,

Lancashire-trained leaders emerged, replacing those men who had left town or been blacklisted, never to be hired again in Fall River. These men were not Irish immigrants with only farming or construction experience. After landing in Liverpool in the early nineteenth-century, some Irish-born had learned the worsted trade in Bradford and others mule spinning in Lancashire cotton mills before emigrating to America.[114] Aware of the hostility created by the 1850–51 strike, the mule spinners' union held its 1858 meetings in secret, in some farmer's field or behind the mills. The members wanted an increase in wages and drafted a petition to the manufacturers, but none wished to sign at the top and risk the blacklist. The wife of one suggested a customary solution. The signatures would appear in circles rather than on a list.[115] To their surprise, the Fall River manufacturers in 1858 agreed to one-third of this wage request but only for the mule spinners.

The depression had eased, and as the market for print cloth rose, the other two-thirds of the requested increase was granted before the outbreak of the Civil War. Skilled spinners, dispersed by hard times and nativist politics, were in short supply. But English and Irish immigrants continued to face the hostility of this manufacturing community. When the war began, pro-ten-hour lawyer Lapham, former editor Webb from the 1850–51 strike, and Father Edward Murphy of St. Mary's Church encouraged the formation of a volunteer Company H. composed of foreign-born citizens, but the city turned them down. Company H. headed by Lt. Patrick Desmond disbanded, while Desmond became a private in one of the two native-born volunteer companies.[116] These companies marched off in July, dressed in uniforms sewn by the ladies of Fall River, organized by Colonel Borden's wife.

Governor Andrew quickly intervened to rescue Desmond and reinstall him as the first lieutenant of a reorganized Company H., locally known as the "adopted citizens" company. The governor had actively recruited reformers and prominent abolitionists into the Republican Party and used military commands to advance the careers of Democrats, such as Desmond and ten-hour advocate Butler of Lowell.[117] A whole contingent of British-born naturalized citizens enlisted in the predominately Irish Company H., renamed the Union Guards. But instead of the generous bounty per soldier paid by the city in 1861 to the two native-born volunteer companies—that cost the city ten thousand dollars—these volunteers got only twenty cents a day for subsistence until ordered to leave for military camp.[118] Adopted citizen meant second-class.

Later, when Fall River became pressed for recruits, many foreign-born working-class men enlisted or were drafted in July 1863, despite great fears in Fall River and in the draft center of New Bedford about the violent antidraft rioting in New York City. When a number of muskets were stolen from an incoming Boston train, wealthy Fall River families hired armed guards. New Bedford officials feared a riot, as in New York City, directed at its large black community by Irish immigrants coming from Fall River and other towns. New Bedford turned itself into an armed camp, but nothing happened.[119] Fall River's first draftee was John Sullivan, a foreign-born citizen.[120] These men may have suffered a disproportionate number of casualties and deaths compared with middle-class, native-born combatants.[121] Among the largely Irish-born draftees in 1863, however, there were at least nine Bordens, one a lawyer, and a scattering of other eminent family names: Chace, Anthony, Eddy, Earl, Davol, Almy, Brayton, and Durfee. After the war ended, the surviving members of these powerful families would control the local Grand Army of the Republic Lodge and Fall River's Republican Party.

In 1861, the mule spinners' union books were closed, and when reopened in 1866, many who had volunteered or had been drafted into the Union Army were dead.[122] This had dire consequences both for the spinners' union and for the veterans' families. The loss of her father in battle forced eight-year-old Mary Ann Burke, the oldest child in her family, into the Watuppa mill, where in September 1865 her left hand was crushed in an accident. The doctor amputated one of her fingers but feared the onset of lockjaw. She and her six-year-old brother Willie who worked with her were the sole support of her widowed mother and a younger child.[123] Severe labor shortages, especially of skilled workers, were common in New England textile mills during and after the Civil War.

Wartime inflation created high prices "for the necessaries of life," prompting a meeting of the Fall River weavers on February 25, 1864.[124] Whether or not they got the wage increase that they sought, the weavers demonstrated renewed interest in organization and activism. Expectations of a postwar boom in the cloth market encouraged the surviving mule spinners and new men in the trade to press successfully for a 15 percent increase in 1865 just to cover wartime inflation.[125] Higher wages were being granted in virtually all textile centers in New England. Skilled workers were at a premium, and the mill agents pleasantly agreed to wage increases as long as profits continued to soar. Meanwhile, Fall River agents hired men to scour the New England countryside for workers. One traveled to Glasgow, Scotland, where about fifty workers agreed to make the trip back.[126] Labor scarcities and pressing demands for goods encouraged textile operatives to agitate for further reforms. Lancashire and Yorkshire immigrants would provide the most eloquent testimony on the need for a ten-hour day in Massachusetts. Both English-born and American middle-class reformers backed them vigorously. The pre–Civil War labor politics that had swirled around the ten-hour movement was about to have its day.

4

WAIT, AGITATE, WORK, AND WAIT
Gender Politics and Ten-Hour Reform,
1865–1874

FOR MANY Massachusetts labor reformers, the passage of the ten-hour law in 1874 seemed the crowning jewel of their movement: the culmination of over thirty years of political agitation. As Charles Cowley, veteran ten-hour reformer from Lowell, wrote: "No sooner was 'all quiet on the Potomac,' than the ten-hour agitation was revived on the Merrimac."[1] Labor reform survived the crisis of the Civil War and gained new momentum toward victory during the postwar years.[2] But whose crown bore that jewel? During the pursuit of shorter hours, skilled male textile workers mobilized politically, held strikes and mass demonstrations, and successfully crafted state regulation of factory work limited to women and children. Their friends and allies in the labor reform movement, more than well acquainted with the firmly entrenched notions at the State House about freedom of contract for adult males, jumped at this solution. This restriction of ten-hour reform to workers, thus made legally dependent, ignored the intense, long-term involvement and lively interest in shorter hours among women operatives, the less skilled, and youngsters. This reshaping of post–Civil War reform politics, however, failed to stifle female political activism.

Charles Cowley's family had emigrated from Glouchestershire, England, to manufacture textiles in Lowell. When only thirteen years old in 1845, Charles attended a workingmen's convention in Woburn, Massachusetts. Admitted to the bar in 1856, he served four years in the Civil War, gaining a naval judgeship to become Judge Cowley. When he returned from service, Cowley became president of Lowell's Ten-Hour League. The passage of the ten-hour bill required an enormous effort,

including the coordination of statewide activities by middle-class labor reformers like Cowley and Boston's Eight-Hour men, such as Ira Steward
and George McNeill, with male and female operatives' petition drives and
agitation. Native-born and British immigrant male workers in the major
centers of textile production mobilized by conducting ten-hour strikes in
1866, 1867, and 1868. During the major depression that began in 1873,
labor activists bombarded the state legislature with demands for the ten-
hour day, backed by votes and noisy street parades. Especially important
to these political activities were Irish-born and English-born immigrants
from the woolen and cotton districts of Yorkshire and Lancashire who
worked and voted in Lawrence, Lowell, Fall River, and New Bedford.
Their experience with ten-hour regulation in England helped define the
Massachusetts law of 1874.

DAVID MONTGOMERY'S *Beyond Equality: Labor and the Radical Republicans,
1862–1872* remains a key early work in the reformulation of the field of
American labor history. In his study of Reconstruction in the North, he
builds on Norman Ware's earlier work to explore, in addition to national
and state politics, politics within industrial communities.[3] Following labor
politics through the Civil War and Reconstruction, Montgomery questions why and how the Radical Republicans, working-class activists, and
their middle-class allies, including eight-hour advocate Ira Steward also of
the Boston Ten-Hour movement, failed to advance labor reform as part
of Reconstruction policy in the Northeast and Midwest. Montgomery lays
out the struggle of capital and labor in the 1860s and early 1870s, using
aggregate economic data from the 1870 manufacturing census, which indicated that the most intense economic development occurred primarily
in mining and iron manufacturing.[4] This source, however, obscures the
tremendous growth in Fall River print cloth production within the less
striking figures for overall textile activity in Massachusetts.[5] Furthermore,
industrial growth in post–Civil War New England—especially in print
cloth production—occurred, not state by state, but regionally. This chapter will augment Montgomery's work by analyzing the economic and cultural dimensions of regional textile production and industrial politics in
southeastern New England, especially the reform politics which led to the
passage of the ten-hour law.

Differences among workers nationwide, based on skill, gender, and
nationality, as well as a prevailing belief in a free labor ideology and individual freedom of contract, Montgomery argues, led to divided efforts
which foundered in the morass of Republican politics. He cites the "blun-
ders" that occurred during a 1868 strike in New Bedford and the "failure"
of the ten-hour day movement in Massachusetts as two illustrations.[6] The
New Bedford strike in 1868, however, proved only a short-term setback
and did not slow down labor reform in Massachusetts, as Montgomery

argues. New Bedford represented a sideshow to the more important later efforts of labor reform activists in other Massachusetts textile centers, especially Fall River, Lowell, and Lawrence.

In these cities, the political activity of native-born and Irish-born workers, native-born and English-born middle-class supporters, such as Steward and Cowley, and working-class Lancashire and Yorkshire immigrants carried the ten-hour law to victory.[7] Radical Republicans may have failed to press their cause beyond legal equality for the freedpeople, but there was another significant attempt to "impose moral order on the market economy."[8] English immigrants brought to New England a heritage of popular radicalism and anticapitalist values based on their experiences in the English industrial order and in nineteenth-century factory reform agitation. Their political activities in Massachusetts made the difference for the ten-hour law. This initial success was, nonetheless, limited. The 1874 statute contained a major loophole, finally plugged in 1879, but, regardless, the textile mills as a rule ignored or evaded the law for decades. The lessons of the limits of the popular franchise and state regulation in the face of concentrated economic power were painful. Still, the political mobilization behind the passage of the ten-hour law in 1874 established the groundwork for more intense political activism and class conflict in 1875. That mobilization began in Fall River in 1867 and erupted in New Bedford in 1868.

Revival of Ten-Hour Agitation

In the spring of 1865 a legislative committee investigating the issue of shorter hours endorsed, surprisingly, an eight-hour day, but recommended no immediate reform legislation at all.[9] The legislature then created a special Public Commission on the Hours of Labor to take lengthy testimony and make recommendations. Meeting between October and December of 1865, the commission heard the testimony of shipwrights, leather workers, carpet weavers, printers, textile workers, farmers, and one textile employer, Edward Atkinson, who ran a small mill in Springfield. The most riveting testimony on behalf of a ten-hour day came from workers in the textile factories of Lowell, Lawrence, and Fall River.

One key witness was Robert Bower, a Lancashire immigrant who had worked before the war in a Lawrence cotton mill. Born in Stockport, England, in 1828, he began work at seven years of age for fourteen hours a day. At fifteen in 1843, he joined the Stockport ten-hour association. He emigrated in 1856 and got a job in the Pacific Mill in Lawrence as a dresser-tender, a skilled but hot and arduous job, applying starch to the warp yarns that were wound on the huge beams inserted in power looms.

In 1862 he enlisted in the Fiftieth Massachusetts Regiment and served for the duration of the Civil War, returning to Lawrence to work and agitate for ten hours. He was fired from the Pacific mills but managed to learn the printers' trade while continuing to organize other textile operatives for what English workers had enjoyed since 1847, including factory schools for children. Lawrence activists also contacted Lancashire immigrants in Fall River, and in 1864, they formed English-style Short Time Committees.[10]

Bower's testimony in late 1865 centered on the extra hours worked in the Lawrence cotton and woolen mills. The usual day was eleven hours, but in response to the postwar demand for cloth, weavers worked an additional two to three hours, three nights a week. Young women often did this work, receiving a twenty-cent bonus per night in addition to wages for each piece or "cut" of cloth, forty-five yards in length. Bower estimated that among these night weavers, one-third were minors under the age of eighteen.[11] Although they were required by law to be sent to school for three months each year, "a great number" between the ages of twelve and fifteen worked at night, earning from one-third to two-fifths the wages of adults. The Massachusetts statute forbidding factory work for children under twelve was totally ignored in Lawrence, as elsewhere in the state.[12] No one would dream of prosecuting the corporations for violations of state law. As Bower shrewdly put it, "what is everybody's business was nobody's business."[13] Charles T. Crane, head of the state carpenters' union, who had worked for six years in one of the Lowell mills, corroborated Bower's testimony. Working thirteen hours a day not only exhausted him physically but so strained his eyes that he experienced blinding headaches. In his opinion, no one lasted in the mills beyond the age of forty.

By 1865 the ten-hour movement had enlisted forceful, ambitious political advocates. Eight-hour supporter Ira Steward of Boston regularly attended the commission hearings. Although Steward advocated an eight-hour day, he supported ten-hour legislation as a first step, joined by antislavery champion Wendell Phillips of Boston and Gen. Benjamin F. Butler. Butler had defiantly run his small woolen mill in Lowell on the ten-hour system since the 1840s. Addressing a Workingmen's Meeting at Faneuil Hall in early November 1865, Phillips pointed out that the people of Massachusetts had no more right to say how a laboring man shall spend his leisure time after ten hours of work than tell a millionaire how to spend his money.[14] At a meeting in Fall River on October 30, 1865, Steward insisted that capital controlled both the press and the pulpit, which together formed public opinion. Capital, therefore, was the power with which organized labor had to contend. "If American laborers knew the strength that the ballot gives them they would soon give to the whole world an eight hour system." He specifically challenged those who claimed that fewer hours for workingmen would result in more drunkenness and vice. Long hours actually produced ignorance and "a chronic helplessness [that] sustained the rum traffic. . . ." The same arguments, he maintained, had been used to defend the system of slavery. He concluded by stating his philosophy that fewer hours at higher pay would produce more demand for manufactured goods and more jobs, a situation economically and socially beneficial to all.[15] For Steward, mutual benefits shared between capital and labor were possible with proper state regulation.

In response to Steward's Fall River speech, editor Thomas Almy of the *News* opposed the ten-hour reform for industrial workers. "The employer has rights," he argued, and his obligations should not be made statutory. Defending an informal system of mutual recognition of interests in the mills, Almy insisted that a legal limit to the working day would degrade "the working man in the best elements of his nature. . . ." It lowers down his manhood, and makes him just that thing which he believes the employer takes him to be,—a mere tool, to be used for the purpose of advancing the fortunes of others." A real man did not depend on estimates by his employer or the state. "As soon as the laborer shall vindicate his moral manhood by industry, sobriety and intelligence, he will have less cause for complaint, and more power to make his voice heard when he speaks."[16] Correct behavior and patience, as defined by middle-class standards, would create respect toward workingmen—however long that took and whatever the result. For Almy and the textile interests in Massachusetts, the protection of contractual rights and republican manhood were both integral to correct state policy.

On November 19, Ira Steward announced to the state commission that twenty operatives from Fall River had been scheduled to testify but that eighteen had withdrawn, threatened with dismissal. Two mule spinners, remaining anonymous, told the Fall River story. The first was a Lancashire immigrant mule spinner who had worked in the Fall River mills for eight years. "He worked harder here," he testified, "than he did in the old country." In Fall River he walked twenty-five miles a day back and forth at his mules and was forced to clean the cotton lint from his machine during mealtimes. He stated that he would willingly accept a wage reduction for reduced hours of work. As in Lawrence, the child labor laws went unenforced. The second spinner himself had two children in the mills, ages seven and nine, earning two dollars each week to help support the family. He testified that labor reform activists among the operatives were summarily dismissed and blacklisted by the mills.[17]

The testimony of Edward Atkinson, the treasurer of a small mill in western Massachusetts with only 650 workers revealed some support for limited reform, although Atkinson was hardly a typical mill owner. While opposing the ten-hour day, he advocated the adoption of the half-time system used in English mills, where children worked full-time for six months and then attended school for the rest of the year. As for adults, Atkinson criticized any state limitations on the hours of work, which would deprive a man of his opportunity to "dispose of the greatest amount of labor at the highest price . . ." during the current prosperity.[18] Labor was after all a commodity. The whole matter of hours and wages, he argued, was regulated by the natural laws of supply and demand. Ignoring the ten-hour proposal, Atkinson concentrated on refuting Steward's eight-hour day. If an eight-hour limitation on the working day should become law in Massachusetts, Atkinson predicted, capital would leave the state and invest in places where there is "shrewdness enough" not to limit daily hours. Massachusetts textile manufacturers agreed with Atkinson's views that the laws of supply and demand determined both wages and hours. Believing that an oversupply of workers would in fact hold down wages, they were hurriedly rounding up as many rural workers and immigrants as they could persuade to join their workforce.[19]

The commission adjourned in December 1865 and sent a report to the two legislative committees on labor in the house and the senate, advocating no action. But the postwar drive for ten hours continued, led in part by British immigrants such as Robert Bower of Lawrence and the mule spinners of Fall River working in coalition with prominent politicians and reformers, middle-class supporters, and with the eight hour men of Boston. In 1866 a major confrontation between all the cotton operatives and the mills of Fall River would produce a voluntary but significant *local* concession: a ten-hour day beginning on January 1, 1867. Those who knew the Bordens, Durfees, and Braytons suspected a direct connection between their willingness to grant a ten-hour day in a scarce labor market and their postwar plans to dominate the domestic market for print cloth.

THE MASSACHUSETTS EIGHT-HOUR MOVEMENT

Skilled white male workers in trades and crafts had by 1864 won their fight for ten hours in the Boston area and in most urban areas in the Northeast, including the machine shops and building trades in Fall River, Lowell, and Lawrence. But labor reformers, centered in Boston and surrounding towns, agreed that working over eight hours deprived craftsmen of time to exercise genuine republican citizenship. The first issue of Boston's *Daily Evening Voice,* on December 2, 1864, put out by members of the local printers' union, some of whom were on strike, asserted the ideology and politics of labor reform. The *Voice* sponsored the developing eight-hour movement in Massachusetts.

On March 8, 1865, Maj. John W. Mahan of the Ninth Massachusetts Regiment, the representative from Boston's Ward I still wearing his Union blue, proposed that the House of Representatives "inquire into" the "expediency" of reducing the hours of labor by law to eight for mechanics and ten for factory operatives.[20] What politician could deny a uniformed veteran this respectful request while the war raged on? Mahan and others were building a Democratic coalition of Civil War veterans eager for state bonuses and Boston workingmen interested in shorter hours.[21] They would not leave the "Boys in Blue" to the Republicans. A similar political coalition of veterans and workingmen appeared in Lowell in late 1865. With the support of labor reformers such as Charles Cowley, John T. Lee, a master blacksmith, won a seat on the Lowell common council and Lorenzo D. Cogswell, a journeyman carpenter, went to the state House of Representatives. By December 1865, Boston boasted eight-hour men as one-third of the aldermen and one-fourth of the common councilors.[22]

Major Mahan's Special Joint Legislative Committee, heavy with labor reformers such as Sen. Martin Griffin of Suffolk County, quickly reported in late April 1865, just days after Lincoln's assassination.[23] The joint committee recommended the formation of another special investigating commission, to be appointed by Gov. John Andrew, a pro-labor reform Republican.[24] Action, Senator Griffin urged, was immediately required to protect the rights and respectability of workingmen. Mechanics regarded themselves as mere slaves with time for nothing but their work. Major Mahan and other Massachusetts men had risked themselves to free southern slaves, but white workers also needed to be freed. An eight-hour law was essential to guarantee their independent, republican manhood.

An alarmed Griffin, a former journeyman printer, had witnessed "cringing servility and supineness" where he once had seen the manly, sturdy independence of the mechanic and workingman, the result of the growing political power of industrial interests.

> Instead of self-respect and intelligence, we have want of confidence and growing ignorance. . . . Instead of honest pride, . . . the consciousness of inferiority . . . [and the] loathing and disgust of . . . drudgery and degradation. . . . Instead of labor being the patent of nobility, it is the badge of servitude.[25]

Post–Civil War Massachusetts workingmen agreed with Griffin's remarks, and regarded the terms *slavery* or *servitude* as condemnatory and politically denigrating. Accordingly, the editors of the *Voice,* endorsing both Griffin's report and the ten-hour movement in September 1865, linked state regulation of working hours, respectable freeborn manhood, and republican citizenship.

After a disappointingly light vote (except in Boston) in the November 1865 state elections, the *Voice's* editor explored the meaning of slavery for northern workingmen.[26] The growing power of capital was fundamental to the decline in their status and prospects. The control of their hours, their wages, and their very survival by arrogant "tyrants" who also monopolized land, commodities, rents, and access to knowledge was the essence of slavery. Perhaps shaken by the failure of the statewide ballot in 1865 to forward the reform cause, the editor of the *Voice* began to recognize growing signs of "bondage" and "degradation." Even among sturdy mechanics, continued threats to their livelihoods from corporate power led to submission.

> A few months ago, Mr. [John B.] Ham of East Boston [an eight-hour man], could not get a single signature to a respectful petition to the legislature for a reduction in the hours of labor among a hundred men in a machine shop in this city, though every one of them desired the reduction, but was afraid of losing their places if they asked for it! This tameness of spirit is the first sign of degradation and the invariable badge of the slave.[27]

This form of slavery, although different from that experienced by the "African race," was a sign of the increasing influence of concentrated capital in politics and in the economy. The eight-hour day was the answer. Senator Griffin and the *Voice* confined hours reduction primarily to white male mechanics. But, as in the 1840s, other broader conceptions of reform politics were emerging during the postwar years.

Ira Steward, the most thoughtful eight-hour advocate in Massachusetts, insisted that an injury to the "humblest" citizen was an injury to the state. He thus enlarged the scope of political responsibility far beyond the needs of respectable, white, skilled men, including women workers in his proposals for hours reduction.[28] In contrast, the editor of the *Voice* argued that the natural laws of supply and demand would work only for capitalists unless all male workers organized, voted, and used the state to right the balance.[29] But Major Mahan's legislative proposal asking for eight hours for mechanics and ten for factory workers, plus his political coalition between veterans and workingmen, indicated the broader base of organization toward which the Eight-Hour Movement and the *Voice* were turning. The editors had already endorsed the ten-hour movement stirring politics in textile cities, but the dismal state elections in 1865 indicated that labor reform candidates had to attract more working-class voters, and, if necessary, organize an independent political party.

Political mobilization on a wider scale seemed the only possible response to the March 1866 report of Governor Andrew's special commission which recommended that the state take no action on the eight-hour day. Both conservative and reformist members agreed that natural laws controlled the workings of supply and demand, but they disagreed over the role of the state to protect individual men. The protection of property rights by the state, the commission reported, was appropriate, but only God possessed the power to make men good. The unimpeded workings of supply and demand and the manly exercise of freedom of contract would protect both wages and the workingman. Eight-hour advocates argued that state intervention would give a man the opportunity "to show himself a man" and a fair chance to use his brains as well as his muscle. To dignify work, they insisted, the law must dignify the workingman. Most of the commissioners rejected state involvement in such individual matters and agreed that "when the goal of manhood is reached, then it is for the *man,* and not the State," to say how many hours he worked. The best interest of the laborer, the commission report concluded, lay in an increase in capital investment and new corporations.[30] Representative Ham of East Boston, still put the issue of eight hours to a vote in the state legislature where it was soundly defeated on April 20 by 109 to 32.[31]

The special commission investigating hours regulation expressed more interest in child workers than in adults. Although pre–Civil War state law set the age of working children at twelve and made provisions for six months of schooling, the responsibility for enforcement lay with local school committees.[32] During the 1866 commission hearings, mule spinner T. J. Kidd of Fall River testified that when "small help" became scarce, overseers raided the schools for children as young as seven, like a military draft. The school committee did nothing.[33] These child workers performed a number of dirty and dangerous tasks. "Lowell Loom" described in 1869 the duties of "little baby oilers," children between six and eight, working among the "flying pickers and wheels to clean and oil the [running] machinery."[34] Small help could squeeze into places where no adult dared to go, risking their limbs and lives. They also scoured floors and wound yarn on bobbins. Mill accidents to children under fourteen were common. In 1867 Katie Lyon, working at the Fall River Linen mill, caught her arm in the machine gearing. "The flesh was stripped from her arm in some places to the bone, and many of the arteries and sinews were severed." She was eight and a half years old and had just been beaten for "carelessness."[35] The use of child workers around dangerous machinery such as pickers, mule spinning frames, and carding machines resulted in amputations or crippled hands and arms. Occasionally a child died. Peter Shay, age eleven, fell into a cauldron of boiling liquid at the Globe Print Works in Fall River. His skin came off with his clothing, and he died three hours later.[36] The state education law, however, included the legal loophole of the word *knowingly,* through which the mill managers evaded prosecution by denying knowledge of child employment.

Most of the public commissioners were associated with state charities, schools, and health agencies and recognized the dangers of child labor and the loss of education. Arguing that "childhood [is] nature's own season of preparation for manhood . . . ," they advocated an American version of the English half-time system. Instead of full-time attendance for a period of months, children would work the first half of the day and then attend school. The report also supported the appointment of state inspectors to replace local enforcement and the prohibition of any child under ten in factory work. And in a significant move, the commission recommended the annual collection of statistics on employment, an idea that led in 1869 to the creation of the Massachusetts Bureau of the Statistics of Labor. However welcome the commission's recommendations for child labor laws, eight-hour men concentrated their energies on politics outside of the Boston area, organizing rallies and promoting their cause. Mule spinners and weavers were already demanding shorter hours.

Postwar Ten-Hour Agitation Among Textile Workers

Some New England mills had experimented in the 1850s and 1860s with a ten- or eleven-hour day. But even if the mills in one city, such as Fall River or New Bedford, granted a shorter workday voluntarily, they could withdraw the privilege whenever they decided that the market required it. Without legal coercion, they could and did lengthen the hours per day at will. Other textile centers in Massachusetts, such as Lowell, insisted that a ten-hour day was impossible to adopt unless their competitors did the same. To resolve both issues, ten hours had to be statutory law.

In this political fight, mule spinners provided the working-class leadership, often cooperating with other operatives. In April 1866 and March 1867, the mule spinners' unions of New England held their first formal regional conferences in Lewiston and Biddeford, Maine, to promote the ten-hour day. Isaac Cartnell, a delegate from the revived post–Civil War organization, represented Fall River. William Isherwood from Lowell attended the 1867 ten-hour conference in Biddeford. Then he was blacklisted and moved to Fall River. Patrick McHugh from Lawrence, Richard Barlow from New Bedford, and others from Manchester and Salmon Falls, New Hampshire, joined the Maine spinners, but there were no delegates from Rhode Island or Connecticut.[37] Both conferences backed regional labor reform activity, and in the late fall of 1866, the Fall River operatives led the way.

A public attack on the Fall River school system by the aggressive eight-hour supporter, John B. Ham, appointed by Governor Andrew as a deputy state commissioner of education, stimulated this rising reform agitation. At an open meeting on October 1, 1866, attended mainly by operatives, Ham blasted local authorities for defying the 1866 state education law which prohibited children under ten from factory work and mandated six months of schooling for those fourteen and younger.[38] Ham announced dramatically that he had seen a mill boy of fourteen who looked seventy-five; "dwarfed and distorted by early toil and with the prospect of a life before him not worth living." Low wages and a needy family left him without time to attend school. The deputy commissioner threatened the school committee and the mill owners with stricter enforcement of truancy laws by state-appointed officers, but ended with a few soothing words.

"Educated labor," he promised, "was above taking advantage of its employers . . . ," in the mills or at the ballot-box.[39] For weeks, the Fall River superintendent of public schools scurried about trying to satisfy the State Education Commission, while the operatives decided to take full advantage of this embarrassing exposure of municipal laxity.[40]

A few weeks after the public meeting, Fall River textile workers at all skill levels, led by the mule spinners, petitioned the mills for a ten-hour day, requesting an answer by October 29, 1866. Already on the defensive, the mill agents cited the "difficulty" of adopting the ten-hour system when the rest of the Massachusetts mills ran at least an hour longer. But rather than refusing outright, the mill agents made an offer to begin the ten-hour day on April 1, 1867, if half the mills in New England did the same.[41] This of course was no offer at all. The operatives insisted that they would all stop working after ten hours each day, beginning on November 31, 1866. This threat prompted another offer from the employers: they would adopt ten hours on January 1, 1867, if the mills in Lowell and Lawrence also did so. Again, with no hope of compliance by these textile centers and in response to threats by the employers to fire anyone leaving work after ten hours, all of the operatives simply walked out. The Fall River mills fell silent, as other New England mills quickly moved into the prosperous print cloth market. The competitive pressures of the market yielded results. The mills agreed on November 2 to begin the ten-hour day in January, and the operatives returned to work the next day.[42] Militant, united action among the operatives had accomplished what state commissions and the legislature could not.

Mule spinners led this work stoppage, but significantly they did not act alone, but with the weavers, carders, and all other textile workers.[43] The political tone of a November 3, 1866, letter to the *News* signed anonymously by "The Cotton Operatives of Fall River" was adamant. Expressing continued hostility at the overweening power of the mills, the letter exposed the employers' offers as "very indefinite," no real guarantee of anything. While the workers were obliged to give two weeks' notice or face the blacklist, the employers could fire labor at will. In bitter language reminiscent of the early 1850s, these inequities were denounced as "most *unjust* and *tyrannical*. . . ."[44] The operatives also warned the agents that whatever was decided in their own meetings was just as binding as the secret decisions made in countinghouses. Finally, they promised that agitation would continue until they had some kind of legal guarantee for a shorter workday.

Unwilling to face new legislation on either truancy or ten hours, the Fall River agents experimented with the ten-hour day, fully capable of either speeding up machinery or withdrawing the privilege whenever they chose.[45] The Atlantic mills in Lawrence and the Wamsutta mills in New Bedford later followed this policy. But the Lowell mills refused to cut hours, and the local leaders among the protesting mule spinners were fired and blacklisted. In New Bedford, the Wamsutta adopted the ten-hour day on January 1, 1868. Then after only one month, Agent Thomas Bennett Jr. abruptly rescinded it. In retaliation, the textile operatives led by the weavers struck the mill immediately.[46] Ten-hour politics reverberated across the region.

A WINTER OF DISCONTENT AND DEFEAT

The whaling industry had long dominated the early nineteenth-century economy of New Bedford, attracting to its busy port a large community of Irish immigrants and free blacks, such as Frederick Douglass, to build ships and to work aboard them.[47] Textile development, handicapped by the lack of water power, began in 1848 with the organization of the steam-powered Wamsutta mills. Thomas Bennett of Fairhaven, Massachusetts, had learned the textile business in the mid-1840s in a Wymansville, Georgia, mill while straightening out its accounts on behalf of Fairhaven investors. For the Wamsutta he obtained the financial backing of Congressman Joseph Grinnell of New Bedford and the expert assistance of mill engineer David Whitman of Warwick, Rhode Island.[48] The Wamsutta produced fine shirting and sheeting which required skilled mule spinners, among them experienced workers from Lancashire. Many Irish immigrants and native-born workers (but no African Americans) were employed as weavers and other workers in the mills. When the Civil War cotton embargo shut down Wamsutta completely in 1864, the jobless faced the Union Army or the scrutiny of the Overseers of the Poor.[49] Some sought work in the Fall River mills.

During the struggle in 1868 with Bennett over ten hours, "A Working Man" pointed out: "It was not the operative who first asked for ten hours. It was given to them by the agent."[50] Bennett's swift, arrogant, and arbitrary reversal of his decision led to the firing of any operative who dared question the return to eleven hours. The first was weaver John Hanover, chair of a worker delegation sent to speak with the agent. When Hanover asked why he had been let go, Bennett told him to go to "Fall River" because he was "a ten hour man." Feeling insulted, Hanover gathered his tools and left the mill like a "gentleman," but stayed on the strike committee. At one meeting he called Bennett, "an almighty dollar man," but predicted that the strikers should remake him into a "ten hour man." Debates over definitions of manliness and its rights became commonplace in the strikers' language and in Bennett's intransigence. They said he had a gizzard (like a vulture) but no human heart.[51] One local observer warned that public ridicule of Bennett would only bring out "all the devil" there was in the man.[52]

Another strike leader, weaver Robert Slattery, had worked for Wamsutta since 1848 and operated looms "along side of John Hanover." If Bennett thought his firing of a few would control the rest, he said, "it could not be done." When Bennett discharged Hanover and thus deprived him of "his liberties," Slattery went on, "he [Bennett] deprives every man in the mill likewise. . . ." At another meeting, Slattery went further:

> [It was] dangerous [for Hanover] to look at a mill superintendent. Though ignorant and poverty-stricken, they [the workers] had the spirit of liberty in their breasts, and some of them had shown it on the [Civil War] battlefield."[53]

In addition to the agent's reversal on ten hours, Hanover's unpleasant experience with the stubborn, unmovable Bennett became a focus of worker anger. Regardless, Bennett alone controlled negotiations with the operatives.

Once the strike began, it became general across skill, gender, and ethnic lines, but divided piece workers from day workers. Using a shrewd managerial policy, Bennett employed two distinct groups at the Wamsutta: 1,050 factory workers paid by the rate set for each piece of work produced and eight hundred job and day workers, many of whom were either on contract or worked as unskilled laborers paid by the day. About nine hundred or about 86 percent of the piecework operatives struck, including carders, female throstle spinners, mule spinners, men and women weavers, and assorted other categories of mill workers. The job workers in the weaving and spinning rooms joined them.[54] Letters signed "Day Worker," supporting Bennett and published in the local press, kept the division between strikers and non-strikers public and embarassing. Efforts by the strike committee to draw the day workers into the movement failed.

The strikers and their leaders were a mix of nationalities. Opponents claimed that "a hundred Englishmen," mule spinners and weavers, were "behind" the strike: "a few bullies with the aid of a few natives."[55] But both English and Yankee names were prominent among the leaders. Women workers also attended meetings and watched for strikebreakers at the railroad station and on the roads. Augusta Luther, Johanna Maher, Ann Gurney, Susan Renshaw, and Ellen and Mary Killigrew—an assortment of American, German, English and Irish last names—canvassed as a committee for relief money. But other women workers refused to strike and returned to the Wamsutta at the first opportunity.[56] As the strike was in its last days, an Irish immigrant strikebreaker and his family fought a group of ten-hour supporters. Two women were injured.[57] Clearly, no one nationality or gender dominated the protest.

In an unusual gesture of interracial unity at one of the citizens' meetings on behalf of the strikers, an African American lawyer and former slave, William H. Johnson, supported the strike and ten hours "as a lover of freedom," pointing out in gratitude that "the Irish had helped fight the battles that set the colored race free. . . ." He continued,

> Some of the speakers . . . have advised you to be quiet and patient, and deliverance would come; that is what my old master used to tell me. . . . The Bible says, Ask, and ye shall receive, but you asked and were kicked out.[58]

Community support for ten hours, labor reform, and public agitation ran deep in antislavery, reform-minded New Bedford. Local citizens accepted political agitation based on moral right. The potential of support from these political groups helps explain the willingness of the strike committee to compromise and conciliate the issue, even to the point of experimenting again with eleven hours. While David Montgomery regards the strike committee's concessions as grave errors, in the context of local politics they seem reasonable. Agent Bennett thus became the target of public criticism by influential middle-class supporters of ten-hour reform.

The Rev. Isaac Knowlton, an active labor reformer, questioned the morality and manliness of the agent's decision. If ten hours seemed right on January 1, why now abandon it? "Is it manly for a person or a corporation to say: I will do right if others will?" Knowlton demolished Bennett's claim that his return to ten hours was an issue of competition with Lowell and Lawrence.

> Are you aware that nobody but yourselves can see any competition between your mills and others? Your stock sells at a premium of 25%, your cloth commands the highest price in the market, your dividends are large; your officers have fat salaries.[59]

Knowlton, like other middle-class citizens, opposed a strike but wanted the adoption of ten hours. Bennett admitted Wamsutta's only real competitors for its fine goods were small Connecticut mills that ran eleven and a half hours.[60] One resident pointed out at a public meeting that the permanent adoption of ten hours would attract the most skilled workmen in New England to New Bedford, thus securing the high reputation of Wamsutta's goods. Another citizen, "Cynic," writing to the *Standard,* insisted that the agent managed Wamsutta poorly, and the stockholders should act.[61] To many local investors, Bennett's willfulness seemed unmanly and his stubbornness threatened New Bedford's prosperity.

A few New Bedfordites, remembering their antislavery days, equated the strike with the oppression of William Lloyd Garrison in the 1830s at the hands of a Boston mob. The moral issue was far more important for them than business strategy; the strikers had their sympathy as "northern slaves."[62] "D. H." supported ten hours and admired the strikers, many of whom were

> exiled from their native land. . . . Am I not a man and a brother [to them]? . . . [Y]ou are not strikers but like the abolitionists, petitioners. . . . Let your manly and womanly conduct . . . put to shame all reproach.[63]

Despite claims of middle-class labor reformers that the strikers represented respectable, moral manhood and womanhood, the strike committee was in fact planning to use women to jeer at and humiliate strikebreakers, believing that no man could stand such treatment by females in public.[64] Respectable and moral conduct could differ with the requirements of class politics.

New Bedford's state representative, the Reverend Isaac H. Coe, had sat in 1866 as a ten-hour man on the legislative committee on the hours of labor. He impressed the strike committee with his political status and his desire for reform through conciliation with Bennett. Suggesting that the stockholders might themselves adopt a ten-hour day, he proposed a citizens' committee headed by himself to talk to Bennett. This the strikers refused at a February 20 meeting as untrustworthy, although they organized a committee of two strikers and Knowlton to seek a compromise. In a swift preemptive move on the following morning, Bennett announced that Wamsutta would reopen on March 1 on an eleven-hour day.[65] There would be no negotiations.

New Bedford's prominent and wealthy Quaker philanthropist Rachel Howland, a key investor in Wamsutta, appeared at a strike meeting and also tried to persuade Bennett to compromise. But her efforts to influence the agent were regarded by the strikers as useless, unless Bennett actually signed his name to an agreement. He would not. The strikers voted unanimously to hold out. During her appearance at a March 4 strike meeting, Rachel Howland firmly opposed strikes as damaging to the operatives' respectability but supported agitation for ten hours. Her appearance at this meeting proved irrelevant. Workers had already begun to show up in numbers at the Wamsutta mills. Bennett's "high feelings," obstinacy, and control of the mill had won.[66] The strikers—first the weavers, then the mule spinners—voted to return to work.

How much did labor reform suffer from this lost strike? Not much in the eyes of English immigrants used to many such defeats. "A Working Man" wrote: "Is John Bright a bully to advocate the rights of English workers?" Ten hours works in England. We will "wait our time, agitate, work and wait."[67] "Anthropos" characterized New Bedford in 1868 as full of "indignation" over Bennett's spite in refusing to rehire many of the strikers, pointing out that hundreds of blacklisted workers were leaving the city.[68] Perhaps some went to Fall River to work a ten-hour day. William McCauley of the Fall River Short-Time Committee had addressed New Bedford strike meetings and promised support. Blacklisted weavers, such as John Hanover, could join a Fall River weavers' union organized in 1867. Mule spinners were also welcome in the city. Representative Coe was reelected in 1868, but New Bedford reformers and workers would have to wait until 1874 for the ten-hour day.

ATTACKS AND COUNTERATTACKS

Meanwhile, the textile corporations of Massachusetts demonstrated their deep hostility to state labor reform on Beacon Hill and in their communities. The members of a Joint Labor Committee in 1867 appointed by Republican Governor Alexander H. Bullock opposed hours reduction. Most corporations outside Fall River resisted a reduction to ten hours, but there were few exceptions: the progressive Pacific and Atlantic mills in Lawrence and the carpet mill and the bleachery and dye works in Lowell. For the operatives, the collusion of the vast majority of the agents and treasurers in rejecting their ten-hour petitions was maddening and discouraging. The power that the textile capitalists wielded in state politics made matters worse.

In an effort to unite the eight-hour and ten-hour movements, "Short-Time Committees," borrowed from English usage, papered over the divisions between mechanics and operatives in Lowell, Lawrence, and Fall River. For example, Lowell's Charles Crane of the carpenters' union announced at a ten-hour meeting: "I am here to help and get eight hours later."[69] Boston's eight-hour advocates Ira Steward, John Carruthers, Ezra Heywood, Rufus Wyman, and A. J. Wright spoke at mass ten-hour rallies in major textile centers, including Manchester, New Hampshire, a state with a ten-hour law that included a loophole—big as a barn door—for any previous contract between individuals. Agitation by influential and articulate men centered on encouraging operatives to sign ten-hour petitions. After their expected rejection by local treasurers and agents, the petitions would be presented to the legislature. This pre–Civil War strategy, along with a proposed independent Workingmen's Party for the 1867 elections and the organization of a New England Labor Reform League, highlighted the most active, but in the end, most discouraging, year for Massachusetts labor reform.

As labor reformers struggled on, mechanics and textile operatives in Connecticut, beginning in December 1866, organized in the mill towns of New Britain, Rockville, and Willimantic near Hartford, in Taftville and Baltic near the Massachusetts border, and in the cities of New Haven and in Hartford. Like New Hampshire, the state had an unenforced ten-hour law. Angry Connecticut workingmen crowded local Democratic meetings and received a promising response by the party during the 1867 spring state elections. Democratic gubernatorial candidate James E. English, once a journeyman carpenter and a popular New Haven businessman who advocated ten hours, became the workingmen's candidate, campaigning for eight hours for mechanics and the enforcement of the ten-hour law for operatives. English was no Copperhead Democrat; he served in Congress during the war, supporting the Lincoln Administration. Workingmen deserted the Republican Party in 1867, and English carried New

Haven and Hartford, sweeping in three Democratic congressmen out of four.[70] The rejection by workingmen of the party of Lincoln made waves that rippled into Rhode Island politics, where it was suppressed, and into Massachusetts. Meanwhile, Connecticut employers took their revenge, beginning with the textile operatives in Rockville. The mills fired any worker who voted for Governor English and starved the rest by running halftime. A call went out for funds to support the local protective union and to warn all men to stay away from Rockville where political opinions could not be openly expressed.[71] Still, in several Connecticut mill villages, ten hours became the rule.

Massachusetts mill agents copied the vindictive measures of the Rockville mills. The Lowell Machine Shop fired and blacklisted short-time committee leaders William Marks and Louis Flynt. Treasurers and agents in Lowell refused to accept the ten-hour petitions, while overseers insulted the petitioners. Lowell mill agents labeled T. C. Constantine, an eight-hour man and former mechanic in the Lawrence Bay State mills, a "conspirator, fanatic." In response, Lowell city councilman J. T. Lee pointed out that "Mr. Constantine" has been called "a fire brand," but who cares what you are called as long as you aren't called in "at half past six [on] winter mornings."[72] Other activists continued to circulate petitions and rally the operatives.

Many in Lowell and Lawrence were English immigrants. P. S. Butterworth, an English-born foreman in a small Lowell bolt factory working on a ten-hour day, had immigrated to New England early enough to join the 1840s labor reform movement. He advised carrying the petitions to the legislature and voting Democratic if the Republicans refused to act. He spoke of prolonged and continuous labor agitation in England as the key to success in Massachusetts and heralded the names of English reformers, Richard Ostler, Fielding of Todmorden, and John Bright. "John Bright," he recalled, "is a townsmen of mine . . . ," but admitted he was fonder of Jacob Bright, the father who influenced his son to vote for the English ten-hour law in 1847. The prominence of English immigrants and their retelling of the English reform story brought many of their countrymen and women to ten-hour meetings in both Lowell and Lawrence.[73]

Public ridicule was a well-used weapon of English agitators and some Americans, such as Seth Luther. Charles Cowley, who had worked for years with Butterworth, admonished the operatives not to be afraid of the power of the mills. At rallies, he ridiculed the tiny brains and feeble physiques of the most obnoxious agents and overseers. About a dozen treasurers and agents, he estimated, blocked legislative reform. What success had emboldened them to such action? Treasurer Henry B. Ward had run both the Tremont and Suffolk and the Lawrence mills of Lowell "into the ground," yet had the "damnable impudence" to reject the petitions. F. B. Crowninshield, treasurer of the Merrimack, often laughed at Ward's "folly and silliness" but lost even more money by unsound decisions. Compared to the founders of Lowell, Cowley charged, these men are "pygmies," with "a record of unparalleled stupidity, ignorance, and obstinacy." They should not stand in the way of fifteen thousand operatives who wanted ten hours. Cowley's insulting personal attacks on lofty, even unnamed, powerful male figures as weak and unworthy fools undermined their public status and power. He was encouraging operatives to testify before the legislature, an act feared by most.[74]

The Lowell mills usually fired any operative associated with or testifying for ten hours. Furthermore, the agents toyed with rent hikes of 25 percent and wage cuts, targeting the most vulnerable workers: women and children. Without any warning, a mill agent announced a pay cut one morning with unconcealed delight, breaking the custom of advance notification. The women workers grew livid at such "barefaced robbery."[75] At the Hamilton Mills, overseer Levi Waterman grabbed a petition out of the hands of a female operative, although he was forced by the agent to return it with an apology for breaking mill rules against rudeness. When Waterman fired Emma Whitcher, an English Canadian immigrant, for testifying at the 1867 legislative hearings, she appealed to the Hamilton's agent who reinstated her in another weave room. Most mill managers were less kind. Another woman who testified in 1867 did so only with the support and protection of her father, Abraham Kershaw, a ten-hour activist and a supervisor at the Lowell carpet mill where she worked. But the father of one nine-year-old girl who worked illegally in the carpet mill with Helen Kershaw refused to allow her to testify for fear that both he and his wife would be fired.[76] Most of these threats worked.

Only three brave women weavers of English, English Canadian, and Yankee backgrounds dared to testify in February 1867 to a Senate legislative committee on "Questions of Labor" chaired by Boston labor reformer Martin Griffin. Miss Helen F. Kershaw, Miss M. S. Burdock, and Miss Emma Whitcher described the exhaustion of working eleven hours and the "general debility" of their health. Two presented petitions from their workrooms signed by almost all the women workers. One described the use of the "kiss of death" shuttle: the weavers rethreaded the shuttle by mouth, thus inhaling the cotton lint. They agreed that the eleventh hour was "very tiresome," leading to serious breakages in the cloth. Burdock, an operative from Maine, regretted that she had to stay on in the mills, because she knew no other work.[77] A well-educated Lowell operative who called herself "Equality" and identified herself as a supporter of women's rights and racial equality wrote to the Boston *Voice* that when she had "expostulated" against overwork, an overseer had told her: "The work must be done. If this set of girls tire out, I must get another."[78] Councilman Lee of Lowell called for woman suffrage as a goal of labor reform, but his stance was exceptional. In both Lowell and Lawrence, separate short-time committees were organized for women workers, and during public meetings at Manchester, New Hampshire, females were seated together in the galleries, apart from workingmen. Their leaders' names, their debates, and their arguments were seldom reported.[79] They could not vote.

White, native-born workingmen remained the focus of many labor reformers. A. B. Plympton, a Lowell lawyer, announced that he had been an antislavery man for thirty years and could predict that the employers' counterattack on the ten-hour movement would bring on a political crisis. If capital interfered with the rights of labor, the result would be a "tornado of dissent." Capitalists would face,

> not the negro . . . , but intelligent white men with Anglo-Saxon blood in their veins, . . . not a race with almost every trace of humanity and spark of manhood trodden out; but . . . men with the terrible power of mind. . . .

Do not be afraid of capital, he counseled the Lowell operatives—oblivious to his racist belittling of the former slaves for whose freedom he had supposedly battled. Even with the welcome commitment of antislavery advocates to the battle for hours reduction, racial denigration, often taking the form in the nineteenth century of applying the category of race to national groups (such as the Irish and French Canadians) made allusions to *slavery* a divisive swamp for labor reformers.[80]

Lowell councilman Lee, encouraged by Cowley's recent attacks on prominent mill men, condemned them during a February 1867 ten-hour rally as "upstarts, [the] codfish aristocracy of Lowell." The real reason, he explained, that the corporations would not grant ten hours was not that an additional hour's leisure would lead to intemperance and "immorality," but that granting ten hours would be a "concession" to workingmen from the corporations determined to keep "us under their heel and to keep us under their power." The issue was the dominance of one class of men over the other at the workplace and in politics. This was white slavery, as the editors of the *Voice* had argued in 1866. Lee insisted that workingmen must "rise in their might" and protect their rights. Pay cuts were a "feint" to undercut ten-hour agitation, which the Lowell mills had decided "must stop." The corporations had amassed great profits in 1866 and were rebuilding and expanding rather than paying higher wages. They blame the "market," Lee pointed out, but if the price of cotton cloth is down, so is the price of raw cotton.[81] Contrary to the belief of many middle-class labor reformers, including Steward and Griffin, in the ideology of supply and demand as economic laws, Lee pointed out that those same economic laws served corporate power. Race and economic ideology remained potent obstacles to labor reform politics.

The Senate committee on labor continued its hearings through February and March 1867, taking testimony and debating the ten-hour bill.

Abraham Kershaw of the Lowell carpet mill testified that he had worked in English factories, beginning at the age of thirteen in 1817, knew the factory laws, and often wrote to friends in the old country. Kershaw spoke of the hardships of long hours on the predominately female and child workforce in the carpet mill, including his own daughter. Robert Bower of Lawrence, just fired from the Pacific mills, read a petition for ten hours signed by three thousand workers and agreed with Kershaw on the effects of overwork for women and children. James Holdsworth, formerly of Lawrence, had left England in 1865. He had worked both the long- and short-hour system and could testify to the positive effects of the English ten-hour law. Immediately targeted for his activities on the short-time committee, he was "forced to leave Lawrence and get a job elsewhere.[82] Bower and other English immigrants in Lawrence would keep agitation for ten hours going until the passage of the law.

The Griffin Committee also heard former deputy state commissioner John Ham, fired by Governor Bullock for trying to enforce the 1866 school laws. He had visited at least one hundred mills that ignored state laws, but his report remained unprinted, buried by the new administration. Ham also raised the issue of the relationship between manhood and power that concerned both workingmen and middle-class labor reformers: "A large portion of the opposition to the ten hour law by factory managers arises from their apprehension that if the manhood of the workmen were elevated, they will be less under the control of employers."[83] Ham also referred to the divisive *race* issue, predicting that Yankee workers could not work the eleven-hour system and that even the Irish would soon be replaced by French Canadians, as in western Massachusetts mill towns. Bower agreed that the threat of workers from Quebec already existed in Lawrence. Ten hours represented a standard of respectable manhood and a bulwark against a tide of non-English speaking, inexperienced Canadians who, as a "race," it was widely believed in 1867, would—man, woman, or child—gladly work an eleven-hour day. Still, in 1870 the Lowell Short-Time Committee organized about seventy French Canadian female and child operatives to sign a ten-hour petition sent to the legislature.[84] Racial categories and narrow definitions of manliness would continue to plague broad-based reform politics.

Before Griffin's Senate committee ended its hearings, the labor committee in the House reported that the legislature had no right to regulate contracts made by adults, eighteen and over. While the debate went on in March and April, the mule spinners of the New England region, following the Fall River example in 1866, went out on strike for the ten-hour day. In a move supported by the Biddeford spinners' meeting in March, 1867, on April 1 mule spinners in Lawrence and Lowell, in Manchester, Salmon Falls, and Great Falls, New Hampshire, and in Lewiston, Maine, left work. In Biddeford, the mills granted ten hours, but only to the mule spinners, thus astutely dividing the operatives.[85] Only statue law could defeat this strategy.

Lawrence mill agents fired the leaders of the spinners' strike to prevent a feared general uprising of the operatives. The strike committee defended its action by insisting that at the 1866 Lewiston conference the mills had been given one year's notice of their intent to work only ten hours but had ignored it. The committee claimed "a right to a voice in the fixing of these things [hours and wages], or are we mere machines . . . ?" After the failure of public moral suasion or attempts to talk with the mill owners, and with the refusal of the legislature to act, only a regional strike remained as a means of protest. The strikers drew their rallying cry from the mid-1850s' Preston strike in Lancashire. Instead of Preston's "Ten Percent and No Surrender," in Lawrence they called for "Ten Hours and No Surrender." As the mule spinners were leaving the mill yards, a large portion of the "female help" left too. The mills identified these women and evicted them from corporation housing to control the rest. The strike committee announced:

> They turn the daughters and sisters of the men who shed their blood [in the Civil War] and left their bones to whiten on a southern soil into the streets, because they will not allow themselves to be ground down to the same object—slavery. . . . This, fellow-citizens, . . . this your reward for fighting the enemies of your country while they sat home in opulence and ease.[86]

In 1867 the mule spinners were brewing a rich political broth of allusions to slavery, suffering women, Civil War sacrifice, English labor reform, and hostility to those who had bought themselves out of the draft and then helped defeat the veteran's bounty bill.[87] But the legislature ignored this activity, rejecting an eight-hour bill and refusing to act on ten hours.

Indeed, the mule spinners' strike for ten hours did not win the support of many middle-class labor reformers. After rumors that about one hundred striking mule spinners in Lowell were advocating physical confrontation, John Carruthers of Roxbury, an eight-hour man, hurried to a ten-hour rally to denounce violence as un-American. In the United States, he insisted, every man had a vote, and workingmen should use the ballot box, not the streets. Carruthers, like many other middle-class labor reformers in New England, cautioned patience. Citing Ira Steward's ideas about decreases in hours worked and increases in wages and worker consumption as the key to the resolution of strife between capital and labor, he insisted that progress toward reform must be slow. The political process was the key; a republic depended on enlightened male voters.[88] But the striking spinners were in no mood to wait. The legislature and the political parties did not seem to recognize that they had the vote and routinely ignored labor reform. The English experience was to agitate and strike, not accept Carruther's disheartening suggestion that even he might not live long enough to see a ten-hour law.

During the Senate debate, S. Angier Chace of Fall River's Third Bristol District attacked the state law on child labor passed in 1866, expressing his opposition to the use of the state constabulary to enforce compliance with any law. The corporations, he argued, "did not like the idea of having State Constables go mousing around the factories. . . ."[89] Chace claimed the law mandating the education of factory children discriminated against textile mills. Three months of schooling, rather than six, seemed perfectly adequate to him. Indeed destitute French Canadian families would starve on arrival in Fall River, he insisted, without the immediate help of their children's wages. Chace argued that to be fair the ten-hour law should be made general in rural as well as urban areas, a proposal certain to maximize political opposition. Senator Griffin rallied the reformers to continue the ten-hour debate, while the House defeated the eight-hour bill on April 19, 147 to 49. A few days later, the *Voice* indicated it was nearly bankrupt. Massachusetts labor reform was in crisis.

Labor reformers and eight-hour men rallied to save their newspaper and called on a wide New England base of support: from Portland to Providence, Worcester to New Bedford, Manchester to Fall River. Attention turned to fund-raising meetings, as labor reform collapsed on Beacon Hill. In Boston, Lowell, and Lawrence, supporters organized Voice Clubs to raise money to sustain the paper for six more months. One prominent leader was Robert Bower who, after the *Voice* folded, became determined to set up a labor reform paper on a smaller scale in Lawrence to fight for ten hours. In Lowell a slate of workingmen's candidates ran in the fall elections, while the Republicans renominated Bullock for governor and the Democrats chose a gubernatorial candidate regarded by workmen as opposed to labor reform.[90] Well before the discouraging electoral results were known, the *Voice* printed its "Valedictory" on October 16, 1867.

In bankruptcy, the editors assumed a moral righteousness that may have eased their regrets but, like the defeated mechanics' movement in the 1840s, included a string of accusations against their "lukewarm supporters." They "without manliness enough" killed the paper. Many middle-class sympathizers, such as Ezra Heywood, had been drawn away into anarchism, temperance, or peace campaigns, while the "dependent masses" failed to respond. For the editors, busily closing up their print shop, the "servility, ignorance, distrust and meanness" of the workers were the inevitable fruit of oppression. Workingmen did not understand reform, nor were they free to act.[91] Feeling beaten, the editors blamed political defeat on failed working-class manhood, not on the power of capital. But this was not the case among the mule spinners, either in Lawrence or Fall River in 1867, nor during a mule spinners' strike in 1870. The *Voice* had been stilled, but ten-hour reform and labor agitation had not ceased.

THE REVIVAL OF TEN-HOUR POLITICS IN FALL RIVER

The Fall River mills were determined to dominate the post–Civil War print cloth market through capacity: producing massive quantities of the cheapest goods and undercutting all competition. This strategy involved both cutting wages and adding hours. In 1869 the mill agents returned to an eleven-hour day and began a series of wage cuts.[92] But the political atmosphere was turning against them. In February 1867, the Merchants Manufacturing Company had sought a new state charter with stock shares beginning at one thousand dollars. The company managers were furious at being forced to accept a legal limit of one hundred dollars per share in the projected $1.5 million, so that "operatives of the mill might be enabled to purchase an interest in it." The Senate voted by a large majority for this arrangement.[93] Chagrined, the Fall River mills singled out a local political scapegoat, Louis Lapham, a popular police court judge who like Charles Cowley of Lowell, had been a long-time advocate of ten-hour legislation. In April 1867 the mill owners and their lawyers tried to unseat him for malfeasance, thus defaming a prominent labor reformer.

A delegation of Fall River citizens descended on the House judiciary committee to demand the police court's abolition on the grounds of Lapham's misconduct. James M. Morton, later appointed to the state Supreme Judicial Court, represented the petitioners. Lapham defended himself. Walter Paine III, Jefferson Borden's son-in-law and the treasurer of the American Linen Company, laid out the complaints. Lapham, he claimed, handled cases involving violations of the law by liquor dealers and businesses of "ill fame" operated by men to whom he owed money. Other prominent citizens testified to the judge's "bad character" in the community, but Lapham assembled his own group of respectable citizens, including lawyers, court clerks, and the Republican Mayor, George O. Fairbanks. Although Lapham was often unable to pay his taxes, the mayor testified that he was an honest, moral man and a well-known temperance advocate who had been an efficient judge for over twenty years. Lapham not only remained on the bench, but he became increasingly active on the Democratic city committee. In 1873 he became editor of the first Democratic newspaper in Fall River, *The Border City Herald,* and in 1874 defeated Republican Congressmen Buffinton in the city, although the incumbent eked out reelection in the district.[94] After his fine showing in the election, Lapham ran as a strong but unsuccessful Democratic candidate for mayor between 1876 to 1879.

Lapham's career after 1867 seemed a weathervane for labor reform and the Democratic Party in the city and the state. The municipal elections of 1868 and 1869 in Fall River produced Republican majorities, but the contest for mayor in 1868 was close. Still, only one Democrat, Daniel Conroy, an Irish American grocer, sat as an alderman. Republican

John B. Hathaway, former state representative for one term, a prosperous merchant, and a director in the Mechanics mill, replaced the busily pre-occupied S. Angier Chace in the state Senate for one term.

There were other important political stirrings in 1869. The small French Canadian community objected strongly to the invasion of their homes by the city missionary, who distributed Protestant Bibles and tracts to their families. Three hundred members of the "Canadian Committee" met to protest this "insult" to their religion and culture. Furthermore their children who attended the city's special factory school, established in 1867, understood little because their teachers knew no French and regarded them as "difficult."[95] Cultural nationalism had drawn this least-advantaged and most-feared "racial" group together for their first public protest. After the Civil War, St. Patrick's Day celebrations became open political gatherings for middle-class Irish American citizens including Democratic alderman Conroy and the Reverend Edward Murphy, a tem-perance priest who had run the first parish since 1840. At the 1869 ban-quet, attorney William M. Connally called for the disestablishment of the Anglican Church in Ireland and attacked landlordism. Wendell Phillips, promoting the labor reform ticket, attended a meeting of the Knights of St. Patrick to support the reelection of alderman Conroy.[96] Fall River's French Canadian and Irish communities were developing their own politi-cal grievances, ambitions, and objectives.

In addition to labor agitation for ten hours, English operatives brought other reform ideas with them. In March 1869 immigrant English and Irish mule spinners reorganized a cooperative grocery store in Fall River on the English Rochdale plan, based on cash payments, no credit, and shared profits. Jonathan Biltcliffe, a Lancashire immigrant who re-sided in and supported a similar cooperative store in Olneyville, Rhode Island, advised them, praised their efforts, and criticized American-style competitive individualism.[97] Biltcliffe would later move to Fall River and become politically active. Weavers in one mill protested the assignment of finer work, requiring more time and effort but without higher wages, and later they too planned a cooperative.[98] When the Fall River mills an-nounced in April 1869 their return to eleven-hours, an outburst of ten-hour activity among the textile operatives, in the opinion of Charles Cow-ley, revived a dying statewide movement.[99]

Business in the cloth market that spring had been dull, except in prints, where "excitement" led to frantic selling under cost. The editors of the *Providence Journal* scolded the print cloth industry, largely centered in Fall River, to keep the supply down to meet the demand. "If too many prints are sent into the market, some of the machines must be suffered to rest."[100] They missed the point. The Fall River mills decided to increase production by returning to eleven hours per day and cutting wages, thus underselling their Rhode Island competitors and seizing control of the market. As long as the Bordens, Durfees, and their in-laws drove production, this remained their policy, whatever happened in the cloth market or to the regional and national economy.

Meanwhile, mill workers and labor reformers organized to restore the ten-hour day in Fall River by law. Accepting the legislature's refusal to interfere with adult male rights to individual contracts and making an important shift in strategy, reformers proposed ten-hour legislation in 1869 that applied only to women and children. This politically, ideologically, and culturally significant move reflected the gender politics behind the English Ten Hour Law in 1847, while recognizing the American belief in individual liberty for adult white men. It also reinforced the stereotype of workingwomen as helpless childlike victims. This decision emerged after several meetings in April 1869 to organize a new ten-hour association for Fall River, headed by the blacklisted Lowell mule spinner, William Isherwood. "To the Operatives and Working Classes of Massachusetts," a broadside issued by the association headquartered at Spinners' Hall in May 1869, made the argument.[101] This key proposal shifted the political and ideological debate over the relationship between manhood and the state from adult men victimized and enslaved by their oppressors and in need of legal protection to workingmen as active, family protectors. Citizens would use the ballot, a republican prerogative of manhood, to gain ten hours and defend their dependents. Ironically, a ten-cent levy on all adult textile operatives, whatever their skill, sex or job, funded this new activity. A ten-hour law, given the integration of production in New England mills, would force managers to limit the workday for male operatives too. Labor reformers in Lawrence and Boston quickly embraced the solution.

The vivid rhetoric of the 1869 mule spinners' broadside reflected this shift in strategy. Eleven hours was termed "an unjust exaction" on "our wives, our sisters, and our daughters. . . ." The long-hour system led to "wearied limbs, the sunken eye and hollowed cheeks," and "pallid countenances of the little ones whom we love, as they stalk half-stupified from the mill. . . ." "The lordly and aristocratic corporations" were scorned as oppressors of the weak: women and the small help. Female and child health and vitality, not republican manliness, were the issues. The ten-hour campaign had become "a God-given right; we [the male operatives] are compelled to take the matter in our own hands. . . ." Yet many native-born female operatives, such as Mary E. Wendell of Lowell, would refuse to accept such imposed images of dependency and victimization. Like the female activists led by Sarah Bagley in the 1840s, she and others would insist on shorter hours to improve their minds. For her, "the masses should be intelligent" rather than have "the few . . . live in luxury and idleness.[102] The decision by Fall River mule spinners and their supporters to avoid the issue of adult male freedom of contract with a strategy to protect workingwomen would collide with female independence and activism.

Agitators in 1869 promised a thoroughly organized state movement as "a tower of strength" so that the legislature, especially the representatives of textile centers, would fear it. Male voters would claim state protection for their dependents, but, as in England, the law would necessarily cover all operatives working in integrated, centralized production. A day of retribution was promised to opponents, although eight- and ten-hour men had made similar threats many times before.[103] An immediate political test came in a vote on May 19 on a new city charter for Fall River in which the school committee was to be chosen by the city council. Workingmen, as the rumor went, would rally to keep the schools in the hands of the people. They did, by a vote of eight to one.

Labor reform reemerged in June 1869 on Beacon Hill. The house committee on the hours of labor supported the recommendations of Henry K. Oliver, a former Lawrence mill agent and a state deputy constable keenly interested in factory schools, for the establishment of the first state "Bureau of Statistics on the Subject of Labor."[104] But few imagined that Oliver himself would be appointed chief of the bureau or that his four annual reports would include a factual, balanced account of the 1870 mule spinners' strike in Fall River and strongly advocate English-style labor reform. Rallies continued in Fall River with appearances by Jonathan Biltcliffe of Olneyville, George McNeill, Oliver's deputy at the Bureau of Labor Statistics, and labor reformer, Jennie Collins, who had worked as a textile operative and ran a home for Boston's workingwomen. Collins, an experienced and effective speaker, mourned the hard lives of the operatives as well as the poverty-stricken widows and children of the Civil War dead.[105] She quickly recognized that limiting shorter hours to women and children was an English-inspired strategy.

The Fall River mills provoked more agitation by flaunting their economic power. In 1869 the Mechanics mill introduced four new slasher-tender machines, designed to prepare warp for looms and replace well-paid skilled dressers. Twelve experienced men were fired and four others reassigned to the newly mechanized work, reducing the workforce by three-quarters. Then all of the mills in late August cut the work week to three days but at eleven hours a day, a decision intended, as in Lowell, to choke off political activity. At one local ten-hour rally, Charles Cowley increased the general anxiety by inciting racist fears over the notorious hiring in 1869 of Chinese workers in a western Massachusetts shoe factory. Cowley predicted that if Chinese workers came to Fall River, the issue of ten hours would be dead. The moves of the mill agents only stimulated political agitation. Mayor Samuel Brown, running for reelection, began to show up at ten-hour meetings. Labor reformer Thomas Webb announced that Fall River led Lowell and Lawrence in the number of spindles and in fervor for ten hours.[106] City politics reflected this new momentum for shorter hours.

In the fall of 1869, the voting strength of workingmen and labor reformers in Fall River centered on the campaign for state senator in the Third Bristol District. Attorney Nicholas Hathaway, nominated as the Workingmen's Party candidate at its Worcester convention, persuaded the local Democrats to endorse him. Having faced Republican domination of Fall River politics for years, the Democrats gave his candidacy a try. Hathaway carried the working-class wards 1, 2, and 3 heavily and easily defeated Republican George H. Eddy, a young retailer. Local Democrats did not, however, nominate the Labor Party's candidate for governor, E. M. Chamberlain of Boston. With the vote split, Fall River went for Republican William Claflin for governor. Democrats made gains statewide in the House of Representatives, especially in Boston where Democratic coalitions with the Workingmen's Party were popular. Nine new senators, among them Hathaway of Fall River, supported ten hours.[107] The stunned, local Republican Party moved to whip up its sixteen hundred party members to defeat Hathaway in 1870, running wealthy mill owner, Charles P. Stickney, who claimed to support ten-hour reform. Democratic attempts in late 1869 to build a stronger coalition in city politics in alliance with disaffected middle-class Republicans by forming a Citizen's Party led to disaster. Edward P. Buffinton, their candidate for mayor and the son of the Republican congressman, insulted local veterans by sharply criticizing the proposed state veterans' bounty and was immediately denounced by a hastily organized "Soldiers' Committee." Republican candidate Samuel Brown, who attended ten-hour rallies and kept quiet about veterans, won easily.[108] Still, the new volatility in city politics in 1869 invigorated reform efforts in the state House.

MOBILIZATION TO PASS THE TEN-HOUR LAW

By the early 1870s, the House of Representatives passed the ten-hour bill year after year, but the Senate, bolstered by the promised veto of Republican governors, remained the stronghold of the textile interests and blocked passage of the bill. Conservative senators from the Boston area and from rural constituencies joined their ranks.[109] In order to change the die-hard opponents to ten hours in the Massachusetts House and Senate, Boston's eight-hour men Steward, McNeill, and Chamberlain developed a statewide coalition to organize the votes of native-born and naturalized immigrant workers to achieve a final victory in 1874. Immigrant textile workers from the woolen and cotton districts of Yorkshire and Lancashire became crucial to this coalition. They were most active in Lawrence and Fall River with their own labor press: the *Lawrence Journal* and the Fall River *Labor Journal.* Four senators from heavily populated Essex County districts supported ten hours, responding to the influence of the pro–ten-hour Knights of St. Crispin at the peak of their power in the early 1870s.[110] In addition, Henry K. Oliver of Salem, and his associate George McNeill used their positions at the Bureau of Labor Statistics to advocate ten hours and other factory legislation. As a result, Republican Governor William B. Washburn fired McNeill in 1873 and Oliver in 1874. Conservative Senator Carroll D. Wright of Reading, who had just been defeated in 1873 for voting against the ten-hour bill, replaced Oliver at the bureau. Both McNeill and Oliver returned to full-time agitation. In recognition of the growing political strength of labor reformers, the governor placed William Bower, brother of Robert Bower of Lawrence, at the bureau, while the new chief, Carroll Wright, called on the textile industry in 1874 to observe the ten-hour day voluntarily.[111] Labor reformers began to threaten politicians at the highest state levels.

The ten-hour movement had able publishers and politicians, Robert Bower and Richard Hinchcliffe—the latter a popular workingman, agitator, and poet, who also helped edit the *Lawrence Journal*. Bower had kept the original Ten Hour Association's records and formed a second one in 1869, serving as its president. In 1871 Bower began to publish a small advertising sheet that evolved into the *Lawrence Journal* and served two terms as a Democratic state representative from Lawrence.[112] Hinchcliffe, born in Bradford, Yorkshire, in 1834, emigrated with his family in 1849. At sixteen, he wrote a poem denouncing the Fugitive Slave Act of 1850 and continued throughout the 1850s to champion the workingman against class oppression. In the preface to his collection of poetry published by Bower, *Rhymes among the Spindles* (1872), Hinchcliffe credited his father and mother for teaching their children basic literacy and arithmetic after both parents and children had worked a thirteen-hour day in Bradford's woolen mills. A poet from his youth, he pleaded, "the cause of justice to the poor and oppressed whatever may be their color or nationality." One of his poems, "Lines, Written on seeing a young Student of Andover Theological Seminary push a ragged cripple from the sidewalk," reads,

> Thou proud, pampered fool, though thy father inherit
>   His thousands in gold and his palace of pride,
> Thou still has no right thus to trample on merit,
>   Nor spurn the poor beggar in rags from thy side.
>
> Though want may be marked on his pale, sunken features,
>   Though poor as the poorest in poverty's clan;
> Though spurned and despised, he is one of God's creatures,
>   And owns what thou hast not—the soul of a man![113]

Hinchcliffe joined Bower's Ten-Hour Association in 1869 and became president in 1873, editing the *Lawrence Journal* for a year, until he replaced Bower in 1874 on the State Central Labor Reform Committee in Boston.

Bower and Hinchcliffe did not always agree on the type of political activity most likely to promote labor reform in Massachusetts. Hinchcliffe supported English-style strikes and direct confrontation between labor and capital. He defended the noisy demonstrations for the ten-hour law in Fall River that Bower deplored, insisting that their open displays of anger were justified.[114] When Hinchcliffe died of pneumonia at forty-one on May 8, 1875, the leading Boston labor reformers Ira Steward and Edward Chamberlain eulogized him at his funeral as a family friend, and: "a Christian, but one that did not think it possible to worship God and Mammon."[115]

The most experienced ten-hour activist in Fall River was Thomas Webb, born in Ireland in 1818, whose family traveled to Lancashire when he was two years old. Trained as a cardroom worker, he became deeply involved in the Chartist-linked Irish independence movement led by Fergus O'Connor. Webb took part in the defeated Irish rebellion of 1848 and fled to New York City, reaching Fall River a few days later. He worked for a while as a carder, then briefly served as the editor of a labor journal. He regarded himself as an old-fashioned Jacksonian Democrat.[116] Fall River also had several equally active, but much younger, English immigrants, among them Henry Sevey who would found the Fall River *Labor Journal* in 1874. Born in 1839 in Shrewsbury, Shropshire, to a middle-class business family, he left in 1860 for the cutlery manufacturing center of Sheffield, possibly to be employed by one of the firms. Then in 1871 he wandered to France for a few months, finally landing in Boston. Arriving in Fall River in 1872, he learned the printing trade, like Robert Bower of Lawrence, probably with the *News*. On January 1, 1874, the year of the passage of the ten-hour law, he began the *Labor Journal*. According to one key labor reformer, George Gunton, Sevey was the "ablest and most eloquent speaker the labor movement in New England ever had."[117]

Thomas Stephenson, a textile operative, organized another labor newspaper called the *Fall River Citizen* upon his arrival in the early 1870s, but it did not thrive.[118] Stephenson did not approve of Lancashire-style labor politics in New England. After his paper folded in 1874, he accompanied Robert Bower on a tour of the Pacific Mill in Lawrence. Stephenson admired both the mill and the "high-spirited determination [of the work people] to make the most of the world as they find it and not to be growling all the time about the rapacity of capital and the helplessness of labor."[119] He dismissed Sevey's *Labor Journal* as unworthy and badly edited, later joining forces with Bower's publication.

Mule spinner Robert Howard of Stockport, Lancashire, arrived in Fall River in 1873. Born in 1844, Howard worked at the age of eight as a piecer in a Macclesfield silk mill and two years later moved with his Irish-born family to Stockport to work as a bobbin boy. At fifteen, he began to serve his apprenticeship. Refusing an offer in 1870 to be an overseer, Howard became the president of the Stockport Mule Spinners' Union. He was an active participant in Lancashire spinners' strikes between 1867 and 1872. The reasons for his emigration remain unclear; he did not seem to have been blacklisted.[120] After his arrival in Fall River, he worked in the Flint mills and did not take a leading role in labor politics until June 1878 when he became the secretary of the Fall River Spinners' Union.

In contrast, the experienced Lancashire agitator and weaver George Gunton came to Fall River in 1874 and immediately plunged into labor reform activities. Gunton was born in Cambridgeshire, England, in 1845, the son of a farm laborer and a Chartist mother. He began working in a textile mill near Rochdale, Lancashire, in 1856 when he was eleven-years-old. He was unschooled but, like many Lancashire lads, steeped himself in radical literature. During the American Civil War he participated in the political agitation opposing British recognition of the Confederacy, while he, his family, and many others subsisted on a scanty diet of oatmeal porridge during the "Cotton Famine" that stagnated the English textile industry. When the war ended, Gunton joined the successful agitation for household suffrage that gained the vote for part of the English working class. In 1868, Gunton also participated in the fight to disestablish the Anglican Church in Ireland.[121]

By the early 1870s the New England cotton textile industry was expanding rapidly. Northern city dwellers, Western farmers, and the freedpeople of the South demanded Fall River's cheap calico. British unions, eager to relieve an over-crowded labor market, encouraged workers to leave, believing that wages, according to the immigrant grapevine, were higher in the U.S. than in Lancashire. At the age of twenty-nine, Gunton caught "American fever." Leaving behind a wife and five children, he emigrated for the same reasons that many Lancashire operatives had: high wages and plenty of work. When in late 1874 he landed in the Tecumseh mills in Fall River, the ten-hour law had just gone into effect. Fall River teemed with Lancashire people. Along with his fellow and sister weavers, Gunton quickly learned that the city was notorious as "the hardest place for work and the meanest place for wages" in New England.[122]

Lawrence activists Bower and Hinchcliffe, working closely with Boston's eight-hour men, provided the final impetus for political lobbying on Beacon Hill that led to the passage of the ten-hour bill in May 1874. Fall River's Sevey, Howard, and Gunton arrived too late, but later they took leading roles in the passage of amendments to the law and other labor legislation. The coalition of Lawrence labor activists and Boston reformers tied to their supporters in Lowell and Fall River had endured years of false promises, a tenacious strategy of delays, and ineffective leadership, especially in the Senate. After these organizational and political setbacks, the 1873 state elections produced solid results for ten-hour reformers. The Republican Party had to take notice.

A strategy of targeting ten-hour opponents and appealing to voters to ignore their usual partisan loyalties worked in 1873. Although the hostile Republican governor William Washburn was reelected for a third term, ten senators regarded as useless, politically ineffectual, or outright opponents of ten hours were defeated in 1873, including the chair of the labor committee, Martin Griffin. Editor Hinchcliffe named them all as "enemies and traitors to the cause."[123] Opponents and even supporters of reform measures that had failed were defeated, including the hostile Carroll Wright of Reading along with senator and long-term state representative Isaac Coe of New Bedford. Other losers included incumbent senators from districts representing Boston, Lawrence, Cambridge, and Worcester. Republican Senator Charles Stickney of Fall River, who endorsed the ten-hour bill, survived for a third term, although he was known for his absences at crucial votes and his encouragment of senators from rural districts to oppose the measure.[124] The affable Stickney proved the most slippery opponent to the bill, serving for four terms as chair of the powerful Senate finance committee that shielded banks from taxes. Labor reformers celebrated their 1873 electoral victory at Faneuil Hall on November 6 by lionizing Joseph Arch, the leader of the English Agricultural Labourers' Union. On this occasion E. M. Chamberlain, Wendell Phillips, and Benjamin Butler among others encouraged trans-Atlantic cooperation of the working classes and the emigration of English farm laborers to the free soil of America.[125]

Fall River politics between 1870 and 1874 demonstrated the increasing divisions within the local Republican Party and the growing coalition between the Democrats and the labor vote. One indicator was the popularity of former mayor George O. Fairbanks who ran successfully for several terms as a pro-ten-hour Republican for state representative. Republican George Eddy announced himself a supporter of ten hours and served two terms in the state House. In 1871 the local Democratic Party joined the labor reform party, probably encouraged by Judge Lapham, to nominate for state representative a ticket of alderman Daniel Conroy, union mule spinner James Cordingly, and physician Isaac Smith. None of these candidates won, but the worried editors of the *News* protested that temperance Republicans, not the proliquor Democrats, represented the true party of reform. The anti-ten-hour Republican candidate for governor in 1871 carried Fall River by only thirty-three votes, while statewide the Republicans possessed a bare nine thousand vote majority.[126] The Democrats then seized the opportunity of a light Republican vote in 1873 and 1874, with many Republicans disgruntled over scandals in the Grant administration, to win big. In 1873 they elected Democrat Daniel McGowan, a twine manufacturer, as a state representative and reelected pro-ten-hour representative Fairbanks. Senator Charles P. Stickney won his most narrow victory in the city but easily carried the rest of the district. He was paying a price for his evasive tactics on ten hours. Ten of his conservative friends in the Senate had been defeated. The path to victory seemed clear.

While labor reformers lobbied tirelessly in the spring of 1874 on Beacon Hill, ten-hour demonstrations erupted in Lynn, Lawrence, Lowell, Newburyport, and especially in Fall River where activists held a sensational mass labor demonstration in early April.[127] The targets were Senator Stickney and his anti-ten-hour colleagues. The spirit of Lancashire protest culture and the use of "rough music"—the public humiliation of lofty or corrupt public figures—animated the widely reported event. Speeches by Judge Lapham, labor reformer Webb, Lancashire activist and former hand-loom weaver Biltcliffe, and Sevey, editor of the *Labor Journal,* attacked the five senators, including Stickney, who had just voted to recommit the ten-hour bill to committee, trying to kill it. An evening torchlight parade of workingmen featured bands and banners labeling Senator Salmon of Lowell a "dead fish," Senator Lovering of Taunton a skunk, and attorney M. R. Dickinson—pictured with a bankroll of ten thousand dollars from western Massachusetts textile interests to buy Beacon Hill votes—a donkey. Other banners revived the mule spinners' 1867 adaptation of the Preston strike slogan: "Ten Hours and No Surrender." The shocked Boston press reported five thousand marchers and fifteen thousand spectators, cheering at the scurrilous caricatures and scenes of blazing torches that seemed to threaten the State House, all carried by "redcapped agitators."[128] These caps may indeed have been hand-made versions of the caps of liberty or *bonnets rouges,* one of the great icons of popular radicalism in early nineteenth-century England. The streets of Fall River were filled with restless, angry people. One motto painted on a ten-hour clock with its hands at six read;

> The patient dint [effort] and powder shock,
> Will blast an empire like a rock.[129]

In early 1874, the Senate had stalled and stalled on ten hours until with unforeseen good timing, U.S. Senator Charles Sumner died in March. After weeks of political skirmishing, during which the House and Senate passed an identical version of the ten-hour bill, anti-ten-hour Governor Washburn emerged on April 12 as the compromise candidate to replace Sumner as senator, leaving Beacon Hill for Washington.[130] Sumner's death saved the ten-hour bill from veto. The new governor, Thomas Talbot, who owned small woolen mills in Billerica, near Lowell, signed the law in May for implementation on October 1.

Before its enactment, however, Senator Stickney of Fall River successfully inserted the legal term *willfully* into the bill in three different places. As all lawyers knew, proving intent beyond a reasonable doubt was formidable. Using this loophole, Fall River manufacturers and many others ignored ten hours until amended legislation passed in 1879 struck *willfully* from the law. In addition, the wording of the bill made it possible for employers to require more than ten hours a day when machinery was stopped for repairs—a commonplace occurrence in weave rooms—providing that sixty hours per week remained the maximum. These provisions in the law, however, were not enforceable.[131] The statute provided no inspection force, only local police, and the fine was unspecified, to be assessed "upon complaint." Still, at a ten-hour celebration in Lawrence, labor reformer Jennie Collins congratulated the local labor reformers, especially Bower and Hinchcliffe, for their tireless efforts.

> Were American agitators for this measure? No! I am ashamed to confess it. The men who have worked and struggled for this law . . . were of British birth, born under a monarchy. I have seen them, a little noble band, day after day, during the past session, filling our legislative halls, keeping Senators to their pledges and in their seats. . . . [N]o graduates of Harvard came to help these men.[132]

The Lawrence labor reformers were overjoyed by the ten-hour victory. The pages of the *Lawrence Journal*—and presumably of the *Labor Journal*—were filled with the language of early nineteenth-century English agitation.

> Might has succumbed to Right. The first link of the chain forged by cupidity to abase and degrade the toiler has been broken, and Labor, now showing its strength, will not be quiescent again in bondage to Mammon.[133]

Eager to continue the coalition with Boston's eight-hour men and the still active Henry Oliver, they planned to introduce the English half-time system of education for factory children—six months of work followed by six months of school—and legislation for weekly wage payments. Still the old disagreements over styles of protest continued. The Bower brothers believed that cooperative stores, not strikes, were the answer to low wages. Richard Hinchcliffe favored street demonstrations and labor protest, while Robert Bower saw the political process as centered within the party system on Beacon Hill, lobbying with the eight-hour men. He regarded noisy agitators, torchlight parades, and confrontational strikes as dangerous to the enactment of additional factory legislation. In October 1874, Thomas Stephenson, who agreed that agitation was useless, joined the Bower brothers to reorganize their paper into the *Lawrence Journal and Citizen,* claiming to represent Fall River, Lowell, New Bedford, Providence, Andover, and many mill villages in Rhode Island. By 1875, serious divisions in style, politics, and goals had emerged among English immigrant labor reformers.

During the 1874 fall elections, the unthinkable occurred: a heavy

Democratic vote in Fall River and across the state. Democratic candidate for governor, William Gaston, won statewide and carried Fall River. Democrat Robert H. Pitman, a printer at Lapham's *Border City Herald*, defeated Stickney, running for his fifth term. The entire delegation of state representatives from Fall River in 1874 were Democrats: a very happy Nicholas Hathaway (who had been defeated in 1870), grocer William Carroll, and Southard H. Miller, a carpenter and an engineer with the fire department. Judge Lapham, running for Congress, carried the city of Fall River and almost beat Republican Buffinton who had served since the 1850s. Lapham then ran for mayor against incumbent Republican John S. Davenport, losing by only 625, or 16 percent, of the total vote.[134] The political mobilization for ten hours had changed the landscape of Fall River politics.

Meanwhile Boston's eight-hour men joined the International Labor Union to promote the philosophy of eight hours as a solution to class conflict. Richard Hinchcliffe's death in 1875 deprived Lawrence of a beloved rank-and-file reformer and a man who had well understood the English political legacy of popular radicalism. One of his last entries in the *Journal* sharply attacked the obstinacy of mill owners such as J. P. Stevens of North Andover who refused to obey the ten-hour law. Hinchcliffe asserted he was close to advocating "knock-down arguments" and "for labor to take capital by the throat."[135] Henry Sevey and George Gunton of Fall River lost a valuable potential ally.

THE GRANITE MILL DISASTER

The celebration of the ten-hour victory was dimmed in Fall River by the terrible loss of life when Granite Mill # 1 burned in September 1874. The list of the forty dead revealed that children under ten were commonly and illegally employed as back boys or as spoolers on the top floors where there were no fire escapes in the dangerously ill-equipped mill built in 1860. They died of burns, or from suffocation, or by jumping from the fifth floor of the mill, about sixty feet to the ground. The surviving injured numbered at least eighty, many never able to work again. Of the four hundred operatives, nearly one-third perished or were maimed. Those who barely escaped the wildfire that destroyed the building in seventy minutes and those who watched helplessly from the nearby Merchants mill never forgot the tragedy caused by mismanagement that had allowed the common occurrence of flames in a cotton mill to lead to an inferno. The fire was visible to at least ten other textile complexes clustered around the Quequechan millpond, the heat from which fused the minerals in the granite block walls of Mill # 1.

When the fire broke out on the north end of the third floor mule room, the first spinner who saw it, Matthew Dillon, rushed to the burning cotton and tried to drench it.[136] Because fires were so frequent in cotton mills, each pair of mules had water pails, usually kept full, but not that morning. There was no additional water in the room's standpipes or pails stored in the central tower. No one had inspected or reported this. Meanwhile, the oily belting that powered the machinery carried the flames swiftly upward, filling the top floors with flame and smoke. Most of the sixteen spinners on the third floor hastily left by the stairs in the mill's central tower. Seven stayed to help, and two died on the fourth floor. Dillon himself left when the empty water hose in his hand began to burn. Smoke and flame rose into the central tower that connected the five floors, cutting many operatives off from escape. The freight elevator did not work. A confused alarm signal sent fire engines to the wrong place for precious minutes, while the hook and ladder companies had difficulty reaching the third floor. Efforts by workingmen to help the firemen splice ladders to reach higher were refused with contempt. The outside fire escapes located near the one central tower proved useless; there were none on the ends of the building and only one tower.

Some men who worked on the fourth floor lowered themselves with ropes or strong coils of warp. Young women who tried either fell to their deaths as others grabbed on to them or suffered rope-burned hands and broken bones. Other operatives on the fourth and fifth floors desperately tried to reach the ladders held out by firemen. Trapped in the sixth-floor attic, terrified women and children, blinded by smoke, pushed their arms through the tightly shut panes of glass and wooden frames. As the smoke and fire filled the top floors, spectators on the ground tried to break the leaps of burning and choking women and children with make-shift heaps of mattresses and hand-held blankets. Many workers on the fifth floor and in the attic who were too paralyzed by fear to jump were "roasted alive," while many who jumped died from spinal injuries, crushed skulls, and broken necks.[137] The youngest of the operatives worked on the highest floors. Among them were the dead Murphy sisters, Bridget, Mary, and Kate, the only children in their fatherless family.[138] The names of the victims on the top floors included young French Canadian girls and boys, Irish American girls and boys, and adult English and Yankee women doing the skilled work of drawing-in.

Fall River workers blamed the policies of mill managers for the fire. In Mill # 1, overseers had denied mule spinners their customary time to oil and clean their machines by setting the piece rate for spinning yarn so low as to require almost total concentration on machine operations. The accumulation of cotton waste on and near mules whose unoiled gears scraped metal against metal caused the disastrous fire. The young spinner whose unoiled machine parts had produced the sparks that ignited the cotton waste was a half-trained fellow, whom Sevey described as "only a boy not yet as thoughtful as a man." The novice spinner had neglected his duties to clean and oil his mules trying to keep up with the movements of the older, experienced men in the spinning room. Granite mill overseers posted the daily work records of each mule spinner in order to create competition among them. As the editor of the *Labor Journal* put it; "If a man is not able to get as much off his mules as the others, he is, of course ashamed, and becomes a butt of ridicule to his fellow-workmen. A boy of seventeen likes to feel like a man . . . and will be tempted to neglect his machinery. . . ."[139] By encouraging competition among mule spinners over their productivity, the power of the mill agents to define this measure of manhood assumed a deadly potential.

At the coroner's inquest and later during a civil trial, mill owners, testifying as a group, denied responsibility for the deaths and injuries. The agents and overseers argued that panic-stricken women and children died needlessly, while cowardly able-bodied workingmen saved only themselves. The overseer in the attic had tested the stair tower and, nearly suffocated from the smoke, then lowered himself by rope. No one accused him of cowardice. Speaking in one voice, they blamed the operatives and testified that because all the mills were poorly equipped to fight fires, no particular mill should be blamed. The Granite mill company suffered no financial loss; it was fully insured.[140] The mill owners paid for funerals and doctors' bills, but the jurors absolved them. The other Fall River mills hurriedly completed the installation of additional outdoor fire escapes required by insurance companies after the 1874 disaster. This added fuel to the operatives' rage.

Operatives' committees responded immediately to the injured and the bereaved, building a local coalition among the various nationalities through a citywide relief committee. Perhaps the most significant participant in the relief work was Honoré Beaugrand, a well-educated immigrant from Montreal, editor of Fall River's *L'Echo du Canada,* (founded in July 1873), a notary public, head of the French Canadian Chamber of Commerce, and the husband of a Yankee wife, Alice Walker of Providence. Beaugrand also supported French Canadian businesses and French Canadian workers, protesting the inability of experienced mule spinners from Montreal to gain work in the Fall River mills.[141] By the early 1870s, there were 3,646 French Canadians living in Fall River. Beaugrand intended to make his newspaper the voice of French Canadian interests in New England, collaborating with Sevey of the *Labor Journal*. He endorsed the ten-hour law in early 1874 and urged the few naturalized French Canadians to vote for Republican Governor Talbot that fall. He encouraged more naturalization and political activity for the French Canadian community. Beaugrand served on the city's fund-raising committee for the Granite mill fire victims and organized benefits in the French community, many attended by Yankee Republicans. At the dedication of the first French Catholic church, Notre Dame de Lourdes, in November 1874, an event crowded with French Canadians and Yankees, the most senior pastor, Rev. Murphy of St. Mary's, called for the union of all Catholics, whatever their nationality.[142] If this were to prove possible, a coalition of nationalities in Fall River could be organized to support higher wages and better working conditions in the mills and defend the Catholic faith.

THE STRUGGLE to gain ten hours in Massachusetts textile mills reveals much about the political dynamics of New England industry, its workforce and their communities, their definitions of manhood and womanhood, and the various uses and sources of power. Since the 1840s skilled workingmen and labor reformers defined manhood as the right of white male mechanics to exercise republican citizenship, guaranteed by a shorter working day. Workingwomen joined the ten-hour movement, convinced that traditions of republicanism also applied to them. Seeking a political coalition with other workers to mobilize political power, eight-hour advocates embraced the ten-hour movement and thus confronted the political and economic power of the textile industry on Beacon Hill. Political opponents defended freedom of contract for adult males, regardless of the inequities of power. Somehow, proper assertions of republican manliness would right the imbalance. State regulation of the working day for men raised difficult ideological and political questions about the meanings of legal dependency and even servility in the American republic. Associating white native-born or immigrant workingmen with any sort of subordination necessarily linked them with lesser races, the new foreign nationalities. While many workingmen and labor reformers charged employers with tyranny, they defined females as dependent children and regarded Chinese and French Canadian immigrants as subordinated races, lacking manliness and whiteness. Ten-hour politics in Massachusetts sustains the arguments of historian David Roediger on the centrality of race to nineteenth-century, working-class identity but adds the issue of the disputed nature of manhood and womanhood.

English immigrant textile workers provided reform language in 1869 that sidestepped some of these political and ideological dependencies and racial denigration. This represented a deft shift in gender politics and organizational strategy for the Massachusetts ten-hour movement as well as the rising influence of English immigrant labor activists. The decision to target women and children for state protection had serious implications for activist women, for working-class understandings of womanhood, and the potential for isolating women workers in labor politics. The legacy of pre–Civil War female labor reformers plus the involvement of women in the 1868 New Bedford strike and the ten-hour petition drives belied these definitions. However, the appalling losses in the 1874 Granite mill disaster confirmed images of women and children as weak and helpless, foolishly and fatally panicking, while hardy, cool-headed men saved themselves. Even workingwomen who actively participated in the ten-hour movement and in labor militancy between 1866 and 1874 could be placed under the control of the male leadership in labor politics. This exclusionary strategy proved to be a powerful force in the developing New England labor movement.

But three brave female operatives had given convincing testimony in 1867 for ten hours, at the risk of their livelihoods. Thousands of other women, including some French Canadian immigrants, signed petitions under the threat of being fired. Letters from others denounced injustice, inequality, and overwork. Lancashire and Yorkshire women in particular possessed a strong legacy of labor activism. Former textile operative and reform agitator Jennie Collins of Boston became the most visible woman activist for ten hours in labor party circles. Thus legal definitions of womanhood conflicted with female activism and female agency would contest them. Yet the New England heritage of female protest demanding equal rights for workingmen and women seemed familiar to a only minority of native-born female operatives in the post–Civil War years and alien to French Canadian women from rural Quebec. Labor politics in England had restricted the activism of Lancashire and Yorkshire women in Chartism, ten-hour reform, and strikes. Still, to define females as legal dependents would prove potentially dangerous to skilled male operatives as employers adopted new technology to deskill work and hired low-paid women. The legacy of gender politics in ten-hour reform added female dependency to race and nationality as divisive to class unity, contradicting more inclusive ideas of organization.

The contest over the passage of the ten-hour law also involved the question of who controlled the state. Labor reformers and working-class voters mobilized to undercut the political weight of textile capital on Beacon Hill. By 1873 efforts on the municipal and the state level had made progress, interested Democrats, and alarmed the Massachusetts Republican Party. Labor reformers and some working-class activists, especially in Lawrence, insisted on the slow, frustrating, and uneven march through hearings, debates, lobbying, and the creation of a third political party. Other English immigrant workingmen tried the more confrontational tactics rejected by many of their allies: strikes, shows of anger and contempt, and noisy mass demonstrations of public ridicule. They were paying homage to the culture of English radical politics. These traditions of disruptive protest would later collide with different cultural meanings for respectable manhood and womanhood among the native-born and immigrants. Meanwhile, factory owners and their agents would fashion new political and workplace tactics to challenge the skill and strength of workingmen and workingwomen. The passage of the ten-hour law opened new arenas of conflict over the uses of power to enforce state regulation and establish political control and personal identity.

During these years of struggle, labor reformers based their power on the pre–Civil War reform movement, republican and Christian values, some measure of success for shorter hours in Fall River, the cultural nationalism and popular radicalism of immigrant groups, and the political heritage of the eight-hour movement in New England. For English immigrants, the willingness of employers to play heavy-handed politics in the mills and on Beacon Hill encouraged mass political mobilization of male voters and summoned protest legacies from Lancashire and Yorkshire. These helped mobilize electoral power, but different cultural values and political heritages could prove seriously divisive. The economic power that backed textile manufacturing remained strong on Beacon Hill, even to the final wording of legal loopholes in the ten-hour law and later in the almost universal refusal to obey it.[143] Capital could easily get state charters for new corporations, control taxes on banks, defend the right to freedom of contract, and attack opponents. During strikes, whether in New Bedford or by the mule spinners of the Merrimack Valley, the mill agents as a group demonstrated their power, locally and regionally, by refusing to respond or negotiate. Most mill agents believed that any negotiations or political concessions would encourage working-class activism.

Experienced English immigrants had seen it all before and dug in for the long term, seizing political leadership from native-born working people. Still, the ability of the mill agents to ignore, punish, blacklist, fire, evict, lower the piece rate, raise rents, and rearrange working conditions were all expressions of corporate power. Behind these lay the strategy of the Fall River mills to dominate the national print cloth market, while paying lip service to the natural laws of supply and demand, which they meant to control and use. American capitalists advocated the ideology of supply and demand, like the legacy of republican individualism and freedom of contract, to block reform. Lancashire people rejected these laws, also alien to French Canadians, but many eight-hour men, such as Ira Steward, and most middle-class labor reformers in Massachusetts accepted supply and demand. For them, state regulation would guarantee that the laws of the marketplace worked for the mutual benefit of all. This was strange stuff for many English labor activists, such as Richard Hinchcliffe from Yorkshire, a strong ally of the eight-hour men. To Hinchcliffe, these so-called natural laws had been put in place by "mammonites," worshipers of golden idols, and used to oppress liberty and justice. The power of the mills on Beacon Hill and in the cloth market would test the political coalitions forged among textile workers and labor reformers in the ten-hour movement. As the mills expanded during the post–Civil War years, textile workers in Fall River and the surrounding region would grow more defiant.

5

To Dominate the National Market, 1866–1878

As THE PRINT cloth market was reviving after the Civil War, two devastating events destroyed most of Fall River's capacity to print. One of the steam boilers at the Bay State Print Works blew up in the early morning of December 5, 1867. The main building with all of its machinery and inventory burned. The fire, caused by a series of explosions of all the boilers, began when the first burst and filled the boiler room with huge chunks of metal that ripped apart the other seven and blew the roof off the boiler house. Boiler parts pierced the dye house roof, destroying it. Another piece weighing three tons ripped a four-story-high gaping hole in the two-foot thick granite wall of the main works. Neighboring cottages were demolished by flying shrapnel that ended up deeply embedded in the frozen ground. Windows, doors, chimneys, and roofs were shattered or sheared off. Most of the print workers escaped serious injury by fleeing when they heard the explosion, but many lost their precious tools. The body of the steam fireman sitting in front of the boilers was never found.

Ten days later, another fire broke out on a Sunday afternoon in an older part of the expanded, just finished, grandly designed, and uninsured American Print Works. Jefferson Borden, the largest investor, planned its great capacity to dominate the postwar production of print cloth. The new structure, valued at a million dollars, was gone in four hours. A northeast storm had just dumped a heavy snowfall, and as the winds from the storm backed around, howling northwest gales fanned the blaze. The intensity of the fire melted the tall snow banks. The municipal volunteer fire fighters, with only hand-operated force pumps, turned away to save surrounding structures. Six printing machines and the entire inventory were destroyed. The *News* called the loss of the new building and its potential "the greatest calamity that has ever befallen the city."[1]

After the Fall River fires, the postwar market seemed securely in the hands of other large New England print cloth works, such as the A. & W. Sprague Company at Cranston, Rhode Island, and the Goddard Company at Lonsdale, Rhode Island, the Merrimack corporation in Lowell, and the Pacific Mill in Lawrence.[2] Even the burning in 1865 of the Arctic Mill in Warwick, the largest cotton mill in Rhode Island, another mill owned by the Sprague interests, proved no long-term setback to their development. Along the seven miles of roads connecting Providence with Woonsocket, paralleling the Blackstone River, other Rhode Island investors in 1866 were building new mills in the small villages of Olneyville, Manville, Albion, and Ashton. By late 1866 Ashton became the site of a large Goddard mill, a branch of the Lonsdale Company, controlled by Brown and Ives of Providence.[3] These Rhode Island mills in particular would become the competitive nemesis of Fall River.

Jefferson Borden's activities after the 1867 devastation reinforced his personal legend for vigorous resolution. On the day after the second disaster, following a night of anxious decision-making, he announced the rebuilding of the American Print Works to a relieved community.[4] He put several hundred men to work that morning, December 16, to clear and scavenge the smoking ruins and debris. Within two years, another American Print Works was open for business, equipped with twenty printing machines, more than three times those destroyed by fire. With his "extraordinary capacity for recuperation" he reopened the boiler-damaged Bay State within six months, while rebuilding the American works with Fall River granite and re-equipping and expanding the whole operation.[5] Jefferson Borden did it by using the assets of the Iron Works as well as those of Borden family members and his closest associates. Contingencies in the development of nineteenth-century business firms sometimes presented challenges that embellished reputations.

ALFRED CHANDLER'S 1977 study, *The Visible Hand: The Managerial Revolution in American Business,* analyzes the rise of modern managerial techniques and distribution processes in the developing mass market of the late nineteenth and early twentieth centuries. Chandler's views on modernization reveal his confident faith in the evolving system of twentieth-century capitalist enterprise. For him, the words *enterprise* and *corporate structure* are interchangeable.[6] Replacing small family-owned businesses and partnerships with incorporated institutions meant economic progress. But Chandler studies institutional development, not specific entrepreneurs, such as Jefferson Borden. "Men came and went," he writes. "The institution and its offices remained."[7] *Visible Hand* does not examine in detail any particular business concern, although Chandler called for such studies. Nor, as he states, was he interested in the workplace, the workers, their organizations and aspirations.[8] Politics and social life are not part of his story. Yet all are important to the dynamic of industrial change.

Chandler's *Visible Hand* explores the way Adam Smith's "invisible hand" of market forces directing the early American economy was transformed by the late nineteenth-century managerial revolution. In his brief discussion of textile capitalism prior to the Civil War, Chandler maintains that market, not human, forces directed the national and international workings of supply and demand. His description of how raw cotton was delivered to the early textile mills and finished cloth to the consumer, however, contradicts his argument. The human players were many, and the hands coordinating those early market operations are clearly discernible. Pre–Civil War cotton buyers for commission houses, financiers in London and Liverpool, mill treasurers, and cotton brokers brought together cotton seller and textile purchaser, all for hefty commissions or percentages of the sales.[9] These men and their relationships, not economic laws, constituted and constructed the market.

Chandler notes that traditional mercantile methods did not give way easily to the new managerial techniques, even in the textile mills with the most technically advanced and integrated production. He admires technological innovation and the beginnings of mass production, but most textile firms did not manage their accounts uniformly or try to determine a unit cost of production. Many of the New England mills may have been incorporated, but they were run like partnerships.[10] Although Chandler does not mention Fall River, New Bedford, or Rhode Island in his treatment of the textile industry, his argument about the persistence of old managerial methods generally fits. Indeed, whenever competition during the expansive post–Civil War period cut into profits, mill agents did not consult their accountants. They simply ran shorter hours to limit production or more often cut wages to reduce costs.

Chandler's *Visible Hand* provides an excellent analysis of the developing post–Civil War mass distribution system, involving railroads, telegraphy, warehouses, and, most important, the commodity exchanges, such as the New York Cotton Exchange and others in New Orleans, Savannah, Liverpool, and London. Eliminating the middlemen who had run the pre–Civil War market on long-term credit and countless transactions, the new system both lowered transportation costs and lessened financial risk. The cotton exchanges also standardized the grades of cotton for the buyer and, significantly, offered a new trading option in cotton futures. Dealing in future contracts in raw cotton appears to Chandler to have been a blessing to modern managerial institutions.[11] Contemporary observers were not so sure. The editors of the *Providence Journal* denounced speculation in commodity trading financed by firms or banks, charging that the futures market in necessities, such as coal, grain, and even railroad stock shares, constituted dangerous gambling and oppressed "the people."[12] Furthermore, during the postwar depression years of the mid-1870s these new practices offered some Fall River treasurers an irresistible temptation. Rather than maintain harmonious labor relations or well-managed mill operations, they could cover any losses from low prices and indiscriminate, costly borrowing through profits from speculation in cotton or in cloth futures. Even the remaining partnerships of the older Bordens and the Durfees did not intervene to prevent these practices. Instead, they covered any speculative losses or new loans by endorsing or cosigning notes that incurred more debt and built more mills. The Borden and Durfee families thereby underwrote and encouraged overbuilding. The bankruptcy and collapse of the Sprague print cloth interests in Rhode Island in 1873 cleared the way for more risky expansion.

Several trusted sons, sons-in-law, and their protégés became entangled at enormous losses in the new cotton and cloth futures markets. The postwar inflation, the frenzied speculation in land to expand mills, the vast wealth and unquestioned credit of the Bordens and the Durfees, and their powerful position in the print cloth market persuaded those who knew about these irregularities to remain silent, hoping that all would turn out right. The public and the shareholders knew nothing until 1878. Then, when these "men came and went," as Chandler put it, it was usually to bankruptcy court, attempted suicide, state prison, or into exile to avoid arrest and prosecution. The unstable mix of new financial institutions and post–Civil War inflation followed by depression, in addition to Jefferson Borden's imperative to dominate the market, would bring out the worst in the second generation of Fall River capitalists. Control of partisan politics and local government also encouraged the Fall River mill interests to construct ideologies and policies that defined their own sense of destiny, manhood, and citizenship, specifically excluding any class antagonists. Because their dominance of politics and government on the local level helped them to accumulate capital for their own purposes, these arenas became a crucial part of industrial development.

EVEN BEFORE the great postwar boom in mill-building, the Borden and Durfee families and their kin controlled most of the income and assets in Fall River, acquired through business activities prior to the Civil War. According to an 1867 list of taxable personal income chosen from those with incomes over $15,000 a year (see table 1), they controlled approximately 70 percent ($598,000) of the total personal taxable wealth ($849,000) in the city. Backed by these assets, the new American Printing Company became the largest in the nation with a yearly capacity of one hundred million yards of print cloth. By 1869 the Fall River cotton mills and print works were again almost miraculously positioned to dominate the post–Civil War print cloth market. To protect these costly investments, Thomas J. Borden, Colonel Richard's son, supervised the planning in 1871 of a modern water works to feed fire hydrants, replacing the scattered covered water cisterns located near the mills. He also headed a municipal fire service equipped with several steam-propelled pumpers and hooks and ladders until he retired in 1873.[13] As chief engineer, Borden appeared at every fiery disaster, in uniform and mounted on a black charger. For financial protection, the mill interests organized the Fall River Manufacturers' Mutual Insurance Company in 1870.[14] The losses in 1867 had taught a hard lesson.

Jefferson Borden's determination and faith in the future of print cloth as the premier money-maker in post–Civil War textiles was not generally shared by Rhode Island textile manufacturers, headquartered in Providence. They worried about the scarcity of raw cotton and the ability of the southern economy to support the planting of a crop in 1865 or 1866, much less send it north. With former Tennessee Democrat Andrew Johnson in the White House and Radical Republicans dominant in the Congress, the reconstruction of the defeated South appeared even less certain than the cotton crop. Postwar consumption would have to be carried on in Union greenback dollars, unbacked by gold. Inflation was a certainty. In Providence financial circles, caution was the byword through 1869: "In times like these men wear their old clothes, and women turn and make over even their calico dresses."[15] Jefferson Borden's daring gambles to rebuild Fall River's capacity to print did not influence most Rhode Island banks or investors.

In contrast, Fall River millowners and investors were optimistic about postwar economic and political prospects. The whole region of the South had returned to the Union and the "destitute population. . . , black and white . . ." needed every article of "comfort and convenience."[16] New England businessmen faced "a golden harvest" and envisioned southern fields full of cotton in 1865 to pay for northern goods. Railroads would have to be rebuilt, but the cotton bales would soon flow north. The Lowell mills increased production in 1865, and throughout the region experienced textile workers, dispersed by the wartime shutdown of mill operations, were in very short supply. With the terrible bloodshed over, southern markets reopened, and with the general population growth in the North and West, countless customers appeared ready to buy print cloth.

This general optimism, expressed in the *Fall River News*, supported local postwar expansion even when the political scene grew more grim and "chaos brood[ed]" over the South during the fall of 1865. A New York organization of growers, middlemen, and textile manufacturers, a "Cotton Congress," was proposed to stimulate production without waiting for demand, thus—in an important ideological aberration—frankly exempting cotton from their professed confidence in supply and demand forces.[17] In the fall of 1866 the physical chaos of the defeated South intensified as a result of devastating floods in the Mississippi River Valley that washed away weakened levees and with them up to three-quarters of that region's cotton crop.[18] But the near collapse of the South's economy in 1866 did not halt the expansion of many New England mills. In late April

1868, a new National Association of Cotton Planters and Manufacturers met in New York City to pressure Congress to reduce taxes and cut expenditures, especially revenues for the occupying Union Army and the Freedmen's Bureau, while raising the protective tariff on cotton goods. New England, the Middle Atlantic states, and the Cotton South were all generously represented. Thomas J. Borden of Fall River joined the committee on raw materials.[19] By 1869, the New York Cotton Exchange had begun to coordinate buying and selling activities.

The expansionist mood in Fall River did not rest solely on hopes for the future. The mills had made money consistently through the war years. With the southern market closed, coarse cotton goods had few buyers, but the steady demand elsewhere for the limited supply of print cloth brought very high prices. Government contracts for the Iron Works also helped the Fall River economy. Anticipation of a small cotton crop in 1861 had led many New England mill owners, including those in Fall River, to stuff their warehouses in 1860. Some mill centers, such as Lowell, curtailed, then halted production, and sold off this precious raw cotton at rising prices.[20] During the war, Fall River seemed untroubled by labor shortages and disrupted markets compared with other textile centers. The Civil War Congresses raised the tariff higher on textiles, adopting a protectionist policy that would later dominate Gilded Age politics. A writer for the *Washington Tribune* later recalled that the market had been very dull in 1865 but the Fall River mills ran steadily. When demand returned, the cloth "sold for more than double the cost of production, realizing fabulous profits. . . . This great source of wealth becoming known to outside parties, new companies were formed. . . ."[21]

Between 1865 and 1869 the steady demand for print cloth and rising profit margins encouraged the organization of five new textile corporations in Fall River, although this growth was halted temporarily by a slump that lasted through 1870. Then prices rose again.[22] The Bordens had chosen their staple product wisely.

New York Speculators and the Fall River Line

In June 1869, the Fall River Steamboat Line, originally organized by Colonel Borden as the Bay State Line to link Fall River with New York City, reopened under the control of Jay Gould and Jim Fisk with a glorious celebration on the bedecked wharves of the American Print Works. The services of its steamers had been disrupted during the war, while other lines sponsored by New York investors threatened competition. One of these, the Narragansett Steamship Company, with its terminus at Newport, was acquired in early 1869 by Jim Fisk, one of the notorious directors of the infamous, ill-managed Erie Railroad.[23] Fisk fell in love with his steamships, the *Providence* and the *Bristol*, and fitted them out as "floating palaces" in the gaudiest carpets, gilded statues, fantastic decorations, and countless brass spittoons. He installed 250 caged canaries, naming them, variously Jay Gould, William Marcy Tweed (the boss of Tammany Hall), Jeff Davis, and General Grant. His tailor made him an admiral's uniform including regulation gold stripes and stars but with the Narragansett emblem on its gold buttons and lapels and room for the largest shirtfront diamond stud in the nation. With his plumed hat and resplendent costume, the rotund Commodore Fisk personally presided over the daily debarkations from New York harbor. Two new bigger vessels, the *James Fisk, Jr.* and the *Jay Gould,* were being built.[24]

Fisk and Gould represented all that was corrupt and scandalous in the feverish speculation following the Civil War, especially in the manipulation of railroad stock and outright embezzlement.[25] Fisk added to his unsavory financial dealings, a well-developed taste for female flesh. As he told his old friend, Daniel Drew, himself a wild speculator and notorious bettor: "... there isn't any hope for Jim Fisk. ... I like these scarlet women–they're approachable."[26] Fisk did not care what was said about him or his affairs, embroidering the stories with outrageous wit. Ministers nationwide cited his lusts as horrid examples of the times. His Vermonter's aphorisms enriched the American voice. "To indicate something that had vanished without a trace, such as money in the stock market, he would say 'It went where the woodbine twineth.' "[27] On that splendid early June morning in 1869, the manufacturers and residents of Fall River excitedly awaited their first glimpse of the reopened steamship line and its new commodore.

The new generation of sons-in-law, conspicuously led by S. Angier Chace and Charles P. Stickney, headed the reception committee that included the older Bordens and Durfees. As the *Bristol* hauled into view, gloriously rigged with streaming flags and pennants, the old Bay State steamer *Canonicus,* which had served in the Civil War navy, fired salutes, while the elegantly trimmed yachts of Matt Durfee and his cousin George B. Durfee stood by as escorts. On the *Bristol* ready to receive the elite of Fall River were Fisk, Gould, and their entourage. No female members of the Borden or Durfee families attended the festivities. Fisk was properly snubbed, but he did not care. A few days after the ceremonies in Fall River, he escorted President Ulysses S. Grant to a Peace Jubilee in Boston.

An enthusiastic S. Angier Chace presided over the lavish Fall River reception and introduced Fisk and Gould to his straw-hatted, stiff-necked in-laws. One well-wined and dined clergyman finally broke the general solemnity with a remark about Fall River being "well Fisked." Voyagers to Newport, he noted, would now dine in the calm waters of Mt. Hope Bay rather than face the nauseating swells of Rhode Island Sound off Point Judith. As everyone relaxed, ate, and drank, they listened to an expanding chorus of praise for Fisk and Gould. Even Colonel Borden, Dr. Durfee, and Jefferson Borden said a few kind words. After loud applause, Fisk told the long, intricate story of his acquisition of the Fall River Line to much appreciative laughter.[28] No Fall River money had been used. The Bordens and Durfees had turned their overnight transportation connection to the New York market entirely into the hands of two of the greatest financial scoundrels of the Gilded Age. Why? They had a textile empire to build.

THE RACE TO DOMINATE THE MARKET

Between 1869, when the American Print Works reopened, and the collapse of Jay Gould's financial empire in 1873 that brought on a severe depression, Fall River expanded spectacularly as a textile center, eclipsing both Lowell and Lawrence in capacity for cloth production.[29] Total assessed investment more than doubled from twenty one million dollars in 1869 to forty seven million dollars in 1873. By 1875 the city boasted thirty-four corporations or companies, each with several mill buildings that employed nearly 12,000 workers: 6,047 women and 5,467 men. Ten years earlier, when the Civil War ended, the total mill workforce had been only a quarter of that number (see table 2).[30] The established textile machinery companies of Hawes, Marvel, and Davol produced self-acting mule spinning machines and Kilburn, Lincoln specialized in plain looms and steam turbines, filling the needs of the boom in local mill construction. Kilburn, Lincoln built a large, new machine shop in 1866 to turn out a high-speed loom built solely for print cloth, but local machine shops were still unable to fill the demands for machinery that slowed the opening of the many new mills. The treasurers imported large quantities of English mules and carding equipment and many experienced English operatives to run them.[31]

The debts for this headlong industrial expansion in an era of inflation began to pile up. In 1870 a piece of land outside of the city center with enough water to supply steam engines, assessed at twelve hundred dollars in 1855, sold—to the owner's delight—for thirteen thousand dollars, or over ten times its former value. High interest loans, materials (southern pine beams and planking, iron posts, brick), all kinds of machinery, contractors, and skilled construction workers were scarce and expensive.[32] Corporations such as the Border City in 1872 sold shares based solely on the highly inflated value of its land and the credit—not the invested capital—of its directors. Small manufacturers and merchants organized additional print cloth mills, for example the Merchants Manufacturing Company in 1867. Treasurer William H. Jennings raised the original $800,000 for shares from local residents in two days.[33]

The Borden family did not hang back. Twelve stockholders controlled the Richard Borden Company, organized in 1871 with the Colonel's son Thomas J. Borden as treasurer. The first mill was built in 1873 on land owned by his son Richard B. Borden, just one year before the Colonel's death. When Fall River mills needed to bleach their goods, they used the Fall River Bleachery, incorporated in 1872 as a strictly Borden operation with Jefferson Borden's two sons, Spencer and Jefferson Jr., in charge. Dr. Nathan Durfee and his cousins followed the lead of his son-in-law S. Angier Chace and his associates in building many new mills. Local and even regional boosters began to call Fall River "the Manchester of America," ignoring that English city's 111 cotton mills and over twenty thousand textile operatives.[34]

No city in New England grew as fast as Fall River, more than doubling its population from 13,240 inhabitants in 1860 to 27,191 in 1870 including 7,140 operatives. Within five years the city's residents nearly doubled again to 45,260 in 1875, with 17,525, or 38 percent, foreign-born: one-third English and Irish from Lancashire, one-fifth Irish-born, and less than a fifth from Quebec. The workforce in the cotton mills had quadrupled between 1865 and 1875 to 11,514 (see tables 2 and 3). Fall River was also distinguished by the source of its mills' capital. Non-residents invested only 8 percent in contrast to the outright dependence of Lowell, Lawrence, and other textile centers on Boston capital. By 1870, the Quequechan River had been buried, lost from sight by the distinctive granite mills of grayish yellow blocks cut from the construction sites. Only those mills built north of the city's center in Mechanicsville used cheaper brick bought in nearby Taunton. By this time, the editors of the *Providence Journal* may have regretted their conservatism, for they reported only solid growth in Fall River and sensible leadership in the old style of Bradford Durfee, David Anthony, and the other men of steady application. Truly, the Providence bankers believed that Fall River could become the "Manchester" of America, but they failed to recognize the rise of speculators and younger men with unworthy "business cunning."[35]

All of this growth during the 1870s stimulated rapid construction in neighboring Rhode Island and eastern Connecticut as well as in New Bedford. By 1880, southeastern New England textile centers made 57 percent of the print cloth produced in the United States. Fall River mills produced well over half of this. Southeastern New England, however, possessed only 37 percent of the national print works capacity.[36] Fall River and other centers sent excess print cloth or "grey goods" to printers in New York and Philadelphia. The other 43 percent of total print cloth in 1880 was produced in mills scattered in various locations between Maine and Pennsylvania (see table 4). With Fall River the leading center of print cloth manufacturing, control of the national market in the 1870s seemed within the grasp of the treasurers and agents of the mills. During the mid-1870s their road to dominance was, however, obstructed by serious labor unrest, economic depression, mismanagement, overproduction, and heavy debts.

One investor, looking back to the heady years of the early 1870s, revealed the extent to which this expansion was based on speculation, high interest rates, and inflated values. In 1871–72, eleven mills had been built in six months on money borrowed at 18 to 24 percent interest. Those with parcels of suitable land organized textile corporations and exchanged the land at hugely inflated prices for stock shares. Dividends were thus paid out on those shares based on the original, absurdly high land prices. Everything else, machinery and the mills, was financed by local credit. "The mills were built on speculation rather than on capital." Prior to the "flush times of 1871," mills such as the Merchants, the Granite, the American Linen, and others were backed by capital, not credit, and paid out consistently higher dividends to investors. A "dead-weight of over-valued real estate which [was] put in as so much stock at its original and inflated valuation" thus created so much debt that lower wages for operatives became the only solution to maintaining dividends.[37] And the debt load in turn, enticed speculation in the futures markets. This was part of the financial dilemma of post–Civil War development that created constant turmoil in the region during the late nineteenth century.

A New Social Elite for Fall River

By the early 1870's, the first generation of Borden and Durfee textile manufacturers had begun to give way to a second generation. Their patrimony included the invention of a local privileged social set and municipal political dominance, which they had the wealth and power to defend. These men were largely responsible for the postwar expansion. Jefferson Borden's financing of improvements and recouping of disasters out of operating funds and the unpretentious living style of the older Borden families stood in distinct contrast with the more spendthrift ways of their successors. Colonel Borden and his sons seemed to share with other Gilded Age businessmen, according to historian Edward C. Kirkland, the fear that luxurious spending on houses and entertaining might tempt men to "speculation and peculation."[38] The activities of the first generation of capitalists seemed a world apart from postwar debt and ostentation. Family style and cultural values among the Fall River elite were being reshaped by a new generation of acquisitive younger men who enjoyed their treasures behind massive granite walls and spiked fences.

Nonetheless, the first generation of leaders bore their share of responsibility for encouraging and financing rampant postwar growth. Every time one of Jefferson Borden's daughters married, the groom received a handsome gift in gold dollars from what seemed an endless line of credit. Borden vacated his relatively plain Greek Revival style house for a lavish Second Empire-style residence with a four-story tower on fashionable Rock Street. Nathan Durfee was regarded in local circles as fabulously wealthy. Until he died in 1873, Matt Durfee's yacht and trips to Newport and Europe financed by his father's estate made him a real catch on the marriage market. Backed by the Borden and Durfee wealth, the second generation showed no fear of material display. They used the power and money accumulated before 1870 as a blank check to make themselves into a conspicuously wealthy social elite. Key members indulged themselves and their families in lavish consumption, unquestioned credit, risky enterprise, speculation in land values, and endless mill building that resulted not only in enormous corporate indebtedness but also in the more ominous threat of overproduction. S. Angier Chace's hero among the first generation, Holder Borden, was the risk-taker and big spender. Before Colonel Richard Borden died of a stroke during the early morning of February 25, 1874, he never imagined the future damage that the financial collapse in 1873 would bring to Fall River's overvalued property, its stock, or print cloth prices.

The evening before the Colonel died, Charles P. and Anna Davol Stickney threw a "freedom party" for their son, Charles Jr., to celebrate his twenty-first birthday. Senator Stickney, born in Newmarket, New Hampshire, was then fifty years of age. He had been introduced into Fall River society after working as a purser on the Bay State Line and a conductor on the Old Colony Railroad, enterprises promoted by Colonel Borden. Stickney married into the Davol family of textile machinery manufacture and cotton mills. Anna Davol was the daughter of William C. Davol and the sister of Stephen. In addition to their shared manufacturing interests, the Stickney and Davol men sat on the board of directors of at least six textile corporations, including the Borden-run Bleachery. Stickney served as president of the Massasoit National Bank and the Davol mills and was a key figure at the Manufacturers' Gas Company. He was also a very politically active Republican and a popular and influential member of the state Senate.[39]

On the night of the freedom party, two hundred richly dressed guests flocked to the Stickney mansion from Boston, Providence, Taunton, New Bedford, New York, and Brooklyn. The front of the house sported two fountains, bronze figures, and a high wrought-iron fence to insure privacy. Huge signs of "Welcome" and "1874" were fashioned out of hundreds of red carnations. The guests danced to orchestral music in halls and parlors choked with twelve hundred tea roses, numerous lilies and camellias, and draped lavishly with greenery. They paused at eleven to consume a sumptuously catered collation of oysters and desserts, then resumed the dance until 2:00 A.M.[40] When Colonel Borden's death was discovered the next morning, they were all asleep.

S. Angier Chace, who along with Stickney, was the most trusted and respected of the sons-in-law, was a man of extremely luxurious tastes. He was born in Freetown, Massachusetts, in 1821, and studied law briefly in

Fall River before working as a clerk on the Bay State Line. He married Mary Maria, a daughter of Dr. Nathan Durfee, the wealthiest man in town. Chace had also become the executor for the large inheritance of Durfee's niece, Sylvia. These resources allowed both men to venture into the flour-milling business as well as investing in textile mills. Chace's mansion stood on over two acres of lawn, its buildings positioned to savor the pleasant views and refreshing breezes from Mount Hope Bay. An observatory to enlarge the bay view topped the large house and gilded weathercocks perched on the vast stables. The windows were illuminated with colored glass but shaded during the hot humid summers by richly colored awnings. Dozens of baskets of blooming plants hung from the balconies supported by Corinthian columns. Rare ornamental trees and shrubbery, little summerhouses, and an archery court dotted the lawn and grounds.[41]

Sociologist Michael Kimmel analyzes the tendency of the heirs of early nineteenth-century "Self-Made Men" to establish their manhood through endless cycles of conspicuous consumption.[42] Consumption, Kimmel argues, measured the man, producing a group of "parasitic" upper-class men and effete upper-class boys. The second generation of textile capitalists in Fall River, however, was also deeply involved in the development and management of the post–Civil War expansion. They displayed their wealth lavishly, but they worked hard and schemed to increase it. The meaning of their manhood was embellished by their residences, expenditures, and family style but not wholly defined by them. More important were their positions of economic and political power that allowed them to make decisions shaping the future of Fall River industry.

The other rising members of the second generation of textile capitalists, except for Thomas J. and Richard B. Borden,—apparently influenced in their mode of living by their more staid father—indulged themselves in similar ways. George B. Durfee, son of Dr. Durfee and son-in-law of Jefferson Borden, lived on Rock Street, "the Fifth avenue" of Fall River. A costly stone fence topped with bayonets and spikes defended Durfee's mansion. Both the house and the stables had tall, sloping mansard roofs that overlooked the city and the bay. Large maples shaded the front yard, and the garden was crowded with the finest fruit trees. George T. Hathaway, Chace's cousin and business associate, also lived in a large residence on Rock Street. He had come to Fall River from nearby Assonet, Massachusetts, with no experience or prospects until he became a clerk in Chace's flour mill. He married the daughter of Iram Smith, a dry goods merchant and mill shareholder. Walter Paine III, the son-in-law of Jefferson Borden, lived down the street from Hathaway in a mansion that from a distance seemed to resemble a feudal castle, so massive were the house, conservatory, stables, and balconies.[43] The view was of course superb. These men from small rural communities, who had limited opportunities until they married into wealthy families, built the new social elite of the city. They also made every effort to dominate local politics through enterprising allies and fellow shareholders.[44]

PARTISAN POLITICS IN POST–CIVIL WAR FALL RIVER

Economic expansion and post–Civil War politics solidified the domination of local Republicans, but in the streets during the 1868 elections some Democrats challenged the public celebrations of triumphant war victories.[45] They disrupted parades and behaved even more provocatively during the Republican nomination caucuses in 1868 for municipal office. The challengers were determined to embarrass those men who expected local politics to be their uncontested arena of control. On the night of October 26, 1868, in a sweeping display of self-righteousness and moral authority, Fall River Republicans organized a torchlight parade supporting the candidacy of Ulysses S. Grant led by the city's four companies of "Boys in Blue." The procession, commanded by Union Army veteran Thomas J. Borden, seemed ready to vote as they had fought. Company A carried a sign that read on one side: "The Border City intend [*sic*] to fight it out on this line," and on the other: "Let those swap horses who will, we will drive the old team."[46] Forming up before the city hall, they marched through the main streets of the city, cheering for Grant and his running mate, Schuyler Colfax. They arrived at Colonel Richard Borden's residence, his lawn lit by Chinese lanterns, there drank coffee, and then marched back through streets illuminated by Roman candles and exploding rockets. But throughout the march, the veterans found themselves under fire from a pack of rowdy boys, aged from thirteen to eighteen years old, who battered the signs and the torch-bearers with stones and sticks. The young ruffians were deplored, identified, arrested, and fined.

To celebrate Grant's election in November, another torchlight parade brought out a more subdued demonstration by the young rowdies to tarnish the sweeping Republican victory. Windows in residences along the parade route were stoned by those who yelled for Horatio Seymour, the defeated Democratic candidate.[47] No one was foolish enough to get arrested. The Democrats had shown themselves as rebels still, but Fall River had gone for Grant with 72 percent of the votes cast. By the same majority Republicans also elected their candidate for governor, William Claflin, over Democrat John Quincy Adams Jr. John B. Hathaway, the brother of George T. Hathaway, became state senator, while mill owners and investors Weaver Osborn, Abraham Hart, and Iram Smith were elected to the state House of Representatives. All had claimed during the election to support the proposed ten-hour law.[48] After the election, they did all they could to block it.

Quickly recovering from this overwhelming defeat, the Democrats in 1868 engaged in some real mischief during the December ward caucuses, nominating candidates for aldermen, councilors, and ward officers. Sick of Republican landslides and torchlight parades, Democrats nailed up placards throughout the city inviting all citizens, *"irrespective of party,"* to meet at the Republican caucuses called for the night of December 4. In Ward 2, where Democrats out-numbered Republicans, the nominations went to Democrat incumbents, routing the Republicans completely in their own caucus. In other caucuses, Republicans close to mill interests such as John S. Davol Jr., Charles O. Shove, C. V. S. Remington, and Weaver Osborn struggled to maintain control. Their reactions ranged from polite but obviously enraged indignation at the unexpected Democratic invasion in Ward 3 to threats to adjourn to secret meetings in Wards 1 and 4. Republicans in the Ward 1 caucus did adjourn to the nearby house of representative Weaver Osborn for refreshments and a closed-door decision on nominations. Ward 5 Republicans deadlocked, even without the interference of Democrats.[49]

The Democrats harassed the Republican men most openly during the Ward 3 and 4 caucuses. In Ward 3 John S. Davol called twice for all Democrats to remove themselves, but only a few did so. Retailer John F. McDonough rose and stated that he had come in response to the placard inviting all "citizens," but he would leave if Davol absolutely insisted. Michael W. Brennan, a clothing store owner, then stood up and asked Davol to explain the word *republican* in the light of a public invitation to all citizens to attend the caucus. Davol icily pointed out that he presumed Brennan knew when a gentleman was asked to a private parlor and when he was not wanted. Brennan countered by offering to help pay for the hall. Content with shattering the chairman's nerves and disrupting the proceedings, all of the Democrats then walked out. To the extent that partisan politics, especially in municipal elections, was a proving ground for manliness, as historian Paula Baker argues, then Davol had lost both his manly composure and his public face.[50]

In Ward 4 Charles Shove presided. Police court judge and ten-hour reformer Louis Lapham, a well-known Democrat, rose from the audience and announced that more people were present than the number of Republicans in the ward. He then moved to adjourn the meeting to the next afternoon, setting off great excitement among the Republican workingmen at the meeting who could not leave their jobs at that hour. As a result of Lapham's well-timed provocation, the meeting degenerated into various motions and shouted votes of "ayes" or "nays" and challenges to the chair that the vote was "doubted! doubted!" The Ward 4 caucus was called off entirely that year. To prevent future disruptions, the Republican City Committee organized a closed citywide nominating convention for 1867. The editors of the *News* denounced the disruptive boys at the veterans' parades and the Democratic pranksters at the caucuses as the modern prototypes of the vandals who sacked Rome.[51] To their great pleasure, the Fall River Democrats had disconcerted their rich and powerful rivals on their own turf, although the Republicans still controlled the mayor's office, the aldermen, and the common council. But these maneuvers in 1868 forecast renewed energy in partisan politics that had nothing whatever to do with Civil War memories. In the spring of 1869 Irish American Democrats, English immigrants, and ten-hour reformers organized rallies that signaled changes for the future.

The Republicans held on tightly to state as well as municipal offices. State representative Weaver Osborn, whose mother was a Durfee, was born in Tiverton, Rhode Island, and as a young militiaman had assisted in crushing the Dorr Rebellion. He joined the Republican Party in 1856. After the war, he was elected to the Massachusetts House for several terms and served on the committee on the hours of labor that reported the ten-hour bill to the full House where it was routinely defeated in the state Senate. Later in 1872, he organized the Osborn mills and become a director in the Pocasset National Bank and the Montaup, Union, Granite, Merchants, and Slade mills. Osborn failed to gain his party's nomination in 1873. After the ten-hour bill became law in 1874, he then joined the rest of Fall River mill owners in evading it.

The career of another Republican, Crawford Lindsey, provides an example of the way tight Republican control of municipal politics served industrial expansion. Lindsey was born in Fall River in 1838 and at the age of nineteen in 1857 became a clerk at the American Print Works. He married the daughter of Oliver Chace, one of Fall River's small but thriving bankers and mill owners, serving as the direct selling agent for the American Print Works until 1879. Lindsey joined a number of small merchants and manufacturers in organizing the Merchants mill and the King Philip mill but also was a shareholder in the Bordens' Fall River Bleachery. In 1869 he became involved in city politics, gaining extensive experience on the common council, the school committee, and the board of aldermen as the city grew to meet the needs of textile expansion.[52] His political life was topped by two terms as mayor in 1878 and 1879, distinguished by his determination both to protect the reputation of the city from its critics and to defeat an important mule spinners' strike. After one term in 1854 as the city's first mayor, Republican James Buffinton had served in Congress for twenty years until 1874, when a New Bedford mill owner replaced him. The roster of state senators from the Fall River district between 1854 and 1874 featured many well-known, mill-connected men: Nathaniel B. Borden, the Reverend Orin Fowler, Colonel Richard Borden, S. Angier Chace, John B. Hathaway, and Charles Stickney, passing on the honor from hand to hand. Controlling the Bristol County district in congressional elections, the state house delegation, and the municipal government with its expenditures and tax policies was part of the Fall River Republicans' strategy of market domination.

Municipal Fire Service, Manly Citizenship, and Class Politics

Municipal policy remained financially tight-fisted but eagerly responsive to the needs of textile mill expansion. The politics of fire fighting, however, developed early into a protracted contest between the rights of male residents serving the town and the growing influence of the mill owners. Native-born volunteer firemen with their own sense of manly citizenship protested against an unrepresentative and class-dominated town fire service. Just as class power wielded by mill interests had encouraged divisive, patriarchal, and nativist attributes for male citizenship during the unsuccessful ten-hour movement of the 1840s, struggles over control of the fire service led by men who cherished their rights as republican citizens symbolized the issue of who controlled Fall River's government.

In 1843, after a disastrous fire ruined the town and killed Major Durfee, Fall River citizens discarded their bucket brigades. A Board of Firewardens organized volunteer fire companies to protect the Iron Works and the growing numbers of mills. The town's fire service was always held in check by the desire of industrial interests to keep taxes low. For example, it took a special state law in 1832 with punitive fines to force the town to establish a fire department. The town government resisted, then grudgingly acquiesced. Antiquated fire equipment and low-paid volunteer companies composed of native-born Yankees appointed by the firewardens were expected to do the job. As town citizens, they were willing to try. Meanwhile, the mill interests set up a private system of fire protection called Forcing Pump Companies, using hosing attached to the mills' stationery steam engines. The firewardens approved these firemen and taxpayers provided part of their wages, but they were mill employees.[53]

The Borden family of Fall River acquired the Globe Print Works in 1854, located in Globe village within the town of Tiverton, Rhode Island. The Tiverton taxpayers, however, opposed providing any fire-fighting apparatus to protect outsiders' property. When in the 1850s the town of Fall River attempted "in secret connivance" with the Bordens to extend the responsibilities of its fire service over the Massachusetts state border into Rhode Island by moving a Fall River hand pumper to Globe village, two of the four fire companies rebelled, refusing to cross the state line in what they called "open warfare."[54] They were citizens of Fall River, not mill employees. During these struggles with the mills, the volunteer fire companies had the support of local labor reformers, some clergymen, and temperance advocates, as did the 1840s movement for ten hours.

In the early 1850s, Jonathan E. Morrill, a newcomer to Fall River, became the foreman of Niagara Company No. 4. He brought with him a love for volunteer fire company rituals, including pell-mell races to a fire for the achievement of "first water" between companies of red-shirted men dragging their hand-pumping engines through the streets and occasionally colliding, sometimes fatally, with an unlucky onlooker. According to the 1854 city charter, the aldermen appointed firemen from each ward. Thomas E. Lynch later recalled a common understanding that *not* to be a volunteer fireman raised questions about a young fellow's spirit and manly qualities.[55] Daring strength, reckless youth, and political clout defined male citizenship for these Yankee men, but they remained sensitive to the heavy-handed influence of the mills.

An element of defiance was added to manly citizenship in 1857, when the city government, trying to control mounting municipal expenses, harassed the six highly competitive fire companies. Each company paid their volunteers sixteen dollars a year, but the city government reduced each company's total wage fund, thus intending to force a reduction in membership. Five of the six companies promptly disbanded but remained intact as social organizations. During that year, thirty-two "incendiary" blazes destroyed private property, while "vandals" (probably former firemen) cut hoses, both at fires and in the engine houses. At their social gatherings, Niagara Company No. 4 sang in defiance, their republican response to the city fathers, to the tune of "Root Hog or Die."

NIAGARA'S BOYS

Come listen, gallant Firemen, brave true-hearted boys,
And every native freeman, who liberty enjoys;
I'm going to tell a story, and tell the reason why,
Niagara's boys so proudly sing, "Root hog or die."

We had as brave a company as in the land was seen,
Each member did his duty, and ran with "der machine,"
But when our city Fathers to touch our rights did try,
Niagara's boys began to sing, "Root you hogs or die."

Our worthy City Fathers did in their wisdom say,
Should a member miss *one* meeting, he's miss his yearly pay,
But for this mighty wisdom we had but one reply—
"Mayor, Chief and Aldermen, 'Root you hogs or die. . . .' "

. . . .

Our Clerk, he called a meeting, we took the case in hand,
And each and every member there, voted to disband,
And every hill and mountain now echoes back the cry—
"Niagara's boys are freemen! 'Root you hogs or die. . . .' "[56]

. . . .

During the crisis in 1857–58, the city marshal, also the head of the police, became the chief fire engineer. But one year later, Jonathan Morrill of the Niagara Company triumphantly succeeded him and successfully reorganized the fire companies. During this protracted struggle, the city of Fall River refused to celebrate the explosive-ridden Fourth of July in 1858. The manly republicans of the Niagara Company took up the challenge. Dressed in splendid new uniforms of red jackets and white trousers, they paraded conspicuously past the city hall and held a festive dinner, listening to patriotic speeches and songs.[57] Seizing the definition of citizenship from the municipality, they presented themselves as loyal sons of America, standing ready to quench fires in locations that they and their chosen members, not the city government, selected.

After the 1867 mill fires that seemed to thwart the city's future and during the tremendous postwar expansion of mills in Fall River, the Borden and Durfee families took over the public volunteer service, arranging for the appointment of Thomas J. Borden and Holder Borden Durfee, successively, as fire chiefs between 1870–77.[58] They continued to improve their own system of forcing pump companies, while the city continued to pay the mills' private firemen. The corporations organized their own fire insurance company but also took out insurance from mutual companies in other cities, especially after the great loss of life in the Granite mill in 1874. The mills built wooden and iron ladders installed near windows, but Rufus R. Wade, the chief Massachusetts factory inspector in 1878, urged the use of railed stairways, to little effect.

Expenditures on new equipment remained tight. A hand-pumped fire engine, purchased in 1818, served until 1853, while a hand-drawn hook and ladder bought in 1826 operated with modifications until 1871. Following the Granite mill fire, however, the city acquired seven steam-powered fire engines, built several fire stations with a total of three permanent city firemen, and replaced cisterns inside the mills and on the streets with a system of hydrants filled with municipal water. New state laws pushed by insurance companies also mandated fire escapes and sprinkler systems, and the mills readily complied. The city water works was completed in 1873. According to one local historian: "the cost was great, but the people had to have it. . . ."[59] In this case the needs of the residents and the mills appeared in retrospect to coincide. The real glory of the city of Fall River in the mid-1870s was the thirty-four gigantic, granite-block textile mills that employed over ten thousand and produced miles of print cloth.

The election in 1872 of the first Democratic alderman, James E. Cunneen, opened the way for a few Irish immigrants or their sons to enter the fire service by appointment. But pitting ethnic groups in the workforce against each other had become a successful strategy of textile capitalism, now used in municipal politics. The mill agents decided in the mid-1870s to rid Fall River of the most experienced English labor agitators and divide them from their Irish allies. One way was the familiar blacklist for prominent strikers and union leaders. Another way was to rid the fire department in 1877 of all Irish members, a kind of blacklist for public servants. The expulsion of an immigrant fireman from his company by a municipal government in thrall to the corporations was another way of defining—by exclusion—respectable manhood and citizenship in public service.

One long-time English resident reacted to these divisive policies based on class power in a letter on July 18, 1877, to the *Fall River Herald* satirizing the Yankee fondness for using Indian names for their mills, such as Massasoit or Wamsutta. The writer signed the letter "Watchemukett." "Muck it" was and is English slang, common among Lancashire and Yorkshire people, meaning to make a mess, create dirt, or disorder. It also carried connotations of filth, foulness, and excrement.[60]

THE BLASTED *Furriners* HAVE GOT TO GIT.

There was a time, not long ago, when the same *furriners* were very useful to have around. Then it was [Civil] war times; and the number of natives who were afflicted with some peculiar physical disability was astounding. Trusses and doctor's certificates were as plentiful as blackberries. But time brings many changes. The truss and certificate are laid carefully away, probably to be used in some future contingency, and the wearer, who could not serve as a soldier, can now perform the arduous duties of a fireman.... The Annawam Company, having been purged of this despised class [the Irish immigrant], the Niagara [Company] now comes to the front, and the solitary *furriner* in that company must git. The weeding out process is being quietly carried out, and soon the [Fire] Department will have gained ... the watchword of the old Know Nothing Party.... true inwardness."

The fire services, private and public, were thus scorned by various groups of textile workers for bigotry and toadyism. Blocked from public service and its social activities, by the 1870s they were organizing their own culturally specific athletic, social, and political activities. The English American Club set up cricket matches, fraternal orders, and debating societies for the Lancashire and Yorkshire immigrants. Democratic Party politics, St. Patrick's Day parades, and marathon walking or "pedestrianism," served the Irish, while French Canadians celebrated New Year's Day and cultural nationalism, while organizing mutual benefit societies. Marathon walking and baseball also became popular spectator sports for all ethnic groups.

The Fall River firemen's musters in 1872 and 1878 were essentially Yankee social affairs. One city leader congratulated the fire department in 1873 as a group "composed [not of roughs as in other cities] but of our best citizens," whose duties ranked even above service in political office or on juries.[61] The purge of 1877 failed, however, to eliminate all Irish from the fire service, some saved by the new chief engineer William C. Davol, formerly with the Niagara volunteers, and two Democratic aldermen.[62] In spite of the political conflict, it is hard to imagine that immigrant residents, youngsters or adults, could stay away from those Yankee-dominated fire musters. Spectacular demonstrations of the manly throwing power of water cascading from the hoses of both hand and steam-powered engines, events sometimes called the "squirts," drew great crowds, even if many had been excluded by class politics from participation in the musters. At the 1878 muster, an Irish immigrant, Patrich Roach, burning with anger over the attempted purge of Irish firemen the year before, arrived with some friends, intent on making trouble. Confronted by the city's police force determined to protect both the peace and cultural purity of the muster, he was clubbed and left with a bleeding head.[63]

At this muster, the Yankee "fire laddies" embodied brave, noble, self-sacrificing duty and devotion to public interest.[64] All but three of these men, however, were not permanent city employees; they also helped manage the textile mills, clerked in retail stores, or lived on their rents and dividends. Corporate power influential in the politics and culture of mucnicipal service had successfully invested manly citizenship in a pro-manufacturing Yankee middle-class. Not until the 1880s with the election of the city's first Democratic mayor, John W. Cummings, did the fire service employ ten permanent firemen. The last two, appointed in 1886, were Capt. Thomas E. Lynch, the historian of Fall River's fire department, and a hoseman, John F. O'Brien. Still, police stations shared quarters with fire stations and the city stables.[65] As Irish-American Democrats came to control the fire and police service at the turn of the century and held their own musters, they would acquire the power to redefine on their own terms the meaning of manly citizenship.

EDUCATION POLICY AND FEMALE BENEVOLENCE

When state law mandated the creation of high schools in all towns in the Commonwealth in 1849, Fall River resisted the expense, as the town had refused to establish a fire department in 1832, by insisting that its grammar schools taught the equivalent of a high school curriculum. But when an alarmed citizenry at the 1850 town meeting protested heavy state-imposed fines for noncompliance, Fall River officials relented in their own way. The school committee rented a small building, called it a high school, and assigned a grammar school principal to run it. After 1854 city authorities continued to starve education and moved the high school from one rented location to another, providing annexes for surplus students. Finally in 1883, Mary Brayton Durfee Young donated the land, money, and a trust fund to build and equip a splendid building, the B. M. C. Durfee High School, in memory of her dead son. Municipal policy in the nineteenth century produced low taxes for the textile mills but meager public services. In the case of education, what the city authorities refused to provide, upper-class women used their private wealth to accomplish. Throughout the late nineteenth century, educational philanthropy in Fall River remained the domain of powerful women, who identified and resolved a pressing social need. Sometimes their gifts bore their own high price.

Mary B. Young negotiated the conditions of her donation directly with the city government without consulting the school committee. The carefully designed building was completed and dedicated in 1887. A clock tower with belfry and bells and an astronomical observatory topped the lavishly equipped four-story granite building in neo-Romanesque style. The structure complied with the best mill construction fire codes, including staircases made at the Iron Works. The entrance hall with marble floors and oak wainscoting gave the appearance of a bank. The mayor quickly obtained special legislation to exempt the deal from state education regulations.[66] All teachers hired had to be approved by persons appointed by Mrs. Young. The curriculum, which she helped design to serve the needs of local industry, emphasized chemistry and "physical and mechanical sciences." At her insistence, military training was made compulsory for boys. The school bells rang only with the permission of a special committee and then always tolled out the twenty-nine years of her son's life.[67] The female heirs of Young continued to honor her public contributions.

In 1861 the city inherited the small private library set up in 1835 by Holder Borden and run as a private corporation by shareholders and subscribers.[68] The public library acquired a little space in the new city hall in 1873. After the building burned down in 1886, the rebuilt, expanded city hall had no room for the library. Finally in 1895 the heirs of Mary Brayton Durfee Young sold part of her homestead property, the old Mansion House, the former site of Major Durfee's tavern, to the city at half its value to build the first respectable city library. Later Sarah A. Brayton, sister-in-law of Mary B. Young, gave the remainder of the homestead to the state-sponsored Bradford Durfee Textile School, founded in 1896, to stimulate innovations in textile production.[69] Municipal benevolence became a tradition of the Brayton women, while other Fall River families of the social elite interested themselves elsewhere.

MUNICIPAL SERVICES AND LOW TAXES

The old Market Building, built of granite blocks in 1844 and later used as the city hall, was a multiple-purpose structure. In addition to containing the town and, after 1854, city offices, the building offered for rent a large public hall, twelve business offices usually occupied by lawyers, a barbershop, and in 1862 three banks. In the cellar a fish market and a lockup shared the space with three undesirably damp rooms for rent.[70] In 1873, instead of building an entirely new structure or moving the city hall to another location, the town had the burned-out building gutted and topped with two additional floors, a mansard roof, and a clock tower. This thrifty plan updated the style of the building and required no new expensive land.

Local taxpayers were spared the burden of educational and other public improvements. Almost every major building or structure in the city was funded elsewhere: the post office, the state armory, the bridges across the Taunton River, many of the wharves on the bay, and the court houses, except for the police court which was housed for several years by the city in a mercantile block. Similarly, any sessions of the superior court convened in rented rooms until 1889 when the state built a courthouse. Property taxes, corporate and residential, remained undisturbed. Throughout the nineteenth century, the city's streets, except for those around city hall, remained unpaved. The rural practice of watering streets and roads, some of them by specially outfitted and privately owned horse-drawn trolley cars, momentarily kept down the blowing dust. Residents had to pay private contractors to oil the streets in their neighborhoods. The city purchased the cinders from the textile mills' coal-fired steam engines to surface the sidewalks.[71] Two privately owned gaslight companies in the city, Fall River Gas Works, organized by the Iron Works in 1847, and Manufacturers' Gas-Light Company, created in 1866, served the mill interests, but neither supplied the city streets with gas lighting.[72] Kerosene lanterns lit all the dusty streets and cindery sidewalks until 1883 when three electric lights were installed on Main Street. Low-wattage electric bulbs finally replaced many of the kerosene lamps in 1908. By 1913 the city paid the privately-owned Fall River Electric Light Company to install powerful arc lights to illuminate the downtown shopping area.[73] The two exceptions to keeping taxes low were the expensive purchase of services from privately-owned local companies and the financing of the municipal debt through local banks controlled by mill interests.

In contrast, New Bedford during the height of prosperity from commercial whaling set a much faster pace of municipal improvements. Flickering lights illuminated flagged sidewalks in the center of town as early as 1832, while water reservoirs supplied some areas of the town. The needs of the whaling industry in the 1840s required granite-paved streets and special granite ramps to move whale oil casks near the waterfront. The new city government, organized in 1847, flagged, curbed, and graded twenty miles of road. Areas near the massive granite temple of the city's Free Public Library opened in 1853 were gaslighted. During the Civil War, the city planned, commissioned, and opened in 1869 a public water works by damming a nearby river. In the late nineteenth century, the expanding fine cotton goods industry in this once prosperous seaport supported a city budget for sewer development, the lighting and improvement of roads and thoroughfares, a public high school, and a street department employing twenty-seven men.[74] Different perceptions of economic needs by the dominant industries in the two cities shaped the municipal environment.

The granite ledge on which Fall River and its factories were built complicated the issue of sewers and drains. Although Mayor Nathaniel B. Borden insisted in 1857 that a sewage system be built, municipal officials decided that blasting through the rock was too costly even to contemplate. By 1860 pollution threatened most of the city's shallow wells. As streets were extended, the engineering design, overseen by Philip D. Borden as city engineer, directed the drainage from cesspools and vaults into Mount Hope Bay via the Quequechan River. The pure spring waters of lakes and ponds in the eastern portion of the city that fed the river flushed the makeshift sewer system, but they too became polluted for lack of proper sewage treatment. The associate judge of the Massachusetts supreme judicial court, James M. Morton, was forced to give up fly fishing for black bass in North Pond. State law in Massachusetts and New Hampshire backed the use of waterways for whatever purposes served the interests of textile corporations.[75]

MIDDLE-CLASS REACTIONS TO FALL RIVER'S POSTWAR EXPANSION

The enormous growth of the city and its textile mills, the influx of a immigrant working-class population crowded into hastily built corporate and private tenements, plus the appearance of a new social elite with powerful political allies in state and municipal government alarmed parts of Fall River's middle class. The more affluent organized their own mills to share in the wealth of the postwar years, but many small shopkeepers, contractors, wholesalers, and professionals worried about the pace of growth. Appropriating the language of industrial development and supply and demand ideology, the middle-class critics of the textile mills shaped a powerful moral critique of corporate power, unleashed speculation, and overproduction.[76]

The most articulate blast at the course of events that was introducing uncontrollable and divisive changes into the city came in the spring of 1872 from the pulpit. The Reverend A. A. Wright of the First Methodist Church, who had earlier attended and addressed a local ten-hour rally, issued the moral indictment. In his sermon on April 5, Wright sternly predicted "a first class pandemonium" rapidly approaching. The city census of March 15, published on the previous Saturday, indicated that 3,646 French Canadian, non-English-speaking Catholics had come to Fall River, with more certain to follow. Wright regarded this ominous influx of a "foreign population," in addition to the rapidly growing numbers of English and Irish immigrants, as a threat to American values. His views were alarmist. "Vast masses of ignorance" must be incorporated into moral and civil society at the peril of the "free air of this Commonwealth." Wright feared that working-class poverty plus overwork in the mills would deepen misery and provoke useless strikes. A commercial panic or widespread strikes caused by "the wicked folly" of overlong hours of work or by "the stupidity of the working classes" bent on "the insanity of rebellion" would destroy Fall River.[77] The middle class had to act.

Wright also hit more lofty targets: the practices of textile capitalists, their economic ideology, and the immoral results. He spoke grimly of the "lewd companionship" that strolled the downtown streets on a Saturday night and of the moral wrong in a city "whose mills keep little children in the street school till nine o'clock in the evening." The new social elite bore its full share of Wright's wrath. He especially feared the disappearance of traditional moral and Christian values among the privileged ones engaged in the pursuit of pleasure and plenty, the "young men [who] speculate in land and drive fast horses." Meanwhile, "young women on the streets wear their loose virtue, shawl-like, shamelessly. . . ." Most of all, Wright was afraid of the temptations of postwar prosperity on middle-class men. "This city," he warned,

> will put its price on you—it has, and your price at which you can be bought
> or sold, the price of every business or professional man in this place, en-
> ters into all the calculations of possible business success; of mill stocks,
> house lots, and is as much a term of speculation as is the price of grain
> or granite.[78]

Supply and demand ideology and the reduction of everything and everyone to commodities ate away at moral and Christian values. Some middle-class members of the congregation must have squirmed in their pews.

This damning criticism of the postwar expansionist era was echoed in calmer tones by those who were more fearful of a collapse in property values fueled by overspeculation. If such a crisis should occur, especially one brought on by the speculator or reckless profiteer, middle-class Republicans who voted for the Weaver Osborns and Crawford Lindseys might feel the urgency for genuine reform, such as state regulation of overwork. The most immediate, pressing problem of headlong mill expansion for most middle-class residents was the acute housing shortage for "skillful mechanics and intelligent traders" who needed and wanted "tenements, shops, and stores."[79] High interest rates and scarcities of materials and capital had created the shortage. About half of the textile operatives lived in corporate housing with a reputation for filth and disease, and Fall River was second only to New York City in overcrowded conditions.[80] Many mills required residence in their tenements as a condition of employment, but any form of trouble from the operatives resulted in eviction within twenty-four hours. With ten new mills planned for the spring of 1873 and more to come, six thousand newcomers in 1872 never found suitable places to live. But, Thomas Almy, the editor of the *News,* concluded that the residents of the city must bow to the laws of supply and demand: "the great see-saw of commerce." Rents would be high, even exorbitant. "One cannot blame the owners of real estate or house owners for high rents. . . . It is the universal custom, whether right or wrong. . . ."[81] The editor insisted that economic laws recognized neither moral nor Christian values, and human nature was weak and unable to resist opportunities for profit. So mills were built, and rents were high.

By early 1873, middle-class disapproval, based on those same laws of supply and demand, shifted into public criticism of too much corporate expansion. With four more mills being planned, the wise investor, the editor of the *News* now cautioned, will buy stock in the established companies, "unless he has a mill site to sell." Serious thought somewhere, Almy wrote, should be given to the dangers of "overdoing matters."[82] These worries were reinforced the following day in a letter from "E. N. S." boldly stating that "mill stock is over subscribed." Build no more new mills, he argued. Machinery, building materials, and workmen are scarce and too expensive. The markets are full of print cloth. There was no reason for further expansion in Fall River. The danger lay in overproduction.

A similar letter from "Remember" agreed, quoting the old proverb: "that whom the Gods would destroy, they first make mad." This writer feared the coming day of not 20 percent, or 10 percent, but 5 percent dividends when demand faltered from too many goods. His advice was to complete the mills under construction, project no more, pay for them, and get on even ground before "a really tight money market emerges."[83] These middle-class investors believed that textile development was out of control and in actual violation of the sacred economic laws, thus jeopardizing their investments. These exchanges occurred just six months before the onset of the business depression in 1873 and the long-feared "really tight money."

To counter this call for restraint, a person identifying himself only as "Tall Oaks" sent a "private and confidential" letter to editor Almy. The writer was a member of the second generation of textile capitalists, and the letter may have been a joint effort. Almy published this confidential letter without comment in the February 25, 1873, edition. "Tall Oaks" regretted any attempt by the *News* to "repress the spirit of enterprise" or the confidence that feeds upon growth until it seems "as though our special mission in this world is to provide its inhabitants with print cloths." That such success in Fall River had come as a surprise to the "more sedate and calculating among ourselves" led to envy and jealousy, all "very inopportune." The writer claimed well-known "antecedents," suggesting a connection with either the Durfee or Borden families, whose members, he claimed, had always put the general welfare above private gain. He then announced his involvement in a number of new enterprises open to potential investors. Although a business contraction was possible, "Tall Oaks" argued arrogantly, those "who take a broad and intelligent view of the whole field" know it will be short, time enough for "small shareholders to be weeded out" and taught to keep their precious money locked up in savings banks. "It is important to our enterprise," the writer instructed Almy, that no adverse criticism be printed in the pages of the *News*. "Tall Oaks" wrote that he did not like to say it but he regarded "an independent press as a public nuisance" and bad for business.

"Tall Oaks" bragged that "a member of my family" was prominently connected with the Credit Mobilier, revealed later in 1873 as a corrupt organization which had drained the profits of post–Civil War railroads through bogus construction companies and political corruption. The writer planned a smaller version of the "C.M." for Fall River: "We propose to purchase a large tract of real estate at a low figure, and sell it to the corporation for a mill site . . . at a correspondingly high one, thus realizing a magnificent profit on our investment." The writer claimed to have put aside in secret some shares in the enterprise in the editor's name until a division of profits took place. He stated his price openly, "in consideration of which I trust the public spirit and indomitable energy of the . . . enterprise will receive due recognition and commendation" in the pages of the newspaper.

The final bribe offered in the "Tall Oaks" letter for editorial silence bordered on the immoral, if not the illegal: "As the dividends of the [Fall River] C. M. will be paid in stock of the corporation, you will see the propriety of [postponing] doing what you can to 'kill' it, in order to enable us to unload while the demand for mill stock is active." The letter's writer was never identified, nor was there a follow-up story or even a letter or comment printed in the *News*. The *Border City Herald* probably denounced this letter, whose writer was undoubtedly well-known in the city. The nonchalant tone of the letter suggests either S. Angier Chace or George B. Durfee and their highly dubious promotion of the Border City Mill based almost entirely on the value of the land on which it was built. The printing of this private correspondence was the editor's rebuke to the writer and his rejection of the offer. Many middle-class shareholders and small investors must have felt both enraged and powerless.

When the financial markets collapsed in New York and Philadelphia in September 1873, the editor of the *News* remarked "that crowding speculation beyond the lines of actual supply and demand only brings ruin and disaster," especially to small investors. In October the newly formed Fall River Manufacturers' Board of Trade, chaired by Charles O. Shove of the Granite mill, and including S. Angier Chace, Thomas J. Borden, and Walter Paine met to survey the prospects of production and sales. They admitted to "the almost entire falling off in the demands for goods," the high price of borrowing money, and the necessity to curtail production. Corresponding with all other print cloth mills in the region, board members found that if a firm had no contracts to fill, they intended to shut down or severely limit production. A general agreement prevailed that while business remained depressed, a reduction in the hours of labor might be a good idea.[84] Even the corporations in Fall River would no longer totally resist, as they had stubbornly and by various subterfuges for decades, a state ten-hour law. For the present, they would run on "short time" or for fewer hours, only a few days a week, although Senator Stickney would still ensure that evasion would be possible under the law passed in May 1874. During the November 1873 municipal elections, a movement among mechanics and workingmen called for a halt to all construction of roads for projected new mills, while a letter from "Mechanic" noting the political disintegration of the old parties in Fall River, called for municipal reform.[85]

Meltdown for the Durfee, Chace, and Stickney Families

S. Angier Chace was a cool, cunning manipulator of men and money. Endorsed promissory notes on the credit of mills controlled by Chace or by men who trusted or feared him allowed him to steal $600,000 over a period of years. His relationship to Dr. Durfee, both as his son-in-law and partner in the Massasoit Steam Flour mill, his status as a church deacon and Sunday school teacher, his unruffled manners when challenged, and his calm reassurances kept many suspicious directors from questioning his activities closely. When the president of the Union mill discovered on Wednesday, April 11, 1878, that there was no money on hand to meet Friday's payroll, the directors, unwilling or afraid to believe the loss or to have it publicly known, put together the amount themselves. Elijah Kilburn of the Kilburn, Lincoln Company, learned by telegraph from Boston that notes drawn on the credit of the Union mill were being protested. Banks in Boston, New York City, New Bedford, Taunton, Lowell, Providence, and elsewhere wanted their loans repaid. Kilburn asked Chace if this were true, and Chace lied. When Kilburn confronted him with a list of notes that Chace had signed personally and demanded his resignation, Chace coolly told him that "he wanted a few days to think it over."[86] The distraught directors agreed. Meanwhile, the clerk at the flour mill had been ordered to burn the books.[87]

The lenient treatment of Chace, and later of George T. Hathaway and Charles P. Stickney, reflected the fears of all directors that not only were their own personal assets at stake but also the reputation and value of all Fall River business. The local, Boston, and New York newspapers filled with speculation, while members of the Union board feared ruin. The directors, thinking they would be held personally liable for the illegally endorsed notes, searched the books to find out how bad things were. While they deliberated and worried, Chace remained in his mansion, saying nothing. Until the directors decided to bring charges, he would not be arrested. They finally acted on April 14, after the Massachusetts attorney general threatened to intervene. After being placed under arrest, Chace, conspicuously well dressed and with great self-possession, was driven by his sons, accompanied by two policemen, in the family carriage to Taunton Superior Court, where he pleaded not guilty. He was then driven back to his home in Fall River to bid his family goodbye and returned to Taunton Jail.[88] Hathaway and Stickney were later treated the same way; their class position delayed legal action and incarceration. A letter from "Justice" to the *Herald* grumbled that if a poor man had stolen a loaf of bread to feed his family, he would have been behind bars immediately.[89] The word *defalcation* applied to their numerous illegal acts was too polite for many ordinary citizens to accept. Why not, wrote the editor of the *Herald* use the "good, old-fashioned Saxon style" *theft?*[90] The Union mills remained closed until 1879.

Other mills and banks became involved. Chace was also the treasurer of the Border City mills and at one time the Fall River Manufactory. When the suspicious Union mill director tried unsuccessfully to fire him, Chace had pressured treasurer Hathaway into signing notes for twelve thousand dollars on the Border City mills' credit and then bought controlling interest in the Union mill. Later Chace warned Hathaway that if he were discovered, others would go to prison with him. Chace also served on the boards of two local banks: the Fall River Savings Bank and the Second National Bank, both of which held some of their assets in Union mill stock or endorsed notes. When Holder B. Durfee, son of Fidelia Borden Durfee, married Chace's niece Sylvia, he believed, as did many, that the Durfee estate was "a gold mine."[91] Then in 1874 he was shown the empty books of the flour mill. For two years, after Nathan Durfee died in 1876, Holder B. Durfee served as the major trustee of a bankrupt estate, but the other trustee, M. C. D. Borden, the son of Colonel Borden, was in New York City and seemed unaware of these developments.[92]

As the treasurer of the Fall River Manufactory, Holder B. Durfee had given Chace an unauthorized twelve thousand dollars loan that had never been repaid. Chace had also threatened him, and Durfee knew the sorry state of the Durfee family assets. Still, in the midst of so much financial grief, the directors of the Fall River Manufactory decided that Durfee's loan to Chace had only been a "mistake."[93] The Durfee family lost heavily as a result of Chace's defalcations. Chace had unlimited access to Nathan Durfee's credit, and although Dr. Durfee knew very well what Chace was up to, he made no move to stop him. Even with the family facing ruin, Durfee gave heavily to the Fall River Central Congregational Church,

Andover Theological Seminary, and Yale College just before he died. As the uncle of Sylvia Borden Durfee, Nathan Durfee's niece, Chace was the guardian of the estate. All that money, along with his wife Mary Durfee Chace's inheritance, was gone. Holder B. Durfee borrowed from his mother, Fidelia, to try to save the flour mill and almost ruined her.

Chace had toyed for at least a decade with the character of two men: his father-in-law, the egotistical, self-righteous business failure, Nathan Durfee, and his inexperienced, easily dazzled, and as easily frightened cousin George Hathaway.[94] In 1868 Chace had brought the young man from rural Assonet, Massachusetts, to work at the Massasoit Flour mill which he owned with Durfee. The business was a sinkhole, and neither partner knew anything about the practical side of textile manufacturing or flour milling. But for some reason Durfee loved it and would not allow it to go under. Hathaway was sent to Providence to learn the fundamentals of bookkeeping, and Chace taught him the rest. Hathaway became the treasurer of the Sagamore mills and the Border City mill, organized in 1872 as "the Peoples' Mill," to entice small businessmen and mechanics to invest their savings.[95] When the stockholders at the Sagamore paid in their share money, Chace helped himself to forty thousand dollars. Hathaway, married and living well by doing his cousin's bidding, was threatened with exposure and ruin if any scruples emerged. He knuckled under and did as he was told.

A week after Chace's arrest, the notes of both the Border City and the Sagamore mills faced legal action from banking institutions and lenders. Hathaway, like Chace, lied to the directors for as long as possible, but eventually confessed that the money from the loans had gone to Dr. Durfee and to Chace. He had also lost money speculating in real estate and in print cloth futures in an attempt to cover the loans, thus raising the total sum close to Chace's thefts of over half a million dollars. Hathaway was not arrested until open threats of lynching by outraged small investors forced him to seek refuge in Taunton Jail. Leaving behind a fainting wife, he left in tears, sobbing all the way to jail. Chace would have been contemptuous, but the Durfees and the Chaces were finished. With Chace in jail and the Durfees bankrupt, Mary B. Young bought the Chace mansion and gave it to her old friend Mary Durfee Chace as a lifetime residence.[96] Concerned members of the Senate judiciary committee reported a bill to the floor in early May that regulated the issue of notes, bills, and drafts on Massachusetts corporations.[97] It quickly became law. On June 26, Chace pleaded guilty to three counts of embezzlement and received a twelve-year sentence in Concord State Prison. Fall River opinion suspected that others had been involved, but Chace did not reveal anything more or further implicate anyone. Perhaps Hathaway would confess during his trial.

An alarmed David A. Brayton of the Durfee mills wrote his brother

John, begging him not to try to save any of the mills involved in the defalcations. This unusually blunt rare document reflected the charged emotions inherent in the situation.

July 30, 1878

D[ear] Brother [John S. Brayton]

In regard to the matter that must make you anxious. I wish again to say, *in no way connect yourself with it*—You are out of it. Keep out—I have been looking for the end for the last two years. What little I know about printing [cloth] teaches me that it is impossible for them to go on under the present management—They do not accept the fact that business is not done in the same manner of years ago. [U]ndoubtingly [*sic*] they could do well enough if business was as good and no more competition than there used to be. [B]ut business is different—people must keep their business in hand. [A]nd manage it and in no way be managed by the business. I suppose from what you write the New York Commission house is not willing to advance any more. [P]robably they feel the thing [the Union mill] is sucked about dry. They know. They feel that they cannot get any more out of it unless you come forward and pool in either with money[,] cloth[,] or endorsements. Money will be the most acceptable to them as it is so easy divided. Cloth next[,] endorsements last—A very heavy pressure will be brought to bare [*sic*] on you for endorsements. They will say to you that you should consider your place. That you should be willing to carry part of the load: and everything else will be said that can be said to bring you in—I tell you unless you wish to go to the pok [jail] with them[,] keep your hands off—Let them remember what they have had from the [print] works. . . . —And I do think that the Borden family has directly and indirectly within the last 15 years [1863—1878] received from the works $1,500,000 of dollars—you on the other hand have paid in about $160,000. And they will not be willing to give you up so long as anything can be squeezed out of you—You must tell Mrs. Young [the Braytons' sister] just how the matter stands. She must not endorse or make any kind of a promise as they will catch at straws— . . . Should they . . . get an extension. it will only put the evil day a little way off. . . . You may wish to know what—I think the effect will be on us. [I]t will only make us stronger as soon as people learn that we and the bank [M. B. C. Durfee Trust Company] is [*sic*] in no way linked up with them. [T]hey will have unlimited confidence in the bank and those connected with it—but for that end you must keep out—When the crash comes and come it will[,] people must know that [neither] the bank [nor] Mrs. Young nor any of us are under the rub[b]ish—[P]eople have known for several years that the end was only a question of time and many[,] very many will not be surprised—All you have to do is to stand firm on the solid ground that is under you—
David[98]

The Braytons waited.

On September 9, 1878, and before Hathaway's confession, Charles P. Stickney was exposed as a defalcator. Stickney sat on the board of directors of both the Border City and the Sagamore mills, and he quickly resigned when Chace and Hathaway were arrested. He also served as the president of the Massasoit National Bank and of the Davol mills. Stickney, who as a state Senator had crippled the 1874 ten-hour law and saved banks from state taxes, was the treasurer of the Manufacturers' Gas Company, where Chace had been president. The association between the two aroused suspicion among the board members, and Stickney resigned. Not only had he dipped into the gas company's assets, but he also had embezzled thousands of dollars from the Border City mills to pay for an extravagant private life, including a much discussed fifty thousand–dollar European family tour.[99]

In all Stickney too had stolen nearly a half-million dollars. Stickney took his exposure hard and was observed drunk in public. Deeply depressed, he was unable to sleep and used so much chloral, an addictive derivative of chlorine and alcohol, that his doctors suspected a suicide attempt. He remained at his mansion with a doctor in attendance. Again, class position stayed the hand of the law. A large crowd gathered outside his home, but the gas company board had hired guards to protect him. Finally, a state marshal read an arrest warrant to a silent, stricken Stickney as he lay stretched out in his elegant bedroom. His doctor feared an aggravated heart condition, but it was more likely acute shame. Stickney would be sentenced in March 1879 to five years in state prison, joining Chace and Hathaway. Family life was shattered. Stickney's father-in-law, William C. Davol, declared bankruptcy in 1879, assuming Stickney's debts of $600,000. In January 1884, after he was released from jail, his wife, Anna Davol Stickney, burned to death under odd circumstances involving a naptha lamp—either an accident, as the family insisted, or suicide. Stickney was badly burned trying to save her.[100] His son, Charles D. Stickney Jr., had fled to London where he pursued what was politely called, "a checkered career."[101]

George Hathaway was sentenced on October 14, 1878, to ten years in state prison. As he began to read his lengthy confession, he struggled to gain control of himself, then broke into sobs. Utterly humiliated and "terribly agitated," Hathaway slowly read the long narrative. The *Boston Herald* reported with disgust his "womanish weakness."[102] Better the cool contempt and flinty self-control of Chace than an open and tearful expression of grief and shame. Hathaway portrayed Chace as a man with a "heart of steel" and himself as a once honest country boy who had been drawn into illegal activity by his reverence for the reputations of Chace and Durfee. Neither man would help or protect him; he had fallen under their power and was now "a wreck." Four days later, Chace and Hathaway both testified in probate court on the Nathan Durfee estate.[103] Chace protected Holder B. Durfee from any accusation of wrongdoing in connections with the management of the estate. Throughout Chace's appearance in court, Durfee sat beside him. The *Boston Herald* reporter noted that Chace testified without showing any feeling, with a strange inward smile, shrew and crafty, betraying nothing. At fifty-seven, he would survive his prison sentence and return to Fall River, having revealed as little as possible and blaming no one. His loyalty to the remaining Durfee family paved his way.

THE RUIN OF THE BORDEN FAMILY

In 1879 the second great family pillar of industry and finance in the city, Jefferson Borden, his sons, sons-in-law, and nephews collapsed in a spreading scandal of speculation, fraud, deceit, bankruptcy, and flight from prosecution. Some of these activities stretched back to 1860 and had been encouraged by the heavy load of debt and inflated values of the postwar boom in mill construction. The depression of 1873–79 and the glutted cloth market had encouraged unauthorized speculation in cotton futures by mill treasurers who needed to appease complaining shareholders and querulous directors. In June 1879, George B. Durfee, Nathan Durfee's nephew and Jefferson Borden's son-in-law, secretly bought twenty thousand bales of cotton on margin from a New York commodities firm. When the price of cotton fell, Durfee had to put up more money on margin but was forced to sell and lost $35,000 of the Mechanics mill's assets. He also lost $100,000 on his own account.[104] The editor of the *Providence Journal*, who disapproved of futures buying as gambling, pointed out that "a call to make good 'margins' on a falling market is withering to personal integrity."[105] The mill directors were secretive, but rumors flew about Boston, New York, and Providence and forced them to disclose the loss. With the debacle of Chace, Hathaway, and Stickney still fresh, the Mechanics directors feared ruin. George's mother, Fidelia, already hard pressed from the collapse of Nathan Durfee's estate, paid off her son's debt to the mill with the last of her valuable property, a seashore summer home in Westport, Massachusetts. That money, Durfee's abject apology to the directors, and his resignation as treasurer of the Mechanics and of the Montaup mills seemed to close the matter quietly.

Dissatisfied shareholders of the Mechanics mill called on the state attorney general to investigate Durfee's alleged defalcation. One Fall River resident observed that while the honest, industrious, half-starved operative, who asked for a small wage increase, is

> denounced, execrated, and threatened ... [with the law], the well-connected mill treasurer who helps himself to advance pay is "pitied, condoled with" and escapes any just punishment when his family makes good his thievery.[106]

A local banker told the *Herald* editor that "We had better move the State Prison [from Concord] down ... [to Fall River] at once," fearing a general loss of confidence in all Fall River credit. The editor agreed that the "small pox of speculation and financial dishonesty" was far worse than strikes.[107] The commission house of Low, Harriman of New York City, where Durfee once worked and to whom he owed $100,000, acted. On August 11, a federal marshal attached the household goods in Durfee's mansion, including paintings, other works of arts, and "costly furniture," forcing him into bankruptcy. One day later, Walter Paine III from Providence, the treasurer of the Linen mill controlled by the Borden family and another son-in-law of Jefferson Borden, was exposed as dealing in unauthorized buying of cotton futures and stealing from the company. The family, who had known this since July 26, clamped down a lid of silence and planned Paine's escape.

On August 19, director Philip D. Borden, a nephew of Jefferson Borden, presented a report prepared by the family on Paine's activities to the Linen mill directors confirming that the directors had no knowledge of the transactions. Then director John S. Brayton read Paine's confession of wrongdoing to the board. Paine had been treasurer since 1860 when the mill was converted to making print cloth. He held twenty-three valuable shares in the company, but the policy of passing dividends and reinvesting profits meant he had to live on an annual salary of $2,500. Jefferson Borden had given the newlywed couple land and a sumptuous house; both remained the sole property of his daughter. The usual one thousand–dollar wedding gift in gold was probably spent furnishing it, among other expenses of the socially prominent young Paines. In his August confession to the board, Paine insisted that he simply could not live on fifty dollars a week. As treasurer of the Linen mill, he had immediately begun keeping a set of secret accounts and withdrawing company assets for his personal use. His intention had been to put all the money back once the dividends started rolling in. This practice became routine, although on occasion he paid some of the money back. Paine rose quickly to other positions: president of the Board of Trade; a director at the Metacomet, American Print Works, and the Granite mills; and a trustee of the Fall River Savings Bank. An active member of the First Baptist Church where the Jefferson Borden family worshiped, he and George Durfee were, like Chace, Sunday school teachers. In the end, he expressed great sorrow and contrition, but the Linen mill had lost over $150,000.

On the same day that Paine's confession was read to the board, George Durfee was arrested for his previous embezzlement of thirty-five thousand dollars from the Mechanics mill. Durfee made bail, astonished at being arrested at all after his family had paid off the mill for his losses. He was indicted in September. A warrant for Paine's arrest for taking twenty thousand dollars from the Linen mill had also been issued on August 12, but Paine had not attended the board of directors meeting at which his confession was read. He reportedly had gone to Providence to say goodbye to his mother and brother and then disappeared. Rumors pointed to Cuba or Canada. Fall River police officers made visits to Boston, New York City, and Providence, but Paine successfully fled arrest. The headlines read, "Where, Oh Where, is Paine?"[108]

For years Paine had concealed the real value of the Linen mill's assets from the shareholders.[109] Jefferson Borden, a major stockholder in the Providence Tool Company, had kept it afloat in 1876 with his own credit and notes on the Union and Linen mills.[110] On Borden's advice, Paine had sold $120,000 worth of print cloth at advantageously low prices to the American Print Works, from which Borden had retired in 1876. As Paine put it in his confession, the resources of the Linen mill had been locked up, and only luck in the futures market could help the mill's financial problems. In early 1879 he began to play the cotton futures game seriously, using the mill's credit to acquire forty-six hundred bales for the mill and ninety-seven hundred bales for himself, all without the authorization or knowledge of the directors. But, as with Durfee, the cotton price dropped, and both Paine and the Linen mill lost. Dipping into a mill's assets as many had done before was overlooked by Jefferson Borden's family. Certainly Jefferson Borden himself had used the credit of the Linen mill for his own purposes, and Paine had been more than willing to help him. Perhaps out of gratitude, a Borden family conference held on the night of August 11, including Jefferson Borden, Philip D. Borden, and Richard B. Borden, planned and financed the escape of Paine, his wife, and two children to Montreal, where he could not be extradited for embezzlement. After brief legal skirmishes with Canadian courts and Fall River law enforcers, the family left for England.

Condemnation and ridicule of Paine and Durfee poured out of the community, especially directed at the notion that in 1860 Paine could not possibly live on $2,500 a year.[111] The *Herald* printed on August 21 a parody of Edgar Allen Poe's *The Raven,* summing up the disgust of many.

"Futures" and "Margins"

Once upon a midnight dreary, while I
pondered weak and weary,
Over many a quaint and curious volume of forgotten lore—
While I nodded, nearly napping, suddenly there
   came a tapping,
As of some one gently rapping, rapping at my chamber door.
"Tis some new 'Futures' I muttered, tapping at my
chamber door,
    Only this and nothing more."

. . . .

Presently my soul grew stronger; hesitating then
no longer,
"Futures or margins, yes truly, your forgiveness

I implore;
But the fact is I was napping, and so gently you
came rapping,
And so faintly you came tapping, tapping at
my chamber door,
that I scarce was sure I heard you"—here I opened
wide the door.
    Darkness there and nothing more.
"Prophet," said I, "thing of evil–prophet still,
marginal devil!
By that heaven that bends above us, by the dollar
we adore,
Tell this soul with sorrow laden if, within
the distance radiance,
It shall steal enough to pay off
that old score—
Bust another corporation with the same old score."
    Quoth the Margin, *Nevermore.*

No one blamed Jefferson Borden. Many in the community and the business and financial world regarded him as an honorable, feeble old man who had suffered greatly at the hands of his guilty sons-in-law, especially from the "depravity" of Walter Paine. In fact, Jefferson Borden was a vigorous man of seventy-eight years, "hale and hearty," dying eight years later in 1887.[112] His style of business management, the futures' losses, and his own flagrant endorsement of promissory notes on his own credit without collateral cost him and his family dearly. After Paine's hasty departure, Philip D. Borden was elected treasurer of the Linen mill, but his appeal in September to the Providence creditors to renew their loans for six months was met with punitive terms, including a mortgage on the mill and bonds at 6 percent semi-annual interest.[113] At the board meeting in October the Linen mill's directors replaced him with an ally of John Brayton's, Robert C. Brown, and then added a new director, David A. Brayton.[114] Out of courtesy, Jefferson Borden remained the president, but the Borden influence was gone. The Braytons were on the rise, buying the Union mill in 1879.

Jefferson Borden declared bankruptcy in early September 1879. The *New York Times* pointed to the "fabulous" liabilities of the Print Works and the Borden family.[115] The editor of the *Boston Globe* reported that Borden's $250,000 in American Print Works shares had gone, in Jim Fisk's words, "where the woodbine twineth."[116] As the biggest shareholder in the Linen mill, his losses were great. As its largest creditor, the Fall River Savings Bank attached his property. His sons, Spencer and Jefferson Borden Jr., lost their entire inheritance. The Metacomet bank was expected to fail as a result of holding Linen mill shares and freely loaning the Bordens money without collateral. In early October, Thomas J. Borden and Richard B. Borden, Jefferson Borden's nephews, declared bankruptcy. Only Colonel Borden's youngest son, M. C. D. Borden of New York City, managed to stay solvent. As treasurer of the American Print Works, Thomas Borden and his brother Richard of the Troy and the Richard Borden mills sought protection in a trusteeship. Their liabilities were in the millions, principally from the debts of the Print Works, backed only by Jefferson Borden's personal credit. The editor of the *Boston Globe* grumbled about Jefferson Borden that "for years he has not been worth a dollar," although his influence on corporation policies remained very great. One Boston clergyman had no pity for him, "He who endorses for more than he is worth is a thief, or in a fair way of becoming one."[117] When the Fall River Savings Bank passed its dividend in October 1879 because of its losses in Borden notes, the widows and spinsters who besieged the bank managers likewise had no pity.

The collapse of the Borden family brought out the risks inherent in concentrated authority held by treasurers and the hiring of close relatives, largely to control corporate and market policy. The Lowell mills, in contrast, usually had three officers with independent responsibilities reporting to the directors: the treasurer, the selling agent, and the buying agent. "In Fall River all is done by the treasurer, and the chief requirement is that he must be a Fall River man."[118] And not any Fall River man would do; family connection and loyalty were crucial. In Rhode Island, conservative financial policies made sure that no mill would issue notes or paper in the open market or to banks. Their loans were always secured with collateral and were regarded as mortgages. In Fall River, as Providence mill interests observed, business had been built largely on borrowed money, and the mill owners had put their whole future in the hands of one fallible man, the treasurer. But then the Providence mills and banks were not attempting to dominate any particular sector of the cloth market.

The *Herald* published the embittered view of many English immigrant textile operatives toward the Borden family's inordinate power in "Six Degrees of Crime" on September 9, 1879, as Jefferson Borden's legend turned to ashes.

> He who "minches" a million is a shrewd financier. (And takes the cake.) . . . [119]
> He who "skips" with a hundred thousand is a rogue. (Sure hit him.)
> But he who "grabs" a pair of boots or a loaf of bread is a scoundrel of the deepest dye, and deserves incarceration in prison, for the remainder of his (un) natural life.
> (If not longer.)

6

They Have Brought Their Horns with Them

Deference and Defiance, 1868–1875

WHILE ANGERED by the crimes and injustices committed within the Fall River mills, the operatives also faced serious divisions within their ranks which had to be surmounted before successful opposition to the mill managers was possible. Wednesday, November 26, 1874, was payday in the Border City mills. The paymaster delivered the operatives' wages to the superintendents at the company's two mills. The overseers in each room paid off the help. Pat Madden, a robust, muscular weaver, watched all afternoon for the paymaster's appearance at Mill #2. Madden had quit two weeks before, but his wife still worked in the mill. The company owed him twenty-nine dollars and paid only once a month. This was the day. Madden watched until the paymaster had disappeared inside the mill tower. There were two women waiting outside. Neither recognized him. After a few minutes, he approached the mill tower.

Herbert Lasalle, the mill watchman, had stationed himself at the tower leading onto the winding staircase that connected with the workrooms. A French Canadian immigrant, he had four daughters working at the Border City mills. His job was to guard the staircase. On payday, no outsider was allowed in the mill. As Madden watched, Lasalle conferred in French with Clara Blais, a warper who spoke no English. She wanted him to contact her dressing room overseer. Julia Bricking, the wife of an Irish American weaver, asked Lasalle if she could collect her husband's wages so she could pay off a grocery bill rather than the debt he owned for beer. Lasalle expressed sympathy and allowed her to enter and speak to the weave-room overseer.

Lasalle left his post only briefly, assigning it to a mill painter. When he returned, Madden had entered the tower and begun climbing the stairs to the weave room. The younger, "stout" Irish weaver then confronted the older French Canadian watchman. Lasalle grabbed a hard maple lapstick, four feet long and three inches in circumference, to even the odds.[1] The two argued, then struggled on the stairs. The women heard the noise and yelled that the men were fighting. Madden ran out from the tower, shouting "Why didn't he let me in?" and leaving Lasalle collapsed on the stairs, bleeding from his ear. Lasalle died later that day from a fractured skull, the lapstick smeared with his blood. The editor of the *News* immediately informed the middle-class public that a drunken Irish weaver, fired from his job, had struck and killed a Border City watchman. The faithful Lasalle whose large family worked in the mill was simply doing his duty.[2] Until the coroner's inquest, readers might have sighed over yet another example of Irish intemperance, slackness, and violence in conflict with French Canadian patience, obedience, and desperate need for work. Ethnic rivalries as well as class tensions were increasing in the Fall River mills.

The testimony at the coroner's inquest revealed a different story. Pat Madden had not been fired; the superintendent testified that the mill had his back wages ready on November 26. Lasalle had allowed one woman into the mill and had left his post to intervene on behalf of a country-woman. In and out of consciousness as he lay dying, Lasalle accused no one of striking him, and no one had seen Madden with the lapstick. But he had run from the mill tower to Patrick Mullen's grocery, seeking a ride out of town. Mullen, who had known Madden for years, testified that he had been in the grocery all morning, waiting for the right time to approach the mill but had drunk nothing. Later he appeared frightened and sorrowful, saying he had pushed the watchman but never struck him. The grocer suggested an explanation. The tower stairs were plated with iron; he himself had slipped on them. Madden had probably pushed La-salle aside to get to the weave room, but the watchman had fallen down the stairs, striking his head on an iron plate. Blood dripped onto the lap-stick still in Lasalle's hand as one of the overseers lifted and placed him in a wagon. The coroner's jury concluded that Lasalle died "in the discharge of his duties" when "forcibly" pushed down the stairs by Madden.[3] No charges were brought; Madden had fled to Rhode Island.

Lasalle, frightened of big Irishmen like Madden, refused him entrance at the order of the superintendent. But Madden saw the watchman relax the rules for the women. Why not for him? Lasalle appeared to represent both the arbitrary power of the mill in denying him his rightful wages that day and also the invasion of French Canadian immigrants who worked for low wages and protected their own. Described by grocer Mullen as quiet but "apt to be impulsive if crossed," Madden expected to brush the little Frenchman aside to get paid, but underestimated Lasalle's determination to carry out his duties. Power relations within the mills, intercultural rivalries, and workplace misunderstandings had produced this tragedy.

DIVISIONS AND RIVALRIES AMONG NEW ENGLAND TEXTILE WORKERS

For many native-born textile workers and some labor reformers, the post–Civil War influx of immigrants from Lancashire and Yorkshire appeared even more threatening than the one from Ireland or Quebec. In 1869, a woman weaver, assessing the hard conditions in the Lowell mills, stated her fears in the *American Workman:*

> Great numbers of skilled English operatives are on their way to compete with us for bread. The capitalists are bringing . . . [them] from the ends of the earth, to still further lengthen our hours, or reduce our pay.[4]

Although highly skilled English printers, dyers, machinists, and second hands were commonplace in New England textile centers, the post–Civil War waves of Lancashire and Yorkshire mule spinners, weavers, and carders seemed a new danger. They entered the New England mills to join the general mixed workforce of Yankees, and Irish, Scottish, and Canadian immigrants, both English and French speaking (see table 5). Their growing numbers and the extent of their industrial experience appeared ominous.

Nineteenth-century New England textile centers had been organized specifically to avoid replicating the terrible conditions in early English cotton mills. American patriots believed their own institutions, political and economic, had to be superior to the defeated, corrupt Mother Country. Textile capitalists, building in Waltham and Lowell, assured the public that the American republic would be served by a different, far more benign, system of industrial production. Wage cuts and turn-outs during the early 1830s and 1840s called this into question. Still, the high turnover rates among the native-born workforce helped the Massachusetts mills maintain a paternalistic image until the strikes in 1848 and 1850. Those strikes also revealed that native-born and Lancashire immigrant workers had different ideas about labor protest. Prior to the Civil War, most American operatives seemed unaware of the English struggle for ten-hour reform or the 1847 law passed by Parliament. Despite the successful agitation in the late 1860s and the early 1870s by immigrant mule spinners and English-born middle-class activists for ten hours, lingering suspicions about the moral character of British operatives haunted both American labor reformers and textile workers.

Henry K. Oliver's 1868 report to the Massachusetts Senate on the employment of factory children concluded with a warning about the immorality of English textile workers and his alarm at "the swarm of ignorant

workmen . . . introduced into our State from England. . . ."⁵ Oliver was
particularly offended by the appearance of sexual looseness among English factory women, who lived without the discipline of corporate boardinghouse regulations. In his 1868 report, Oliver cited the excursion of a
fellow mill overseer, John Aiken of Lowell, into the streets of Manchester,
England, in 1845.

> You pass gin-shops and beer-shops, oft frequented and well patronized,—
> and it would be well if bold unblushing sensuality were confined to the
> men,— . . . but gross and disgusting profligacy are discovered among the
> women. . . . Multitudes of women are seen [in the market at night], . . .
> many of them without bonnets . . . forcing their way through the throng,
> . . . returning the joke, or open-handed slap to the passer-by of the other
> sex. The American eye has never seen such a sight at home.⁶

Oliver worried that the "youngling-operatives," who came with their
"degraded" families and worked with them in the mills, would become
part of the "swelling wave of an untaught, immoral class" unless the state
acted promptly. He also wrote of the "cholera of ignorance," and the necessity for "sanitary measures," thus associating female sexuality with disease and uncleanliness, not unlike the 1840s mechanics' movement. Oliver wished to educate the children,

> so that they shall shrink away, with a sort of moral shudder, from intemper-
> ance, licentiousness, debauchery, gin-shops, dancing-saloons and nasty
> homes,—from hatred of employers, strikes, and the festering immorali-
> ties, which seem to be the normalisms of English manufacturing towns.

He seemed particularly concerned about the boys, who if correctly educated would accept the employer's contract, feel its "sacred nature," and
work faithfully and productively, until each one "too becomes A MAN, in
all the elements of a manly manhood, and he and his employer, standing
within nearer reach of each other, may commune as man with man for
each other's good."⁷ For Oliver, as for many middle-class labor reformers,
true men accepted the mutual interests between employer and worker
and would naturally avoid class strife.

Oliver admired the English factory schools and advocated their adoption while chief of the Massachusetts Bureau of Labor Statistics. Admitting
that he had "factory children on the brain," Oliver lobbied hard for this
reform in coalition with Robert Bower of Lawrence. Much in his 1868
report, however, fed the pre–Civil War stereotypes of English operatives,
especially the workingwomen, as immoral and dangerous to the Commonwealth. An 1865 essay in Boston's *Atlantic Monthly* anticipated Oliver's
observations, smugly contrasting the gentility of American factory girls to
the filthiness and coarseness of many English workingwomen. Both their
"half-naked" condition in cotton spinning factories and the male garb of

The Park Meeting: Thomas Evans rallying strikers in 1894, *Fall River Herald*, October 19, 1894. Courtesy of Paul Coppens

Jonathan Thayer Lincoln
after retirement from
the Harvard University
Business School, c. 1938.
Courtesy of Louise
Kittredge

Mrs. George Borden,
mother of Holder Borden,
with her second husband,
Bradford Durfee. Courtesy
Collection of the Fall River
Historical Society

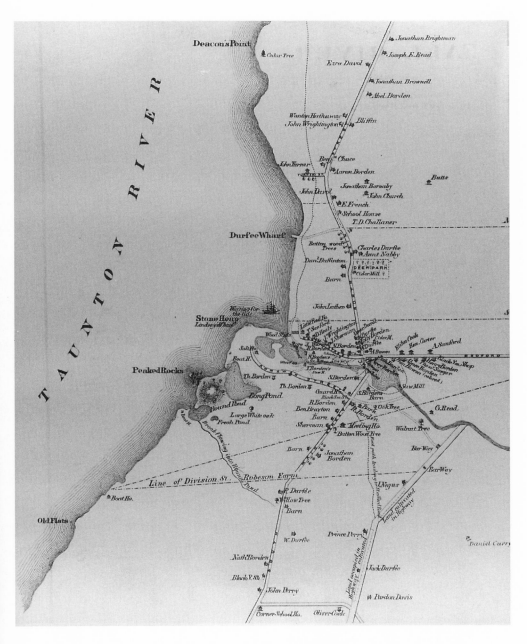

Town of Troy (later Fall River) in 1812 before the organization of the first cotton mill.
Reprinted from Earl, *Centennial History* (1877)

The Annawan Mill, c. 1830. Courtesy Collection of the Fall River Historical Society

Engraving of Fall River mill
girl Sarah Maria Cornell.
Reprinted from the *Brief
and Impartial Narrative of the
Life of Sarah Maria Cornell*
(New York, 1833)

Thomas Almy, ten-hour reformer and Editor of the *Fall River Mechanic.*
Courtesy of the American Antiquarian Society

Conscience Whig Hon. Nathaniel Briggs Bordon, 1801–1865.
Courtesy Collection of the Fall River Historical Society

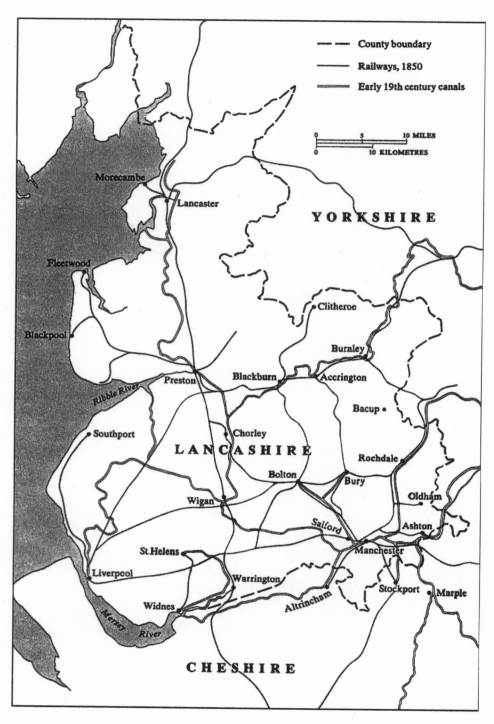

Mid-nineteenth-century Lancashire, England. Courtesy of Paul Coppens

Fall River's Granite Mill disaster, 1874. Courtesy of Cornell University Libraries

Jefferson Borden.
Reprinted from Earl, *Centennial History*
(1877)

American Print Works, Fall River,
as rebuilt by Jefferson Borden in 1869.
Reprinted from Earl,
Centennial History (1877)

Richard Colonel Bordon. Reprinted from Earl, *Centennial History* (1877)

Dr. Nathan Durfee. Reprinted from Earl, *Centennial History* (1877)

Fall River Town Hall and Market Building, 1845. Courtesy Collection of the Fall River Historical Society

The Fall River City Hall, 1876. Reprinted from Earl, *Centennial History* (1877)

The defalcators exposed in 1878: S. Angier Chace, George T. Hathaway, Charles P. Stickney, and Walter Paine III. Courtesy Collection of the Fall River Historical Society

John Summerfield Brayton. Courtesy Collection of
the Fall River Historical Society

the pit-brow lasses in the Wigan coal fields of Lancashire distorted their womanliness in ways the female writer regarded as incomprehensible.[8] For American middle-class observers and reformers, these displays of un-womanly and unmanly behavior as well as Lancashire-style labor protest were profoundly alien to New England. Continuing coalitions between immigrant workers and labor reformers would have to overcome great cultural and political difficulties.

NEVILLE KIRK'S 1985 study of the mid-Victorian compromise in Lanca-shire explores the kind of harmonious labor relations that Oliver hoped for in New England. In 1994 Kirk undertook a massive comparative study of the British and American labor movements in the nineteenth and twen-tieth centuries. In the introduction to his first volume, *Labour and Society in Britain and the USA: Capitalism, Custom and Protest, 1780–1850,* he carefully assesses the strengths and weaknesses of comparative labor history. Kirk cites the American workingman's possession of the ballot, the possibilities of geographic and social mobility, the damaging legacy of slavery and rac-ism, and the "deep imprint" of capitalist values on the working-class popu-lation. Nonetheless, he firmly rejects any notion that the experience of labor protest in the United States was fundamentally different from or exceptional to the British. Indeed, he argues that the two national tradi-tions "coexisted and interacted" and that, nineteenth-century immigra-tion to America created ties and sustained strong mutual influences.[9]

Kirk regards American labor relations during the post–Civil War pe-riod to the 1873 depression as similar to England in general moderation and conciliation. He also views the eight-hour movement and German radicals as the only groups interested in class politics, overlooking British immigrant radicals and former Chartists. The influx of immigrants from Lancashire and Yorkshire after 1865 with their high expectations about wage standards and working conditions reshaped New England labor poli-tics. The years between the depressions of the 1870s and 1890s, unlike in England, were times of recurrent, severe crisis. Kirk notes that no period in American labor politics seemed to have been so different in the depth of class consciousness and conflict compared with the British, although his conclusions lack a specific comparison of the textile industry in Britain and America.[10]

Ironically, Kirk's key sources on the nature of English immigration and its contribution to American labor politics, Clifton K. Yearley Jr.'s *Britons in American Labour* and Roland Berthoff's, *British Immigrants in Industrial America, 1870–1950,* are national overviews that generally confirm dif-ferences between the American and British experience.[11] For example, Berthoff primarily emphasizes the conservative contribution of skilled British workingmen to the rise of the wage-conscious and apolitical Amer-ican Federation of Labor. Yearley's ambitious, well-researched survey of

British influences, focusing on the period between 1850 and 1900, cites institutions, such as trade unions, cooperatives, fraternal organizations, and friendly societies, to demonstrate the significance of English and Irish immigrant leaders, especially in the mining and metal industries and in New England textiles. To Yearley, Robert Howard's conservative career as the leader of organized mule spinners in New England is "typical" of British immigrant textile workers, but this view ignores the post–Civil War decades of struggle over labor politics within the contingent of British immigrant mule spinners and weavers in the Northeast, not unlike similar Lancashire conflicts over strategy, tactics, ideology, and objectives. Yearley contrasts the conservatism of trade unionist Howard with more radical German immigrants but does not investigate many other British immigrants, such as Richard Hinchcliffe, Henry Sevey, George Gunton, and a multitude of lesser known men and women who advocated more radical, inclusive policies. Yearley's conclusions about the nature of American labor—the powerful nature of capitalist opposition, a less homogeneous workforce than in England, "less class consciousness," "fierce economic nationalism," "instinctive pragmatism," "incorrigible optimism," and a "myopia" about funding amalgamated unions—does not support Kirk's arguments on essential similarities.[12] Furthermore, Kirk ignores evidence in Isaac Cohen's work on vast differences between mule spinners in Lancashire, England, and New England as well as the unique complexities of post-1880 textile labor politics in Fall River as explored by historian John Cumbler.[13]

A study of southeastern New England textile centers provides crucial evidence between 1848 and 1905 to test Kirk's analysis. The influence of popular radicalism, the salience of class consciousness among Lancashire and Yorkshire workers, the strategies and rituals of radical labor protest, and the transmission of English culture and customs to the New England industry remained significant political and cultural issues throughout the late nineteenth century. Much of this evidence supports Kirk's argument about similarities. But when, as he argues, English-inspired idealism, moral dignity, "affirmative Christianity," and "God and vision" give way to "the cost of living index" in the United States, it is important for historians to analyze the working-class politics that explain this development.[14] As Kirk writes in his introduction, historians should investigate both division and community among working people and detail the ways that fragmentation and unity interact "at specific points of time and over time."[15] A study of post–Civil War labor politics in the southeastern New England textile industry deepens an understanding of the conflicts, complexities, and differing outcomes in Old and New England.

LABOR AGITATION linked with the ten-hour movement survived the Civil War years, reemerging with vigor. Successful strikes by a Fall River weavers' union in the early 1860s took advantage of the pressures of wartime inflation and labor shortages. In the fall of 1865, the reconstituted mule spinners' union took the lead in a general strike that advanced their wages 15 percent to meet the swollen costs of fuel and provisions. By 1866, new immigrants from England asserted their presence in labor politics, agitating for the ten-hour day as "in the Old Country."[16] Pressure mounted until the Fall River mills, prodded by the booming cloth market and labor shortages, finally granted the ten-hour day on January 1, 1867. Strikes for ten hours, supported by Fall River mule spinners, broke out at the Wamsutta mills in New Bedford and in Lawrence, Lowell, Manchester, and Lewiston, although this regional uprising did not succeed. Even in Fall River, mill agents started squeezing an extra thirty minutes per day out of the operatives by starting the steam engines early, a practice begun in 1867 that they continued long after the enactment of the ten-hour law. The only authority they recognized was the market for cloth and their pressing need for "help."

The general booming condition of the textile industry soon glutted the market. A surprise wage cut in early 1868 of 18 percent for the weavers and lesser cuts for other operatives threw labor politics into frenzy. Recently arrived English immigrants became divided from older operatives, both immigrant and native-born, while middle-class sympathizers worried about the style and direction of agitation. Weavers defied their employers; mule spinners tried a more deferential approach. W. B. Mc-Auley spoke for those weavers who wanted to strike against "a grasping set of men" who had cut wages outrageously for "honest, hardworking men and women" from "the old country." But the mule spinners' union distrusted the excited weavers and sought a compromise by either reducing the wage cut or by working shorter hours, a policy preferred by many Lancashire immigrants. The weavers refused to cooperate with the spinners and returned, determined to "fight a running battle. . . ."[17] In 1868, the mule spinners union tried compromise, moderation, and arbitration with the "masters," a policy that had characterized mid-Victorian labor politics. Based on their experience in Lancashire, deference worked better than defiance.

Divided from the mule spinners over strategy and tactics, the male and female weavers, faced the deepest wage cut and rallied to form a union in February 1868. Some male weavers feared that undependable women members might undermine the union, while others insisted on including the female weavers, arguing that they made the best collectors of union dues. Irresistible or unreliable, no women spoke out at the meeting. McAuley became the union's secretary, but his defiant words about freedom of speech and tyranny meant that no mill supervisor would negotiate with him. He proposed resistance to time stealing, a letter-writing campaign to warn all Lancashire of the oppressive nature of Fall River, and a threatened mass return of weavers to England. McAuley, blacklisted and victimized in his words by "the caprice, wickedness, and covetousness" of the managers at the Union mill, had been told by his overseer: "Your tongue is too loose. You had better go somewhere else."[18] Veteran labor reformer and former carder Thomas Webb dismissed McAuley as an impractical dreamer to expect Lancashire-style standards in New England.

The mule spinners' union, pursuing a policy of deference based on a strong organization, began a general strike of spinners and weavers in early March 1868 to get back their old wages.[19] The spinners' union with one hundred seventy four members attempted to consult with their employers to settle the situation "amicably and honestly." The weavers joined the work stoppage, but when the negotiations failed they returned to work, while the spinners voted to continue the strike. It lasted only two weeks. By May, part of this spirit of resistance shifted into the organization of the Fall River Ten-Hour Association.[20] The weavers and spinners continued to jockey over the leadership of local labor politics.

THE FALL RIVER MULE SPINNERS STRIKE OF 1870

As the result of a wage cut in Lancashire in 1869, a massive contingent of weavers and mule spinners from Preston, Blackburn, and other Lancashire mill centers left for New England, where, they believed, "work is plentiful, and where they are abundantly paid for their labor."[21] Reinforcements were on the way, easing the Fall River labor shortages but increasing union membership (see table 3). But in 1870 Fall River managers cut wages 10 percent, attempting to flood the print cloth market with cheap goods and drive out their Rhode Island competitors, a policy they would continue throughout the late nineteenth century. Using carefully considered deference rather than outright defiance, the mule spinners stopped work followed by other Lancashire immigrants and, orchestrating their public images as respectable, skilled workingmen, tried to maneuver their employers into face-to-face negotiations. Representatives of the 420 spinners, speaking for the seven thousand other operatives thrown out of work with the stoppage of yarn production, requested a compromise through a series of formal letters. The mill agents never responded. Strike leader William Isherwood, blacklisted in Lowell as head of the ten-hour association, regarded this as "silent contempt."[22] Instead, the managers attempted to provoke reactions from the striking spinners to make them appear reckless and irresponsible. Massachusetts labor reformers as well as the general public abhorred both violence and strikes, but for Lancashire immigrants not all expressions of resistance could remain polite or electoral. Still, uncontrolled confrontations might justify a refusal to negotiate. The strikers became determined to prevent any association of violent acts with male unionists. The union stated its position as "repeatedly and respectfully" entreating the mill owners to negotiate, while peaceably offering any arriving strikebreakers train fares back home. Wage levels and union negotiations had symbolized the relative strength of the workforce in Lancashire, and both operatives and agents regarded their contest in New England as an issue of power, of who would "rule." If the strikers won, one mill agent remarked, it would be "England right over again."[23]

Meanwhile, the mule spinners enlisted sympathetic weavers, men and women, who refused to weave any filling yarn purchased outside of Fall River, as well as their own wives and children to confront strikebreakers. The union thus implicitly endorsed rude and violent public behavior for females: yelling, pummeling strikebreakers, and throwing stones, activities inappropriate for respectable working-class men and illegal in England. Women could—at the direction of the men on whom many depended for support—use violence and intimidation against strikebreakers in cooperation with male and female weavers. Portrayed as victims and dependents during ten-hour debates after 1869, workingwomen, at the same time, became protagonists in ways crucial to the strikers' strategy.

The only incident of open violence during the strike toward a "knobstick" illustrates how the spinners' allies assumed responsibility for intimidation. A Scottish immigrant farmer who had worked as a mule spinner for only three years, Isaiah Sanderson, refused to join the spinners' union but expected trouble and afterwards would name no attacker. To make an example of him, noisy members of a crowd waiting outside the Durfee mill kicked, stoned, and gave him "a tremendous pounding" as he quit for the night after two days at work. The crowds surrounding Sanderson were mostly women and children, and his attackers were probably adult weavers who supplied the howls and jeers, the fists and blows, to humble a disloyal male. These crowds were backed up by the tenants of corporation housing nearby, armed with stones and dirt clods ready to shower the strikebreakers at a signal. Women sat at their windows, the objects concealed in their aprons.[24] The mule spinners controlled and directed these events, while their peaceable manly behavior and female rowdiness served class politics.

Women's involvement in the 1870 strike sometimes represented more than simple support for their husbands and families. In Lancashire mule spinners' wives were not usually employed, but some spinners' wives and daughters in Fall River were weavers.[25] Women, married and single, represented about half of the Fall River workforce of eight thousand weavers by 1875, and the number of working wives in cotton goods was the highest in the state (see table 6). In 1870, an English-born spinner described to a state investigator a pattern that he claimed was familiar to the families of Fall River mule spinners. Each working day, he rose at 5:00 A.M. and while his children and wife slept, started the breakfast and put the dinner into the pails. After work, he "help[ed] along supper until she gets home."

On Sundays he and his wife, who had been a factory girl in England, cooked and cleaned the house together and took a "nap" after dinner, the only chance for intimacy during the workweek of nearly seventy hours. His wife had worked as a weaver since their arrival in Fall River, except for periodic intervals of six months to bear and care for a new child. Shared housework made it possible for his wife and her twelve-year-old daughter to tend ten looms, more than the usual six to eight looms of women weavers, and thus earn more for the family.[26] Luckier families immigrated with kin who eased the burden on working parents. As the mills expanded production and supplied plenty of factory work for immigrants, some wives and daughters of mule spinners who worked as weavers, generated support for the mule spinners' strike within the working-class family. This public testimony by a mule spinner about his voluntary participation in routine housework alongside his working wife did not contradict his sense of manliness as head of the family. Still, the involvement of women in strikes and unions remained controlled by workingmen.

During the strike, mill agents tried to denigrate the respectable manliness of the mule spinners by claiming that elsewhere in the industry, "girls run mules easily and successfully."[27] In Salem's Naumkeag mills, Taunton's Whittenton mills, and others in Newburyport, Biddeford, Lewiston, and in Rhode Island, the agents claimed young women worked on small mule spinning or "jack" frames. Thus managers tried to undermine their skilled male workers by feminizing mule spinning. Denying this, mule spinners argued that they worked harder and faster at their machines than anywhere else in New England, walking twenty-five miles and more per day over eleven hours with only one young boy to help them: "a pretty good day's work for any man." Strikers insisted that this exhausting work was "not a fitting employment for females."[28] The mill agents also used their economic power during the 1870s to invest in developing a primitive technology: ring spinning machines to replace mules for the production of warp yarn. Arguments over male control of spinning operations in New England mills would continually divide men and women operatives and pit nationality against nationality in the late nineteenth century.

In addition, New England mill agents had refused to supply their mule spinners with the assistants customary in Lancashire, thus increasing the burden of work and depriving, spinners of the manly authority of hiring and supervision. A Fall River mule spinner had only one "back boy" to help piece up or repair any broken strands yarn spun out during the back and forth motions of the huge frames. Other boys worked as "doffers" and "tubers," whisking the spun yarn away in boxes and replacing empty tubes on spindles, often suffering from splinters in their bare feet as they scrambled to do their work.[29] The spinners' twenty-five miles each day produced what was known as the "Fall River walk," brisk and quick. Few mule spinners, even the younger, vital ones, had the stamina to work out a full month of six day weeks at eleven hours a day without dropping out as "sick" for several days to rest and regain their strength. The mills kept a list of "sick spinners" who were called in routinely to fill the jobs of exhausted men for several days each month. For the employer to define a spinner's work as just beyond the extent of a man's physical powers, an abuse the operatives called the "grind" or "lashing the help," was intended to undermine a man's pride in strength, authority, and skill. Mule spinners in Lancashire never accepted such working conditions, and many immigrants returned to England in disgust.[30] Other late nineteenth-century New England textile centers adopted Fall River practices, which became an industry standard.

Furthermore, the mill agents justified the use of strikebreakers in Fall River by utilizing the language of supply and demand. Market forces, they insisted, shaped the local labor supply that in turn set the wage level. If a spinner's wages were too low, he should go to another mill center where there was a demand for his skills. The agents argued that any opposition to market forces by workers in America represented coercion and interference with individual rights of contract and natural economic laws.[31] Their ability to frame these arguments and impose their version of market terminology as a defensive ideology reflected their economic power. Strike leaders knew that any dispersal of union men to other textile centers would cripple resistance. They sought instead to fix the responsibility for the wage cuts on decisions made in Fall River countinghouses by the mill agents, not by any so-called impersonal market, decisions that could be changed by negotiation. This struggle over the meaning and validity of supply and demand ideology characterized Fall River labor politics throughout the 1870s.

The mill agents usually remained cool-headed during their confrontations with their workers, relying on their combined power and vast inventories to intimidate. David A. Brayton, treasurer of the Durfee mill, broke ranks with this practice, to his regret. Raised on a farm and trained as a lawyer, Brayton was relatively new to the textile business. In 1866 he began to run the first Brayton family mill. In 1870, with markets widening, he was supervising the building of a second mill and personally owned nearly one-third of the company's stock. The 1870 mule spinners' strike, which threatened his business expansion, became his first confrontation with politically experienced, skilled workingmen. Unlike the other textile managers who always refused to speak directly with any strikers, Brayton reacted with passionate anger to the situation.

In early July, two striking spinners, trying to get Brayton to compromise on the wage cut, approached him in the millyard as he was climbing into his carriage. He talked with them for a while but then said,

> I think you should be thankful we don't have to cut down [wages] again;
> . . . One of them commenced arguing the case. . . . Finally he spoke of the
> high price of beef here and in England, to which I replied that it was very
> high here, but not so high as to prevent any honest laboring man from
> having it on his table three times a day. "Well," said he, "we can't have
> salmon." At that I got a little excited and answered: By thunder! if you are
> going to count on salmon I can't stand here to argue with you.[32]

Increasingly offended, Brayton found himself discussing inside his own
mill yard what was likely to appear on his workers' dinner tables, and his
remark about beef three times a day indicated his growing excitement.
Goaded by his anger and responsibilities, Brayton attempted to reopen
the Durfee mill long before the strike ended. He and his mill became the
target of the strikers and their supporters. This also got him into trouble
with the mayor and the other mill agents. After his employee, Sanderson
had been severely beaten, Brayton notified the police to escort him home
and gave the injured man a pistol. Then after conferring with Thomas
Borden, head of the fire department, Brayton went to the city hall, insisting on action. Mayor Samuel Brown tried to calm him down, but Brayton threatened to go to the governor's office for state troops if the city
authorities failed to act. The next evening as the Durfee workers were
leaving the mill, the city marshal, armed only with a little whip, tried to
part the jeering crowd to let the workers through. Brayton was disgusted:
"It was like switching grasshoppers."[33] If the city would not act decisively,
he would.

In his own words, "now greatly excited," Brayton, armed with a loaded
pistol, set off the municipal fire alarm, bringing onto the scene the volunteer fire-fighting force. He and the city marshal directed it to drench the
crowd of about two hundred strikers, driving them away from the front of
the mill. His forthright action turned ridiculous: the firehoses' stream of
water reached only about one hundred thirty feet. The crowd, after much
hissing and hooting, simply stood in defiance beyond the water's reach.
Thrown into a rage by the impotency of his actions, Brayton drew his
pistol, intending to force his workers through the line of strikers. Before
this could happen, the mayor, prodded by the mill agents in a city "all
astir," arrived and, ignoring Brayton's pleas for mass arrests, ordered the
strikers in the name of the Commonwealth to disperse. They did. The
next day, in an overwhelming show of force, two hundred special police,
four city companies of militia, and a contingent of state police arrived to
control both the strikers and Brayton.[34] He had learned that hard way
how Fall River managers effectively handled strikes: refuse to talk, sell
their inventories, starve out the strikers, and blacklist the leaders. Thereafter, Brayton fell into line. Quiet reliance on the class power of the mills
allowed the agents to display their own dispassionate and respectable
manliness and defeat the strikers. Protest strategies based on mutual rec-

ognition of manly respectability and deferential behavior might have offered hope in Lancashire, but they did not work in Fall River.

The editor of the *Providence Journal* provided an additional rationale for breaking the 1870 strike. A "simple and obvious law of labor," freedom of contract supplemented supply and demand theory. In the United States, the editor argued, there is no lawful power to compel men either to pay or to accept a fixed rate of wages. Every man must judge for himself what is in his own best interest. Describing a fancied economic realm without markets or mills, poverty or wealth, vulnerability or power, the writer insisted that it was the duty of the state to use "military force" to secure to American citizens this "unquestioned right."[35] In fact, the publishers and editors of the *Providence Journal* were advocating freedom of contract in their own interests, because they owned many mills in villages adjacent to the city, especially those to the north along the Blackstone River.

After two months, textile workers slowly returned to the Fall River mills. Union leaders were blacklisted and forced from their corporation tenements, while other strikers reluctantly signed anti-union contracts.[36] Those blacklisted union leaders, such as Isherwood who stayed on in the city as a storekeeper, had lost their status as craftsmen. Others forced to leave the city lost contact with their fellow unionists. The attempt by the spinners' union to link respectable masculinity with craft and union proved vulnerable to the determination of Fall River managers to tame their Lancashire workers by blacklisting their leaders and destroying the union's membership. Fall River strikers behaved in 1870 as respectable, deferential union men in ways that rejected their employers' disparagement of their skills and manliness. Women and weavers had harassed and humiliated strikebreakers, but this strategy of separating activities during strikes based on sex and skill did not empower them in 1870 nor had it in New Bedford in 1868. The employers, backed by ideological, economic, and political power, had to be forced—somehow—to negotiate. Meanwhile, the spinners organized in secret, and the weavers regrouped, waiting for increasing numbers of immigrants from the old country. Together, goaded by another wage cut and an increase to an eleven-hour day in December 1873, they poured their energies into the successful political campaign for the ten-hour law in 1874.[37]

LANCASHIRE POLITICAL HERITAGES IN POST–CIVIL WAR NEW ENGLAND

The decade of turmoil in the 1870s peaked during a year of open defiance in 1875. English immigrant textile workers, who had immigrated in successive waves before and after the American Civil War to the textile cities of Fall River, New Bedford, and to the mill villages of Rhode Island, seized control of labor politics in southeastern New England. Unlike

many immigrants to nineteenth-century America from preindustrial societies, these people came with industrial skills, urban experience, class-
consciousness, and a rich heritage of the customs and traditions of popular radicalism.[38] These included rituals of public demonstrations and community censure; varied uses of respectable deference and radical defiance
as demeanors in labor politics; measures of bodily strength and food preferences; expectations about manhood and womanhood; and the responsibilities of sons and daughters to the ideals of their parents and of workingmen and workingwomen to their Lancashire heritage of labor politics.
At the same time, Fall River capitalists were attempting to dominate the
American domestic market for cotton print cloth and purge their English
workers of "their chronic insubordination."[39] These conflicting politics of
industrial life significantly influenced the direction and content of late
nineteenth-century New England labor activity.

English mule spinners and weavers had developed different organizations and strategies to defend their interests. The strikes of 1868 and 1870
reflected these differing policies. Mule spinners sought to build powerful
organizations of skilled male workers in key textile centers to counteract
the mill agents' argument that market forces determined wages. In contrast, the weavers' organizations accepted both men and women who
tended the looms at equal piece rates. Their immediate goal in New England was the establishment of a standard list of wages, as in Lancashire.
For men and women weavers, strong and inclusive regional organization
was far more important than the sex or skill of union members in anyone
textile center. Definitions of manhood and womanhood also became central to specific struggles in the 1870s among various groups of men (employers and workers, mule spinners and weavers) and among the various
ethnic groups of working-class men and women in Fall River. One crucial
element in this conflict was the class power used by mill agents to determine market strategy for their goods. This power, if unopposed, gave employers the authority to alter wages and working conditions in the mills
that influenced working peoples' understanding of manhood and womanhood as well as the effectiveness of union strategy. During this decade
of conflict with the power of capital, relationships among working-class
men and women and between mule spinners and weavers were openly
contested.

Between 1865 and 1873 Lancashire men and women, many from
Preston and Blackburn, immigrated to Fall River as individuals, as brothers and sisters, and as husbands and wives, usually leaving behind networks of kin who formed such an important part of Lancashire culture
and politics (see table 5).[40] Those who chose to emigrate and did not
return also left behind them the reformist moderation and general stability of the mid-Victorian textile industry.[41] In addition, the structural elements of Lancashire work and life that underlay patriarchal union organi-

zation and family wage rhetoric in England barely survived the voyage to New England. The issues of ideology, strategy, and gender relations in labor protest required reconsideration, negotiation and reformulation.

From the moment that Lancashire workers landed in Fall River, the managers of the mills treated them with a mixture of contempt, arrogance, and fear, systematically challenging their customary measures of skill and strength based on wages and working conditions. The mill agents used the cheapest raw cotton and the best machinery, paid the lowest wages in the region, and demanded ever more intense physical exertions from their operatives, especially from mule spinners, to produce massive quantities of inferior cloth, the defects in which the printing process would conceal. They controlled the domestic market for print cloth by having the capacity to glut it with the cheapest possible goods, regarded by Lancashire operatives as "shoddy," unworthy cloth. As a result, many Lancashire and Yorkshire workers despised the agents in the Fall River and Lawrence print cloth mills, as "shoddyites" and promoters of "shoddyite morality."[42] A letter signed, "I Want to Know," dismissed the "bosses" at the Washington mill in Lawrence as ignorant even about bobbins, calling them "do-nothings" as well as "know-nothings." Coworkers agreed, suggesting that the old "drones" be confined to the Tewksbury Asylum for the deaf and blind.[43] The weavers at Fall River's Chace mills criticized the superintendent in 1874 as responsible for intolerable conditions out of stubborn ignorance: bad yarn, "clouds of dust and steam," and dishonest measurements of the cuts of cloth, which determined the weavers' wages. "People say he does not know anything, and what is worse, can never be taught. . . ."[44] Irish-born David Lawlor who immigrated in 1872 became a doffer in the Granite and the Davol mills. He observed stolen worktime, arbitrary measurements of weavers' cuts, and regarded the Fall River mill agents as "mad on production . . . at low cost." The weavers of Lawrence grew restive in 1874, complaining of tyrannical practices and wage cuts without proper notice. Their experiences in English cotton and woolen mills provided the measure for their contempt and discontent. These Lancashire mills, usually run by partnerships and devoted to a single process of textile production, contrasted sharply with the huge integrated mills of New England.[45]

English immigrants also faced ruthless American managers intent on paying off—during the industrial depression of 1873 to 1879—very heavy corporate debts for overvalued land, new buildings, and machinery. Unlike mill owners in Lancashire, they often relied on men with managerial and financial skills acquired in commerce, such as S. Angier Chace at the Union, or on attorneys, such as David A. Brayton at the Durfee and Charles O. Shove at the Granite mills. These men were unfamiliar with English work traditions and styles of labor protest. Both William Jennings of the Merchants mill and Robert B. Borden of the Crescent feared and despised their English workers and regarded their doffed caps, politeness, and references to their employers as "masters" as marks of unmanly servility.[46] In England, this courteous behavior had reflected conciliatory relationships between employers and union men. In Fall River, however, Lancashire men faced both their employers' immense market power and a dismissive, open contempt for their deferential, respectable manhood.

Inexperienced, arrogant Fall River agents believed that they could dominate these historically unruly people as easily as they dominated the national market for print cloth. The tide of immigration in the early 1870s swelled the numbers of Lancashire workers resident in Fall River, quadrupling the workforce from 2,654 in 1865 to 11,514 in 1875. The social dislocations of a rapidly expanding city and a depressed economy created opportunities for a new impetus in labor politics. Weavers such as George Gunton entered the Fall River mills and faced working conditions, long hours, and opposition to labor protest unheard of in Lancashire since the 1840s. Intensified workloads and additional wage cuts during the depression years further undermined male workers' craft standards and respectable manhood. Working-class men regarded these pressures on their bodily strength and stamina as an assault on their physical capacities to support their families. The pace of work drove them beyond endurance, and the ten-hour law remained unenforced. Fall River managers had responded to statutory limitations on daily labor by significantly speeding up work processes and pushing daily operations beyond the legal limit. Protecting their capacity to produce the cheapest print cloth in New England remained the Fall River mills' key to dominating the domestic market.

Wage cuts during hard times also meant less income to spend on food to sustain overtaxed strength and vitality. English spinners and weavers had legendary appetites for beer and beef. After a sweating spinner had walked his daily twenty-five miles or more back and forth at the mules in a brutally hot spinning room, lager beer supplied carbohydrates for a thirsty body and anesthetic for overstrained muscles and nerves. But middle-class temperance organizations in Fall River categorized all alcohol consumption as drunkenness and all beer halls as "rum-shops." These attitudes encouraged mill agents to castigate English workers as drunkards and to claim that "more sickness is caused by beer than by overwork."[47] A typical mule spinner's dinner at noon was meat, potatoes, and ale. During hard times, embarrassed workers concealed dinner pails with only cheese and bread rather than the customary cold meat, and in 1870 striking mule spinners had refused to substitute salmon for beef, that perennial New England means of feeding apprentices cheaply.[48] A workingman's physical well being, especially under the exhausting terms he faced in Fall River factories, required red meat and plenty of beer. Eroding wages and working conditions circumscribed the consumption choices of skilled workingmen. They may have measured themselves against the English "bread-winner" ideal, but they defined their status in accordance with their right and their ability to eat meat. Tensions over beef-earning reflected the limited choices of immigrant men beset with both economic depression and the power of American textile capitalism.[49]

THE REVOLT OF THE WOMEN WEAVERS

In late 1874 the Fall River mill agents decided to stimulate prices in the depressed print cloth market by limiting production. In response, Rhode Island textile mills, especially the Bristol Steam Mill Company in Providence and other mills in Central Falls, Newport, and Pawtucket, shifted to print cloth production to meet the shortfall. Their market for sheets, shirtings, and wide goods was even more depressed than the market for print cloth. Some mill villages, such as Lonsdale and Ashton on the Blackstone River, used their wide looms to produce narrower cloth by manipulating the harnesses on the loom to produce 28-inch widths. Print cloth, especially calicoes, remained popular. "Their cheapness" the *New York Times* reported, "created an unprecedented demand for them in every nook and corner of the North and the liberation of the slaves created a very great demand for them in the South." Freedwomen refused to wear coarse, hot "nigger cloth" made of linen and wool, just as freedmen rejected unlined work shoes or "brogans" as symbols of slavery.[50]

Fall River factories returned to full capacity in late December 1874 and cut wages by 10 percent, intending to flood the market and undercut their upstart competitors. This second wage cut, on top of a similar cut in 1873, made hard times worse. The mule spinners reluctantly accepted it, vowing a strike the following spring and threatening to withdraw all savings from local banks.[51] At two weavers' meetings held on January 3 and 6, 1875, gatherings that excluded workingwomen, restive male weavers initially accepted the additional cut until the cloth market improved. Shouts of "strike," "strike" from the floor were outvoted. The weavers' union then held a general meeting on Saturday night, January 10, which included both women weavers and French Canadian operatives. Lancashire weaver George Gunton and his allies urged a vote not to strike which passed two to one. But in response to Gunton's speech cautioning restraint, one woman weaver reportedly "brought down the house" with her fervor for a strike.[52] Still, the majority agreed that the print cloth market was too depressed for a strike.

Women weavers acted to prevent this acquiescence by the male weavers and mule spinners. Inspired by their sense of connection with Lancashire popular radicalism, they organized an all-female meeting on January 13 to oppose vehemently any further capitulation to the mills. Excluded during the 1850s from the deferential politics that characterized the mid-Victorian compromise in Lancashire with its language of paternalism and the family wage, the women shamed and pushed their reluctant male coworkers into the only successful general weavers' strike in Fall River in the nineteenth century.[53] During two major strikes in 1875, the first begun in January and the second in August, labor politics in Fall River focused on the emerging disagreements among workingmen and -women, mule spinners and weavers, over the nature and direction of labor protest. The successful challenge of activist women to male leadership and the different priorities given to regional organization and standard wage lists by weavers and spinners produced intraclass conflict over the definition of respectable working-class manhood and the desirability of female activism. The traditions, customs, and history of popular radicalism in Lancashire provided the cultural and political framework.

Female operatives organized themselves across skill and ethnic lines. As one activist, a Mrs. Pendlebury, later put it: "We have not been men or women enough to stick to our rights . . . and must sink all national differences in the one great question of [their] preservation."[54] While women weavers from Lancashire provided much of the leadership, the meetings also included female cardroom workers, native-born Americans, and Irish and French Canadian immigrants.[55] The leaders demanded that the men, both weavers and mule spinners, act quickly and decisively to prevent a pattern of recurrent wage cuts. These rebellious Lancashire women denounced conciliation and deference as cowardly and unmanly. They were reaching back to early nineteenth-century popular radicalism as more appropriate than deference and moderation to the ruthless nature of Fall River textile capitalism. They cited historic examples of the long-term effectiveness of resistance—win, lose or draw—on the relationship between labor and capital in Lancashire. The lessons of history and politics were plain to them and informed their expectations about working-class manliness.

After their January 13 meeting, activist workingwomen issued public statements revealing the sources of their anger: their exclusion from the first weavers' meetings and their disapproval of the men's decision.

> Writhing under the cruel and oppressive effects of the late reduction, and dissatisfied with the dilatory, shilly-shally and cowardly action of many of the chief conductors of our late meetings, we, the female operatives, have decided to meet together and speak and act for ourselves. . . . We realize vividly the fact that we must resist this tendency on the part of the combination of mill owners to cut down our wages, and that every reduction they succeed in establishing renders us less able to resist the next.[56]

Their second meeting, held on January 17, reverberated with direct challenges to working-class manhood. Insisting on anonymity, they addressed their complaints to the only man present, Henry Sevey, editor of the *Labor Journal* who reported the story for the *News*. They shouted insults: "Come on, you cowards! You were [be]got in fear, though you were born in England."[57] The male weavers were being reminded in public that they were the sons and grandsons of the hand-loom weavers of Lancashire who had fought tenaciously and boldly for their rights. One woman told a story of having overheard a manufacturer inform an overseer that

> a number of Lancashire operatives had landed in New York, 'Well, we shall have a lot of greenhorns here to-morrow.' To which the overseer replied: 'Yes, but you'll find that they have brought their horns with them.' "

Because American manufacturers hold us in contempt, she insisted they had to be shown that English workingmen "had [indeed] brought their horns with them, and that they meant to use them."[58] This story, directed at the male weavers, challenged them to use those manly "horns" with bold action and imaginative strategy or face public ridicule and humiliation. The assembled women weavers were ascribing to working-class manhood the qualities that they themselves were exhibiting: aggressiveness and defiance. In return, Lancashire women promised to sing ballads in the streets for bread, not to be beaten. For them, New England was a new Lancashire where the old battles needed to be refought by workingmen and workingwomen together.

The women weavers also debated strike strategy. In their view, the depressed print cloth market was not be feared but rather to be used to pressure the mills and to further the strike. On January 16 a committee of the weavers' union reluctantly approved a strike, but only at three mills: the Merchants and the Granite, whose agents had instigated the wage reduction, and at the Crescent where weavers were already on strike over the disputed length of the cloth cut, another trick to lower wages. But one woman pointed out that the mills all had contracts to complete and were anxious to fill their orders for the spring trade. If they failed, competitors in Rhode Island would fill them. She urged a general strike, recollecting, that "in England, on one occasion," closing only a few mills for three months did not work, but a general strike won in three weeks. "It may be cold, . . . but it is warm and comfortable in bed, and we shall have no occasion to rise early." Still, to many this seemed risky. Some women weavers urged cooperation with the union's strategy of targeting three mills, even though the leaders had displayed a lack of courage that overestimated the power of capital. Still, if the male weavers finally had some spirit, it was best to cooperate. They would begin at the Merchants, the Granite, and the Crescent. If nothing resulted, then "they could make the strike general."[59] A committee of four women met with the weavers' union, urging cooperation and action.

Before accepting a strike, some male weavers, discouraged by past failures and hard times, took their hats in their hands and tried once again to negotiate with their employer. On January 17 a group approached Robert Borden, treasurer of the Crescent mill. They presented their demands to him, witnessed by a *Boston Globe* reporter.

> A delegation of 6 tall, blond, blue-eyed Englishmen, they held their hats in their hands and their tongues in their mouths until the Treasurer spoke to their leader when he stepped respectfully to the counter and said in a marked North Country accent: "Wael, I suppose ye're awaere we are come to see ye, sir, about our little grievances, and thaet's about the figger thaet we think will bring us back t'our looms."

When Borden protested that the manufacturers suffered more than the weavers from the depression, their barely concealed anger flared briefly.

> "More of a hardship, sir?" interrupted a giant bearded Yorkshire man, with flushed pale face and tears standing in his eyes, "more of a hardship, sir? Ah if ye knew—" "We haeve to live upon our daily wages," another said in a low suppressed voice, "and back of thaet we've no money, sir; while you've plenty to back-set you, I hope. . . ."

As the men went away disappointed, the reporter remarked to Borden: "That's a gentlemanly set of strikers." "Yes," Borden replied, "I make them gentlemanly."[60]

Some of the more radical weavers during the 1875 strikes were men who had emigrated in the 1840s and 1850s, thus less familiar with the mid-Victorian rituals of paternalism and deference. They had accepted the leadership of the mule spinners during the strikes of 1868 and 1870 but had been disappointed. That deference ended. The day after the Borden interview, the male weavers joined the women on strike, followed quickly by the mule spinners, carders, and pickers.[61] Meanwhile, a transformed, convinced Henry Sevey hurried to Valley Falls, Rhode Island, where he urged the cotton operatives to organize support for the Fall River strike among the other working people in the Blackstone Valley: Central Falls, Lonsdale, Berkeley, Ashton, Pawtucket, and Woonsocket. Many were English immigrants. Another delegation obtained the support of operatives in the Potomska print cloth mill in New Bedford.[62] A new Lancashire was in the making.

THE FIRST 1875 STRIKE

Robert Bower and his associates in Lawrence seemed cool to Fall River's January strike, expecting "trouble ahead."[63] Little appeared in the *Lawrence Journal and Citizen* until February. When the strikers showed both unity and peaceable determination, Bower organized a mass meeting with speeches by his journalistic rival Henry "Seavey" and local sympathizers. Sevey argued that the Fall River strike concerned all textile operatives in New England mill centers. Adopting the arguments of the women weavers, he insisted that the first wage cut in 1873 should have been resisted so that the owners would not have dared to act even more aggressively. Sevey finished by urging the women operatives of Lawrence to organize and "assert their rights as workingwomen." "A Laborer" agreed that the fight touched all textile workers in the region. Fall River was becoming the key to prevailing wages and working conditions. He denounced the employers as a "monied aristocracy" who accepted "money as a God," yet treated their workers as "heathens and infidels." The writer had overheard a Lawrence mill owner describe his working people as "a pack of fools," but what, he asked, would the agent do "without the aid and assistance of his foolish friends."[64] The Lawrence meeting endorsed the strike, but sent no money. The rivalry between Bower and Stephenson's labor newspaper and Sevey's *Labor Journal* for leadership of New England textile workers made generous support unlikely.

Still, as the strike spread and the prospects for a settlement brightened in March, Bower relented in an editorial significantly titled "No Surrender," echoing the cry of the 1854 Preston strikers. The Fall River strikers must hold out; the future welfare of all textile workers is at stake, he wrote. This strike was justifiable "resistance to oppression. . . ."[65] Meetings supporting the Fall River strike spread to Newburyport, Lowell, and Taunton. The mule spinners of Lowell struck in mid-March. In Lawrence, the Pacific mills promised no similar wage cut and announced the possibility of weekly wage payments. Operatives in Lonsdale, Rhode Island, a center of print cloth operations, were notified of a contemplated wage increase by April. The agents at the Wamsutta in New Bedford and in the Newburyport mills promised to reverse wage cuts made in late 1874. Mass meetings were held in Pawtucket, Newport, and Providence. Eastern Massachusetts and Rhode Island had come alive.

Bower recognized that the irresistible forces of victory led by activists he opposed might undercut his position of leadership. A mid-April editorial urged the Lawrence operatives to form strong unions in order to

> be prepared for the day of trouble should it arrive. Such action would not mean defiance; it would simply mean defense. . . . If the operatives of Lawrence united together they would soon be in a position to resist successfully any encroachments capital might attempt on either their time or pay. . . . Strikes would not occur. If, however, strikes become necessary the chances of their being successful would be multiplied.[66]

The following day, Bower wished the Lowell mule spinners well in their fight. The Fall River strike was sweeping aside cautious labor reformers.

The involvement of Fall River women weavers in the two 1875 strikes significantly expanded their traditional participation in labor protest. The female weavers organized workingwomen across skill, ethnic, and religious lines. The workforce in Fall River in the mid-1870s consisted of one-quarter native-born (25.2 percent); one-third English immigrants, including Irish-born, Lancashire-trained operatives (33.9 percent); one-fifth Irish immigrants (20.7 percent); and less than one-fifth French Canadian immigrants (17.3 percent).[67] Fall River had the highest percentage of foreign-born workers in Massachusetts: 52.64 percent and more working wives than any other cotton textile center.[68] The presence of mature women workers seemed to provide leadership for the women's meetings as well as political connections among working-class families. Many of the most outspoken activists were married or perhaps widows: Mrs. Elizabeth Fleet at the Merchants mill and the outspoken Mrs. Ashworth, Mrs. Pendlebury, Mrs. Ogden, and Mrs. Worley. Single women were also prominent, especially Cassie O'Neill, an Irish American weaver, and a French Canadian weaver, Miss Bergeron.

In contrast with their subordinated role in many Lancashire strikes, women appeared regularly on public platforms with men, agitating at strike meetings, and traveling to other textile cities in southern New England to raise money. Cassie O'Neill accompanied Sevey, Hinchcliffe, and Hiram Coffin, a Fall River labor reformer and retailer, to Newburyport to urge support for their strike and encourage local organization.[69] She later spoke twice in April to mule spinners' strike meetings in Lowell with Sevey and Boston labor reformer E. M. Chamberlain, urging the men to organize any young women, being trained on ring-spinning machines that produced coarse warp yarn.[70] She also encouraged any female ring spinner to "knock on the door" of the mule spinners' union and refuse to be a knobstick. O'Neill called on women weavers to form unions, join the strike, and ask for equal wages. "[L]et it not be said that the women are a dead weight to the mule spinners of Lowell."[71] Most provocatively, striking women weavers urged the mule spinners of both Fall River and Lowell to organize those young women recruited by the mills to operate the first, very primitive, ring spinning frames.[72] Mule spinners regarded the inclusion of women as a threat to male control of spinning as well as to the mule spinners' leadership in local labor politics. The weavers might share their union with women; mule spinners would never do so.

Speaking for themselves as workingwomen and for children, women strikers defined new ways to represent joint family interests in labor protest, apart from the family wage ideal. Many women strikers, such as O'Neill, were calling eloquently for the removal of all children under fourteen from the mills. No child would have to work in a mill if both parents earned enough to sustain family life. In all of this, they were questioning whether an adequate family wage was an issue only for men. And they were also challenging the domination of respectable, deferential men over the conduct and direction of labor protest in Fall River. Many activists in Fall River, including George Gunton, were the sons of Chartists. Memories of the activities of their own mothers and grandmothers in support of the Chartist movement (however limited) may have inspired some of these Lancashire immigrant women.[73]

Many women spoke defiantly at public meetings. Mrs. Ashworth told a February 14 meeting about her interview with one of the agents.

> I told him I would not go back for 24 cts. a cut; I should stand it out. He said, "I suppose you have something to fall back on." I told him "No, I had scarcely a penny to keep myself with." He asked, "What would you do, then?" I replied: Do as the Yankees do, live on baked potatoes! But "suppose you couldn't get the baked potatoes?" I said, "So long as I live I am bound to get something!"[74]

If the agent was testing the will of the women strikers, she was giving him a dose of Lancashire courage.

Her speech inspired a Yankee female weaver at the Davol mills, who was paying a percentage of her wages based on the number of her looms to the strike fund. She announced,

> We mean to *have* the 27 ct. a cut. That's the way to talk it. . . . The manufacturers say they are determined to fight it out to the bitter end. Let them know that we are on the same track! . . . Never did the help seem in better humor for giving. . . . With determination the right shall conquer. . . . It sometimes takes time, perseverance, hard work, and much self-denial. This contest is equal to that waged a few years ago at the South. . . . [75]

References to Yankee baked potatoes and the Civil War indicate the inclusive nature of the women's organization. At an earlier meeting, appealing to the local native-born operatives, Henry Sevey had compared the strike to the sacrifices made by New Englanders during the American Revolution, when they were subjected to "oppressive burdens" by the British government.[76] These explicit appeals to American political heritages helped the foreign-born strikers avoid nativist responses from some operatives, a problem that had weakened pre–Civil War activism.

FRENCH CANADIAN TEXTILE WORKERS AND *LA SURVIVANCE*

French Canadian participation in the January 17 meeting encouraged about 20 percent of the two thousand immigrant workers from Quebec to support the strike.[77] At an early March meeting, four hundred French Canadian male and female weavers and carders, working in mills not being struck, formally voted to support the English-speaking strikers and raised twenty-two dollars on the spot. Led by L. C. H. Archambault, a local photographer, they adopted the motto of the weavers' committee: "Stand to the last." Both male and female operatives made short speeches of support in French.[78] In the Fall River village of Bowenville, Irish and French Catholics shared a church with a bilingual priest, an arrangement that might have encouraged this cooperation, although the French parishioners always insisted on a priest from Quebec. The support of these immigrants for the first 1875 strike—and even the complex behavior of Herbert Lasalle, the watchman at the Border City mills in 1874—questions the centrality of the concept of *la survivance* to French Canadian working-class life in nineteenth-century New England.

Historians of nineteenth-century French Canadian immigrants to the Northeast have defined *la survivance* as an heritage of conservative rural peasants in early nineteenth-century Quebec whose leaders accepted a political accommodation with English ruling authorities to keep their religion, language, and culture intact. Unsuccessful Quebec rebellions in 1837 and 1838 and the union of all Canadian provinces in 1841 had strengthened English rule. The development of *la survivance* as a cultural and political response in Quebec rested on the isolation of French Canadian Catholics in rural areas, distant from urban industrial life. These areas became cultural bastions, although agricultural depression, scarce arable land, and subsequent overpopulation plagued the region. By the 1850s, overworked land and crowded farms threatened the very physical survival of the large rural families who had become the major prop of *la survivance*. Emigration, beginning before the American Civil War, seemed the immediate solution, but how would Quebec's cultural politics be transmitted and preserved in a new country?

Historian Richard Sorrell argued in 1981 that the historical "destiny" of French Canadian immigrants, based on their political and cultural heritage, the closeness of the homeland, and the concentrations of immigrants in certain industrial cities and towns, guaranteed the continuance of *la survivance*. "The French Canadian Church elite directed this fierce, often fanatical, struggle to maintain *foi, langue,* and *moeurs,* . . . in New England." Indeed, a description of institution building in the seemingly classless "p'tits Canadas," especially in the textile centers, became Sorrell's measure of the "success" or "loss" of *la survivance*.[79] But Irish control of the New England Catholic Church, which promoted assimilation and opposed culturally distinct parishes, delayed for a time the introduction of French-speaking priests with their own churches. Meanwhile, many early secular leaders, according to Sorrell, felt they had betrayed their culture by plunging into a materialistic and individualist American society, thus accounting for their vehement promotion of *la survivance* for the masses. Some historians of French Canadian immigration confine much of their analysis during the initial period of settlement, 1865–1900, to the elite leadership, relying on the cultural politics of *la survivance* to explain working-class French Canadian experiences. Immigrant families sent their family members as soon as possible into New England textile mills and shoe factories. There, according to the *la survivance* paradigm, they passively took orders and worked harder than other groups, undercutting wages and breaking strikes opposed both by their parish priests and the community's conservative middle class. Historian André LeBlanc insists, however, that French Canadian life prior to 1900 remains part of a "mythic" past based on prosaic studies and in need of more solid research.[80]

La survivance for Quebec immigrants to New England meant a defensive clinging to language, religion, and culture in the many virtually ideologically indistinguishable "Little Canadas" of the region.[81] Leaving rural Quebec, however, set in motion economic and social challenges to the French Canadian elites' ideology. These post–Civil War ethnic enclaves in Fall River, New Bedford, and Rhode Island did not provide jobs for the majority of immigrants, forcing them to enter the urban, industrial world and later partisan politics, which they had avoided in Quebec.[82] French Canadian textile operatives, largely women and girls, left their neighborhoods six days a week to work in mills and factories with other nationalities. Involvement in the industrial life of Fall River and other textile and shoe centers, as well as intense geographical mobility among those cities and towns, mitigates the idea of cultural isolation in Little Canadas.[83] Herbert Lasalle's willingness to leave his post to aid an Irish American woman and his stubborn, tragic resistance to interference with his duties contradicts the reputation of French Canadian workers as docile, submissive, and faithful only to their own. A few apparently brought industrial experience from textile mills in the Montreal area, but the majority of rural immigrants were learning how to be textile workers, often through their kin like the Lasalle family.[84] The world of industrial work thus complicates French Canadian cultural experience in New England. In early 1875, four hundred in Fall River supported the labor politics of other nationalities and later developed their own. Class analysis can reveal additional dimensions to conflicts within French Canadian culture.

Furthermore, discourse analysis of *la survivance* as a political ideology and social system reveals much about gender and class relations implicit in the collective preservation of *foi, langue,* and *moeurs.* This belief system in Quebec, sustained by the middle-class immigrant elite in New England, placed French Canadian women at the center of *la survivance.* They would be the bearers of many children, the caretakers of large families, and the leaders of home devotions and language instruction. Mothers and wives in the domestic sphere or "holy environment" provided the foundation to sustain *la survivance* for the community.[85] Male immigrants as heads of families appeared to have fewer explicit responsibilities in maintaining conservative cultural politics. As naturalized citizens, according to historian Ronald Petrin, they embraced by 1895 "recognition politics," efforts to advance the interests of the community, not through defensive isolation, but in partisan political activity.[86] The immediate necessity, however, for women and girls to move into unskilled positions in New England textile mills and shoe factories to provide for the economic needs of their newly immigrated families conflicted with their other burdensome domestic duties. Immigrant mothers with large families might support *la survivance* in Little Canadas, but their daughters and granddaughters faced more complex experiences. Reliance on the wages of working-women and girls to sustain the family economy undercut their ability to sustain high population growth and thus undermined "the revenge of the cradle" as a political and cultural strategy against a hostile, alien world. Indeed, the active involvement of some young French Canadian women in Fall River labor politics in the late nineteenth century suggests a generational shift that failed to sustain the cultural politics of the elite leaders. Furthermore, the implications of revenge through incessant childbearing led to severe physical hardship for mothers and economic distress in rural Quebec, not community empowerment.[87]

In April 1875 when French Canadian textile workers struck the Ponemah mill in Taftville, near Norwich, Connecticut, their compatriots in Fall River, in contradiction to *la survivance* passivity, contributed to the strike fund.[88] The Ponemah mill, built in 1872, was the largest cotton mill in Connecticut and produced fine cloth like that of the Wamsutta in New Bedford. Shifting to coarser goods during the depression years, the mill had cut wages 24 percent over two years. The workforce consisted of Rhode Islanders as supervisors, skilled English and Irish mule spinners, and small numbers of Germans and Poles among more numerous Irish and Quebec immigrants. Along with the rest of the operatives, about six hundred French Canadian workers in Taftville objected to reduced wages and an 11¾-hour day, in defiance of the state's ten-hour law. Clerks in the company's store paid operatives what was left of their wages, after deducting, often erroneously, food, rent, fines, and other charges. This demeaning treatment, as if they were "children," resulted in a total walkout, the most impressive in the state for several years, and the organization of a union that included all nationalities.[89] On May 11, the French Canadian weavers of Fall River listened to the pleas of "Thomas Paine," a Taftville striker. Radical politics may have had a strong appeal to rural Quebec immigrants with memories of their own rebellion against the English. In response, the weavers assessed each of their looms 12½ cents to support the strike. All members of the Taftville union, including French Canadian workers who obtained support from Fall River and New Bedford, were blacklisted and evicted, but the strike lasted at least six months. Many skilled English and Irish workers and their blacklisted French Canadian allies left after the strike, relocating in New Bedford, Fall River, Lowell, and other textile centers. The Ponemah mill hired additional French Canadian immigrants.[90] Other small mill towns in Connecticut (probably with French Canadian workers), were also on strike in 1875: 150 operatives at the Union mills in Norwalk and at the Meriden mill at Meriden, near Hartford, as well as the woolen weavers at the Mill Brook mill at South Coventry, Rhode Island.[91] Eastern Connecticut textile centers with French Canadian operatives were being drawn into regional labor protest.

Philip Silvia argues that French Canadian immigrants to the textile industry in Fall River declined to participate in labor protest in the 1870s and that as potential strikebreakers became the chief target of antagonist labor activists. He confines his analysis to the relationship of the Quebec people with the English and Irish mule spinners led by Robert Howard, but noted that "a small body of weavers" were an exception during "the 1875 strike." Although acknowledging that French Canadians could not move into skilled work and that the majority were young female unskilled workers, Silvia argues that the mule spinners and weavers such as Pat Madden still feared these immigrant workers as conservative anti-unionists.[92] Certainly many French Canadian middle class leaders in Fall River advocated *survivance* and labor conservatism, as Sorrell insists, but not all. Honoré Beaugrand, the Quebec-born pro-ten-hour editor of *L'Echo du Canada,* supported the early 1875 strikes in Fall River and Taftville, urging the formation of unions and cooperative mills while complaining about the difficulties encountered by Montreal mule spinners in getting jobs.[93] A liberal secularist and Francophile with connections to the anticlerical Institute Canadienne in Montreal and with the Masonic Order, Beaugrand despised French Canadian conservatives who cooperated with the English as much as he deplored the domination of French Canadians by Quebec priests and notaries. He had begun *L'Echo* in 1873 in competition with two more conservative French-language newspapers in Fall River, H. R. Benoit's *L'Ouvrier Canadien* and P. A. Morin's *Fall River Charivari.* His ambition was to become the leading French Canadian newspaper editor in New England.[94] His prominence as a secular middle-class leader of the French community in Fall River and his liberal politics supporting both naturalization and the preservation of French culture through special schools encouraged links with other working-class ethnic groups.[95] Thus for Beaugrand cultural preservation became mixed with the desire for social justice, political power, and working-class organization. In *L'Echo* he printed the words of one immigrant mule spinner, "Coeur du Fer," who urged the formation of "a serious and tight-knit union" for all ethnic groups—French Canadian, Irish, and English—against "the oppression of capitalists."[96] Beaugrand supported organization with other nationalities, urging, with Henry Sevey of the *Labor Journal,* the naturalization of both the English immigrant and his own countrymen.[97]

In the late 1870s the Rhode Island branch of the New England Ten Hour Association put French Canadian textile workers in contact with Lancashire activists in Olneyville, Lonsdale, Valley Falls, and Central Falls. Labor activity during the New Bedford Wamsutta strike in 1877 and later in the 1880s and 1890s by many French Canadian men and women in New England may have flowed from these earlier connections with their compatriots in rural mill villages.[98] Although many French Canadians left textile centers during strikes to return to their homeland or to seek work elsewhere, this behavior was not singular to French Canadian immigrants;

Lancashire workers sometimes did the same thing. And Quebec operatives later conducted their own strikes, for example in Suncook, New
Hampshire, in 1881, where they kept their eyes on wage levels and daily
hours in Fall River, as the industry's regional standard.[99] Thus French Canadian activism in southeastern New England challenges the beliefs of
both nineteenth-century textile operatives who feared conservative and
passive Quebec immigrants and ethnic historians who accept without
question *la survivance* as the essence of working-class immigrant life.[100] *La
survivance* should be further explored as a cultural and political construction and as a response to shifting power relations within the ethnic community and the textile region.

THE PATH TO VICTORY

At a February 14 meeting, John Smith, secretary of the weavers' union,
admitted that the strike had been "inaugurated" by the women weavers
and asked them to expand it. "The committee followed you. They now
ask you to follow them." Three more mills must be struck. Smith had
immigrated in 1862, "believing it [the United States] to be the home of
the oppressed of every land."[101] He had also served in the Union Army.
The strikers were now enlisted to save the rights of labor. He urged if
necessary, a return to Montreal or England to thin the local labor supply.
His references to the mills of Montreal indicate that some experienced
French Canadian operatives worked in Fall River. Perhaps one was the
female weaver, who spoke both in French and English at this meeting, demanding 27 cents per cut. One voice at the meeting insisted: strike the
ones that are in debt![102] The weavers' committee voted to strike the Sagamore, the Stafford, and the Chace mills.

The mule spinners also expanded their activity in cooperation with
the weavers. Believing that the Osborn mill was selling yarn to the Merchants operation, they walked out until convinced that the yarn actually
went to a mill not struck by the weavers.[103] The next day, ten mule spinners
and their families returned to the old country in Lancashire style, their
fares paid by the union. Before boarding the train to Boston to catch
a ship to Liverpool, they were escorted through the streets from union
headquarters by a procession of strikers conspicuously circling the be-
sieged Merchants mill while playing music and carrying American flags
and a banner: "I'm Going Home."[104] Emigration became a collective act
of protest.

The issue of supporting the women's strike in January and thereby
tolerating their assertive, independent activism alarmed some Lancashire
men. Thomas Stephenson of the *Lawrence Journal and Citizen* sharply criticized Sevey's conversion during the all-female meeting on January 17 as
another "Adam in the garden of old" who had been manipulated "as the

weaker vessel" by "babbling Amazons." He wrote to the *Boston Globe:* "Let us have family altars, not demoralizing harems." True men, he implied, controlled their women and female sexuality within the privacy of the family. Stephenson insisted that the desperate weavers' strike, as conducted, would prove "suicidal." His belief that Sevey lacked "ordinary manly courage and determination" may have echoed the views of many male workers.[105] At issue were the prerogatives of sober and careful men weighing the possibilities and tactics of labor protest against men who might be misguided and potentially emasculated by emotional, rebellious Eves.

Other Lancashire men agreed with the workingwomen's reading of the lessons of history and politics. They found in female strikers' challenges to their respectful and deferential behavior a satisfying, if more unruly, physical core. As Sevey voiced it: "If a man cannot knock down his oppressor, you at least like to see him try; and if you cannot knock the tyrant down who would oppress you, you can at least give him a welter!"[106] Sevey cautioned against violence, but the weavers' committee, as in the 1870 mule spinners' strike, condoned intimidation. At the Merchants mill, one female strikebreaker had her dinner pail torn from her grasp and kicked out of shape. She did not return to work the next day.[107] Jonathan Corkhill, a Lancashire immigrant weaver, told a story reported in the *News* about one mill owner during the Preston strike who returned from church and was asked by his wife how he liked the sermon and the text? He replied that he "hadn't heard a word of the sermon for thinking of the d—d weavers!" When hard-pressed manufacturers began to swear in public, as in Fall River, the strikers knew they were winning. Corkhill reminded them that the results of the hard-fought but lost Preston strike was a decision by the mills in 1869 to consult the help about their narrow profit margins. Agreements followed suitable to all parties.[108] The weavers must resist.

Another rousing weavers' meeting on February 27 symbolized how far workingwomen had come during the strike. On the platform along with Louis Lapham, George Gunton, Jonathan Biltcliffe, Simon Morgan, James Sellers, the president of the weavers' union, and secretary John Smith, were Mrs. Elizabeth Fleet, Mrs. Ashworth, and Cassie O'Neill. Mrs. Fleet admitted she subsisted on the goodwill of her storekeeper, but if he refused to give her any more credit, she would still hold out. Declaring herself unafraid, Mrs. Ashworth, who had canvassed in Rhode Island mill villages, urged others to work harder for the cause. Cassie O'Neill insisted on an end to child labor, rebuking the striking weavers for the "sin" of too much patience.

> What have we seen the recent cold mornings this winter? Little children in flocks are on the road as I go to my prison. It is our fault that this is

done. The mechanics' children go to school but the operative's children must go to work. We ought to be united, throw off the yoke, and defy our opponents.[109]

In addition to the female speakers, Archambault, a friend of Beaugrand, reported to the strikers that the French weavers were united with all other nationalities and that their motto, like the weavers' committee's, was "Stand to the Last." Their key activists were a Mr. Brouillette and a Miss Bergeron.

Despite early incidents of violence by men and women strikers against knobsticks, the strike was generally peaceable. Seventy city police and fifty state police patrolled the streets. Mary Sullivan and Mary Grear got arrested for shouting insults at them. Defended by attorney Lapham, they were convicted of disturbing the peace. They were only two out of hundreds, expressing their views against police surveillance. Jonathan Biltcliffe approved of these verbal insults, calling them an assertion of manhood and womanhood.[110] E. M. Chamberlain, Ira Steward, and other labor reformers lent their aid by holding a series of public hearings in Boston to air the facts about wages in Fall River compared to other cities. On March 5, their Labor Council issued a widely-publicized report, supporting the strikers' views that the mills could well afford 27 cents a cut and admonishing the agents for acting as "haughty aristocrats."[111] On March 6, the editor of the *News* used the supposedly inescapable laws of supply and demand to counter the well-received report.

> We all live in a world where imperfect laws control society. The working people have chosen their employment subject to these laws. Among them are the chances of high or low wages, kind and unkind overseers. . . . We all have to succumb to the inevitable. . . . To live is a battle and we must consent to the hard discipline of small pay when the current price says so.

Within days of this statement, the mill owners offered their first concession to the strikers—to cut the wage reduction by one-third and then examine market conditions once the operatives returned to work. The key issue, however, was not the price of print cloth, but Fall River's policy of dominating the market by glutting it.

At a weavers' meeting on March 7, editor Lapham of the *Border City Herald* dismissed the mill agents' proposal as "an insult." The weavers' rejected it and continued their meetings, listening to inspirational stories from Jonathan Biltcliffe and Elizabeth Fleet. In his seventies, Biltcliffe was a former handloom weaver. He described the sufferings he and his family had endured in England in 1826, during a year of great hardship and scarcity. He learned as a boy that "a half loaf [such as the agents' offer] was worse than no bread." He contrasted the decent treatment of operatives in Derbyshire mills—dry stockings provided for wet feet and a light lunch before their customary dinner hour at noon—with Fall River hardships and unrelenting discipline. Fleet recalled that as part of a group of textile workers recruited in 1864 by the Emigrant Aid Society of Boston, she and her cotravelers came close to being defrauded on the cost of passage but resisted successfully. After a speech on labor and wages from a member of the John Swinton section of the Labor Vanguard of New York, Sevey announced the imminent departure of many English immigrant weavers. He read a letter from one already in Blackburn, Lancashire, insisting that the purchasing power of workers in England was much greater than in New England. In response, one weaver rose and said he was ready to go back. "He did not like America one bit. There were no social privileges, and the employers were tyrants."[112]

Then Henry Sevey announced the weavers' counter offer. If the employers announced publicly that they would pay 27 cents a cut beginning April 1, the strikers would return to work, not to England. The weavers agreed to work for two weeks at the 10 percent wage cut to get their 27 cents a cut.[113] Within four days the strike was over. Even the openly hostile, contemptuous William Jennings, the Merchants mill agent, who had instigated the wage reduction, agreed to rehire all strikers. The weavers had won. Only George Gunton was blacklisted, but he had regional agitation, not weaving, on his mind.[114] Whatever the rancor or misgivings about female activism among male weavers and spinners, once the battle was over on April 1, the weavers controlled local labor politics. Their aggressiveness and unexpected success had empowered labor protest and defeated the arrogant employers. The editor of the *News* complimented the victorious strikers.

> They have as good a knowledge of the markets as anyone; they know the sources of supply and the costs of materials, transportation and working machinery, and of course they understand equally well the average profits. . . . [A]s long as capitalists in American persist in importing or employing the shrewd operatives from Lancashire, Eng., they cannot expect them to forget or to refuse to use the intelligence acquired at home, after they get here.[115]

NEW ENGLAND AS A NEW LANCASHIRE

Contemplated wage cuts were dropped or rescinded throughout the region. A four-week strike in Newburyport led by English immigrant weavers ended with success. In other mill centers such as New Bedford and in some Rhode Island mill villages, the mill agents, fearing the establishment of unions, granted the operatives their demands. In doing so, they helped establish Fall River's reputation as the center of wage standards for New England. Quickly the weavers began to organize a regional association of all textile operatives in coalition with labor reformers to agitate for a standard list of wages and ten-hour laws that would make New England the

Lancashire of America. Meeting with delegates from the New Bedford mills on April 4, Henry Sevey, sitting on the platform with weavers including Elizabeth Fleet and Mrs. Ashworth, announced that "the establishment of a standard list with the basis of 30 ct. per cut for all New England states could be as effectually carried out as in England. . . ."[116] By late April the date for a cotton operatives' convention had been set for May 20. No delegates from Lawrence came forward; Richard Hinchcliffe had died of pneumonia on May 7. After his political achievements in 1874 Robert Bower did nothing to support the new organization. The *Lawrence Journal* remained silent on the convention and activities of the New England textile workers' union. After mourning the loss of Hinchcliffe, the editorials concentrated on demands for public bathhouses and biweekly wage payments, on temperance and the question of free trade versus tariff protection.[117] Within a year, Thomas Stephenson moved to New Bedford.

In New Bedford, however, a meeting of operatives listened with sympathy as weaver Thomas Evans denounced the dominance of capital in the mill villages of Rhode Island, especially the mistreatment handed out by the Lonsdale Company. Evans, who had lived in the Lonsdale's corporation tenements and traded at the company store, had moved to Fall River in 1875, where agitators seemed more welcome and the future of labor politics looked exceedingly bright. The May 20 convention held by the New England Weavers' Association organized an inclusive new Amalgamated Cotton and Woolen Operatives' Association. Heady notions emerged about regional agitation from secretary Gunton, but the more cautious D. G. Harriman, a Fall River store owner, served as treasurer. With the *Labor Journal* as the official newspaper of the organization, Sevey became an important influence, urging the convention delegates to organize the region. Their goal was "to establish a union in every village where the spindles revolve or the click of the busy shuttle is heard."[118] Gunton, who could not be fired or intimidated, would help create well-run locals. Unions, Sevey went on, were political instruments to lobby for labor reform legislation, such as the 1874 ten-hour law. The immediate agenda included factory inspectors, schools for mill children, protection from dangerous machinery, and mandatory fire escapes. Mill agents were becoming alarmed throughout the region.

Even lost strikes, such as the Lowell mule spinners' strike in April, were always useful, Sevey argued, in demonstrating resolve and self-sacrifice to the employers. That Lancashire lesson should never be forgotten. Reaching out to the various nationalities, Sevey compared the Lowell strike to the Battle of Bunker Hill and the rebellion of the Irish people against English rule. The chief goal of a union was to "enable their members to negotiate with their employers on an equal platform."[119] On the other hand, ill-considered strikes could prove damaging if newly formed locals became "too anxious to fight." Sevey, no doubt unwittingly, chose as his model union the New York City's Typographical Union which excluded women. The convention ended with speeches by Boston labor reformers George McNeill and Charles Stewart and from several Fall River weavers, none of them women. The new amalgamation would sanction all strikes, work for a New England ten-hour law, and press for legislative reform. The two major political parties were dismissed as useless. Male members would form unions, become citizens, and vote for labor reform candidates. The amalgamation would use its political power primarily on Beacon Hill and at the bargaining table. The influence of middle-class labor reformers on Gunton and Sevey helped shape the new organization and its strategies.

TEMPTATIONS AND DIVISIONS

For mule spinners, prospects of a standard wage list and a powerful regional organization were tempting, undermining the threat of the blacklist and the opposition of strikebreakers. But regional organization required sharing the direction of labor protest and the definition of its goals with the weavers and their contingent of activist women. Spinners had tolerated female participation in strike activities, as in 1870, only as long as they directed labor protest and controlled spinning. The success of the first strike in 1875 created a dilemma for mule spinners. An alliance with the weavers represented a tantalizing vision of powerful combinations against the mills that might lead to union recognition. But this approach might also undercut the mule spinners' dominance of their trade with the acceptance of female ring spinners and challenge their leadership of labor activities. The March mule spinners' strike in Lowell had been defeated with strikebreakers, while the ring spinners remained unorganized. Cooperation with the weavers' strike in Fall River had advanced the cause of workingmen but raised vexing questions about the subsequent role of workingwomen. Throughout 1875, the mule spinners' union did not alter its organization; neither did the male card strippers and grinders. They stayed aloof from the weavers' amalgamated union and made their own decisions. The mule spinners had allies among the weavers, most importantly George Gunton, who wanted the family wage for men so that wives would not have to work. Others suggested that married women might be prohibited from working in the mills.[120] Activists Mrs. Ashworth, Elizabeth Fleet, and Mrs. Pendlebury would be relegated to their kitchens. These issues remained unresolved.

Furthermore, many New England–born textile workers, male and female, valued geographical mobility—not organized strength in one textile center—as a measure of personal liberty. Movement, initially from farm to factory and now from factory to factory, signaled an individual's right to seek economic opportunity. New England mill agents would strongly reject any obstacle to market forces as coercion and any interference with both the individual rights of Americans and natural economic laws.[121] New England textile workers had been told that their industrial experience and political rights were superior to those of the factory slaves of England. As one Fall River operative critical of English ways said in 1875, "Individual ideas, rather than the collective, rule in this country."[122] Other New England workers, whether as Civil War veterans or just dreamers about the western frontier, rejected as spiritless and unmanly the claims of English spinners and weavers to a right to work in their chosen community. Charles Nordhoff, labor reporter for the *New York Herald,* contrasted the attitudes of English-born and American workers.

> [Lancashire weavers] know only weaving, and nothing else, and regard it as their only work . . . and they will starve rather than do anything else. . . . He remains in Fall River; he does not attempt any other work; . . . They will work and growl, and when they can they will strike again. . . . I cannot help but think the American would show the greater pride and independence in his course.[123]

Many American textile and shoe workers, especially females, were young, single boarders in New England cities, more easily able to relocate than members of resident families.[124] As one Lancashire weaver put it in 1875, "Ay, but we are too poor to move away; we owe money, mayhap; and where shall we go?" Some English workers viewed the Yankees' willingness to move about the region looking for better work as playing into the hands of hostile employers. Lancashire operatives described the byword of Fall River: "If you don't like it, get out," and spoke of the American as "proverbial for his submission."[125] In contrast to American attitudes toward individual mobility, Lancashire people regarded many of their emigrations as collective, not individual, acts.

Those English immigrants who had served in the Civil War and participated in the ten-hour movement, had developed connections with native-born workers and labor reformers. They also learned a new rhetoric of American individual rights and republicanism. In contrast, immigrants who arrived after 1865 had endured the shortage of Confederate cotton in England, called the "cotton famine" by English textile interests. In Lancashire, the handling of unemployment relief during the famine both maintained public order and avoided any form of payment that appeared to middle-class observers to undermine a work ethic. Oakum picking and stone breaking in the workhouses was part of those relief efforts. Discontent in 1863 led to a short riot in Stalybridge, Lancashire, blamed on youthful Irish immigrants, which, frightened the authorities into encouraging emigration for such activist weavers as Elizabeth Fleet.[126] The distress was severe, made no easier by the antislavery sentiments of many in Lancashire. Among the well-known songs of distress was "Th' Shurat Weaver's Song," by Samuel Laycock:

O dear! Iv yon Yankees, could nobbut jus see,
Heaw they're clemmin' and starvin' poor weavers loike me
Aw think they'd soon sattle their bother, an' strive
To send us some cotton to keep us alive.[127]

The famine taught bitter lessons to Lancashire operatives about their position in the world market of textile production. The pre–Civil War immigrants, especially the mule spinners, had served as mediators between American labor reformers and textile workers and the newly arrived English people. But the victory in April 1875 by the Fall River weavers added a volatile new element to this coalition: the new arrivals now heady with success.

TEXT AND CONTEXT

As they organized regionally, the male weavers published a short history of the "labor troubles" between 1873 and April 5, 1875, *A History of the Fall River Strike*. This forty-page reminiscence by "A Workingman," edited by the secretary of the weavers' union, John Smith, gave the New England public what the union leaders believed would be potent arguments in defense of their successful actions and persuasive reasons to advance textile unionism.[128] The text also disclosed tensions over class and gender relations during the strike. The writer denied any intent to create class antagonism or to advocate strikes, defending those who chose not to contribute to the strike fund as exercising American-style personal liberty. For two years, the history stated, the weavers had acted together, observing the variations of the prices of print cloth and the effects of regional competition, accepting wages cuts when essential but checking market conditions. These were the actions of calm, reasonable men. The powerful, united board of trade, "a Manufacturers' Union," organized in 1873, was cast as the aggressor; in 1874 the weavers' organization had formed for self-protection.[129] When in March the Boston labor reformers had offered to mediate the strike, the employers as a group boycotted the local hearings, explaining that the issue was not money, but "*discipline.*" As the weavers' history recounted, "And this was in a Christian country, whose citizens had fought and bled to abolish slavery." Only the disgruntled Thomas Stephenson had disputed the weavers' figures on wages, rousing great local "indignation."[130] The weavers' history concluded by advocating, as a solution to future disputes, binding arbitration or a standard list of wages and negotiations between employers and workers when the cloth market fluctuated. The tone was confident and moderate, containing no reference to Lancashire-style labor protest.

The text of the weavers' history minimized the participation of women weavers. None was named, their activities equally ignored. According to the official history, when the all-male weavers' committee had held very large, public meetings in January and voted to accept the 1874 reduction, "*under protest,* . . . only "one little thing" was "overlooked"—"the consent of the females." The text diminished the numbers of women weavers, the women's rebellion, and the divided reactions of male workers to that "little thing."[131] Complimenting the women on the effective handling of their own meetings but expressing relief that they had not been too "bold" or headstrong to advocate a general strike, the weavers' history represented the successful strike as managed by experienced labor activists, relegating the women to a very minor role.[132] The weavers' history thus erased the contribution female weavers made to starting the strike, creating a strategy, and sustaining the momentum. Even after it was won, female activism appeared dangerous to the management of affairs by calm, reasonable union men. To whom was this text addressed?

The weavers' union presented itself to the New England public, the established mule spinners' union, and the mill agents as a group of cautious, moderate, restrained, generous men, eager to go back to work. "A lover of *law* and order," Judge Lapham, had presided over some of their strike meetings. The board of trade, not the strikers, held out for "honor," a refusal to be beaten in public, and the chance to dominate their "hands." Male workers asked for a family wage and the "best of food," not "porridge twenty times a week," to sustain them. The press reports, especially in the *Border City Herald* and the *Boston Herald,* praised the honorable conduct and "manliness" of the weavers, arguing that the operatives were "men and brothers" and must be so treated by their employers.[132] These comments thus also erased the sexual identity of a major portion of the weaving workforce. The decision to sideline the women's actions and their political rhetoric was expected to play well with those weavers and mule spinners, as well as the middle class, who believed in restricted spheres for female activism and male control of labor politics. This account was neither generous nor accurate. Only Henry Sevey of the *Labor Journal* paid tribute in the weavers' history to the activities of men and women strikers as partners.

Careful not to claim provocative Lancashire legacies, the weavers' history nonetheless drove home the major points of English labor protest on which the women weavers had insisted. Indeed, they agreed with Mrs. Pendlebury that all national differences "must be sunk" to gain working-class rights.[133] Refusing to recognize their contribution, the weavers' union nonetheless advocated the women's stance in January that "it must be shown to the employers that there is a stopping place in the reduction of wages, and past that they cannot go, and we think it [the strike] will make them pause. . . ."[134] Still, strikes must give way to standard wage lists and arbitration. To New England operatives eager to organize, the weavers' union urged avoiding strikes but building up a strike fund, as the mule spinners had done. First, try persuasion, talk to sympathetic gentlemen, keep control of decisions in the hands of the strike committee, and if defeat should result,

> it will be an honorable defeat. . . . So Long as Capital shall make itself the greatest enemy to Labor so long shall Trades Unions be required to protect Labor. . . . We hope the time may soon arrive when Capital and Labor shall walk hand in hand. . . .[135]

All would be well, provided moderate and cautious male leadership remained in control to deal with employers with mutual concerns.

The moderation of the weavers' history could not erase the bad feelings coming from the board of trade after the strike was over. William Jennings at the Merchants mill, known for petty tyrannies and mistreatment of his help, tried hardest to hire replacements to break the strike. He supported calling in extra police and the militia, but the strikers gave them nothing much to do. Jennings was an angry man. The mill agents stubbornly failed to observe the agreement to end the 10 percent wage reduction on April 1, delaying until April 5 when it was more convenient for their paymasters. The strikers raised no objection, but the lesson was plain. Nothing had changed the minds of the board of trade men.

Only union organization in the region could make things different. This the weavers set about to accomplish, concentrating on Rhode Island. The list of financial contributions in the strike's history indicated uneven depth yet a fairly wide breadth of support for the weavers' strike. New Bedford was the largest contributor, Lowell and Lawrence both disappointments. Seventeen Rhode Island mill villages sent money, most generously Ashton, Berkeley, Lonsdale, and even beleaguered Taftville, Connecticut. Four New Hampshire mill towns, including Manchester, contributed a little, while the donations from the unorganized granite cutters of Dix Island, Maine, and the silk weavers of Paterson, New Jersey, proved surprising.[136] During the summer of 1875, the weavers organized throughout southern New England, holding mass rallies. Operatives in eastern Connecticut from Taftville, Norwich, Greenville, and Wauregan held demonstrations in support of the amalgamated association.[137] The political opposition in Connecticut abolished the state's bureau of labor statistics in 1875. Bower and the *Lawrence Journal and Citizen* lent little organizational support; Lowell had no weavers' union. This was a southeastern New England movement.

THE LONG VACATION IN AUGUST 1875

The editor of the conservative, pro-manufacturing *Commercial Bulletin* of Boston concluded that the weavers had managed the January strike "admirably from first to last," forcing the textile managers to retreat. The mill owners had become deeply embittered, while the weavers' union obtained "very great" prestige. Fall River seemed like an English cotton mill center. "Operatives elsewhere always look to Fall River for the first effective protest against a reduction in pay."[138] From the mill villages of eastern Connecticut and Rhode Island to the mills in Providence and New Bedford, operatives waited eagerly for leadership. Despite the moderation of the weavers' union, there was a good chance for a new Lancashire in New England.

One of the key elements in the success of the January strike was a clause in the manufacturers' contracts with cloth brokers that canceled any agreement if a strike disrupted production. This pressure on the mill agents to settle the strike or lose business to their competitors would not be repeated. The print cloth contracts for the fall trade were rewritten to remain legally valid despite strike or lockout. The Fall River mill agents were determined to use their productive capacity both to break the unions and undersell that "cankering sore," their Rhode Island competition.[139] Their objectives persisted: discipline in the workplace and control of the market. The weavers' association in Fall River and its plans for regional organization and an amalgamated union had become obstacles to control and dominance. The English-style unions were getting stronger as a result of the summer organizing drive, but hard times meant they had no strike fund. Still, in early August, feelings of strength and confidence among the union operatives hit their highest point. The weavers had proved unyielding and "dogged," but the mill owners too were "obstinate" and had "plenty of money and credit."[140] The issue as they saw it was control of their property and thus the market, nothing less. Other New England mill owners supported them. The unions had to be broken, whatever the cost.

In July the mill owners decided that continuing competition from Rhode Island firms required them once again to glut the market with cheaper cloth. Issuing the unions a direct challenge, they reduced wages between 10 and 20 percent, back to the January figure of 24 cents a cut. If the weavers struck any mill, they would face a lockout.[141] The operatives responded by continuing their political and organizational activities, while rejecting the wage cut that would have canceled their April victory. In addition, they challenged the moral right of the employers to make self-serving decisions based only on their own perception of the market. Who defined the condition and direction of the market became contested. In doing so, the operatives were resurrecting the Lancashire tradition of a "moral economy" that in 1875 rejected the employers' total control of the language and rules of the marketplace and the ideology of supply and demand.[142] Instead, the workers would attempt to influence the market price of cloth by collectively withholding their labor. This, added to the board of trade's chagrin over the defeat in April, represented an extraordinary challenge to the power of the mill agents to control production and dominate the market. A showdown was at hand.

Weavers, mule spinners, and carders, men and women, met at the local Opera House on the sweltering night of July 31 and decided to stop work. Secretary John Smith, Jonathan Biltcliffe, and Simon Morgan presided.[143] These men had met with the mule spinners' and carders' unions, all agreeing on a shutdown. The meeting was packed with enthusiasts; only two out of the hundreds voted against the proposal. Conspicuously absent were George Gunton, Henry Sevey, and Louis Lapham. D. G. Harriman attended but urged cautious deliberation. All four had strong reservations about this work stoppage. The leaders announced to the operatives that they would use the English term for a late summer holiday and call the strike, the "long vacation." Protection against strikes and lockouts had been built into the fall contracts, but what about a "vacation" or work stoppage? The operatives meant this withdrawal of their labor to be seen as a conscious policy to influence the print cloth market for their own purposes. It made no sense to them, to other New England print cloth producers, or to public observers to flood the already depressed market with huge amounts of even cheaper goods. The best solution would be a curtailment of work, not a wage cut and continued production. Many New England mills had already shortened the workweek or closed down. In Lawrence, the Atlantic mill, lacking contracts, released the workforce for six weeks in July.[144] The reasonable solution, given Fall River's gigantic productive capacity, was to stop production to give the market a chance to rise. In Lawrence, Robert Bower advocated a ten-hour day for Rhode Island and running on short time until the market began to rise.[145] Then the wage cut would be unnecessary.

The decision by the Fall River spinners, carders, and weavers reflected their acceptance of the mills' boasted key position in production, their understanding of how the mills manipulated the cloth market, and their determination that supply and demand would not be used against them. But for the operatives, this issue went further than a reasoned attempt to intervene in the workings of the market. At the Opera House meeting on July 31, the sweating, enthusiastic operatives wildly applauded a statement by Simon Morgan that if the Fall River mills could not pay decent wages for weaving, they had no moral right to the print goods market. They agreed that if other manufacturers could pay more for the work, then "they have the best right to it," and the Fall River mills "must stand their chance of being burst up." Convinced that at some point the mills would inevitably be forced to halt overproduction, the operatives seized control of the timing of the shutdown for the summer months when their costs in food, fuel, and clothing were relatively low.[146] They, not the mill agents, would decide. This defiant act denied the validity of a morally neutral market run by natural economic laws, which masked the powerful position of the Fall River mill agents. As historian Marc Steinberg argues, English workers often fought back by borrowing justifying language from their opponents.[147] Seizing the initiative, the operatives decided whether

or not the mills would run. To William Jennings and the other mill owners, the basis of their power seemed at stake. For the board of trade, the
only logic they saw in supply and demand was to assure market power.
They would use the market first to destroy their competitors, then use
their control of the mills to kill the unions.

Debates at the spinners and carders' meetings revealed opposition to
the vacation plan. The key opponent was George Gunton, secretary of the
amalgamated union, who feared that a failed strike would endanger the
regional ten-hour movement. He argued that one month's vacation could
not possibly alter the price of cotton goods; inventories were too full.
Many others with knowledge of the industry agreed. One retired Rhode
Island mill agent said, "You might as well throw a stone in a mill pond and
expect to see a rise in the water. . . ."[148] But to most operatives, the victory
in April was still fresh. Few were anxious to toss it away by accepting the
wage cut they had so gloriously defeated regardless of market prospects.
This was a fundamental issue of power for workingmen and workingwomen.

Other commentators, such as the pro-labor editor of the *Providence
Sun,* Lester E. Ross, agreed with Gunton and insisted that only a regional
shutdown would work. A walkout in Fall River alone was not the solution
to depressed cloth prices. But to Ross, it still seemed reasonable to try.
The reputation of the Fall River weavers with other New England operatives, especially in Rhode Island, as the main hope against their own wage
cuts would bring in donations to provide a strike fund. Everyone agreed
that overproduction was the basic problem. By early August, thirty-four
mills and nearly fifteen thousand operatives stood idle, while political activities, opposed by manufacturers but led by Fall River weavers for a ten-
hour day in Rhode Island, intensified.[149] The struggle with the unions
over the market blinded the board of trade to the competitive advantages
in a regional extension of the ten-hour day. Instead the mill owners became absolutely determined to crush this unprecedented threat to their
power at all costs. This ferocious conflict over the vacation strike subsequently exposed the mule spinners and the male weavers to damaging
charges of recklessness and irresponsibility and seriously divided the
strikers.

August 2, the first vacation day, was a success despite drizzle and chilly
northeasterly winds blowing inland from the Atlantic. August 3 brought
steady rain; a mass demonstration and procession were canceled. Still,
hopes and resolution remained high. For Gunton, the key event to help
the Fall River shutdown was an August 16 mass ten-hour rally of southeastern New England textile operatives, staged at a popular recreational spot,
Rocky Point, Rhode Island. Shore dinners of lobsters and clams, music,
dancing, and other amusements would tempt working people to make
this a resounding political success. Gunton's hopes were reasonable.

Rhode Island operatives had already staged a general strike in 1873 for the ten-hour day.[150] The steamship *Canonicus* carried the Fall River day-trippers to the spot well known for its refreshing breezes on hot days and well-appointed facilities. But August 16 proved a washout: chilly, windy, and drizzling. Attendance was down; speakers were forced inside a dance hall above the bowling alleys. Still, delegates came from Taunton, New Bedford, and from Olneyville, Lonsdale, and Central Falls, Rhode Island.[151]

As the key agitators for the amalgamated union, Gunton and Sevey had maintained a strong relationship with Boston's eight-hour men and labor reformers. Chamberlain, Steward, McNeill, plus former Democratic state Senator Hathaway roused the crowd that responded with resolutions to organize torchlight parades in front of the statehouse in Providence and adopt the political tactics that had worked in 1874 in Massachusetts. Vice presidents for the amalgamation represented constituencies in mill villages of Rhode Island and Connecticut, as well as the key textile centers in southern Massachusetts.[152] The standing committee for ten-hour agitation was a mix of experienced labor reformers with rank-and-file speakers from Fall River, Providence, Lonsdale, and other centers of activity.

During the first vacation week, all the cotton mills in Fall River were sufficiently crippled by labor shortages to force a general shutdown. Many operatives still needed persuading. A reporter for the *Providence Sun* was addressed by one young woman weaver who had just talked to another: "See here, sir, this girl has a soft place under her hat. She is afraid that she cannot afford a month's rest, and I am telling her that I could stand on my head for a month."[153] Signs of division emerged quickly. After only two weeks, D. G. Harriman sponsored a straw vote on the vacation at his dry goods store. When he had reportedly collected nine hundred "yes" votes to return to work, his opponents rallied, defeated the question, and denounced him as "Satan at work again!" and "a traitor in the camp."[154]

During the first strike, the French Canadian operatives organized, contributed to the Taftville strikers, and had the support of *L'Echo du Canada,* Honoré Beaugrand's progressive newspaper.[155] Beaugrand pushed hard for their participation in the new amalgamation, but by August their organization and French Canadian activists had disappeared. Pursuing political ambitions in Montreal, Beaugrand sold *L'Echo* in mid-June to the conservative editor of *Ouvrier Canadien,* a storekeeper whose politics reflected his precarious position in a community whose residents often returned to Canada leaving unpaid debts. H. R. Benoit advised his country people throughout the vacation to accept what the mills offered, go back, and work hard.[156] Hundreds of French operatives refused, many choosing to return by rail to Montreal. They would not break the strike. Instead, they left town for home or for other New England mill centers. This would become a persistent pattern for many French Canadian operatives during late nineteenth-century textile strikes. By the fall of 1875, Beaugrand's political influence and many experienced operatives from Quebec were gone from Fall River.

After four weeks of no work and no sign of market improvement, the operatives began to abandon their vacation. First the carders and mule spinners, holding separate meetings, voted to return to work and accept the wage cut. Urged by Secretary Morgan, the weavers discussed a return to work, after serious dissension over the merits of holding out to the bitter end for the 27 cents. Gunton warned the operatives about the "iron-handed and iron-willed" nature of the mill owners. If they voted to continue to stay out, the prospects were grim.[157] As their resolve weakened, weavers' meetings held on September 11 and September 15 exposed their outrage against the traitors, Harriman and Gunton. An angry Mrs. Ashworth began to denounce Harriman but was pulled away from the speaker's platform.[158] The weavers voted to accept the wage cut, but many would never forgive Gunton's caustic attacks on the failed leadership of both Morgan and Biltcliffe. To many moderates such as Gunton, Sevey, and Cassie O'Neill, the New England ten-hour fight, not the vacation strike, seemed the better course.

The mill agents were not finished with the operatives. Eager to demolish any hope for a Lancashire in America, the board of trade decided to lock out their employees for another month, threaten more wage cuts, and starve them into giving up their unions. Fearing, as in 1870, that secret unions would flourish despite the anti-union contracts operatives were forced to sign, mill owners particularly wished to destroy Lancashire-style union discipline: "Up goes a hand and out goes the help!"[159] One "well-known mill owner" spoke to the reporter of the *Commercial Bulletin*, explaining their objectives.

> We strike at the root of the matter and oblige all who work for us to cut loose entirely from organizations that adopt such objectional methods. . . . The nature of the work is such that the whole factory can be stopped by, and they have been, continually stopped during the past year or two, by the hands in one department suddenly leaving their work. . . . As it is a matter of vital importance to us that these methods be stamped out, and [if] we can see no other way of doing so, than by breaking the unions, can you blame us for breaking them?[160]

The mill agents' solution was to forbid more than one-eighth of the workforce in any workroom to leave without forfeiting their month's pay. This, the board of trade believed, would end the disruptive annoyance of "petty strikes." But just as important was preventing any repetition of the January strategy of striking only a few mills at a time, . . . "the success of which made such a profound impression upon the manufacturers."[161] Still, as the editor of the *Bulletin* later observed, the older corporations, including

Jennings' Merchants mills, dominated the board of trade, while the newer mills, heavily in debt, were under tremendous pressure to sell goods. Some had made money running between January and April, but the two-month vacation and lockout threatened ruin. Despite these divisions on the board and among the two generations of mill owners, in September they acted together to crush English-style unionism.

After several weeks of trying to live on potatoes and bread, the operatives gave up and accepted the wage cut. Then the conditions of the anti-union contract leaked out from a printer's shop. On September 27, the mills finally reopened, but enraged workers were informed that they could not enter without signing these contracts. As one spinner put it, this was unthinkable: "We mun ask for oor roights the same as thae gie em in Englan'." He characterized the mill agents' response: "Noo, mind ye, thae toorn upon em and insoolt em by declarlin" thae'll never soobmit to the rooles here as thae ay doone in England'." A weaver from Burnley put it more bluntly. "When they get Ben Wilkins to creenge an' bow for a livin'[,] it'll be on the hoighway and not in a mill . . . me'd leike to poot a few o' them dommed buildings to the torch."[162]

The weavers, the mule spinners, and the carders rallied to act in concert to this threat. They would accept the wage cut after being beaten but not the destruction of their unions. As the editor of the *Commercial Bulletin* pointed out,

> The wonderful success of trades unionism in England . . . is being tried in Fall River. The spinners at Lowell so sorely beaten had not $\frac{1}{10}$ the strength, money, brains or feeling of unity possessed by the Fall River spinners' association.[163]

This assumption that the mule spinners controlled labor politics also made them appear responsible for anything that went wrong. The editor's conclusion was that a one-month vacation was "absurd" and that overproduction and underconsumption remained the basic problem. Then the editor advised producing even cheaper goods to stimulate consumption, thereby supporting the Fall River managers.

On September 27 when the mills reopened, the operatives flocked to the mill yards, willing to work but refusing to sign the contracts that would both cripple any short-term, disruptive strike action and destroy their unions. The overwhelming majority who would not sign—although some did out of desperation—were turned away into the streets. There, they would decide what to do next. Hunger and the knowledge that the mills would employ only the utterly defeated inspired a response by angry Lancashire operatives that reached back to the atmosphere of late eighteenth-century bread riots.[164] This response, specific to Lancashire people, contained the seeds of cultural and political dissension.

Thousands of disappointed workers left the mills and marched to a nearby city park. As they waited and growled, a delegation sent to city hall to ask for public relief returned without success. As a body, they cheered proposals to demand bread from the mayor, then the governor, and if refused to take it wherever they might find it. Two days earlier, the elderly Jonathan Biltcliffe had reminded a mass meeting to great emotional response about late eighteenth-century food riots in England and Wales and told them that "as good men as you have been unable to contain themselves in times past. . . ." To the over ten thousand strikers in the city park, an enraged Biltcliffe now insisted that "while there was bread in the town I would go take it."[165] The Lancashire tradition of manliness, Biltcliffe insisted, meant public action against injustice.

Ignoring the moderate leaders' feeble plan to organize support from labor reformers and the general public, hundreds of men and women strikers filled the streets and marched to city hall, cheering and yelling "Bread!" "Tyranny!" Twenty boys carried poles bearing loaves of bread stolen from a bakery, symbols for the bread riot.[166] Bobbins and operatives' work tools tied to other poles were also customary rituals of Lancashire radical politics. An American flag, upside down as a distress signal, preceded a sign that read: "15,000 white slaves for auction," topped with a loaf of bread. British immigrant workers had long been incensed by American pretensions to freedom and civilization in contrast with the tyranny that thrust submission on them. To underscore their anger at being told to return to work or face the misery of the state poor farm, one woman striker hit the mayor on the head with a loaf of bread.[167]

The historic and cultural significance of the bread riot rituals that gave form and direction to the angry turmoil in the streets was clear to Lancashire people but baffling to many others, including the mayor, who knew neither literally nor figuratively what hit him.[168] Only the editors of the conservative press in Boston and Providence recognized the rebellious implications of Manchester-style riots in New England, while labor reformer Jennie Collins observed appreciatively the "extraordinary proof of English cool-headed control" that indicated disciplined, ritualized crowd action during the tumult.[169] But others saw only potential mayhem. A notice scrawled on a mill building had been found inciting the burning of the mill agents' lavish homes on Rock Street. Their destruction, the note added, would at least give someone work. The city responded by summoning the state militia.

The spectacle and hostility of the ritualized demonstration split the textile operatives into confused, alienated camps and alarmed many labor reformers. Native-born New England women reportedly returned to their rural homes by the hundreds. Mill windows had been smashed. Showers of stones, bread, and brickbats had fallen on arresting police. To the editor of the *News*, these customary rituals were "hideous" and "incendiary" conduct by a riotous "mob." Editor Benoit's French-language newspaper denounced the demonstration as a "ridiculous" mob led by "poltroons," but the responses of Quebec operatives are unknown.[170] The Reverend Jesse Jones, a labor reformer from Abington, Massachusetts, rushed to Fall River and lectured the defeated workers that "rioting and violence are not the true American way of settling a difficulty." Robert Bower of Lawrence scolded the operatives for becoming pitiful "poor dupes" of demagogues, but also pointed out that small shareholders, at the mercy of the board of trade, "bitterly" opposed the wage reduction, blaming it on poor management.[171] Popular opinion held the mule spinners responsible for the debacle. These class and cultural divisions plus the crushing defeat of the vacation strategy convinced the spinners that the weavers' union with its contingent of female agitators had led the strikers into disaster. The 1875 struggle in Fall River shattered the fledgling amalgamated union and undermined its regional vision.

The collapse of the weavers' strategy, the loss of the strike, and the activities of the bread rioters resolved for some the contested meanings of working-class manhood and womanhood. The mule spinners concluded that uncontrollable women had instigated riotous actions by strikers and that their emotional, public displays of anger had emasculated the male weavers. Indeed, the press described the behavior of the women strikers on that day as "the most excited," "more violent and vulgar than the men," and their language as "coarse . . . to indecency."[172] Public expressions of desperation and rage unsexed both men and women. In addition, Simon Morgan, the son of Irish parents and a self-taught labor reformer and activist, had already been exposed to press attacks for "loafing," although he had been blacklisted. More seriously for his reputation among the operatives, Morgan had been arrested for a drunken spree around the Fourth of July. Although he remained sober throughout the vacation and lockout, the mule spinners could not forget the newspaper accounts of Morgan's wife calling the police twice to put him in the lockup.[173] For the spinners, Morgan represented the measure of the weavers' manhood. Begging city authorities for bread backed with threats of violence and the prospects of the state poor farm as a last resort was no manly way to behave in public or deal with their employers. Passion had overcome reason.

The misguided efforts by unruly male and female weavers to wrest away the mills' market power resulted in a concerted attack on all union activity. For many mule spinners, this failure tainted, undermined, and feminized Lancashire political traditions, making them a dangerous burden in New England. Mill owners cited the disorderly conduct of bread rioters in the streets of Fall River to label both the spinners and weavers as Lancashire brutes and later to characterize all union men as "English and Irish scum."[174] Female activists such as Mrs. Atherton and Cassie O'Neill had threatened male control of the spinning trade, challenged the authority of spinners in labor protest, and now undercut the respectable manliness of mule spinners by associating them with public riot. Worst of all, workers were forced to sign away their union memberships, while the local weavers' organization disintegrated and the spinners' union went underground. Spinners were thus forced to sign the hated contracts, an act that threatened to turn them into the "slaves" and "serfs," the common rhetoric of labor reformers and activist weavers.[175] With the Lancashire past rendered passionate and perilous in 1875, the spinners recaptured the leadership of labor politics in Fall River, turning toward moderation and caution.[176] But the long-term struggle over these two conflicting approaches to labor politics by the weavers and the mule spinners after 1875 undermines what some historians regard as the inevitable rise of conservative leadership among New England textile workers.

Mule spinner Robert Howard watched these events in 1875 but took no known role in them, except as a member of the spinners' union. In his later 1887 review of the textile trades, he ignored any reference to female activism or the bread riot but described the events leading up to the vacation as "embers of discontent, which had been smoldering all summer [and] burst suddenly into a blaze." Excluding the involvement of mule spinners in rejecting the anti-union contract and in the march on city hall, Howard represented the weavers as a dangerous "conflagration" that raged out of control, consuming and destroying.[177] The fiery metaphor suggested that unseemly, effeminate passion endangered labor politics and required extinction by powerful, reasoned manly action.

After 1875 Lancashire radical politics and customs lost some of their power to unite English mule spinners, carders, and weavers. Ethnic divisions in Fall River intensified and became increasingly institutionalized. By the 1870s, separate communities had organized around religious and cultural difference and ethnic advantage in municipal politics. Nonetheless, the process by which Lancashire immigrant textile workers came to perceive themselves separately as Irish Americans and English Americans represented a cultural transformation, signaling the results of class defeat. As English Americans began to mourn a lost Lancashire; as Irish Americans joined the American Land League and came to believe themselves exiles from "Holy Ireland"; and as many middle-class and some working-class French Canadian immigrants put their faith in conservative, defensive politics of cultural and economic survival, the events of 1875 can recall under what dramatic circumstances both their class and ethnic identities had shifted to support the rise of ethnocultural politics.[178]

THE CONTESTED meanings of working-class manhood and womanhood remained central to labor politics as conditions of work and life changed in New England textile centers throughout the late nineteenth century. Between 1868 and 1874 mule spinners and their male weaver allies attempted to transfer the deferential politics of industrial relations from England to New England. In doing so, they protected their respectable masculinity in ways that they believed served class interests. This included some flexibility in the relationships between men and women during labor protest and within their households, as long as the leadership of male workers remained unquestioned. The traditions and customs of popular radicalism adopted by rebellious men and women during the 1875 weavers' strikes revealed serious conflicts among the operatives over what should inspire and who should direct class activities in Fall River. The success of the first weavers' strike in early 1875 offered potential solutions to the dangers of a geographically mobile labor force in New England. A regional ten-hour law and a standard wage list would prevent blacklisting and strikebreaking, while an amalgamation could openly challenge the mill agents' ideology of supply and demand and their power to manipulate the market. But this inclusive activism of the weavers associated with public disorder and feminized passion also might threaten male control of the mule spinning trade, the authority of men in labor politics, and the respectable manhood of skilled workers and unionists. For many non-English textile workers, the ritual mass demonstrations on September 27 in the midst of defeat seemed alien and futile. The failure of the vacation strike laid bare the cultural divisions among textile workers in ways that eager employers and their middle-class supporters hastened to exploit. The defeat slowed additional emigration from Lancashire and no doubt revived old country tensions between the English and Irish, the mule spinners and the weavers.[179]

The struggle in Fall River over gender meanings took place in two overlapping arenas: the working-class community and the textile mill. After years of defeat, the weavers seized control of labor politics in 1875 and struck defiant blows at the mills' control of the print cloth market. Initial success repudiated the past failures of deferential policies. The operatives' perceptions of power proved as significant as those of the mill owners. Later this strategy of defiance produced a humiliating defeat and the destruction of established unions. Dissension within the working-class community in late 1875 seemed almost as serious a threat to labor politics as the power of the mills. How to be a Lancashire immigrant in America yet remain loyal to the old country heritage became one key issue while Irish and Quebec immigrants had their own political and cultural problems. In the meantime, activist women and their views on politics and ideology were suppressed.

Struggles over the meanings of manly and womanly behavior in Fall River factories and in labor protest provide evidence of powerful intraclass conflict and cultural discontinuity in the meanings of working-class gender and ethnicity that generally remain unexplored in the history of people caught up in immigration, industrialization, and acculturation in late nineteenth-century America. The ways in which working-class masculinity and femininity took different, contested forms during the labor politics of the 1870s demonstrate the contingencies, not the inevitabilities, in the meaning of gender, the direction of labor politics, and the definitions of appropriate working-class family relations in nineteenth-century America.[180]

After 1875, mule spinners and weavers in New England went their own ways in labor politics. Memories of the 1875 defeat haunted later strikes in Fall River, while confused recollections and deliberate erasures undercut the potential of activist women weavers, their male allies, and Lancashire-style militancy. These struggles, however, clearly demonstrate both female agency and its role in defining the meaning of manhood and the significance of gender to working-class politics and culture. It is important to historicize gender for both sexes and to identify those moments of conflict, choice, and possibility before gender meanings hardened and sexual difference became rigidly embedded in discourse and institutions. In doing so, historians can uncover how and why the meanings of masculinity and femininity are made and remade in a changing world.

The turbulent decade of the 1870s also reminds us that immigrant cultures transferred vital traditions of radical politics to industrializing America. English influences, while important in terms of skills and institutions, also offered alternative protest politics, cultural forms, and gender ideologies. Evidence on the activism of working-class emigrants from Lancashire and Yorkshire in New England can contribute to reexaminations of English working-class popular radicalism, reformism in mid-Victorian England and the rise of working-class conservatism thus supporting but also complicating comparative studies like the works of Neville Kirk. In what might be a commentary on this chapter, Geoff Eley argues that the crucial strategic problem in English working-class formation was—as in New England—

> how to mobilize the maximum solidarity from a socially defined constituency which has no essential unity in the sphere of consciousness, but on the contrary a series of particularistic loyalties and preferences and a widely differing experience of everyday life, a mosaic of individual histories. The analysis of working-class politics begins with this dialectic—the contradictory and dynamic intersection of unifying and fragmenting tendencies within the class as a whole. . . .[181]

The shock waves that fanned out across the region's textile centers between 1876 and 1878 provide the best assessment of the political and cultural ramifications of defiance and defeat in 1875.

7

A New Lancashire for
the Northeast, 1876–1878

ONE WINTER day in 1884, a Rhode Island farmer watched the struggles of a thinly clad man trying to negotiate a huge, iced-over area in a road that ran between stone fences. The ice was too thin to support his weight. Again and again, his steps broke through to the puddle below. Finally, he gave up and splashed his way through. It was January, no time to be walking the roads with soaked boots and stockings. The farmer called to him and let him dry his feet in the kitchen before setting out again. While the man's belongings dried, he told his story.[1]

He was a Fall River weaver, disgusted with conditions in the city's mills, especially at the Laurel Lake mill built in 1881. He declared that he would rather spend five years in prison than work there. So he was on a tramp, searching for better employment in some mill village in Rhode Island or Connecticut. He had been sizing up the conditions and wages at the villages of River Point and Phenix, Rhode Island. At Phenix, where he stopped to buy some tobacco, the storekeeper scrutinized him so closely that the weaver asked what he wanted. The man replied that his duty was to watch for suspicious persons. The weaver grew angry and told the storekeeper what he thought of being spied on in a free country but left the village quickly.

The weaver had grown weak from lack of food and shelter, but told the farmer he had once crossed a railroad bridge on his hands and knees, despite the risk of an oncoming train. Along the road he had met two French Canadian peddlers, one of whom had worked in the Fall River mills, and told them where they could find their countryfolk in the area. He had searched for decent work at Taftville and in other Connecticut mill villages where he checked the prices in the company stores and concluded that the operatives were being swindled. He found that the Connecticut mills operated from 5:00 A.M. to 7:00 P.M. and were "nothing but slavery and oppression." He stayed for a time with a mule spinner and his wife. In debt to the company store, the spinner offered to join him in his search for work, but the weaver insisted that tramping was no "pleasant thing," advising him to stay where he was. During his tramp, he met many other weavers like himself. Continuing his journey to rural Quidnick, Rhode Island, on a branch of the Pawtuxet River, southwest of Providence, he finally returned to Massachusetts, convinced that he had no better alternative. After the defeat of the weavers' strike in 1875, George Gunton too had tramped southern New England, but found he was blacklisted everywhere.

This tramping Fall River weaver knew where to look for work in southeastern New England and how to judge its possibilities. His wanderings, his knowledge of the region and what working conditions to reject, and his discovery of a network of contacts indicate that histories of single communities are inadequate to capture the experience of this textile workforce. The industrial power of New England textile capitalism and the economic conditions of the post–Civil War expansion and depression had created a regional labor market. As operatives searched for work in the reviving economy of the late 1870s, this regionwide work culture suggests the basis for an inclusive labor politics of all textile workers, regardless of skill and nationality—the dream of the Fall River strikers in 1875.

JOHN T. CUMBLER's comparative study of two different industrial cities, Fall River and Lynn, is an example of the depth and richness but also of the narrowness of the community study approach that was common among labor and social historians in the 1970s and 1980s. In *Working-Class Community in Industrial America: Work, Leisure, and Struggle in Two Industrial Cities, 1880–1930* (1979), his comparison of the political geography of the residences, workplaces, and leisure centers of working-class life in two communities yields important conclusions about social cohesion and labor activism. Cumbler's study has great strengths as the most lively account and important analysis of late nineteenth-century Fall River labor politics, including the conflicts between mule spinners and weavers in the late nineteenth century. Especially valuable is his appreciative handling of the active role of many French Canadian textile workers during the strikes of 1884 and 1894. His analysis, like that of Daniel J. Walkowitz in *Worker City, Company Town: Iron and Cotton-Worker Protest in Troy and Cohoes, New York, 1855–84* (1978), undermines the persistent stereotypes about immigrant workers from Quebec as passive, anti-union, priest-ridden, and politically conservative. Any study of French Canadian working-class life and culture in New England should begin with Cumbler.[2]

Cumbler's study of the labor politics of Fall River does not include, however, the formative struggles of the 1860s and 1870s and their contribution to the late nineteenth century. In addition, his emphasis on one community misses the powerful reach of New England textile manufacturers, the regionally contested ideologies and labor politics of English immigrant workers, and the mobility of the workforce. Studies of industrial life should follow as widely as possible the lines of economic, political, and cultural experience. The politics of New England industrial life must give due attention to the competitive drives within the New England textile industry and the conflictual dynamics of regional labor politics.

THE IMPACT OF DEFEAT IN FALL RIVER

When the Fall River operatives struck selected mills in January 1875, their actions reverberated throughout New England, especially in the mill villages of Rhode Island. In these villages were many cotton mills that produced goods of better quality than print cloth, such as shirting and sheeting, and attracted skilled English workers. The immigrants quickly found that the mill villages, clustered in an alley along the Blackstone River between Woonsocket and Providence, and governed by the large towns of Cumberland, Providence, and Smithfield, were, in the words of the *Providence Journal's* editor, "owned" by the local mills.[3] As immigrants, English workers faced the same restrictive property qualifications for voting as the Irish. Until the depression of 1873, Brown and Ives, the Goddard family at Lonsdale and Ashton, and the Chace family in Valley Falls and Albion provided their mill villages with housing, a water supply, Protestant churches, schools, and skilled work at good wages. Then faced with the same wage cuts as Fall River workers, the Rhode Island operatives in many of these mill villages supported both Fall River strikes in 1875, protested against the tyranny of their employers, and conducted strikes of their own. The editor of the *Providence Sun,* Lester E. Ross, became the voice of Rhode Island's working class. Recognizing the regional nature of these labor troubles, he wrote: "The cause of Fall River is Rhode Island's cause."[4] Operatives by the dozen wrote to the editor about their grievances, and hundreds read their words. When the Fall River strikers won in April, Rhode Island workers expected—and sometimes received—wage increases.

Many of the operatives in these Rhode Island mill villages of Lonsdale, Olneyville, Valley Falls, Central Falls, Ashton, Albion, and Berkeley, and in the mills in Providence and Woonsocket spoke the same dialects and shared the same political heritage as the Lancashire and Yorkshire people of Fall River. In early 1875, woolen weavers, including female activists, led a strike and formed a union at the Wanskuck mill in Providence.[5] When the company's managers insisted that the cloth market was saturated and that they could chose either to accept a wage cut or face a total shutdown of operations, the skeptical weavers wanted to run half-time on the old wages. They agreed with Fall River operatives that it made no sense to produce more, cheaper cloth in a glutted market. In Providence, the weavers at the Aquidnick mill struck against a wage reduction and demanded the return of a popular former superintendent.[6] The Sovereigns of Industry at Olneyville, Lonsdale, Ashton, Valley Falls, Warren, Woonsocket, Pawtucket, Bristol, and Providence had organized many English-style cooperative stores by the summer of 1874. In December 1874, they met as a council representing twenty-two cooperatives and twenty-five hundred members.[7] Fall River strikers, including female agitators, had visited the tiny village of Hope, owned by the Lonsdale Company on the Pawtuxet River and Valley Falls on the Blackstone, where they met with textile workers from nearby Lonsdale, Ashton, and Berkeley to solicit support and funds.[8] Throughout the region operatives who dared purchase copies of the pro-labor *Providence Sun,* either in the Pawtuxet region, in Berkeley village or just over the border in Dodgeville, Massachusetts, faced dismissal. Trading in Providence rather than at the mill company store also meant trouble. Yet in spite of all this intimidation, "even Canadians who can't read English buy the *Sun,* and have it read to them," the editor reported proudly.[9] Operatives living in Baltic, Connecticut, River Point, Rhode Island, and Hebronville, Massachusetts, complained and grew restive.[10] Various national groups at Taftville were already on strike. The first Fall River strike in 1875 incited labor protest throughout southeastern New England.

Furthermore, many English operatives in Rhode Island had grown disillusioned with their choice to immigrate. At Lonsdale, attempts to prevent them from reading the *Sun* produced open indignation among them. Unable to vote, they grew contemptuous of Rhode Island–style democracy. From Berkeley, "Lancashire Lad," a famous pen name from the cotton famine years, sent the editor of the *Sun* an article from the *Preston Herald* in Lancashire titled "A Warning Voice from America." Thousands of English immigrants to the United States "have, ever since they landed, cursed the unlucky hour they first thought of crossing the Atlantic." Wages in New England were low, he complained, and the cost of living high. "A disappointed Englishman" living in South Providence wrote, "I with my family left the old country for, as I thought, a better; but I find that this place is worse than England. . . ."[11] He predicted a mass exodus if conditions did not change.

After the first Fall River strike was won, some Rhode Islanders eagerly joined the weavers' Amalgamated Textile Workers' Union and participated during the summer of 1875 in the revived ten-hour movement, promoted by Fall River's George Gunton, Simon Morgan (formerly of Merinoville) and Jonathan Biltcliffe (formerly of Olneyville). In 1873 Rhode

Island workers had organized a general strike for the ten-hour day which involved Morgan, Biltcliffe, and Jonathan Corkhill (formerly of Merino-ville), but nothing had happened.[12] Perhaps now in coalition with the victorious Fall River operatives, a ten-hour day in Rhode Island could become law. Organizers of the mass meeting at Rocky Point on August 20 expected that a huge turnout might influence some Providence politicians, although because of dismal rain only a few delegations, primarily from Lonsdale, Pawtucket, Olneyville, and Providence, showed up. Still, James Austin of Woonsocket became president of the New England ten-hour movement organized at Rocky Point with numerous vice presidents selected from Newmarket and Great Falls, New Hampshire, Taunton, Fall River, and New Bedford, Massachusetts, ten from the Rhode Island centers of Lonsdale, Warren, Providence, Pawtucket, River Point and Olneyville, and one each from Taftville, Norwich, Greenville, and Wauregan, Connecticut.[13] Lowell, Lawrence, and Manchester sent no delegates. This was overwhelmingly a southeastern New England drive.

The long vacation strike in Fall River in August proved less popular with Rhode Island operatives and labor reformers than the January strike. The editor of the *Providence Sun,* along with Lapham of the *Border City Herald,* thought the weavers were wrong to believe that shutting down Fall River's productive capacity alone would influence the cloth market.

> Could the Fall River operatives have combined with the operatives in other mills [in other villages and cities] to vote themselves a vacation, the other mills could not have run, and the stock [of cloth] would inevitably have gone down.... Unless the stop can be made general, it will hardly be a success.[14]

Still, it was hard for editor Ross to criticize the operatives for "taking the bull by the horns." Their admirable and "sensible" attempt to stop work seemed the "wisest course under the circumstances [of a glutted market]." Even Henry Howard, the former governor of Rhode Island, a ten-hour man who owned a mill in Providence, wrote to the *Sun* that "the operatives of Fall River have shown themselves wiser than the manufacturers."[15]

As events in Fall River turned against the strikers, mill owners in Rhode Island responded by announcing unspecified wage cuts beginning in mid-September that spread throughout the region. Meanwhile at Valley Falls, the operatives, who had been cut down 13 percent in late 1874, sent one hundred dollars to Fall River with the belief that "if they fail to make a success of their strike, God help us, for then the mill-owners will have it all their own way." Already Valley Falls overseers had taken over the Sovereigns of Industry cooperative, undermining its credibility, and the owner of the mills, Samuel Chace, refused to let any workers go to the Rocky Point ten-hour demonstration in August. He told them that "if Fall River gave twenty-seven [cents per cut], he would, but if they only gave twenty-four he should give the same."[16] The discouraged president of the local weavers' committee resigned to go west.

The Valley Falls mills, according to operative Jane Dwight, constituted a "complete system of tyranny" with a spy network that prevented the "help" from reading the labor press and a practice of fining weavers for the smallest imperfection. "Daily overworked women fainted. . . . We are working the 'poor' cotton now [making print cloth]. . . ." The Providence Steam mill required weavers to use wide looms to produce narrower print cloth. The work became much more difficult, and the compensation for the extra effort proved negligible. Wages had been cut 30 percent since January 1874. At the River Point mills, owned by the proprietors of the *Providence Journal,* the worst of Rhode Island working conditions prevailed. "Small help," as young as eight, worked eleven hours daily with no schooling, while the weavers worked from twelve to fourteen hours a day. There were many French Canadians among the operatives, and all used the mill's store for supplies.[17] This was what Fall River mill owners called the "canker sore" of Rhode Island competition.

Even weavers in the Berkeley mills, who made fine cloth of high quality requiring great skill and exacting watchfulness, faced wage cuts. Their supervisors told them that their New Bedford competitors had cut wages after the Fall River defeat. In Providence, weavers found their piece rate cut 10 percent. Overseers required the looms to run during their dinner hour and imposed fines on operatives for talking or combing their hair. "Sary H. and Mary B." at the Oriental mills warned that the best weavers are "thus driven away disgusted." Meanwhile, the editor of the *Providence Sun* defended the September 27 bread riot in Fall River as fundamentally a calm and deliberate procession led by a majority of sober, intelligent, and industrious operatives. He attacked the mill owners: a victory over a starving people beset by the cries of their hungry children was no achievement. The operatives were heralded as "manly and worthy of the highest commendation" and as a people of "terrible earnestness."[18] But in Fall River, there was only defeat, despair, and recrimination.

Things did not seem quite so bad in late October 1875 to labor activist James H. Hargreaves of Olneyville, who supported trade unions and producer cooperatives. He believed that strikes could not led to meaningful wage increases until the New England textile mills reorganized into producer cooperatives as in Oldham, England, with whose members he corresponded. Such cooperatives had thrown off the yoke of industrial tyranny by shifting capital into the hands of the many, not the few. Hargreave thought that the Fall River defeat confirmed his views, although the vacation strike had prevented cloth market prices from dropping even further. "Let us remember," he wrote, "the suffering people of Fall River, who, from sheer necessity, were compelled to sign away" their liberties, and let us organize to "prevent a similar injustice to ourselves in Rhode Island."[19] Cooperative mills funded by union treasuries were the answer but none emerged.

At Valley Falls, the village run by the former antislavery advocates, Samuel and Elizabeth Buffum Chace, women operatives not only endured wage reductions but also sexual harassment from mill managers. Insults and the possibility of either having "their persons outraged" or being discharged became important grievances. One operative became "enciente" [sic] after being seduced by a supervisor promising marriage. Her complaints to his mother only got her into deeper trouble; she was fired. Elizabeth Chace, who ran the local aid society, intervened in this particular case and had the mistreated young woman (likely a Yankee) rehired and relocated to living quarters under the Chace family's protection. The mill's overseers ceased spying on workers who read the *Sun,* but at the same time the length of the cut was increased from 40 to 46 yards, and the work intensified. Whatever moral responsibilities the Chaces felt toward the operatives did not extend to the imperatives of cutting costs. In Lonsdale, female operatives with infants had insufficient time to nurse and care for their children. Management permitted only five minutes twice a day. Expectant mothers in all stages of pregnancy worked a twelve- to fourteen-hour-day or were fired. The "lying-in bed vacation," the period of labor, childbirth, and recovery, was the only vacation workingwomen got if they wished to continue weaving.[20]

Still, one contented male weaver with the pen name "Eng" insisted in early November 1875 that working conditions and wages in Lonsdale were acceptable, even admirable. The operatives, using the best machinery imported from Scotland, made the finest cloth in the United States. The workforce in the mills owned by Brown and Ives with the Goddard brothers as agents were "very contented" and treated well. A man tending six looms could earn between thirty-six dollars and forty dollars a month. Rent was reasonable, no overseer spied on readers of the labor press, and the Sovereigns of Industry, numbering 250, ran a successful cooperative grocery. Working ten and one-half hours per day with Saturday afternoon off, the male operatives organized the Lonsdale Cricket Club whose season of nine wins and one loss had just been celebrated at their second annual ball.[21] But his contentment did not last. In January 1876, the Lonsdale company cut wages, and the mill village exploded with its first strike.

THE LONSDALE STRIKE OF 1876

The Lonsdale company, located about seven miles north of Providence along the Blackstone River on the Smithfield town side, had begun production in the early 1830s with three small mills. A bleachery built in

1844 served the needs of the company's other mills in Blackstone, Ashton, and Hope and other factories in the vicinity. Added in 1860, Mill # 4 with its own "new" village sat in the town of Cumberland, but the political power of Brown and Ives and the Goddard family prevented any serious problems with either town. Both mill villages contained operatives' tenements, a library, a school, and churches. No one sold liquor. All four mills made fine sheeting, shirting, muslins, and other high-quality cloth. In 1870 a workforce of thirteen hundred used brand-new technology, such as the slasher-tender and the latest bleaching apparatus. The Lonsdale company also built the mill village of Ashton, located in the town of Cumberland, three miles away from its main operation in Lonsdale village, just beyond Albion village, owned by the Chace family of Valley Falls. The scattered locations did not, however, prove as ideal as planned. In May 1870 the Lonsdale operatives struck the mills over a 10 percent wage cut. Labor reformer Thomas Webb of Fall River visited the village and promised support, but the mule spinners' strike that summer in Fall River undermined these efforts.[22] Both strikes were lost. However, southeastern Massachusetts operatives were forming a network of connections with their coworkers in Rhode Island.

By 1876 the workforce in Lonsdale had grown to three thousand, half English immigrants and the other half Irish. The Irish operatives believed that management always favored the English, and ethnic rivalries plagued the Lonsdale strike. When informed on Monday, January 10 of the expected but unspecified wage cut, the weavers at Mill # 4 poured out at noon and refused to go back. No one knew exactly how much their monthly pay would be reduced; this proved "the feather that broke the camel's back," according to one striker. After a hastily called meeting, the strike committee spoke with the assistant superintendent, G. W. Pratt, seeking a compromise. George Kilburn, the superintendent, refused to talk with them. That evening the committee reported to a meeting crowded with operatives from both the old and the new mill villages. Pratt had received them "kindly" but yielded nothing. He insisted that the company had delayed the cut as long as possible, hoping the depressed market would rise. Either the operatives accepted a cut or the mill would shut down. Perhaps, Pratt suggested, the wage reduction might soon be rescinded. The company also promised to cut the price of meat at its store, but when the strike committee reported this to a general meeting, they were greeted with open disbelief and ridicule. When the committee members recommended that the operatives go back the next day, the hall rocked with laughter and cries of "Out!, Out! Out!"[23] All the operatives, except the committee, voted to strike.

The next day, word spread quickly about the weavers' strike at Lonsdale's Mill # 4. The strikers gathered in front of the other three mills, calling out the hands. Then someone shouted, "Let's go to Ashton." A large group of men, women, and children walked the three miles to seek the support of the operatives in the company's other major mill. As they passed out of Lonsdale, cheers came from windows and doorways. They were well aware, as was everyone else in the region, of the dangers in any public disorder. "Quietly and orderly the large body marched past Berkeley to Ashton," but for any Rhode Island mill village this march was sensational. When the jovial crowd reached Ashton, the superintendent threatened to have them all arrested. Since these mill villages maintained only one policeman at best, his remark caused a "great deal of merriment," while some of the female weavers called him, "a sweet old man" who wouldn't hurt anyone. The strikers marched around the mill several times. The operatives inside rushed to the windows, but the sweet old man had locked and bolted all the doors. Satisfied that they had demonstrated their determination to strike to the Ashton folk, the marchers went home, singing "merry English songs."[24] The Goddard brothers decided not to cut wages at Ashton, but that night they sent for police from Providence.

As in Fall River, female weavers in Lonsdale goaded their male coworkers into action. During the first strikers' meeting, Kate Reevey, who along with her sister and two brothers supported her family, denounced "the cowardly action of the men," some of whom had returned to work at Mill # 4. Her "eloquent" and well-received speech prompted one striker to remark, "If the strike is successful they will have to thank the women, for it has been their pluck and perseverance which made the present movement thus far a grand success."[25]

As the meeting broke up, Providence police were seen marching from the depot "with a conquering air," some to be stationed at the company headquarters at Mill # 4 and the rest at the other mills. The mayor of Providence, Thomas A. Doyle, backed politically by Brown and Ives, defended his decision by insisting that the business interests of his own city depended on the growth and prosperity of neighboring villages. Therefore his duty required the Providence police to protect property and preserve "good order." They attended the strikers' meetings to intimidate them, but the operatives' speeches grew even more "emphatic." Many thought "the bringing of a police force into the quiet village was an act of arrogance, power and nabobism well worthy of the Lonsdale Company."[26] One boy was arrested for calling the Goddards tyrants, but the strikers made sure the Providence police had nothing much to do. Mayor Doyle was the treasurer of the Atlantic Delaine mill in Olneyville, only two miles north of Providence, which had shut down in January 1874. Its seventeen hundred operatives had been unable to collect the two weeks' pay owned them.[27] The Goddards had a good friend in Providence city hall.

On the third day of the strike, the bleachery workers decided to join in. Their skill and importance to the area's mill operations made them even more crucial to sustaining the strike than the mule spinners, carders,

and loom fixers, who also supported the weavers' actions. Along with the
bleachers came the rest of the help from Mill # 4 and the other new buildings. Then the weavers placarded the area around the old mills, calling
on their coworkers to "Strike for your rights this afternoon" and demand
"Liberty for the white slaves." The bleachers left fifteen thousand dollars
worth of cloth soaking in chemicals. This, they believed, would "fetch em
to their oats," and bring the company to terms. Their boss at the bleachery, Peter Byrne, wanted them all back regardless of the outcome, but
they insisted they would not be back, "not even to save the cloth in the
pickle."[28] First, the company would have to restore wages.

The Lonsdale strikers quickly became divided between the cautious
strike committee and those more boisterous and defiant who attended
the strike meetings. Differences had already emerged between men and
women weavers over the depth of their commitment to the strike. Irish-
born weaver and ten-hour reformer John Mooney, one of the regional
vice presidents chosen at the Rocky Point ten-hour meeting and the
elected chair of the strike committee, must have been puzzled over the
denunciations of him by female weavers who nonetheless had voted for
him. From the platform, Mooney called for calm, caution, and the end of
demonstrations and "unnecessary excitement." When a voice proposed
voting by secret ballot to avoid the hissing and jeering of those in opposition, the general view prevailed that such persons needing secret votes
were "moral cowards." Women strikers gave "the best" speeches that
roused "the faint-hearted" men who, in the opinion of one striker, had
been "weak in will and vacillating in their actions."[29] The conciliatory
Mooney had reason enough to be angry with the Lonsdale company; no
Irish weaver had ever been promoted to the skilled position of loom fixer.
The agent always chose English immigrants.

The Lonsdale strike began to spread to Berkeley, Phenix, Blackstone,
and Hope, all mill villages "owned" by Brown and Ives, the most influential men in Rhode Island textiles, especially since the downfall of the
Sprague family mills in 1873.[30] The operatives at Rockville, Connecticut,
near Hartford, also went on strike.[31] The pages of the *Providence Sun* filled
with letters from operatives exposing bad conditions in Blackstone, Pawtucket, Berkeley, Woonsocket, Albion, Providence, Warren, and Warwick.
All Rhode Island mill workers seemed ready for another general strike.
To gain support, the Lonsdale strikers decided to go again to Ashton to
call out the operatives. Tipped off, a large force of police struggled
through falling snow at dawn to get to the village, but the march was canceled because of the storm. The strikers, "feeling jolly," had a good laugh
at the expense of the "Lonsdale peace preservers."[32] For their next march,
they decided to request a police escort. All of these activities and merriment, recorded in the *Providence Sun* as "the bubbling up of fun in the
crowd" kept alive the spirit and concealed the disunity within the strike.

The editor of the *Providence Journal* observed darkly that "exactly as was the case in Fall River, we see the intelligent, prudent, thoughtful . . . minority overruled by the impulsive majority."[33] The leaders of the strike committee denounced the most boisterous, including Kate Reevey, as "girls and boys," and admonished all strikers to remain in their homes and wait.[34] Disorderly, passionate behavior might signal a failure of manhood and womanhood, but most of all, the committee was afraid of repeating the Fall River debacle.

Memories of that humiliating defeat were fresh as Mooney led a committee of three, unauthorized by any vote of the strikers, to seek a compromise. Significantly, the meeting was held in Providence at the headquarters of the Lonsdale company. The committee came as lambs to the slaughter and reported back to a strike meeting on January 26. Mooney, Patrick Bolen, and Michael McCarty had met Col. William Goddard and Robert H. Goddard in their elegant Providence offices. The committee asked for a compromise. The managers replied, "The Lonsdale Company cannot recede from the stand it has already taken." The committee asked whether the wage cut would be restored if the strike ended. "As the Lonsdale Company has not the governing or controlling of the market, it can make no promise for the future." As in Fall River, the Goddards argued that it was a question of supply and demand. Mooney reported to the strikers' meeting William Goddard's insistence that although "the company was rich and powerful," it was losing money. Operations had to be curtailed or wages reduced. Mooney recommended a return to work. The assembled strikers received the report with "great disfavor" and "disapprobation," while an exasperated Mooney threatened to use the police to throw out troublemakers.[35] The meeting adjourned in disorder and division.

Dissenters questioned the extent to which a depressed cloth market threatened profitable production. The Goddards usually got $12\frac{1}{2}$ cents per yard for their finest cloth, which was reportedly selling in 1876 for $9\frac{3}{5}$ cents per yard. When in January 1875 the company had eighteen hundred cases of fine goods held off the market in storage, the agents had not cut wages. In early 1876, with no inventory, the company, which had signed contracts with the commission house of Woodward, Lawrence and Company of New York City, still reduced wages. As in Fall River the company, not the market, made the crucial decisions to withhold goods or produce them. Rumors put the price of the cloth under contract at 11 cents, but without access to the yardstick of a working cooperative mill, the operatives had no information on profits except from the company or the press.[36] The company valued the skill of its "help" that determined the high reputation of its product, but when "the operatives believed that they have a moral right to share in the benefits" of production, this was "heretical."[37] Particularly for the Lancashire English of Lonsdale, as for those in Fall River, customary moral right measured the justice of textile operations. Nevertheless, the committee of three, all Irish-born immigrants, conferred without formal authority in Providence and favored of any kind of compromise.

Another tradition dear to Lancashire hearts was to stand and fight for their rights against "tyranny." The editor of the *Providence Sun* denounced the Goddards as men who would not condescend to negotiate with the operatives, expecting "blind, unhesitating obedience," as if from a workforce in a state prison.[38] But many Lonsdale operatives were leaving the village, certain that with their skills and experience they could easily find jobs elsewhere. Some returned to England. Others contemplated travel to Texas or Arizona, based on fantastic descriptions of the climate and cheap land. Rumors circulated about the preparation of a blacklist, another incentive to leave. The departure of Lancashire people thinned the number of strikers until the amalgamated union in Lonsdale fell apart, and the mule spinners and bleachers voted to return to work. At the last strike meeting on January 27, the 341 strikers, only 10 percent of the workforce, voted 209 to 132 to return to work. Some charged that the Mooney committee had been paid off by the Goddards to undermine the strike. One English striker insulted those who did not wait for the official vote as acting like a "parcel of idiots" to "sneak back . . . a few at a time."[39] No Lancashire workers would do this; win, lose, or draw, they would return in one body. The strike had lasted only three weeks, but defeat in this key Rhode Island mill village reinforced the Fall River defeat.

Meanwhile the Goddards, who had contributed $250 to the Providence police fund, publicly thanked the police for controlling "a mass of men and women, who were acting under a fancied sense of injury, stimulated and kept alive by foreign influences."[40] In October 1876 Lonsdale physician Lucius F. C. Garvin reported to the annual meeting of the American Public Health Association in Boston on the condition of cotton operatives in the Lonsdale factories and proposed necessary reforms. Garvin did not mention the strike, the wage cut, or the depression years as factors in his investigations and cautiously avoided blaming Goddard policies, but he concluded with an appeal for a ten-hour law as the most fundamental step toward bettering the health of Rhode Island workers.[41] Garvin later became an active Democratic political reformer, pushing a ten-hour law for Rhode Island.

In the aftermath of the defeat in Lonsdale that reflected divisions among English and Irish immigrant strikers, contentious letters in the *Sun* debated the political and cultural position of the Irish-born citizens of Providence. One issue became the celebration of St. Patrick's Day in 1876. Many felt that during hard times the money should go to the poor. In defense, supporters of a grand march and supper insisted that these activities represented the achievements of the Irish community in Providence. Let those who supported charity, they insisted, cancel the Fourth of July or the 1876 Centennial celebration. The St. Patrick's Day festivities went off as planned by the middle-class Irish of Providence led by Mayor Doyle.[42] As the Rhode Island state elections in April approached, critics of the dismal state of the Democratic Party blamed qualified Irish residents for selling their votes or refusing to assist the campaign to overturn property qualifications for the foreign-born. As one wrote, "I am a Democrat in politics." If the "foreign element [meaning only the Irish] . . . would manfully go for their rights," they could overturn the property qualification. The writer advised, "Keep cool, try and unite your people, don't be clannish, rely for strength on your own resources, deposit your ballot like men, don't sell your vote, manfully seek your rights."[43] Such public criticism of the political behavior of Irish men, alone among the other foreign-born nationalities, further threatened whatever cohesion had survived among working people after the Lonsdale strike.

Ethnic division remained a problem, but experience in the Lonsdale mills still provided a powerful ground for class unity. In the spring of 1876, "Rory" of Lonsdale applauded the bleachery workers who were trying to organize a union and to join with the weavers and mule spinners in a restoration of the amalgamated union. He further hoped that the carders would organize the young girls employed in carding operations. Rory "wished to see a union in every town and village [in the Blackstone Valley] from Providence to Worcester. . . ." Verifying the mistreatment of Irish Catholic workers in preference to English operatives, he listed the names of those discriminated against, including John Mooney.[44] But another Lonsdale operative, "Good Deposition," the village correspondent for the *Sun,* insisted that the Catholic religion should not become an issue in labor politics and that a good six-loom Irish male weaver could out-earn any English-born loom fixer any day. Compliments to the Irish weavers' capacity to produce cloth did not lessen the sting of a policy of bigotry in the mills. "Rory" retorted that "Good Deposition" might be bucking for an overseer's job.[45]

Outside of Lonsdale, "Mickle Gow" of Warren, Rhode Island, southeast of Providence, complained in the *Sun* about the poor wages and other common grievances in the print cloth mills that paid 19 cents a cut, measuring 46 yards. The yarn was "impossible" to weave, and the machinery was old. The unpainted, damp tenements had water "unfit to drink, cook or wash with." The superintendent of the Warren Manufacturing company, Eliphalet P. Emery, distinguished himself for "ignorance, mendacity and brutal tyranny." One of his favorite tricks was to deduct from the wages of departing families charges for alleged damages to their decaying tenements. Mickle Gow had known Emery for years and believed he had "not one manly principle." Some of his Lancashire weaver friends, he wrote, turned Eliphalet into "He'll-lie-for-it." The family who managed the company boardinghouse also supplied spies and "lickspittles" and served hash and "messes." Gow ridiculed one family member employed in the mills who chased the female operatives, looking for "some 'doosed' [devilish] fine gal with no nonsense about her. . . . How these artful factory girls do stuff the poor goose." As in Lonsdale, the Irish in Warren had it hard. The boss weaver of the three mills at the Warren company despised the Irish operatives and "fires them to get English help. . . . " But Mickle Gow stated with admiration, "those sturdy Lancashire weavers don't stay long, they object to starvation wages, . . . hash, Warren mud, and poisonous water . . . , and the small-change knavery and slave-driving tyranny of 'He'll-lie-for-it.' "[46] As long as Irish and Lancashire operatives in Rhode Island shared such conditions, they could speak a common language of class oppression.

Strikers Challenge the Wamsutta in New Bedford

Another test of the vitality and unity of southeastern New England labor protest came in early 1877. William Bennett, the superintendent and agent of the Wamsutta, retired in April 1874 after twenty-seven years. The directors selected as agent and treasurer Edward Kilburn, whose father George had once worked for the New Bedford-backed Robeson mill in Fall River and then helped manage the Lonsdale, Berkeley, and Ashton mills in Rhode Island. George Kilburn was a brother of Elijah Kilburn of the Kilburn, Lincoln textile machinery works in Fall River.[47] The Kilburn family provided a network of regional connections among the textile mills of southeastern Massachusetts and Rhode Island.

The Wamsutta directors charged Edward Kilburn in 1874 to sustain stock dividends during the deepening depression. He saw many ways to achieve this, altering working conditions and buying expensive new machinery but cheaper cotton, coal, and oil. The cheaper lubricating oil, contaminated with bacteria, caused the death of Mrs. Thomas Sharples, who pricked her finger while cleaning her looms. First her hand, then her arm swelled, and she died a few days later of blood poisoning.[48] Other weavers recovered from similar cases, and they all blamed Kilburn. He also assigned operatives more work with no additional pay and fired "spare hands." Kilburn altered the cloth's quality by decreasing the strength of the yarn through manipulating the drafting process. This made weaving more difficult. Cloth buyers quickly recognized that Wamsutta cloth was being cheapened, and its price on the market dropped.[49] The mills now competed with makers of cheaper goods. When Bennett was agent, Wamsutta cloth had been second to none.

Kilburn also cut costs by reducing wages twice between 1874 and early 1877. In a policy unusual for New England mills, he pitted the operatives against each other by slowly introducing between October 1876 and January 1877 different wages for the same work, for no stated reason. This system of unequal pay, deliberately divided the workforce. Operatives in Mill # 5 built in 1875 faced the lowest wages. In early January, the agent announced an unspecified wage cut beginning February 1. As in Lonsdale, anger among the workforce increased at the uncertainty of the reduction. Meanwhile, the wages at New Bedford's Potomska mills, built in 1871 and expanded in 1877, remained unchanged.[50] To the operatives, who avidly read newspaper accounts of the cloth market, Kilburn's policies and the threatened wage cut during a rising market for fine goods sparked the first strike in ten years at the Wamsutta. They had actively supported strikes in Fall River, Lowell, and Taftville in 1875. A large demonstration in New Bedford by those who could not go to the Rocky Point meeting in August 1875 had rallied for the passage of a ten-hour law in Rhode Island. The lost strike at Lonsdale must have been unsettling, but the operatives in New Bedford expected strong regional support, especially on the new issue of unequal wages for equal work. If the strike was not successful, Edward Kilburn's policy could be adopted by any mill in the region.

During the third week in January, the Wamsutta mill agent made the wage cut specific: between 7 and 10 percent, depending on the job. Given press reports on market conditions, many had expected an advance in early January, but, as in Lonsdale, the managers alone interpreted the movements of the cloth market. At an operatives' meeting on January 21, few men were bold enough, fearing the blacklist, to join a delegation to meet with Kilburn; the workforce was already hesitant and divided. When a weaver suggested that two women be included in the delegation, all those asked refused. But resolutions passed unanimously expressing "our astonishment" at the wage cut and arguing the "we ought to receive the benefit of the improved state of the market."[51] Finally, a delegation of men agreed to talk with the agent.

Borrowing the Goddard brothers' tactics, Kilburn met them at the Wamsutta offices along with former mayor Andrew G. Pierce, the company's salesman, and with the impressive, venerable president of the company, former congressman Joseph Grinnell, the original investor in 1847. Before anyone could speak, Kilburn insisted that no resolution or argument would change the minds of the directors about the wage cut. Citing Pierce as his authority on the cloth market, he discounted the published reports on prices as incorrect. When members of the delegation quoted wages paid in other mills in Massachusetts and Rhode Island, Kilburn dismissed them as irrelevant. The eighty-eight-year-old Grinnell then gave a short speech on the Wamsutta's poor financial condition, backing Kilburn and his policies. He stated further that once the current dispute in the electoral college over votes in the Tilden-Hayes 1876 presidential race was settled, the market would probably rise and wages could be raised.[52]

Following the Lonsdale pattern, the managers proved united and unmovable. When the delegation reported back to a mass meeting of the operatives, some questioned the losses that Kilburn and Grinnell claimed the Wamsutta had suffered. Many believed that Kilburn himself had wasted $250,000 on new machinery and that wages were being cut to pay for it. Others cautiously insisted that all operatives be canvassed and that a secret ballot be arranged. Those who counseled against a strike were frequently interrupted, and the idea of a secret ballot was rejected. Signs of division had emerged quickly, but by January 30, fifteen hundred operatives, mostly weavers, were calling for a strike.

The strikers gained the support of Daniel Ricketson, a prominent labor reformer and a vice president chosen by the 1875 Rocky Point ten-hour rally who also symbolized the attachment of New Bedfordites to the Garrisonian antislavery movement, to the Concord Transcendentalists, and to the earlier ten-hour mechanics' and operatives' movements in Massachusetts and Rhode Island. He addressed them at city hall, mentioning Kilburn's "certain extravagances" to loud cheering.[53] Ricketson stated that the Wamsutta did not want a strike; their "pockets were tender." Furthermore, the Fall River operatives would support their protest. As testimony to that, Henry Sevey denounced the wage cut as unnecessary and an "infernal shame," pointing out that in late 1876 Fall River operatives obtained a small advance. Sevey believed that the Fall River mills and the Wamsutta were conspiring in 1877 to hold down regional wages.[54] If Kilburn succeeded, the Fall River operatives would soon feel it. But Sevey did not recommend a strike. Wait, he argued; work at the reduced rates under protest, organize, build a strike fund, and then take on Kilburn. Still, if the operatives voted for a strike, he would join Fall River's state representative Hiram Coffin, labor reformers Lapham and Harriman, and James Langford, leader of the mule spinners' association, to help them. Hissing at dissenters, the majority of operatives voted to turn in their two-week notices in preparation for a strike if the wage cut was not withdrawn.[55]

For legal advice, the Wamsutta operatives turned to lawyer William H. Johnson, the former slave who had strongly supported the 1868 strike. Nine years in New Bedford had not changed his views. The Wamsutta, he argued, was on strike against the operatives. He knew all about oppression and, to the satisfaction of the English immigrant operatives, "remembered when his race was shelterless except under the British flag [in Canada]." At this moment, Johnson helped class interests to overcome racial prejudice. As a former slave, he could denounce wage slavery to a white working-class audience without arousing bigoted, divisive responses. The audience gave him a great English-style acclamation: three cheers and "a tiger."[56] As their lawyer, Johnson made sure that the operatives' notices were correctly prepared.

Weaver Thomas Maloney, chair of the operatives' committee, read a long, technical list of inequities in the work and wages among all the operatives.[57] Starting with the weavers, he announced that 223 cuts woven in Mills # 1, 2, and 3 over the past month had been "black-crossed" or fined for defects, costing each weaver responsible 33 cents a cut, *more* than they received per cut. Maloney knew very well how difficult it was to run eight looms and avoid minor mistakes. Other grievances involved wage differences among the five mills for the same work and speed-ups or extra work for no extra pay for card grinders and strippers, spoolers, warpers, mule spinners, doffers, and back boys. In addition, the mule spinning machines had been enlarged by one-third with no additional compensation for the spinners. Kilburn's policies encouraged some overseers to invent their own ways of humiliating the help and getting at their wages. One overseer, nicknamed "the bulldog," required his "employes" to buy their milk and cabbages from his farm or lose their jobs. He also refused to allow the operatives to use soap, towels, or mirrors, forcing "the help" to walk to their homes, covered in cotton lint or smeared with grease. Within a few days, given the prospects of getting Kilburn to change his mind, Maloney, considered one of the most effective members of the operatives' committee, left New England for good. A sympathetic grocer, John Smith, who could neither be fired nor blacklisted, replaced him. Meanwhile, the New Bedford city government considered selling the well-managed, comfortable City Almshouse, situated on beautiful Clark's Point, to summer resort developers.[58] There would be no coddling of strikers in local charitable institutions.

After the operatives first week's notice had passed, Kilburn extended his divide-and-conquer policies. Citing a little rise in the market, he would reopen the mills on March 1 at January 1 wages, rescinding the wage cut, but he would not budge on the issue of unequal pay.[59] When questioned by the workers' delegation about the mule spinners' specific grievances, he responded, "No matter, it must stand as it is; we cannot make any alteration whatever. . . ." His position was the same on all other jobs. Having made one concession, Kilburn remained unmovable on all other points. When this was reported at the operatives' meeting, they cried, "Strike! Strike!" from all parts of the hall.

Again the labor reformers, including Sevey, were cautious, recommending that the operatives accept the wage restoration and return to work under protest, provided Kilburn promised to change the unequal wages by April 1. Sevey had received letters from Lonsdale, where mule spinners' wages had been targeted, fearing that if Kilburn won and "was allowed to grind down the operatives . . . , another Kilburn would try the same experiment here." A few days later, the Lonsdale operatives reported that, "Father Kilburn has been down from Ashton, and on his return had put up notices for a reduction." The Wamsutta battle combined regional and family ties among mill agents in southeastern New England to counter the operatives developing regional network. In Fall River Hiram Coffin warned, "The eyes of the operatives of New England are upon the work [to support the New Bedford strike]. . . ." James Langford of the mule spinners' union urged the New Bedford strikers to stand firm. His association sent them five hundred dollars, the highest sum donated. The vote for the strike had been unanimous, but the next day Kilburn locked out all of his employees.[60] He also withdrew his wage concession.

Gathering a relief fund and maintaining unity represented the most troublesome problems for the strikers. A chilling east wind off the cold Atlantic blew for weeks on end, delaying spring, while the soup kitchen run by strikers at Smith's grocery store tried to keep stomachs warm and full. A number of strikers tried to collect their two weeks' back pay from the Wamsutta's countinghouse. Kilburn told them in person that they would have to wait until March 1 when the payroll was drawn up. Some wished to leave town and needed the cash. Many believed "that they were entitled, both as a matter of right and in a legal sense," to this pay. Kilburn was toying with them, forcing them to live on credit or the soup kitchen and making it impossible for them to go elsewhere. Five went to their lawyer, Johnson, who notified Kilburn that the operatives were entitled to their pay and that the company would be held liable. Nothing happened until March 1. Before then, thirty families gave up, and using their savings, returned to England, while a dozen others left for Quebec.

For those who remained, the issue of the strike had been blurred. Kilburn might restore wages to January 1 levels for most of the workers, but those who faced unequal pay, especially in Mill # 5, wanted the others to hold out until that issue had been settled. Daniel Ricketon insisted that both issues were equally important. He believed that Kilburn's single concession revealed his determination to control the workforce through differential pay. When asked about the possibility of further wage increases, Kilburn had replied evasively, "the future must take care of itself." When questioned about an end to the injustice of unequal pay, he gave them no hope at all. Ricketson believed that if the strikers accepted Kilburn's terms, "they would not have been worthy of the name of free men."[61] This middle-class reformer thus equated working-class manhood with acts of courage and defiance, even under the harsh and unbending industrial regime in New Bedford. For many, especially those with families, this was too much to ask.

Monthly paydays coincided throughout Massachusetts and Rhode Island. Donations to the Wamsutta strike fund in March and April remained meager. The weavers in Fall River, disorganized and dispirited, sent little, compared with the generosity of the mule spinners. One Fall River weaver complained that New Bedford operatives were coming to Fall River to replace them at lower wages.[62] Rhode Island operatives, except for those in Lonsdale, did not do much better. The strikers had to rely on donations from the Potomska mill workers and from other symphatizers in New Bedford. Some canvassed the region; others begged on the streets. Grocer Smith attended two weavers' meetings in Fall River, praising the mule spinners' donations but asking, where are the weavers?[63] Divide-and-conquer spread through the operatives' regional network. Many workers believed the New Bedford press reports, reprinted in the Fall River press, about the strikers' weak organization and internal dissension. Walter Scott, the new English immigrant editor of the *Fall River Herald* replaced the politically active Lapham, but, although he had witnessed the Preston strike in the 1850's and had been involved in the English male head-of-household suffrage movement, he sent no special correspondents to nearby New Bedford and became increasingly hostile to the strike.[64] When it ended, he denounced the Wamsutta defeat as a disgraceful rout that would paralyze labor activity in the region. "It is time to give over fooling. . . . What has been gained from all the strikes and vacations, but loss, disappointment and bitterness of feeling."[65] Scott intended to run the paper as a professional journalist, turning it into an efficient joint-stock company, supporting the prosperity of the city, and, while serving as the official Democratic newspaper, "honestly" examining all sides of public questions. By mid-May, the editor had distanced himself from everyone but the mule spinners' association: from Lapham, labor reform "as conducted in Fall River," Sevey, Gunton, and the *Labor Journal.* He regarded the mule spinners' organization as conducted on the best, old country principles of high dues paid by skilled men. This stance alienated the Fall River weavers and undermined the New Bedford strikers.

In early April an "independent committee" approached Kilburn. He had succeeded in dividing the strikers. In addition, two letters appeared in the local press which damaged the strike. One from "E," stated simply, "I am a Wamsutta operative and I will go back to work" next Monday, believing that "Mr. Kilburn" will advance the pay when the market revives.[66] Thomas Stephenson, who had briefly joined Robert Bower's efforts in Lawrence, signed the other letter. Already viewed by many in Fall River as a traitor to his class and to Lancashire traditions during the 1875 strike, Stephenson announced on April 10 that the New Bedford strikers were desperate and the "end was near."[67] Indeed, many operatives talked openly of accepting whatever terms Kilburn offered.

A meeting of strikers at city hall on April 24 considered what to do. Stephenson took a seat in the front of the hall. "In a minute nearly every woman in the meeting was on her feet, crying 'Put him out!' " Slowly the men came forward, surrounded him, and then hustled him out of the hall to the women's loud applause. Ricketson complimented the strikers in terms that appealed to English immigrant weavers, admiring them "as noble examples of manhood and womanhood . . . suffering for their rights. . . . Whether you succeed or not, you have demonstrated that corporations cannot deal harshly with their help without making trouble." As the ballots on continuing the strike were distributed under the watchful eye of attorney Johnson, German and French-speaking interpreters explained the situation to the two national groups among the strikers which included about twenty German immigrant families.[68] Denying allegations in the local press that the French Canadian workers were about to return to work, weaver John Smith from Fall River declared, "It is a favorite game of capitalists to set different nationalities among the help to opposing each other." The vote was 105 to return to work and 458 to continue the strike, but this meant little. The total number voting represented only 23 percent of the twenty-five hundred Wamsutta workforce. Most were weavers.[69] Both the strikers and Kilburn expected many workers to return on Monday, April 29.

On that morning, the striking weavers demonstrated that their spirit had not been broken. The police department of eight men tried to keep order and arrested several strikers for threatening those returning to work. When Stephenson showed up, he received an especially "vociferous" reception by the women operatives, who, it was reported, could be heard a mile away. Stephenson went home. One woman carried a black doll hung by the neck and tied to the top of a long staff labeled "nobbstick." Another shook a handkerchief full of nickels at the returning help.[70] In a gesture of shaming, she indicated that she could hold out if they would not. Later Kilburn was burned in effigy, but the police would not permit the figure to be carried through the streets. Most of the noise on Monday morning came from the women weavers who were in the majority, while the men remained quiet spectators. They may have remembered the defeat in Fall River and the role of female agitators. The press reported that about two hundred operatives showed up for work that morning and another three hundred in the afternoon, about a quarter of the workforce. The next day, the striking women too fell silent.

On April 30, the strikers met on the city common, where grocer Smith congratulated them on their spirit and characterized Kilburn as a member of a family "who believed in crowding down the people." But he expressed disappointment at those French Canadians who had returned to work, having been "bull-dozed" or coerced from "a quarter he did not expect." When the French Canadian strikers met on the previous Friday, led by a physician, Joseph D'Audray, who translated for them during strike meetings, the vote to stay out had been unanimous. On April 28, the following Sunday, after mass at the Church of the Sacred Heart, Father Paget left the pulpit, removed his cassock, and spoke to his congregation, man to man. He advised them to act as seemed best to each individual. Go to work and ignore the taunts or stay at home and do not cooperate with other people who opposed a return to work. Father Paget's words divided the French workers. Those who stayed on strike when the mills reopened on April 29 met on the city common with the other strikers and heard D'Audray urge them to stick with their English-speaking brothers and sisters and make the strike a success. Significantly, he spoke to reassure both groups, first in French, then in English.[71] His words were not enough. On May 2, large numbers of weavers—the backbone of the strike—returned to the mills. Kilburn prepared a blacklist for the strike leaders and for those who had "most violently abused" him personally at the strike meetings. The most stubborn still refused to work, including those French Canadians, loyal to D'Audray, who listened as one of their countrymen, a Fall River operative, encourage them to hold out.[72] Workers from Quebec continued to be divided until the bitter end between those responsive to secular leadership and others loyal to the church, but *la survivance* had not dominated the response of either group, nor would it in future strikes in southeastern New England.

The cooperative store in New Bedford collapsed as its members were blacklisted or left the city.[73] The strike failed, but the pattern of New England labor protest continued to reflect the influence of popular radicalism of English immigrants in coalition with native-born, Irish-born, Quebec-born, and a few German-born operatives. The memories of the Fall River disaster in 1875, however, had reshaped the style and terms of protest. Strikers in Lonsdale and New Bedford had avoided noisy demonstrations and disorder, but both losses greatly strained the regional, inclusive idea of amalgamation. Still, female weavers continued to play decisive and provocative roles in both strikes. And the presence of different nationalities within the workforce did not necessarily lead to strikebreaking. Immigrant workers from Quebec remained divided between secular and clerical leadership, while others, like the English, chose to return to their homeland. The decisions to strike in both Lonsdale and New Bedford reflected the defiant code of the English weavers to resist wage cuts and denounce what every Lancashire worker called "tyranny," "slavery," and unmanly behavior. This style of labor protest would emerge again in Fall River in 1878.

Meanwhile, Edward Kilburn convinced the Wamsutta's directors in 1878 to purchase the Potomska mills. Andrew Pierce became the treasurer and Hiram Kilburn, Edward's brother, the superintendent. In 1879 Edward Kilburn became president. Another brother, John Kilburn, was employed at Lowell. The Kilburns now "owned" New Bedford as well as Lonsdale, Berkeley, and Ashton. Edward Kilburn managed the New Bedford mills and organized local banks until he retired in 1887, remaining on various boards of directors. Kilburn frequently testified as an expert witness on cotton manufacturing.[74] His stand during the 1877 strike established his reputation and extended anti-union policies in the New England cotton industry.

A consistent managerial policy in New England textile operations was taking shape in Fall River, New Bedford, and in Lonsdale and surrounding Rhode Island mill centers. This policy developed local and regional control essential to market domination over various elements in industrial life: the workplace, partisan politics, ideology, and culture. One primary goal was to divide the nationalities and skill groups in the workforce either through preferential treatment, unequal wages, denunciations of English radicals, or demonstrations of absolute managerial power through wage cuts to humble or disperse the malcontents. State regulation was opposed or ignored. The assertion by mill agents of superior knowledge often deprived the operatives of reliable information on either cloth prices or the direction of the market, leaving them nothing to bargain with. Announcements of unspecified wage cuts demonstrated the power of managers to manipulate through fear and uncertainty, while dangling the possibilities of advances if the market, as they judged it, improved. The cloth market was fast becoming an arena where power and capacity determined relative position and profit. Finally, an informal network of agents and owners in southeastern New England became bound together in the 1870s by both depressed markets and kinship ties. Although often competitors, they worked together to undermine regional wage levels and labor protest. Once textile interests dominated both the community and the workforce, they competed for market shares. But only the Fall River mills pursued the policy of continually glutting markets in a depressed economy using their unparalleled capacity. The Lonsdale and Wamsutta defeats reverberated through New England. In January 1878, the Fall River corporations stunned the workforce by announcing a shocking wage cut of 15 percent, while continuing to ignore the ten-hour law and supporting its repeal. George Gunton led the agitation. The New Bedford strike had failed; the line had to be drawn in Fall River.

George Gunton and the Renewal of Labor Reform Activity

Fall River operatives regrouped after 1875. Some had supported the strikes at Lonsdale and New Bedford in 1876 and 1877, but James Langford and the mule spinner's union provided the leadership. The weavers had little organization. Meanwhile, in an effort to stimulate cloth prices, George T. Hathaway, agent of the Border City mills, had left for Manchester, England, in late 1875 to explore the possibilities of an export trade for Fall River prints.[75] Thomas Almy, editor of the *News*, who sat on the boards of directors of banks and mills, welcomed the return of "reason" to the operatives but ridiculed the weavers in New Bedford and Fall River for trusting demagogues and "knavish agitators" who had duped them into the sufferings of strikes. He let his vision of exports as a solution to the severe depression soar to global proportions. "Fall River ought to take the lead," he wrote. American prints should be pushed into the markets of England, the Continent, the Middle East, Africa, Asia, and Latin America. The mills of Fall River, he argued, "ought to print every yard woven here, and market it [from our own wharves] without any interven- ing agency in New York. . . . [It] can be done and must be done. . . ."[76] English textile manufacturers ridiculed the idea of American imports, holding them to a minimum. Nonetheless, cloth prices generally, and print cloth prices especially, inched up during the summer of 1876 from 3 cents per yard to 4½ cents. This market activity also revived the hopes of Fall River operatives for an end to the punitive August 1875 wage cut.

Treasurer Langford of the mule spinners' union chaired a mass meet- ing of eighteen hundred operatives on August 21, 1876, to send an offi- cial appeal to the mill owners. The operatives and their leaders had watched market conditions carefully. They argued that since prices had risen and the agents had promised that when that happened "they should feel the benefits," the operatives demanded a restoration of the wage scale of April 1875, when the weavers had won their first strike. Furthermore, they insisted that the rise in the market was neither speculative nor short- lived and pointed out that the mill agents were eagerly contracting with cloth printers for the next three months. The agents refused to respond. Indeed, even the threat of a strike in Fall River seemed to depress activity on the cloth exchange. There was no strike.[77]

By January 1877, after a year-long drought had halted production at many New York and New England mills powered by water turbines and even curtailed operations at steam-powered mills, the print cloth market slowly advanced to a steady a 4¾ cents per yard. The Fall River mills ran full time, six days a week, while wages rose 10 percent compared with January 1876. As the largest cotton textile center in the nation with nearly as many spindles as the entire state of Rhode Island, Fall River's capacity seemed to defy hard times elsewhere. But managers used potential divi- dends to pay off heavy indebtedness and meet secret obligations to cred- itors. The shareholders would have to wait. These policies appeared sound, cautious, and unimpeachable.[78]

In the spring of 1877, editor Almy, unaware of the great financial scan- dals concealed by the Borden and Durfee interests, scoffed at reports that Boston investors controlled Fall River industry. He bragged that since 1870 outsiders had held only 5 percent of the stock and industrial indebt- edness amounted to only a small percentage of asset valuation. "Our busi- ness is done economically, and by men without fat salaries. There are no $20,000 agents to swallow up half the profits of a year's work." With Fall River business based on local money and brains, Almy envisioned an expansion from thirty-four to one hundred mills. Fall River would supply the world with print cloth. Ironically, Almy concluded his glorious vision on a note of warning: "The basis of this prosperity is already laid, and only terrible misfortune, unlooked for and impossible to avoid, will prevent it."[79] The concealment of the embezzlements kept most stockholders, including Almy, in the dark until 1878.

Complaints by small shareholders about scarcity of information and limited dividends became public as early as the fall of 1875. In an investigative report in the *Providence Sun,* many shareholders admitted they had never seen a balance sheet or an audit of the accounts and were not even sure that the books were in fact being audited. They agreed that the annual shareholders' meetings proved useless, as the clerk "mumbled" the annual report in such a way as to prevent any information from being heard.[80] By the mid-1870s, the wealth and power of the thirty-four Fall River mills rested in the hands of seven families, connected by intermarriage: the Bordens, the Durfees, the Chaces, the Davols, the Slades, the Braytons, and the Osborns. Jefferson Borden, the "patriarch of the profits," headed the most powerful family. Next came the Durfees and the Chaces. These few controlled power and patronage within most mill offices. On their decisions rested the prosperity and future of the local industry. As for the shareholders, one reporter expressed the hope: "may their faith never bring them to repentance."[81]

The unease began to mount. First, the Providence Tool Company, one of Jefferson Borden's favorite investments, came close to bankruptcy in January 1876. The company persuaded many employees to return their month's pay to save it. They never saw those wages again nor, for many, another company payroll.[82] Borden put his personal credit behind saving Providence Tool as well as the credit of the Borden-controlled Linen mill. In March, young Moses B. I. Goddard, of the Goddard family in Lonsdale and Ashton and the Brown and Ives families in Providence, had to be rescued from his creditors by an infusion of $600,000.[83] This was shocking news. Then Dr. Nathan Durfee died on April 7, 1876, and his heirs found his estate had been emptied by S. Angier Chace. All this bad news and much more was not made public until April 1878, when Chace and Hathaway were arrested for embezzlement.

Meanwhile preventing the repeal of the 1874 ten-hour law and attempting to get it enforced became the focus of reviving labor activism in Fall River. During a typical case in January 1878 against the Union mill, the defense relied on the legal loophole of the word *willfully* while Democratic state representative John W. Cummings presented the case for the prosecution. Two state detectives testified in second district court that the overseer of the weaving room had admitted to them that operatives worked over sixty hours per week. Called for the defense, female weavers responded that they simply did not know whether or not they worked more than a ten-hour day. Clara Brown described her working day as beginning at 6:25 A.M., starting again after the dinner break at a few minutes before 1:00 P.M., and ending at a few minutes past 6:00 P.M. Brown testified that the overseer did not force her to start up her eight looms. In effect, the overseers stole minutes each day by manipulating the starting and stopping times of the steam engines, but at the trial, the operatives were not willing to admit it. The defense called the Union mill treasurer, S. Angier Chace, who swore that he did not know "of a single instance of any person working over that time [sixty hours]." He, the superintendent, and the weave room overseer simply had no knowledge of any "willful" overwork.[84] Stickney's loophole in the 1874 law worked well; case dismissed. Given this outcome in ten-hour violation cases, it was widely believed that many Massachusetts textile manufacturers did not care whether the law was either repealed or not.

George Gunton led the labor reform activity over ten-hour violations. Historians know Gunton as a colleague of labor intellectuals Ira Steward and George McNeill, men active in the Massachusetts eight-hour movement in the 1870s and early 1880s. Later Gunton became a man distanced from labor conflict who, in David Montgomery's words, "ground out books and pamphlets for the A. F. of L."[85] Before that, Gunton was a committed fighter for an amalgamation of all textile workers in the northeast, spearheaded by the weavers. He had, however, vehemently opposed the vacation strike in 1875 as politically unwise. After that defeat, many Fall River weavers scorned him, while the mule spinners' recaptured control of Fall River labor politics. The dispirited weavers focused their anger on Gunton who was forced to leave the city and moved to Cambridge in December 1875. One of those irate weavers was Thomas Evans who, "as an unfortunate victim," suffered with his family months of unemployment and privation.[86] As a result of his unpopularity, the momentum of Gunton's amalgamated union halted in Fall River, staying barely alive in Rhode Island. During the long vacation strike, Gunton had toured the Northeast to raise strike funds and promote organization. The textile workers of Paterson, New Jersey, responded.[87] Later in 1877 Lancashire immigrant Simon Morgan, blacklisted in 1875 as the head of the defeated Fall River weavers' union, relocated to Paterson along with other Fall River operatives. This network of support and communication provided the basis of Gunton's plan for an amalgamated organization of all textile workers in the Northeast.

Ira Steward and George O'Neill rescued Gunton in 1875 by persuading Benjamin Butler to use his political clout at the Boston customs house where Gunton was hired as a day laborer. His wife and children traveled from England to join him in Cambridge where he continued to work with the eight hour-men, many of whom were joining the International Labor Union (ILU), a coalition of American Marxists and eight-hour men.[88] Not yet a citizen, Gunton got involved in the successful 1876 state campaign to defend both the ten-hour law and the Bureau of Labor Statistics. His activities distributing handbills for pro-ten-hour labor candidates angered the Democratic politicians at the customs house who fired him. Gunton and his family returned to Fall River in 1877 where he became the associate editor of Henry Sevey's *Labor Journal.* He also wrote for the ILU's *Labor Standard* in New York City and for any English newspapers that would print his warnings to textile workers not to leave Lancashire for America.[89]

The increasingly discouraged Sevey had tried and failed to turn the *Labor Journal* into a Democratic paper to replace the *Herald,* making an enemy of its editor Walter Scott. Sevey's office was attached in a libel suit in 1877. By July 1878, despite his labor reform activities that year, Sevey gave up and became the local correspondent for the conservative *Providence Journal.* An outraged Gunton never forgave this act of betrayal until Sevey died in a horrible elevator accident in 1880.[90] He continued to edit the *Labor Journal* until with the backing of the Boston eight-hour men in December 1877 he became the Fall River editor of the New York *Labor Standard.*[91] In 1878, Gunton also plunged again into labor politics, agitating to strike the term *willfully* from the ten-hour law and to get enforcement. Before the worst about the defalcations was known in Fall River, however, the state House of Representatives easily defeated an amendment to strike *willfully* from the ten-hour law.[92] Gunton also took the lead against the Fall River mill owners' reaction to the defeat of the Wamsutta strike, the unexpectedly harsh 15 percent wage cut, to take effect on April 1, 1878.

Recognizing the weakness of the weavers, carders, and most operatives, except the mule spinners, the labor reformers sadly but insistently urged them not to strike against the 1878 wage cut. At a March 25 mass meeting, Democratic state representatives Hiram Coffin, John W. Cummings, and Patrick M. McGlynn, standing with George McNeill of the ILU, Sevey, and Gunton, denounced the wage cut but recommended a strict adherence to the ten-hour day. Accept the cut but refuse to overwork; be peaceable but do not yield an inch on hours.[93] The operatives realized, however, that they would lose their jobs if they did not let the overseers steal nearly sixty minutes a week. Agent Jennings at the Merchants mill had already fired one male and two female weavers for refusing to work overtime. Most acknowledged that the mills "hold the winning cards." One weaver advised, "Don't strike . . . , but work on and watch . . . , your time will come . . . , striking now is impossible." Hoping for some kind of concession, Gunton and his ally James Langford approached S. Angier Chace, the secretary of the board of trade, at the Tecumseh mills where Gunton had worked in 1874. Chace refused to discuss anything with the two men, but asked Gunton, what he was? Gunton replied, "I was a weaver and remained at this mill until I was blacklisted."[94] Chace dismissed both men.

The men and women weavers at the Chace mill, however, would not accept any more mistreatment. The overseers promised 22 cents a cut for weaving piqué cloth, paid at 25 cents before the wage reduction. On April 1, the weavers were informed that the price would be 21¼ cents. Other mills in Fall River paid more than 22 cents for piqué. As a former weaver, Gunton immediately understood the injustice of 21¼ cents a cut for a weaver who had to run eight looms, making difficult piqué cloth, which had parallel ridges running lengthwise. In addition, the weave room overseer, Joseph Baker, inexplicably would not pay for cuts woven the week before. The weavers refused to start their looms until they had seen the agent, but Baker told them to get their pay and leave. When they tried, they received nothing. Enraged at the arbitrary treatment that seemed to follow the general acceptance of the wage cut, the Chace weavers went out on strike and sent delegations to the other mills.

At a mass weavers' meeting on April 4 with Gunton and D. H. Harriman presiding, a confrontation occurred that indicated that the youngest male operatives had either forgotten or had come to disapprove of the active role of women in previous conflicts. Or worse, having observed defeat after defeat they had simply lost interest in attending labor meetings except to make trouble. When one woman weaver at the Chace mill rose to speak, "boys shouted, 'sit down . . .'" and made other rude remarks. "She sharply responded, 'who do you want to sit down? You don't seem to have as much manners as Joe Baker.'" She expected to get blacklisted, but refused to work at the very lowest paid mill in Fall River. Other women recounted Baker's response to their protests: "We have fixed our prices and won't change them." Thomas Webb, the veteran agitator, scolded the boys for being noisy, while another operative, annoyed by "the wicked boys in the gallery," suggested that if they had no more money in their pockets than brains in their heads, "they had a damned small amount of capital."[95] Then one of the offenders turned out the gaslights, disrupting the meeting. He was seized and ejected, the lights turned on, while Gunton apologized for their insults to the female weavers. Generational divisions had begun to emerge among the operatives.

Feelings were soothed when the Chace mill agent relented. The weavers went back to work the next day at 22 cents, "colors flying," and everyone was rehired.[96] Gunton also supported the Robeson mill women weavers on April 4 for refusing to resume work before 1:00 P.M. Walking back and forth with them during the noon hour in front of the mill, he was harassed by police. Gunton insisted, "I have a right to tell people not to break the [ten-hour] law, and if you see fit to arrest me for that, you can do so." A state detective, a relative of the politically well-connected Buffinton family, told the women to go into the mill; they were not breaking any law. In a standoff, the women walked in at 12:55 P.M.[97] Grievances and mistreatment after the acceptance of the wage cut seemed likely to increase. The defalcations of Chace and Hathaway, announced in April, followed in September by the revelation of similar criminal acts by Stickney and Paine provided a rare opportunity for radical agitation.

ROUGH MUSIC IN THE STREETS OF FALL RIVER

Gunton quickly seized on the April announcements of the defalcations to turn the mill owners into the targets of a mass English-style public demonstration of shaming and humiliation, laced with mottoes reflecting the operatives' many grievances and slogans of the eight-hour movement and the ILU. Gunton and his supporters had planned this parade carefully, postponing it once because of rainy weather. He wanted a spectacle that would bring out crowds and attract the press. Three major concentrations of English and Irish immigrant mill workers in the city, Flint Village, Bowenville, and Globe Village, contributed nearly seven thousand marchers watched by a "seething mass" of twenty thousand spectators.[98] Music bands from the French Canadian community, from the predominately Irish St. Mary's Church, and from the English weavers' band supplemented by New Bedford musicians represented the various nationalities followed, as a symbol of unity, by the amalgamated union band. Unemployed operatives from the bankrupt Border City and the Sagamore mills marched together. Historian Brian Palmer argues that working-class cultural formation involves processes "as a complex blend of [both] residual and emergent strains," adaptive reactions borrowed from customs and blended with popular politics.[99] James Langford represented the mule spinners' association, but this was Gunton's show.

The procession began at 5:30 P.M. on a warm Saturday evening led by Grand Marshal Gunton riding a borrowed gray charger and dressed in a military uniform, complete with sword and—instead of a plumed hat—a coal scuttle tilted on his head. He was mocking the Republican-dominated Grand Army of the Republic. Behind him in an open carriage rode labor reformers and representatives of the mule spinners and weavers. Among the slogans and mottoes carried by parade wagons were quotes from Mary and Ira Steward on the need for, and blessings of, an eight-hour day along with Gunton's inflammatory personal attacks on mill agents. He scandalized the community that day by labeling William Jennings, the most despised mill agent, Fall River's Lord Leitrim, a hated English landlord in Ireland who had just been brutally murdered. As the march passed Jennings' house, women hooted and sang a parody of a Civil War song, "We'll hang Bill Jennings to a sour apple tree." This procession was Gunton's last public hurrah in the streets of Fall River, his last British salute to American textile capitalism.

Among the major purposes of this demonstration was a protest against the 15 percent wage cut and the continual violations of the ten-hour day by Fall River supervisors. The operatives also demanded weekly rather than monthly wages to avoid credit charges that reduced income. Monthly wages involved many workers in the hated trustee system that turned their earnings over to mill clerks who, after deducting a heavy service charge, paid off their creditors. This aspect of the march, combined with sympathy for the unemployed workers at the three bankrupt mills, was warmly welcomed. Chace and Hathaway were targets in cartoons, "Whom the Lord loveth he Chace-neth." A last minute entry of a wagon carried a jail containing two boys with the words, "Taunton Jail, the Home of the President of the Board of Trade," and slogans, which the *Herald* editor regarded as unprintable. The whole board of trade came in for a lambasting, the strongest words written by Gunton: "The Board of Trade—Qualification for membership: Fools in business management, asses in statesmanship, idiots in political economy and traitors to Republican institutions."[100]

Other themes in the mottoes and cartoons appeared more controversial and even painful. References that stirred memories included an imaginary scene of militia firing into a crowd of operatives, labeled "the 27th of September 1875," perhaps a visual reference to the Peterloo Massacre or the 1876 Tompkins Square shootings in New York City or both. Other operatives would recall that in 1875 they had been beaten into signing away any association with a union. The theme of the factory slave was also prominent, linked to the Civil War. A young white slave stood manacled to a veteran's tomb with an inscription, "Boy I died to free you." In another cartoon, a female operative also manacled was pictured with the words, "I appeal to my maker. Who'll buy?" The racism implicit in references to factory slaves also arose in vicious depictions of Chinese workers as an employers' threat to working-class living standards. One cartoon read, "Cheap Labor. Our future dinners rice and rats." On another banner, a Chinese man was portrayed next to cats, dogs, and rats in a cage. The bill of fare read, "Bow-wow stew, 1 cent; me-eow hash, ½ cent, rat-tail soup, 0 cent." This was followed by a motto signed by Gunton: "If cheap labor be the basis of prosperity, why is China not the head of civilization?"[101] Other images on banners and placards included avenging angels in sunbursts or with swords, bidding the operatives to cut their bonds as well as scenes of idealized family life under the eight-hour day.

As the most prominent agitator in the procession, Gunton provided much ammunition for his critics because of his provocative mottoes:

> Reform saved England from Revolution.
> Revolution saved France from ruin.
> Which are we to have, reform or revolution?

and "The daily press, the organ of the capitalist class." Banners urging the unity of the ILU and the Workingmen's National Party spelled out its political platform: "Eight hours and greenbacks for money; no more [gold-backed] bonds; free land with Government Aid; land thieves and Shylocks, railroad and cotton kings, disgorge your plunder."[102] All this was exciting and colorful, although it reduced controversial, divisive political issues to mere slogans. For example, many English operatives believed the gold-backed pound was superior in purchasing power to greenback paper dollars.

The procession ended with speeches in a city park to an audience of about four thousand. Harriman saluted the ILU brotherhood coast to coast and denounced the defalcators. Gunton followed, congratulating the marchers on the orderliness of the proceedings. The operatives, he insisted, must demand a return of the 15 percent cut. The mill agents would blame the thefts of Chace and Hathaway and claim they could not afford it, but with the falling price of raw cotton, they could give it back. Gunton then boosted the Democratic labor reformers in the Fall River state house delegation, Coffin and McGlynn, but criticized Cummings as "slippery" and not to be trusted. Sensing partisan danger, Harriman interrupted, proposing three cheers for the seventy-nine members of the House who had voted to strike the word *willfully* from the ten-hour law. Henry Sevey, still at the *Labor Journal* in May, defended Gunton from those who had victimized him in the past, while Webb attacked the defalcators and Jennings' avarice. A unanimous vote to demand weekly wages and an end to the wage cut ended the day with a show of unanimity. But in 1878 no progress was made in Fall River on ten hours or on wages. The mass demonstration that pilloried the defalcators reflected spirit and outrage but also dredged up memories of failures and provided no immediate solutions.

Dangerous Female Sexuality

The 1878 procession drew Unitarian minister Jonathan Baxter Harrison from Boston to Fall River to assess certain dangerous tendencies in American life among the operatives in a representative textile center. His interest in female sexual morality among immigrant operatives, English, Irish, and French Canadian, who were unconfined in protective corporation-owned boardinghouses, reflected the perennial fascination among self-appointed moralists and middle-class reformers, such as Henry Oliver in 1868, with sexual scenarios involving vulnerable young women at work in mills surrounded by predatory males. Indeed Harrison judged many of the male workers "coarse and sensual." Surmounting hostility and suspicion from both the "hands," who distrusted all but those of their own class, and the mill owners, he watched the operatives in the mills and scrutinized their recreations. The older female operatives restrained the younger women inclined to be "forward and impudent" and taught them "to take care of themselves," a phrase Harrison quoted from working-women's culture.[103] As in Valley Falls and Lonsdale, young women dealt with the advances of male workers and supervisors and, "were not at all ignorant of evil. . . . The mill girls are familiar with coarse and vile language, and can hear it unabashed and without blushing; they can answer in like terms." Still, Harrison observed no inclination to "unchastity" except among the older English and Irish immigrant females, "as [he insisted] one can plainly see."[104] For most workingwomen, "toil represses passion." Female exhaustion protected their morality, providing Harrison's strongest argument against the eight-hour day, one of the many political issues which he discussed with Gunton, Lapham, and Robert Howard.

After work most mill girls, except for the French Canadians whose families refused to let them go out at night, flocked into the streets and met young men, "our fellers," at candy stores and small music halls. Fall River had several of these English working-class institutions, owned by former mill operatives, where beer, a piano, a stage, and willing customers supplied melancholy songs and recitations from the old country. Harrison's interest in their potential for immorality led him to visit half a dozen, where he observed signs of bodily movements, tones of voice, glances and expressions, and "spontaneous mental action" among both young men and women that gratified his search for suspected sexuality. Young women called loudly to their fellers to "shout," to treat them to beers. Harrison thus transformed the courting customs of English and Irish operatives into dangers to the republic, centered on perceived aggressive female behavior. He also noted to his surprise, that a young "colored man" from Boston, an accomplished song writer, was a well-received and respected singer of popular music and spirituals, regarded as the "best performer in the city."[105] Temporarily in Fall River, the black musician spent most of his year traveling with a negro minstrel show. The appreciation of his art by the music-loving Lancashire audiences in Fall River's music halls, represents a nineteenth-century theatrical experience to contrast with historian Alexander Saxon's view of the minstrel show as reflective of working-class racism.[106] These elements of an inclusive Lancashire culture surfaced here, indicating a potential for broad political amalgamations.

GUNTON, PATERSON, AND THE AMALGAMATED TEXTILE WORKERS

As editor of the Fall River *Labor Standard* between 1878 and 1881, Gunton reached out to all weavers in the Northeast, including those in Cohoes, New York, and Paterson, New Jersey.[107] Gunton's activities in support of the 1878 Paterson strike shift Herbert Gutman's community focus on Paterson to a wider dimension.[108] Like Fall River, New Bedford, and the mill villages of Rhode Island and eastern Connecticut, Paterson was linked to the labor politics and the regional system of textile production in the Northeast, including the influence of interstate labor markets, regional employers' associations and their market strategies, and systems of production in rural areas subsidiary to urban industrial centers. A strictly community focus conceals such networks of industrial workers with similar politics and ideologies who raised strike funds or prevented strikebreaking.

The Lancashire and Yorkshire textile workers in New England and the Northeast could well appreciate the situation of the silk and cotton weavers who immigrated to Paterson from Macclesfield in Cheshire, from Coventry in Warwickshire, and from Krefeld, Germany. They too had brought with them industrial and urban experience. Their immigrant cultures had not been cruelly uprooted or carefully transplanted, but transferred as a resource for labor politics and as an ideological and moral refuge against the dominant political culture of textile capitalism.[109] The silk weavers of Paterson, like the Lancashire immigrants, English and Irish-born, tried to remake the American textile industry, using their own political traditions for agitation and confrontation.[110] The central lesson of Lancashire experience, spoke to them. Win, lose, or draw, organized resistance operating in the broadest possible arena was the key to obtaining power in any single community and essential to counteracting the cultural fragmentation inherent in American industrial life. Gunton believed that Lancashire labor politics contained values and strategies relevant to all textile workers. For him, much like for Seth Luther in the 1830s and 1840s, the entire textile world was Lancashire. In the late summer of 1878, Paterson became one of the sites of agitation.

Gunton was briefly in Paterson during the strike to promote the amalgamated weavers' branch of the ILU with J. P. McDonnell and McNeill.[111] He used the *Labor Standard* to make the weavers' strike at a mosquito netting factory infamous among the wider community of textile workers in the Northeast and to raise strike funds and warn away strikebreakers. He alerted the operatives in Fall River to the presence of an agent hiring strikebreakers and demanded that the local ILU weavers prevent it. He assisted in drafting a standard list of wages for New Jersey weavers and encouraged the women weavers in Paterson who became the heart and soul of the strike. Gunton threatened to identify any strikebreaker who went to Paterson to every union organization in the United States and send the traitor's name to the Lancashire mule spinners' and weavers' unions.[112]

While McDonnell became increasingly immersed in the day-to-day activities of the strike, Gunton and McNeill kept the *Labor Standard* going. Gunton exulted over a series of grand demonstrations similar to the Fall River activities in May, but soon the strike committee dropped these tactics as harmful to the cause.[113] He cautioned the silk workers in Paterson to wait until the weavers' strike had been won to press their own grievances. Gunton also used his considerable skills at ridicule. For example, when one of the mill agents had a female striker arrested for yelling "scab," Gunton threatened a countersuit for public obscenity against the hot-tempered agent, who frequently raged at the strikers in the streets. But to Gunton's great embarrassment, that scab was from Fall River. Despite his efforts to prevent it, five women and thirty men from Fall River went to fill the jobs of striking weavers in Paterson, although all but eight returned.[114] Turning his invective against those traitors, Gunton characterized Fall River operatives as "the worst" in the treatment of Paterson strikers, both for failing to send financial aid and for being the only textile center to send strikebreakers.[115] He may have been developing regional contacts, but his local support in Fall River was dwindling. Gunton labeled one strikebreaker, Thomas Bolton, a "treacherous" toady and memorialized him in the lines of Irish poet Tom Moore:

> Oh, for a tongue to curse the slave
> Whose treason like a deadly blight
> Comes o'er the counsels of the brave
> And blasts them in their hour of might!
> Just prophet, let the damned one dwell
> Full in the sight of paradise,
> Beholding heaven and feeling hell![116]

The attempt by Fall River manufacturers to resume an eleven-hour day beginning at the Robeson mill on October 13, 1878, in defiance of state law shifted Gunton's attention to Fall River and partisan politics. McDonnell became the man of the hour in Paterson, establishing in October 1878 a Paterson edition of the *Labor Standard* and surviving a libel conviction that endeared him to New Jersey textile workers who promptly paid his fine and costs.[117] McDonnell's popularity with the strikers in 1878 must have made Gunton uneasy about the decline of his own fortunes in Fall River. Finally in late December 1878 with the Paterson strikers still holding firm, the ILU held its first convention, not in Massachusetts, but in New Jersey, and for very good reasons. The vitality and success of the labor movement in Paterson contrasted sharply with the disarray in Fall River. Still, Gunton's dream of an American Lancashire seemed partly vindicated as the ILU resolved to work in cooperation with British trade unions and to send delegates to the next English trade union congress.[118] But Gunton's weakening position in Fall River led him to make some serious political misjudgments.

PARTISAN POLITICS AND LABOR REFORM

The state and municipal elections of 1878 ended the coalition in Fall River between labor reformers, the eight-hour men and supporters of the ILU, and the local Democratic party, further undermining Gunton's position. This alliance, which had won passage of the ten-hour law in 1874, operated in the legislature to protect it from repeal and lobbied to strike the word *willfully* as a loophole. Labor reformer Louis Lapham had received the Democratic nomination for mayor in 1875, 1876, 1877, each election increasing his percentage of the vote and giving the Republican nominees James Davenport in 1875 and 1876 and Crawford Lindsey in 1877 some close races.[119] By 1877 all three state representatives from the Eighth Bristol District were Democrats: retailer Coffin, an eight-hour man close to Gunton and McNeill; storekeeper McGlynn; and attorney Cummings who had prosecuted ten-hour violation cases, always losing them to the loophole. But in 1877 Republican state Senator Charles J. Holmes carried Fall River by only 364 votes. Democratic Party fortunes were on the rise. The local state representatives lobbied hard with other Democrats and labor reformers to get the ten-hour law enforced, but in the spring of 1878 Gunton openly opposed Cummings and wanted another man nominated.[120] Cummings, however, had the strong support of editor Scott of the *Fall River Herald,* who had tired of the influence of labor reformers in local Democratic nominations and refused to back the former editor Lapham for a fourth try for mayor in 1878. The focus of this partisan political infighting became George Gunton.

Gunton had planned, organized, and led the spectacular demonstration against the defalcators in May. In October he walked the street in front of the Robeson mill in support of the striking operatives and ten hours. The Robeson mills' managers backed down from their plan to run an eleven-hour day under citywide pressure from operatives and their supporters. French Canadian operatives attended labor rallies.[121] Gunton was Fall River's premier agitator, but many had come to view him as an outsider with his primary interests elsewhere. Cummings criticized Gunton's self-appointed leadership of the operatives and challenged his calls for labor meetings without consulting either the mule spinners' or the weavers' associations.[122] The 1878 candidacy of Benjamin Butler on a Greenback-Labor Reform ticket against the former Republican governor Thomas Talbot, who had signed the ten-hour law, split the Democratic Party in Fall River and statewide. Butler won the support of most of the city's textile workers, but representative Cummings, sensing an impending defeat, held off endorsing Butler, fearing that many party Democrats would vote for Talbot. Cummings did not even attend the Butler Democrats' convention that nominated him for representative over Gunton's objections. He accepted their nomination only four days before the election. Meanwhile a Democratic/Labor Reform convention nominated Coffin and McGlynn, but not Cummings, replacing him with a laborer, Marcus Leonard.

Butler was beaten badly statewide in 1878, carrying Fall River by only 575 votes. In 1874 Democratic Governor Gaston had done much better. Many Democrats supported Talbot and split their tickets, electing

McGlynn, Cummings, and to his surprise, the late nominee Leonard over the incumbent labor reformer Hiram Coffin. The coalition between labor reformers and Democrats had come apart. The Democratic candidate for state Senate, Jonathan L. Hilliard, an old-line Democrat, carried Fall River over Republican Weaver Osborn, but Osborn, an opponent of the ten-hour law, won the election by 35 votes in the senate district with no provision for a recount. Those who feared a mass defection of Democrats to Talbot were right. The editor of the *Herald* used both the defeat of Butler and the election of Cummings to vilify Gunton, McNeill, and Coffin with a bitterness that focused on their personalities and failings. The *Herald* had championed the Robeson strikers and demanded enforcement of the ten-hour day, but letters to the editor before and after the election heaped blame on Gunton, the "fraud," the Boston labor reformers, those "dangerous wire-pullers," and the *Labor Standard,* that "labor rag."[123] One invited Gunton to depart:

> Gunton[,] weakest of the biped race,
> Leave Fall River with disgrace.
> Never again to show the face
> of yourself, McNeill or Coffin[124]

It would take more than invective to get rid of Gunton or the Fall River *Labor Standard.*

On November 27, the city Democratic Party decided to nominate Republican Crawford Lindsey for mayor. Lindsey, president of the well-regarded King Philip mill, had never violated the ten-hour law since its passage in 1874 and was popular with the operatives. Lapham, running as a labor reformer, received only 227 votes. One politician tried to connect Lindsey with the defalcators, but the key issue was the disruption of the Democrats and labor reform coalition, symbolized by the derisive attacks on Gunton. This breakup reflected the rise of new ethnic leadership in the Democratic Party and the declining fortunes of labor agitation by the ILU or Gunton as a voice for Fall River workers. At one 1878 labor rally, George McNeill of the ILU had hailed Fall River as the "Lancashire of America, where Irishmen and Englishmen join hands in unison." Meanwhile, Irish American Democrats were making deals with willing Republicans for patronage. An English American Club organized in 1876 tried to do the same thing. Unity in 1878 had given way to fighting among ethnic groups over control of the local Democratic Party and municipal politics. Even in Lancashire, depression, wage cuts, and "dark days" marked 1878.[125] Labor politics seemed stymied and in need of a some new direction and leadership.

8

STRUGGLING OVER AMALGAMATIONS OR TRADE UNIONS, 1879–1884

IN 1879 the Fall River mule spinners had the only viable union in New England textiles, but it was beset with trouble. The biggest threat to its existence was the systematic blacklisting of its members and sympathizers. During the winter of 1881–82, Robert Howard of the mule spinners' association brought social reformer Lillian Chace Wyman of Valley Falls, Rhode Island, the daughter of Elizabeth Buffum Chace, to Fall River to interview blacklisted mule spinners. Howard and Wyman visited the home of an "elderly" English spinner, "Mr. W." His little house represented the best of Victorian working-class domesticity, clean, neat, with pictures on the wall, crochet-edged towels, and a stack of firewood that promised "good cheer." During the visit, his "old wife" rose from her easy chair to serve tea after the interview in which she took no part. Mr. W appeared be the sole support of his large family until the children could work in the mills. Before he was blacklisted, he had antagonized his supervisor by objecting to violations of the ten-hour law and the speeding of machines, complaining that the additional strenuous physical effort would be "the death of me yet." His overseer timed the motions of the spinning frames with his watch to keep them going at full speed until the old English spinner "cursed him in his heart for the fatigue and pain that he was suffering as he toiled."[1]

In answer to Wyman's questions, Mr. W characterized his experiences with the mills' secret blacklist as an assault on his manhood. His choice seemed to be to stay in the city and find other work, losing his place among his brother spinners, or take to the road looking for a mule spinning job in a distant town far from his friends and union. "It was a heavy heart I had that night—for I'm gettin' to be an old man, and my old woman . . . , she broke down a-cryin'." Like other union spinners, Mr. W had been told that he was being fired for poor work, forcing him to spend weeks seeking another place, only to be discharged again and again until by chance he discovered his name on the blacklist in some mill office. He was relieved, however, to find that union activity caused his censure, not a judgment on his spinning ability. As Mr. W put it: "You may think it a weakness in me but that pleased me, and it pleased the old woman, and made her proud to think they couldn't find fault with me."[2] Husband and wife shared the view that—despite his age—strength and skill measured his worth as a workingman.

Mr. W had been proud of his activities as a union leader in Lancashire and spoke with great bitterness about the New England strikebreakers who defeated the 1879 mule spinners' strike. But after months of being blacklisted, poverty forced him to sign away his union membership and return to work, promising to remain silent about grievances and never again participate in strikes. This act signaled a shameful abandonment of cherished Lancashire traditions that had formed the basis of his resistance. Remembering the sting of this, he sprang to his feet and cried out, "I'm humiliated,—I'm less of a man than I was!"[3] His respectable manliness rested both on his estimation of his skills and physical ability to spin to his satisfaction and on his right to work as a mule spinner in Fall River. Mr. W's sense of humiliation and loss of manhood also reflected the weakening of popular radicalism and organized resistance, the aftermath of that bitter decade of class strife in New England.

In spite of a keen sense of loss among some mule spinners like Mr. W, who as strikers in 1870 had rejected the mill agents' use of market forces as the measure of a skilled worker's wage, the mule spinners' union in the early 1880s began to accept a definition of wages as a function of price fluctuations on the cloth market. Their bargaining included demands for higher wages for mule spinning as the most skilled work in textile mills, but the union did not challenge working conditions except for overtime. Adopting as their motto, "Defense not Defiance," the union advocated a family wage paid to respectable and dispassionate men who controlled their exclusive organization. This, Robert Howard believed, was the way to win strikes. Howard corresponded with English mule spinners' unions to stop the flow of emigration and control the local labor supply, while weavers and carders continued to immigrate to Fall River during the 1880s and 1890s.[4] The Fall River spinners' union was pointedly abandoning Lancashire protest traditions for participation in American-style electoral politics as the key to labor reform. The involvement of potentially unruly, disenfranchised workingwomen in labor protest thus appeared both undesirable and irrelevant. Furthermore, the mule spinners would refuse to organize female ring spinners. Womanhood for the unmarried came to mean youth, low skill levels, and high turnover in the workforce, while wives represented domesticity and economic dependence. Respectable, skilled, and cautious union men would operate effectively for themselves within the new economic and political context.[5] The national mule spinners' union would later become central to craft conservatism in the American Federation of Labor.[6]

COMPARATIVE STUDIES of industrial development and labor protest in different communities or regions offer ways to trace parallel circumstances and highlight differences. The key problem in effective comparisons remains the research design. Daniel J. Walkowitz's *Worker City, Company Town: Iron and Cotton-Worker Protest in Troy and Cohoes, New York, 1855–84* (1978) focuses on the differences between labor activism in two adjacent industrial centers in the Hudson River Valley. He compares each community's industries, workforce, politics, and industrial development. His main interest is to explain the contrasting patterns of labor protest. Skilled white male workers in Troy's heavy industry emerge as the carriers of class-consciousness and the instigators of protest in both communities. Troy's ironworkers, led by skilled men of Irish, Scottish, English, and American backgrounds, became well organized by the late 1850s and early 1860s. Their major battles with management occurred during the depression years of the 1870s. The operatives in the Cohoes textile mills, including British immigrant mule spinners, lagged far behind, staging strikes in the early 1880s that led nowhere.[7]

Isaac Cohen compares the labor politics of nineteenth-century New England mule spinners with their counterparts in Lancashire in *American Management and British Labor: A Comparative Study of the Cotton Spinning Industry* (1990). He also ranks immigrant mule spinners, their strikes, and unions as second-rate in their ability to sustain craft control over working conditions as compared with mule spinners who remained in Lancashire mills. Cohen argues that after key setbacks during the 1870s in Fall River, New England mule spinners as a skill group declined into mere machine tenders in mass production.[8] The comparative research designs used by Walkowitz and Cohen, which contrast two different industrial communities and the fortunes of craftsmen in New England and in Lancashire, produce a limited grasp of the dynamics of industrial life. By omitting regional economic contexts for the industries and the workforces in Troy and Cohoes and by dismissing the importance of labor politics among mule spinners and other groups of New England operatives, the studies by Walkowitz and Cohen tell only part of the story. A comparison of Troy and Cohoes with other centers of iron and textile production in the Northeast would alter the picture of uniqueness and interdependence. Both historians argue that significant labor activity among textile workers ended by the early 1880s, but textile workers in the Northeast continued their agitation and strikes vigorously into the 1880s and 1890s.

Walkowitz's study rests on social theories about the vital necessity of adaptation to factory life by preindustrial, immigrant workers as a precondition to labor protest. Thus the timing and circumstances of adaptation account for the contrasting developments in Troy and Cohoes. The need for adaptation before labor activism suggests that many newcomers to industrializing America brought no culture of political protest either to hasten the process or substitute for it. Indeed, Walkowitz recognizes only one significant immigrant heritage in Troy, that of Irish peasants in rebellion against and in flight from British oppressors. These Irish immigrants combined with Yankee and English immigrant ironworkers with artisan backgrounds to organize an industry yet to be mechanized or its workers deskilled. In comparison with the ironworkers, English, Irish, and French Canadian immigrants working in the textile mills of Cohoes seem not to have possessed viable protest traditions. Yet, Lancashire and Yorkshire textile workers brought distinct heritages of labor politics, while mule spinners, according to Cohen, possessed a preindustrial artisan legacy and status as craftsmen. In addition, Quebec revolutionary politics in the mid-1830s produced memories of rebellion and hatred toward the English Protestant ruling class among many French residents of the province, similar to those of Irish immigrants.[9] Quebec immigrants to New England textile mills brought these memories with them. The political legacies of all immigrant groups in industrial settings deserve evaluation.

According to Walkowitz, ironworkers provided "a cadre of male leadership" for male and female workers in both diversified industrial Troy and in one-industry Cohoes. They alone possessed a vital artisan work culture and the labor politics to organize and confront employers. Furthermore, Walkowitz claims that "adolescent" Irish and French Canadian female workers dominated the workforce in Cohoes, delaying significant protest until the early 1880s because of their social and cultural characteristics of dependency and passivity. Thus, Walkowitz's research design produces overt dichotomies: Troy/Cohoes, male/female; skilled/unskilled; artisan/factory worker; heavy industry/light industry; and protest/passivity. An analysis of the diversity and complexity of gender relations and ethnic culture are essential to understanding the politics of labor protest and to provide an inclusive picture of both communities. When labor protest emerged in Cohoes during strikes in 1880 and 1882, women weavers, like those in Fall River and Lonsdale, initiated the activities supported by former weaver and labor editor Louis Sault from Quebec. Regional contacts and amalgamation with textile workers in other centers of print cloth production in the late 1870s and early 1880s, specifically in Cohoes, became the primary commitment of George Gunton and the ILU. On these issues, *Worker City* is silent.

Cohen's comparative study rests on erroneous assertions about the activities of immigrant mule spinners in Fall River. By conflating the events in 1870, in January 1875, and August 1875 with the mule spinners' strike in 1879, he argues that British mule spinners alone organized and led all Fall River strikes in the 1870s.[10] Cohen assumes furthermore that all these strikes were attempts to retrieve craft control over mule spinning operations. In contrast with the success of Lancashire spinners, their efforts in New England ended in failure. Cohen transforms any references to "control" or assertions of power by either strikers or employers during the 1870s into a "retrieval" of customary craft traditions, even when the strikers cited wage cuts and other grievances. But even the earlier mule spinners' strike in 1850 did not attempt to restore the piecer and minder system of helpers or regain the authority exercised by mule spinners in Lancashire spinning mills. In the 1870s, mule spinners along with other operatives fought arbitrary wage reductions and anti-union contracts. By 1879 higher wages for skilled male spinners and the exclusion of outsiders from the craft—primarily French Canadians and women—had replaced craft control retrieval, which had been long lost in the integrated cotton mills of New England.

Cohen ascribes the failure of the mule spinners to regain their craft customs to the power of American managers, largely exercised by interlocking corporate directorates—not unusual in New England but organized in an exaggerated form in Fall River. He fails to grasp that those Fall River managers used "cohesion" and capacity for only one reason: domination of the print cloth market. This drive for market control made it impossible for post–Civil War mule spinners to dream of regaining the craft status they enjoyed in Lancashire but lost before the Civil War in New England. Craft retrieval required a return to Lancashire, and hundreds of mule spinners did just that. Rather than exploring the involvement of New England mule spinners in labor politics with other textile operatives during the strikes of the 1870s or examining their choices about strategy and tactics during and after the 1879 strike, Cohen portrays them simply as the victims of ruthless, indomitable American mill agents, much as Mr. W did in 1881.[11] His focus on mule spinners alone, like Walkowitz's emphasis on Troy ironworkers, results in a limited picture of the politics of industrial life.[12]

THE MULE SPINNERS TRY MODERATION

With the militant Lancashire heritage regarded as dangerously radical and feminized after 1875 and regional labor amalgamations a dissapointment, the mule spinners recaptured the leadership of labor politics and advocated moderation and caution. Secretary Howard replaced the blacklisted James Langford, who with a handful of others had kept the union alive in late 1875. Langford had supported the unsuccessful strikes led by weavers in Lonsdale and New Bedford, while Howard stayed out of public activity. By 1879 he won acceptance as a union leader whose goal was to make his members "as obedient and docile and harmonious as the parts of a mule frame."[13] The union adopted objectives that tried to restore a sense of respectable working-class manhood: recognition of their union by the mill managers and higher wages for themselves, paid weekly and based on calculations of costs and profits. But their employers refused to negotiate, controlling both wages and working conditions. Even as the new technology of ring spinning began to threaten their craft, the mule spinners distanced themselves from the young ring spinners, while working-women, and working wives in particular, became the target of the mule spinners' insistence on a family wage for men. Howard saw no future in cooperation with a weavers' amalgamation or with any other operatives. His national union exclusively for skilled, white, English and Irish immigrants became George Gunton's nemesis.

Howard dramatically shifted the strategy of Fall River labor protest in an important confrontation with the board of trade over the 15 percent wage reduction announced in 1878. In close association with the editor of the *Herald,* the spinners' union in February 1879 first requested weekly rather than monthly wage payments to avoid buying staples on high-priced credit that usually led to the despised "trustee" system.[14] At the request of creditors and for stiff commissions, mill clerks withheld "in trust" the operatives' wages to pay their debts, often resulting in empty wage packets. The mill agents did not respond.

Howard then notified the managers in April that the mule spinners would hold them to a promise made in 1878 to restore wages when the print cloth market improved. The disorganized, dispirited weavers and cardroom workers were not involved. The union made its case for an restoration of wages, citing figures from New York City's *Journal of Commerce* on print cloth market inventories which had fallen from 818,000 pieces in March 1878 to 101,000 pieces in March 1879. They argued that supply and demand would quickly increase prices. Now was the time to give back the 1878 wage cut.[15] In 1879 the spinners' union had many members and a strike fund. Sensing the opportunity for renewed labor activity, Gunton and veteran activist Webb called the weavers together to form a union to push for a similar wage advance, but only 150 responded. This suited Howard who wanted no amalgamation. He also pointedly ignored local labor reformers and Gunton's ILU-backed *Labor Standard.* Later, Howard bypassed Gunton entirely and contacted the ILU's New York City headquarters directly for financial support. Cut out of these activities, Gunton still supported the mule spinners' strike and urged other operatives to contribute to the strike fund.

The Fall River manufacturers were divided over the prospects of the market in April, but they generally opposed advancing wages. The board of trade dismissed the promise made in 1878 to restore wages as "the merest twaddle."[16] Yet Howard's statements appeared sweetly reasonable and even sympathetic to the financial difficulties of many mills. Heavy debts, made worse by the Chace, Hathaway, and Stickney defalcations, plagued some mills, while other agents thought the price of raw cotton too high. Over a third of production was under contract with the cloth printers until July 1, 1879, at 3⅞ cents a yard, too low a price, most treasurers agreed, for a wage increase. Some agents cited 4 cents as high enough to advance wages, but others held out for 4½ or 5 cents or higher. The mills analyzed all figures on the cloth market themselves, and they would not be cornered into negotiations by the mule spinners' interpretations of market statistics. Meanwhile, the board of trade met to coordinate the mill owners' response to the spinners' proposal. They refused to meet with any delegation to compare figures on prices or wage advances for mule spinning in Lonsdale or Blackstone, Massachusetts.[17] Howard counted on the stubbornness of the Fall River mills to contrast with his strategy of patience, forbearance, and moderation. This behavior contradicted everything the weavers had done in 1875. The spinners were in charge and meant to win.

On May 4, 1879, the spinners' union voted to strike at five unnamed mills, while Howard went to Lowell, Lawrence, New Bedford, and Rhode Island mill towns to organize support among the spinners. The Fall River weavers vowed never to weave any yarn produced by strikebreakers in those five mills. The *Providence Journal* forecast a lockout if any mills were struck to prevent a repetition of the successful limited strike against six mills in early 1875. The editor of the *Herald* opposed a strike as did many storekeepers and retailers.[18] To keep their sympathy, the spinners also talked compromise: one half of the wage reduction restored only to them for six months, awaiting changes in the market. Howard's strategy was to appear flexible on timing and tactics yet adamant about the need for the restoration of wages. Most citizens of Fall River, except for mill agents, treasurers, and shareholders, believed the operatives deserved higher wages, especially after the scandalous embezzlements revealed in 1878.

Howard summed up the mule spinners' position in early May with an argument he would take from Paterson and Newark, New Jersey, to Cohoes, New York, Lewiston, Maine, Lynn, Massachusetts, and New York City between May and October. Over the last five years, wages in Fall River for spinning had declined 45 percent. Nearly all of the mule spinners were in debt, their wages trusteed by creditors. In April 1878 when wages were cut 15 percent, cloth was selling at 3¼ cents per yard. In May 1879 the mills were refusing offers of 4 cents, holding out for 4⅛. The mills were running at full production, their stock shares were climbing in value, and cloth inventories were low. These signs of returning prosperity had led the union to seek an interview with the board of trade to compare information and negotiate a compromise. If the agents proved the union's figures wrong, Howard argued, the spinners would submit. A delegation from each mill had sought a meeting with the agents. They were all refused. Howard insisted that the mills' reports on high wages for mule spinning in Fall River were falsely inflated. Fall River paymasters put the wages of back boys into the mule spinners' wage packets, while in other textile centers the back boys were paid separately. An agent in 1878 had told them: "We are all sailing in one boat and if we go down, you go down." Fair weather and good sailing had returned, and the spinners wanted inclusion in that boat.[19]

Howard specifically repudiated the Lancashire model of labor protest. We understand, he wrote to the *Herald* on May 8, that the manufacturers wish no repetition of 1875, "when whole rooms were stopped by the raising of a finger." None of this "annoyance," he argued, had come from "the spinning branch." The source was always the "boys and girls" in other departments. Young people, he stated, typically earned higher wages than mule spinners with families. Howard used the equal piece rates of weavers to argue for a special family wage for mule spinners. "There are spinners working in this city for less pay than girls in other departments [weaving], 18 or 20 years of age in many instances. . . ." For Howard, young single women of twenty were "girls," whatever earnings they might be supplying for themselves, dependents, or family, while married men with four or five family members deserved more as responsible heads of families. Howard made it clear that the spinners' union did not want a strike in 1879 but reconciliation with the mill agents, perhaps leading to arbitration.[20] The agents opposed this proposal as stoutly as any of the weavers' demands in 1875. Still, the goal of arbitration, the agents' refusal, the arguments about the family wage, and the direction of market prices set up a different political and ideological framework for the bitter contest in 1879. The mule spinners wished only to sit down as reasonable men and compare facts. The mill agents would never sit down with them.

Howard's waiting game established his reputation as a dispassionate man of reason. On May 11, the spinners postponed the decision to choose exactly which five mills to strike, delaying it again and again to divide the mill agents and to gain public sympathy. The *Herald* praised Howard's decisions as manly and generous, free of bitterness or desire for mastery of the situation. We don't want a strike, Howard insisted. "Strikes do not pay. . . ." Most newspaper editors and reporters reacted to strikes by calculating the losses in wages and profits, making issues of power and justice seem irrelevant. Howard appeared to be embracing this point of view, at least for the time being. Exercising "wise, manly," praiseworthy conduct, the secretary suggested that if some mills had contracts under the current market price until July, then the decision to strike could wait. Meanwhile, all spinners would stand by their union. "Be united as one man . . . ;" avoid all anger or law breaking.[21] Howard's ability to direct the spinners' union and its decisions indicated his powerful control of the organization and its representation of working-class manhood. The 1879 strike would contest all of this.

The secretary continued to disassociate the spinners from labor protest in 1875. Attacking Gunton and Sevey, he insisted that the spinners had never voted for the disastrous August vacation strike or advocated Lancashire moral values as superior to the workings of the marketplace.[22] Instead, Howard relied on supply and demand arguments. He criticized the frenzied activity, harsh language, and "folly" of 1875, supporting instead a concept of mutual interests between employer and employed. We want, he wrote, "to get nearer to them," to gain their sympathy. Let there be no more outside interference from politicians, journalists, or labor reformers without involvement in Fall River industry. "Reverses met in times past should not soon be forgot, . . . [but] let us fight it out on a different basis than we have done heretofore. . . ." He meant a contest carried on by skilled organized workingmen—respectfully, dispassionately, and in the midst of a rising market. If the mill agents would agree to conciliation, he promised, there would be no strike.[23]

The weavers remained almost totally apathetic. Gunton, who featured the spinners' activities in the *Labor Standard,* called another weavers' meeting, but it was canceled when only 50 young men showed up. That same night, about one thousand of the key male militants among the weavers, including the sons of activists Louis Lapham, Jonathan Biltcliffe, and Jonathan Clegg, attended a meeting of the fraternal lodge of the Ancient Order of Foresters, popular with English immigrants. At the small weavers' meeting, "one man said, '[this] means that the spinners will get the advance and the weavers won't.'" One experienced agitator among them had never seen such "disgusting apathy." Someone in the audience denigrated the passive weavers as "half-hearted, milk-sop manlings," in contrast with the mule spinners.[24] Activism, not passivity, still defined the meaning of manhood for these weavers.

Gunton staged another weavers' meeting with two local Democratic state representatives and Charles Litchman, the secretary of the Knights of St. Crispin, centered in the shoemaking city of Lynn. Gunton admitted his shame, pointing out that the weavers far outnumbered the spinners and that Fall River used "to be the banner city in labor matters. . . ."[25] Litchman counseled organization but no strike. Build a union, he argued, during the rising prosperity: be calm, let reason and common sense prevail, and, like the spinners, seek arbitration. A weavers' committee formed, but little action was expected. The spinners' union wished to avoid a lockout, if possible, and urged the weavers to continue to work and contribute to the spinners' strike fund. After the women weavers at the Robeson mill announced they would strike in support of the spinners, Howard advised them not to become "combatants" but to remain passive, implying that, if the spinners' won, weavers' wages probably would be raised.[26] But the mills could much better afford to increase the wages of one thousand men than fourteen thousand operatives. Most of all, Howard wished to prevent any militant weavers' uprising.

The mill agents continued to refuse conciliation or arbitration as unheard of in American business relations with labor. "It is foreign and we will not inaugurate it here." Howard assured them that his organization represented only mule spinners and no other branch or amalgamation. The wage advance would go to "males and heads of families" to shield their manhood from the shame of an empty pay envelope, considered "a disgrace in the eyes of their fellowmen." In response to his appeal, the "ultras," those most opposed to union recognition on the board of trade, decreed that if any mill were struck, there would be a lockout just as in September 1875. Any person who participated would be blacklisted. Ring-spinning frames would be introduced as rapidly as possible to replace mule spinners. Howard expressed no fear of this, insisting that the men would actually welcome the new technology as a blessing.[27] One leading but unidentified employer insisted, "We intend to run the mills as we please; pay what we please; and will not rest satisfied until every vestige of union amongst mill operatives is broken up in this city."[28] Howard desperately wished to avoid a repetition of the 1875 lockout, but he could not back down.

Curious about this new force in labor politics, the sympathetic Boston and New York press interviewed Howard and the Fall River spinners. A reporter from the *New York Sun,* edited by radical John Swinton, spoke in late May with the "moderate and intelligent" leaders of the highly organized and "shrewdly conducted" union.[29] Howard made the most of the occasion. Described as a "sturdy English countryman" with rosy cheeks, the secretary, who had long left his mules, contrasted vividly with the "pale, weak-eyed, hollow-cheeked, cadaverous set" of workingmen. They told the reporter about the system of sick spinners who replaced regular men worn out by "tramping around a narrow alley in a cloud of flying dust and cotton waste, bending over whirring machinery with a deafening racket about one's ears. . . ."—no Sunday stroll in the country. At noon, dinners were swallowed in ten minutes. "Our machines must be oiled, cleaned, and kept in order. . . . It is too risky to clean [them] when the mill [steam engine] is running." They were obviously underpaid, exhausted men. Because most of the mill owners regarded Howard as a "firebrand and a dangerous agitator," the spinners met in private to avoid the blacklist but welcomed reporters. Howard's reputation among the public and other trade union leaders began to rise. The *Boston Herald* called him "one of the ablest if not the very best man, ever connected with labor movements in the United States."[30]

With no positive response from the mills, the mule spinners voted on June 15 to strike, but Howard insisted that each workingman give his ten days' notice. Perhaps there was still time to bargain. Some spinners speculated that if the rest of the operatives would not strike, the conflict would be lost in two weeks. Others expected a lockout. The editor of the *Herald* opposed the strike but endorsed the spinners' view of their manhood as bound up with well-disciplined resistance to injustice. What could the mule spinners do after no progress had been made on conciliation? If they "tamely" submitted or refused to act, this passivity would question their "manhood" and give the employers the sense they "controlled" their skilled workingmen. The spinners had earned the respect of the community with their calm words and behavior and with their willingness to delay action. That patience had been exhausted, thanks to the "family shoddy aristocracy" of Fall River.[31] Manly workmen must resist.

Howard could not dictate what the mule spinners actually thought and felt about their manhood, but a "Spinner" wrote the *Herald* that the manufacturers should remember that "they are dealing with men, who may not possess as much of the world's wealth as themselves, but who, nevertheless are men of thought and feeling, men who have their rights to defend, not "'dumb, driven cattle.'"[32] Male weavers believed that they too had rights. Some envied the spinners' actions and claims to manhood. While the weavers remained disorganized and apathetic, they deplored the wage cut. To depend on the actions of other, more organized men while remaining passive seemed wrong and emasculating.[33] Gunton continually reminded them in the *Labor Standard* that the weavers, men and women, had always been active. Women weavers had initiated the first successful 1875 strike, and females on ring-spinning frames, if organized, would be active too. Both workingmen and workingwomen, not just the mule spinners, could claim respectability and independence through inclusive organization and resistance.

After the strike began, the spinners' union and Gunton told the weavers to stay at work and remain "subsidiary to the actions of the spinners." Weave on, even with filling spun by knobsticks, and in case of a lockout, go to the city for relief.[34] Many weavers remembered, however, that in September 1875, the city had denied them any relief, sparking the bread riot. A weaver, signing himself "Operative," objected to the disgrace of city relief as an alternative to active confrontation with the mills. "I would rather say to my fellowmen and women, come and share with me rather than lose manhood by becoming paupers" or face the dreaded almshouse.[35] "Another Operative," responded,

> I cannot see that a man would, under the pressure of a starving wife and children at home, degrade himself very much by asking assistance from the only source to which he has a right. . . . If we are to so tamely to submit to the mills, it would sink our manhood more.[36]

Still strikes were necessary "after a long continuance of undisputed power on the part of the employers." But the male and female weavers remained at work and kept up production during the three months' strike. Howard feared unruly weavers, especially those from Preston and Blackburn, Lancashire, whom he regarded as "mobbish" and "turbulent." His refusal to involve them placed the burden of winning on the striking mule spinners. They somehow had to keep knobsticks away from the Fall River mills peaceably, while raising enough money to sustain the strike. As in 1870, it proved a formidable challenge. Their powers of endurance and their handling of strikebreakers would test their union and their manhood.

When the spinners gave their ten days' notice, trouble began. Supervisors threatened them. Some, fearing the blacklist, withdrew their notices but were fired anyway. Several mills refused to accept the spinners' notices, arguing that this violated the 1875 anti-union contracts that prevented more than one-eighth in any department from quitting. Philip D. Borden, treasurer of the Linen mill, withheld their monthly wages on these grounds and never paid them off.[37] Two hundred non-union spinners did not agree to strike. There were one thousand mule spinners in Fall River, 15 percent of the workforce. Eight hundred were union members; 788 voted to strike. Most of the mule spinners were English and Irish-born fathers and sons, trained in Lancashire mills as skilled workingmen, who cherished their rights but not all would join the union.[38] Some mills began to offer the non-union spinners incentive pay to remain at work. These divisions added to Howard's difficulties.

An Adamant Board of Trade Responds

One irate treasurer expressed the depth of bitter opposition among the members of the board of trade. He predicted a lockout of four weeks that would exhaust the monthly wages paid in June and that new spinners would easily be found to replace the strikers. After all, "the cravings of the stomach will soon correct the errors of the brain."[39] He blamed the sorry physical state of the striking spinners on drunkenness and dissipation, while claiming that their figures on the market were all wrong. The mill agents decided, as in 1870, to avoid a general shutdown and keep the mills running with recruits. Strikebreakers began to arrive from Rhode Island and Connecticut. On the first day of the strike, fearing attempts at intimidation of new men as in 1870, alderman Philip D. Borden proposed the hiring of special constables to control the striking spinners. But this time the Republicans did not have the votes, and three Democratic aldermen blocked any action.[40] Partisan politics had begun to contest the mills' control of the city. The mill owners became angry, taking their frustration out on Republican Mayor Crawford Lindsey, a mill owner who refused to join the board of trade.

Mill agents clamped down unusually hard, withholding the monthly pay of those who lived in corporation tenements until they had gone. All relatives of striking spinners, men, women, and children, were fired and evicted. Spencer Borden, son of Jefferson Borden and spokesman for the board of trade, demanded that the English operatives and all those who agreed with them must leave Fall River.[41] "One of the Proscribed Race" pointed out to a gratified *Herald* editor that indeed Englishmen dared to assert their rights and that the only political party that represented the foreign-born of all nationalities was the Democratic Party. "Cannot a man or a body of men ask for an increase in wages without being regarded as lawless?"[42] The mills remained open and running, but filling yarn would soon be used up, and the weavers would have to stop their looms. During the first few weeks, second hands, overseers, doffers, back boys, older spinners, and non-union spinners tried to run the mules. One elderly worker was fired for refusing.[43] The agents tried to hire female jack spinners who worked in a Salem, Massachusetts, cotton mill.[44] Could the mills locate sufficient numbers of competent spinners and protect them from intimidation? This would test Howard's policy of strictly avoiding violence.

William Jennings, treasurer of the Merchants mill, showed the other mill agents the way. He provided strikebreaking spinners from out-of-town with beds and meals in a room over the mill office. When word got out, a group of young men threw stones through the windows. Enraged at the use of a mill yard as a sanctuary for strikebreakers, about ten spinners kicked and beat a weaver, mistaken for a knobstick, on "the lower part of his body."[45] Such actions prompted not only disavowals from Howard, but also led the mill agents at the Tecumseh and Slade mills to demand police escorts to corporation tenements for new spinners arriving at the depot. Some mills built barracks within the mill yards for their new spinners and armed them with pistols. This provocative decision suggested that if the mayor would not act to protect property and keep the peace, the spinners could fight it out. Open conflict was Robert Howard's worst fear.

Mid-July became nightmarish. Prices on the print cloth market fell slightly, while production continued in the Fall River mills. The strikers refused to believe the figures. Wages paid in mid-June were running out; funds had to be raised. Howard obtained promises of financial support from the Central Trade and Labor Unions of Boston and New York City and from many textile centers.[46] The Knights of St. Crispin in Lynn came through generously, but every trade union had suffered during the depression years. Contributions from New England textile workers, including the weavers and cardroom workers of Fall River, had to keep the strike going. After the workday ended, the strikebreakers housed at the Tecumseh, Flint, Slade, Granite, and Merchants mill yards, probably out of boredom, used their revolvers for target practice in violation of city ordinance, but no one was arrested. The sounds of gunfire drew neighborhood crowds. The mill agents, it was rumored, supplied the knobsticks with beer and whiskey, fearing to let them walk the streets. Gunton called it "rum and revolver rule."[47] The crowd taunted the strikebreakers. The situation was becoming explosive. Nothing like this had happened during the 1870 or 1875 strikes.

Crowds of strikers began to gather after work at other mills, hooting and yelling. Their intent was to intimidate, but they were clever, careful not to provide any grounds for arrest or any evidence that would stand up in court. The mill agents blamed Mayor Lindsey and the city marshal for laxness, but retired mill owner John S. Davol, a resident of Fall River for fifty years, attacked the agents as a "sham aristocracy of new-fledged upstarts" bent on becoming wealthy and in the process ruining the city. Howard appealed to fathers and mothers to keep their children home, but adults, both men and women, were in the thick of it. A French Canadian woman with two boys working in the mills—probably trying to learn how to spin—was threatened by a group of striking spinners. Later she refused to confirm this to the police, and her boys would identify no one. There were no arrests. The police found it impossible to catch stone-throwers who escaped on foot into the crowds. "Parties unknown to them" made threats of arson to working spinners. Strikebreakers who lived in tenements outside the mill yards faced personal danger from menacing groups of strikers.[48] Working spinners began to quit in small numbers. Bearing the entire responsibility for the strike, respectable union men chose open acts of coercion.

At the Slade mill yard on Sunday afternoon, July 27, gunfire erupted among armed overseers and knobsticks, city police, and striking spinners. This showdown in the crowded streets led to a district court trial that revealed the political influence of the mill agents on the city's legal system. The next day, George B. Durfee's secret speculations on margin in the cotton futures market and the mill's losses were announced, increasing rancor in the tense situation. Judge Josiah S. Blaisdell of the district court, which had replaced Lapham's police court, handled cases of minor assault, drunkenness, and petty larcenies without a jury. The court now began to hear complaints brought by mill agents against strikers of the intimidation of working spinners. Blaisdell openly favored the interests of the mill owners, who were represented in his court by prestigious local lawyers, such as Milton Reed, the city solicitor and assistant district court judge, and James M. Morton. The strikers hired Democrat Nicholas Hathaway and E. L. Barney of New Bedford, a close associate of Democrat Benjamin Butler. Barney challenged the legality of the 1875 employers' anti-union contract on behalf of the spinners' union. Judge Blaisdell heard cases of alleged intimidation, occasionally finding just enough evidence and assigning sufficient bail to keep the suspect, a striker, off the streets and in jail, later to be referred to Taunton superior court. In this touchy situation over the Slade mill shootout, Howard announced that the union would pay no bail for any member arrested.

On that Sunday afternoon, Deputy Sheriff Benjamin Buffinton, known as a bully who ordered operatives into the mills in violation of the ten-hour law, and also an employee of the Slade mills, dragged a young boy into the mill yard. He had hidden his badge that day, but Frank O'Neill, a striker at the Slade mill, recognized both him and the boy whom Buffinton, aided by a Slade mill overseer Alfred Wordell, was hauling away. O'Neill intervened to stop the arrest, claiming to know the boy's father. He put his hand on the deputy sheriff's shoulder, while Buffinton replied, "You get off, you son of a bitch or I will put a bullet through you." As O'Neill tried the rescue, the crowd stoned the mill yard and the shots began. One strikebreaker apparently had a rifle.[49] At Buffinton's order, Wordell fired four shots; others rang out from the mill yard. O'Neill was hit in the hand and the leg. Buffinton arrested the boy, who was later released uncharged, and took him into the mill yard. O'Neill went to a doctor with nineteen holes in his clothing.

The testimony in district court disclosed evidence dangerous to the strikers' cause. O'Neill was charged with interfering with an arrest, while Wordell was charged with assault on O'Neill. This time, there were many witnesses. On that Sunday, strikebreaking spinners at the Slade mill had attracted a crowd of onlookers and strikers by shouting insults to passing women and children, who had often hooted at and stoned them. Some of these spinners were armed, as were at least three of the Slade's overseers. As the crowd surged forward toward the mill yard, the young boy, George Martland, began to ridicule a spinner, yelling that he could not be both a true Englishman and a knobstick. Buffinton then seized him for trespass and disturbing the peace. The prosecution witnesses were Slade mill overseers, who admitted they were armed that Sunday. They all agreed that O'Neill had taken Buffinton by the collar and had shaken him, in effect "hitting" the deputy sheriff. O'Neill's idea was to shake the boy loose to escape into the crowd, but Buffinton was determined to use the mill yard as a police station. The defense witnesses all testified that the overseer Wordell had shot O'Neill. Milton Reed defended Wordell, arguing that he was under police orders to shoot O'Neill who was leading a crowd of nearly five hundred, a "turbulent assemblage." Legally, Reed claimed, the armed overseers were acting as deputy police in the face of a mob, and Wordell fired in Buffinton's defense. Both O'Neill's attorney and Reed agreed the assault on Buffinton was minor, but Barney insisted that O'Neill had done nothing to justify getting shot. The judge discharged both Buffinton and Wordell, but convicted O'Neill of assault.[50] The mill agents had a good friend on the district court bench.

More Violence in the Streets of Fall River

Two weeks later, eight strikebreakers, half of them French Canadian, went on a drunken spree on a Saturday night, firing their pistols in defiance into the air. Among them was William Potts from Middleboro, Massachusetts. When called "knobstick" and stoned by a crowd of men, women, and children, Potts fired, hitting striker Michael Hurley in the leg. Then he and his companions ran into the nearest fire station and hid in the cellar until the police arrived. Judge Blaisdell discharged Potts on the grounds of self-defense, while the injured Hurley, who had an earlier conviction for intimidation, was held for perjury despite six corroborating witnesses. Blaisdell, who could find no trace of evidence to support ten-hour violations before the removal of the word *willfully* in early 1879, became vigilant in cases of intimidation.[51] That same night, ten strikebreaking spinners at the Wampanoag mill got drunk and fired their revolvers into a crowd around Henry McGee's saloon, hitting one man in the leg. There were no arrests. Armed by their employers, the knobsticks freely walked the streets, challenging strikers and their supporters. The district court judge and city solicitor backed the mills' position, despite city ordinances against discharging firearms in the city and disturbing the peace. The strikers could be shot, and if arrested they could not expect a fair hearing but faced fines and jail.

While the press in August bemoaned the escape of defalcator Walter Paine aided secretly by the Borden clan, the strikers worried about continued production in the Fall River mills. At great cost, yarn was either being spun on mules or bought from out-of-town sources. Ring spinning of warp yarn by women and young boys increased in the Pocasset mill during the 1879 strike. But rather than organizing the ring spinners, the mule spinners favored "thinning" the labor market by the withdrawal of all women or at least all married women from factory work.[52] Contributions from the Boston labor unions and from the New Bedford spinners proved disappointing in August and September, while gunfire was becoming a familiar sound at night. Production had to be stopped. The spinners' union began to encourage a general strike by the weavers and cardroom workers, promising them a wage increase. Henry Austin, secretary of the weavers' committee appointed in April, supported a strike, but first he conferred with the striking spinners. The weavers were already deeply divided over taking any action. Gunton urged them to act like the noble spinners, trust their secretary, and build their organization to fight New England's battles in Fall River. The weavers postponed action until their committee had talked with the spinners' union.[53] The results were disastrous to unity among the operatives.

On September 5, the weavers' committee made public its dealings with the spinners' union. They requested a return of the weavers' contributions to the strike fund over the past two weeks in order to begin their own treasury. The spinners refused; the money was gone. Would the spinners help relieve cases of suffering if the weavers went on strike? The union leadership said no. If actual starvation faced striking weavers, what would the spinners' union do? Nothing. The committee submitted the report and resigned. There was no weavers' strike. Meanwhile on the same day, a delegation of union spinners sought a meeting with the secretary of the board of trade, Simeon Borden Chase, treasurer of the Tecumseh mills, and William Jennings of the Merchants mills to negotiate a truce. The delegation would not insist on the 15 percent wage increase but sought an "honorable end" to the strike. The delighted "ultras" on the board insisted firmly on an unconditional surrender of the beaten union men. As the *Herald* editor wrote, the struggle was not over wages but over power: "mastery" for the manufacturers. For the spinners, the confrontation was also an issue of power: their union and "the recognition of their manhood."[54] At no time, contrary to Cohen's claims, was craft control of mule spinning, a retrieval of the Lancashire system, a central issue. Jennings of the Merchants mill suddenly became gentlemanly and reasonable. He would talk individually with his old spinners but would never speak to representatives of the union or fire his working spinners.[55] Mastery had won.

Varieties of Knobsticks

Most of the striking spinners continued to hold out, but a few began to return in small numbers, a sight that sickened and angered the others. The New Bedford spinners, knowing that the end was near, gave little when on September 14, Howard and others made a personal appeal based on their support of the 1877 Wamsutta strike.[56] The sight of eight French Canadian families from rural Quebec, sixty persons in all, being taken from the depot by wagon on September 16 to housing provided by the Crescent and the Stafford mills drove some of the strikers wild. When the families, who had been recruited by Father Pierre Jean Baptiste Bedard, the pastor of Notre Dame de Lourdes, appeared in the streets, a crowd of about two hundred people, men, women, and children, hooted at and stoned them. Several persons were hit. One man, Mazaire Bouche, who spoke a little English, was kicked, and someone knocked down and kicked a woman with a child in her arms. The French families panicked and scattered. Later that night, five of the sixty were still in hiding. These were not armed knobsticks; nor were they any immediate threat to mule spinning jobs. Facing defeat and humiliation, the anguished strikers had abandoned their union leader's ideal of calm, respectable manhood.[57] The angry mill agents pressured the board of aldermen, but again the three Democrats blocked the hiring of any special police.

Father Bedard had brought these families from their Quebec farms into the strike-torn city to expand his parish. In mid-July the mule spinners, fearing such activity, had appealed unsuccessfully to the Bishop of Rhode Island to pressure Bedard to give up his solicitation of what they regarded as potential strikebreakers. The vicious attack on these families in the street of Fall River alienated the few hundred naturalized French Canadian voters from the local Democratic Party. The French middle class in Fall River had supported Bedard, who preached submission and *la survivance*, arranged for jobs, and established a French school.[58] When the Fall River school committee refused in March 1879 to grant French Canadian children work certificates from Bedard's school, he bristled, charging them with "narrow, exclusive, bigoted intolerance."[59] The activities of the highly controversial Bedard represented for the mule spinners' union all that was wrong with French Canadian immigrants. These tensions between the spinners, many of whom were Irish immigrants, and the French Canadian operatives over work, religion, and labor politics would shape religious affairs and municipal politics in late nineteenth century textile centers.[60]

Many strikers believed that French Canadians provided the core of the knobsticks. A few French names appeared among the strikebreakers, but most were Irish, English, and Yankee. Experienced spinners from Montreal had failed to get steady work in 1874 and 1875 and most had left the city.[61] The Fall River strikers were used to working with the other nationalities, but not with French Canadians. One Scottish spinner, who had emigrated in 1869 and participated in the 1870 strike, spoke of his ten years of "slavery" and insisted that only the French and some "bummers" were strikebreaking.[62] The eight families from Quebec provided easy targets for desperate men, even though in August six French Canadian mule spinners from Maine had, at the request of the union, gone home, refusing to go to work.[63] Before the damaging attack of September 14 on the families from Quebec, Howard had admitted his inability to "restrain all the angry passions of a thousand men!" The violence against knobsticks continued. With the failure of his policies of caution and moderation, Howard lost control of the situation. As in 1870 and 1875, fury and passion overcame reason.[64] The suppression of anger in the interests of the union's ideal of manly respectability did not work.

The mills paid whatever it took to beat the mule spinners' union, including the expenses of unruly, lazy strikebreakers. Their objective was power over the workforce, not market rationality, profits, or cloth prices. Managerial policies of the modern business firm remained secondary to control of the workforce, and, having gained that, profits would rise. Two days before the strike began, the board of trade had hired an unidentified French Canadian resident to find spinners in Rhode Island, New Hampshire, and eastern Massachusetts. The mill agents continued to hire, at ten dollars a head for the recruiter, virtually any adult male who showed up. Their costs included erecting barracks, providing meals or paying board, furnishing handguns, beer, and whiskey, even gymnastic equipment, and (it was rumored) women. The knobsticks knew their value to the mills and frequently shirked work. Some played cards at the beginning of the workday to determine who would start up his mules. Others exchanged their pistols for liquor. "Black Tom" Norton, usually drunk and disreputable, walked the streets, bragging that he could beat up any four men. One night he got a well-deserved drubbing from four strikers. In retaliation, knobsticks at the Tecumseh mills descended on a saloon owned by one of the Democratic aldermen who had blocked the hiring of special police, forcing the barkeep at gunpoint to give them beers.[65] The Peter Toomey family became particularly flamboyant and obnoxious. On the other hand, agents in Providence and Lewiston, Maine, eager for their own purposes to provide strikebreakers for the Fall River mills and keep down regional wage levels, were bilked time and time again for meals and railroad tickets by men who never showed up in Fall River. Those who did produced such poor yarn that the mills were forced to buy filling. The overseers had to get them to spin or step up to the mules themselves.[66] The mill agents over-reached, however, when after the stoning of the French Canadian families, they threatened to withhold their property taxes to make up for their expenses in protecting their spinners. Middle-class residents became furious. As the strike collapsed and the old wages prevailed, the knobsticks either took off or staged their own short strikes.[67]

The behaviors and motivations of strikebreakers varied widely. One Rhode Island man who called himself, "A Temporary So-called Knobstick," explained that a Fall River spinner had taken his job when he was absent one morning because of family illness. Hearing about the strike, he became determined to find that particular man's mules and run them. When he noticed the spinner had returned to his old Fall River spinning room, the "So-called Knobstick" went back to Rhode Island. "I never cared to work in Fall River," he wrote, and "I was not fool enough to overwork myself." He bade a public farewell to the agents "who boarded us free," to constables "who protected us," to overseers "who dared not find fault with imperfect work," to "rogues who rob the operatives," to mill engineers "who start up ... long before legal time...."[68] The availability of such a variety of strikebreakers in New England indicated a desperate need for a regional organization for mule spinners.

"A Satisfied Overseer" got the last word about knobsticks, as many of the beaten but valued old mule spinners returned to work in late October.

> Good-bye, knobstick, go hence to whence you came. ... [R]eturn to your old quarters, the jail. Good-bye, knobstick, from Lewiston imported ... , recipient of free grub ... covered with vermin, ... always a stranger to cleanliness ... , whose favorite company and associates are thieves, ... who gloried in your pistol and schooner, ... coward and drunkard, ... old tramp, terror of women and children. Good-bye, jail bird, wearer of chains and shackles, ... If you never return, you're no great loss.[69]

The 1879 strike had been lost, but Robert Howard achieved some public notice as a moderate, capable leader and became a rising man in the labor movement. He rebuilt the union.

THE PARTISAN POLITICS OF DEFEAT AND REVENGE

The startling success of local pro-labor candidates in the 1879 state elections in November jolted the complacent board of trade. In the aftermath of the lost strike, the local Democratic Party, unified statewide behind Butler's second candidacy for governor, nominated a labor reform state delegation. For state senator, the Democrats chose Thomas Webb, the Irish-born, Lancashire-trained carder, former Chartist and fighter for Irish freedom who was forced to emigrate in 1848. The three state representatives on the ticket were two Irish Americans for reelection, Marcus Leonard and Patrick M. McGlynn. The third was James Langford, former leader of the mule spinners' union, handpicked by the English American political club. State representative and Democrat attorney John W. Cummings had his eye on the senate seat but failed to be renominated for a third term. Cummings supported biennial state elections, while Webb campaigned fiercely for annual elections as essential to a genuine republic. Webb's chances in his first run at office were regarded by everyone, including himself, as poor, but Democrat Butler, although losing to Republican Lieutenant Governor John D. Long, carried Fall River by a 1,200 vote majority by bringing out the Democrats and workingmen of all nationalities. In the Eighth District's town of Somerset, local ironworkers rallied against the Republican farmers and townsmen to help elect Webb district-wide by 70 votes, while all three Democratic candidates for state representatives won.[70] Fall River Republicans were shocked into some clever politics for the December city elections.

Although city solicitor Milton Reed badly wanted to be mayor, the Republican city committee carefully chose a more neutral candidate, one uninvolved with defending armed strikebreakers in 1879 or bringing in the state militia in 1875. William S. Greene, the president of the common council and the son of the city's postmaster, appeared, even to Gunton, as distanced from the board of trade.[71] No one named Borden could gain any Republican nomination. More important, the board of trade, run by the shrewd pair of Simeon Chase and William Jennings, announced on November 26, six days before the municipal elections, that they would restore the 15 percent wage cut on January 1, 1880. Howard claimed that his moderate policies toward wage cuts based on successfully predicting the rising market prompted the wage increase.[72] Meanwhile conflicts within the Democratic Party over chances at municipal office split the nationalities. Members of the English American club, having arranged for James Langford's nomination to the state house, turned independent, announcing their support for Republican Greene.[73] Democrat Patrick Lunney undercut the official Democratic candidate for mayor, Jeremiah Leary, by endorsing Greene and was still reelected alderman. He rejoined the two other popular Democrats, John M. Leonard and John A. Connelly, who had blocked the hiring of special police. Three first-term Republican aldermen who were elected included James F. Davenport, the controversial mayor during the 1875 strikes, and John E. Buffinton, the brother of Benny Buffinton involved in the Slade mill shooting. The city election reflected both divided nationalities and opened opportunities for pro-mill Republicans.[74] So badly shattered was the local Democratic Party that Mayor Greene won reelection easily in 1880.

The English American Club of about one hundred men of various occupations had backed Republican candidates before in Fall River. That was no surprise. They carried little weight with English immigrant operatives who were probably more influenced by the announced wage advance. Rival Irish American Democrats had just as often undercut each other in the struggle to win office and patronage. But 1879 produced many political contradictions. The Republicans won a city victory after a Democratic year in the state elections. The lost strike had nonetheless established the reputation of Robert Howard as a trade union leader of reason and caution. A well-timed wage concession from a board of trade, much too slippery and powerful to trust, helped disrupt local Democratic politics. On January 1, the board postponed the wage hike for several days to underscore that point. Ethnic animosity and disarray in city politics, involving immigrant Englishmen, dubbed by Gunton "Tories in clogs," and others who failed to support the Democratic candidate for mayor, replaced the few moments of class and transnational unity during the mule spinners' strike. Another contributing factor to ethnic division was the domineering, envied position of Lancashire overseers recruited for the Fall River mills. Stories circulated among Irish American and French Canadian operatives about those English overseers vowing together early in 1879 that no supervisory job would ever go to other nationalities. In addition, many union mule spinners faced racial insults from these English overseers, who insisted after the strike had collapsed that they preferred Chinese workers. If workingmen refused to see the city elections as "a contest of class," in Gunton's words, these divisions were as dangerous at the ballot box as in the textile mills.[75]

GUNTON'S AMALGAMATED TEXTILE UNION FOR THE EASTERN STATES

The 15 percent wage increase in January 1880 set off a chain reaction of strikes throughout New England and New York textile centers that astonished the board of trade. To textile operatives, Fall River remained the regional trendsetter for wages. The cloth market for all kinds of goods continued to rise; print cloth sold at 5½ cents. In fifteen different locations, operatives in Connecticut, Rhode Island, New York, and Massachusetts demanded wage hikes. Initially refused or shortchanged by Fall River standards, strikes erupted in places that had been quiet for years: in Valley Falls, Rhode Island; at the Harmony print cloth mills in Cohoes, New York; and at the Lancaster gingham mills in Clinton, Massachusetts. The weavers in Valley Falls formed a union, demanding "the same that others are getting in the villages and towns of New England." Operatives in Manchester, New Hampshire, who also produced ginghams, supported the Clinton strike, hoping to benefit from wage increases demanded by the highly skilled weavers in this line of goods. Young women weavers in Clinton, Cohoes, and Lawrence led the way. To prevent a mass uprising, Rhode Island textile manufacturers announced an immediate, statewide wage increase.[76]

The supervisor of the Harmony mills at Cohoes, Robert Johnston, a former mule spinner, faced his first strike. He used as many Fall River tricks as New York law allowed: withholding wages, firing relatives, importing strikebreakers, and legally harassing Louis Sault's *Regulator.* When he finally gave in, Johnston negotiated only with the mule spinners "as men," while two "insolent," "impertinent" (probably female) leaders of the weavers were fired. When the operatives returned to work in mid-March during negotiations, Johnston tried unsuccessfully to blacklist the leading striker. Four thousand operatives, the majority of them women weavers, stopped all the company's mills in less than an hour. One of their slogans was "ten per cent and no surrender," the old motto of the 1854 Preston strike in England.[77] For Gunton, this was the true Lancashire spirit, whoever was involved and wherever it occurred.

Gunton agitated at as many rallies in the region as possible, exhausting himself. The time was ripe to try again for an amalgamation of textile operatives within the ILU from the mills of New Jersey and New York to Maine and New Hampshire to demand a national ten-hour day. With weavers on strike in Valley Falls, Clinton, Cohoes, Lawrence, and by early May in Pawtucket to fuel his imagination, plus a weavers' organization in Fall River to set wages, Lancashire standards could be achieved in America. The ILU, however, especially George McNeill, regarded Gunton's plans as dangerously divisive. Once freed from jail on a libel charge, J. P. McDonnell, went from Paterson to Cohoes to mediate the strike, while Gunton tried to ignore this intervention. At a rally in Manchester on behalf of Clinton strikers, he answered a denunciation of French Canadian immigrants as a threat to jobs, made by the chair of the meeting, John M. Harrington. The French are simply poorer than you are, Gunton argued. The condition of one, as with the gingham weavers in Manchester and at the Clinton mills, was the condition of all. Competing nationalities divided the mutual interests of the operatives. Forget, that there was an England, an Ireland, a Quebec, or an America, he argued heedlessly. Then he criticized the Manchester workers for their own submission to the city's mills which encouraged "tyranny": "[Y]ou stand in the same position toward the operatives of New England that the Frenchmen do toward you."[78] Harrington's reaction is unknown.

The onset of the strike wave in 1880 inspired Gunton's decision to organize a ten-hour convention for the national amalgamated union, set a date in May, and issue a call for delegates. In Cohoes and in Valley Falls, the mule spinners had eagerly supported the weavers' strikes.[79] Gunton made room for them in the new Amalgamated Cotton and Woolen Operatives Association which challenged Howard's ambitions for his own National Mule Spinners' Association. In early 1880 Gunton saw himself as the only man fit to lead the textile operatives of the eastern states. His support in 1879 for Howard and the spinners' union abruptly deteriorated. A letter written by Howard to treasurer Jennings at the Merchants Mills—dramatically introduced by a witness at a state house hearing on tightening the enforcement of the ten-hour law—acutely embarrassed Howard. At first he denied he had written any letter assuring Jennings of his opposition to a planned prosecution for ten-hour violations at the Merchants mills. Once the letter was made public, Howard praised the Merchants mills for "being good to its help."[80] The spinners were treated well, working only ten hours, but this policy applied to no one else. Howard apparently believed that Jennings had been impressed by the strength of the spinners' union during the 1879 strike. They had earned better treatment and ultimately had won the wage increase for all. The overworked weavers at the Merchants became incensed.

This quarrel over Howard's letter revealed the vast differences in labor politics between these two stubborn, increasingly contentious men and between the mule spinners and the weavers. Gunton criticized the spinners' union for dividing their own members. Demanding higher wages for spinning fine filling yarn, admittedly a harder job than spinning warp or yarn with low counts, unwisely divided the craft. Gunton charged that the minority of filling spinners ran the union for their own benefit. An "aristocracy" within one branch of textile operations divided workers and undercut unity for better wages and hours. An independent, exclusive union for skilled male workers would undermine Gunton's dream of a regional organization of all textile operatives from mule spinners and weavers to "crossing [floor] sweepers," the lowest paid job in the mills.[81] The further Howard moved away from the weavers' traditions and interests the angrier Gunton became. He believed that only the energy and enthusiasm of the weavers, as demonstrated by women weavers of Cohoes, were capable of generating the necessary resistance against American textile capitalists. Inclusive unionism involving all trades, levels of skills, and all nationalities was the key to building a strong, regional amalgamation. This had characterized the successful strikes in early 1880, but in Fall River, to Gunton's dismay, the weavers had not formed a union. Only the mule spinners were organized.

Gunton's open anger and barely concealed jealousy revealed a growing contempt for "Bob Howard," the "toady" who had written the controversial letter to Jennings undercutting new legislation raising fines for ten-hour violations. Howard became the target of Gunton's expert, but politically dangerous, uses of vilification. Gunton utilized the weekly *Labor Standard,* the only regional labor paper in New England, as his vehicle to try to unseat secretary Howard. Gunton labeled him a "fraud," "dissembling humbug," "plodding intriguer," and "TRUCKLING TRAITOR."[82] The "accident" of the 1879 spinners' strike had "floated him" into the position as a representative of labor. But his moderate, cautious behavior toward the mill owners and his labor politics based on skill division disqualified him from that leadership. "A Merchants Mill Weaver" questioned Howard's "honesty and manhood," denouncing him as a laughing-stock, "an ass hiding in a lion's skin," and a "great *I am.*" That weaver also charged him with "beastly" public drunkenness on a trip to Paterson, New Jersey, as a delegate to the ILU convention in 1878. He had never arrived in Paterson, but allegedly spent the time sobering up under an assumed name in a Providence jail cell. The exposure of Howard's sporadic bouts of drinking during periods of great stress could undermine his public image of moderation and reason. This became a vital point at which Gunton jabbed again and again. The *Labor Standard* carried the headline, "The Treacherous Trio: Jennings, Howard and Sevey."[83] Howard became a betrayer, a hypocrite, and a sellout to the mills. Whatever their disappointment with their secretary, Gunton's attacks forced the mule spinners to defend him, hardening divisions in Fall River. Howard became even more popular when the mule spinners negotiated another general wage increase of ten percent for April 1, 1880. Then he waited for the right moment to hit back.

Meanwhile Gunton tried to form a power base for his operatives' amalgamation and for labor reform. A convention in May to establish a National Ten Hour League failed. Support came from eight-hour men Ira Steward, John Carruthers, state representative from Somerville, and a Boston physician, E. E. Spencer, but none represented industrial centers. Conveniently, the annual eight-hour convention followed the next day. Clinton, Massachusetts, sent the only operatives' delegation. Two weeks before, Howard had held his own Boston convention to organize an Amalgamated Spinners' Union, which Gunton gamely endorsed. George McNeill did not attend Gunton's convention, while the Paterson *Labor Standard* refused to print the summons until it was too late to send delegates, other than those opposed to its aims. On the floor, delegates from the

ILU in New York City and Paterson questioned the competition from the new league for their own efforts, but the revered Ira Steward was chosen president of the National League, despite his plans to move to Illinois within a month to improve his health. The elected officers, state representative Langford of Fall River, Spencer of Boston, and New Bedford's Hiram Coffin were pro-Gunton men. The key issue was choosing a salaried agitator. Gunton angled for the job to combine with his barely paying editorship of the *Labor Standard*. The convention refused to make a choice, thus failing to accomplish its major purpose.[84] There was too much anti-Gunton sentiment sparked by Howard and the ILU.

Undeterred, Gunton began to plan a summer and fall speaking tour of Maine to establish local ten-hour leagues and promote pro-ten-hour candidates.[85] Strikes by French Canadian weavers in Manville, Rhode Island, and by women weavers in three small mills in Worcester, Massachusetts, encouraged him. Gunton fantasized about ten-hour demonstrations "up the Blackstone stream." He also worked hard to organize the Fall River weavers, insisting that they hire a paid secretary, like Howard, to negotiate with the agents. The man should, he argued, be "warm from the looms," but "cool and level-headed," reluctant to strike, but, pointedly unlike his image of Howard, with more beef than beer in him.[86] One weaver responded enthusiastically to Gunton's agitation for a union: "I began to doubt whether there was any manhood or womanhood left [in the weavers of Fall River]. . . . [B]ut these qualities only lay dormant and can be aroused in their purity, power and force. . . ."[87] Months of organizing in Fall River mills where weavers had special grievances resulted in the formation of a weavers' union, headed in late October 1880 by secretary Joseph Stafford, a former weaver and a temperance man.

During the summer of 1880, the Wamsutta weavers in New Bedford became increasingly angry over continual changes in the type of goods woven that altered both the lengths of the cut and the piece rate. The Fall River mills began to adopt this practice of changing cloth types, resulting in a pattern of alleged confusion among the mills' clerks in computing wages as a way to cut them back from the 10 percent increase in April. This was the sort of dispute that Gunton, as a former weaver, could explain to an audience in detail, using the outrage over cheating to organize weavers. Wamsutta's Edward C. Kilburn purchased the fine goods King Philip mill in Fall River and developed close relations with John D. Flint, treasurer of the Flint mills. Gunton had overheard a conversation during the summer of 1880 between Kilburn and Flint, traveling by train the fourteen miles between Fall River and New Bedford. He hastily wrote it down and later described a conspiracy between the two textile centers to undermine the April wage increase. In mid-September, the Fall River board of trade began to consider a 10 percent wage cut. Since the amendment striking the word *willfully* from the ten-hour law had taken effect in 1879, many mills had been convicted. In response, the treasurers merely paid their tiny fines of fifty dollars and costs, while their overseers continued to harass and overwork the operatives. In mid-September Judge Blaisdell provided another loophole for ten-hour violators. He ruled that posters nailed up by the mills citing the ten-hour limit absolved managers of responsibility for overtime. All his political instincts told Gunton, "This is a good year for Labor."[88] He was a hard head and a true believer.

Gunton did not wait for politics to catch up with him. Langford, the English American candidate for state representative in 1879, refused renomination. Who, Gunton wondered in print, would replace him? Someone sober, respectable, experienced, and clearly identified as a labor candidate. Gunton arranged for Boston's eight-hour men to endorse his candidacy in the *Labor Standard*. Most came through, including Ira Steward writing from Illinois who got Albert R. Parsons of the Chicago Trades and Labor Council to support Gunton.[89] In mid-August a hastily organized, very small Fall River Labor Party nominated George Gunton for the state legislature. His platform contained a list of labor reform proposals for Massachusetts that would provide an agenda for the rest of the nineteenth century. Gunton wanted higher fines and jail sentences to enforce ten hours, with each operative forced to work overtime handled as a separate case, thus making the small fines potentially huge. The trustee system and the truck system of company stores in mill villages would be abolished. The one-sided obligation of ten days' notice for operatives to quit, often used to withhold wages and discourage strikes, would end. Gunton wanted fire stairs, rather than the rope or iron ladders fixed to the mills' outside walls. He wanted employer liability for injuries, an end to the two-dollar poll tax, and the protection of annual state elections. No other candidate issued a statement on which they would campaign. Even the Democratic editor of the *Herald* called Gunton's platform "smart, decisive, and emphatic."[90]

The Democrats, still divided by their defeat in the 1879 city elections, wavered. Louis Lapham announced his candidacy as a labor reform Democrat for state representative. Members of the English American Club had their own candidates and, led by Sandy Harrison, harassed Gunton at Labor Party meetings. In return, they got insulted in print. In late September, the local Democratic organization borrowed an employer tactic and backed efforts to silence the *Labor Standard,* having its offices attached for debts and getting Gunton jailed on a charge of criminal libel. On the advice of his attorney, he slipped over the Rhode Island border until his case was heard and dismissed, then triumphantly published the October 2 issue, exposing all of those behind the plot. He also proclaimed the successful weavers' strike at the Barnard mills as the most unified and swift action in Fall River history, a strike joined by French Canadian weavers, "the black eyes of the damsels flashing defiance."[91] This strike and others over the mills' miscalculation of wages on new piece rates strengthened the weavers' union and prompted the selection of a paid secretary to handle such matters. A clever, determined Gunton would have his way. Both Democrats and Republicans shuddered to think of him representing Fall River at the state house.

The Democrats settled on Robert Howard as their labor candidate for state representative to dispatch Gunton. They chose his old foe, John W. Cummings, to replace Webb in the state Senate. Gunton denounced the ticket as full of anti-labor "Irish Know-Nothings" whose lives are little better than "one continuous drunk." Howard had become an irresistible target for Gunton, regardless of the political damage. The *Labor Standard* joined the local press in mid-August in denouncing a mule spinners' excursion to Rocky Point as a drunken brawl. The *Herald*'s story described the scene at the wharf, which collapsed under the weight of the tumultuous crowds: "Broken bottle, old papers, shirts, corks, pieces of women's clothing; shoes and hats lay on the ground near the wharf giving the place anything but a decent appearance"[92] Gunton did not blame the fighting on the union's executive committee, which had tried to keep the peace, but on a gang of rowdies that attacked the carousing spinners. Still, he argued, a union that keeps a drunken leader could not be surprised when the "scum of the barroom attends its excursions." The union must get rid of Howard. The mule spinners had much to do. The board of trade was threatening a wage cut. It had to be resisted, and only the spinners were organized. While disdaining Howard, Gunton focused on the need to prevent a wage cut with a general strike and uprising, as in 1875. For most, memories of that year focused more on the vacation defeat and the anti-union contract than on the April victory. Gunton pressed on. If the spinners would strike, sixteen thousand operatives would join them. "All the conditions of the vacation will then be upon us. . . ."[93] He meant that this time they would win.

THE DEFEAT OF GUNTON

To his disgust, the mule spinners' union decided on October 2 not to strike. Humiliating Gunton by beating him soundly had become Howard's primary goal. When the spinners' union met, those who supported action were restrained, and a ballot on the question was quashed. All was done in secrecy and with speed. Undeterred, the striking weavers at the Barnard Mill, men and women, began to elect union officers. At one rally, D. G. Harriman, treasurer of the amalgamated union, reminded the crowd of Gunton's and his own opposition to the vacation strike. One weaver responded with bitterness, "Yes, Mr. Gunton and Mr. Harriman were the only two in the whole city, who opposed the 'vacation.' " References to the 1875 strike did not please the weavers, but Gunton ignored this. "This meeting," he announced, "reminds me of . . . '75, when the women struck because the men were afraid to strike." He denounced the board of trade's 10 percent cut as a conspiracy cooked up on July 3 between Flint and Kilburn. This calculated swindle ignored the cloth market and reflected the agents' belief that the operatives had enjoyed enough high wages. The issue for Gunton was a contest between corporate power and the weavers' capacity for resistance. If the spinners, led by the treacherous Howard, submitted, the weavers certainly would not. Dredging up Lancashire-style protest traditions, Gunton insisted that if a man is swindled and submits,

> he is a coward that deserves kicking if he don't resist, success or no success. . . . Resist, resist, resist, poor or not, and if you can't reach him any other way bung his eyes up. Resist at first in a few mills, any way resist.[94]

But neither the spinners, led by their cautious, ambitious secretary, nor the weavers chose to resist in 1880. When the Republican Party abandoned its aspiring candidates and nominated Robert Howard for state representative, all became clear to Gunton. Howard had refused to strike in order to get enough Republican support to humiliate him.

Meanwhile, the Barnard strikers and other fine goods weavers built a union and went their own way. After many attempts at a settlement, the Barnard agents finally relented, and the weavers won. An overjoyed Gunton insisted that their united action reminded him of early 1875, while encouraging the weavers at the Troy mills to join the union and strike over the same issue of cheating on complicated piece rates. After these successes, he believed, the spinners would have to consult the weavers' union before making decisions on strikes. When two weavers' strikes were won and similar trouble broke out at the Globe mill, secretary Stafford negotiated successfully. The cardroom workers also organized, but only the male grinders and card strippers, not the female help. Their model was Howard's trade unions of skilled men.[95] As the weavers and carders organized, so they voted.

In November, Democrat and Republican candidate Howard won easily in the city with 3,342 votes, while Gunton tallied only 304. Ignoring his own embarrassing defeat, Gunton exulted in the major setback for the local Democrats. Only one Democrat won a representative's seat. The rest were Republicans, including Milton Reed who, to Gunton's delight, beat Cummings for the Senate seat. The Democratic Party nationally was overwhelmed by Republican James A. Garfield's policy of high protective tariffs to guarantee workingmen's wages. For Gunton, votes for Garfield only empowered protected manufacturers who imported cheap labor to beat down wages. Putting a spin on his terrible showing at the polls and ignoring the fact that there were far more than 304 organized weavers in the city, the unsinkable publicist tried to make virtue out of defeat. Gunton argued that the abolitionists, the Chartists, the American colonial rebels all started with a few principled men. At a roast beef banquet at the *Labor Standard*'s office for the "noble" 304, some of whom were mule spinners, Gunton imagined the beginnings of a permanent Labor Party for the city.

His personal defeat did not deter the Weavers' Mutual Benefit Association, although it emboldened some mill agents. When the Barnard managers attempted to cut the wages they had just negotiated, the union's secretary had a little talk with them. They reversed their decision. The weavers' union could operate without Gunton in the state legislature. Nonetheless, he expressed delight at their strength, unity, and victory. "How soon they [the mills] learn mathamatics [*sic*] when there is a well organized union and a paid secretary."[96] But he reminded the weavers that their goal, unlike the spinners', should be labor reform, not just wage increases; an organization full of agitation on labor and social questions; not just a well-filled treasury. Gunton still believed that they would be the best leaders for the operatives, but the weavers' union later collapsed during the summer of 1881, and Stafford returned to his looms.

After the elections, Gunton felt beleaguered and embittered. He wrote, "I am crazy. I have been crazy all of my life. As the world goes[,] every man is crazy who won't float with the tide against liberty." He compared himself with Christ, George Washington, Fergus O'Connor, the Chartists, the Russian Nilihists, John Brown, William Lloyd Garrison, and other radicals.[97] Clothed in civic duty and drenched in self-righteousness, he began to investigate Howard's background, his immigration to the United States, his friends, and his naturalization papers. Gunton's unwillingness to let Howard enjoy his victory led to his own tragedy.

GUNTON'S REVENGE AND DOWNFALL

During his search for something incriminating about Howard that would overturn his election, Gunton hinted darkly, "It may require more than [the final tally of] 3,349 votes to give 'a drunken perjurer' a legislative seat."[98] Howard's naturalization papers showed 1861 as the date of his emigration from Stockport, Lancashire. Mule spinner Joseph Houghton, an enemy of Howard's in the union, told Gunton and another spinner that he remembered leaving Howard in Stockport when he emigrated in 1872. When Houghton saw a copy of Howard's naturalization papers, he reportedly laughed, "Oh, what a fraud!" He then recalled years of militia service, workplaces, strikes, and the names of many other spinners who knew Howard well until blacklisting in 1871 forced them to emigrate with the union's help. Houghton agreed to testify and brought Gunton a letter sent to him from a Stockport spinner who was happy about Howard's election to the state legislature and recalled his departure on April 24, 1873, after a "jolly good time" at the Spread Eagle Inn. If Howard had sworn falsely to the naturalization officials, he had committed perjury, disqualifying him from public office. Even if acquitted, no man who was not a citizen could hold a legislative seat.[99] Gunton believed he had his man.

With the help of some Republicans, the Democratic establishment in Massachusetts rushed to save Howard from charges of perjury and illegal voting. The case was tried quickly on December 31, 1880, in United States District Court in Boston. Howard's defense team of Democrat Benjamin Butler and Republican Milton Reed attacked the legality of any oath administered by a naturalization officer. Butler's argument for acquittal meant that the entire naturalization process as it had been conducted for years was invalid. The process, not Howard, was flawed. When Joseph Houghton testified, he contradicted everything he had told Gunton. He admitted that fearing the blacklist in the United States, he himself had sworn he immigrated in 1855, instead of 1872. Two other spinners gave the same kind of evidence, saving Howard from conviction. They too had lied during the process, as had countless numbers before them. For Gunton, Howard had already proved a fraud and a liar, unfit to sit in the legislature, but he took his seat, apparently agreeing not to seek reelection in 1881.[100]

Within the year, Gunton sat in the local district court before Judge Blaisdell on a charge of assault and battery on his wife, Elizabeth Gunton. This was a countersuit to a criminal libel charge brought by Gunton against his antagonist Sandy Harrison, overseer at the Tecumseh mills, Democratic city councilman, and former member of the English American Club. Meeting Gunton in the Common Council chambers in April, Harrison had punched him in the face and then kicked him. Labeled in the *Labor Standard* as a rowdy, a scoundrel, and a blackguard, he was arrested for assault and fined.[101] Gunton's printed insults further incited Harrison to publish a scurrilous letter about Gunton's private life. To add fuel to his anger, Harrison lost his position on the City Council in December. Both Harrison and Gunton stood charged in district court in late December, but fascinated public attention focused on the intimate details of Gunton's private life. He had a strong defense team of Yankee Republican James M. Morton Jr. and the politically rising French Canadian lawyer Hugo A. Dubuque to face the prosecution of an angry Milton Reed, just defeated as the Republican candidate for mayor by a bipartisan citizens' ticket. Morton's father had helped mill agents escape the ten-hour law before Judge Blaisdell. Gunton was desperate.

Testimony during the Harrison case severely injured Gunton and his family. Harrison's letter alleged that Gunton failed to support his wife, was in debt, and had lovers. Elizabeth Gunton, according to the testimony of the older of her six children, was a drunken, abusive mother who frequently hit them and their father, severely neglected them, and often stayed with friends, sometimes with men, drinking until unconscious. Their father, separated from his wife, had taken the children to live with him and a sixty-one-year-old housekeeper during the summer of 1881. Gunton somberly confirmed this. One of his suspected lovers was a woman named M. P. Le Compte, a Nihilist from New York City who had been associate editor of the *Labor Standard* for two years and had written for Swinton's *New York Sun*. She had lived in New Bedford for a while as a correspondent for Gunton, signed her many articles as "Proletaire," and had managed the paper when Gunton was on speaking tours. Gunton's oldest children knew her well, helping her set type by hand and getting out the weekly editions. Aside from her work at the office of the *Standard,* where some witnesses, including several policemen, testified they had been seen together and where there was a "lounge," no evidence linked them intimately. Gunton believed that his wife had become deeply jealous of the younger, well-dressed, politically sophisticated French woman. Le Compte left Fall River in July 1881 for Europe after Nihilists assassinated the Russian czar, Alexander II. Elizabeth Gunton also resented the house-keeper Sarah B. Holbrook, who as a supporter of labor reform allowed Gunton free use of her typographical equipment while caring for him and his children.

On the stand, Elizabeth Gunton told her story of marriage at eighteen in Lancashire and Gunton's departure for Fall River, leaving her with three children to support by working in a cotton mill. He sent small sums of money to her in England, but within a year she and the children had joined him. Elizabeth Gunton was poorly educated and uninterested in the labor politics that consumed her husband. She denied abusing her children, or drinking anything but a little beer, but she was a deeply un-happy woman. Gunton had been a different man, she testified, when liv-ing near their families and kin. "He never used me well here." She insisted that her husband had alienated her six children. Her unhappiness was used by the defense in an attempt to shield Sandy Harrison from criminal libel. Both Guntons were on trial. Milton Reed's summation for the de-fense was lurid and full of contempt. Gunton was a sham labor reformer who slandered everyone in his paper. Elizabeth Gunton was an object of pity. The judge, after listening to Gunton's lawyers, found Harrison probably guilty and bound him over to a higher court. The ordeal of the Harrison trial proved too much for Mrs. Gunton. Aided by her husband, she went to his friends in Cambridgeport and returned to England. In her absence, Gunton's prosecution for assault and battery was dismissed, but the exposure of his family life shattered him.[102] The last issue of the Fall River *Labor Standard* was published on December 31, 1881.

With his political standing in shambles and few friends left, Gunton accepted the offer of the fatally ill Ira Steward and his friends to write a book on the philosophy of the eight-hour movement. His career as a labor agitator was over. This was a great loss for late nineteenth-century New England labor protest, especially for the weavers. Not even Fall River, much less New England, became a new Lancashire. Gunton remained committed to Steward's philosophy, publishing *Wealth and Progress* in 1887 and *Principles of Social Economics* in 1891. He believed these works scientifically documented Steward's arguments that shorter hours of work would result in general economic and social progress. He moved to New York City, establishing the Institute of Social Economics in 1890 and editing the *Social Economist,* later *Gunton's Magazine* between 1891 and 1904. Gunton came to accept large corporations, even trusts, to avoid cut-throat competition and low wages as he had known them in the New England textile industry. He remembered his experiences in Fall River well and occasionally returned to the city as a lecturer.[103] Gunton may have brought Steward's ideas to the attention of Samuel Gompers, first president of the AFL.

New England textile operatives in the late 1870s and 1880s had become deeply alienated from labor reformers, especially the Boston eight-hour men. Historian Larry Glickman argues that Ira Steward's philosophy linking long hours and underconsumption represented a radical nineteenth-century working-class vision of the producer as consumer.[104] But repeated piece rate reductions and the speeding of machinery seriously undercut the consumption standards of both organized and unorganized textile workers in southeastern New England. Many patronized the cooperative stores organized by English immigrants that reduced prices on staples and helped them live a little better. The cooperative system, which lowered prices and undercut small retailers, actually contradicted Steward's view that shorter hours and higher prices for consumer goods would raise wages and create jobs. Steward died in March 1883, but by the early 1880s both Gunton and Steward had been marginalized in New England labor politics.

When George McNeill was preparing a book on American trade unions, he chose moderate Robert Howard, not Gunton, to write the chapter on textile workers. Neither Gunton nor the weavers were mentioned.[105] Still, in early March 1881, Howard and labor agitator Thomas Evans, representing the weavers, campaigned, as Gunton had for years, for the Rhode Island ten-hour day. Later in a private interview, Howard, like Gunton, urged Elizabeth Buffum Chace of Valley Falls to adopt a shorter working day.[106] Legislation finally passed in 1885. Howard's standing in the national labor movement after his politically quiet, single term as state representative began to climb. Historian Martin Shefter argues that trade unions and political machines highlighted the late nineteenth-century labor movement, but New England labor politics also involved crucial ideological, strategic, and deeply personal political struggles over the alternatives of amalgamations or trade unions.[107]

THE HARDENING OF THE FALL RIVER SYSTEM

While Gunton and Howard disputed the future of labor politics, the Fall River mills enjoyed high dividends, rising stock prices, huge production, and large salaries for their managers. They refused to alter the October 1, 1880, wage cut. Gunton had written perceptively, "[W]hen trade is dull they cannot afford to pay and when trade is good they can afford *not* to pay."[108] The aborted early October strike by the spinners was followed in February 1881 by a threatened general strike of the newly organized weavers and the carders and spinners. But by then the volatile print cloth market had fallen to 3¾ cents per yard. Inventories had become glutted with overproduction, and the operatives agreed that it was no time to strike. Fall River's capacity ruined their opportunity. The mill owners, sensing their hesitation and vulnerability, hit back. Targeting the spinners' union leaders, they blacklisted any spinner testifying for the enforcement of ten hours in court or at the state house or seen in deputations, on union committees, or in any capacity critical of the mills. Some mills resurrected the hated, ironclad anti-union contract of 1875 to cripple strikes. The board of trade planned to destroy the mule spinners' union during the summer of 1881, led by agents at the Merchants, Chace, and the Durfee mills. At the Chace mills, John Marland, the spinners' union treasurer, was ordered to live in the notoriously foul corporation tenements. He and his family could be charged high rent and easily evicted. Marland refused and was blacklisted. The superintendent sneered, "Come what may, Marland shall never work here again." Howard rushed to defend his union, and the mule spinners struck the Chace mills. Nearly all the Chace mill weavers were organized, but the spinners, as in 1879, did not involve them.[109] The partial strike did not succeed.

Howard reached out to other labor organizations, as Gunton had, to sustain his amalgamated mule spinners' association, later renamed the National Cotton Mule Spinners Association, which represented the workforce in four states. The ILU collapsed in 1882. The fledging Federation of Trades Unions in New York City provided his best allies, especially Frank K. Foster of the Cambridge typographers' union, later editor of Boston's *Labor Leader.* In 1883, Howard became treasurer of the federation with English immigrant Samuel Gompers as president. He like Gompers testified at the 1883 United State Senate hearings on education and labor held in New York City and in Fall River against blacklisting, overtime, female drinking, and the trustee system, but nothing came of this.[110] Howard's organizational efforts were halted by another strike in 1884.

After the disintegration of the weavers' union during the summer of 1881, the "bosses" or overseers in charge of weave rooms began to harass women and men in unusual ways. The violent boss weaver at the Davol mill, who frequently threatened to hit workingwomen, observed a young man begin to eat his dinner before the machinery had come to a stop. To teach them all a lesson, "Boss Congdon" kicked the dinner pail out of the weaver's hands, spilling its contents over the floor. In another incident, an older weaver, who had witnessed this and decided to weave elsewhere, asked for his back pay after working out his ten days' notice. Congdon refused to pay him, knocked him down, and got the yardman to help him throw the old man headlong into the street. The city marshal said he could do nothing.[111] Old or young, the weavers' treatment worsened. At the Flint mill, one zealous boss weaver introduced a category of "second class goods" in print cloth. Whenever he judged the cut inferior, 50 percent was taken off the wages earned for the cut and an additional fine reduced the piece rate to 5 cents a cut. This practice of fining for minor defects in weaving later spread to the New Bedford mills. The Flint weavers immediately left their looms and talked to the agent who canceled the overseer's order. They all went back to work.[112] Still, disorganization among the weavers encouraged experiments in outrageous mistreatment.

WHY THIS TURMOIL?

The rising tensions in 1880 and 1881 led several observers to wonder why Fall River was so turbulent and convulsed by strikes in contrast with other mill centers in Massachusetts, especially Lowell and Lawrence. According to their analysis, the mills of Fall River operated in specific ways to dominate the print cloth market through huge productive capacity. High inventories quickly glutted the market, forcing prices down and discouraging competition. With the huge granite mills in Fall River pouring out print cloth, any competitors would be forced to consider other lines of goods. This system produced unstable markets, low wages, and labor unrest. The refusal of the Fall River mills to observe the ten-hour law, with the exception of the King Philip and other mills that manufactured finer goods, also reflected the pursuit of market power. Each month, as every operative—sixteen thousand by 1881—worked thirty to forty-five minutes overtime at speeded machinery, the mills gathered excess production. "This little margin," Gunton had observed in March 1881, "just serves as a whip in the hands of the manufacturers to reduce wages and harass the operatives."[113] It also squeezed from the overworked mule spinners and weavers a monthly margin of cloth kept in inventory ready to glut the market. Keeping wages as low as possible but maintaining overproduction required the destruction of all unions, at whatever the costs. Market domination would pay them all back. Not all members of the board of trade agreed with this policy. Some thought the attempt to run the mills during the 1879 strike had been too costly, but others pointed to the profits and dividends that followed in 1880. For the leaders of the board of trade, a turbulent workforce had to be subordinated for their policy to succeed. This was a continuation of the old Borden-Durfee strategy of local and regional domination.

A reporter for the *Boston Herald* in October 1880 judged the mills' policies as the narrow, "sordid" selfishness of petty men. They lacked the paternalistic, high-minded policies of the Boston Associates and others who had capital invested in Lowell and Lawrence. Instead Fall River agents had things their own low-minded, disastrous way, and themselves produced the city's labor turbulence. Lowell and Lawrence possessed clean tenements with good board and provided social services for the health and education of the operatives. These mills paid consistently high dividends, it seemed, because they had a contented workforce and no strikes. In Fall River the rules of the mills reflected "soulless selfishness" and "grasping meanness" that treated the exhausted workforce as refuse. The result was "constant fluctuations; now high dividends and high wages, now distress and a strike." In Fall River, the *Boston Herald* reported, "class distinction" and class conflict prevailed, leading the better centers of production to "despise Fall River." The "diseased" mill agents in turn despised and hated their turbulent operatives and treated them even worse. The more contempt and hate each felt the worse the strife.[114] The reporter blamed the mill agents and their policies for Fall River's constant turmoil, as did others.

A labor reform clergyman, the Reverend J. H. Nutting of Fall River, also blamed the mill agents for mistreating the help and ignoring reason in their "unmanly" and unjust refusal to arbitrate strikes or consider a sliding scale of wages adjusted to the market. His carefully prepared sermon on February 11, 1881, based on comparative statistics and printed in the *Labor Standard*, defended the English operatives against charges of insubordination. Their defiance, Nutting observed, came from a sense of justice, independent spirit, and self-defense, qualities that New England men should cherish. When they felt they had their rights, English operatives became "a peaceable and law-abiding class." This was unlikely in Fall River as the manufacturers believed they were fighting "the battle of their whole fraternity." Fall River set the wage standard and that wage standard must be as low as possible throughout the region. The help and the mills regarded each other as enemies. One threatened a strike, the other a lockout. Passion overwhelmed reason. In a powerful moral indictment, Nutting blamed the mill owners for class conflict. The mill owners believed they had a right to set wages as they liked. What about moral right? "You have this right," he noted, "if the power to do a thing gives you the right to do it, . . . if business is not more than a game of grab. . . . On no other principle do you have the right."[115] Using their influence with the state, the Fall River mills complained to Carroll Wright at the state labor bureau, prompting an investigation of labor turmoil in three centers of the Massachusetts textile industry that was designed to be favorable to the mill owners.

By the early 1880s, the highest percentages of English immigrants, explosive growth, and consistently low wages distinguished Fall River from Lowell and Lawrence, setting the stage for complaints about constant turmoil. Between 1870 and 1880, Fall River had grown three times as fast as Lowell and Lawrence. In 1875 Fall River's workforce contained the highest percentage of foreign-born, including the highest number of English-born immigrants. Boasting the highest annual wage payments, Lawrence had the second highest percentage of foreign-born but the lowest number of Quebec-born immigrants, while Lowell had the highest percentage of native-born in its workforce. In 1880 Fall River still had the highest percentage of foreign-born workers in its total workforce, while Lowell retained the highest percentage of native-born, although by that time, the Irish-born immigrants of the 1840s and 1850s would have raised a first generation of native-born children. By 1880 Fall River continued to grow the most rapidly, had the highest percentage of English immigrants, both in the total population and in those employed in all industries. Both wages (in 1875) and values of product in print cloth (in 1880) were lower in Fall River than in the more diversified manufacturing base in Lowell or the worsted industry of Lawrence. (See tables 7, 8.)

According to the *Thirteenth Annual Report* of the bureau published in May 1882, operatives interviewed in 1881 exposed their worsening position as the Fall River system of regional dominance extended its influence. "Our work," said one, was "coarse and demoralizing." Making only one grade of inferior grey goods for printing led to poverty, low wages, overwork, mistreatment, and tenement life unknown in England. Entire families labored in the mills; mothers could not care for them properly. Print cloth production required only low-grade cotton, miserable for spinners and weavers to work and often illuminated only by flickering gaslight. Their supervisors knew nothing of cotton manufacture only "the business of making money." They wanted first-class goods out of poor quality material and speeded production. While productivity rose 22 percent between 1875 and 1880, through the speeding of machines, working overtime, weekly quotas, cheating, bulldozing, fines, or lengthening the cut, wages had fallen 14 percent, a widening gap between effort and pay of 36 percent. English operatives called these practices "the drive" or "the grind," producing the grueling "Fall River walk." When profits were large, the operative's wages should also rise; "It is one [notion] we have been brought up to, and we cannot very well rid ourselves of it," said one English immigrant. But complaining meant being fired and blacklisted. The byword of Fall River was, "If you don't like it, get out."[116] These Fall River workers in 1881 did not seem to realize that domination of the cloth market was behind everything the mill managers planned. For many, the pursuit of profit, not the drive for market power, caused injustices.

In contrast, both the Fall River manufacturers and the operatives of Lowell and Lawrence interviewed by the state bureau scorned the labor politics of the English and Lancashire-trained Irish workforce. The mill owners charged that they also brought with them their habits of drinking, gambling, striking, and unruliness—stubbornly resisting American ways. As the old images of degraded English operatives reemerged, a Lowell operative blamed the "English help" and their old country ideas for all the trouble. A typical Fall River girl left the mill barefooted with a shawl over her head, caring only for a loaf of bread and a mug of beer. In Lowell and Lawrence, female operatives dressed well, lived in good boarding-houses, and saved their wages. Lawrence was the reverse of Fall River's rough, tyrannical despotism. Many Yankee operatives agreed that "[i]ndividual ideas, rather than the collective, rule in this country." In return, Fall River immigrants scorned the American operative as "proverbial for his submission." One native-born Fall River weaver acknowledged a general degradation among the operatives. "Nearly everybody drinks and gets drunk. We are indeed a very low class of people in Fall River. I believe that the work we have to do, combined with the national tendencies of the English and Irish races, make us so." But others defended drinking lager after the exhausting workday as an appetite stimulant, a relief from crowded, hot tenements, and a man's duty to treat himself and his friends.[117] Perceptions of cultural differences weakened the possibilities for regional organization, but class realities offered hope.

All of the operatives testifying in 1881 wanted weekly wages and an end to the trustee system. They recognized that monthly payments provided extra capital for the mills. Fall River, Lowell, and Lawrence workers alike expected to share in those profits when times were good, and they resented wage cuts. Quality products, decent living conditions, fair piece rates, and low prices for staples determined how well they could live. Some outside of Fall River hoped for premiums on special work, sick benefits paid by the corporations, and even Christmas gifts. These native-born operatives hated outside agitators from Lancashire as well as the rude, burly English and Irish overseers. In contrast, many in Fall River would agree with one operative who stated: "I was brought up in England, where a strike was as natural as a day's rest on Sunday." The divisive cultural and political hostilities among the operatives in these three cities enabled the Fall River mill owners to dismiss "the scum of the English and Irish in our mills and their antagonistic notions. We root out trades union members whenever we find them." Many operatives in Lowell and Lawrence regarded Robert Howard and the mule spinners' union as "ignorant" parasites and strikes as useless and riotous, while Fall River weavers insisted that only numerous informal strikes kept piece rates fair. In 1881 Lowell and Lawrence workers did not strike because they believed they were contented, well treated, and well paid in comparison with Fall River.[118] But when their mill managers adopted the Fall River system with the blacklist, the drive, and the cheating, there was trouble. Operatives began to face falling wages, speeding of machinery, blacklisting instead of the usual "honorable" discharge, and the mistreatment of women workers by male overseers, similar to complaints about Fall River textile mills. In early 1882 an unexpected and unsuccessful strike, led by self-supporting women weavers and ring spinners in Lawrence, an action opposed by the local mule spinners' union, belied all that had seemed different.[119]

THE CHINESE OF THE EASTERN STATES

The experience of French Canadian immigrant workers in the New England textile industry, regarded by most historians as a story of families who clung defensively to their culture in order to survive in an intensely hostile setting, proves far more complex. As supporters of labor activity and ten-hour politics in the 1870s in cooperation with other nationalities, they reached out to their compatriots in other textile centers and mill villages. During the 1879 strike, fresh recruits from Quebec seemed to pose a threat to wages and working standards until they became accustomed to textile operations. The mule spinners remained the greatest working-class rivals of French Canadians, refusing to admit them to the trade but fearing them as strikebreakers trained in western Massachusetts and Maine. Historian Alexander Saxon analyzes the Chinese immigrant as the target of organized racism in nineteenth-century California labor politics.[120] Similarly Quebec immigrants became the "indispensable enemy" of the mule spinners. It was a different story for the weavers and carders who accepted and organized those willing to resist. Furthermore, French Canadian workers dominated strikes in Manville, Rhode Island, in 1880 and in Suncook, New Hampshire, in 1881.[121]

A well organized regional network of French Canadian communities in New England and New York reacted with outrage at the characterization of Quebec immigrants as "the Chinese of the Eastern States" in the section on "Uniform Hours of Labor," printed in the 1881 annual report of the Massachusetts Bureau of Labor Statistics. Led by a politically eager middle class, residents of Little Canadas in New England demonstrated a powerful commitment to aggressive cultural nationalism while claiming the rights of white, Christian male citizens. The *Twelfth Annual Report* released in May 1881 by the bureau's director Carroll Wright had advocated the voluntary adoption of a ten-hour day by all the region's textile mills, making further state regulation unnecessary. Among the major obstacles to this adoption of a regional standard, the report cited "sordid and low" French Canadian textile workers, comparing them with Chinese immigrants in their "beggarly" lives, political isolation, and indifference to American institutions.[122]

> They are a horde of industrial invaders, not a stream of stable settlers. Voting, . . they care nothing about. . . . Rarely does one of them become naturalized. They will not send their children to school if they can help

it. . . . [T]hey deceive about the age of their children with brazen effron-
tery. . . . [If forced,] the stolid indifference of the children wears out the
teacher with what seems to be an idle task.[123]

While blaming the French Canadian operative for indifference to overtime in the widely distributed report, Wright ignored the frequent convictions and fines of mill owners, especially in Fall River, for systematic violations of ten hours.

A respected Republican politician and well regarded statistician,
Wright, nonetheless, became the target of organized, defiant protest
among French Canadian communities from New York to Maine, their first
public upwelling of political and cultural nationalism.[124] Community leaders from Massachusetts, New Hampshire, Rhode Island, Maine, and New
York's Plattsburgh, Glen's Falls, Champlain, and Cohoes, protested the
"calumnious" insult of Wright's comparison of their communities with
low-paid Chinese workers, infamous among Massachusetts shoeworkers.
Gunton, who always followed and highlighted local and regional French
Canadian labor activity, described the community's reaction as "a fearful
storm of indignation among the French all over the city."[125] Yet he accepted Wright's general description of Quebec immigrants, but as an issue of class, not race; like the Chinese they were "poor." Gunton was more
concerned about the failure of the French middle class to support unions
and labor candidates in the Democratic Party. During this controversy,
the issues of class, race, religion, and nationality became central to defining the presence of French Canadians in New England.[126]

In October, French Canadians from Massachusetts and Rhode Island,
mostly shopkeepers, doctors, priests, and lawyers, met for three days in
Fall River to denounce Wright's statements as an unjust defamation but
also to push for political power by encouraging naturalization. The potential political influence of the French Canadian middle class in the Northeast forced Wright to confront them at a State House hearing in Boston
on October 25, 1881. Just days before the meeting, as Republican Hugo
Dubuque of Fall River, counsel for the middle-class petitioners, pointed
out, Wright insisted that the report did not apply to the French people in
Massachusetts.[127] This did not save him from vigorous attacks, especially
from the infuriated Ferdinand Gagnon, editor of Le Travailleur in Worcester who charged the bureau with publishing slander and premeditated
malice. This he traced to "the cupidity and avarice" of manufacturers who
recruited Quebec immigrants and to defeated strikers.[128] French Canadian workers did not oppose ten hours but moved about from place to
place seeking higher wages and the legal ten-hour day. Nevertheless, Gagnon insisted "the Canadians are not wandering Jews," but Christian set-
tlers in the United States. Twenty-five percent of all immigrant families
from Quebec owned a house. Despite serious barriers to male suffrage in

Massachusetts, Rhode Island, and New Hampshire, nearly five thousand French Canadians voted and fifty-three held public offices. The "young [English-speaking] generation," Gagnon predicted, will force politicians to "count with us."[129] Many others argued that Quebec immigrants were highly industrious, thrifty workers who were not inclined to strike, but who strongly supported the ten-hour law. The petitioners defended "our race," describing French Canadian communities as full of loyal, propertied, and naturalized family men.[130] In response to Wright's stern assertion at the hearing that "you cannot be loyal Americans and loyal French Canadians at the same time," the French Canadian middle class spokesmen never mentioned *survivance* ideology. Instead, like other nineteenth-century national groups, they actively claimed the rights of white, Christian male citizens of the United States.[131] During the Fall River strikes of 1884, the French Canadian operatives in Fall River would give their own answer to Carroll Wright, to their middle-class countrymen, and to the mule spinners' union about the nature of their labor politics. If a strike appeared advantageous, the workers would participate wholeheartedly.

1884: STRIKING SPINNERS, STRIKING WEAVERS

In 1884 two separate strikes erupted in Fall River, underscoring the divisions between weavers and mule spinners. The cloth market was seriously depressed in all lines of goods, the result of massive overproduction in those New England mills that followed the Fall River model. The sensible policy, advocated by other New England textile manufacturers, by Fall River businessmen, by George Gunton, and by Robert Howard and the national mule spinners' association, was to curtail production through shorter hours. The board of trade refused, claiming that no other mills would agree to this. Their competitors in the print cloth trade had already cut wages 10 percent and threatened to take over the market if Fall River mills closed down.[132] One Fall River retailer wondered, "For God's sake, what do our agents mean? . . . What sense is there to piling up cloth . . . ?"[133] But this was only business as usual: to protect market dominance with a retaliatory wage cut and massive production. The market would sag further under the glut, discouraging all competitors from print cloth production. Operatives would work harder for less. If there were a strike, the board of trade would pull together and protect its members, while crushing the strikers. The Republican Congress helped with a 40 percent tariff on cotton textiles. These policies represented the Fall River way. Nonetheless, dissension on the board nearly broke up the organization in early 1884. The hard-liners, such as Simeon B. Chase, A. S. Covel, and John S. Brayton, calmly listened to bitter accusations from the opposition, but the manufacturers stuck together, however stormy the decision-making.[134] Any mill still running would contribute financially to those under siege by strikers.

After the rejection of their offer of short time and only a 5 percent cut, the mule spinners' union decided to strike at ten mills where wages were lowest, spinners' grievances the worst, and dividends continued to be paid. Those targeted were the Border City's two mills; the Slade mill; Tecumseh's Mill # 1; the Chace mill; Sagamore's Mill # 1; the Wampanoag; and all three Brayton-owned mills at the Union, whose agent announced the wage cut in the morning and a 5 percent quarterly dividend in the afternoon.[135] Striking at only ten mills meant that union spinners at work in the other forty-four mills, could contribute to the strike fund. But the strike also meant trouble for the weavers and carders at those same ten mills. Unorganized, they were not consulted and could not expect any strike support. Robert Howard would not admit that the 1884 strike resembled the "six mills' strike," begun by the rebellious women weavers in January 1875.[136] He would not involve the weavers directly in the strike, except to urge them not to weave with knobstick filling and to organize a mutual benefit association under his personal guidance.

Howard's rhetoric as he prepared for confrontation with the board of trade turned angry and radical. He sounded like a new man, borrowing phrases and arguments from Gunton and the Lancashire past. Resistance was essential at this moment or a worse situation—industrial serfdom and a reduction to the status of Chinamen—would inevitably follow. The manufacturers displayed "inhuman greed for gain" and "a lamentable lack of common sense and ordinary business tact." They did nothing useful but sit in brokers' offices to earn high salaries. The mills must pay decent wages to the mule spinners or close their doors forever. It was a question of submission or resistance, slavery or manhood. Howard's conviction on a trumped-up charge early in January for public drunkenness fed his anger. The police were after him. Judge Blaisdell found him guilty on the flimsiest evidence.[137] Howard's moderation as union secretary in 1879 and 1880 and his term at the state house in 1881 had not bought protection for his union. Unlike the 1879 strike, the spinners scoffed at any ten days' notice. All these themes echoed down through the last days of the strike and suggest the possibility of a general strike of all operatives. Instead division, disunity, and violence dogged the entire three months' effort, resulting in collapse and failure.[138]

When the specifics of the wage cut became public, the weavers, representing half of the fifteen thousand operatives, got the worst deal: from 21 to 18½ cents a cut or a 12 percent reduction. Spinners and carders faced 10 percent. On February 1, the mule spinners' union of 565 men voted to strike, 484 to 81. They insisted, as did others in Lawrence, that they deserved higher wages than the weavers because they worked the hardest.[139] Divisions among Fall River spinners and weavers reemerged with renewed bitterness. One weaver asked in late January, when did the spinners ever care about the weavers' wages or conditions? On the same day the mule spinners voted to strike, the frozen corpse of a tramping weaver was discovered near Pawtucket, Rhode Island. It was John Wilkinson, born in Blackburn, Lancashire, in the 1830s and naturalized in Fall River in 1881. For ten years he had tramped through Rhode Island mill villages, separated from his wife in Fall River. Just returned from a visit to England to see his relatives, he had earned nothing for six weeks. The body was dressed in striped wool with English hob-nailed shoes.[140] This grim discovery was a bad omen.

Weavers conducted their own strikes against different mills from the ones the mule spinners chose and for different reasons. In February the Bourne mill tried to cut 15 rather than the announced 10 percent. The Barnaby gingham mill had a violent bully as boss weaver. The Pocasset arbitrarily lengthened the cut, and the King Philip tried to cut its most skilled or "fancy" weavers more than the mule spinners. The Linen mill failed to provide warps ready to be woven yet held to strict weekly quotas. The fancy weavers at the Barnaby gingham mill, young men and women who were all children of immigrants, expressed a new but ironic justification for their strike against their tyrannical, Lancashire-trained boss weaver: "For we are almost all of us American born, and won't take that old-country sort of treatment." Within a month they got the agent to fire him.[141] The fancy weavers conducted the longest strike at the Crescent mills, where the strikers not only battled a particularly stubborn and punitive agent, A. S. Covel, but also struggled for weeks with the weavers' mutual benefit association to win strike funds. Under the pressure, the association collapsed, and weavers thrown out of work by the mule spinners' strike got nothing. Efforts to form a Fancy Weavers' Union, apart from the general organization, revealed divisions among different skill levels and nationalities within the weaving workforces.[142] A personal appeal by Howard to the weavers living in the village of Bowenville and working at the Border City and the Mechanics mill to stop weaving for strikebreakers failed. These weavers continued to weave whatever filling yarn became available. Howard continued to urge all the weavers not to use knobstick-spun filling and, in alliance with Frank Foster, encouraged them to join the Knights of Labor where he could control them.[143] Regardless of labor activism by the fancy weavers, the mule spinners' strike remained primary.

The spinners' union also faced troubles from within the craft. Exuberant back boys who walked out of mills not being struck hampered union spinners and had to be restrained. Some of the struck mills began to install ring-spinning frames, conspicuously dumping a few mules in the mill yard, although most rings could only spin warp yarn, not filling which required experienced men. On February 13, a delivery of filling yarn spun by union men at the Barnard mills arrived to feed the Border City looms. Howard threatened to strike any mill that sold filling to the ten struck mills, but the threat proved empty. The market remained too dull to extend the strike. Many Fall River mill agents delivered filling yarn, much of it spun by union men, and Providence firms sent filling to Fall River mills. The struck mills also hired as many knobsticks as possible, mainly from Rhode Island and Connecticut, regardless of any harm done to the mules, the costs of wages and boarding, or the poor work.[144] It was 1879 again.

When the strike began, both French Canadian and English workers prepared to leave Fall River and return home to Quebec or to the more settled labor conditions in mid-1880s Lancashire. The Fall River spinners would not train French boys or accept into their union any experienced French Canadian mule spinners from Montreal, Connecticut or western Massachusetts. Many young men from Quebec became weavers and carders, but the spinners' strike in 1884 at ten mills offered unusual opportunities to learn and practice the mule spinning craft. On February 6, a French back boy was working at the Chace mill. Two French Canadian mule spinners from the Wamsutta in New Bedford found jobs at the Border City mill. Others appeared in groups, sometimes persuaded to leave Fall River but always regarded as a threat to the union. Ethnic exclusivity as a strategy was not working. Some French Canadian weavers voted to ignore the strikes and the union, but other Fall River operatives from Quebec, as in previous New England strikes, joined in and contributed to the weavers' strike. A letter from "Tisserand," (the French word for a male weaver) warned, however, that the fancy weavers on strike at the Crescent were replacing other, less experienced weavers at other mills, leaving them with no help, no sympathy, and no honor.[145] French Canadian immigrants judged labor politics in terms of the direct impact on their own working lives.

Simeon B. Chase, treasurer of the Merchants mill after William Jennings retired, was one of the toughest antagonists of the operatives on the board of trade. His attitudes filtered down the ladder of the Merchants mill management. One day, an "old" French Canadian elevator operator, Onisieme Trottier, confused by orders given in English, delivered a faulty warp beam to a boss weaver, John Gregson. The boss angrily tipped the heavy wooden beam back into the elevator, hitting the old man on the toe. Trottier began to curse in French at the pain. The enraged overseer hit him, and he struck back. Gregson then grabbed the man by his long gray beard, tucked his head under one arm, and punched away. Other weavers quickly gathered, shouting: "Shame! Shame!" for hitting an old man. Judge Blaisdell (who later admitted owning Merchant mill stock) found Gregson's actions "justifiable."[146] When French Canadian immigrants were warned away from Fall River by their countrymen, the reasons included mistreatment and bigotry by supervisors and mule spinners as well as frequent local labor strife.

Howard had trouble with his own union men in addition to the three hundred non-union spinners in the city. In small numbers, some became knobsticks, seeking favor or promotion to second hands. Some sought jobs in the Grinnell mills in New Bedford, thus breaking a mule spinners' strike there. These Fall River "renegades" who produced filling yarn were hard on morale. In addition, New Bedford's Wamsutta and Potomska mills, owned by Edward C. Kilburn, sold filling yarn to the Grinnell. Howard was counting on the print cloth market to rise, as it had in 1879. Instead, prices steadily worsened, encouraging the profitable sale of filling. As the market sagged, desperate union spinners began, as they had in 1879, to attack knobsticks, abandoning their public stance of manly respectability. Beatings, stonings, and exchanges of gunfire became particularly common on Saturday nights.

Two unusually violent acts against knobsticks late in the mule spinners' strike began to erode any existing public sympathy. John Scofield, an "old man," nearly sixty-years-old, worked the mules of striking spinners in the Chace mill. He and his wife lived in poverty; he was literally earning his "bread." On St. Patrick's Day, he and other English immigrants were at work in the mill. James E. Crann, whose brother-in-law's mules Scofield was allegedly running, pulled picket duty that day at the Chace. Pickets, as in the Civil War, watched for and identified the enemy. In the public street of a crowded neighborhood, three men approached Scofield as he left work. They struck him many times, and he fell to the ground. A second hand at the Chace went to his aid, but as he supported the injured man one of the attackers gave Scofield a vicious kick and ran. It opened a two-inch cut behind his ear, and he died days later from a brain hemorrhage. Crann was arrested and jailed.

The only eyewitness, fourteen-year-old Nellie Foster who also worked at the Chace, was scheduled to provide the prosecution's key evidence. James M. Morton Jr. and his partner Andrew D. Jennings, son of William Jennings, were astonished to hear her change her story during the preliminary hearing before Judge Blaisdell. She had initially identified Crann as the cap-wearing attacker to state detectives, but when she saw him in his jail cell, she grew uncertain. It had all happened so fast. There were no other eyewitnesses; she could not be sure. As the only child of an elderly mother, a union spinner had taken her under his protection. The prosecution was livid. Democrat Nicholas Hatheway defended Crann, insisting that there was no physical evidence, no weapon, and no other eyewitnesses. Crann's wife swore that at the time he was at home and always wore a hat. Hatheway argued for a dismissal, but Judge Blaisdell found Crann "probably guilty," bound him over to a Taunton grand jury which later acquitted him, and jailed a quavering Nellie Foster on a charge of probable perjury, bail set at three hundred dollars. Attorney Morton made it clear: the spinners' union killed Scofield. Hatheway snarled back at Morton's summation as "a mean despicable attempt . . . to satisfy the desires of a certain class of this city."[147] After the trial, Howard and his strike committee listed those "renegades and traitors" among union spinners who had taken jobs as second hands. None was French Canadian.

Public sympathy for the operatives faced another severe test in less than three weeks. The Toomey family of strikebreakers, notorious during the 1879 strike, returned in mid-February. Employed after a fashion at Sagamore Mill # 1, Peter Toomey walked the streets, armed and sneering at union men, while Mrs. Toomey recruited other knobsticks at two dollars a head. On April 24, they easily obtained a warrant against union spinner Robert Bowden on a vague charge of using insulting language in the streets. Bowden had shouted, "There's that —— knobstick; ain't he a daisy?" He sat the night out in jail and was later fined. The next day the Brayton-owned Sagamore Mill # 1 burned to the ground. Everyone believed the cause was arson by persons familiar with the mill. A few minutes after 6:00 P.M., the end of the workday, three blazes erupted simultaneously in the basement where raw cotton was stored. The cellar door had been left propped open, providing a strong draft for the smoldering smoky fire that prevented the superintendent from seeing well enough to turn on sufficient sprinkler valves. Confused fire alarms were sent, none from the Sagamore. Where, people asked later, was the alarm key? Mislaid or stolen? Fire fighters arrived late, in too few numbers, and with equipment that failed. The mill filled with flame from tower to basement. In an hour it was gone. "The whole city was illuminated. . . ." Mill # 2 seemed threatened but was saved. The night of the fire, Bowden, free on bail, spoke again to Toomey, "you won't work there anymore."[148] Later the Border City agent cautiously refused to hire any of the displaced Sagamore knobsticks. Many suspected the spinners' union, as in the death of John Scofield, but Howard pointed out that the Sagamore, owned by the Brayton family—who also owned the non-union Durfee Mill— was fiercely guarded by watchmen and hired police. But someone had slipped through.

Only the Crescent strikers among the weavers worked out a compromise in early May that allowed them to return in a body to the mill, rid of the knobstick weavers. Agent Covel gave nothing else. The striking mule spinners trickled back to work in early June. By the time the mule spinners' union officially gave in, even the editor of the *Herald* had lost interest. The cloth market remained severely depressed. After Howard's defeat in 1884 for the state Senate running without the backing of the Demozncrats, he sought some solace briefly in the Knights of Labor, District Assembly # 30 in Fall River, and later in the American Federation of Labor with Frank Foster and his new friend, Samuel Gompers. Historian Philip Silvia argues that the mule spinners dominated Fall River labor politics beginning in the early 1880s and that the mill agents accepted "laissez-faire" economic values, not market domination, a position, he claims, that allowed a measure of "independence" for working-class life.[149] But Silvia ignores the contested labor politics among the mule spinners and the weavers, fancy and plain, and the interference of the mills in tenement living over wage issues, and their threats to fire relatives of strikers. These policies indicated a profound commitment to control even the domestic lives of their workforce in developing the Fall River system.

AFTER MANY attempts to organize unskilled immigrant workers in an intensely hostile political and economic system, the American Federation of Labor concentrated on skilled white men in trades and crafts. Bruce Laurie labels this policy "prudential unionism."[150] The Fall River mule spinners who joined the AFL in 1889 had not, however, found the other operatives working in the cotton industry unwilling to cooperate, strike, or organize, even if they proved less able to keep a union alive. And the mule spinners also experienced great difficulties and setbacks as a result of divisive labor politics in the 1879 and 1884. Still, the fancy weavers in particular had skills, numbers, experience in labor protest, and a spirited tradition of adversarial labor politics. Establishing Lancashire standards in New England became their persistent objective. They and the carders organized new unions in the late 1880s and many French Canadian operatives would join.

On the other hand, the skills of the mule spinners faced the immediate threat of the accelerated technical development of ring spinning. Howard publicly discounted the threat of ring spinning to the craft and decided to ignore the ring spinners. Where Gunton had seen an opportunity to organize an amalgamation, Howard feared weakening his union of skilled respectable men. The mule spinners' union struggled to survive in the early 1880s. If, as Isaac Cohen argues, the mule spinners were actually trying to regain their customary craft position in the mills, they were indeed unsuccessful. In the context of the Fall River system, recognition of their exclusive union and higher wages for skilled men had become primary by 1879. These policies represented the core of their working-class manliness, while humiliating defeats prompted acts of violence and further dissension. Nonetheless, the mule spinners developed the most viable organization among textile workers but failed to recognize that confrontation with the Fall River system required more inclusive approaches. Craft control was long gone, while mill managers continued to discard old mule frames and replace them with rings.

The national mule spinners' organization, like other trade unions that joined the AFL—the cigarmakers, the hat finishers, and the building trades—adopted exclusive policies that were intended to organize and benefit skilled white male workers. Eileen Boris argues that, like the mule spinners who dismissed the weavers and later the ring spinners, union cigarmakers decided after a failed general strike in 1877 to abandon "the unorganized and unskilled, often female, immigrants. . . .[151] To Robert Howard in the mid-1880s, these policies appeared politically wise and potentially empowering, but they excluded too many important allies in the textile mills to help the mule spinners win strikes. The weavers, the carders, the women, the French Canadians, the loom fixers, the less skilled men, the ring spinners, the back boys, even the small help, with all their grievances and interconnecting interests and the potential of their united power to shut down the mills—as George Gunton had dreamed—were either used briefly or simply ignored. Howard's approach proved too narrow to change working conditions for the mule spinners, much less for the vast majority of New England textile workers in the late nineteenth century. In the AFL the mule spinners' union would rely on a special, negotiated position on wages backed by a treasury big enough to threaten the mills with the crippling loss of vital skills. How long this "pure and simple" approach might work would be a contest of technology and organization as the Fall River system matured.

9

PIECING UP THE FALL RIVER
SYSTEM, 1885–1897

ON A STIFLING August day in 1892, the Fall River police questioned Lizzie
Andrew Borden about the hacked corpses of her father and stepmother
found at 92 Second Street. After hiding her bloody dress inside another
one hanging in her closet and using the slop jar for her menstrual linen
to conceal the stained rags that had cleansed her head and hands, she
called for help and later confronted the officers. In her initial panic, she
blamed the deaths on a quarrel she said she had overheard that morning
between her father and a Lancashire man at the front door. She never
repeated her desperate lie, and police suspicion quickly shifted to the
Irish servant, Bridget Sullivan, but the long-term antagonism between English immigrants and Fall River mill men had provided her with an immediate, convenient red herring.[1]

As the word spread of the grisly murders of Andrew J. Borden and his
second wife, Abby Durfee Borden, a thousand textile operatives spontane-
ously walked away from their jobs, closing down work and crowding the
streets around the Borden house. They seemed driven both by curiosity
and satisfaction, knowing Borden as a pitiless landlord who collected his
rents in person. He served on boards of directors and voted his shares
dutifully at the board meetings of various mills and banks, receiving large
dividends. At his funeral parlor, so the rumor went, corpses were "fitted"
to cheap caskets by having their feet cut off. One comment on the street
at the news of his death was "Well, somebody did a good job." He was
called "the sharpest man in town," among some very keen men.[2]

When Lizzie Borden was indicted for probable murder after the district court inquest, Judge Blaisdell wept. She left the city in official custody
for Taunton Jail to wait for her trial in New Bedford. Crowds of mill workers accompanied her carriage to the train station. The defense challenged

all Lancashire names on the jury lists as well as any others not distinctly Yankee. A jury dominated by rural farmers decided her fate. Andrew J. Borden's property, estimated at a half-million dollars bought her special treatment in jail, the silence of Bridget Sullivan, and the legal services of both Andrew D. Jennings and a former Republican governor who personally appointed to the bench the chief judge presiding at her trial. Although shocked by her attorney's bill for twenty-five thousand dollars, she was pleased to be acquitted. As for the Borden money, Lizzie said, "Where would I have been without it?"[3] She loyally invested that money in Fall River mill stock for the rest of her life.

By the turn of the twentieth century, Lizzie Borden's distant cousin (their great grandfathers were brothers), M. C. D. "Matt" Borden of New York City, the third son of Colonel Richard Borden, had built an informal trust or combine to control the Fall River print cloth mills and maintain profits.[4] He began by obtaining sole ownership of the Fall River Iron Works from his brothers in 1886, razing the structures built by Jefferson Borden and building new print cloth mills to feed his American Printing Company. John S. Brayton, president of the B. M. C. Durfee Safe Deposit and Trust Company and the owner of many mills, helped finance part of this expansion and included members of the Borden family as treasurers and directors in his own firms. M. C. D. Borden also had many important connections among the dry goods and banking circles in New York City. By 1901 Borden was setting the price of grey goods and printed cloth. He and the money behind him manipulated the Fall River system and the cloth market. His achievement of the family dream of dominant power was the climax of a struggle that left the Borden family broken and profoundly divided and filled the mill offices in Fall River with jealousy and hate. Also by the turn of the century, the workforce in the mills of southeastern New England included increasing numbers of new immigrants from Poland, Germany, and the Azores of Portugal. They formed labor associations and amalgamations and conducted strikes in response to declining wages and worsening conditions as a result of the long-term battle between the entrenched mills in the city, their allies and competitors in the region, and the new strategies and tactics of M. C. D. Borden.

In *Figured Tapestry: Production, Markets, and Power in Philadelphia Textiles, 1885–1941*, Philip Scranton analyzes the flexible "batch" system for the production of fine textile goods, which employed skilled, union workmen and provided a stable foundation for Philadelphia's prosperity well into the twentieth century. This industrial model contrasts sharply with the well-integrated production of cheap consumer fabrics that poured out of Fall River's huge cotton mills. In Scranton's 1997 study, *Endless Novelty: Specialty Production and American Industrialization, 1865–1925*, he examines the key role of small-scale specialty production, such as jewelry making in Providence, Rhode Island, as central to understanding the complex development of the American business system.[5]

The Philadelphia textile industry relied on partial processes of manufacture conducted by small firms organized more like those in Lancashire than New England. Well-informed buyers carefully guided Philadelphia manufacturers, often experienced in English textile production, to meet middle-class consumer tastes in carpets, upholstery, curtains, laces, fine dress goods, wool suitings, and hosiery. The market for their goods became predictable and stable. Shoe factories in Essex County, Massachusetts, used a similar marketing system of cautious probes in the late nineteenth century, carried out by salesmen or drummers, who traveled by rail with sample cases full of the latest designs in ladies' high-buttoned shoes for retailers to choose. Shoe factories and small textile mills then received those orders by telegraph. Unlike Philadelphia in the post–Civil War years, Lynn and Haverhill in eastern Massachusetts concentrated on mass production of standardized high-buttoned ladies' shoes, then shifted into specialty goods at the turn of the century.[6] Both Philadelphia and Essex County shoe factories focused on quality batches rather than mass bulk production, paid high wages, earned steady profits, employed skilled, unionized workers, and sustained industrial production well into the mid-twentieth century.

In contrast, throughout the nineteenth century and into the early twentieth, Fall River mills used a standardized, bulk approach to the massive production and sale of its staple product: coarse grey cloth, later bleached and turned into calico and other goods at local and other northeastern print works. Run by a second generation of managers largely from commercial or legal backgrounds, the Fall River mills dominated their market sector based on enormous capacity, overproduction, glutted markets, pressure on competitors, and continual wage cuts during the late nineteenth century. The system produced constant turmoil: an unstable market, struggles over industrial production, and frequent strikes in the region. The mills of Fall River often acted together, and by the 1880s and 1890s many Rhode Island, Connecticut, and other Massachusetts mills, such as those in Lowell, had adopted similar wage standards, marketing practices, and techniques in dealing with mill operations, wages, and unions.[7] Scranton's interest in restoring batch production and small-scale specialty production to their appropriate places in American economic history should be balanced by the continued recognition of the destabilizing market power of manufacturers with inordinate capacity in nineteenth-century industrial production.[8]

During the late 1880s, the capacity for bulk production of print cloth set the direction of market prices for all other textile products, including fine goods. Fall River mills had become "the bellwethers for the entire industry," while New Bedford led the fine goods sector.[9] By 1901, M. C. D.

Borden, backed by New York money, controlled the price of print cloth as tightly as if he operated a trust or a holding company. In 1899 other textile men organized the American Woolen Company and the American Thread Company, buying out their rivals and formally merging into single corporations that controlled the price of worsted cloth and cotton yarn.[10] Yet, much of the cotton textile industry outside of Philadelphia continued to compete in unstable markets while attempting to improve the profit position of large corporations by subduing and exploiting their operatives. The Fall River system represents an historically specific form of business "rationalization" that bore little resemblance to Alfred Chandler's model of managerial order and corporate development and Philip Scranton's small-scale batch and peripheral industries.[11] This industrial system and the region it dominated also significantly differed from Philadelphia's placid prosperity.

Scranton presents an inclusive model of interdisciplinary analysis in *Figured Tapestry* and *Endless Novelty*, both of which contain important comparisons of regional competitors and alternative sectors in production. In *Figured Tapestry*, he examines the role of the state, technology, labor relations, managerial innovations, and political issues. His work focuses on the fundamental dynamic between the market and the textile mill but leaves out important issues of social and cultural experience, including the changing meanings of class, gender, and ethnicity. In addition, when contrasting the flexible batch system in Philadelphia and elsewhere with staple bulk production in New England, he underestimates the regional influence in the Northeast of the Fall River system of production. His discussion of "informal leadership" in New England omits an examination of M. C. D. Borden and his crucial role in manipulating the maturing Fall River system.[12]

MULE SPINNERS JOIN THE FALL RIVER SYSTEM

During the decade following the 1884 strike, Robert Howard and the National Cotton Mule Spinners' Association developed a unique relationship with the new Fall River Cotton Manufacturers' Association, which was eager to repress labor strife. Recognized to his great satisfaction as a bargaining agent, Howard negotiated in 1887 a special arrangement for the mule spinners: a sliding scale of wages.[13] Earnings for the spinners would rise and fall based on a formula that involved the price of baled raw cotton, the selling price of 28 inch wide print cloth, and an assured margin of profit.[14] This market-based agreement favored the mills, as the mule spinners quickly learned. The mill treasurers controlled information on profits and provided false data, refusing the leaders of the mule spinners union access to any mill accounts. During the first year, spinners' wages did not budge, while many firms in the city began to experiment with the production of other lines of goods not covered by the sliding scale. The spinners' union and its leader had been lured into a position that assured conservative unionism but failed to raise wages consistently. For example, the mill agents frequently cut wages 10 percent, then occasionally advanced wages at 5 or 10 percent. Any percentage increase was always figured on the previously reduced piece rate, and thus the full cut was never restored. This shaving off the edge of wages, along with the difficulties the workforce faced in gaining any increases at all, became central to the Fall River system. In early 1888, the manufacturers soothed the spinners' anger over the disappointing sliding scale agreement by granting a 9.5 percent wage increase for the spinners but only 4.5 percent for the other operatives. Wage differentials which separated and antagonized various groups of operatives became another fixture of the Fall River system.

The late 1880s and early 1890s brought great prosperity to the print cloth mills and high dividends to their shareholders, but wages lagged far behind, especially for the weavers and carders. The spinners, like Mr. W in 1881, still faced the speeding of the mules, one of their most common grievances. High speed and fatigue meant injured feet and hands from splinters and crushed bones. The "sick spinner" brigade continued to relieve these exhausted men. As dues-paying union members, sick spinners became an integral part of labor-management relations. For lack of apprenticeships in mule spinning, boys were being attracted to the ring-spinning rooms and easier working conditions. The mills began to require that mule spinners provide, as a condition of employment, a back boy from their own family. The special relationship of the mule spinners' union with the Fall River system concerned wages, not working conditions. Faced with continual complaints about "the grab policy" of cheating, speeding, and overtime, Howard controlled all spontaneous strikes through the executive committee, intervening personally to resolve grievances.[15] Usually he succeeded.

Howard also became politically active, serving eight terms from 1886 to 1892 as a state Senator from Bristol's Eighth District. His long-term political commitment to state regulation of industry contrasted with Samuel Gompers' emerging views on the trade union movement as nonpartisan. Julie Greene argues persuasively that for Gompers the term *politics,* pure and simple, meant the power to exclude all but trade unions in the AFL.[16] In contrast, committed political efforts to push labor reform helped make Massachusetts a pioneer in regulation of labor relations. With others, Howard backed important labor legislation, including weekly wage payments, employers' liability for injury, a workweek limited to fifty-eight hours, and prohibitions against nightwork for women and children, blacklisting, and the fining of weavers for alleged defects in the fabric. He initially believed—along with the mill agents—that mandating the shortest workweek in New England might harm Massachusetts industry, although the legislation passed with his support.

Nonetheless, the employers successfully resisted almost all of this state regulation. By withholding vital information, Massachusetts mill agents refused to cooperate with the State Board of Arbitration established in 1887, and textile workers, in contrast with shoeworkers, came to distrust the board's investigations. The spinners' union tried to negotiate an end to the blacklist, because Judge Blaisdell's rulings in Fall River made the blacklist law a dead letter. The Massachusetts Supreme Court ruled the 1891 weavers' fining law unconstitutional as a violation of freedom of contract. Mill agents continued to ignore state regulation or paid the small fines for violations when brought to district court.

Howard's policy of working with the mill managers on behalf of his men remained primary. Whatever benefited the other operatives was not his concern. They could, if they would, form their own unions. Howard criticized the operatives of New England in late 1888 for failing to organize during a time of widespread prosperity. "Operatives of Lowell, Lawrence, Holyoke, Chicopee, wake up and act the part of men," he urged.[17] Howard's idea of working-class manhood meant skilled white men organized into trade unions like his own that tightly controlled the membership from the top. Successful negotiation of grievances, an impressive union treasury—fifteen thousand dollars in 1889 invested in local savings banks—and high wages defined the status of mule spinners, regardless of lost strikes, injuries from speeding, and the declining use of mules.

Influenced by Frank Foster, editor of the Haverhill, Massachusetts, *Laborer,* Howard brought the mule spinners into the Knights of Labor for two years, 1886–88. Leon Fink argues that the Knights of Labor represented the "quintessential expression of the labor movement of the Gilded Age."[18] The Knights were strongest in Rhode Island for a brief period where, according to Paul Buhle, much of the impetus behind the organization came from English and Lancashire-trained Irish textile workers in the mill villages of the Blackstone Valley. The activities of both Gunton and Howard in the late 1870s and early 1880s had encouraged the political mobilization that succeeded in passing an 1885 ten-hour law. In Lawrence and Fall River, mule spinners dominated the local Knights. In the Massachusetts textile industry, the center of the Knights of Labor District # 30 was in Lawrence and Lowell, although Robert Howard was among the leaders. Fall River cooperatives in the 1870s and 1880s supported the Knights' vision of a cooperative commonwealth, but the most active Massachusetts industrial workers in the Knights were Essex County shoeworkers who organized a separate District # 77.[19] The response of Massachusetts workers to the Knights of Labor was scattered by industry and community, less "quintessential" than Fink argues. By 1888 trade unions quickly drew many industrial workers out of the Knights.

Committed to his own approach in dealing with the Fall River mills, Howard rejected the moral idealism and anti-capitalist stance of the Knights and returned in December 1888 to the Federation of Organized Trades headed by Gompers. Under his leadership the National Mule Spinners' Association, covering New England and New Jersey received a charter from the new American Federation of Labor in 1889. The national spinners' union lobbied successfully against any cuts in the tariff schedules on fine yarns made by the Democratic congress in the 1894 Wilson-Gorman tariff bill. Spinning fine yarn had become their most highly paid work, as the technical development of ring spinning advanced to take over the coarser counts of warp and filling yarn.[20] By the turn of the century, the position of the mule spinners in the cotton textile industry, based on exclusive control of skill and high wages, was dwindling, but Howard had carved out a special place for mule spinners in the Fall River system.

THE WEAVERS FIGHT THE FALL RIVER SYSTEM

Angered by the differences between the wages granted in 1888 to the small but well-financed spinners' union in comparison to the wages of the thousands of weavers in the workforce, the Fall River weavers began once again to organize. In February, Thomas Evans, writing to the *Fall River Herald* as the "Old Agitator," argued that high profits in the surging market meant the mills could not afford a strike. Now was the time for the weavers to organize mill by mill into a general union, which specifically recruited women workers who, Evans believed, had proven more spirited, committed, and fearless than many male weavers. Most operatives feared the blacklist, but he argued that the mill agents could be reasonable and responsible if they were not aggressively criticized. During the spring of 1888 Evans chaired one in a series of weavers' meetings that created a new protective association. But he had misjudged the retaliatory temper of the Fall River mill agents in good times or bad. He was immediately blacklisted at the Granite mills. Evans left the city in April but failed to find work anywhere in New England for almost a year, sinking into poverty and longing to return to England.[21] Evans sat out the 1889 strike in the Newburyport Poor Farm.

After nine months of being ignored by the manufacturers' association, the weavers' union, led by secretary Patrick J. Connelly, threatened on January 30, 1889, to strike for a wage increase equal to that awarded the mule spinners one year earlier. Unlike the spinners' organization, the union represented only 14 percent of the seven thousand weavers and could not "act as one man." Everything depended on the support of shop committees organized in each mill. Cloth was at 4 1/16 cents; profits were high. Connelly asked for 21 cents a cut on print cloth, an increase of 2 cents, or 9.5 percent, and a full 10 percent increase on finer goods of higher value. The secretary of the manufacturers' association refused, arguing that competition was too keen. Meanwhile, the Fall River mills advertised in Lancashire for five thousand weavers through the *Cotton Factory Times* of Manchester and in the Burnley *News*.[22] The weavers were outraged and eager to strike. The Fall River mills had stretched their strategy of dominance across the Atlantic.

In 1889, the mill agents made their usual contracts with cloth buyers, fully protected against civil damages in case of strikes or lockouts. The weavers' union was seen as "only a handful of men," unrepresentative and easily ignored. Therefore, the weavers' strike that began on March 11 with the support of the shop committees surprised many. Nearly sixty-five hundred from a workforce of seven thousand men and women walked out. Many non-union French Canadians struck, and some joined the union. The union executive committee welcomed two non-union French weavers as liaisons to the rest. At the Sagamore mills, only one male weaver showed up on the morning of the strike and began reading a newspaper. When the boss weaver ordered him to start his looms, he looked up and replied, "No." Fancy weavers at the King Philip, the Bourne, and the Durfee mills struck, even though they had no quarrel over wages. The new Conanicut mills made fine goods, but their treasurer could not lure the weavers back, even with a 6 percent wage boost. Overseers at other mills fired loom fixers who refused to weave. The weave rooms fell silent. Connelly exulted over the manufacturers' shock; they did not expect such a show of mass support. But the manufacturers knew that the new union's treasury could not last more than a few weeks.[23] These upstarts had to be crushed. This was Fall River.

Beneath a show of unity, boisterous mass rallies, and the solid front of the seventeen-day strike lay conflicting styles of labor protest. Unlike the mule spinners' union which ignored the strike, the weavers were responding to a sense of injustice and inequality, rather than calculating wages against the movements of the cloth market. With the spring trade over and the fall trade yet to begin, this was not the best time to pressure the manufacturers who could easily stop a few weeks to exhaust their cloth inventories and the weavers' treasury. The spinners were still working, and Fall River filling yarn sold for high prices in Taunton, Philadelphia, and throughout Rhode Island. Agents from Maine, New Hampshire, and Rhode Island sought to hire the skilled weavers on strike but had a hard time persuading them to live in isolated rural villages. Sympathetic mule spinners with relatives who were weavers wondered why their union leaders had decided not to support the strike. In the Durfee mills, one mule spinner with eight weavers in his family was ordered to bring them in or be fired. These family connections had brought the operatives together during the strikes of the early 1870s. On the third day of the weavers' strike, James Rooney reminded the operatives of past collaboration and of that infamous anti-union contract they all had been forced to sign in September 1875. In lyrics to a familiar song, he wrote,

> We will show that we are game,
> We'll show them we've not forgot
> The day we signed our name.[24]

After one week of impressive unity, the inability of the new union to support over six thousand strikers led to a quick offer to compromise. Thomas S. Borden, the grandson of Colonel Richard and treasurer at the Metacomet and Annawam mills, made it plain. The weavers must return at the old wage scale and only then would arbitration be considered. No one believed this would happen. But the mills did not threaten a lockout as long as filling yarn sold well, for this might lead to action from the spinners' union. Any negotiation with the weavers would mean union recognition, a privilege reserved for the mule spinners. The mills, Connelly told a mass meeting of strikers, "are trying to crush our spirit and strangle our union." The silenced looms had briefly empowered the weavers with a "bulldog pertinacity." They would enjoy nearly three weeks of an early, warm spring and, according to secretary Connelly, "hang hard."[25] Local opinion hardened against the mills, but middle-class views meant little. A letter from "Business Man" accused the mill agents of telling the weavers:

> You have reached the highest rate of wages that you can ever hope to obtain; consequently you must stay right where you are, while we go on accumulating wealth, living in opulence and increasing our power to crush you still lower whenever we feel disposed to do so.[26]

By March 27 the union treasury was empty.

New issues emerged during the 1889 strike that would reshape the future of unionism in Fall River. The involvement of women workers in union activism sharply declined. With increasing numbers of women, girls, and boys employed in ring spinning, which took over more and more yarn production, training by mule spinners became less and less available to youngsters. Meanwhile, the number of adult men in the weave rooms grew to half the workforce. Like the mule spinners, many weavers who were family men regarded the equal piece rates for weaving as "women's wages," not enough for a man with dependents. Family men needed special rates, more looms, or faster speed. Speeded-up looms, like mules, created new groups of male and female "sick weavers" in each mill, available to replace the exhausted. In early 1888 sixty-three-year-old Thomas Evans had contemptuously described one of these young male weavers in the Granite mill, as "a driver." Arriving early, he started up his ten looms when the belts began to move, hopping about like "a kangaroo," never looking up all week—except to eat his dinner while cleaning the looms and waiting for the belts to start—until Saturday noon. Always on the watch for special treatment from the overseer and better yarn to weave, he used soap to speed the belting and then managed to get faulty cuts accepted. The faster the speed, the more money he earned as well as the chance to boast about his prowess. Evans called such young men—with inexhaustible physical strength, eager to earn a family wage—voluntary slaves who helped drive others. Male weavers totally controlled the union by 1889. Women's voices, except those translating in French, were silent. But one observer warned that to exclude women weavers from the union's leadership would create an large, uncontrollable group that might decide independently to return to work.[27] Women weavers were increasingly viewed as a separate, unpredictable lot.

Male weavers began to debate the crucial importance of the family wage to their own sense of manhood. The Reverend John Brown, a Scottish immigrant and Presbyterian minister, supported the 1889 strike. Totally unfamiliar with the weaving process but sympathetic to the operatives, this eloquent preacher harshly criticized the mill owners and interpreted the meaning of manhood to eager male listeners among the strikers. Brown proposed a workforce of family men with citizenship. Foreign ways, the Scotsman argued without irony, had no "rights" in America. The mills forced poor women "to work so hard and sweat so much that their blood is thin," making them unable to perform their womanly part in family life. The speeded work compelled females to "lie up a week or so every little while." According to Brown, such feeble women, weakened by factory life, could barely maintain their femininity, much less compete with men. Womanhood seemed equated with mere sexual function. Brown argued that the strikers had borne insults and contempt that no man could stand without fighting back, but true manhood, for this middle-class minister oblivious to the implications for labor protest, also required protecting the liberties of other men, including their right to work. He exhorted them to "Be true to your own manhood by recognizing the manhood of every other man." Brown urged the strikers to remain firm, show a manly Christian spirit, avoid violence and intemperance, save their money, and become naturalized, "Americanized" citizens.[28] Several groups of male strikers thanked Brown for his support, and some of the younger weavers might have agreed with his nativist, middle-class view of manly individualism. Many older men, such as Thomas Evans, and many Lancashire-born women weavers would contest these meanings by their actions in future strikes. Reactions to Brown's words exposed the tensions within the workforce of weavers, especially the wish of many male weavers to imitate the mule spinners by pursuing the family wage, while excluding women from labor politics and perhaps even the weave room.

The striking weavers in a body returned to work under protest on

March 28, hoping to build an organization worthy of the respect of the mill owners. The majority of non-union weavers had backed the union enthusiastically; this signaled a potential for organization. Shop committees still functioned, voting as a group to return to work. In reaction, the secretary of the manufacturers' association cautiously made no comment when the strike was over, fearing that his statement might be "misconstrued by the weavers." At the Border City mills, the weavers successfully insisted that sympathetic loom fixers be rehired before they would go back. Others held out to get assigned to their old, familiar looms.[29] The strike seemed to have impressed some mill agents.

From his lofty place as a popular state Senator, Robert Howard reviewed the history of strikes in Fall River to place the 1889 weavers' effort in perspective. Recalling the first 1875 strike as the only successful one in the history of the city, Howard pointed out that during that walkout the mule spinners and the weavers had cooperated to win, but that the spinners had never supported the failed August vacation idea. Since that time, he argued, the spinners' union had to carry on alone—refusing to admit that the spinners insisted in 1879 that the weavers stay at work. He continued to demand the highest wages for mule spinners. The editor of the Lancashire *Cotton Factory Times* surveyed the details of the lost weavers' strike in 1889 with "disgust." It reflected the "usual stupidity" of a new labor association, especially one involving grumblers (the weavers) rather than joiners, such as the mule spinners. There had been "tall talk," but the employers had "laughed at them." In times past, Lancashire textile workers had made the same mistakes as those in Fall River. Perhaps this time, the editor noted, the American weavers had learned their lesson. His correspondent was Robert Howard.[30]

The potential unity demonstrated by the weavers quickly vanished. The divisive issue became the active role of shop unions in specific mills. Patrick Connelly of the protective association insisted on one big union with a general membership. The shop unions wanted to amalgamate but retain their ability to negotiate grievances independently with overseers about the weavers' increasingly complex piece rate system. The Granite mills shop union, organized in 1888 by Eugene Sullivan, had supported the 1889 strike and continued to flourish. Chauncey W. Ruoff, a highly skilled weaver at the King Philip mill, had organized five other mills and sent funds when weavers struck in Berkeley, Rhode Island. Ruoff's informal amalgamation of shop committees had the largest number of members, the largest treasury, and remembered well the fate of the general union with five thousand members in 1875. He pointed out that in contrast to the disunity among the weavers, the "manufacturers have this matter down to a science."[31] The amalgamation of shop committees was strongest in the fine goods mills among the highly paid fancy weavers, but excluded many plain weavers. These divisions kept the amalgamation shop committees and the protective association from merging. Members of the protective association feared that high pay for fancy weaving would result in the decline of the general wage level for less skilled weavers. A mass meeting of the seven thousand Fall River weavers was called for August 19 to decide the issue but attracted less than one thousand. A delegation sent to meet the manufacturers' association combined the leaders of both groups. By default, they had become an amalgamation. But the mill agents would not see them.[32] After 1889 not only the weavers, but also the male carders, loom fixers, and slasher-tenders would consider adopting Howard's model of trade unionism that had achieved a special position within the Fall River system.

WAGES AND TARIFFS: THE ELECTORAL POLITICS OF 1892

After the 1889 strike, the mill treasurers, agents, and directors became a political target for free-trade Democrats anxious to return former president Grover Cleveland to office in 1892 and undo the Harrison administration's high tariff schedules. A New York newspaper described Fall River as "a typical highly protected city." The weavers' grievances over wages had demonstrated that the Republican claim of high tariffs' protecting the wages of workingmen was a political farce. The "mill masters" owned everything in Fall River. Highly protected cotton "has done all this for them." A *Boston Globe* reporter interviewed many agents on March 14, drawing a collective portrait of wealthy, powerful men with "well polished boots, rich clothing and immaculate linen. . . . Jewels of great price flash upon their fingers and shirtfronts. . . ." Conspicuous consumption flaunted on the male body marked successful, powerful, upper-class manhood. One agent called the striking weavers an "unthankful people." The reporter asked whether the new machinery and increased speed did not "fag upon the bodies and minds of the weavers?" He answered, "I never thought of that. People who work for a living have to work hard. . . . The race is to the swift. . . ." He blamed the "pigheadedness of a few people" for interrupting local prosperity. In New York and Boston the free-trade press contemptuously represented Fall River as a city that even "at the best of times [was] the last place God made" and then regretted the whole idea.[33]

The prosperous years of the late 1880s ended in 1891 with a slump in the cloth market caused by overproduction, halting wage agitation from both the mule spinners and the weavers. A minority of organized operatives, however, began to promote an amalgamated association of textile unions, including the weavers, the carders, the slasher-tenders, and the loom fixers, providing a special place for the mule spinners with their AFL charter. Additional state regulation in 1891 setting fifty-eight hours per week as a legal limit failed to guarantee that wages would not be cut, but Fall River accepted the mandated shorter hours without cutting piece rates. This refusal to cut the piece rate amounted to a 3⅓ percent wage boost based on general expectations of higher productivity even with fewer hours to earn it. Lowell and Lawrence did not go along with this wage policy.[34] In 1892 the cotton textile industry revived as a result of the tariff bill of 1890, named after William McKinley, Republican congressman from Ohio, and abundant, cheap southern cotton. As the incumbent Republican Benjamin Harrison and Democrat Grover Cleveland campaigned over tariff protection, this prosperity sent profits and dividends surging in what the Republicans claimed as their boom. The McKinley tariff, they insisted, enabled American employers to pay higher wages to workingmen than in any other nation, including free-trade England. The Yorkshire woolen trade had been hard hit by the McKinley tariff; some mills relocated from Bradford, Yorkshire, to Rhode Island. Democrats retorted that the protective tariff raised consumer prices sharply, cutting workers' purchasing power and actually lowering wages. In this political context, Fall River spinners and weavers began to agitate for a 10 percent increase. Protection became the fundamental political issue in 1892.

After some dispute and much public speculation, the Fall River manufacturers' association voted 19 to 1 to raise wages 7 percent across the board—just four days before the election. Initially the cautious Brayton interests in the association had blocked this move. What if Cleveland were elected? The bolder treasurers called a second meeting. Simeon B. Chase spelled out the many advantages of voluntarily raising wages 6 or 7 percent. The association would head off any operatives' agitation, avoid a strike, help the Republican Party, advance wages less than the 10 percent demanded by the operatives, and continue to run during the prosperity, however long it lasted. Chase and his allies were bullish on Harrison and the Republican boom. These local political maneuvers based on wage advances were one more component of the Fall River system.

The textile workers and much of the public regarded this increase of 7 percent as "the McKinley bluff." The mule spinners' union held out for a full 10 percent increase, while both local party organizations registered as many new voters as possible. Harrison carried Fall River by over three hundred votes and won in Massachusetts and Rhode Island, but Cleveland won in Lowell and Lawrence, in Connecticut, and nationwide. Even McKinley was defeated in Ohio. The editor of the new Democratic *Fall River Globe* blamed misguided workingmen for the local Harrison victory, but the rest of the political news was good. The Democratic governor, who had signed the fifty-eight-hour bill, was reelected by a larger margin in the city than in 1891. The district elected its first Democratic congressman, Charles S. Randall. The five state representatives from Fall River were all Democrats except for Rev. John Brown who ran as an Independent Republican with the strong backing of the weavers. State Senator

Robert Howard, running for his eighth term, proved unbeatable. Simeon B. Chase refused to comment: "I'm very much in a hurry this morning."[35] The stunned, local Republicans could scarcely mount a campaign for the city elections.

The Fall River manufacturers swallowed the 1892 political defeat and immediately began lobbying along with the mule spinners to protect the print cloth market from serious tariff revision under the second Cleveland administration. When the financial crisis began in the fall of 1893, they cut wages 15 percent. The operatives, including the spinners, with no recourse under their sliding scale agreement, accepted this under protest. Just as no one could predict the outcome of the 1892 campaign, no one could say how long the downturn would last. Print cloth production continued at lower wages, flooding a market with little demand. By August 1894, the Fall River mills decided to try another 10 percent cut. The old arguments surfaced over how best to stimulate the market and still hold on to Fall River's dominant position: shorter hours or lower wages. The deadlock resulted in a strike.

TUMULT IN 1894

Unexpected combinations and divisions, haunting memories of 1875, and resurrected Lancashire traditions shaped the surprising course of events. When the mills announced the second wage cut in August, the amalgamated association of textile unions organized after the 1889 strike reluctantly voted to accept it under protest. Headed by Lancashire immigrant James Whitehead, the weavers' union in the amalgamation claimed about three thousand members, less than half of the seventy-five hundred weaving workforce which included some newly arrived Portuguese immigrants. When the wage cut was announced, Robert Howard was in Manchester, Lancashire, at the International Textile Congress, out of touch with events. He also enjoyed a warm reception in Stockport where he had been president of the local union, but warned all mule spinners not to go to America.[36] Still, emigration continued among other English operatives. Historian Maldwyn Jones argues that beginning in 1869 English immigrants to the United States began to outnumber those from Ireland: by 1880 two to one. So many returned, however, that the net emigration from England scarcely changed in the 1870s and 1880s. Late nineteenth-century English emigrants included high proportions of single men and women, "largely temporary and transient." Jones points out that this "impermanence" among these English immigrants was little different from the "new immigration" from southern and eastern Europe.[37] The Fall River system with Howard's help apparently worked to discourage the potentially troublesome English weavers and carders from staying in New England.

When he left for Lancashire, Howard left Thomas O'Donnell, treasurer of the spinners' union, as acting secretary. Both Howard and O'Donnell supported the amalgamated association's decision on August 14, to
accept the 10 percent wage cut. O'Donnell's instructions were to conserve
the treasury, but in Howard's absence his executive committee became
seriously divided. The spinners initially voted 240 to 50 against accepting
the cut, but O'Donnell convinced the general membership to reconsider;
on August 30 they voted by a narrow margin to accept under protest, 407
to 300.[38] This meant trouble for O'Donnell. The spinners suspected that
the manufacturers would welcome a strike, both as a dodge for unprofit-
able contracts and to deplete their union treasury. An uncertain O'Donnell wrote to Howard, expecting him back in October.[39] Certainly a mule
spinners' strike in Fall River that cut off potential strike contributions to
other spinners on strike would be good news for the New Bedford agents,
who also faced profound discontent. O'Donnell and the executive committee decided to wait and suppress dissension among the membership.
The deeply alienated Fall River weavers had other ideas. Later the mule
spinners would follow their lead. It was 1875 again: Robert Howard's
worst nightmare.

The weavers' grievances included more than the 10 percent wage cut.
In 1892, the Massachusetts legislature had passed the weavers' particulars
law which forced textile mills to mark on tickets attached to warp beams
all the specifications in the weaving process, including the length of the
cut, although the length could vary legally within a five-yard margin. The
act forbade arbitrary changes in piece rates on various styles and in
lengths, both profitable and widespread maneuvers intrinsic to the Fall
River system. In response, the mill agents decided to evade the law by
paying the weavers by the pound, weighing the cloth in the cloth room.
At just over 2 cents a pound, the weavers faced a drop from 18 cents a cut
to 16, well over the announced 10 percent. One weaver observed, "next
they will pay us by the quart."[40]

As with the ten-hour law, the weavers' fining law, and the prohibition
against blacklisting, the refusal of the textile mills to obey state regulation
was central to the Fall River system and made political agitation for labor
reform seem useless. For male operatives, native-born or naturalized, the
ballot, so precious to republican traditions of manly citizenship, appeared
irrelevant given the economic power of the textile mills in New England.
Mill agents in Fall River and New Bedford continued to ignore the legal
power of the state and ran their operations as they wished, paying any
fines out of the profits earned through evasion. In 1894 the weavers, organized and unorganized, decided to teach them a lesson about supply and
demand. They bolted the amalgamated association and decided to take a
two-week "vacation." Thomas Evans, just off the blacklist, was one of the
vocal agitators. The weavers in New Bedford, still being paid by the cut,

not yet by the pound, agreed to test in court the mills' evasion of the particulars law.[41]

Many New England mills and operatives, especially in Rhode Island, supported curtailing production in 1894 as a solution to the glutted market. The Fall River mills, as usual, chose to cut wages and keep producing cloth. The editor of the *Cotton and Wool Reporter* in Boston, Frank P. Bennett, denounced the Fall River wage cut as a worn-out, ludicrous way to stimulate the market. New Bedford agents running fine goods pointed out, furthermore, that, "[p]rint goods, as is commonly known, rule the [entire cloth] market." The Fall River system defied product diversification. Following Fall River's wage policy, the New Bedford mills cut their operatives 10 percent on August 14, producing a general strike despite the misgivings of their union leaders. Still secretary Matthew Hart of the New Bedford weavers' union pointed out in sympathy, "When the prices for weaving fine goods and fancies drop below those of prints, it passes the point of endurance for any self-respecting weaver."[42]

Samuel Ross, secretary of the New Bedford mule spinners' association, agreed that print goods had become a barometer of the entire cotton cloth market. When prints declined, all other textiles followed, even those not in direct competition. Such was the power of Fall River's capacity and market position. Against Ross's advice, the 350 New Bedford mule spinners voted four to one to strike on August 16. O'Donnell, supporting Ross, tried to talk them out of this, but one defiant spinner, whose wages had been cut 20 percent in one year, interrupted defiantly, "Agent Kent [at the Wamsutta] could tell us that same thing."[43] The Fall River spinners' union treasury would have to support these strikers. The New Bedford carders representing men and women, some of them French Canadians, followed one day later. The New Bedford weavers were last to act but organized support for the strike among the English, French, and German communities.

With production curtailed in both cities by mid-August, the Rhode Island print cloth mills, especially those in the Lonsdale area owned by the Goddard interests, followed the leadership of the rising firm of B. B. and R. Knight in Arctic, the center of the Pawtuxet Valley. All the Rhode Island mills refused to cut wages further. Unlike the Fall River print cloth mills, those in Rhode Island had contracts that they could not break without liability. They had observed the Fall River system over the years and suspected the Fall River mills of waiting for a rise in the market to dump huge, secret inventories, another feature of the Fall River system. Providence warehouses had their own inventories to sell. Eager to scoop up any unfilled contracts with cloth printers, Rhode Island mills wanted their operatives at work, but a "recent great" strike in Olneyville had produced a Rhode Island District Council of Textile Workers headed by Richard McGuy who offered support to striking Massachusetts operatives.[44] If Fall

River and New Bedford successfully cut wages, the Rhode Island mills would be forced to do the same—if they could. The Rhode Island agents hoped for a lengthy vacation in Fall River and a long New Bedford strike.

Widely condemned in the industry, the policy of cutting wages and making cheaper and cheaper goods had secured Fall River's hold over print cloth production. As usual, overproduction made no sense to the weavers in Fall River who decided to vacation for two weeks. Unlike the long vacation in 1875, the 1894 vacation involved no expressed moral criticism of the market system based on the Lancashire past, whatever the weavers may have felt. Still, the vacation idea represented another attempt by the operatives to influence the cloth market by withdrawing their labor. This effort also successfully united various skill groups, fancy and plain weavers, men and women, organized and unorganized, and the various nationalities. In 1894, the weavers adopted the economic arguments of the mule spinners' union for their sliding scale to defend their vacation: conditions in the cloth market. They met with the spinners on August 18 to argue for a combined vacation. These differences in labor politics between the mule spinners and the weavers over strategy and objectives were also a part of the Fall River system.

The weavers held several meetings on the question of the vacation. Older weavers warned the younger activists about the events of 1875, but James Whitehead himself was swept along into support of the curtailment. The amalgamated association stood repudiated. At one meeting, two thousand men and women weavers listened avidly to Thomas Evans and others advocate the vacation. More cautious advice came from a "thin-voiced weaver" who appealed to the married men to speak out against it. Admitting his poverty, he appealed to those like him with wives and young children to "act as men," not as a set of "rattle-brains." After the last vacation in 1875, he had suffered greatly and "signed away his liberty," but he was frequently interrupted by critics and finally gave up. Thomas Evans too had suffered in 1875 but strongly supported resistance. The family wage argument proved unpopular at this point. Following the vote, the weavers gave "an outpouring of shouts that would have drowned out the noise of a battery of guns at short range."[45] The old spirit of protest was on their lips.

The unorganized weavers became crucial; would they take a vacation? If they did, the weavers could shut down the looms, curtail production for two weeks, and wait for some sign of market reaction. Cheap calico always had customers, even during hard times. If the price of cloth rose, there would be no reason for a wage cut. This time, in contrast to the 1889 strike, the weavers' timing was shrewd. The key period for the spring trade came in mid-August through September. The vacation was technically not a strike and therefore not a drain on secret union funds. The employers might be liable for their contracts. The weavers' enthusiasm acted like a "fever" on the carders and other operatives.[46] If the market failed to budge and the manufacturers' association would not compromise, it could lead to a general strike or a lockout—as in 1875. The secretary of the manufacturers' association, Cyrus C. Rouseville, treasurer of the Shove mills, ruled out any repetition of the 1875 vacation, lockout, and anti-union contracts as "madness," but the echoes of the turbulent past haunted everyone.

On the first vacation day of August 20, only about 25 percent of the looms in Fall River were running. More weavers left during the week. The manufacturers admitted they were astonished at the breadth of the support and depth of the commitment to the weavers' walkout. For years, they had viewed the small weavers' union and its scanty treasury with contempt. The unorganized weavers also walked out, while other operatives, who were still at work, including union spinners, grew anxious to join in. Excitable young doffers and back boys, essential to mule spinning but eager to be on vacation, had to be controlled. Everyone watched the market reports, as angry members of the manufacturers' association condemned the weavers for "deciding that they knew better than the manufacturers what would be for the best interests of all," practically taking the management of the mills into their own hands.[47] The old, profound fear of losing control over the workforce, capacity, and the market initially unified the otherwise increasingly divided manufacturers' association. To many, overproduction seemed a dangerous policy. Still, the interlocking boards of directors made up of the mill treasurers and agents not only protected each other's salaries and positions but also provided solid ground for unity. Before the weavers' vacation could have any direct impact on the market, the small executive committee of the Fall River Cotton Manufacturers Association, meeting in secret, announced a month-long lockout on August 23. Without consulting the membership, the leaders of the association expected all of them to honor this decision and shut down, putting twenty-three thousand operatives out of work. If the market rose, the mills—not the weavers—would claim credit. To O'Donnell's relief, the lockout also headed off a mule spinners' strike that would have depleted the union treasury, and Howard was due to return a month earlier than planned.[48] But to add to O'Donnell's troubles, the mule spinners at the Cocheco print cloth mills in Dover, New Hampshire, went on strike against a similar 10 percent wage cut and expected support from the national organization.

DISAFFECTION AMONG THE MILLS

Divisions among mill agents surfaced quickly in New Bedford after the August 14 wage reduction. The manufacturers' committee waited to cut wages until William D. Howland, the owner of three small yarn mills who opposed a wage cut, was safely out of town. New Bedford mills made print

David Anthony Brayton (below)
on the Quequechan River,
contemplating the Durfee Mills,
c. 1870. Courtesy Collection of
the Fall River Historical Society

"The Labor Riot at Fall River, Massachusetts, "*New York Graphic,* October 2, 1875. Composite scene of the state militia called to restore order after the Fall River strikers' bread riot on September 27, 1875. See (bottom right) placard and boys carrying bread loaves on poles. Courtesy of Cornell University Libraries.

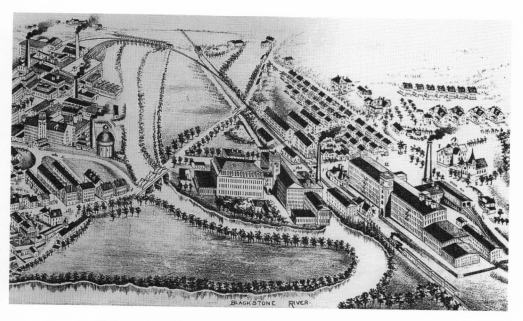

Bird's eye view of Lonsdale village, divided by the Blackstone River and
located in the towns of Smithfield (left) and Cumberland (right), Rhode Island, 1888.
Lithograph by O. M. Bailey & Co., Boston, RHi (X32) 43.
Courtesy, Rhode Island Historical Society

George Gunton, Lancashire immigrant
weaver and labor editor. Courtesy,
Dictionary of American Portraits, published by
Dover Publications Inc., in 1967

Robert Howard, Lancashire immigrant
mule spinner and labor organizer, *Fall
River Globe,* November 2, 1892.
Courtesy of Paul Coppens

M. C. D. (Matthew Chalonder Durfee) Bordon. Reprinted from Speed,
A Fall River Incident (New York, 1895)

The plant of the Fall River Iron Works Company, 1895. Reprinted from Speed,
A Fall River Incident (New York, 1895)

"Matt" Borden starting the Corliss steam engine in Mill #4, 1895. Sketch by W. Louis Sontag Jr.,
reprinted from Speed, *A Fall River Incident* (New York, 1895)

Andrew G. Pierce Sr. as "the Mark Hanna [inside manipulator] of New Bedford,"
Boston Post, January 16, 1898. Courtesy of Paul Coppens

THE GREAT AMERICAN COTTON INDUSTRY.

PAST.　　　　　　　　　PRESENT.

The oppression of women
weavers during the New
Bedford strike as portrayed
in William Randolph
Hearst's *New York Journal,*
January 24, 1898.
Courtesy of Paul Coppens

The key issue in the
New Bedford strike as
portrayed in Joseph
Pulitzer's *New York World,*
January 25, 1898.
Courtesy of Paul Coppens

Mrs. Harriet Pickering, an undaunted activist weaver during
the New Bedford strike, *Atlanta Constitution*, February 10, 1898.
Courtesy of Paul Coppens

cloth, fine goods, and yarn to sell to special customers. The markets for each product were different, and in August the demand for yarn was strong. Fall River's yarn mills—the Globe, the Sanford, the Conanicut, and the Kerr Thread mill—were so eager to run that wages had not been cut. Howland also refused to cut wages in his three yarn mills, the Howland, the Rotch, and the New Bedford, insisting that if he had to choose between the local manufacturers' committee and his help, he would not cut wages. "Our goods have a reputation and we have orders that must be filled . . . I cannot run a mill without the cooperation of the help. . . . [M]y silent spindles will not make money for the stockholders."[49]

The New Bedford yarn mills as a group employed three thousand, while the cloth mills had seven thousand operatives. One "leading mill man" in New Bedford argued that no manufacturers' association should control their decisions. "It is a serious matter for a yarn mill to lose a buyer as its product identity [unlike Wamsutta] is not known to the general public who purchases it under another brand name."[50] Maintaining contracts with yarn buyers was as crucial to the yarn mills in Fall River as in New Bedford. Andrew G. Pierce, on the other hand, the power behind the manufacturers' committee and the treasurer of the Wamsutta, was closely connected with Fall River interests. He dismissed Howland and the yarn mills as unimportant. The Wamsutta directors had already agreed with the other cloth mills as early as 1884 to cooperate, as in Fall River, to compensate any struck mill for fixed expenses.[51]

The Fall River weavers continued to work at several large mills where wages had not been cut in order to pit those mills against the others. Most important were the three Iron Works cloth mills owned solely by M. C. D. Borden and the Union mill controlled by the Brayton interests. Matt Borden, always a loner, did not cut wages and fed his grey goods into his expanding American Printing Company. The Braytons, who also owned the B. M. C. Durfee Trust bank and the Durfee mills, could afford to oppose the "McKinley bluff" in 1892 and run their mills independently of unions or manufacturers' associations. Their opposition to the wage cut meant that other Brayton-controlled mills, such as the Sagamore, the Border City, and the Pocasset might refuse to cooperate. The fancy goods mills also refused to cut wages. Many of these mills had run steadily throughout the depression year of 1893, providing jobs for their grateful workforce.[52] These divisions among the Fall River mills could benefit the strikers.

The prospering Seaconnet yarn mills did not cut wages and continued to run, having "forgotten" to sign their association membership, but the manufacturer's association disciplined its weaker disaffected members. The treasurer of the Sanford Yarn Mills, Arnold B. Sanford, who too had refused to cut wages, quickly changed his mind under the pressure of an agreement signed by all members of the association to abide by a majority vote, representing three-fourths of the mule spindles in Fall River. As a result Sanford lost his contracts but mollified his Fall River colleagues who had threatened him and others with severe retaliation.[53] Most of the other yarn mills in Fall River then caved in and observed the August 23 lockout, while competitors in New Bedford and Taunton took over their contracts. A basic assumption of the Fall River system was that lower wages and weaker unions would make up for all the financial losses during strikes or lockouts. But the largest cloth producers in Fall River, the Iron Works mills and the Brayton-controlled mills, the Durfee, Sagamore, Border City, Union, Pocasset—as well as the independent Seaconnet and the Globe yarn mill—continued to run. These serious divisions among mill managers encouraged the operatives. Jockeying about as in 1894 for leverage by managers and workers alike represented the essential character of Fall River's industrial politics.

The cloth market slowly crept up. After two weeks, prices rose slightly to 2⅞ cents. Baled cotton had never been cheaper during the post–Civil War period. The mill agents dismissed the rising market as "but a spasm." Another week passed. Cloth rose to 2¹⁵⁄₁₆ cents, but the Fall River agents said they wanted 3 cents, then demanded 4 cents and some action in the cloth futures market. The rise could never be high enough. The issue was not profits, but joint action to beat down wages, the operatives, and their unions. Whenever the market rose, the association termed the movement spasmodic, inconsequential, unsatisfactory, or "temporary, owning to artificial causes."[54] The Fall River system gave them the power to define the language of the market. Rhode Island competitors, supply and demand, "unbusinesslike" conduct, criticism from the press, the interests of stockholders, or the local business community—none was important.[55] With the Fall River, New Bedford, and Dover cloth mills shut down and serious drought curtailing water-powered production in rural areas, especially in the Pawtuxet Valley and eastern Connecticut, the other Rhode Island mills grabbed contracts at the highest price available, ran their mills, sold print cloth, and made money.[56] Some Fall River mills with huge, secret inventories unloaded them, gaining considerable profit, although overtly supporting the lockout. When the weavers' vacation ended officially on September 15, cloth sold at a solid 3 cents. There appeared to be no reason for a wage cut in terms of profits, but the mills refused to budge. Confrontation and domination, not orderly managerial decision, were inherent to the Fall River system.

1875 AGAIN?

In response to the rising cloth market, both the weavers and the mule spinners voted to strike. O'Donnell had lost control. When the spinners' union met on August 27, four days after the lockout, disorderly younger men, uncontrollable by the usual means, overwhelmed the old-timers. The spinners agreed not to accept any benefits from the union treasury, voting thus "with the full power of a thousand lungs."[57] By early September, even the union spinners who managed the treasury were in "a fighting mood," provoked by the rising market. A flustered O'Donnell did his best, but admitted that even "the old fellows want to strike and I can't stop them. . . . We don't want strikes. . . . I've done my best to prevent them."[58] He was being swept along by a determined, angry union membership. Howard would return within two weeks but that was too late.

On September 12, the amalgamated unions, revived by the shift of all operatives to support the weavers' vacation, contacted the manufacturers' association at the urging of secretary Whitehead, who was threatening Howard's preeminent position in local labor politics. The weavers, they all believed, had made the market rise. Whitehead claimed that the success of the vacation proved that all the weavers were behind the union and that the rest of the operatives, including the mule spinners, supported his direction of labor protest through the amalgamation. Any reply from the association would imply recognition of the amalgamation as representing the twenty-three thousand operatives in the city. The manufacturers did not respond, thus treating him as a man who, unlike Robert Howard, could not control his own union, much less the other operatives. But they underestimated the angry reaction of the workforce to this insult. Pushed by both the older members and the executive committee, the mule spinners voted on September 15 to support Whitehead and strike.[59] The mule spinners had a strong treasury to see them through, but everyone knew that the weavers' union had little money for their vacation.

Most weavers had some savings to call on, but not a berry or a clam would escape their foraging. Each ethnic community served its version of strike rations: English porridge, Irish boiled salted meat and cabbage, and French Canadian pea soup. One locked-out spinner introduced a dubious Boston reporter to a fish and chips lunch for ten cents at a local shop. The crisp French fried potatoes and the fresh, tasty fish, the local squeteague or weakfish, proved irresistible. "That feed will do me for the day," said the spinner, and still allow him to buy a few beers with his friends.[60] In England, cheap fish and chips prepared in small shops had already begun to replace the red meat preferred by the older generation of English textile workers.[61] With the arrival of cold New England weather, however, all Fall River operatives would feel the need to afford sustaining beef. Cheap flour and local huckleberries produced the strikers' only luxuries, pies and dumplings. The weavers voted to hoard their small union treasury, allowing payments only in the form of store goods and only to members with families.[62]

The National Cotton Mule Spinners' Association met for its annual convention in Boston on September 19, only four days after the Fall River spinners voted to strike. Howard made a dramatic entrance in mid-afternoon, just off the steamship from Liverpool. He commended O'Donnell's leadership but expressed surprise at the concurrent mule spinners' strikes in Fall River, New Bedford, and Dover. He claimed to have expected only curtailment. But his long experience prepared him for a lockout, as did O'Donnell's letters. Howard denounced the weavers' vacation as a "false move" and the New Bedford strike as "a great mistake."[63] O'Donnell had been unable to prevent a Fall River strike; Howard had to find a solution. On September 22, the price of print cloth tilted to $2^{15}/_{16}$ cents. Howard sought some kind of compromise that would reopen the mills. His role in the Fall River system was at stake.

The manufacturers quickly agreed to meet Howard and give him the bad news. The mills would reopen only when all the operatives accepted the reduction. Howard insisted that after the first 10 percent cut in 1893, the mills had promised to sustain wages when cloth reached 3 cents and their profit margin was 77 cents. Quoting the *Providence Journal,* Howard pointed out that the cloth market had reached 3 cents and their margin was 83.74 cents. He offered to compromise on behalf of the mule spinners. They would return to work for one month at the old wage rate, and if the market continued downward, they would accept the 10 percent reduction. The agents refused. Howard then offered to return at a 5 percent reduction. If the market provided a profit margin of over 75 cents, then the mills would pay back the other 5 percent. Some of the agents reacted eagerly to this offer but were silenced by a quick adjournment.[64] Still, Howard felt he would be able to divide the association with the 5 percent offer.

The weavers refused to let Howard speak for them or consider anything less than the restoration of 10 percent. They denounced him for ignoring the amalgamation, but Howard shrugged them off. He represented no group but the mule spinners. The print market remained dull, under 3 cents, and showed little interest in future contracts. The depression of the 1890s was settling in. Negotiations went nowhere, while Cyrus Rouseville organized the support of the most powerful mill agents, the Braytons, Simeon B. Chase, Charles M. Shove, and Richard B. Borden.[65] Freed of dissenters as the market sagged, the manufacturers' association held out, believing that business was seriously depressed and hoping that their competitors in Rhode Island had made no significant inroads into their market control. If the spinners wished to exhaust their sixty-eight-thousand-dollars treasury supporting three strikes, so be it.[66] The weavers counted for nothing; they would return whenever the gates opened.

The mill agents then proposed that the mule spinners accept the 10 percent reduction for two months, while they watched the movement of cloth prices. They wanted to divide the strikers and knew Howard well. Refusing even to try to sell this offer to the irate striking spinners, he countered with a 5 percent cut for sixty days. If the margin rose to 85 cents, the additional 5 percent would be restored. But the mills wanted unconditional surrender on their terms. Accept the 10 percent cut, and we will see. This offered nothing. Then on October 4 the cloth market rose again to 3 cents, resulting in the brisk sale of inventories. Fall River warehouses cleared out 800,000 pieces. In Providence, the Knight brothers sold 150,000 pieces of print cloth, signing contracts at 3 cents until January 1895. Samuel Ross in New Bedford announced that a special committee of mule spinners had compromised with the mills at a 5 percent cut, and he had refused to block the move. This settlement interested both Howard and the Fall River manufacturers' association, and they moved to compromise. The New Bedford weavers also returned to work, assured of the strict observance of the particulars law. After two frustrating weeks but still talking about fighting to the bitter end, Howard and O'Donnell went to New York City to seek support for the three New England spinners' strikes from the American Federation of Labor.[67] Gompers' assurances were widely published but never tested.

On Friday October 12, Howard gave "the speech of his life" to convince the spinners' union to go back to work under terms many considered unworthy. It had taken two hours of "heated discussion" on the previous afternoon just to get the executive committee to support a return for two months at a 5 percent cut. If the profit margin stayed at 85 cents (unlikely in a depressed market), the 5 percent would be restored. When the margin fell below 66 cents, the 5 percent cut would become standard. At the mule spinners' general meeting, Howard called upon his sterling reputation and the reality of a depressed market in a talk laced with both pathos and threats. He knew his men. They had been angry, outraged but now would be reasonable under his guidance. He recalled to them the long weeks of struggle in 1879, his stubbornness during a similar 1884 strike, and how he had finally yielded when one striker begged, "For God Almighty's sake, don't see us starve." That man stood up and said, "I remember" to cheers.[68]

Howard continued. In 1884 we had mules in every mill but, for the first time in public, he announced that ring spinning now threatened to displace all warp and some filling mules. Ten mills in the city had no mules at all. The union had to meet their financial responsibilities to six hundred older spinners, doffers, and back boys or risk seeing them recruited to work the mules. The strike must end to preserve the craft, the treasury, and to prevent general privation. Howard regretted that the compromise would not cover the carders or weavers who had fought an "heroic and noble" battle. Many of the union spinners, however, had wives, sisters, and brothers who were carders and weavers. Left out of the settlement, they believed that they faced starvation wages. Howard spoke of one woman striker who came to his house saying she would be forced

from her boarding place if she did not work, and where would she go?
One "lusty old spinner shouted," why didn't you take her in, man! For a
full five minutes, the hall rocked with laughter at the embarrassed bachelor, blushing bright red.[69] He accepted their laughter as one of them, a
fully sexual man among virile men. Howard then claimed that the striking
spinners had actually won a victory: the treasury was still full, for the first
time the mills had compromised while the spinners were still "in the
streets," and the union stood united. Despite a great deal of criticism
about the profit margin of 85 cents being too high and despite the two
months of waiting which would take them into winter, the members supported their leader. The carders who gained nothing also voted to return
to work. On the Monday when the mills reopened, the district's Democratic Party, meeting in New Bedford, nominated Robert Howard for Congress. His standing in politics reflected his status in the Fall River system.

The "backbone of the strike" was thought to have been broken, but
not for many weavers who refused to return to work.[70] They folded their
overalls and working skirts over their arms and approached the mills on
Monday, but no one wanted to be the first to go in. A spontaneous meeting and demonstration at the park led to an organized march through
the central mill district, calling out the weavers, "in earnest . . . determination to asset their manhood and womanhood and throw back at the manufacturers the lie that 95 per cent. of them will work at starvation wages."[71]
For thirteen more days, over four thousand weavers refused to go back,
and the unorganized followed the organized.

Marching weavers carried the symbols of their job, Lancashire-style: a
reed hook and a steel comb tied to a stick.[72] Orderly and cheerful for the
most part, they waved handkerchiefs and sang songs but also jeered and
shook their doubled fists, especially hooting and yelling as they marched
past the mansions of Simeon B. Chase and Cyrus Rouseville on Rock
Street. One union officer pointed out that the American flag they carried
was made of silk, not print cloth. At the Iron Works mills they cheered
Matt Borden who had not cut wages. Many working weavers left their
looms to join the marchers, some irresistibly drawn by memory and tradition to the mass demonstration. Furious to be back and beaten, it was not
hard for them to decide. This fervor continued, as surprising as on the
first day of the weavers' vacation. More parades followed, some primarily
of women weavers. Mottoes and banners, echoing traditional Lancashire
defiance, read: "We Are Willing to Starve but Not at the Looms"; "Weavers want 5 per cent. or no surrender." Music from bands or single instruments, including raucous fish horns, kept up the pace. One tall, thin gray-
haired woman of about sixty danced happily around in circles to the
music as she marched, a symbol of spirit and perseverance. The weavers
held out, organizing parade after parade as the October weather turned
windy and colder. They kept more than half of the mills' looms silent and

forced some, including Rouseville's hated Shove mill, to suspend operations.[73]

One of the members of the mule spinners' executive committee commented on October 25,

> It ain't the spinners now. They told us we were the only ones who found fault with our wages and I guess they know different now. I'll keep my three girls out till hot soup freezes over before I'll ask them to work for such prices.[74]

His admiration was wholehearted. Based on the strength and vitality of these demonstrations, secretary Whitehead again sent the manufacturers' association a letter and received insults in return. They would never recognize the weavers' union, but Robert Howard, running for Congress, predicted that day would come soon.

> You can't starve people in America and it took our fellows 10 years to prove it. If the weavers can hold together a couple of weeks longer you'll have to give in, and if you don't then you'll have trouble for a long time to come.[75]

One perceptive treasurer pointed out the dangerous contradiction in opposing the weavers' union, while the spirited demonstrations continued.

> Although it does not represent all the weavers in town, it is the best organization they can get, and I don't see any sense in [the mill owners] insisting that [before any negotiations the weavers must] make it more powerful. . . . [76]

On October 27 over a thousand weavers voted narrowly to remain on strike, but the following Monday they were back at work. The weavers had their vacation, relived some of the old-time spirit of defiance, felt the power of united action—and the market had risen. Their final parades were important gestures of courage and spirit, demonstrating that the striking weavers were neither beaten nor starved but remained men and women worthy of dignity and honor. They were experiencing the dynamic of class, culture, and power in their own way.

As the depression deepened in 1894, however, some male weavers continued to develop a different vision of working-class manhood and womanhood and of future policy. Ignoring the importance of women weavers during the 1894 vacation strike, the lockout, and the demonstrations, many male weavers began to demand the same bargain as the mule spinners. "We are men as the spinners are. We have families as the spinners have. Why can't we get the same treatment?"[77] If the weavers' union only had a treasury like the spinners and as firm leadership, they too would gain recognition as union men. The family wage and the exclusive craft union idea seemed the answer. The inclusive traditions of the weavers' union, including female activism, would have to be abandoned. Secretary Whitehead survived these defeats and troubles. During the 1894 election, Howard carried Fall River but was not elected to Congress and retired in 1897. He remained on the executive committee of the national spinners' association that he had built. Samuel Ross of New Bedford, an immigrant from Cheshire, south of Lancashire, took over as national secretary. This trade union model for textile workers, built upon decades of conflict over the issues of amalgamation and inclusion, would be tested again in 1898.[78]

MATT BORDEN BUILDS HIS EMPIRE

During the 1894 strike, M. C. D. Borden acted independently in ways that reflected his past and predicted his future. The third son of Colonel Richard Borden and Abby W. Durfee Borden and born in 1842, he attended Phillips Academy in Andover, Massachusetts, and graduated from Yale College in 1864. A year later he married Harriet M. Durfee, a daughter of Dr. Nathan Durfee. His father appointed young Matthew as the representative of the American Print Works in the New York City dry goods district. Working as a clerk for Low, Harriman and Company, he walked the streets of the dry goods center with rolls of "American Prints" under his arm. In 1867 the firm made him a partner. He had arrived in New York just as the Bordens decided to expand operations in Fall River to achieve a commanding position in the postwar textile world. Young Matt Borden had to deal with the collapse of printing capacity when fire destroyed two Borden works in 1867, but after 1869 production soared. Strikes in 1870, 1875, and 1879 disrupted contracts with printers and commission houses. From the selling end of the business, they made no sense. He and Harriet raised their family of three sons in New York City, not Fall River, although family relations remained close. The notorious embezzlements and personal bankruptcies of the Bordens and Durfees in the late 1870s acutely embarrassed him.[79]

As his family prospered, Borden acquired a town house on West Fifty-sixth Street and a summer place on the New Jersey shore where he kept a steam yacht, his only avid recreation, which he steered, not the winds. During the Spanish-American War, he leased his ship to the U.S. Navy to carry dispatches from Key West and bought a better one.[80] The bankruptcy in 1879 of the American Print Works and the Fall River Iron Works followed by the financial collapse of the Borden family had forced Matt Borden to organize the American Printing Company in 1880. His father had died in 1874, Dr. Durfee left no estate in 1876, and his uncle Jefferson was deeply in debt. Loans from the B. M. C. Durfee bank and trust, owned by the Brayton family and founded on Iron Works shares, put the business back together. His oldest brother Thomas stayed in Fall River as a partner and the agent of the company, while Matthew returned to New

York City. Thomas J. Borden, who at sixteen clerked at the Iron Works, was content to remain a Fall River man, actively involved in the print cloth business that his brother would dominate.

In 1888 Matt Borden began to tear down the old Iron Works foundry and other buildings to construct print cloth mills. His brothers Thomas and Richard B. owned several cloth mills, but his decision revealed contempt for local operations and a desire for independence. These plans had split up a potential partnership among the brothers in 1887. The Fall River Iron Works Company, operating under the original charter with all privileges intact, had a tiny directorship: M. C. D. Borden, the president and director; his oldest son, Bertram H. Borden; and his brother-in-law, A. S. Covel, with William J. Harley as treasurer. Likewise, Matt Borden tightly controlled the American Printing Company as president, with Covel as the treasurer and James B. Harley, William's brother, as the agent. The cloth printing company's directors also included two New Yorkers, Bertram Borden, and Covel.[81] The chimney for the first Iron Works textile mill was huge, 350 feet high, thirty feet in diameter, dominating the skyline and a sign of mills to come. To sell his goods, Borden joined the largest commission house in New York, the J. and E. Wright and Company, later reorganized as Bliss, Fabyan and Company. The *Fall River Herald* in 1888 described him as extremely close-mouthed and shrewd, but as a man who wished to be known as the "grand mogul" of print mills and printing works.[82]

While his cloth mills were being built, Borden had to buy grey goods. In August 1889, the local mills, angry about his contemptuous, expansive plans, tried to freeze him out of the market, refusing to sell their products at anything less than 4 cents a yard. He had to buy in order to make print cloth or lose his customers. They thought they had him "cornered," both in Fall River and in Providence. Borden, however, found sellers at less than 4 cents elsewhere through his New York contacts. He "shipped prints enough to supply [his customers'] demand out the front door, sold cloth in the grey from the back door and made money on both deals."[83] In response the Fall River and Providence firms were forced to lower their price or miss out on the selling season. Matt Borden was speculating in grey cloth even before he could make it. By mid-August, his buying and selling over, he vacationed in New Hampshire's White Mountains, expressing no interest at all in the market he had just upset.

This was only the beginning. In the depressed market of November 1893, he bought five hundred thousand pieces of Fall River grey cloth, clearing out the local inventories and causing the price—after he bought—to jump to 3 cents. He also bought inventories in Providence and Boston of three hundred thousand pieces (about fifty yards per piece), using for the entire purchase over a million dollars in cash. As Holder Borden had used Providence money, M. C. D. Borden used his financial contacts in New York City to shape the 1893 cloth market and production policy. The New England print mills reopened and decided not to cut wages. He seemed a sort of wizard to boards of directors and a hero to the operatives. He accomplished his "master-stroke" in seven days, demonstrating that he had "the power to make prices for commodities."[84] He built three Iron Works print cloth mills in 1889, 1892, and 1893 to assure himself a steady supply of grey goods. No Fall River mill would ever slow him down or charge him too much again. In 1894 he refused to cut wages or join any manufacturers' association and ran his mills throughout the vacation, lockout, and strike. His operatives had stood at the Iron Works mill gates, cheering on the parading weavers. Borden employed union mule spinners, until ring spinners replaced them. He bought enough grey goods locally in 1894 to keep his printing machines active for months. In October, he took advantage of the lowest price for raw cotton since 1849, buying sixteen thousand bales in just a few hours at 5⅝ cents a pound. It cost about a half a million dollars and forced him to build new cotton storehouses.[85] He always refused to talk about his business decisions, but as a director in the Bank of the Manhattan Company, his connections with New York City banks and investors undoubtedly helped finance the deal.

In the fall of 1895, Matt Borden demonstrated how powerful he was becoming. His newest triumph, the fourth Iron Works mill, was ready, equipped with a three thousand-horsepower Corliss steam engine, the largest in the United States. The Corliss Company of Providence had the giant steel crankshaft—two feet in diameter with a nine-inch bore hole—made by the Bethlehem Iron Works in Pennsylvania. The Bethlehem Works was the only steel mill, except the Krupps company in Germany, able to fabricate such a machine part. The custom production of this crankshaft for Corliss supports Philip Scranton's insistence on the key role of specialty production in making mass production feasible.[86] The shaft alone weighed 45½ tons. Starting up such an engine, Borden decided, deserved a public festival for his New York City associates and held in Fall River. Invitations also went out to key textile interests in Providence, Boston, New Bedford, and Fall River. He hired space aboard the *Priscilla*, one of the huge, ornate steamboats on the Fall River Line, and brought his oldest son and sixty-one of his New York and Philadelphia friends and associates overnight to the wharves he maintained under the omnibus charter issued to the original Iron Works. On the way, he showered them with lavish dinners, cigars, souvenirs, soft music, and entertainment. After breakfast the next day, the group inspected the new cotton print mill, and just as the New England guests were arriving, Borden started up the Corliss steam engine. All ran smoothly, the only noise coming from the new belting, one of which measured fifty-six inches across, the widest in Fall River.[87] He employed twenty seven hundred well-paid workers. Later he would build two additional mills.

In early 1895, convinced that sluggish business would rebound, Borden had raised wages 10 percent and ordered the construction of this fourth mill. The depression did not exist for him. Borden's red-brick cotton mills even looked different from Fall River's granite block structures, except for the local granite in the foundations and window sills. His fourth mill was the largest with windows extending almost from floor to ceiling, allowing an extraordinary amount of light to pour in. Electric light generated by each mill's steam engine, rather than gaslight, illuminated the rooms. Both New England and English firms had furnished the machinery. Ring frames replaced all the mules. The freight elevators had been built by his brother-in-law's firm, the local Covel Company and the shafting and pulleys came from Kilburn, Lincoln of Fall River.

The looms in Borden's cloth mills were Mason or plain looms, not the new automatic Northrop looms. George Draper, president of the Draper Company of Hopedale, Massachusetts, believed that his automatic Northrop loom would be quickly adopted in Fall River. With a stop action for serious warp breakages and a round battery of full bobbins ready to replace empty ones automatically in the looms' shuttles without any attention from the weaver, the new loom represented advanced technology for mass production. Agent Alexander G. Cumnock at the Boott Mills in Lowell was among the first to adopt Draper's loom, but in Fall River, they were installed only in the Seaconnet mill where Draper sat on the board of directors.[88] The Fall River mill owners, including the innovative Matt Borden, disappointed George Draper. As Matt Borden might have remarked, why do I need a new loom? I now have the market.

At the champagne lunch to celebrate the opening of his fourth mill, Borden surrounded himself at the head table with New Yorkers representing banking and the dry goods business. There were only three Fall River men: John S. Brayton, Leontine Lincoln, and Mayor William S. Greene. Conspicuously absent from the guest list was Thomas J. Borden. The point was unmistakable; Matt Borden's allies were not Fall River types, including his own brothers. After Borden and his guests dined on little neck clams and oysters, beef filet with mushrooms, capon with truffles, and grouse with cress accompanied by Mumm's Extra Dry and Perrier-Jouet Brut, they listened to seven lengthy, lavish testimonial speeches describing Borden as a Napoleon in his vision, the foremost citizen of the city, the herald of good news during hard times, and a symbol of boldness, aggressiveness, and progress. One New York banker dubbed him "Boss Borden" and challenged anyone to rebel against his "princely rule." Matt Borden responded briefly: "I believe in success—the greater the better. I believe in the accumulation of wealth without any limit, . . . Unusual success in the accumulation of wealth brings with it . . . extraordinary responsibilities. . . ."[89] He then proudly announced his gift of one hundred thousand dollars to Fall River charities.[90] Outside of the Brayton family, public benevolence was hardly a Fall River or a Borden tradition. While the *Priscilla* returned the New Yorkers that night across Long Island Sound, the mansions on the "Hill" and along Rock Street must have resonated with cries of outrage, envy, and alarm.

The Fall River manufacturer's association responded to Borden's moves by forming a selling committee to coordinate their activities within the new market situation dominated by Matt Borden's policies. The mills continued to produce massive amounts of print goods, sooner or later ending in a crisis of glut and falling prices. Matt Borden alone could not change this pattern. The old issue of short time or wage cuts faced them again in early 1897. But some association members figured that if M. C. D. Borden could "clean out" grey goods to boost prices as in 1893, perhaps the print cloth manufacturers in Fall River, Lowell, Rhode Island, Maine, and New Hampshire might raise prices by agreeing finally to curtail production. As competitors, a voluntary agreement would be useless. Robert Knight of the B. B. and R. Knight firm of Rhode Island and Connecticut tried to persuade the key Rhode Island manufacturers—the Chaces, the Goddard brothers, and Brown and Ives—to join an "ironclad, copper-riveted" agreement for three months. They refused. Undeterred, Knight went to Fall River in early February. The Braytons and Borden's Iron Works mill managers agreed, carrying all the rest of the local mills into the three-month curtailment. Fall River's decision later included the Knight brothers' firms as well as the mills in Lewiston and Biddeford, Maine, Salmon Falls and Dover, New Hampshire, and Lowell's Hamilton and Merrimack companies.[91]

Once all had pledged, Matt Borden pulled off the largest raid on grey goods in Fall River, topping even his local purchase in 1893. Following a plan known only to three other mill owners, he slipped into town secretly staying with his brother-in-law Holder Durfee. On February 8, Borden bought up all the grey goods in Fall River at the asking price of 2 $\frac{9}{16}$ cents: 750,000 pieces for $900,000. He then agreed to print all of this grey cloth, keeping it out of the market until it was calico. The curtailment agreement held. For this spring trade season, the American Printing Company was able to undersell all the other cloth printers. Borden even avoided broker's fees by doing the buying himself. It was called another "historic swoop" in the interest of manufacturing stability. The next day he returned to New York City.[92] Cloth printers and brokers panicked, and cloth prices began to rise. Except for the mills of the Knight brothers, many Rhode Island mills went into full production. Once the curtailment ended, the Fall River mills also returned to full production. Fall River's last print cloth mill, the Arkwright, was built in 1897. By 1898, the industry was again severely depressed, and the market glutted. Baled cotton sold for 5 cents a pound, cloth for under 2 cents a yard. Something else had to be done, as mill agents regarded an additional curtailment in 1897 "an utter failure."[93] Still, the agreement among many of the major textile interests in New England to stop print cloth production for three months in 1897 demonstrated the potential of a regional textile manufacturers' organization to curtail production or to cut wages. But now much depended on Matt Borden in New York City.

THE MATURING of the Fall River system during the 1880s and 1890s provides a model of American textile production that stands in contrast to the earlier Rhode Island and Lowell models and with the mature Philadelphia system. There was never any pretense at paternalism. Whole families of immigrants from Ireland, England, Quebec, Poland, Germany, the Portuguese Azores, and Italy worked in huge mills, pouring out cheap print cloth. Working and living conditions worsened. Wages declined; skills were undercut. The national mule spinners' union held its privileged position without seriously challenging the workings of the system. Most other unions bent on resistance, especially the weavers, were crushed. Strikes became opportunities to clear inventories and break unwanted contracts, while emptying union treasuries. Interlocking directorates, backed by mutual interest—kinship and friendship—continued the policy of overproduction and glutted markets. The price fluctuations of print cloth now influenced the market for all other standard goods. The Fall River mills, like others in Lowell and Providence, kept secret, huge inventories and surplus funds hidden in the accounts to pay dividends and to build more mills. Many older mills ignored investment in new machinery except for ring spinning frames. The mill treasurers alone interpreted information about the market, creating a self-serving language shaped for their interests and based on their market power. Unstable cloth markets and managerial arrogance intensified class bitterness but sustained Fall River's position as the market leader. All defied the orderly organization of modern business "rationalization." The men who ran this business culture were not "Titans," "Captains of Industry" or even "Robber Barons." Lacking the stature and acumen of Andrew Carnegie, John D. Rockefeller, or J. P. Morgan, these second-rate men used their advantages to enrich themselves heedlessly, and thus they contributed to the ruination of New England textile capitalism.

Textile mills in New England and New York, despite labor legislation and the resistance of some mill agents, copied many features of Fall River operations. The Arkwright Club of Boston began to lobby on Beacon Hill to protect the interests of the region's cotton mills by repealing labor legislation and opposing additional state intervention, while textile mills ignored labor laws by absorbing any small fines, firing complainers, or manipulating the judicial system. The validity of this regional system based on the Fall River model would be tested in a New England-wide crisis in 1898.

10

THE ASCENDANCY OF TRADE UNIONS AND COMBINATIONS, 1898–1906

ONE DAY before the New Bedford operatives struck in January 1898 against a regionwide wage cut, a reporter for the *Boston Post* investigated the life of weaver Mattin Offinger who worked at the Acushnet mills.[1] He had emigrated as a boy with his family from Germany to New Bedford in 1868 and met his future wife in the mill. They married in 1884. When they wed, Mrs. Offinger earned thirty dollars a month as a weaver and her husband thirty-five dollars. They both tended four looms. She left the mill after the first of her two children was born. As a result of the wage cuts and speed-ups adopted during the depression years, her husband tended eight looms at the Acushnet mills in 1897, earning between five dollars and seven dollars a week or twenty dollars to twenty-eight dollars a month. But his weekly earnings were often cut further by a fining system introduced in the New Bedford mills after the Massachusetts Supreme Court had declared the 1891 weavers' fining law unconstitutional and even though a revised law had been enacted in 1892.[2] Once the weekly fines for imperfect work were deducted, Offinger often brought home three dollars. "Little by little things have been getting worse," his wife stated, "until it does not seem as though it was of any use to try to live." Weekly rent for three rooms was $1.50. Once a week Mrs. Offinger bought soup bones, bread, cheap coffee, sugar, and vegetables. Even potatoes were scarce. For fuel, she and her children scavenged the streets for wood chips and scrap.

> To go hungry and cold is hard to bear. It is so hard to face a dry crust every morning . . . and they expect us to keep our health and strength. My husband can have no meat for breakfast unless it is a small piece of bologna sausage, while the children and I go without.[3]

The *Boston Post* reporter examined the pantry, finding half a cabbage, six potatoes, and a small package of chicory coffee. All the sugar was on the breakfast table. Their crockery was meager, their bedding consisted of straw mattresses and homemade cotton quilts. Mrs. Offinger admitted,

> It's not much after fourteen years of married life and hard work. . . . If a weaver makes a good week he is fined or something is done to cut him down to even it up the next week. If there is a single thread rough the whole cut is taken and he is paid nothing, but the cloth is sold for first class just the same.[4]

Many girls and young women also wove in the New Bedford mills, usually running five looms and earning about 90 cents a day, nearly five dollars a week, before fines halved their wages. The difference between the number of looms run by males and females intensified a sex differential in wage rates, made much worse by overseers' targeting women for the majority of fines.

The system of fines and cloth inspection convinced many New Bedford weavers, led by predominately English immigrants, that the mills were determined to cut their wages down in the most oppressive and arbitrary manner possible. After a strike in 1895 over a 10 percent wage cut, all the New Bedford operatives had compromised on a restoration of 5 percent. The fining system took the rest of that 5 percent back, but only from the weavers—a practice that divided the operatives in local labor politics. Then on December 31, 1897, the cloth mills in New Bedford announced another pay cut of 10 percent. As usual, the Fall River mills had been the first to notify their help of a similar reduction, three weeks earlier. This wage cut and the hated fining system together became the target of the New Bedford weavers' determination to strike in 1898. The issue was regional justice or starvation.

The potential drama of the weavers' plight attracted the attention of William Randolph Hearst's *New York Journal* and Joseph Pulitzer's *New York World*. Sensationalist or "yellow" journalists filed exclusive stories and sketches from New Bedford to seize the attention of the nation's readers with images of starvation, suffering, and grinding poverty as the pitiful lot of weavers like Mattin Offinger. Competition for circulation between the *Journal* and the *World* made these press reports a dress rehearsal for the journalistic frenzy over the sinking of the USS *Maine* in Havana harbor on February 16 and the long drawn-out decision by President McKinley for war in April. As one reporter wrote in mid-January, "The strike of the New England mill operatives, if the country could suddenly awaken to a realization of its significance, would cause us as much alarm as the appearance of a hostile fleet off our coast."[5] The yellow press would have to wait only a few weeks, until February 16, for the opportunity to exploit such a moment.

THE REGIONAL wage cut in 1898 represented a decision made and backed financially by the powerful Arkwright Club of Boston, an exclusive organization of cotton mill treasurers in northern New England. Louis Galambos in *Competition and Cooperation: The Emergence of a National Trade Association* (1966) examines the early years of the Arkwright Club and two other regional associations devoted to the technical and marketing interests of textile manufacturing.[6] All three represent informal groups who used their personal political influence and, in the case of the Arkwright Club, lobbying on Beacon Hill and in other New England state capitals against legislation promoted by labor interests to regulate industry. The successful effort to strike the word *willfully* from the ten-hour law in 1879 had prompted the organization of the Arkwright Club in 1880. The club's political activities against subsequent legislation, including weekly wages and the fifty-eight hour law, remained uncoordinated, however, without a staff and dependent on the political clout of various treasurers, such as its organizer Charles H. Dalton of the Merrimack Manufacturing Company of Lowell. Congressman William C. Lovering of Taunton became the club's president in 1897.

For Louis Galambos, the Arkwrighters represented a dinner club of individual heads of firms seeking market stability through cooperation but without a great deal of success.[7] He regards the Arkwright Club as an undeveloped prototype, pointing toward later, more mature, forms of trade associations representing corporations committed to eliminating destabilizing competition in their industries. *Competition and Cooperation* explores more successful versions of these early trade associations, concentrating on the period 1926 to 1935. But as a recurrent theme in his book, Galambos inserts descriptive snapshots of "Fall River: Spring 1880"; "Summer 1900"; Autumn 1925"; and "Winter 1932": a progression of industrial growth, stasis, decline, and failure. Relying on the personal correspondence of several members for his research, he concludes that the Arkwright Club was only a small group lobbying to prevent state regulation.[8] His view overlooks its impressive influence at the turn of the century on the state, the region, and the nation.

In late 1897, the Arkwright Club galvanized the regional cotton industry by identifying and publicizing the threat to New England of southern competition.[9] Its analysis of southern advantages that threatened to overwhelm the cotton mills of the North became a defensive litany, devoutly sung by the declining industry well into the twentieth century. The southern "menace," according to the Arkwright Club in December 1897, defined the future of political debates over the new, dangerous interregional competition. The active role of this emergent trade association, representing the cotton textile industry north of Boston, recast the meaning of the word *region* into a national context. Fall River's market power now came under siege both in the South and in the North.

NEITHER THE Fall River nor the New Bedford treasurers seemed involved in the formation or activities of the Arkwright Club, but they agreed with and supported its opposition to state regulation. Controlled by over a hundred large but unnamed "northern New England mills," the club represented a counterweight to southeastern New England's economic pre-eminence.[10] The Fall River mills had set the standard for New England textile centers in wages and working conditions. In the 1880s and 1890s the mill agents in Fall River had opposed the production curtailments sponsored by the Arkwright Club, until the cloth market became so over-stocked in 1895 and 1896 that no other course seemed possible. Still, the Fall River treasurers continued to believe that control of competition in the print cloth market was best achieved by dominance through their vast productive capacity. With the exception of Matt Borden, they had little interest in combinations other than their own or cooperation with mills outside of Fall River. Regional wage levels were settled inside their granite-block mills. The December 1897 report of the Arkwright Club on a crisis in New England textile production pointed out that southern textile producers were targeting print cloth, which poured from the Fall River mills. Along with Matt Borden and his manipulation of the cloth market, the South, according to the estimates of the Arkwright Club, was beginning to challenge Fall River's market power.

Another voice for industrial cooperation in the North was Edward Atkinson, an opponent of the 1874 ten-hour law and president in 1878 of the Boston Manufacturers' Mutual Fire Insurance Company. He later became one of the pillars of the New England Cotton Manufacturers' Association, devoted to technical advances in the industry. Although at odds with the Arkwright Club on high tariff protection of textiles, he spoke for northern industrial interests at the 1881 Cotton Exposition held in Atlanta, Georgia, which Atkinson had proposed and helped organize. There he exhorted the South to concentrate on developing and perfecting its agricultural capacities, leaving the North and its superior mills to manufacture cotton fabric. Developers rejected Atkinson's view of their New South, and, according to Broadus Mitchell, the 1881 exposition became the pivotal event that turned the southern economy toward textile manufacturing during the next two decades.[11]

Southern competition in the coarser grades of cotton textiles grew swiftly in the late nineteenth century. Many of these mills also made print cloth and "odd-sized" widths (goods other than the standard 28 inches but of the same quality), the staples of Fall River production. By 1897 this inter-regional competition could no longer be discounted or ignored in the North. Print cloth sold that year for a low 2¼ cents. Organized curtailment among the northern cotton mills had failed in the 1890s, and overproduction continued. In late 1897, the Arkwright Club recommended to the entire New England cotton industry the formula that the

Fall River mills had favored for decades to control the market: continued full production at reduced wages. This time the objective was to meet southern competition.

Creating the Southern Menace

On December 15, 1897, a special committee of the Arkwright Club offered its analysis of and recommendations to address the "hopelessness of prolonged competition between the northern and southern manufacturers."[12] Two unidentified members had investigated the Piedmont region of North Carolina, the Charlotte area in particular. The report acknowledged but generally discounted all southern advantages in climate, cost of raw cotton, low taxes, new machinery, and cheap sources of water power and coal. The three crucial differences between cotton manufacturing in the two regions were lower southern wages, "conservatively" estimated at 40 percent less; longer hours, including an eleven-hour day with two shifts in the Charlotte mills; and southern "freedom from legislative interference" and from "the vexatious restriction upon the freedom of contract" in Massachusetts. The report specifically condemned the fifty-eight-hour law passed in 1892 and called for its repeal. The Fall River policy of overproduction and glutting markets seemed only a minor contributory factor to the southern threat. The club unanimously endorsed the report and issued it immediately to the press.

Efforts to repeal Massachusetts labor laws, however, appeared to the Arkwright Club as hopeless as eliminating southern competition. Labeling their findings on low southern wages for ring spinning and weaving as "astounding," the committee recommended that Massachusetts manufacturers "act for themselves." Wages must be "equalized" with the South, while allowing for the higher costs of living in the Northeast. Overproduction of cotton goods depressed the price and had made profits intolerably low. Even worse, the prospect of a failure to compete successfully with the South in print cloth and the coarser goods would drive *all* New England production into fine goods, the sector of the industry which the Arkwright Club represented. Competition would intensify in the region with those northern mills "already in the field." The report suggested that the cotton industry would change in Lowell, Lawrence, Manchester, New Bedford, and the mill towns in Maine, all centers with substantial fine goods production, and their Boston investors would never allow this.

With the 1897 report, the Arkwright Club thus created a sense of historic crisis and revealed its agenda. The leaders endorsed, as crucial to the survival of the New England cotton industry, a regional wage cut of at least 10 percent for a workforce of one hundred thousand. On December 9, even before the report was made public, the Fall River manufacturers' association announced the reduction to twenty-eight thousand operatives in seventy-five mills.[13] For the print goods industry in New England to survive, production costs had to be cut. By January 1, following Fall River's lead, the mills of New Hampshire, Massachusetts, Rhode Island, Connecticut, and Maine announced a wage cut of 10 percent or more.[14] This action represented more than corporate cooperation or a gentlemen's agreement around a dinner table. Already operating as a regional trade association, the Arkwright Club, it was widely reported, would retaliate financially against any slacker, whether a member or not.

In the fine goods center of New Bedford, the management at the Wamsutta mills, immediately and firmly dismissed the Arkwright report as scare tactics. The New Bedford Board of Trade also rejected any threat of southern competition as meaningless. Pointing out that southern costs for raw cotton and coal meant little, a representative of the prominent Pierce family cited northern advantages. The South had no bleacheries for print goods. Southern mills celebrated as a great achievement the spinning of filling yarn at counts of 50s (relatively coarse) on ring frames, while the New Bedford mules easily spun counts as fine as 200s. Freight rates to northern bleacheries, cloth printers, and New York commission houses also placed the southern mills at a distinct disadvantage. In addition, the total number of spindles in the southern mills was smaller than the total in Fall River. The southern mills could not make fine goods without mule spinning, and mule spinners would bring unions and agitation for labor laws to the Carolinas.[15] In December 1897, the families who dominated New Bedford cloth production felt no threat from the South to their market sector. This dismissal of the southern menace would later haunt the New Bedford mill owners when, under the pressure of the combined New England cotton interests, they gave in and announced their own 10 percent wage cut, effective January 17, 1898. This was no well-considered managerial decision but a response to powerful political and economic pressure from the emerging New England textile lobby led by Boston's Arkwright Club. As a result, New Bedford became the scene of the most significant fight in the nineteenth century over the New England wage standard, which drew the attention of rival editors William Randolph Hearst and Joseph Pulitzer as well as of Samuel Gompers of the AFL and socialists Daniel DeLeon and Eugene V. Debs.

ACQUIESCENCE IN FALL RIVER

The response of the Fall River operatives was crucial to any acceptance of the regional wage cut. In a shrewd move, the manufacturers' association met with all of the union leaders, members of the newly organized International Textile Workers' Union associated with the AFL.[16] The mill managers bestowed on the other unions the privilege, granted previously only to the mule spinners' union, of recognizing them informally as bargaining agents. The gesture cost the mill owners nothing, while the union leaders regarded it as very significant. But was there anything to bargain about? The mill interests had announced a wage cut of $11\frac{1}{9}$ percent, an unusual figure, based on the exact percentage drop that resulted from cutting the weavers' piece rate from 18 to 16 cents a cut. The union leadership countered with three ideas: postpone the wage cut for two months, curtail production to four days a week, and bring in the state board of arbitration. The manufacturers agreed to consider their proposals but during the meeting criticized them as unworkable. The industry's lobbyists had made sure the state board remained powerless to obtain information or enforce its decisions. Impatient during the show of reason and courtesy that barely masked the determination of the mill men, Albert Hibbert of the weavers' union railed against "McKinley prosperity." Fourteen months ago, he admitted, he had voted along with many textile workers for the Republican presidential candidate McKinley. "Like a sucker," he proclaimed, "I took the bait and here I am today with no prosperity." No one responded.[17] The next day the manufacturers' association rejected all union proposals and targeted the fifty-eight hour law for repeal. Their reply was sent only to secretary Thomas O'Donnell and treasurer John Golden of the mule spinners' union, thus excluding and insulting the others. Furthermore, secretary Cyrus Rouseville stated that the manufacturers' association members regarded the wage cut as "very moderate—much less than is thought by many to be necessary. . . ."[18]

Would the nearly twenty-six thousand Fall River operatives strike? O'Donnell expressed shock over the rejection of the union's "business proposition to the men who employ us" that the cut be postponed until March 1 to see if the market improved. He knew that most union operatives in Fall River were eager to strike, but the textile unions organized into the AFL had been exhausted by fighting for several years with Daniel DeLeon's Socialist Labor Party.[19] Furthermore, the workforce faced divisive wage rates. Following a policy as in New Bedford that the operatives called "skinning," the Fall River mills no longer paid the same piece rates for the same work. Each mill used various techniques to cut labor costs. All branches of the workforce faced speeding of old machinery, intensified work on new machinery, and rapidly changing and confusing styles of cloth and piece rates for different types of work. The loom fixers' union had prevented many strikes by negotiating with supervisors over any new work rules, but this regionwide wage cut could not be ignored. Potentially, the across-the-board cut would hit the operatives in different mills and lines of work unequally, but the Fall River mills decided to equalize wages downward to the lowest piece rate *before* the $11\frac{1}{9}$ percent cut in January. As a result, many weavers found their pay reduced by a full 20 percent.[20] This created even deeper anger.

M. C. D. Borden, not a member of the Arkwright Club, telegraphed his refusal to cut wages at their behest. Furthermore, as in 1892, neither the Fall River nor New Bedford yarn mills cut wages, as the demand for yarn in 1898 remained high. The union secretaries decided not to strike but urged the acceptance of the wage reduction under a vague threat of a strike after March 1. Persuading the membership was not easy. A conference committee of the unions presented the enraged operatives with their recommendation. Cutting wages certainly would never cure overproduction or raise cloth prices, but, the union secretaries argued, a strike "would not be good business policy on our part at the present time." Selling this recommendation to the irate mule spinners nearly resulted in O'Donnell's ouster by the union membership. He wisely summoned Robert Howard from Boston to steady them.

At a second meeting O'Donnell pleaded with the spinners not to dismiss the conference committee as the manufacturers' association had done. He warned them against the dangers of a general strike in midwinter, but one spinner asked if he had been reading "ghost stories." Treasurer John Golden urged the members to accept the reduction, but a second spinner, recalling the 1884 strike, pointed out that the union had even less money then and the weather had been just as bad. Another union man detailed what the mills would make in profits from the wage reduction, imagining them on vacation at Saratoga, New York, resorts while the operatives dug clams. But Robert Howard, cheered as "Our Bob," deflected this incipient rebellion. He acknowledged their anger and eagerness to strike and called the reduction senseless and unjustifiable, but he advised them as responsible union men to postpone the vote and think it over coolly and calmly. Would not a strike be more successful in the spring?[21]

Except for the mule spinners, all the union members accepted the wage reduction. Then at a tense meeting of the spinners on December 31, acceptance of the wage cut passed with a majority of only thirty-five votes. Those ready to strike "were beside themselves with rage," yelling, "To hell with the union. Strike! Strike!" Denouncing O'Donnell and Golden as frauds, they created such a disturbance that the leadership summoned fifteen policemen. Still, after this meeting, the union secretaries all expressed relief at the outcome; perhaps they already knew that the strike would center in New Bedford. The spinners had fallen in line with the carders, weavers, slasher-tenders, loom fixers, and the rest of the organized help.[22] Their position was characterized as "Defense, not Defiance," the old mule spinners' union motto from the 1870s. After the operatives decided not to strike, Matt Borden's Iron Works mills also cut wages 10 percent as good business policy. In New Bedford, however, the mule spinners, the weavers, and the carders vowed to strike when their reduction took effect on January 17.[23]

Assessing the Southern Menace

In December 1897, as the wage cuts spread throughout New England and mule spinners and weavers in Lowell, in Lewiston, Biddeford, and Saco, Maine, and in George Draper's Queen City mills in Burlington, Vermont, went on strike, the editor of the *Fall River Globe* assigned reporter Walter N. Caswell to test the validity of the Arkwright report. Travelling widely in the South, he collected opinions, impressions, and whatever data he could squeeze from mill men. Robert Howard, who had attempted to organize in the Georgia textile mills for the AFL, and state representative Samuel Ross of New Bedford, secretary of the National Cotton Mule Spinners' Association, denounced the Arkwright report as highly exaggerated.[24] Organized labor, the operatives, and the public eagerly read their statements, while the Arkwright Club backed their own conclusions. Investigating reporters or union officials had little power to change minds of mill treasurers, but the question of who was right about southern competition could have serious political implications in the Massachusetts state legislature.

After visiting mills centers in Charlotte, North Carolina, Spartanburg, South Carolina, and Atlanta, Augusta, and Columbus, Georgia, Caswell denied the key claim of the Arkwright report. Wages were not 40 percent lower than in northern mills, but rather averaged 15 percent lower. Wages in the country mills in the Piedmont region near Charlotte, North Carolina, which made wide sheeting and print cloth, were decidedly lower, but in the Georgia mills, only 5 percent lower and some wages were equal to northern wages. Hours were longer, especially in the Piedmont region, where mills operated two shifts of eleven hours, six days a week. The average workday in the South was eleven hours. Caswell observed that all textile manufacturers, North or South, wished to produce as much as possible each working day, noting that the Fall River mills ran overtime whenever the machinery stopped for mechanical failures to make up for any lost time on a fifty-eight hour work week, whether the market was overstocked or not. Their decision to cut wages, he decided, was "radically wrong."

Caswell also found that the country mills in the South did not have natural advantages in lower costs for raw cotton. Competition among small mills in a particular district, especially in the Piedmont region, bid up the price of local cotton, whereas northern mills could buy cheaper cotton shipped from Texas. Lower taxes were also a myth. Country mills escaped town taxes but faced county assessments. In addition, southern mills had significant disadvantages in high interest rates on money borrowed from New York commission houses and high costs of shipping their goods by railroad to bleacheries, print works, and the New York market. And southern mills suffered just as much as northern mills in 1897 from the severely depressed cloth market. Caswell concluded that the Fall River idea of driving the southern manufacturer out of the print cloth business by cutting wages was an illusion. The South, with its lower living costs would retaliate by reducing wages. Do not believe the alarmists, Caswell wrote on December 29, just before the Fall River unions voted. If northern mill interests would just keep their investments in New England and not cut their own throats by building southern mills, the Arkwright Club pessimists would be proven wrong.[25]

Caswell's image of the southern mill worker as a shiftless, submissive, poverty-stricken resident of a broken-down shanty was shattered during his visit.[26] He talked with overseers and operatives as well as mill managers, who praised their workforce but absolutely refused to give him any data on production costs. During his trip through the textile South, Caswell met many operatives from rural areas who were uneducated but intelligent and very quick to learn. He came to believe that southern operatives when properly taught would be capable of producing fine goods. Naturally courteous, strictly temperance, and deeply religious, they had an inclination when faced with strikes or wage cuts to move about from mill town to the mill town, not unlike French Canadian and Lancashire operatives. The high turnover rates among the workforce reflected a southern spirit of independence but also indicated a refusal to join trade unions as alien to rural life. Union organizers had better opportunities in cities such as Atlanta, Augusta, and Columbus, Georgia. The southern mills used no mules, only ring spinning frames.

One overseer with experience in the north claimed it was impossible to "drive" the southern textile worker to equal New England's productivity. Southerners were touchy, stubborn, and walked out at the use of harsh language. Any overseer who spoke contemptuously to a female operative was likely to face her father or brother after work. Most of the workforce in the Columbus, Georgia, mills lived across the state line in Phenix, Alabama, in a small town controlled by textile workers. The owner of the Louise mills in Charlotte, North Carolina, well acquainted with conditions in Fall River and Providence, claimed that he did not need and would never hire New England workers. He had a "superabundance" of the kind of men who made the best fighters for the Confederacy, even if they refused to volunteer and had to be drafted. He had commanded sixty such men in his own military company. They cared neither for unions or strikes. As former farmers used to working long hours for little return, cash wages were a great boon. Many sent their whole families into the mills.[27]

The Louise mill owner blamed the 1896 elections for producing a North Carolina legislature full of Populists and Republicans, the latter the "worst elements" in southern life, who had already cut one hour from the twelve-hour workday. In retaliation, he eliminated free rent at his cottages, blaming the labor reformers. But in South Carolina and Georgia, the eleven-hour day with only one shift was law. Furthermore, the southern mill managers knew precisely which northern mills they competed with in garment linings, wide sheeting, odd plain widths, print cloth (woven on automatic Northrop looms in the Spartan mills of Spartanburg, South Carolina), or ginghams (made near Charlotte). Their targets were the markets of Fall River, the Amoskeag mills in New Hampshire, and New England in general. Why, many southern mill owners wondered, didn't the northern print mills use their mules to make finer, superior print cloth and recapture the dress goods market? Generally, they agreed that overproduction represented the worst problem for both North and South. Why, one mill owner in Augusta, Georgia, asked, did the Arkwright report not mention this?[28]

The housing provided by textile operations located in Atlanta was like the privately owned tenements of Fall River: crowded, ill kept, unsanitary, and located on dirty streets. There Caswell found the urban poor white class, the Georgia "cracker," especially at the Exposition mills. The Georgia mill owners in Atlanta, Augusta, and Columbus laughed at the Arkwright report but refused to tell Caswell where it was wrong on production costs. For the northern trade journal, *Textile World*, the "only bright spot" in southern competition was potential racial strife between white and black operatives, which probably would spark labor agitation by whites, strikes against the introduction of black workers, and all-white unions lobbying for labor reform. Some northern mill owners, however, feared that the reserve of black labor meant that wages in southern mills had virtually no bottom. In August 1897, the hiring of black workers at the Fulton Bag and Cotton Mill resulted in a strike in Atlanta that caused the union membership to jump into the hundreds, including many white women operatives. When the AFL convention met in Nashville, Tennessee, in late 1897, the organization voted to contribute funds and send Samuel Ross from New Bedford to investigate. The Fulton mill strikers were well dressed and religious, running their meetings with prayers and union chaplains. When he found that the strike was overhiring black operatives rather than a wage cut, Ross returned to New England. The National Union of Textile Workers led by P. W. Greene of Columbus, Georgia, organized six unions with a combined membership of about two thousand. In 1897, the entire South had no other textile unions. A decade earlier, the Knights of Labor in Augusta had been active in a lockout and unsuccessful strike between July and November 1887, but labor activity continued unsuccessfully until 1905.[29]

Regardless of the dismal prospects for unionization, Caswell insisted that his travels revealed the Arkwright Club's report as highly exaggerated.[30] Nonetheless, in Fall River the operatives all voted on December 31 to accept the wage reduction. In New Bedford, where the "English outnumber[ed] all the others together," the mule spinners voted unanimously in early January to strike the fine goods mills, busy with orders, well protected by tariffs, and with no acknowledged competitors outside of Lancashire. The weavers and the carders joined them in a strike against the nine cloth mills with nine thousand operatives, expecting to be backed by a New England textile workforce of ninety thousand. Some strikers began to purchase flour by the barrel, indicating their expectation of a long struggle with the stubborn Pierce and Knowles families. The regional wage cut and the future of labor politics in New England rested on the outcome of these events.

Yellow Journalism and the 1898 Textile Strike

An outbreak of violence on the first day, January 17, brought reporters from Boston and New York to New Bedford, intrigued by the stoning of the nephew of John F. Knowles, treasurer of the Acushnet and Hathaway mills, where the system of fining weavers for defects in the cut had been introduced and was most blatantly unjust. At the Bristol mills strikers had smashed windows, although after these initial outbursts, they remained very orderly. Journalists from New York's *Journal* and *World,* and from Boston's *Post* and *Traveler,* predominately female, created their own sensational images of the strikers. The reporters described the New Bedford strike as an uprising of women weavers with their own outrageous grievances, independent leaders, and confrontational labor politics. Highlighting the activities of women weavers in the press accounts, whatever the motives, contributed to tensions within the weavers' union.

Eva McDonald Valesh and Anne O'Hagan for Hearst's *Journal,* Elizabeth L. Banks for Pulitzer's *World,* and Lizette LeBaron-Cotton for the Boston *Traveler* were among the first wave of women reporters representing the New Journalism of the 1880s. Valesh had come to New York City as a labor reporter after her involvement in Minnesota's agrarian politics of the late 1880s and early 1890s. In 1891 she was an active presence at the AFL convention, where she and other female labor delegates were successful in persuading Samual Gompers to hire a female organizer, Mary Kenney of Chicago, who concentrated her efforts in Massachusetts. In 1896 she was a national organizer for the Peoples' Party and campaigned for William Jennings Bryan. After two years writing articles for AFL's *Federationist,* Valesh in 1897 joined the staff of the *Journal.* During the early weeks of the 1898 strike, she quickly identified Mrs. Harriet Pickering as the leader of the four thousand striking women and seized upon her as a dramatic symbol of the women's struggle. Pickering stated, "We are striking against a trust that controls the whole textile industry of New England," while Valesh extravagantly promoted Pickering in the free-trade *Journal* as "New Bedford's Joan of Arc."[31]

Born in Blackburn, Lancashire in 1865, Harriet, an independent, rebellious child, ran away from her father's farm and began to work at eight in a weave room. She married at eighteen and bore a son at twenty, but six years later her mule spinner husband died. In 1889 she and her boy immigrated, first to Fall River, staying briefly, then settling in New Bedford. The last eight years, she reflected, "have worn and aged me more than all the rest." Pickering refused to live in mill tenements, renting an attic in a respectable middle-class neighborhood and denying herself food and new clothing to keep her son in school. She intended that he become a lawyer. Pickering read books on economics and called herself a Christian Socialist, a respectable movement in England but one opposed by the AFL. She became a naturalized citizen and participated in the labor reform activities that successfully backed the particulars law of 1892. Pickering's overseer at the Hathaway mills caught her writing down as evidence for the violation of the particulars law the specifications posted for the cloth she was weaving. She was fired and blacklisted. She found work at the Wamsutta under another name but was discovered and fired again. Finally, a Grinnell mill overseer gave her some looms. Pickering believed that the New England textile workers must form an amalgamation like the cloak makers of New York City. "If we are to fight a combine, we must do it with a combine."[32] A tall, slender, pale woman with piercing brown eyes, she became the controversial champion within the weavers' union of abolishing the fining system. This became the key divisive issue during the strike. Eva Valesh upstaged Elizabeth L. Baker of the *World*, who never found a Harriet Pickering but concentrated on exposing the miserable housing in New Bedford and the wretched lives of the striking operatives. Baker had been a reporter for a London paper, and her exploits, bravado, and persistence won her a job at the *World* and the assignment in New Bedford. After the strike, she criticized yellow journalist editors for offering women reporters dangerous, difficult, and demeaning assignments.[33]

But Valesh out-maneuvered all her rival journalists, quickly proposing that state representative Samuel Ross, also head of the national mule spinners' union, introduce legislation to investigate the causes of the regional wage reduction. Although Senator Joseph J. Flynn, Democrat of Lawrence, decided to sponsor a similar measure, Valesh and Hearst's *Journal* grabbed the credit.[34] Later Valesh, a hard-working self-promoter, had legislation drafted and introduced to reform the fining system, while taking a leading part in both subsequent hearings. Her great coup was an interview at the White House with President McKinley who, she claimed, endorsed the proposed state investigation, immigration restriction, and a shorter working day. Valesh also questioned Republican Nelson Dingley of Maine, chair of the House Ways and Means Committee, about the influence of the Dingley tariff, which Hearst strongly opposed, on the New Bedford strike. Major centers of production in Maine were erupting with strikes, but Dingley denied any direct connection. Meanwhile Hearst's editorials denounced the Dingley tariff and the McKinley administration which many New Bedford operatives had supported against Democrats and the Populists in 1896.

While Valesh was in Washington, the rival *World* sent Minnie R. Rosen, a twenty-five-year-old "Hebrew" labor organizer from the lower east side of New York, the secretary of the Women's Branch of the United Garment Workers. Rosen spoke eloquently to mass meetings of New Bedford strikers, lamenting their condition as "white slaves" in the mills and interviewing many operatives about their privations. William Foley, vice president of the weavers' union, speaking for many operatives, begged Rosen and the other women reporters not to portray the proud strikers as broken-down miserable people living in hovels. Many articles contained comparisons of New Bedford weavers with southern slaves and Russian serfs and portrayed the enormous, oppressive power of the New Bedford mills, sketched in such outlandish ways that many textile workers became offended. One example was a Hearst editorial titled, "The Lashing of White Women," illustrated by a black female slave being whipped by a white overseer next to an emaciated white woman weaver closely watched by her overbearing boss weaver holding a book marked "Fines." Even in a former center of antislavery agitation, no white worker in New Bedford wished their conditions described as worse than southern slaves. In late January, Hearst's staff located the son of a slaveholder and a former slave living in New York City. Both visited New Bedford, looked around, and declared that southern slavery had been a more benign system. James Copeland, the former slave, insisted, "No, I wouldn't be one of those weavers, nohow."[35] Such sensational reports, however, attracted great public attention and potential strike contributions.

Valesh, Baker, Rosen, O'Hagan and LeBaron-Cotton looked for picturesque poverty to expose the dismal situation of women workers in the New Bedford cotton mills. Low wages, further cut by the fining system for weavers, frequently forced female workers into the workforce, regardless of age, marital status or number of children. Young single men and women boarded in private homes and company houses. Married men and women workers also boarded until they had families. Then, like the Offingers, they rented rooms in tenements. Some mothers stayed in the mills, taking a little time off to care for newborns but soon returning to their looms, leaving their infants with others. No male weaver earned a family wage. "How can I live on the wages my man earns?" asked one working wife. Most of the female reporters' attention focused on women who supported others as the working heads of families: widows with dependent children, such as Harriet Pickering, or young single women supporting their widowed mothers, disabled fathers or young siblings. Many of these female-headed families and the less skilled French Canadian weavers felt they could not afford even 10 cents a week in union dues. As times grew even harder during the strike, families of working women and married couples doubled up in rooms to save rent and fuel. The "canary" press headlined many stories of hardship, some so exaggerated that workers complained of the hideous rendering of their appearance in sketches or the demeaning descriptions of their poor food and housing. Valesh and Baker were especially scorned for making up statements that many called outright lies. The strikers' greatest fear, however, was having their names appear in print along with their grievances, notoriety that was sure to land them on the blacklist or in trouble with the union officers for unauthorized statements.[36]

FINING WOMEN WEAVERS

The New York and Boston reporters revealed that the fining system, most onerous at the Acushnet and Hathaway mills owned by the Knowles family, targeted women and teenaged weavers as less likely to complain or to be able change jobs than male weavers. All weavers were fined, but many male weavers believed themselves more capable of resisting, while the women were too "meek." The fining system thus became regarded as a workingwoman's problem. These perceptions fed male and female conflict within the local union, while the New England Federation of Weavers-AFL agreed that fining was primarily a woman's grievance. Still, many male weavers, such as Mattin Offinger, were victimized during the depression years, and the union was reluctant to admit that their male members were forced to submit to an abuse that had become feminized. Some women weavers stated that the distractions of family life and housework made them careless and too exhausted to complain but not to feel angry disgust at the rampant cheating by the overseers. Other women insisted that the looms ran so fast and the filling yarn was so fine that it was impossible to avoid slight errors, such as a single hanging thread or a tiny spot of oil. What weaver was ever hired to produce perfect cloth? In New Bedford, complainers were fined more often and threatened with the blacklist to shut them up. Weaver Lola Minet at the Hathaway, the sole support of her dying mother, lost control one day and asked her critical overseer, "Sam, don't you call that good cloth?" Sam sneered, "Oh, don't try to get rich so fast, miss." She struck him as hard as she could, several times, and found herself blacklisted as a "vixen." Female weavers had to submit to hold on to their jobs. Despite their denials, so did male weavers, English and French Canadian. Leon Chevier got so angry that he snatched the allegedly "blemished" cloth from his arbitrary overseer and ran. He spent thirty days in jail for theft.[37]

The 1891 weavers' fining law, making the deduction of penalties from a weaver's wages illegal, had been declared unconstitutional by the state supreme court for violating freedom of contract. In 1892, legislation permitting the "grading" of cloth contained a section setting strict conditions under which an employer might fine a weaver. The imperfection had to be the fault of the weaver, not the result of stains made by loom fixers, oil dripping from machinery, flawed filling, or poor warp on the loom's beam. Before this fine could be imposed, the weaver had to examine the cloth, accept responsibility, and negotiate the amount of the fine with the superintendent. As usual, the New Bedford mills ignored state legislation that had no meaningful enforcement. The Acushnet and Hathaway mills not only violated the provisions in the 1892 law in outrageous ways but also mended and cleaned so-called blemished cloth and sold it as first-class goods. Many disgusted weavers simply refused to examine the cloth as a waste of their precious work time. Some weavers believed that the cloth room workers, who inspected and cleaned or repaired each 60-yard cut of fine fabric, were actually paid out of the fines. The strikers also suspected that treasurer John F. Knowles had hired a cloth room inspector who earned a commission on every defect found. After the strike began in January, Knowles persuaded the cloth room women at the Acushnet to inspect and pack up the last of his orders and then rewarded them by paying for this work at the 10 percent reduction. The gross violations of the 1892 law had sufficiently aroused the New Bedford weavers' union members to consider a strike against the abuses, but the system of grading and fining was less harsh at other New Bedford mills, and the practice had not been adopted in Fall River.[38]

Anne O'Hagan of the *Journal* discovered Jane Gallagher, who in 1897 quit her job in protest against fining at the Hathaway mills, and turned her into "the bravest woman in New Bedford." Jane Gallagher possessed an Irish face and temper combined with a Lancashire dialect and doggedness. Like so many others in New England, her Irish-born parents had brought her to English mills where she worked as a weaver until widowed. There was no system of punitive fines in Lancashire. She was thirty-six-years old when she and her daughter emigrated in 1893.[39] Like Harriet Pickering, Jane Gallagher represented the continued immigration of Lancashire weavers to New England, even after the flow of mule spinners had ended. Each fresh wave of immigrants brought with them the old country standards and practices which they compared with conditions and labor politics in New England. They judged the New England mills as badly managed, too large, and extravagant in paying generous dividends to shareholders. In January 1897, Gallagher was working on plain looms at the Hathaway mills. One Saturday, she collected full pay for a cut she had woven, but the following week found that her pay had been reduced 58½ cents for that same cloth now judged imperfect. No one had informed her, and she never examined the cloth. Regarding this treatment as unjust and a violation of Massachusetts law, she took her hat and shawl and told her overseer, "I will not be fined." He laughed at her. Labeled an anarchist and a firebrand, she had difficulty getting work, but her skill as a fine goods weaver helped her find a new place. She sued the Hathaway mills with the union's help but had no money to proceed until editor Hearst offered to pay her legal bills in a typically grandiose gesture.[40]

Trouble in the Weavers' Union

When the New Bedford mills cut wages, secretary Matthew Hart of the weavers' union had already decided to strike over the fining system. To combine the two issues of wage cuts and fining was potentially divisive during a general strike of all operatives. Only the weavers were fined, and not all mills in the city fined as severely as those run by the Knowles family. Cleverly, the mills fined no one on their last payday. Yellow journalists portrayed the fining issue as a woman's problem, and many male weavers thought so too. The union's executive committee wanted to separate the wage cut from the fining issue, believing that the strike offered a unique opportunity to organize all the weavers into the AFL-backed federation. The executive committee would not act, however, unless the general membership agreed, although to abandon the issue might prove just as divisive within the New Bedford union. Jane Gallagher's case based on the 1892 law, if sustained, might resolve this difficult issue. Until then, the fining system remained controversial, especially as the blacklisted Harriet Pickering began to challenge the union leadership over strike objectives. When the general membership met on January 19, the unorganized strikers had already voted by the hundreds to keep the abuses of the fining system central to their strike. At the union meeting, the well-publicized Pickering made her first appearance as a vocal supporter of keeping both issues as strike goals. One third of those at the meeting were women.

Speaking nervously at first, Pickering stubbornly talked down the men who tried to interrupt, arguing that, "the 10 percent reduction is an insult added to the fining. . . . You must remember that in this country the manufacturers are all combined . . . , only last week . . . Horatio Hathaway was married to one of the daughters of [Congressman William C.] Lovering," president of the Arkwright Club. Her shrewd observation about the combined political and social power of the mills symbolized by a wedding was met with derisive male laughter. In a parting shot at the executive committee, she warned, "if you fight against this reduction alone, you are going to get grandly left." The specter was a return to work by the women and the non-union weavers. Using a secret ballot, a two-thirds majority of union members supported Pickering's position, and the executive committee reported to the general strike council that they would not give up the fining issue. Then Pickering tried to meet with the women weavers separately, despite the objections of the executive committee.[41] They gave her a lesson about who was in charge.

Pickering's first meeting to organize a female branch of the union featuring Eva Valesh, an experienced AFL organizer, was canceled for lack of an audience. Male weavers crowded the second meeting, declaring that they would not be "led by the nose," by any upstart female. Then they left. With anger illuminating her thin white face and flashing eyes, she addressed the remaining small number of women.

> Down with the fines system. You call yourselves Americans. You are slaves—white slaves, slaves as nowhere exist in England. I have worked in the Lancashire cotton mills and know what I am talking about. I have become a citizen of the United States and an inhabitant of your town and State, and I am going to do my duty by you and myself and abolish the slavery of the fining system.

"Yes," remarked one woman to a reporter, "perhaps she will, but we'll starve to death in the meantime."[42] Furthermore, by the 1890s, a number of investigating reporters had transformed the meaning of white slavery from a fundamentally racist term into forced prostitution, an association that morally respectable workingwomen wished to avoid. Pickering was raising some difficult, divisive issues for the weavers.

Other women weavers favored loyalty to the executive committee and the single issue of the wage cut. One was Yorkshire-born and Lancashire-trained Mrs. Maria Hindle, a critic of the fining system but the leader of the anti-Pickering female weavers. Out of eighteen mills in New Bedford, only those owned by the Acushnet and the Hathaway fined outrageously. First, Hindle argued, get back the wage cut; then make war on those two mills. At a third meeting, Pickering was prevented from speaking, her podium whisked away by the janitor while noise filled the hall. Withdrawing in disgust at the cheering and hissing she was forced off the platform by a very large audience of union men and women.[43] Still, the unorganized strikers represented a serious problem, and Harriet Pickering was not silenced.

In an obvious move to divide the strikers, the New Bedford mill owners asked to meet with Pickering and a delegation of women weavers. They had always refused to deal with secretary Hart, treating him with a total lack of respect. Backed by women's rights activists from Providence, Harriet Pickering called a meeting to select a female delegation to confront the treasurers on the issue of the fines. Both men and women weavers appeared, but none would go with her. Leave this to the men, women strikers insisted. Despite her sense of the gross injustice in American mills, Pickering now appeared a divisive dupe of the mill interests. Whenever she showed up at union meetings, she was greeted with loud derision meant to drive her away. She stood her ground. In failing to utilize the strength and purpose of Harriet Pickering and Jane Gallagher, famous victims of the fining system, the striking weavers were losing two valuable if difficult allies. Both women needed the guidance and support of the union, but Pickering's public challenge to secretary Hart as a man who was leading the weavers into "a ditch" and the lionizing of Jane Gallagher by the *Journal* had turned them into untrustworthy malcontents. Female dissidents were not welcome in a union increasingly dominated by male interests.

There were other deep divisions among the nine thousand New Bedford strikers. The mule spinners' union, with sixty thousand dollars in the local treasury and the backing of its national organization, supported just over three hundred strikers. The yarn mills in New Bedford had not cut wages and were running at full production and those yarn mill spinners were paying both dues and strike assessments into the union treasury. Sharing sentiments often expressed in Fall River, one striking New Bedford weaver remarked, "What do the spinners care for us?" About twenty-five hundred carders and one hundred loom fixers in AFL-affiliated unions were out on strike. The mill owners knew that the weavers, carders, and loom fixers had small union treasuries and expected the four thousand striking weavers to break first. Union weavers received only tiny amounts of strike pay, as little as one dollar a week, in accordance with a descending scale of dues between 25 and 10 cents a week. One man who had paid his 10 cents for nineteen weeks found himself just one week short of qualifying for strike pay. The executive committee could not budge; there was not enough money to support union members for long. All outside contributions, including a vigorous campaign for the "Funeral of the Arkwright Club" sponsored by the *Lowell Sun,* theatrical benefits in Boston and New York City, and huge contributions of bread, sponsored by the *Boston Traveler,* went to non-union strikers. But at the first distribution of benefits, each received only 6 cents, an untimely move much criticized as deeply discouraging.[44]

Local tradesmen offered credit and specially low-priced groceries to strikers, some landlords refused to evict their tenants, and fish dealers contributed five hundred pounds of fresh cod each week. Beef for boiling sold for 5 cents a pound, but most strikers purchased cheaper fish, liver, hearts, and salt pork. A soup kitchen, set up by a sympathetic storekeeper and former operative, distributed quarts of soup each day to families and pints to individuals. Chicken, tripe, pea, chowder, and always fish soup on Fridays fed those not too ashamed to be seen in public with empty pails and cans. Many of the English operatives preferred cooperative housekeeping, pooling what they had with their fellow workers.[45]

The state board of charities sent its director, who personally surveyed the New Bedford scene after Mayor Charles S. Ashley had expressed sympathy for the strikers. But the state prevented the local overseers of the poor from granting relief to any union members. The dismal state alms-house at Tewksbury was the only other option. Local poor relief for non-union strikers, limited to eight weeks, depended on several years' residency in New Bedford and on citizenship. In addition, only heads of families could apply, usually placing the shame of accepting charity on men. Although French priests assisted strikers in their community, many French Canadians left the city, some to return to Quebec. A French Canadian operative said he was leaving New Bedford because

> I am poor. I cannot stay idle. I do not belong to any union, and therefore cannot expect them to look out for me when funds get low. I am not a citizen of New Bedford, and if I ask for aid I must go to Tewksbury. . . . I can go home now and get work in the [Quebec] lumber camps. It is hard work but I would rather do it than work in the mill at the rate they want to give us.[46]

The Primitive Methodist Church, packed with an English immigrant congregation, was influential with both New Bedford and Fall River trade unionists and supported the strike. One immigrant, desperately trying to return to Lancashire, stated, "This country's no good for a weaver." Many hoped to return as quickly as possible, once they had money for their passage. Unmarried men and women boarders also left the city in large numbers.[47]

The weather turned bitterly cold with nights of below zero temperatures. Windows frosted over in the tenements. A major blizzard on January 31, in addition to snow, sleet, and rain blown by icy winds off Buzzard's Bay, required the city to hire men to clear the streets. The city paid strikers $1.50 per day, more than a weaver could earn at his looms. A non-union striker was reduced to occasional shoveling, charity, begging, the soup kitchen, and a pittance from the unexpectedly meager contributions from New England textile operatives to the strike fund. Women strikers had fewer options to earn money. One Staten Island woman wrote to Elizabeth Banks of the *World*, offering a position as a domestic servant in her household to a "friendless," strong, English or American girl. Banks found that most female strikers lived with their families, none knew the fundamentals of middle-class housekeeping, and all preferred mill work to being servants.[48] Striking women took in washing and ironing and went out scrubbing but wished to stay in New Bedford. Mill work was their life. Meanwhile, the press printed the salaries of the treasurers and the dividends paid by the New Bedford mills in 1897. The Acushnet and the Hathaway led with 16 percent and 10 percent, respectively, with lower rates for the rest. The Wamsutta paid 6 percent. Treasurers' salaries averaged fifteen thousand dollars annually. The mill owners believed that at some point the non-union help in their desperation would clamor for work. According to Otis N. Pierce, the second son of Andrew Pierce and treasurer at the Grinnell mills, the "wretches" would break the strike sometime in mid-February.[49] Despite the divisions within the weavers' union and difficult times, the Pierces were wrong.

THE STATE INVESTIGATES THE REGIONAL WAGE CUT

In mid-February a joint labor committee investigated the regional wage cut, targeting the Arkwright Club's role in the decision and exposing its political power on Beacon Hill. With so many textile operatives affected, the Flynn-Ross bill sponsoring the investigation, backed by Hearst's *Journal* and the pro-labor Boston press, became politically popular in January, especially in the state house of representatives, even though it represented an unprecedented attempt by the state to examine managerial policy. The Republican majority in the state Senate fought back and struck the words *and papers* from Flynn's original bill, which had called for "full authority to send for persons and papers." No mill treasurer could be forced to supply the committee with documents, and testimony would not be taken under oath. Once the investigation had been hobbled, the Republican governor urged the senate to pass the bill quickly in response to public interest. But the Boston *Post* insisted that without access to papers and account books, the real story of why the mills cut wages would never be known.[50] The hearings became a stage for the conflicting views of mill owners and operatives, while the committee's only charge was to produce a report on the hearings. Still, the Arkwright Club and its analysis of the threat of southern competition became the focus of this state investigation.

Before the mid-February hearings began in New Bedford, the joint labor committee briefly considered new regulatory legislation. The proposals included bills to prevent both the fining of weavers and overtime to make up for machine stoppages in textile mills, as well as the Arkwright Club's proposed repeal of the fifty-eight hour law and a Massachusetts AFL-backed proposal for a fifty-four hour workweek. Eva Valesh had her version of a weavers' fining bill prepared by a former state senator and filed by state representative Ross of New Bedford. The committee allowed her to cross-examine witnesses with the same freedom of the Arkwright Club's three attorneys, headed by Fall River lawyer Milton Reed. Valesh claimed her proposal had the backing of Robert Howard, who had sponsored initiated the original fining law in 1891. But most weavers and their union leaders opposed the Valesh bill. Her draft made both fining and the grading system (in the revised 1892 law) illegal and also required overseers to provide notices of any imperfection to the weavers in writing so that operatives could have grounds for a lawsuit. Jane Gallagher's lack of money—not evidence—had delayed her case, which was being heard in the superior court at Taunton.[51] Valesh's bill did not address the issue of freedom of contract, nor did written notices of fining empower the weaver to sue the mill. Most weavers simply wanted the 1892 law enforced.

Many legislators regarded the Valesh fining bill as interference from a reporter employed by a notoriously self-promoting New York newspaper. Valesh herself was personally criticized as a chattering, "new woman," a pushy, "nervy" female with little knowledge of the textile industry or Massachusetts politics. Valesh sweetly ignored this male hostility and combined smiling and gracious charm with unrelenting pressure on witnesses to get information. Milton Reed tried to undercut her aggressive questions by pointing out her lack of knowledge about weaving or the fining system. Valesh retorted that Reed himself knew nothing of weaving, and as an expert on labor legislation she was as qualified as any attorney. In his summation, Reed dismissed her bill as a "raw, crude, fungus law," while Valesh called the 1892 law a "dead letter" in need of change. According to Mary Louise Roberts, "New Women" journalists played with gender identity, exploiting the "multiple sites and workings of power."[52] So too did activist women weavers.

Although Valesh was treated with courteous indulgence by the committee, male reporters criticized her activities at the hearings as damaging and ridiculous.[53] Organized labor, however, lined up to support changes in the fining law but gave higher priority to the bill to prevent working overtime when mill machinery was stopped. Samuel Gompers, the state AFL officials, representatives of the New England Federation of Weavers, and the weavers' unions from Fall River and New Bedford attended the hearings. Opposing the fining bill were the Fall River manufacturers' association, the New Bedford mill treasurers, three lawyers representing the Arkwright Club, and surprisingly, Mrs. Harriet Pickering. She rejected the Valesh bill because it did not simply abolish fines. Pickering faced merciless ridicule at union meetings for her appearance at the state house but was not expelled. Ignoring her opponents and her critics, she stubbornly drafted her own bill to make all fines illegal. After three days, the labor committee closed the hearings on new legislation to proceed with the investigation of the regional wage cut. The committee began to hear witnesses in New Bedford on February 15 and 16, just as public interest became riveted on events in Havana harbor, Cuba.

The pattern of testimony in New Bedford would be repeated as the joint committee moved at a leisurely pace on to Fall River, Lowell, and Lawrence. The mill treasurers read prepared statements in response to the committee's list of questions. The key ones for the New Bedford fine goods industry were the sources of its competition, the amounts of dividends paid, the workings of the fining system, and the influence of the Arkwright Club on the decision to cut wages. Many believed that whatever the New Bedford mills lost financially during the strike, the members of the Arkwright Club had pledged to make up. The Fall River manufactur-

ers' association had followed this practice since the 1880s. Andrew D.
Pierce, the president of the New Bedford manufacturers' association, confirmed that when he was the Wamsutta treasurer he had been an Arkwright member and had attended the December 1897 meeting when the
report on the southern competition was approved. He said that at the
time, he had ridiculed the contents of the report on southern competition but now insisted that the Wamsutta competed not only with the South
but with all American mills. He had found curtailment of production "impractical"; the Wamsutta had paid 6 percent dividends for several years;
and he would give no information on salaries, costs of production or payrolls. Pierce insisted that he expected no financial aid from any group.
That was it "in a nutshell," and all the committee got. In response to some
of his curt answers, the audience laughed openly. When one committee
member asked him about Matt Borden's ability to raise wages and create
a boom in cotton cloth, Pierce replied that no one else would be willing
to take such a chance.[54]

The responses of his son, Otis Pierce of the Grinnell mills, echoed
those of his father. Otis Pierce defended the wage cut as a business necessity, entirely justifiable, and no business of the legislature. He made it
clear that he would refuse requests for any data to back his statements.
"You must take my word for it." More forthcoming on the Arkwright Club,
Pierce stated that "New Bedford has been made the fighting ground [for
wages]. I think we will get some help from other sources. . . . It is no more
than fair."[55] But he denied he was a club member. When Pierce insisted
that the Grinnell mills never fined their weavers, the audience uttered,
"Oh!" at the lie. Representative Samuel Ross, the chair of the labor committee and head of the national mule spinners' association, was sick that
day and unable to challenge the Pierce testimony. Subsequently, the mill
owners would be allowed to say anything or nothing as they pleased; the
state investigation would uncover little that was not well known. State laws
would continue to be ignored or evaded.

The most important witness in New Bedford was expected to be
John F. Knowles, treasurer of the Acushnet and the Hathaway, where fining was most oppressive. Knowles treated the hearing as a joke. In "great
good humor," he read his prepared statement. Southern competition for
New Bedford goods had become "very serious," but he denied that the
Arkwright Club report had anything to do with the wage reduction. Dividends, paid mostly to dependent women and trustees of estates—the
widow and orphan defense—were 5 percent, not the reported 16. When
asked about fines, he replied, "I don't care to go into the case at all."
Commenting on the grading system for weavers, he expressed ignorance
of any state law regulating such a practice. After all, he said, "We have a
right to contract with anyone as to what we shall pay him."[56] With Milton
Reed, counsel for the Arkwright Club, at his side, Knowles lived up to

expectations. Valesh had already left for New York City, and the *Journal* sent no reporters to cover the hearings. No one in the audience was allowed to pose questions. The character of the investigation reflected the political and economic power of the Arkwright lobby.

The New Bedford strikers, who attended the hearings, grew suspicious and angry. Many believed that the senate labor committee planned to meet privately with the mill owners at the state house and ignore the unions' views altogether. The joint committee chair would not permit union leaders to question the mill owners, although the Arkwright lawyers were allowed to. Otis Pierce insisted that he would not be questioned by "every Tom, Dick and Harry." The chair overruled objections from pro-labor members. Still, the secretary of the local carders' union with over two thousand out on strike stated to the press that the manufacturers had formed a "combination . . . to enforce the cutdown." Samuel Ross of the mule spinners' association insisted that southern competition was not a threat because of the higher productivity of northern workers. Matthew Hart for the local weavers pointed out that the New Bedford mills profited more from fining than from firing operatives and that the weavers had no confidence in the Massachusetts Supreme Court's handling of the Jane Gallagher case. When Senator Joseph Flynn, the chair of the joint labor committee, interrupted Hart to explain that fining weavers for poor work not their fault was illegal under the 1892 law, Hart replied that no weavers had the time, given the speeding and the low piece rates, to examine all the materials, the warp or the filling, much less oversee the work of the loom fixer or the looms.[57] The state, not the weaver, had to find the means to enforce the law. Many Boston newspapers denounced the hearings as a useless whitewash, a waste of time, and an expensive farce.

Testimony at the New Bedford hearing from weaver Jim, "not James," Green revealed the growing conviction within the local weavers' union that women like Harriet Pickering and her supporters were simply impulsive, embittered, and divisive victims of the fining system, whose campaign contradicted the growing support for the family wage among the majority of the male weavers in the union. Hart had testified during the hearings that of thirty-eight hundred weavers on strike, nearly 40 percent were men. Speaking quietly and earnestly, Jim Green concluded, "the present wages of a weaver are not sufficient for a man to support his family in respectability." From the audience, someone broke in, "he has to send his wife into the mill to help him out." But this common practice had deep roots in the nineteenth-century textile industry, and mule spinners also sent their wives to the looms. Under the pressures of the textile depression and devastating strike, male heads of families with empty pockets watched their wives and children endure hunger in bitterly cold weather. The male weavers' support for a family wage for men was hardening. A reporter from the *Boston Globe* found Green's words deeply moving, spoken by a "broken-voiced man" who "evidently felt it an outrage to his manhood and his soul that he could not support his family. . . . It was a confession of personal shame that his wife must work because he could not otherwise feed his children."[58] Green's remarks also called forth the English "Hear, hear" from the audience, voiced in bitter, ominous tones. As workingmen, they understood his shame. With the state uninterested and labor politics pointless, the trade union model of the mule spinners' union now seemed the only respectable goal. The New Bedford strike council began to consider dropping the fining issue entirely as a barrier to a compromise that might end the strike. This courted open conflict with the general membership of the weavers' union.

Making matters worse, Samuel Gompers instructed all AFL unions to send contributions, not to weaver William Cunnane, secretary of the New Bedford strike council, but to H. S. Mills, organizer for the International Textile Workers Union-AFL. The weavers' union in New Bedford became furious with this diversion of strike funds, and the strike council began to dissolve. Cunnane's Christian Socialist views, combined with his influential position in the weavers' association, stirred his opponents to force his resignation from the strike council. Matthew Hart, an AFL loyalist close to Ross, replaced him. Cunnane also lost the support of the AFL's weavers' union when he arranged an unauthorized meeting with the manufacturers to negotiate the fining issue. Seeing a chance to divide union and nonunion weavers, the mill treasurers agreed to talk but nothing else. The union repudiated Cunnane's action, and his activities also angered the mule spinners and the carders who decided to take over direction of the strike. Many AFL unions regarded any support for socialism, either Christian or the Socialist Labor Party, among New England union textile workers as nearly as dangerous as the power of the New Bedford mills. The main issue was becoming the direction and ideology of labor politics, not the regional wage cut or fining system. Still many hungry weavers wondered why they were striking against the 10 percent wage cut alone, when the "unholy" fining system left them vulnerable to even worse losses.[59] Again, the mule spinners and weavers, as well as the workingmen and workingwomen, had become deeply divided.

GOMPERS, DELEON, AND DEBS DEBATE LABOR POLITICS

When Samuel Gompers came to New England during the second week of February to encourage contributions to the New Bedford strike, he did not expect that his appearances in Lowell and New Bedford would reveal significant support among textile workers for Daniel DeLeon, the head of the SLP, because his supporters had been formally expelled from the ITWU-AFL in 1897. At a meeting on February 8 in New Bedford, Gompers lost his temper over an invitation offered by a local SLP member to

debate DeLeon at the city hall. Perhaps surprised earlier by criticism of
the AFL from SLP members in the mule spinners' and weavers' unions in
Lowell and that night in New Bedford, Gompers made some angry remarks, leaving his face reddened and the veins in his forehead pulsing.
He called DeLeon a traitor, a Pinkerton agent, and a tool of the corporations. He refused to debate such a man or accept an immediate offer to
debate James T. Hancock, the local SLP member who sat conspicuously
on the mule spinners' union executive board. Gompers described the SLP
as a "red button brigade" of hopeless idealists. How dare the strikers attack the AFL at their time of need, Gompers fumed? Where was the promised financial backing of the AFL, one member of the audience retorted?
Insisting that he would be back, Gompers left the hall that night in a
hurry to catch his train to Boston. Hancock was severely criticized for
daring to challenge the head of the AFL in public.[60] The New Bedford
audience remained divided, as in Lowell, between the strikers loyal to the
AFL and those who considered themselves socialists. Things had gone better for Gompers in Lowell where he attacked the Arkwright Club and
dismissed the menace of southern competition as a lie. Still, Gompers
must have been alarmed to find SLP members in Bob Howard's organization and a Christian Socialist as president of the New Bedford Weaver's
Protective Association.

The following Friday night Daniel DeLeon, editor of New York City's
The People and head of the SLP, spoke at city hall to the assembled strikers.
His carefully prepared speech captured the attention of the largely anti-
socialist audience. He did not attack Gompers or Ross until he had explained clearly and graphically the labor theory of value and the necessity
for political action to control the state and the court system. Then he
asked the strikers: whose wages had increased or whose fines had disappeared as the result of trade unionism or the 1892 fining bill of Ross? No
one in the hall raised a hand. Then he attacked Gompers as a willing tool
for both political parties and criticized Ross for failing to demand the
impeachment of the Massachusetts judge whose opinion had killed the
original 1891 fining law. DeLeon was illustrating that capitalists controlled the legislature and the courts. Politics, he insisted, was the arena
to fight the capitalist oppressor.[61]

Harriet Pickering answered DeLeon's call for questions. She was
jeered and hissed, prompting DeLeon to intervene and ask the audience
to behave like men and let the woman speak. She then asked if DeLeon
believed that Ross "was in alliance with capital?" He relied, no, but Ross'
clear responsibility had been to call for that judge's impeachment. Gompers was his target, not Ross. DeLeon compared his own reasonable,
decent manhood in giving the audience the facts, drawing conclusions,
and allowing questions with the behavior of Gompers, the unmanly name-
caller, who had run from debates over essentials and dodged questions.

Then DeLeon himself called a few names. Gompers was his enemy and a "labor fakir." He concluded by urging the strikers to join the SLP and have the manly courage to come out of their houses and hold massive demonstrations in the streets against the local capitalists, a move the strike council strongly opposed.[62] DeLeon's vision of socialist men marching courageously through the streets and to the ballot box, presumably with their women left at home, contradicted all the journalistic images of wretchedness and desperation as well as the AFL's policy of controlled, cautious family men. Contesting the meaning of working-class manhood and the best strategy to win political power became central to this debate.

The response to DeLeon came from the executive committee of the national mule spinners' association, meeting in Boston on Sunday, February 13. At Gompers' request, the committee announced a general textile strike in New England, thus taking over firm control of decisions and making New Bedford a side-show.[63] The mule spinners and the New England Federation of Weavers-AFL had full treasuries. The delegates rushed home to consult with their locals without acting on any further aid for the deserted New Bedford strikers. But this move by Gompers failed. The vast majority of New England operatives rejected the general strike idea as utterly impractical. New Bedford remained the battle-ground over regional wages.

On Wednesday, February 16, every newspaper in the nation headlined the explosion of the USS *Maine,* an armored cruiser dispatched to Havana harbor on January 24 to protect American interests. From that moment, the yellow press forgot New Bedford. War fever even crowded the strike from the front pages of the pro-labor *Fall River Globe.* Jane Gallagher lost Hearst's backing. Nationalism overwhelmed any public interest in New Bedford's despair. Throughout March and April, tensions over Cuba governed circulation. Only the Boston *Traveler* continued to cover the strikers' plight in detail, largely to advertise their own contributions to prevent starvation, but on March 18 it mourned, "the cry of Cuba Libre drowns out the cry of the New Bedford operatives."

Encouraged by Ross of the mule spinners' association, Gompers returned to New Bedford on March 4 in an attempt to prevent the SLP from gaining control of the local labor movement and persuade the strikers to compromise. Gompers faced many opponents. Thomas F. Connolly of Lowell, a socialist who organized a steady stream of contributions for the New Bedford strikers, refused to shake Gompers' hand because the AFL was trying to take over the New England Federation of Weavers that Connolly had organized. Gompers refused to debate Thomas A. Hickey, organizer for the SLP's Socialist Trades and Labor Alliance. Meanwhile, Ross was trying unsuccessfully to convince the weavers' union to drop the fining issue to settle the strike. The strikers listened to Gompers' speech with "general coldness and one or two interruptions" as he attacked both

DeLeon and the local socialists. He continued to label any anti-AFL strikers as "traitors" in the battle against capital.[64] What Gompers had to say that night was not well received in New Bedford.

Forgetting his mission to heal local divisions, Gompers let loose at DeLeon, denigrating him as less than a man, a professor who never worked one day in his life and whose newspaper was "a rag." "DeLeon runs amuck through the country with stiletto and dirk to cut the hearts out of any man or woman who dares to speak a word for labor."[65] Most of the strikers were unimpressed and more concerned with the promised AFL funds. Gompers admitted to the surprised audience that the federation had no magic strongbox to dip into, claiming that 95 percent of all the strike contributions came from AFL members. But weaver William Cunnane then pointed out that many heads of AFL locals were socialists. Another voice raised the issue of the recent failure of the English engineers' strike, although that trade union had resources of more than three million dollars. Ignoring this challenge, Gompers insisted that strong unions with full treasuries were the only means to power for the American workingman and continued to attack DeLeon. After Gompers left, it was announced that Eugene V. Debs, leader of the Social Democracy, would speak in New Bedford the following week. After Gompers' unpopular March 4 appearance, SLP organizer Hickey quickly formed a fourth local of the ST and LA, while DeLeon claimed to have organized one himself in New Bedford.[66]

Debs addressed the striking weavers on March 11, after signing up Harriet Pickering as a member of the local Social Democracy. Trying to heal the breach between the mule spinners and the weavers, he defended "Sam" Ross as a good, honest man. One capitalist trick was to undermine strikers' faith in their leaders. The audience agreed. Debs also warned the union men to keep the support of the unorganized and especially the women. "Men get their courage from their wives," he argued. Women make the best fighters because they realize the dangers to family life. Defend your manhood, he urged. "This manhood once gone, it's lost forever." Debs judged working-class manhood based on his own harrowing experiences of strikes and prisons in the 1890s as a test of individual integrity and family loyalty.[67] Unlike DeLeon's battalions of marching men, he was calling for a show of manly courage based on moral respectability.

Debs criticized capitalism for driving workers through the competitive system into a state of degradation. Describing his involvement in the 1894 Pullman strike, he suggested, scratch a capitalist and you will find Uncle Sam. You cannot get an injunction against a "blue tailed fly," but capitalists can get anything they want. He counseled the strikers to combine politically, recalling DeLeon's advice and endorsing a SLP rally in New Bedford. Trades unions are not enough, he argued, until the workers control the state.

There is a lot of patriotic talk now over Cuba and about fighting for her liberty. . . . The workingmen [will do the fighting]. . . . Just think of [railroad magnate] Chauncey DePew on the battle field. Imagine [Western Union tycoon] Russell Sage dying of patriotism. . . . While you are issuing the bullets, they will be issuing the bonds. . . . War is murder, wholesale national murder.[68]

Sharing the platform with Debs were the secretary of the loom fixers' union and the local secretary of the Social Democracy movement. The SLP and Debs' organization were both attracting adherents in New Bedford and Fall River.

By early March, New Bedford had four locals of the SLP's Socialist Trade and Labor Alliance, representing mule spinners, weavers, mixed trades, and one exclusively for Bohemian and German immigrants, a total of one thousand members.[69] The growing popularity of socialism complicated regional labor politics. The weavers in Pawtucket, Olneyville, and Central Falls, Rhode Island, began to join Thomas Connolly's New England Federation of Weavers made up of SLP locals. This move left the AFL-backed International Textile Workers Union to try to organize the rest of the Blackstone and Pawtuxet valleys.[70] The Rhode Island state elections held in early April 1898 indicated support for the SLP among former Democratic voters in Providence, Pawtucket, and Woonsocket. In Central Falls in the Blackstone Valley, the SLP won more then 15 percent of the total vote.[71] On March 27 John Simpkins of the thirteenth Massachusetts congressional district died at thirty-six of peritonitis. Postmaster William S. Greene of Fall River, a popular former mayor, won the Republican nomination over district attorney Andrew D. Jennings. During the general election in late May, Greene won the light vote in the district easily, while the Socialist Labor Party nominee, Walter P. J. Skahan of New Bedford, beat an unpopular Democratic candidate in his own city, 731 to 128. Discontented socialist voters in New Bedford and Rhode Island and among the Lowell weavers were challenging the AFL in New England. In Fall River, however, the SLP won less than 100 votes in the 1898 congressional race, but in 1900 Fall River socialists in the SLP and SD cast 614 ballots or about 6 percent of the total vote.[72]

THE VIEW FROM THE SOUTH AND FROM LANCASHIRE

P. J. Moran, a reporter for the *Atlanta Constitution,* Henry Grady's voice for the economic development of a New South, traveled in February to New Bedford, attracted by the images in the yellow press of starvation among northern operatives. Moran saw no sign in the North of the "superior wages which the Arkwright Club thought so exorbitant."[73] He observed the high cost of living in New England in coal, flour, meat, and warm clothing. He interviewed Harriet Pickering, who described the weavers' union membership as equal in numbers of men and women and detailed the grievances of New Bedford operatives. The overseers fined women, she said, and all operatives during winters. When help was scarce, fining eased up. "They fine when they think they can do so with the least danger of trouble," she observed. A cut of cloth revealed any previous mistakes by other operatives and flaws in materials and machinery, but only the weavers were fined. On second-class goods at the Wamsutta, the overseer stamped a blue mark of "shame" which Pickering felt as a "perpetual brand." New England weave rooms commonly listed on a blackboard the names of weavers judged incompetent, a practice similar to posting mule spinners' daily quotas. To Pickering, vigilance forced the weavers to become part of the machinery; the "hard, grinding work" left her with no soul or feeling. Women weavers fainted in the mill and at home. Based on his interviews, Moran concluded that the talk from the Arkwright Club or "trust" on southern competition was "a farce."

Others agreed. Edward Kilburn of the eminent New Bedford family, former agent at the Wamsutta, told Moran that there was no such thing as southern competition in fine goods. The Arkwright Club's report was "all talk." Kilburn portrayed the northern mills as the reverse of what he regarded as southern paternalism. Here, he insisted, "the two classes stand separate and apart. . . ." Perpetually suspicious and combative, Kilburn believed that the operatives intentionally damaged the fabric to injure the mills' profits. The system of grading and fining was essential given the turbulent labor politics of New England. But Moran's southern eye saw in Kilburn an apologist for a system of "filching" and robbery, typical of Yankee hypocrites who had defended an industrial system of white slavery while attacking chattel slavery in the pre–Civil War South. For Moran, both the Republican and Democrat tariffs protected those "shoddy" manufacturers who had fattened on war contracts and bought government bonds which they insisted be redeemed in gold. The mill owners were in alliance with the "money sharks," while U.S. Representative Dingley of Maine, standing in debate on the House floor with the Arkwright report under his arm, blamed the textile depression of the 1890s on low southern wages, an attitude "so . . . characteristic of moral New England!" Moran and his editor blamed underconsumption for hard times and the Dingley tariff for raising the cost of living for American workers. The old sectional political wounds throbbed.

The Arkwright Club, according to Moran, had ordered a reduction of northern wages to southern standards, dubbed by the *Boston Globe,* a "hog and hominy" standard. The club's report claimed that wages were 40 percent lower in the South, using data, Moran pointed out, from isolated, poorly paying mills to compare with the highest northern wages. Where, he asked, were the progressive mills of Columbus, Georgia, which made carpets, curtains, and toweling? Meanwhile, the club's president, Republi-

can congressman Lovering of Taunton, was lobbying for a federal constitutional amendment to allow Congress to create a standard working day
for the textile industry. "Lovering's Folly," his scheme to nationalize the
length of the working day, was in effect an internal protective tariff for
the Northeast, supported by Dingley, Samuel Ross, president of the national mule spinners' union, and New York economist George Gunton.
To Moran, the amendment would threaten states' rights and undermine
southern enterprise. After observing northern mills, Moran concluded
that shorter hours only meant speeded machinery. He envisioned a conspiracy of active, young workingmen with great physical endurance pushing for a fifty-four hour day in 1898, after a fifty-eight hour day had
wrecked the vitality of women workers, such as Harriet Pickering. He contrasted the image of the nerve-racked, worn-out Pickering with the white-
bonneted, graceful southern mill girl working at a slower pace on longer
hours. These images updated the pre–Civil War arguments about the nature of slavery, North and South, and the images of female textile workers.

Moran also exposed the Arkwright report as a cover for northern investment in southern textile expansion. New England machine works had
been pressured to demand cash instead of stock in payment for southern
purchases to hold up development. Meanwhile, the Massachusetts mills
in Lowell made higher profits from their new mill in Lindale, Georgia,
than at home. Moran's interview with Arthur Amory of Boston focused
on his family's mill at Cordova, Alabama, close to cotton fields and coal
beds, hindered only by the southern railroads' high short-haul rates. Untroubled by "foreign labor," Amory's southern investments depended on
keeping the white native-born people in the cotton mills and the blacks
in the cotton fields. Henry T. Shaw, treasurer of Lawrence's Pemberton
mills, admitted that capital would best be invested in the South but not
for the reasons set forth in the Arkwright report. There was no direct
competition between northern and southern mills. For Shaw, overproduction in the North had created the textile depression. The real competition
occurred among the New England corporations, aggravated by lack of
investment in new machinery and labor agitation. Overproduction, the
traditional Fall River practice, lowered dividends. Lancashire-born James
Tansey, secretary of the Fall River carders' union, believed that northern
mill owners invested in southern mills and then used the threat of competition to cut wages in New England.

Rumors early in the 1898 strike that the New Bedford mills would
buy English yarn and reopen after the expected collapse of the weavers'
resistance prompted secretary Ross of the mule spinners' association to
contact the Lancashire unions. Both the English union leaders and the
editor of the *Cotton Factory Times* remained unmoved and unimpressed
with the progress of trade unionism in New England.[74] In early February,
Thomas Ashton of the Amalgamation of Operative Cotton Spinners ex-

pressed complete indifference as to where English yarn was sold as long as wages and working conditions in Lancashire were acceptable. The chief worry for the American spinners, he cautioned, should be the unorganized weavers. The secretary of the Master [or fine yarn] Cotton Spinners' Association denied that English spinners could prevent the sale of yarn if New Bedford buyers wanted it. He sympathized with the strikers, but the more important problem was the high protective tariff that reaped profits for the New England mills and delivered high living costs to the operatives. Free trade, he argued, would equalize wage differences between England and America. But he seemed unaware that the New England mule spinners voted Republican in 1896 and had lobbied in 1894 for better protection against English fine yarns. In the *Cotton Factory Times*, James Mawdsley, secretary of the Amalgamated Association of Cotton Spinners, wrote off the future of the Massachusetts cotton industry unless there was a national standard for hours and the development of an export market. The editor of the *Cotton Factory Times* had long been convinced that the American weavers were hopelessly disorganized. The complexities of American government and politics made all this advice useless to the New Bedford strikers.

Would Lancashire operatives send contributions to New Bedford? English immigrant spinners and weavers in New Bedford, especially weavers from Blackburn like Harriet Pickering, had contributed funds to the Lancashire textile strike of 1892–93 and to the failed engineers' 1897–98 strike. The leaders of the organized carders and weavers in Oldham, however, had not been formally contacted about contributions. The carders' secretary dismissed the New England contest: "it's nothing to do with us." Thomas Birtles of the Oldham weavers' association urged stronger organization and fuller treasuries but expressed interest in sending help if properly approached. When in late March a circular printed in English arrived in Lancashire from New Bedford asking for contributions, the union leaders were astonished to read on the other side a similar appeal written in French. The informal nature of the appeal and its expression in a "strange" language, was enough to "damn it." The American workforce was too "cosmopolitan." Follow the British example, and in the future strikes might be won. In March the Lancashire unions remained uninformed and uninterested, viewing the New Bedford strike "as dead as Queen Anne." The *Cotton Factory Times* pronounced the strike a testimony to the silly effort of a single center of production, ignored by the press, to resist a wage cut that all other mills in the region had accepted. The English never grasped the regional strike strategy.

One Lancashire leader among the mule spinners' associations admitted to the Oldham correspondent for the *New Bedford Standard* that the English unions were feeling too superior. They measured the strength of their own organizations by numbers and treasuries, not political or ideological power. Divisive hierarchies among various skill groups and organizations should be dealt with, this man insisted, to put their own house in order before lecturing to Americans. Trade unionism had failed the English engineers. British pure and simple unionism faced the challenges of a "new unionism" led by Tom Mann, Keir Hardie and others, emphasizing independent political action by labor, while in Germany, Italy, and France, socialism grew.[75] Furthermore, in February 1898 Manchester capitalists W. H. Houldsworth and W. H. Holland, both members of Parliament, had organized a combine that controlled all English spindles capable of producing the finest yarn counts. Fine yarn spinners called it an American-style trust and looked forward eagerly to higher yarn prices and wages.[76] The power of the new combine did not seem to bother them. After all, English yarn already had a monopoly on the world market. Coates & Clark Ltd. had bought out sewing thread makers in Scotland, England, and the United States, creating another trust. So much for free trade doctrine, wrote the correspondent for the *Standard*. Lessons preached about tariffs and stronger organization were all the New Bedford strikers received from their compatriots in Lancashire during the critical weeks of February and March.

During the tenth week of the strike, the New Bedford mule spinners' union heading the strike council offered to compromise at a 5 percent cut. The manufacturers refused. When the market in their judgment warranted it, the New Bedford mill treasurers would grant an increase, but not without "the others."[77] They would stand by the Arkwright Club. With the New England mills at full production, the market declined further in March to 2 cents for print cloth. Many agents agreed that the 10 percent wage cut had not been enough; curtailment was next. The New Bedford strike council, rid of the socialists, now faced the responsibility for the strike's outcome and aftermath.

HOLDOUTS IN MAINE AND FALL RIVER'S DILEMMA

The textile workers' strategy to oppose the 10 percent wage cut in 1898 had rested on the potential financial support of ninety thousand New England operatives for the nine thousand strikers in New Bedford. This promising plan had been immediately violated in January by a number of stubborn strikes in Maine, but more importantly in Fall River with a mule spinners' strike against the King Philip mills. Lowell mule spinners and weavers had agreed most reluctantly to call off any strike action. As the King Philip strike continued, they charged the Fall River spinners with "treason" for violating the regional agreement to fight only in New Bedford. Disorganization and fragmentation continued to divide and weaken the efforts of New England textile workers to oppose the Arkwright lobby.

When the Maine fine goods centers in Lewiston, Biddeford, and Saco

cut wages 10 percent, organized workers struck against this needless reduction. As in New Bedford, there was no southern competition for their
products. At the Pepperell and Laconia mills in Biddeford, a few skilled
warp dressers began the strike, followed by the AFL locals of mule spinners and slasher tenders headed by Irish Americans. French Canadian
immigrant Noel Beaupre led the unorganized weavers, carders, and pickers. As in Fall River and New Bedford, the unorganized operatives in Biddeford remained out on strike or left town. AFL policy had rejected the
unorganized as weak, uncontrollable, and potentially treacherous, but local businessmen, farmers, and the priests of the Biddeford Irish and
French churches helped the multinational strikers by keeping them fed.
After eight weeks, the well-regarded agent in Biddeford promised the
strikers to restore wages as soon as possible if they would return to work.
The dressers agreed, and the unions and unorganized workers accepted
the compromise. The Biddeford mills began to take over New Bedford's
market for fine goods.[78] The workforce in the York mills at Saco and the
weavers and spinners in the Androscoggin mills at Lewiston distrusted
their agents and held out until April. These strikes drained support away
from the New Bedford effort.

The King Philip strike in Fall River proved more significant to the
future of New England labor politics than the regional wage cut, by raising
the issue of admitting ring spinners into the mule spinners' union. The
national mule spinners' association began to seriously to consider organizing ring spinners, mostly young French Canadian females. To do this
would redefine the culture and politics of this union of adult English and
Irish men, for whom exclusivity remained fundamental to their sense of
skill and manhood. In addition, the carders' association in both Fall River
and New Bedford faced growing numbers of young people from Portugal,
who were replacing the French Canadians as pickers and carders, as the
French had replaced the Irish and English. Secretary Tansey of the carders' union called this generation of new immigrants "a menace."[79] The
political implications of both gender and nationality became crucial issues for labor politics in the Northeast and later in the South.

The King Philip strike on January 16 was a mule spinners' event. The
weavers and the rest of the operatives accepted the wage cut and continued to work. But the spinners' union had an agreement, hammered out
by Robert Howard with Simeon Chase, to receive higher piece rates for
finer counts of yarn, equal to the wages being paid in the New Bedford
yarn mills. The New Bedford cloth mill workers were on strike, but the
local yarn mills ran at the old rates. The Fall River manufacturers' association, promising to provide financial aid to the King Philip, insisted that
Chase cut their spinners, on both mules and rings, $11\frac{1}{9}$ percent, along
with the rest. For the first time, the ring spinners went on strike in support
of the mule spinners. Meeting in the carders' association rooms to make

their decision, the ring spinners heartily responded "Oui!" All the spinners, adult men and women, girls and boys, had come out together. With
the ring spinners came the doffers and sweepers who worked with them.
In a political gesture, agent Chase had fourteen pairs of old mules junked
in the mill yard, destroying the jobs of the spinners who ran them.[80] For
the mule spinners, the King Philip strike symbolized formidable difficulties in maintaining the basis of their organization as technical developments in ring spinning raced ahead.

Many ring spinners in Fall River, New Bedford, and Lowell had become members of the carders' union that also organized female card
room workers. The slasher-tenders' associations admitted the drawing-in
girls, who skillfully drew each piece of warp yarn, prepared by the slasher-
tenders and wound on wooden beams, through the loom harnesses before the beams were inserted into the looms for weaving.[81] Piecers, doffers, and back boys, who helped the mules spin, formed a separate union.
Although many expected to become mule spinners, none was admitted
to the national mule spinners' union.[82] Sixteen-year-old Al Priddy, a Lancashire immigrant and back boy in New Bedford, supported the union's
strike, hoping some day to become a mule spinner.[83] In Rhode Island, the
mule spinners' association considered admitting nearly 450 back boys
who were willing and eager to pay dues, but as members they would have
the right to draw strike pay and other benefits. The back boys would have
to go it alone. But as railroad carloads of ring frames arrived at the King
Philip mills, the striking mule spinners had no option. They offered "assistance," but not strike pay, to the ring spinners to stay out.[84] Could this
lead to a powerful new combination?

Secretary Thomas O'Donnell of the Fall River local quickly met with
the national union's executive committee in Boston. Chase had obviously
planned for months to put in the ring frames, "to do away with men in
the mill." What could the national union do? The mills apparently preferred to deal with "children," even if this meant inferior cloth.[85] Honor-
ary member Robert Howard defused O'Donnell's sense of crisis. He insisted that many mule spinners were already seeking other kinds of work,
such as jobs with city government, reducing their numbers and thus increasing the ability of the national union to pay benefits to the current
membership. In addition, Howard announced with pleasure that the unorganized ring spinners and back boys in other mills were sending strike
contributions; there was no need to organize them. But in New Bedford
back boys were receiving only fifty cents a week in strike pay and threatening to run the mules as strikebreakers.[86] Clinging to his old exclusionary
policies, Howard missed the point. If the "children," actually teenaged
girls, women, and boys working as ring spinners and back boys, returned
to work, the men were through.

The mule spinners ended the King Philip strike after five weeks. Those men whose mules had been junked joined the list of sick spinners. Everyone expected the ring spinners to return, but they had other ideas. As one remarked, "the mule spinners said the strike was over, but they found out they were mistaken." The ring spinners and the back boys in Fall River, New Bedford, and in Pawtucket, Rhode Island, wanted to become part of a powerful, national, protective union. When the carders returned to the King Philip, one adamant ring spinner told secretary James Tansey of the carders' union that they were willing to fight "their battle alone."[87] In 1898 the people from Quebec numbered thirty thousand in Fall River and worked in every department but mule spinning and loom fixing.

The ring spinners wanted their wages restored, even though the mule spinners and the carders had accepted the cut. Agent Chase fired carder Leon Cote whose two daughters were ring spinners. The idea was to pressure the fathers to get their children to drop the strike. Tansey told Chase, "these days a man cannot always control the actions of his grown-up daughters." The Cote girls stayed on strike; some second-generation immigrant daughters had their own ideas about labor politics. The Godreau family faced a crowd of striking ring spinners, hooting and yelling the English word knobstick as the father accompanied his two daughters to the King Philip. Three strikers were arrested for assault. Mrs. Malvina McKay threw whitewash over the Godreaus, ruining their clothes. Emma Bouchard tossed a paper bag at Godreau, hitting him in the chest. It contained salt, pepper, and peas, the ingredients for pea soup, the mainstay of French Canadian strikers. The district court charged fifteen-year-old Emma Bouville with assault and battery on Mary and Emma Godreau. All charged were found guilty.[88] These acts of spirited resistance, plus the growing substitution of ring frames for mules, made the organization of ring spinners essential for the long-term survival of the national mule spinners' union.

Meeting in early April, the annual national cotton mule spinners' convention headed by Samuel Ross voted to support the proposed Lovering amendment to the United States Constitution for a national standard on daily working hours but only debated admitting the ring spinners. Technically, the carders' union would have to agree to release them, but that proved unnecessary. Instead of organizing the ring spinners, the convention decided to recruit into the national union the mule spinners in the northern woolen and worsted industries where ring spinning did not yet threaten spinning operations. To do so, the national union voted to change its name, dropping both Cotton and Mule to become the National Spinners Association. Each district was instructed to "look after the ring spinners," but organizing them was not compulsory, and each local could decide for itself. That meant following the example of Fall River where the carders' union was recruiting ring spinners.[89] Male spinners in woolen and worsted were welcome in the national union; female ring spinners were not. The mule spinners continued to regard them as "children" and reserve their organization for skilled adult males. The national union remained as it had been under Robert Howard, an exclusive organization distanced from the more inclusive labor politics of the textile workers federation. Control over the expansion of ring spinning was left in the hands of mill agents who increased their hiring of Portuguese immigrants for this work, setting up conflicts with the French Canadians. The new national spinners' union, rejecting any attempt to organize ring spinners, would become totally irrelevant to the growing southern textile industry where spinning was done only on ring frames. Although the reorganized union would remain a force in the North, this key decision meant the organization had abandoned any effort to exercise national influence in the cotton textile industry.

COLLAPSE IN NEW BEDFORD

By early April, the New Bedford mill agents, feeling the competition from the Biddeford mills in fine goods, planned a showdown with the strikers. The mills tried to starve them out. State aid to the board of overseers of the poor ceased. Local grocers and merchants cut off donations to the soup kitchens and credit to the strikers. Contributions continued from Lowell and Fall River to the weavers, but many strikers subsisted on hasty puddings of boiled milk and flour and on dried herring. Responding to their own working-class customers who were donating to the strike, grocers in Providence and Boston sent fish to the soup kitchens, while Pawtucket merchants provided potatoes, onions, beans, oats, coffee, and ham. But the three French Canadian priests in New Bedford carefully prepared their congregations to face the reality of no credit. Church funds were exhausted, but the pastors refused to give any direct advice. If the strikers could "continue the battle against capital, all well and good," but with the soup kitchens struggling, families should not allow themselves to starve. The priests had supported the strikers in their congregations, and the manufacturers knew it.[90] Two hundred French Canadian families had already gone, a serious loss to the parishes. Violence at cotton mills still on strike at Lewiston and Saco, Maine, prompted the president of the Wamsutta mills, William Crapo, a former congressman, to get Mayor Charles Ashley to use military force to keep order when the mills reopened on April 11.

The New Bedford strikers remained deeply divided. The strike council without the weavers had offered unsuccessfully to compromise at a 5 percent cut and, fearful of uncontrollable demonstrations, boycotted a weavers' parade on April 4, cutting the number to about five hundred marchers. The mill agents laughed at the poor show. Still, union weavers in their protective association, many loyal to the socialist New England Federation and joined by fifty SLP men in the "Red Button Brigade," marched to make their grievances clear. They carried mottoes: "Abolish the de-Grading System," "Strike at the ballot box," and "Whilst There's Soup There's Hope."[91] Matthew Hart joined them to soothe the bad feelings among the weavers toward the AFL textile workers who dominated the strike council. The weavers voted to stay out on April 11, while many went to Lowell on April 12 to join delegates from Manchester, Lonsdale, and Fall River to transform themselves into an anti-AFL National Federation of Textile Operatives.[92]

When the mills opened their gates, a gauntlet of strikers—English, Irish, French, Bohemian, and German—met the returning workers with yelling, hooting, blasts from fish horns, rotten eggs, and stones. Women on bicycles, trying to escape the strikers, had their wheels seized and ended up on the street. A boy kicked one man and had his face slapped hard. Then the crowd of strikers turned on the knobstick and punched him in the face. Although these actions were mild compared with the violence of Fall River mule spinners' strikes, the mayor called out the state police and read the riot act, making "congregating, collecting, assembling, and gathering together" almost anywhere in public illegal. This show of police power worked. After a week, on April 22 the loom fixers voted to return to work. The next day as the city of Fall River sent off its first volunteers to the Spanish-American War, the weavers gave in. Harriet Pickering returned to the Grinnell mills but quit after she was fined for defects in damaged warp yarn caused by the long shutdown. She announced she would look for work as a bookkeeper. Finally, on May 21, the mule spinners voted three to one to go back, while in Fall River, four large corporations including the Iron Works mills began to curtail production.[93] The market remained seriously depressed until 1899.

NATIONALISM, WAR AND GENDER RELATIONS

Oh, what a night! ... It ... was the departure of the first installment of the quota which Fall River stands ready to contribute for defense of the national honor and the preservation of the freest, noblest and grandest republic the sun shines on.[94]

The editor of the pro-labor *Fall River Globe* paired his growing enthusiasm for war with Spain with continual, daily announcements during early April that the New Bedford strike was over, even though the mule spinners held out until May. Kristin Hoganson argues that the public eagerness for war in 1898 as a guarantee of vigorous manliness reflected cultural tensions over gender relations in late nineteenth-century America.[95] Class issues in the New England textile industry reinforced these gender tensions. Nationalist fervor offered relief from the tormenting images of New Bedford hopelessness, the bitter divisions among men and women strikers, and the apathy of Fall River workers. Leading Fall River mill owners seemed threatened by new state regulation, by the crisis over southern competition and control of the cloth market, and by the rising local Democratic Party. But on April 22, rich and poor, young and old, male and female mingled together in the streets of Fall River, "thoroughly representative" and entirely united in an outburst of national pride and fervor that swept the strikes over the regional wage standard into oblivion. Eleven naval volunteers in Company F, assigned to the coastal defense of Boston harbor fought their way through the crowds to the wharf. "[T]he grandest, wildest, and most enthusiastic demonstration the city has ever seen" dimmed memories of nineteenth-century labor demonstrations. Workingmen and women leaving the mills, carrying their dinner pails, stopped to watch the flags, the skyrockets, the assembled Grand Army of the Republic veterans, and the frenzied goodbyes. Young men envied the honor shown to the departing volunteers. Everyone wanted to shake their hands in farewell. "The women seemed especially desirous of doing so." These middle-class volunteers in 1898 had already become masculine heroes.

Historian Gail Bederman analyzes a shift in nineteenth-century meanings of manhood from an ideal of behaviors, customs, and duties associated with artisanal and republican values, to the social construction of masculinity, tested by virility and physical prowess, especially as measured against other races.[96] Bederman has little evidence on working-class men in the 1880s and 1890s, focusing her attention on the middle class. Physical displays and virile combat among working-class men of differing ethnic backgrounds, however, had a long history in southeastern New England. Sporting contests that pitted nationalities or "races" against each other, the continual tests of physical prowess by the mule spinners' twenty-five mile daily walks, and young weavers turned into "drivers" prepared the way for shifts in meanings of manliness. The weavers, both men and women, advocated a manly political stance, including muscular resistance: giving the boss "a welter" or "bunging up" eyes. George Gunton rejected male workers who refused to confront their adversaries physically as individuals or in mass demonstrations. Respectable mule spinners frequently engaged in angry acts of aggression, especially when strikes went awry and damaged their sense of respectable manhood invested in their trade union. Even workingwomen contributed to this definition of virile manhood during the strike of 1875 with their reference to manly "horns." They sometimes led the way, labeled "amazons" for taking initiative and "vixens" for striking their overseers. All this supports, as Bederman argues, the long, contested nature of the emergence of the concept of masculinity in the late nineteenth century.

On that night of April 22, the volunteers for war with Spain broke into the song "America," the crowds joined in, and the evening ended with a mighty cheer. This was no British salute, but a signal of the end to anxious weeks of congressional debate over the loss of the USS *Maine*, reams of inflammatory yellow journalism, unremitting pressure on the president, and deepening fervor for war. The New York *World* announced on April 19 that chairman Dingley of the Ways and Means Committee would introduce a special tariff bill to raise millions to fight the Spanish, not through taxes but by increasing the protection of American industry.

After the splendors of the little war with Spain, New England industrial politics grew more conservative.[97] Labor legislation came to a halt on Beacon Hill, although the repeal of the fifty-eight hour law failed. All other legislation on weavers' fining, the proposed fifty-four hour week, and a bill making overtime illegal for machine stoppage remained buried in committee. On May 18 the joint committee on labor issued its report on the investigation of the regional wage cut, calling only for the adoption of Lovering's national standard for hours and no action on proposed labor legislation, labeled "further limitations on the rights of capital." The report cited only the low dividends paid in Fall River, not the higher New Bedford figures, and accepted the Arkwright report's estimates on southern wages as lower by thirty to forty percent. The committee members faulted underconsumption, not overproduction, as the cause of textile troubles. The report concluded that depressed markets and "competition" had forced the northern mills to cut wages.[98] On March 14, to great applause on the floor of Congress, a member of the Massachusetts delegation officially welcomed southern competition in textile production as a symbol of the end to sectional political division: "the cementing of the common country we love so well."[99] When the New Bedford strike officially ended in late May, so did any opposition to the regional wage cut. The Arkwright Club had successfully acted, not as a prototype as Galambos argues, but as a powerful trade association in its own right.

The Arkwright Club, while opposing further labor legislation and lobbying for the repeal of labor laws, had seized the initiative in the 1890s by recasting labor relations into an inter-regional economic and political setting. Moving labor-management issues out of the hands of the state government and into the realms of supply and demand economics, this textile lobby constructed the first widely recognized crisis over southern competition to New England textile production. Grossly overestimating cost advantages and potential product competition in southern mills, the Arkwrighters, led by Republican William Lovering of Taunton whose family controlled key Lowell mills and their southern subsidiaries in Georgia and Alabama, called on Congress in 1898 to amend the United States Constitution to set a federal standard for the working day. This politically hopeless proposal, dubbed "Lovering's Folly," not only required a vast extension of federal power but more importantly shifted labor reform issues into congressional politics, out of the grasp of Massachusetts and Rhode

Island labor reformers. The Arkwright Club and its supporters thus defied state regulation and redefined the arena of political contestation to shore up the most profitable sectors in the New England textile industry. Regional corporate resistance had successfully moved the venue of labor politics onto much more hostile political grounds. Representatives of northern and southern textile interests joined hands as a national political lobby to defeat "Lovering's Folly" in the Congress and pursue their common interests.

Reduced wages and the fining system in New Bedford continued to force skilled weavers to relocate. In the textile centers of Lowell, Fall River, New Bedford, and Manchester, the total number of immigrants from Greece, Italy, Polish areas in eastern Europe, and Portugal rose from 3,581 in 1890 to 15,589 in 1900, increasing the cultural diversity of the workforce. French Canadian immigrants and Franco-Americans began to assume a dominate position in the Massachusetts textile workforce, as the numbers of English and Irish-American workers declined.[100] Trained in large numbers as weavers, Franco men became loom fixers and organized strong unions.[101] By February 1899, the market improved. Print cloth, still the "barometer" for all other goods, rose to 2½ cents.[102] On March 1 the Fall River mills announced the restoration of the 10 percent wage cut. The Iron Works mills had already raised wages three months earlier. New Bedford mills waited until April 3. Then the agents simply announced their decision without bothering to confer with the unions, even with the mule spinners. President McKinley had no trouble carrying both cities in the 1900 elections, especially after the successes in war and empire building in addition to the wage restoration. When the organized weavers in Fall River found space for their union, they named it McKinley Hall.

WORKINGWOMEN AND LABOR POLITICS

Better markets between 1900 and 1903 did not resolve the divisions among New England textile operatives or draw the weavers and spinners into one union. Working conditions continued to deteriorate. "A Cotton Factory Girl" in New Bedford complained to the *Boston Globe* in December 1900 about high speed, deafening noise, too many looms, and heavy fines. Her lungs ached from sucking the bobbin thread into the shuttle, a practice well known to weavers but popularized as "the Kiss of Death" by Hearst's *Journal* in early 1898. Many of her friends among the weavers became sick, then died of consumption. Wearing their greasy, dirty work clothes, female weavers, whatever their age or size or strength, now had to carry their lengthy, heavy cuts to the cloth rooms for the feared inspection. Young male weavers could handle this new task with more ease. The fining system, so successfully defended during the New Bedford strike, spread to Fall River. Work had become so hard that this careworn, worried

"Cotton Factory Girl" actually envied the cleaner, safer life of domestic servants, an idea utterly rejected by nineteenth-century women weavers.[103]

The second generation of American-born workers of Irish background lived and worked like their parents but at lower wages and with the women weavers facing severe fines for defects. In 1903 James Carroll and his wife worked as weavers in Fall River to support their six children. Both had entered the mills at fourteen, married in their early twenties, and Mrs. Carroll had born ten children in fourteen years. In mid-December 1903, the Fall River mills announced a 10 percent wage cut. On their old wages, the Carrolls could afford butter, milk, bakery cookies, and meat once a week. Their oldest son, Jimmy, carried dinner pails to the mills, earning enough to buy his own shoes and pay his ten-cent monthly dues to the Fall River Boys' Club built with Matt Borden's 1895 gift to the city. James Carroll carried a little life insurance on his family and, as a member of the Ancient Order of the Foresters, had some burial money. The union did not seem to exist for them. A weaver's cut had grown to 54 yards, still woven on plain looms. Times were getting worse, and new immigrants crowded the workforce. Still, when Mrs. Carroll thought about her children, she believed, "they'll all be weavers when they're old enough."[104] She was sure that the mills would go on forever.

The declining status of women workers in the textile trades of southeastern New England had been developing since the battles of the 1870s and 1880s and the growing prominence of the exclusive mule spinners' union in New England labor politics. As Robert Howard and his successors negotiated their special position for skilled men and provided a model for other unions, the ring spinners had been siphoned off into the carders' union where their interests were ignored. They had little influence in labor politics, remaining largely unorganized and increasingly drawn from young women of the newer immigrant groups. But on the new twentieth-century ring frames, the ring spinners would produce more and finer cotton yarn for the industry, North and South. In all this, there was little room left for trade union cooperation with workingwomen or collaboration with socialist politics or with the new immigrants flooding the workforce.[105]

Aggressive, assertive Eva Valesh, the labor reform journalist, briefly created a public stage in 1898 for weavers Harriet Pickering and Jane Gallagher. Neither was well received by organized labor. These two stubborn, vocal female heads of families, fresh from Lancashire, contradicted the direction of the New England weavers' organization. Many male weavers in New Bedford had adopted the trade union ideal of a family wage. Wives appeared out of place even at the looms. Pickering and Gallagher, who represented the fining issue and embodied female activism, could find no place for themselves in politics as the leaders of workingwomen or as representatives of Lancashire militancy.[106] Workingmen had convinced

themselves that fining weavers was only a woman's issue, arising from female vulnerability and a need for additional state protection of women,
not an exercise of corporate power that required combined resistance. As
a result, the practice of fining spread. Two scales of wages increasingly
divided men and women weavers. The mill owners had triumphed in this
and in the regional wage cut. In Fall River, the two most conservative
unions of skilled men would back the local mills against the continuing
ambitions of Matt Borden to control the cloth market. Some women weavers might well envy any kind of work outside the mills. Mrs. Carroll in Fall
River and Mrs. Offinger in New Bedford continued to work, scrimp, and
send their children into the mills, seeing neither the family wage nor
much hope in trade unionism.

William E. Forbath's *Law and the Shaping of the American Labor Movement*
(1991) represents recent efforts by labor historians to explore the influence of court decisions, political institutions, and state policy on the late
nineteenth-century labor movement. Many argue that legal constructions
proved more influential on organized labor than issues of class and culture, criticizing the Marxian concept of law and the state as the super-
structure of economic power. Forbath insists that the specific structures
and traditions of American law, both as a discourse and as power, shaped
the labor movement "and its members' identities, material interests, and
capacities for collective action." He admits that the process of how "the
discourse of law enters ordinary people's social experience is, largely, an
empirical question," which he does not seek to demonstrate.[107] New England industrial workers in textile and shoe production and the consistently radical *Labor Standard* and socialist press do not fit this analysis.

Forbath's primary interest lies in the response of Gilded Age labor
leaders, not the rank and file membership, to battles with the courts and
the state, but the conflictual politics of the ascendance of a conservative
labor leadership remains a key historical issue. This legalist approach to
labor history ignores the persistent power struggles carried out by New
England textile operatives over the ten-hour day, the underlying shifting
gender and ethnic coalitions, changing protest heritages, the setting of
industrial development and technical innovation, and the challenge of
monopoly capitalism to regional competition. The law and the courts did
not alter the communities or ideologies of southeastern New England textile mill owners or their workers, although the mill owners refused to obey
the law and clung to freedom of contract as their ultimate defense. Many
operatives resisted—win, lose or draw—and maintained their own culture
of local and regional protest despite court rulings and state policy. For
example, when the weavers' fining law was declared unconstitutional in
1891, labor reformers in the legislature quickly passed another in 1892.
The enforcement of state policy, however, became a power struggle conducted through labor politics in the industrial centers and throughout

region, regardless of legal jurisdictions and political demarcations. Class, culture, and labor politics remained the bedrock of their industrial experience.

MATT BORDEN'S COMBINE IN THE MARKET

Many Fall River mill treasurers and large shareholders recognized that the success of the regional wage cut in 1898 did not solve the problem of market instability from overproduction. Gentlemen's agreements to pool market shares through the manufacturers' associations did not work, because competitors could not resist underbidding each other to cloth brokers, dragging down the market price. In September 1899 the leaders of the Fall River manufacturers' association proposed strengthening the selling committee by assigning it additional powers to curtail production, thus placing key management decisions in the hands of one local group. These men believed that the depressed market in 1899 called for curtailment and yet another 10 percent wage cut, and they also realized that continued cutthroat competition would endanger many of the older firms. Although backed by the "big men," Dr. Robert T. Davis, Simeon B. Chase, president of the association, John D. Flint, who owned shares in all the city's mills, and Richard B. Borden, the idea failed. Any reluctant agent in the association could veto the scheme, an indication of the fear of loss of corporate control to a larger body. One did.

The Fall River treasurers also considered offers from outsiders to form a national cotton trust, one from William M. Wood who had just put together the American Woolen Company. Other offers came from the backers of the New Bedford–centered New England Cotton Yarn Company, a trust financed by Kidder, Peabody of New York City, as well as offers from groups with dubious financial backing. The treasurers refused to consider any proposal that undermined local control of production or failed to provide cash to stockholders instead of new stock. They refused to abandon their traditional approach to market dominance. While this debate in 1899 continued, Matt Borden acted, making another large purchase of a half million pieces of grey goods in Fall River. There was no question about Borden's financial connections. The market for grey goods rose; no wage cut seemed necessary. Borden's "raid" in a depressed market with print cloth at a low 2⅞ cents meant he could again undersell many other cloth printers. His maneuvers caused "some annoyance" in Fall River. He could act, but they could not. In late September 1899, the association discarded the idea of a cotton trust and resumed full production.[108] Borden remained a powerful factor in setting the market price of print cloth and influencing regional wages. Borden was no humanitarian; cheap wages cheapened the product.

The cotton crop in 1900 was the smallest in ten years, creating a nation-wide crisis in the textile industry. All cotton mills faced sky high prices for their raw material. The bad news trickled out in August and September. Drought in some areas shriveled the plants, especially sea island cotton essential for the finest goods. In other parts of the South, flooding rains and muddy fields prevented cultivation; grass choked the buds as they tried to flower. A tropical storm in mid-September ruined most of the southeast Texas cotton. Wild speculation seized the cotton futures market, but many buyers sat on their money, refusing to pay 10 cents a pound yet fearing even higher prices by December. Most mills kept only a thirty-day supply of bales on hand. Print cloth made with cheaper 1899 cotton was offered at 2⅞. The Fall River warehouses were still full of grey goods from nonstop production. The mill treasurers in July finally agreed to a four-week curtailment and by September decided to cut wages 10 percent. Lowell, Manchester, New Bedford, and the Rhode Island mills were expected to follow. The operatives and their unions preferred shorter hours, as they were already trying to live on reduced income cut by months of curtailment. No one suggested a union-backed vacation; that idea was long dead. The Southern Cotton Spinners' Association, a manufacturers' organization, supported curtailments and shutdowns in the Carolinas, where the crop had failed badly, and throughout the South.[109] Cotton remained too expensive for anyone to make a profit in textiles.

On September 5, Matt Borden bought at the going price of 2⅞ cents a yard another half million pieces of grey goods, clearing out one-third of what the Fall River manufacturers' selling committee controlled. Being as usual "long-faced pessimists," they sold gladly. The Borden purchase or "plunge into a stagnant . . . market" buoyed the print cloth price and all others, killing talk of curtailments or wage cuts. According to the *Providence Journal*, Rhode Island operatives, who knew him no better than the Dowager Empress of China, thought of Matt Borden as another George Washington.[110] He was trying to manage the unmanageable: the uncontrolled overproduction that drove the Fall River system. His massive purchases made when overproduction had driven the price down to its lowest point allowed him to undersell other cloth printers. If he could not stop overproduction, he meant to make use of it. Borden's access to New York banks and dry goods houses made this possible. His manipulation of the system did not, however, mean he accepted its policies of glut.

Cotton prices in 1900 stayed high. No region was spared; national production suffered. The only solution would be a rising price for cloth that would permit manufacturers to make a profit using ten-cent cotton. By September 14, print goods sold at 3 cents but sellers waited, holding on to their grey goods and any cheaper cotton in their warehouses, hoping for a downturn in the chaotic cotton futures market. Then, demand for American cotton textiles collapsed. China's Boxer Rebellion in 1900 against foreign interference shut down the South's market for cheap goods. Meanwhile European textile producers turned to Indian cotton, driving up the price. Lancashire interests regarded the Nile delta in Egypt as a prime area for growing long staple, well-irrigated sea island cotton. Poor weather and a bad crop in the southern United States became involved in a global context. Bales of 1899 cotton, whatever the quality or condition, squirreled away in southern barns and warehouses, emerged on the market.[111] Most important, cloth prices rose slightly, and production resumed.

Not content with setting the price, Matt Borden attempted in the fall of 1901 to corner the print cloth market. He was determined to control the policies of the Fall River mills. The manufacturers' association fiercely resisted. The mill treasurers faced "the greatest struggle they ever encountered."[112] In mid-September, Borden raised wages 5 percent. The other mills ignored this. After four weeks, he raised wages another 5 percent, while the other treasurers were discussing a wage cut of 15 percent. Wage levels manipulated by Borden appeared irrelevant to decision-making in Fall River. The operatives immediately demanded an increase to match the Iron Works piece rates. Borden's moves as a "hustler" upset the mill agents' calculations, coming as usual at "the most inopportune time."[113] The print cloth market was still unmoved at 2⅞ cents, glutted by overproduction and the prospect of cotton prices nearly as high as in 1900. Borden gave an unusual number of interviews to the New York press, manipulating the fears growing in Fall River that he intended to form a combine to eliminate the position of the local treasurer. Reporters described Borden as abrupt, blunt, quick in mind, speech, and action, an aggressive "man who controls the cotton cloth market of America." The man was "a law unto himself. . . ."[114] Interviewers, portrayed Borden as a vital warrior and masculine man, as eager to take on his competitors as to send his steam yacht against the Spanish navy.

With uncharacteristic openness, Matt Borden made war on his rivals in Fall River, including his only surviving brother, Richard, regarded as a local elder statesman. He dismissed them all in one interview as either too selfish or incompetent to give the operatives a share of their profits. First, he bought all the Fall River grey goods that he could find, outright or through contracts, at 3 cents, but turned down offers from Connecticut print cloth mills. Borden explained, "Oh, we don't care for your goods, we want Fall River goods."[115] Then in late October he announced his second 5 percent wage increase, effective on November 4. This pushed weavers' wages at the Iron Works mills to nearly 23 cents a cut, unheard of since the early 1870s, and put the city into "an uproar." The manufacturers refused to discuss any wage increases. After they had sold Borden their contracts through January, any wage advance would cut seriously into the mills' profits. They were beginning to realize what he was up to: gaining control of their ability to make decisions. A strike would shut down the city, boosting the price of the print cloth already in Borden's hands. Most treasurers were furious at being squeezed, but some thought that if the price went to 3½ cents a wage increase might be possible. These men missed the point. Whatever it cost him, Borden was trying to fix regional wages and the cloth price. He was fulfilling Fall River's tradition of market dominance. The pressure on union leaders to strike became immense, but the newly formed Fall River Textile Council, representing all five unions, required a four-fifths vote to strike. The mule spinners had a veto.

The treasurers turned to the "more conservative," although numerically minor, groups among the unions to help them fight Borden. The sliding scale system now applied to all operatives' wages but became a source of continual discontent. The agents supplied outrageously false data, such as figuring 45 yards to a cut when the local standard measured 54 yards and longer. Their power to shape the meaning of statistics and wages and interpret the "rationality" of market behavior had earned them the union membership's deep animosity. The members would decide which way the union would go; their leaders cautiously refused to take a public position. Pressure from the manufacturers' association on the business community, the clergy, and the unions intensified as they urged all groups to oppose Borden and back the mills. Borden, they argued, was an enemy who threatened prosperity and steady work. The mills had not been doing well, they insisted, allowing two Catholic priests and two Protestant clergymen, equally bewildered, to examine their accounts. If the market advanced, wage increases might be considered by January 1902. No one believed this.

On October 31, the mule spinners' membership and the loom fixers' membership voted narrowly against a strike. The mule spinners' rules required a two-thirds majority vote to strike; support for a strike among the 333 members lacked forty-eight votes. The total number of mule spinners in the Fall River workforce was less than 1 percent. The small loom fixers' union also decided against a strike but by only four votes. The carders, the weavers, many of them women, and the slasher-tenders voted overwhelmingly to strike, but the textile council refused on the three-fifths vote.[116] The cost of this outcome was continuing, deepening division among the unions and their members. The treasurers could not have been more grateful. Still, for many angry, disillusioned operatives, an historic opportunity for class action had eluded them. When textile workers met in Washington, D.C., in November 1901 to amalgamate with the AFL, the Fall River loom fixers and weavers tried unsuccessfully to retain their local autonomy and then bolted from the organization. The new head of the United Textile Workers' of America was Fall River's James Tansey of the carders' union. In 1903 John Golden, the former assistant to Thomas O'Donnell, became president.[117] Fall River conservative unionists controlled the UTW.

Matt Borden was not through. On November 5, 1901, he cut wages for his mill workers by 10 percent, defending his decision as business-like and reflecting the prevailing rates set by the Fall River mills and, most of all, accepted by the unions. He was teaching both of them a lesson about power and labor politics. But most treasurers felt lucky in early November and wished "no war of any kind" with Borden. He then stopped buying grey goods and allowed the market price to stabilize at 3 cents. Everyone knew he could upset it again whenever he chose. He possessed unexcelled resources and a hostility to the Fall River system that would ultimately undermine its cotton industry along with independent treasurers, over-production as a business policy, and constant struggle with skilled opera-tives over wages. But this would take more time. On November 19, 1901, without warning or explanation, Borden cut the price of printed goods, underselling his competitors in the dry goods trade. Grabbing the mar-ket, he got the bulk of the orders, but appeared to lose an estimated half million dollars in the process. His purchases during the Fall River fight proved costly, but Matt Borden remembered that when a president died, as Garfield had in 1881, everyone wore mourning and cloth printers made immense profits. As McKinley lingered and seemed to rally after being shot by an assassin in early 1901, Borden gambled on death. In addition to his usual orders, the American Printing Company sold 2.5 million yards of black and white prints. His bleacheries also prepared cloth, anticipating the heavy demand for commemorative draperies.[118] He was therefore able to absorb his losses. As one dry goods trader remarked, Borden thought in the long run. Although Lovering's proposal for a na-tional textile workday had gone nowhere in 1898, this unprecedented proposal reflected the Republican Party's growing emphasis on a stronger and mildly regulatory federal government, especially during the years of Theodore Roosevelt's presidency from 1901–8 after McKinley's death.

The repercussions of the November 1901 decline in print goods hit the grey cloth market; the price fell to a low of 2¾ cents. With raw cotton prices still high, the Fall River mills would lose money filling any contracts other than the ones they had signed with Borden at 2⅞ cents. Their profits now depended on collaboration with him. The issue had become his power over the cloth market and the Fall River system, not short-term losses. The Fall River treasurers would not give in easily. In a final gesture of contempt on December 24, Borden gave his workforce at the Iron Works mills a Christmas "offering." This bonus was figured on what they might have earned between November 18 and December 30, if the wage cuts set by the Fall River treasurers and backed by the textile council had not required him, as a good businessman, to reduce wages 10 percent. The labor leaders replied lamely that they wished the other mills might be as generous for the holidays.[119]

In 1902 T. M. Young, reporter for the *Manchester Guardian,* visited Fall

River, New Bedford, and some Rhode Island mills to evaluate the threat to Lancashire production of George Draper's Northrop loom. Fall River boasted eighty-seven mills held by forty-one corporations and employed thirty thousand "hands," a term Young used for his British readers. He toured the Fall River Iron works mills among others, noting the production entirely by ring spinning of a hard twist warp and weft which the plain looms banged out as print cloth, "reedy" and "bare," not equal to the quality of print cloth made in Burnley, Lancashire.[120] But this "inferior," even shoddy, product, which continued to dominate production in Borden's mills, had a well-protected American home market. Cloth printers knew that market well and produced bright prints in vivid colors, vulgar by European standards but the mainstay of American and Canadian consumption. Matt Borden's ambitions did not include producing better cloth, advancing weaving technology, or developing a foreign market for American goods. In this respect, he remained a Fall River man. He spurned what Young termed the "Unknown God" of American manufacturing, the constant search for a new invention to reduce costs of production and increase salaries.[121] Borden's ultimate concern remained the domination of the print cloth market.

As that market became glutted again, the New England mills cut wages 10 percent in 1903 and increased the speed and number of new automatic looms assigned to weavers. The old plain looms ran at top speed. Lowell operatives struck unsuccessfully in 1903 led by Golden of the UTW-AFL. Then another staggering cut of 12.5 percent precipitated a gigantic, unsuccessful Fall River strike in 1904–5, resulting in a mass exodus of strikers, mostly Irish and English activists.[122] Typically, the Iron Works mills and the American Printing Company, the largest textile corporation in the United States owned by one family prior to World War I, paid the old wage rates throughout the strike. The ramifications of this severe defeat forced the Fall River weavers in January 1906 to reconsider their distanced relationship with the UTW-AFL. Trade unionism and combinations had become the dominant expression of industrial politics. This ongoing debate within the weavers' union drove the "Old Labor Agitator" Thomas Evans to his death in the Taunton State Asylum.

Despite Evans' fears about the weavers' surrender to conservative trade unionism, the UTW-AFL leaders did not succeed in organizing the weavers of Fall River and New Bedford. Constantly withdrawing from, then rejoining the national textile union over problems of local control and high dues, the weavers, the loom fixers, the slasher-tenders, and even the mule spinners of Fall River and New Bedford never became dependable AFL members. In 1909 the weavers resurrected the old New England Federation of Weavers and tried to make it a national federation. A more inclusive National Amalgamation of Textile Operatives formed in 1916. In Lawrence, some English operatives abandoned trade unions entirely in

1905 to form a branch of the Industrial Workers of the World.[123] But this industrial unionism largely came to represent those emigrants from southern and eastern Europe, new to New England textile mills and so feared by craft unions, carrying their own ideas about the politics of industrial life.

DURING THE last decades of the nineteenth century and into the early twentieth, the policies and market strategies of the New England textile industry, labor protest and union organization, partisan politics, gender meanings, family dynamics, and ethnic identities—all were contested and transformed on a field of shifting power relationships. Trade unions and combinations became major forms of the expressions of power relations. The constant turmoil experienced by the people of southeastern New England in the overlapping realms of class, culture, and power represents a fundamental element in the history of nineteenth-century American industrialization and labor politics. These changing meanings and relationships, as well as the struggles to sustain the values inherent in differing memories, legacies, prerogatives, and entitlements, demonstrate the conflicts and contingencies in the creation and exercise of power.

EPILOGUE

The Escape of Al Priddy, the Death of M. C. D. Borden, and the Burnley Reunion

THE YEAR 1901 marked the peak of Matt Borden's ascent to domination of the print cloth market, an aim of the Borden family since the 1830s. He fulfilled that legacy by manipulating the late nineteenth-century Fall River system from his headquarters in New York City. Until 1910, Borden continued to be "the unquestioned power in the print cloth markets." With "little respect for the old fashioned customs," he meant to make them obsolete. His methods involved "making no one his confident until like a general, his plans . . . [were] complete." Then he left the rest to his subordinates.[1] Among them were his sons with whom he formed a partnership, M. C. D. Borden and Sons, in 1910 to finance the sales of the American Printing Company. He knew that he had intestinal troubles and was putting his business affairs in order. When the Fall River mills offered a 5 percent wage increase to the operatives in early 1911, the seriously ill Borden made it 10 percent. He prevailed.

As Borden struggled to retain his hold on the market, a 1911 autobiography of a Lancashire immigrant back boy and doffer indicated that young English immigrants were rejecting textile work in New England, even highly paid mule spinning, to search for a better life elsewhere. *Through the Mill*, a collection of articles first published in *The Outlook*, told the dismal story, under the pseudonym "Al Priddy," of the early years of Frederic Kenyon Brown in the mills of New Bedford.[2] Fred Brown had immigrated in 1892 as a boy of ten with his aunt and uncle, both habitual drunks. His dependence on them as his only kin and their reliance on his wages to stave off creditors made the textile mill seem his destiny. Later as a college student, Brown remembered that he had thought of himself as a "hand," convinced that the "*mill* was the measure of a man" and a test of his personal "moral capacity."[3] As a youth of sixteen, he supported the 1898 New Bedford strike, more as a release from drudgery than out of any political commitment to resistance. Socialism meant nothing to him, and the likes of activist weaver Thomas Evans failed to capture his imagination. Furthermore, becoming a mule spinner like his uncle no longer defined manliness for him or offered a respectable skill. While working as a "joiner," sharing the operation of a pair of mule spinning frames in the city's worst mill, Brown concluded that

> the labor was, after all, a wild frenzy, a race and a stab and a sob for ten and a half hours! I can never think of it as anything more. . . . And, added to all this, there was the constant depressive contact with unsympathetic and foul-mouthed desecrators of ambition.[4]

When he was twenty, it dawned on him: "*Leave the mill at any cost. . . . quibble* no more, offend all, risk all, but *get away from the mill!*"[5] After this crucial decision, Brown regarded his last days of work, and indeed all his days in the mill, as a time of waiting, not his true destiny. He had "mastered" the control of his life and felt "jubilant."[6] In 1902 he left New Bedford to seek an education. From his train window he watched the mill crowds at the grade crossings and mused,

> I saw them as I had walked with them—women in shawls and looking always tired, men in rough clothes and with dirty clay pipes prodded in their mouths, and girls in working aprons, and boys, just as I had been, in overalls and undershirts. And I was going away from it all, in spite of everything![7]

Increasingly during the early twentieth century, the youngest generation of English immigrant textile workers abandoned the New England mills.

The sons of M. C. D. Borden, Bertram Borden and Howard Borden, remained the treasurers of the American Printing Company and the Iron Works mills. His namesake, Matthew S. Borden, had trained as a physician and fell in love with a young woman who was an actress. In 1903 they married secretly in defiance of Matt Borden's wishes. He refused to see them. When Borden made his last will in 1904, he attached a codicil, not revealed until the will was probated in July 1912, cutting Matthew off from his expected one-third of his father's five-million-dollar fortune. M. C. D. Borden died at his summer residence in New Jersey on May 27, 1912, with his three sons in attendance. He never informed Matthew about his disinheritance, the result of that "unfortunate marriage."[8] His only other bequest went to Yale University. The two heirs could not sell their stock shares and much of the estate remained in trust. They would try to continue to buy and sell print cloth as their father had done. The man, who like his Borden relatives remained obsessed by market control, left them no choice.

Overproduction ceased to be the key policy of the Fall River mills, although wage cuts and strikes continued. Throughout New England, the textile industry diversified and declined. Southern competition intensified (see table 9). After World War I, silk and artificial silk or rayon became the fashion rage. Stylish young women in the twenties considered clothing made of print cloth old fashioned and dowdy. The American Printing Company hired Hollywood actresses of the silent screen era to wear dresses of print cloth and held contests for the most fashionable gown sewn of the material, but this did not work. Consumer demand had shifted to ready-to-wear silk and rayon dresses, some of them stitched in converted Fall River mills.[9] New forces drove the cloth market. All cotton textile production in New England in the 1920s became seriously depressed, while production in the South continued to grow. Aware of his district's economic decline, Republican Congressman William S. Greene strenuously promoted a remarkable scheme, to be funded by the War Department, to dig a canal using small rivers and ponds that stretched between Fall River and Boston, from the Taunton River to Massachusetts Bay.[10] Numerous, well-populated towns stood in the path. Nothing happened.

Just before Matt Borden's death, emigrants and their children from the weaving center of Burnley in Lancashire organized reunions in 1911 and 1912 as celebrations of their ties to the old town. By 1905, more British immigrants were settling in Canada than the United States (see table 10). Franco-American workers had replaced them as the most numerous national group among Massachusetts textile workers. The great nineteenth-century English immigration to the New England textile industry was over. The most successful Burnley reunion occurred in Fall River on April 27, 1912, at McKinley Hall, Weavers' Building. Eight hundred people from Fall River, New Bedford, Pawtucket, Providence, and smaller mill towns attended the occasion, as reported in the Burnley press.[11]

> The gathering was a memorable one, and the souvenirs were suggestive of the love ex-Burnleyites have for the old Lancashire borough. . . . [A] specially designed programme, with the embossed and coloured American and English flags crossed; contained particularly appropriate items. . . . "To our Burnley lasses"; . . . "To good old Burnley"; . . . "[T]o our Burnley chaps!"

The reunion began at four in the afternoon with a dinner of cold meats, celery, jam and apple tarts, and "steaming hot coffee." A concert of popular and comic songs and Lancashire dialect readings, which were "particularly well received," preceded a grand march and dancing until eleven.

Everyone greeted everybody else with the heartiest welcome, and the spirit of joviality characterized the affair throughout, and made it one of the merriest and most enjoyable events that have held sway in McKinley Hall in many a season.[12]

This was a nostalgic moment for people who regarded themselves as New Englanders but still Lancastrians. Politics, especially labor politics or memories of strikes, demonstrations, and hard times, did not appear on anyone's program. Even the 1912 strike in Lawrence, where the English immigrant branch of the Industrial Workers of the World became involved, the New Bedford strikes in 1910 and 1912 led by the IWW, or the revival of militancy in Lancashire prompted no public comment at the reunion.[13] It seemed enough that evening to eat, laugh, dance, remember a well-loved birthplace, and be with people, who had perhaps once been labor activists but now wished to forget the past and be Burnleyites again—at least once a year.[14] It was Yankee mill owner Jonathan Thayer Lincoln of Fall River who preserved the political heritage of Thomas Evans and his Lancashire-style labor politics, while Fred Brown studied and the people from Burnley enjoyed their reunions marked only by fond remembrances.

CRITICAL ASSESSMENT OF PRIMARY SOURCES

HISTORIANS MAKE sense of their research and thinking by evaluating the quality, perspective, and context of the evidence they seek, discover, and choose to use. Assessing the nature and ideological construction of primary resources materials, such as diaries, newspaper accounts, government reports, and manuscript collections remains essential to the process of developing analysis and argument.

CHAPTER 1

Primary sources on the early industrial development of Fall River are scattered, lost, or incomplete, especially business records and manuscript collections on major figures. Obituaries in local newspapers offer important information. The standard nineteenth-century books on Fall River history by Henry H. Earl, D. Hamilton Hurd, and J. D. Van Slyck are essentially commemorative but provide numerous useful details. Alice Brayton described her two-volume collection of primary sources, *Life on the Stream,* smugly but shrewdly as "a written portrayal of our way of life." The work includes her rich, imaginative speculation on the private lives of the early generation of industrial founders.

Like many other historians, I have relied heavily on the research in primary sources found in Robert K. Lamb's 1935 Harvard dissertation on Fall River. His study of early textile development rested on published and unpublished memoirs and diaries, business records at Baker Library for which he became a major interpreter, a thorough search of the remaining copies of early newspapers, and a few unpublished papers at the Fall River Historical Society. Lamb's dissertation remains the most important source on pre–Civil War industrial growth in Fall River. It is an unparalleled study that puts together the complex story of families, investments, and industries.

CHAPTER 2

The key primary sources on the labor politics of artisans and operatives are Fall River newspapers: the Whig *Monitor,* 1830–57 (with the most complete collection at the Boston Public Library), the ten-hour reform paper, *The Mechanic* (1844–45) and its successor, *The Fall River Weekly News,* which became a daily Republican newspaper in 1859. *The Voice of Industry* (Lowell, Fitchburg) contains material on labor activity in Fall River in 1845 and 1848. Most of these sources (with the exception of the *Voice* and other scattered periodicals) were written primarily for and about craftsmen and artisans who viewed factory operatives and workingwomen with condescension. The Fall River *Mechanic* contained no letters from factory girls, although the editor became indignant at charges of immorality against them. The *Awl,* published in the early 1840s by activist Lynn shoemakers occasionally reprinted an article from the *Voice,* but none from shoebinders. Except for the *Voice,* workingwomen remained silent in the New England labor press. Other sources reveal the activities of workingmen and workingwomen in the late 1840s. For example, Thomas Almy, editor of the *Mechanic,* 1844–45, became the coeditor of the *Fall River News* and continued his interest in the ten-hour day and labor activism including coverage of the 1848 and 1850 Fall River strikes in which women participated both as strikers and as strikebreakers.

Also useful are the published speeches of Seth Luther in the early 1830s; the published diary of Benjamin Wood Pearce (1890), the memoirs of Hannah Borden, *FRGlobe,* February 27, 1889; obituaries in the local press; the broadside, "To the Employers of Fall River, October 11, 1841," and the unpublished "Life of Benjamin Wilbur," the latter two at the Fall River Historical Society.

CHAPTER 3

Evidence on English immigrant workers between 1840 and 1865 in Fall River, New Bedford, and in Rhode Island is found in the newspaper collections of both the labor and the commercial press. These include the extant copies of the *Fall River Weekly News, The Monitor, The Voice of Industry,* and Boston's *Daily Evening Voice.* Historians should use with care Robert Howard's chapter, "Progress in the Textile Trades," in *The Labor Movement: The Problem of To-Day,* ed. George E. McNeill (Boston, 1887), except as a primary source on Howard, who emigrated in 1873, and on his leadership of the Fall River mule spinners' union after 1878. His account, which ignores or underplays the many political battles with the weavers, apparently used oral tradition, as well as whatever mule spinners' union records remained but did not cite the labor press as a source for events before his arrival. Howard's essay provides an account almost wholly dedicated to mule spinner activities. Its uncritical use by the editors of *The Encyclopedia of the American Left,* (1990) led to errors; see chapter 8, note 105.

CHAPTER 4

Work on post–Civil War labor reform begins with the Boston *Daily Evening Voice,* published between December 1864 and October 1867. Primarily the voice of Boston's Eight-Hour Movement among mechanics and skilled tradesmen, the paper's editor quickly recognized the importance of the ten-hour movement in the state's textile centers. Regular correspondents reported on labor reform from Lowell, New Bedford, and other cities in the Northeast. The Boston *Voice* printed transcripts, often the only published accounts in the New England press, of legislative and commission hearings and speeches given at labor conventions and rallies in New England cities. The coverage, however, concentrated on skilled workers and physicians and often gave only brief mention of textile operatives' testimony, better covered in the local press of textile cities. The *Voice* also printed news of other labor conflicts in the United States and Europe. Lowell's popular press, *Vox Populi,* (1841–91) supported labor reform but exists only in extremely scattered editions. A scant two issues of Fall River's *Labor Journal* (1873–76) remain in the Fall River Historical Society. A search for this invaluable source aided by English labor scholars in manuscript and archival collections in Lancashire, England, where it was reportedly sent on a regular basis, and in London's Colindale Library proved fruitless. Also see in the Rare Book Collection of the Boston Public Library, a circular of the Ten-Hour Association of Fall River, "To the Operatives and Working Classes of Massachusetts," May 8, 1869. Robert Bower's *Lawrence Journal (1871–73),* later *Lawrence Journal and Citizen,* (1874–77) in the Essex Institute, Salem, Massachusetts, was until recently too fragile for use. It is now available on microfilm, thanks to the efforts of archivist Richard Fyffe and the Boston Public Library. The *Bradford Observer,* Yorkshire, England, carried letters from English immigrants as did other Lancashire newspapers. When the *Voice* folded in 1867, the local, Boston, and New York press (especially the *Boston Herald* and the *New York Herald*) filled the gap created for press coverage on the ten-hour movement until Robert Bower's *Lawrence Journal* began publication in 1871. In 1900, Charles Cowley published his short reminiscences of the Massachusetts' ten-hour movement in *Lowell: A City of Spindles.* A collection of radical poetry by an English immigrant textile worker and ten-hour activist, Richard Hinchcliffe, *Rhymes Among the Spindles* (1872), is in the Rare Book Collection, Concord Public Library, Concord, Massachusetts.

On Fall River and New Bedford, the *News* and the *Evening Standard* and *Mercury* carry accounts of the strikes of 1866, 1868, and 1870. The *Border City Herald,* later the *Fall River Herald,* began as a ten-hour paper in early 1874 but existing copies start in 1876. The French-language newspaper, *L'Echo du Canada,* edited by Honoré Beaugrand (1873–76) supported ten hours and was for a brief time the paper of reform for the local French Canadian community. Although Taunton, Massachusetts, had textile mills and an activist workforce, the *Taunton Gazette,* owned by the *Fall River News,* is not a good source of information on labor conflict. Henry K. Oliver's *Report to the Massachusetts Senate,* no. 21 (1868) is a gem of information on ten hours and child labor. Oliver became the head of the Massachusetts Bureau of Labor Statistics created in 1869. The bureau's reformist annual reports begin in 1870 and contain a balanced investigation of the 1870 strike in Fall River, and others contain valuable evidence on labor reform ideas, working conditions, and standards of living. For a recent selection from the reports, see *Their Lives and Numbers: The Condition of Working People in Massachusetts, 1870–1900,* ed. Henry F. Bedford, (Ithaca: Cornell University Press, 1995).

Philip S. Foner and Brewster and Angela Chamberlin translated and edited German Marxist Friedrich A. Sorge's *Labor Movement in the United States: A History of the American Working Class from Colonial Times to 1890* (Westport, Conn.: Greenwood Press, 1977). This problematic version of Sorge's work written in the 1890s represented efforts by Foner to reconstruct Sorge's life in a biographical essay (3–41) and to correct errors in the work. Some glaring errors on New England textiles remain, such as the identification of mule spinner Robert Howard as "an old weaver," (83), and there is serious confusion over the Fall River strikes of 1875 and 1879, (172, 186–88). Sorge, who lived in New York and New Jersey and traveled frequently to Europe, described the American working class in 1872 as constituted of Irish, Germans, "Negroes," and (white) Americans, underrating the contributions of English immigrants to the labor movement, except in organizing miners, (19–20, 111). Sorge used as one of his two key sources on New England, Howard's essay in McNeill's 1887 book and the volumes of the Massachusetts Bureau of Labor Statistics. Foner updated Sorge's notes, but this editorial decision obscured rather than clarified the sources on which Sorge's book was based. Although now available in English, this translation of a primary source should be used with care.

CHAPTER 5

Records on the development of most Fall River and New Bedford mills have vanished, except for the Baker Library collection on the Fall River Iron Works, 1821–1909, and the small Annawan mill, and some scattered records at the Fall River Historical Society. At Baker, these include day-books, journals, ledgers, invoices, accounts receivable and payable. The payrolls of the cotton mills run by the Iron Works such as the Metacomet and Annawan are very scattered after 1881. The Annawan Manufactory records are more complete between 1825–99, but the operation was small compared to the larger postwar print cloth mills. The Metacomet Mill records also are fairly complete, 1846–1903, but payrolls and the names of operatives are scattered, while Letter Books, 1846–81, contain both general correspondence and incoming letters from agents. The American Linen Company records are meager and not useful. The memorandum of J. T. [Jonathan Thayer] Lincoln for Baker Library provided a very short history of the Iron Works. The American Print Works records, a key firm owned by the Iron Works since 1835, are not contained in this collection. John Cumbler examined the business records at Baker Library for a later period, but their importance appeared slim in his work.

The Fall River Historical Society has a few letters of John S. Brayton, but no diaries, memoirs, or reminiscences of the key families engaged in the postwar expansion of the print cloth industry. Alice Brayton's work referred to a diary of Mary B. Young, but none has emerged. The society has some scattered records of the Richard Borden Manufacturing Company (1873–98), the Durfee Mill (1870), the Troy Cotton and Woolen Company (1868–78) and the American Linen Company (1852–84) during the relevant years of expansion. The local press and coverage of the economic development of Fall River by the press in interested cities, such as Providence, Lowell, Boston, and New York are invaluable. Had Robert Lamb been able to extend his analysis into post–Civil War Fall River industry, more of the business records might have been preserved.

The Old Dartmouth Historical Society in New Bedford has one volume (the second) of the Wamsutta's Board of Directors' minutes, 1874–1901. These minutes occasionally addressed wage issues, but they ignored the 1877 and 1898 strikes, dwelling on real estate transactions, machinery purchases, yearly profits, and the fixing of dividends. The rest of the Wamsutta papers were transferred to New York City, subsequently damaged by flooding and discarded. Also see in New Bedford the very scattered correspondence from the personal papers of Thomas Bennett Jr. (1821–1898).

CHAPTER 6

Despite the loss of the Henry Sevey's *Labor Journal* and the early issues of the *Border City Herald,* newspaper reportage in the *Fall River News* is detailed and rich, while the first several reports of the Massachusetts Bureau of Labor Statistics cover the 1870 strike and other labor activity in textile centers. A one in ten sample of two "mill villages" within Fall River, as identified in the 1945 dissertation of Sylvia Lintner, provide contextual material on family structure in 1870 among the diverse working population as reported in the federal census of population manuscripts (see table 5). Beaugrand's *L'Echo du Canada* (1873–76) reflected the opinion of the progressive segment of the city's French Canadian population, while H. R. Benoit's *Ouvrier Canadien* (1875) the more conservative. Special correspondents from Boston and New York reported the events of 1875. Especially useful and detailed in their analysis are the *Boston Herald* and the *New York Herald*. Massachusetts newspapers generally carried news of these events and of ensuing labor activity in their areas. Many also reported on the English textile industry and significant labor strikes. The *Providence Sun*, a Democratic, pro-labor alternative to the conservative *Providence Journal*, is a rich but greatly underutilized source on Massachusetts, Rhode Island, and eastern Connecticut labor politics. The *Lawrence Journal and Citizen* spoke for Robert Bower and his colleagues but also printed many letters from working people. The *Workingman's Advocate*, the *American Workman*, the *Boston Pilot*, the *Commercial Bulletin*, and Patrick Ford's New York *Irish World* carried comments. The Massachusetts Bureau of Labor Statistics' *Seventh Annual Report* (1876) and the *Eleventh Annual Report* (1880) covered the events. The published three volumes of the 1875 Massachusetts Census provide comparative data on textile centers and their populations. The Massachusetts manuscript population census for 1875 is lost. Fall River *City Directories* for scattered years have been helpful. Both Robert Howard's account of the 1875 events and the *History of the Fall River Strike*, by A Workingman, edited by the secretary of the Weavers' Union, John Smith (Fall River 1875), should be used with caution as primary sources. Also see "The Strike At Taftville," Connecticut Bureau of Labor Statistics, *Second Annual Report*, May 1875 (Hartford, Conn.: 1875), State Archives, Connecticut State Library.

The memoirs of David S. Lawlor, *The Life and Struggles of an Irish Boy in America* (Newton, Mass: Carroll Publishing Co., 1936), described the life and work of the son of a skilled machinist in a Waterford textile mill in County Tipperary who brought his family to Fall River in 1872. The father became a mule spinner and David a tuber and doffer in the Granite mill and later the Davol mills. He described the operatives' work clothing and witnessed the Granite mill fire in 1874. Lawlor left the mills in 1889 at twenty-four, unable to stand the noise of the weave rooms where he worked as a second hand.

CHAPTER 7

For labor protest in Rhode Island, Connecticut, and Massachusetts, the weekly *Providence Sun* is the most valuable source, 1875 to 1876. The editor, Lester Ross, printed countless letters from Rhode Island operatives and commented vigorously on strikes, such the 1875 events in Fall River, and on Providence politics. He saw his circulation as including not only Rhode Island, but also eastern Connecticut, and southeastern Massachusetts, where the paper was widely read despite the opposition of many mill agents. When Ross ceased to be editor in January 1877, the focus on labor protest diminished, and the paper became the organ of the Rhode Island Democratic Party. Between 1878 and 1882, the Fall River *Labor Standard*, edited by George Gunton, took over the job of reporting regional textile news as well as national and international material on labor issues. In the absence of copies of the *Labor Journal* of Fall River and the increasing conservatism of the *Lawrence Journal*, the researcher is forced to rely on the more conservative, pro-manufacturing press, such as the *Providence Journal* and the *Providence Star* (for which Sevey and Gunton were Fall River correspondents), the *Fall River News*, the *New Bedford Standard*, and the *New Bedford Mercury*. Both the *News* and the *Border City Herald*, later the *Fall River Herald* (existing copies begin on February 16, 1877) carried the stories from the *Mercury* on the New Bedford strike. I used only the *Standard*. Wamsutta workers viewed both papers as indistinguishable. Carl Gersuny's article, "A Unionless General Strike: The Rhode Island Ten Hour Movement of 1873," *Rhode Island History* 54, 1 (February 1996): 21–32 is a fine example of the utilization of the conservative press of Rhode Island for evidence on labor protest.

Government documents on Rhode Island reflect the tense political situation in the 1870s and 1880s over the ten-hour movement and the establishment of the Bureau of Labor Statistics in 1887. Strong political opposition in the Rhode Island General Assembly meant that commissioners were fired annually and deprived of authority and staff. In 1889 the general assembly made a serious attempt to abolish the bureau, then starved it of funds, while Rhode Island industry refused to cooperate with the commission. For the commissioner's complaints, see Commissioner of Industrial Statistics, *Second Annual Report* (Providence, 1889), 140–41 and *Third Annual Report* (Providence, 1890), 3–4. In the first report in 1888, statistics from employers omitted information on the production of specific goods "to prevent exposure of their business" (*First Annual Report* [Providence, 1888], 19).

Manufacturers boycotted the state census in 1885 (*Rhode Island State Census*, 1885 [Providence, 1887], 601–3), furious over the passage of the ten-hour law and the disclosure of their assets in the 1880 federal census to local government scrutiny. The state census reported industrial information in the aggregate for the state and only for towns and counties, thus obscuring data on specific firms and mill villages within the large towns of Cumberland, Smithfield, and Providence. For its third report focused on workingwomen, the bureau relied heavily on random samples of "employes" opinion in various occupations (a total of 1,430) but had to dispatch special agents in 1889 to gather responses. In carefully edited "remarks," anonymous workers demanded weekly payment of wages and accused the manufacturers of ignoring the ten-hour law, child labor laws, and unsanitary and hazardous working conditions, all issues guaranteed to stimulate opposition in the general assembly. The reports also briefly listed annually the location and outcome of strikes.

The Lonsdale Company Records (Rhode Island Historical Society, Providence), especially the letter copybooks 1857–75, provide some evidence of regional coordination of wage levels in 1875.

CHAPTER 8

Fall River newspapers carried detailed accounts of politics, strikes, court cases, and economic news, often reprinting stories from Boston, Providence, and New York papers, especially when focused on Fall River. The *Labor Standard*, 1878–82, is an enormously rich source on the city, region, national, and international news about labor, politics, and the economy. The *Fall River Herald* and the *Fall River News* are rich on the local scene, representing the Democratic and Republican parties, respectively.

One of the most well known sources on Massachusetts workers is the annual reports of the Bureau of Labor Statistics beginning in 1871. These reports were, however, highly selective and produced in an intense political context. For example, the surveys and conclusions in the comparative study of Fall River, Lowell, and Lawrence in the *Thirteenth Annual Report* (1882) are biased. Earlier assessments of conditions in Fall River in 1880 and 1881 reported in the press blamed the mill owners for local labor turmoil and probably prompted both the shaping of the investigation and the conclusions (see "Part III, Fall River, Lowell, and Lawrence," 195–415). The gathering of data and interviews occurred between June and November 1881, a period of an employers' assault on the mule spinners' union and the collapse of the weavers' union. Much of the collected data was never published in the report.

This MBLS study was a response to a question put to bureau head Carroll D. Wright in April 1881 from an unidentified state representative from Worcester, Massachusetts: "Why is it that the working people of Fall River are in constant turmoil, when at Lowell and Lawrence they are quiet?" (195). The answer given in the report pointed out the different working conditions and behaviors of the mill operatives in the three cities, especially the turbulent English immigrant operatives in Fall River. Some questions were posed in opposites: are you content or discontent, do you experience labor convulsions or equilibrium, and if so why? Operatives were also encouraged to choose their own topics to relate. They were few, but they had their say. Their comments describe a particular Fall River style of textile management. The investigation claimed to be exhaustive and scientific, not based on opinion, although opinion was the basis for the findings. Those opinions were largely middle class and male.

Anonymous mill operatives, manufacturers, and "leading" citizens were questioned, and tenements and boardinghouses visited. A total of seven hundred persons gave testimony, of which 447, or 64 percent, were directly connected with textile manufacturing. Thirty-six percent of those questioned were middle class, including clergymen, grocers, lawyers, physicians, city government officials, bankers, and other "well-informed parties," in addition to manufacturers. Only 10 percent of tenement dwellers interviewed were operatives. In Fall River, 9 percent of the total interviewed were operatives, in Lowell, 6 percent, and in Lawrence, 16 percent. In Fall River, eight mule spinners, four weavers, and three "others" were interviewed; in Lowell, three mule spinners, three weavers, and four others; in Lawrence, seven mule spinners, five weavers, and nine others. Eighteen mule spinners, or 39 percent of a total of forty-six operatives, gave recorded testimony. The Lawrence weavers were probably female, as women dominated the weave rooms. Of the total number of operatives interviewed, Lawrence provided the largest number (45.6 percent), followed by Fall River (32.6 percent), and then the smallest, Lowell (21.7 percent). Of the total of seven hundred persons interviewed, the operatives represented only 7 percent. In the report, all workers were described as above average in intelligence; their language, concise, discreet, and well-chosen; their average ages between thirty-five and fifty; and the majority temperate, family men (197–201). Their nationality was not uniformly identified nor were their occupations. This report must be used with caution.

The primary source on Gunton's activities is the relatively under-used (especially by historians of New England textiles) *Labor Standard*, (1878–82) published in New York City, Fall River, and Paterson, the voice of the International Labor Union. Unitarian minister Jonathan Baxter Harrison spent time in Fall River in 1879, observing the operatives, their recreations, and housing. He also interviewed Gunton, Lapham, and Howard, although they are unnamed. His report appears in *Certain Dangerous Tendencies in American Life, and Other Papers* (Boston, 1880), 157–202.

Chapter 9

The key newspapers that covered labor activities, partisan politics, and strikes are the *Fall River Herald* and after 1885 the *Fall River Globe*, the latter an excellent source on New Bedford, Rhode Island, and Connecticut labor politics. On M. C. D. Borden, newspaper coverage of key events and items from trade journals, especially his obituaries in 1912, are the only existing sources as Borden, a secretive man, left no papers except for an inventory of his library. The Baker Library, Harvard University, collection of the Fall River Iron Works Papers concentrates on the pre-1887 period. There are some payrolls, construction accounts for the new cotton mills projected by Matt Borden, incoming correspondence, and an accident file in the 1890s and 1900s as well as some materials on the Borden-owned Annawan and Metacomet mills. Press reports of Borden's decisions give an overall picture of how he operated and what he accomplished. Also useful is Jno. Gilmore Speed, *A Fall River Incident or A Little Visit to a Big Mill* (New York, 1895). The typescript reminiscences of Frank Bennett, editor of the *American Cotton and Wool Reporter,* at the American Textile History Museum, Lowell, Massachusetts, are impressionistic and vigorously opinionated. My thanks to Claire Sheridan for access to the typescript.

CHAPTER 10

On the 1898 strike at New Bedford, the key source is the invaluable scrapbooks of clippings donated to Harvard University by Henry B. Hough, Edgartown, Massachusetts, former editor of the *New Bedford Standard* and author of *Wamsutta*. The scrapbooks consist of four handmade volumes marked 1–2, 3, and 4, unevenly paginated, usually with datelines but often out of chronological order. In addition to the various clippings and many illustrations, especially from *The New York Journal* and the *New York World*, are a few unpublished letters from operatives. The newspapers include Boston's *Post, Traveler, Globe, Herald, Record, Journal, Advertiser, Transcript;* the trade journals include *Wades' Fibre and Fabric, Textile World*, the *Cotton and Woolen Reporter,* and *New York Dry Goods Record;* there are also clippings from *Providence Journal, Taunton Gazette, Fall River Herald* (by then acquired by the pro-corporation publishers of the *News*), some English newspapers (including material from the *Cotton Factory Times* and others), the *Atlanta Constitution*, the *New Bedford Standard* and the *New Bedford Mercury*. The scrapbooks are stored at the New England Deposit Library, Allston, Massachusetts. My thanks to manager Charles Montalbano for his courtesy and permission to copy the scrapbooks. For the larger political and economic context, I used the *Fall River Globe*, December 8, 1897 to June 1, 1898. On Matt Borden, see above.

The *Manchester Guardian* reporter T. M. Young, perhaps attracted by the controversy over the Arkwright report in 1898, observed in 1902 the major centers of textile production in the United States, North and South, except for Philadelphia and cities in New Jersey and New York. The Lancashire textile interests enlisted him to evaluate the developing southern industry in the Carolinas, Georgia, and Alabama, but more important, to assess the competitive threat of the Northrop loom with its automatic bobbin changer. Young, well conversant with the practicalities of textile production, visited Fall River, New Bedford, and centers in Maine, New

Hampshire, and Rhode Island. His firsthand accounts appeared in *The American Cotton Industry: A Study of Work and Workers* (New York: Charles Scribner's Sons, 1903) and remain a major source on the Lancashire view of American competition in technology and managerial practices in the early twentieth century.

Appendix

Table 1

Personal taxable income in Fall River, 1867

$161,732 J[efferson]. & P[hilip]. D. Borden Trust (Valentine estate of Providence, Rhode Island)

$144,657 B. M. C. Durfee (son of Major Bradford Durfee and Mary Brayton Durfee Young)

$78,678 Colonel Richard Borden

$63,806 Jefferson Borden

$49,000 Hale Remington (textile chemicals)

$46,912 Dr. Nathan Durfee

$40,861 S. Angier Chace (son-in-law of Nathan Durfee)

$39,503 David Anthony (Troy, Pocassett, and Union mills)

$36,897 Stephen Davol (textile machinery)

$35,477 Foster Stafford (small manufacturer and merchant)

$29,812 William Mason (small manufacturer and merchant)

$26,260 R. K. Remington (textile chemicals)

$21,523 Fidelia B. Durfee (youngest sister of Holder Borden, mother of George B. Durfee, the son-in-law of Jefferson Borden)

$20,292 Holder B. Durfee (son of Nathan Durfee)

$18,768 Charles O. Shove (Union and Granite mills)

$17,811 Mary B. Young (mother of B. M. C. Durfee)

$15,380 Augustus Chace (yarn manufacturer)

Figures are for individuals with at least $15,000 and over from a total of 235 taxpayers. Source: *Fall River News*, May 25, 1867.

TABLE 2
Cotton manufacturing data for Fall River, 1865 and 1875

Population	1865	1875
	17,525	45,260
Population increase		27,779 or 159%
Total adults employed in cotton mills	2,654	11,514
Males employed	1,037 or 39%	5,467 or 47%
Females employed	1,617 or 61%	6,047 or 53%
Employment in cotton mills increase		8,860 or 228%

Sources: *Fall River News,* September 30, 1865; Peck and Earl, *Fall River and Its Industries* (1877), 68, 112. Massachusetts Census of Population, 1865 and 1875.

TABLE 3
Comparative nativities of population, 1870

Fall River	Lowell
Total population: 26,766	40,928
Total Native-born: 15,288 or 57%	26,493 or 65%
Total Foreign-born: 11,478 or 42.9%	14,435 or 35%
Ireland: 5,572 or 49% of foreign-born	9,103 or 63%
England: 4,042 or 35% of foreign-born	1,687 or 11%
Canada: British, 1,324; French, 1,129 or 21% of foreign-born	British, 414; French, 2,620 or 18%
Scotland: 382 or 3.3 % of foreign-born	469 or 3.2%
Total from Great Britain: England, Scotland, and Ireland: 10,012 or 87% of foreign-born	11,282 or 78%

Source: *United States Census of Population for 1870,* v. 1, 380–91 from "Nativities of the Population of Fifty Principal Cities" (does not include data on Lawrence).

TABLE 4
United States cotton mills producing print cloth, 1880

City or Regional Mills	Total Spindles	Pieces* per Week
Fall River	1,239,000	155,000
Southeastern New England	984,000	125,000
Total and Percent	**2,223,000**	**280,000 or 64%**
North of Boston	944,000	105,000
Western Massachusetts and Vermont	300,000	37,000
Hudson and Mohawk Valleys	326,000	41,000

Table 4 *(continued)*

City or Regional Mills	Total Spindles	Pieces* per Week
Philadelphia and Vicinity	100,000	12,500
Total and Percent Outside		
Southeastern New England	**1,670,000**	**196,000 or 43%**
Grand Total for U.S.	3,893,000	476,500

*Fifty yards to a piece. Source: Smith, *Fall River Industry,* 65–67.

TABLE 5

Characteristics of 153 "works in a cotton mill" families, Fall River: Globe Village and Little Canada in Ward 1, 1870

The sample suggests that the vast majority of English and Scottish immigrants in Fall River lived in male-headed families, half of them living in nuclear family groups and the other half in extended families including boarders and/or relatives. This reflects the general pattern in male-headed families of all nationalities except the Quebec-born. Total immigrants from Lancashire or Yorkshire (including Irish and Scottish-born with English-born children) represented 43 percent of the sample. Kinship did not seem to provide the networks of support in New England in 1870 as in English cotton districts. Female workers slightly outnumbered male workers in the sample but well over half of them were twenty years old or younger. The majority of male workers (63 percent) were over twenty years old.

An analysis of family structure based on the average number of children in the family and the average number of children working in the mills suggests that Irish-born and Quebec-born families were most similar, although the Irish-born represented the largest segment and the Quebec-born the second smallest in the 1870 sample. Quebec-born families were largest in number of children with the youngest and most numerous children at work in the mills. English and Scottish-born families had lower numbers of children in the family and at work than the Irish and Scottish-born families who had trained in Lancashire. Native-born families had the highest percentage of female heads and the highest average number of children in the family but the lowest number of children working in the mills.

Age ranges of "works in a cotton mill" by sex:

Males	Females
Total in sample: 73 or 48%	80 or 52%
Age range: 9–65 years old. Under 20, 37%; 20–45, 51%; over 45, 12%	10–45 years old. Under 20, 65%; 20–35, 31%; over 35, 4%

Composition of male-headed families:

Total in sample	135 or 88%
Nuclear families	67 or 49.6%
Extended families with relatives and boarders	13 or 9.6%

Table 5: *(composition of male-headed families, continued)*

Extended families with boarders or domestics	49 or 36.2%
Resides in large boarding house	7 or 5.1%
Occupation of male head of family	25% works in cotton mill; 75% other.

Composition of female-headed families:

Total number in sample	18 or 12%
Nuclear families	6 or 33.3%
Extended families with relatives	4 or 22.2%
Extended families with boarders	7 or 38.8%
Living alone	1 or 5.5%
Total number of male- and female-headed nuclear families	73 or 48%
Total number of male- and female-headed extended families	79 or 52%
Others	8 or 5%

Family composition ranked by size and nationality in sample:

Irish-born family composition in sample	56
Extended families	56 or 100%
Male-headed families	77%
Female-headed families	23%
Timing of emigration	Pre-1860 55%; post-1865 14%; unknown 31%
Average number of children in family	3.6
Average number of children in family works in a cotton mill	2.4; age range 9 to 35 years old
English and Scottish-born family composition in sample	50
Nuclear families	48%
Extended families with boarders or relatives	54%
Male-headed	92%
Female-headed	8%
Timing of emigration	Pre-1860 14%; post-1865 44%; unknown 42%
Average number of children in family	2.2
Average number of children works in cotton mill (second smallest)	1.4; age range 10 to 23 years old
Irish and Scottish-born via England (English born children in family)	16
Nuclear families	44%

Table 5: *(English and Scottish-born via England, continued)*

Extended families with boarders and relatives	56%
Male-headed	81%
Female-headed	19%
Timing of emigration	Pre-1860 19%; post-1865 50%; unknown 31%
Average number of children in family	3.6
Average number of children works in cotton mill	2.5; age range 9 to 30 years old
French Canadian–born family composition	16
Nuclear	100%
Male-headed	100%
Timing of emigration	Pre-1860 6%; Post-1865 94%
Average number of children in family	7 (largest in sample)
Average number of children works in cotton mill	4.8 (largest in sample); age range 8 to 29 (youngest in sample)
Native-born family composition	12
Nuclear	33%
Extended with boarders or relatives	66%
Male-headed	58%
Female-headed	42%
Average number of children in family	3.8 (second highest in sample)
Average number of children works in cotton mill	1.3 (lowest in sample); age range 12 to 27 years (oldest in sample)

Total immigrants from Lancashire or Yorkshire in sample including Irish and Scottish with English-born children: 66 or 43 percent of sample: pre-1860 15 percent; post-1865 45 percent; unknown 40 percent.

Method: Source of boundaries of Globe Village and Little Canada, Ward 1, from Lintner, "Social History of Fall River," chapter 2. One in ten sample of occupation: "works in a cotton mill" from the 1870 United States Census of Population manuscripts; my thanks to Jean Sherlock and Marion Mollin for compiling the sample. As the 1870 census lacks information on the relationship to head of household, inference is necessary.

TABLE 6

Fall River, Lowell, and Lawrence, 1875:
Persons employed in cotton goods

Fall River	Lowell	Lawrence
Total employed 14,216	9,960	8,585
Males: 6,644 or 47%	2,661 or 27%	3,448 or 40%
Females: 7,572 or 53%	7,209 or 73%	5,137 or 60%
Married Females: 882 or 12%*	315 or 4%	169 or 3%

*highest in any Massachusetts cotton textile city

Source: *Massachusetts State Census, 1875*, v. 3, 442–43. No data for New Bedford.

TABLE 7

Total population: Percentages of foreign-born in leading
Massachusetts manufacturing cities, 1875

City	Total Population	Foreign-Born	% Foreign-Born
Fall River	45,340	23,866	52.6%
Lawrence	34,916	15,546	44.5%
Lowell	49,688	17,778	35.8%
New Bedford	25,895	5,947	22.8%

Source: *Massachusetts Census of Manufacture: 1875*, prepared by Carroll D. Wright
(Boston, 1877), 49. Fall River ranked the highest in number of foreign-born as a
percentage of total population. Second was the mixed industrial city of Holyoke
at 52.0 percent.

TABLE 8

Comparative data on Fall River, Lowell, and Lawrence,
1870–1880

Census data reveals distinct differences among the three communities. Between
1870 and 1880, the population of Lowell and Lawrence both grew 21 percent,
while in Fall River, the growth was three times as much, 69 percent. In 1870, Fall
River's total population contained 57 percent native-born and 43 percent foreign-
born; in Lowell, 63 percent native and 35 percent foreign; no data listed for
Lawrence. In 1875 Fall River's total workforce contained the highest number of
foreign-born at 53 percent, including 36 percent English-born. Lawrence had 45
percent foreign-born with the lowest number of Quebec-born and paid the
highest annual wage, while Lowell had the highest number of native-born and of
Irish-born, 60 percent in a foreign-born workforce of 36 percent.

Table 8 *(continued)*

City in 1875	Fall River	Lowell	Lawrence
Total workforce	15,095	13,941	10,899
Native-born	47%	64%	55%
English-born	36%	13%	22%
Irish-born	38%	60%	53%
Quebec-born	21%	21%	12%
Average annual wage	$266	$340.46	$349.25

In 1880, Fall River's total workforce in all occupations contained 52 percent native-born and the highest percentage of foreign-born at 48 percent. Lawrence, a center of worsted production, had a total workforce of 56 percent native and 44 percent foreign-born. Lowell retained the highest percent of native-born at 61 and 39 percent foreign-born, although by 1880 Irish and English immigrants of the 1840s and 1850s produced a second generation of native-born children.

City	Fall River	Lowell	Lawrence
Total employed in all industries	16,753	21,819	14,840
Native-born*	34%	51%	44%
Foreign-born	66%	49%	56%
English-born	40%	16%	30%**
Irish-born	25%	42%	42%
British Canada including Quebec-born	33%	40%	20%
Capital invested	$22,707,043	$11,279,011	$5,350.400
Value of product	$14,510,007	$19,500,955	$5,059,400
Numbers of corporations	33	11	5

*By 1880 this number would include the children of immigrants.
**By 1880 Lawrence had become a center of worsted production, drawing immigrants from Yorkshire.

Fall River had grown most rapidly by 1880, had the highest percentage of foreign-born, especially English immigrants both in total population and in employed in all industries, and possessed the largest number of corporations and capital investment. Wages in 1875 and the value of product in print cloth in 1880 in Fall River were lower than more diversified textile manufacturing in Lowell.

Sources: MBLS, *Thirteenth Annual Report* (1882): *Statistics of Population of the United States, Ninth Census, 1870* (1872), v. 1, 380–91; *Statistics of Population of the United States, Tenth Census, 1880* (1883) v. 1, 536–41; *Report on the Manufactures of the United States at the Tenth Census* (1883), xxvi–xxxviii, 402–14. Also see "Rank of Seven Leading Cities in Cotton Goods (Value of Product): Lowell, Fall River, Philadelphia, Manchester, Lawrence, New Bedford, Holyoke," xxvi.

TABLE 9

Southern competition and the Massachusetts cotton textile industry

In 1905 and for the first time, southern competitors appeared in the manufacturing tabulations of the Massachusetts state census. Overall national cotton production increased between 1900 and 1905 by 32.80 percent. Massachusetts ranked first both in 1900 and 1905 in value of goods produced, but had dropped from 32.57 percent of the nation's total product of cotton goods in 1900 to 28.68 in 1905. Second, third, and fourth place went to South Carolina, North Carolina, and Georgia with Rhode Island and New Hampshire in fifth and sixth place. Connecticut ranked eighth behind Pennsylvania and Maine tenth behind Alabama.

United States: Total value of goods, 1900, $339,200,320
Total value of goods, 1905, $450,467,704
Percentage increase in total value of goods, 32.80

State	1905 percentile rank	Percent of U.S. goods, 1900	Percent of U.S. goods, 1905	Percent increase 1900–1905
Massachusetts	1	32.57	28.68	16.92
South Carolina	2	8.76	10.97	66.32
North Carolina	3	8.36	10.49	66.53
Georgia	4	5.44	7.81	90.57
Rhode Island	5	7.09	6.80	27.32
New Hampshire	6	6.78	6.56	28.45

In 1905 the three southern states together produced more in value of cotton goods product 29.27 than 28.68 percent in Massachusetts. In addition, percentages of increase in those three states rose dramatically in comparison with the top three producing New England states. Some mills in Rhode Island and New Hampshire may have been shifting into fine goods production, while the southern mills were building capacity.

Source: *Census of Massachusetts, 1905*, v. 3 (Boston, 1909), xix–xx.

TABLE 10

British immigration to the United States, 1840–1905

A key shift in *annual average rates* of immigration toward English over Irish to the U.S. occurred in the years after 1870. The figures exclude Scottish immigration and the data excluded Irish residents in England.

1861–1870	English to U.S. 35%	Irish to U.S. 65%
1871–1880	English to U.S. 55%	Irish to U.S. 45%
1881–1890	English to U.S. 59%	Irish to U.S. 41%
1891–1895	English to U.S. 60%	Irish to U.S. 40%
1896–1905	English to U.S. 57%	Irish to U.S. 43%

Total immigration of British (English, Scottish, and Irish) between 1840 and 1905 peaked during the 1862–1872 period, then declined slowly to 1905.

Table 10 *(continued)*

1840–1850	Total immigration to the United States, 1,135,198	Percentage of total 1,739,509 immigration to British North America, the U.S. Australia and New Zealand
1851–1861	Total immigration: 1,545,007	66%
1862–1872	Total immigration: 1,807,292	87%
1873–1883	Total immigration: 1,954,999	82%
1884–1894	Total immigration: 2,550,160	78%
1895–1905	Total immigration: 2,201,975	75%

Data for 1906–1911 indicated a shift of immigration from the U.S. to British North America (some to settle the potential wheat-growing areas of western Canada) and rising numbers to Australia and New Zealand. By 1911, 69 percent of British emigrants headed for destinations other than the United States.

Source of data for percentages, see tables 1, 2, 4, "Destinations of Emigrants Sailing from the United Kingdom (only to British North America, United States and Australian Colonies and New Zealand," in Stanley C. Johnson, *A History of Emigration from the United Kingdom to North America, 1763–1912* (London: George Routledge & Sons, Ltd., 1913), 344–47. No account of the nationalities of British emigrants was kept before 1853, 348.

Notes

Prologue: Unlikely Acquaintances

1. Obituary, *Fall River Globe* [*FRGlobe*], Jan. 25, 1906. The writer acknowledged that "few in this vicinity could make a better speech off hand than Thomas Evans in his day and his arguments were always strong and forcible...." As he aged, Evans claimed to have been in his youth a disciple of anti-Chartists, John Bright, Richard Cobden, and the Manchester School of Liberals.

2. Robert G. Hall, "Tyranny, Work and Politics: The 1818 Strike Wave in the English Cotton District," *International Review of Social History* 34 (1989): 433–470. The July 1818 strike, according to Hall, was the first for the powerloom weavers. On Bolton as a center of adamant resistance, see 465.

3. The Chartist movement in the 1840s advocated many other political reforms, see chapter 3. Thomas Evans was not found in Fall River during a search of the Index to the federal census of Massachusetts in 1840 and 1850. In 1850 he would have been twenty-three years old. In 1855 he submitted naturalization papers, suggesting a post–1850 immigration but did not become a citizen until 1862, one year after he unsuccessfully volunteered for the Union Army, *Fall River News* [*News*], Nov. 25, 1878.

4. *FRGlobe*, Dec. 11, 1905.

5. Jonathan Thayer Lincoln, *The City of the Dinner Pail* (Boston: Houghton Mifflin, 1909) 52–59.

6. On Thomas Evans' death, see Commonwealth of Massachusetts Vital Records, *Returns of Death*, vol. 85, (1906), 431. Fourteen days after his commitment to the Taunton Asylum, he died on January 25, 1906 with his age recorded as eighty-three although he was born in 1826. The cause of death in the physician's certificate is listed as "rupture of the left cardiac ventricle" with contributing factors of degeneration of the heart and senile dementia. I believe this to be the medical equivalent of a broken heart. According to the current Taunton State Hospital, the asylum kept no record of his admission or treatment (correspondence with author, March 11, 1993). For Bridget Evans' obituary, see *FRGlobe*, Sept. 16, 1908. On the weavers' union debates and decision to join the AFL, see *FRGlobe*, Dec. 10, 1905; Jan. 8, 10, 12, 29, 31, 1906.

7. Jonathan Thayer Lincoln, *The Factory* (Boston: Houghton Mifflin, 1912) 95. On Lincoln's life as remembered by his daughter, Victoria Lincoln, see Vicky L. to Agnes de Mille, c. 1966, Harold Ober *Collection,* Box 55, Folder 2, Manuscripts Division, Department of Rare Books and Special Collections, Princeton University Library. My thanks to Louise Kittredge of West Newton (granddaughter of J. T. Lincoln), her family, the Harvard Archives, and Baker Library, Harvard University for granting me permission to examine the surviving records of Jonathan Lincoln Thayer.

8. Lincoln, *City of the Dinner Pail,* 57–58.

9. Ibid., 56–59.

10. Lincoln was the firm's president and Israel Brayton, of another prominent Fall River textile family, was the treasurer. Orra L. Stone, *History of Massachusetts Industries* v. 1, (Boston: S. J. Clarke Co., 1930) 180.

11. Jonathan Thayer Lincoln, "Trade-Unions and the Individual Worker, *Atlantic Monthly* 104 (Oct. 1909): 469–76; "The City of the Dinner-Pail," *The Outlook* 85 (Feb. 9, 1907): 317–24; "The Sliding Scale of Wages in the Cotton Industry," *The Quarterly Journal of Economics* 23 (Nov., 1908): 450–69. His daughter Victoria became a writer in the 1930s and 1940s, winning the Edgar Award for mystery literature in 1967 for *A Private Disgrace: Lizzie Borden by Daylight.* (1967, reprint, New York: International Polygonics, Ltd., 1986). As a child she had once met Lizzie Borden, and her book argued that Borden murdered her parents (see below, chapter 9). She deeply admired her grandfather Leontine Lincoln as "not primarily interested in business" (Vicky L. to Agnes de Mille c. 1966, Harold Ober *Collection*). On Jonathan Lincoln's life, see obituaries, *Boston Transcript,* Jan. 30, 1942; *Boston Post,* Feb. 13, 1942; *Providence Journal* [*Providence*] Feb. 11, 1942.

12. Lincoln, *The Factory,* 109.

13. "Labor and Life," unpublished manuscript, 1. Copy in the possession of the author, courtesy of the Kittredge family.

14. On the Sears family, see Edward Pessen, *Riches, Class, and Power Before the Civil War* (Lexington, Mass.: D.C. Heath and Company, 1973), 110–20.

15. See letter of Sept. 12, 1961 (Box 37, File 14, Harold Ober *Collection*). All quotations published with permission of the Princeton University Library.

16. Leontine Lincoln also devoted himself to the support of a leprosarium and countless other charities. For a portrait of another model employer in nearby New Bedford, Massachusetts, who operated yarn mills in the 1880s and 1890s, hired union spinners from Lancashire, and provided some corporate housing, see Thomas A. McMullin, "Lost Alternative: The Urban Industrial Utopia of William D. Howland," *New England Quarterly* 55 (1982): 25–38.

17. Vicky L. to Agnes de Mille, Jan. 13, 1966 (Box 55, Folder 2, 3, Harold Ober *Collection*).

18. Ibid., 5, 10.

19. Class notes, Jonathan Thayer Lincoln File, Harvard University Archives. The Kittredge family possesses copies of the unpublished "Labor and Life" and "The Age of Power," which they kindly permitted me to copy. During the early thirties, Lincoln also worked at Harvard on the history of textile machinery: "Material for a History of American Textile Machinery," *Journal of Economic and Business History* 4 (Feb. 1932): 259–80; "The Cotton Textile Machine Industry," *Harvard Business Review* (Oct. 1932): 88–96; "The Beginnings of the Machine Age in New

England: David Wilkinson of Pawtucket," *New England Quarterly* 6, 4 (1933): 716–32; "New Light on the Development of Early American Power Looms," *Textile World* (Jan. 1933): 46–8. He worked with and encouraged Robert Keen Lamb, a graduate student in the Division of History, Government, and Economics at Harvard who earned his Ph.D. in 1935 with a well-documented study, "The Development of Entrepreneurship in Fall River: 1813–59."

20. "Labor and Life," 2.

21. Ira Berlin, "Herbert G. Gutman and the American Working Class," in Herbert G. Gutman, *Power and Culture: Essays on the American Working Class* (New York: The Free Press, 1986), 56. For my attempt to analyze Fall River labor protest in 1875, see below chapter 6.

22. For a similar approach to the definition of the "*political*, understood in the broadest sense," including working-class variations on a moral economy, see, Lizabeth Cohen, *Making a New Deal: Industrial Workers in Chicago, 1919–1939* (Cambridge: Cambridge University Press, 1990), 5–9.

23. Berlin, "Gutman and the American Working Class," 3–69. A 1998 survey of recent work in labor history, *Labor Histories: Class, Politics, and the Working-Class Experience*, ed. Eric Arnesen, Julie Greene, and Bruce Laurie (Urbana: University of Illinois Press, 1998), divides its essays into separate categories "Politics and the State," "Class and Culture," and "Labor Activism and Workers' Organizations." In the introduction, 1–15, the book's editors explore the interrelationships among these three themes, but they define politics fairly narrowly as collective public expressions, excluding the politics of identity and the private sphere. For a classic critique of labor history on these grounds, see Ava Baron, ed., *Work Engendered: Toward a New History of American Labor* (Ithaca: Cornell University Press, 1991). Walter Licht's, *Industrializing America: The Nineteenth Century* (Baltimore: Johns Hopkins University Press, 1995) remains the most successful effort to include multiple analyses in an interpretive overview.

24. "Edward Thompson, Social History and Political Culture: The Making of a Working-class Public, 1780–1850," ed. Harvey J. Kay and Keith McClelland in *E. P. Thompson: Critical Perspectives,* (Philadelphia: Temple University Press, 1990), 12–49. Eley argues that the Thompsonian approach explicitly links class and cultural analysis with the political by examining the function and changing forms of state power and developing a concept of the public, plebian domain which is political in its very nature.

25. The quote is from Berlin, "Gutman and the American Working Class," 15. For an example of Gutman's flexible use of politics and power, see "Workers' Search For Power: Labor in the Gilded Age," Gutman, *Power and Culture,* 70–92.

26. Berlin, "Gutman and the American Working Class," 57. English immigrants were well known for their growling, see below chapter 6, and David R. Roediger, "What Was So Great About Herbert Gutman?" *Labour/Le Travail* 23 (Spring 1989): 255–261.

27. Federal census manuscripts for population in 1870 and 1880, crucial years for understanding conflicts in Fall River labor politics, list occupations for textile workers as only "works in a cotton mill," thus making skill categories unavailable to the researcher.

28. As Herbert Gutman stated in an interview for *Radical History Review* in 1983: "Events illuminate changing structures and processes at work over time. . . .

The central value of historical understanding is that it transforms historical givens into historical contingencies. It enables us to see the structures in which we live and the inequality people experience, as only one among many other possible experiences," Gutman, *Power and Culture*, 345–6.

29. One example is the characterization of Quebec immigrants by the Massachusetts Bureau of Labor Statistics in 1881 as the "Chinese of the Eastern States," see below chapter 8.

30. Gutman and Ira Berlin were extending the boundaries of class formation and development, see "Class Composition and the Development of the American Working Class, 1840–1890," in *Power and Culture*, 380–94. I shift the emphasis slightly. In the New England textile industry the key periods of class formation and class development were pre-1850 and 1890, rather than pre-1840 and 1880.

31. "Review Essay: Expanding the Boundaries of the Political: Workers and Political Change in the Nineteenth Century," *International Labor and Working-Class History* 32 (Fall 1987): 59–75. Bernstein advocates the analysis of "the interplay of authority and resistance," and Thomas Bender's "multiple vision" of investigating "the centers of authority, in the public forums where power is tested, and at the edges of the regime, in the cultures of its constituent groups," 62. Bernstein's goal is "a political history of class relations that preserves the richness of analysis of consciousness and culture found in the best of the new social history," 71. He cites chapters from his *The New York City Draft Riots: Their Significance For American Society and Politics in the Age of the Civil War* (New York: Oxford University Press, 1988), on changing definitions of political boundaries. His definitions include "complex quotidian rendering of work, community, gender, racial, ethnic, geographical, and party values and interests . . . ," 62.

32. Baker calls for such research to broaden the definition of the political by nineteenth-century men in "The Domestication of Politics: Women and American Political Society, 1780–1920," *American Historical Review* 89 (June 1984): 620–47.

33. Joan Scott in her introduction to *Feminism and History* (Oxford: Oxford University Press, 1996) expands her categories of difference to include gender, sexuality, race, religion, ethnicity, class politics, and ideology or discourse. Scott's great contribution to historical analysis has been to focus the attention of historians on the linguistic methods by which meaning is constructed and power revealed as well as the importance of gender as a universal yet contingent category of historical analysis. For an analysis of the changing meanings of emotions, see Introduction, *An Emotional History of the United States*, ed. Peter N. Stearns and Jan Lewis (New York: New York University Press, 1998).

34. Eleni Varikas discusses "the tension between the attempt at rational explanation and the role of the fortuitous," in "Gender, Experience, and Subjectivity: The Tilly-Scott Disagreement," *New Left Review*, 211 (May 1995) 100.

35. On the perennial crises over the politics and meanings of political history and a defense of the vital importance of revision as central to historical understanding, see Mark Leff, "Revisioning U.S. Political History," *American Historical Review* 100 (June 1995): 829–53.

36. Steven M. Gillon, "The Future of Political History," *Journal of Policy History* 9 (1997): 240–55. Political historians have been eager to appreciate and integrate into their thinking the work of social historians such as Paula Baker, Lizabeth Cohen, and Sara Evans. Sessions on the future of political history at Organization of American Historians conventions in 1995 and 1999 have continued the debate.

37. Gillon defines the new social history rather narrowly as an emphasis on private spheres and intimate personal behavior, Ibid., 242, 251.

38. In studies greatly admired by political historians, Paula Baker, Lizabeth Cohen and Sara Evans analyze social, cultural, gender, and class issues as underpinnings to political activity in Cohen's *Making a New Deal* and Evans' *Personal Politics: The Roots of Women's Liberation in the Civil Rights Movement and the New Left* (New York: Knopf, 1979).

39. For example, see Peter H. Argersinger, *Structure, Process, and Party: Essays in American Political History* (New York: M. E. Sharpe, 1992). Leff defines political history simply as "the development and impact of governmental institutions, along with the proximate influences on their actions, "Revisioning," 829. He cites the work of social historians on the development of the twentieth-century welfare state and on the centrality of race to politics, the implication being that social historians, not political historians, are actually rewriting political history, 850–53.

40. For a vigorous defense of the new political history from reductionist charges concerning the primacy of the ethnocultural interpretation of nineteenth-century political parties and voting, see Ronald Formisano, "Invention of the Ethnocultural Interpretation," *American Historical Review* 99 (1994): 453–77. Interestingly, Formisano insists that the most class-conscious political groups were elites.

41. "Urban Working-Class Political Behavior and Theories of American Electoral Politics, 1870–1940," *Journal of American History* 74 (Mar. 1988): 1257–86, esp. 1270, 1283, 1285. He questions "the widespread existence of a class-conscious artisanal republicanism in nineteenth-century America" and calls for studies of labor politics that reach beyond the community or case study and link up with the long term national political shifts of majorities that interest political historians, 1265, 1267. He concludes that "the structure of [presumably class] power in American society limited the translation of [working-] class sentiment into political consciousness," 1286, and regards the experience of immigrant workers as essentially one of survival, defense, and adaptation, 1274.

42. Varikas terms power as the "relations of forces" in "Gender, Experience and Subjectivity," 99.

43. For that initial call, see Louis Galambos, "What Make Us Think We Can Put Business Back Into American History?" *Business and Economic History* 20 (1991): 1–11. Galambos challenged business historians to contemplate the uses of deconstructionism, neo-Marxism, gender analysis, and nineteenth- and twentieth-century progressive critics of American business to probe the meaning of its central ideas and myths, rationales and emotions in order to formulate a new synthesis. On the early work of Galambos, see below chapter 10.

44. See Kenneth Lipartito's analysis of how business culture reveals the uses of customer relations as symbolic displays, conceptions of power, and social practices in "Culture and the Practice of Business History," *Business and Economic History* 24 (Winter 1995): 1–42. Lipartito writes, "Culture I define as a system of values, ideas and beliefs which constitute a central apparatus for grasping reality," 1–2.

45. Ibid., 33.

46. Many biographers of American business leaders do not confine themselves to the firm. See Ron Chernow, *Titan: The Life of John D. Rockefeller, Sr.,* (New York: Random House, 1998) and his biographies of J. P. Morgan and the Warburg

family. In addition, American fiction has many examples of businessmen set squarely in their social, cultural, political, and economic contexts.

47. See Alice Kessler-Harris, "Ideologies and Innovation: Gender Dimensions of Business History," *Business and Economic History* 20 (1991): 45–51; Angel Kwolek-Folland, "Gendered Concerns: Thoughts on the History of Business and the History of Women," *Business and Economic History,* 23 (1994): 129–40; Wendy Gamber, "A Gendered Enterprise: Placing Nineteenth-Century Business Women in History," *Business History Review* 72 (1998): 188–216; and Kathy Peiss, *Hope in A Jar: The Making of America's Beauty Culture* (New York: Metropolitan Press, 1998).

48. For one example, see Louise M. Newman, "Critical Theory and the History of Women: What's At Stake in Deconstructing Women's History," *Journal of Women's History* 2 (Winter, 1991): 58–68.

49. For work on the family wage, see Hal Benenson, "The 'Family Wage' and Working Women's Consciousness in Britain, 1880–1914," *Politics and Society* 19 (1991): 71–118, and Wally Seccombe, "Patriarchy Stabilized: The Construction of the Male Breadwinner Norm in Nineteenth-Century Britain," *Social History* 11 (1986): 53–76. Anna Clark in *The Struggle for the Breeches: Gender and the Making of the British Working-Class* (Berkeley: University of California Press, 1995), successfully transcends class and culture to investigate gender conflicts over access to power. Clark, for example, locates the vanguard of English class formation, not in the urban culture of violent gender antagonism among Edward Thompson's London radicals and artisans but in early nineteenth-century Lancashire textile communities that integrated men and women workers into a culture of resistance.

50. Anthony Rotundo, *Manhood in America: A Cultural History* (New York: Free Press, 1997), 20, 23, 33, 37, 44. Other cultural standards observed by Kimmel in 1995 include the responsibility of the male breadwinner as head of family, the fear of property loss, the rage of skilled white workers against all others, and the manipulation of masculinity in politics. For an appreciative review of Kimmel's work with similar reservations as mine, see Robert Griswold, *Journal of Social History* 30 (Summer 1997): 999–1002. The literature on American artisans has paid little attention to gender analysis. For a recent example, see Howard B. Rock, Paul A. Gilje, and Robert Asher, eds., *American Artisans: Crafting Social Identity, 1750–1850* (Baltimore: Johns Hopkins University Press, 1995), except the essay by Teresa Murphy. On nineteenth-century middle-class manhood, Anthony Rotundo's *American Manhood: Transformation in Masculinity to the Modern Era* (New York: Basic Books, 1993) is based on personal papers of white middle-class men in the Northeast. Few papers have survived for the mill owners in Fall River, while the scarcity of such sources on the private lives of working-class men suggests that the public record of tensions, conflicts, strike behavior and rhetoric, and political debates is crucial to understanding the connotations of working-class manhood.

51. See below, chapter 10.

52. From her comment on the session "Citizenship, Manhood, and the Performance of Public Service in Nineteenth-Century America," Organization of American Historians conference, April 1997.

53. The introduction to *Manful Assertions: Masculinities in Britain since 1800* (New York: Routledge, 1991) sets a high standard of historicizing manhood, not always achieved in the other essays. Tosh's analysis of the psychic dimension of masculinity, formed within the family as the child matures, is a class-bound ap-

proach, dependent, like Rotundo's, on diaries and correspondence, rare for working-class people. On the other hand, Tosh insists on the need to examine "the structures of power that often remain hidden" in the social and psychic dimensions of masculinity in "What Should Historians do with Masculinity? Reflections on Nineteenth-Century Britain," *History Workshop Journal* 38 (1994) 198.

54. Tosh, "What Should Historians do with Masculinity," 192.

55. "The Gendering of the British Working Class," *Gender & History* 9 (1997): 333–63. Those studies include the recent work of Anna Clark, Sonya Rose, and Deborah Valenze.

56. See Charlotte Erickson, *Invisible Immigrants: The Adaptation of English and Scottish Immigrants in 19th-century America* (Ithaca: Cornell University Press, 1990 reprint of a 1979 edition).

57. "Americanization from the Bottom Up: Immigration and the Remaking of the Working Class in the United States, 1880–1930," *Journal of American History* 79 (Dec. 1992): 996–1020.

58. "Putting 'Capitalism' in Its Place: A Review of Recent Literature," *William and Mary Quarterly* 52 (1995): 315–26 especially 322.

59. For an overview of the development of social history, see Peter N. Stearns, ed., *Expanding the Past: A Reader in Social History* (New York: New York University Press, 1988) and *That Noble Dream: The "Objectivity Question" and the American Historical Profession* (Cambridge: Cambridge University Press, 1988), 178–80, 440–5. Also see the call for an analysis of the spatial in "the next social history" by graduate students in the 1998, "Conference Report on 'The Next Social History': Practicing Space, Time, and Place," in *Perspectives,* (November 1998): 47–9.

60. For example, see the response by Geoff Eley and Keith Nield to Patrick Joyce's dismissal of social history, "Starting Over: The Present, the Post-Modern and the Moment of Social History," *Social History* 20 (October 1995): 355–64. For Joyce's essay, "The End of Social History?", *Social History* 20 (January 1995). Social history has had many critics, conservative and poststructuralist, including Eugene Genovese and Elizabeth Fox-Genovese, Laurence Stone, Gertrude Himmelfarb, and Joan Scott, who produce lengthy, contentious, and polarizing debates over its merits and politics. See Genovese and Fox-Genovese, "The Political Crisis of Social History," *Journal of Social History* 10 (1976): 205–20; Stone, "The Revival of Narrative: Reflections on a New Old History," *Past and Present,* n. 85 (1979): 3–24; Himmelfarb, "Denigrating the Rule of Reason: The New History Goes Bottom-Up," *Harper's Magazine* (April 1984): 84–91; and Scott, "The Evidence of Experience," *Critical Inquiry* 17 (Summer 1991) 773–97. My major concern about postmodernist theory is a nagging fear that the lure of linguistic analysis will distract researchers' attention from the laborious search for new evidence, including empirical data and texts, to throw new light on historic meaning.

61. Marc Steinberg, "Culturally Speaking: Finding a Commons between Post-Structuralism and the Thompsonian Perspective," *Social History* 21 (May 1996): 193–222, especially, 204–6.

62. In "Gender, Experience and Subjectivity," Varikas refers to "the relationship of forces in which . . . discourses are established and . . . the extra-discursive conditions which might possibly transform them." For example, Varikas cites political experiences among Saint-Simonian feminists in the 1830s, which she argues might provide a different understanding of the discourse of working-class

French women in 1848 than that provided by Scott in "Work Identities for Men and Women: The Politics of Work and Family in the Parisian Garment Trades in 1848," in *Gender and The Politics of History* (New York: Columbia University Press, 1988). For an examination in this study of a discursive text in 1875 within its political dynamic and the analysis of the discourse of *la survivance*, see chapter 6.

63. One example is the destruction of local union records after the violent Cripple Creek strike in 1904, see Elizabeth Jameson, *All That Glitters: Class, Conflict, and Community in Cripple Creek* (Urbana: University of Illinois Press, 1998), 13.

64. One of the pitfalls in ignoring chronology and historical context is conflation, overgeneralization, and questionable conclusions. For example, see my critiques of the work of Sonya Rose and Isaac Cohen below chapters 6 and 7.

65. *Home To Work: Motherhood and the Politics of Industrial Homework in the United States* (Cambridge: Cambridge University Press, 1994), especially chapter 1. Also see a similarly inclusive political analysis in Jo Ann E. Argersinger, *Making the Amalgamated: Gender, Ethnicity, and Class in the Baltimore Clothing Industry, 1899–1939* (Baltimore: Johns Hopkins University Press, 1999).

66. For a different argument stressing the continuities among craft unionism, the Knights of Labor, and labor radicalism, see David Brundage, *The Making of Western Labor Radicalism: Denver's Organized Workers, 1878–1905* (Urbana: University of Illinois Press, 1995).

67. See Herbert J. Lahne, *The Cotton Textile Worker* (New York: Farr & Rinehart, 1944) and Ardis Cameron, *Radicals of the Worst Sort: Laboring Women in Lawrence, Massachusetts, 1860–1912* (Urbana: University of Illinois Press, 1993) and Melvyn Dubofsky, *We Shall Be All: A History of the Industrial Workers of the World* (Chicago: Quadrangle Books, 1969).

1. THE FALL RIVER PATRIMONY

1. *Fall River Daily Herald*, [*FRHerald*], Mar. 23, 1901. The Holder Borden clipping is in the Fall River Historical Society Scrapbook. Chace died on November 1, 1900. His reminiscences of Holder Borden were based on the September 16, 1837 obituaries in the *Monitor* and the *Providence Journal* [*Providence*] and various conversations with those who had known Borden personally.

2. *FRHerald*, Mar. 23, 1901. In 1878 Chace was charged with embezzlements that bankrupted the Union mills. See below, chapter 5.

3. Most prominent was Henry H. Earl, *A Centennial History of Fall River, Massachusetts* (New York, 1877). Earl was the son of Benjamin Earl, who had known Holder Borden in the 1830s. See also D. Hamilton Hurd, *The History of Bristol County* (1883) 408–10; J. D. Van Slyck, *New England Manufacturers and Manufactories* (Boston, 1879) v. 1, 114–15; and Alice Brayton, *Life on the Stream* (Newport, RI: Wilkinson Press, 1962), "The Legend of Holder Borden," 9–29. Twentieth-century writers on Fall River have forgotten Holder Borden, crediting his uncles with the early development of the local industry; for example, see Stone, *History of Massachusetts Industries*, 160–88.

4. Robert E. Dalzell Jr., *Enterprising Elite: The Boston Associates and the World They Made* (New York: W. W. Norton, 1993). I rely heavily on Robert K. Lamb, "The Development of Entrepreneurship in Fall River: 1813–1859," (Ph.D. dissertation,

Harvard University, 1935). One of Lamb's advisors at Harvard was Fall River's Jonathan Thayer Lincoln. Rejecting economist Joseph Schumpeter's entrepreneurial theories on the market as a mechanism that produces equilibrium, Lamb defines the market as an instrument for rationalizing men's desires for creating economic "flexibility." This concept allows room for human agency and can account for the pursuit of controlling power and wealth by ambitious men in Fall River. Lamb criticizes a strictly economic analysis of industrial development and stresses the importance of "the social element," defined as family structure, "nonhomogeneity," and "social atomization," see chapter 15 and the conclusion. Robert Keen Lamb was born in 1905 of a Washington D.C. family and attended Phillips Exeter Academy and Harvard University. He received his Ph.D. at Harvard in Economics in 1935 and became an assistant professor at Williams College. From 1938 to 1940 he worked as a special investigator for Senator Robert LaFollette's labor committee on violations of civil liberties. Between 1940 to 1947, he served in Washington as staff director for House and Senate committees investigating migration and the problems of small business and as legislative representative for the United Steel Workers of America. When he died in 1952, he was teaching at the Massachusetts Institute of Technology (*Harvard Class of 1928: Twenty-fifth Anniversary Report* [Cambridge, 1953], courtesy of Harvard University Archives). He never was able to finish his study of Fall River in the post–Civil War period, his only publication being "The Entrepreneur and the Community," in *Men in Business: Essays on the Historical Role of the Entrepreneur,* ed. William Miller (Cambridge: Harvard University Press, 1952), 91–119.

5. Dalzell in *Enterprising Elite* analyzes the motives of Francis Cabot Lowell, speculating persuasively about Lowell's concern for a safe and lucrative alternative for his family's commercial investments and his search for a secure social position among the established Boston elite. Many of the Boston Associates shared his concerns. Having the luxury of paying consistently high dividends, the Boston Associates had no trouble selling shares for ventures in transportation, banking, and insurance companies. But an essential conservatism and the search for security, both socially and financially, meant a halt to technical innovation by 1840. Betty Farrell in *Elite Families: Class and Power in Nineteenth-Century Boston* (Albany: State University of New York Press, 1993) analyzes the social world of the female members of the Boston Associate families and discusses their later investments in telephones, electrical equipment, and overseas agriculture. For a critique of the "postulate" Boston Associates, see François Weil, "Capitalism and Industrialization in New England, 1815–1845," *Journal of American History* (March 1998): 1334–55.

6. Charles Sellers, *The Market Revolution: Jacksonian America, 1815–1846* (New York: Oxford University Press, 1991). See also "Symposium on Charles Sellers, *The Market Revolution: Jacksonian America, 1815–1846*" in the *Journal of the Early Republic* 12 (Winter 1992): 445–76 with essays by Richard Ellis, Mary Blewett, Joel Silbey, Major Wilson, Harry Watson, Amy Bridges, and a response by Sellers. Also see Melvyn Stokes and Stephen Conway, eds., *The Market Revolution in America: Social, Political, and Religious Expressions, 1800–1880* (Charlottesville: University Press of Virginia, 1995).

7. See Sellers' response, *Journal of the Early Republic,* 473–76.

8. Mary Blewett, "Symposium on Sellers," *Journal of the Early Republic,* 451. My critique was shared by Daniel Walker Howe, "The Market Revolution and the

Shaping of Identity in Whig-Jacksonian America," in Stokes and Conway, *The Market Revolution in America,* 259–81.

9. Bordens had been in Rhode Island since 1635, *FRHerald,* Mar. 23, 1901. Thomas Russell Smith, *The Cotton Textile Industry of Fall River, Massachusetts: A Study of Industrial Localization,* (New York: King's Crown Press, 1944) provides a motive for the break away from Freetown in 1803: the distance to the town hall was too far for people with few horses (5). In *Centennial History,* (238) Earl tells the story of a "prominent citizen" who visited Troy, New York, and persuaded his fellow-townsmen to adopt the Homeric name.

10. Brayton, *Stream,* v. 1, 9–10. Neither of the daughters lived to adulthood. Earl described Durfee as an "active, stirring man," *Centennial History,* 27.

11. Brayton, *Stream,* v. 1, 13–14.

12. Dexter Wheeler of Rehoboth, Massachusetts, helped run a cotton yarn factory in "Swansey" (neighboring Swansea), but joined his cousin David Anthony to build the Fall River Manufactory in Troy. Both were blacksmiths, Lamb, chap. 4, 1–5.

13. Ibid., 5–8. For a comparative discussion of the differences between pre–Civil War textile managers' decisions on technology and industrial organization in New England, Philadelphia and Britain, see Isaac Cohen, *American Management and British Labor: A Comparative Study of the Cotton Spinning Industry* (Westport, Conn.: Greenwood Press, 1990), 28–54.

14. The length of the drop of the stream is variously described as 132, 130, and 127 feet.

15. Lamb, chap. 5, 1–3.

16. James B. Hedges, *The Browns of Providence Plantations: The Nineteenth Century* (Providence: Brown University Press, 1968), 165–66. For the transfer of textile technology that made much of this development possible, see David J. Jeremy, *Transatlantic Industrial Revolution: The Diffusion of Textile Technologies Between Britain and America, 1790–1830* (Cambridge: Massachusetts Institute of Technology Press, 1981).

17. Smith, *Fall River Industry,* 22–23. For an overview of the final triumph of industrial development despite all of the individual losses and failures, see Caroline F. Ware, *Early New England Cotton Manufacturing* (New York: Russell and Russell, 1966), especially chapter 6 on "Capital." Ware emphasizes changes that capitalist development brought to relations among farmers, merchants, workers, and textile developers. She agrees with Lamb and Sellers that these changes created class divisions that threatened democratic institutions. Her classic 1931 study, reprinted in 1966, remains the place to begin.

18. Earl, *Centennial History,* 25. Her willingness to sell was a major coup for the New Bedford investors.

19. Chace's son, Harvey, in charge of marketing at the Troy, later became the owner of the Albion Mills in Valley Falls, Rhode Island, Ibid., 17–18.

20. Ibid., 23. Rodman kept a detailed diary, making a few references to trips to Fall River to attend the quarterly meetings of the Pocasset Company, Zephaniah W. Pease, ed., *The Diary of Samuel Rodman: A New Bedford Chronicle of Thirty-Seven Years, 1821–1859* (New Bedford, 1927). Many sources on New Bedford overlook the early investments in Fall River and cite the organization of the Wamsutta Mills in 1846 as the first New Bedford experience in textiles; see Ware, *New England*

Cotton Manufacture, 107–8. See also Henry Beetle Hough, *Wamsutta of New Bedford, 1846–1946* (New Bedford, Mass.: Wamsutta Mills, 1946).

21. Almy and Brown of Providence marketed the products of Slater's mill in Philadelphia. As Alfred Chandler points out, the Blackstone River's limited water power held back the introduction of the power loom in Rhode Island mills, *The Visible Hand: The Managerial Revolution in American Business* (Cambridge: Harvard University Press, 1977), 525, note 32. On Slater, see Barbara Tucker, *Samuel Slater and the Origins of the American Textile Industry, 1790–1860* (Ithaca: Cornell University Press, 1984) and Sellers, *Market Revolution*, 27–28. Tucker's analysis emphasizes the fundamental harmony of Slater's paternalistic operations in Pawtucket, arguing that the patriarchal and hierarchical values of the New England family and village coincided with the discipline of the spinning factory. In contrast, Jonathan Prude's *The Coming of Industrial Order: Town and Factory Life in Rural Massachusetts, 1810–1860* (Cambridge: Cambridge University Press, 1983) reveals Slater's high-handed, much-contested role in economic development and local politics. In addition, the high turnover rate among female textile operatives indicated a rejection of the Rhode Island system. Prude examines local conflicts and the desire for domination—the darker, imperious side of textile capitalism and patriarchy—as well as the negative response from village residents and workers to the imperatives of the small company mill town. Like Prude, Gary Kulik's work on the conflicts between artisans, farmers, and textile workers who fought the Wilkinson and Slater developments in Pawtucket argues that class politics were central to early Rhode Island industrialization. See "Pawtucket Village and the Strike of 1824: The Origins of Class Conflict in Rhode Island," *Radical History Review* 17 (1978): 5–37 and "Dams, Fish, and Farmers: The Defense of Public Rights in Eighteenth Century Rhode Island," in *The New England Working Class and the New Labor History*, ed. Herbert G. Gutman and Donald H. Bell (Urbana: University of Illinois Press, 1987), 187–213.

22. In competition with Newport, Providence began to develop connections in the 1790s with eastern Connecticut and southeastern Massachusetts, establishing banks and insurance companies, building turnpikes, and deepening its own harbor, John S. Gilkeson Jr., *Middle-Class Providence, 1820–1940* (Princeton: Princeton University Press, 1986), 18. Weil argues in "Capitalism and Industrialization" that the concept of "local dynamism" explains the development of industry in New England, not the early dominance of Boston's capital assets or the political influence wielded by Boston investors (named the Boston Associates by historian Vera Shlakman in 1935). Weil studies textile development in Springfield, Massachusetts, but by the 1840s, other Boston capitalists [not the Boston Associates] controlled Springfield's mills, attracted to the profits and potential begun by local investors. Boston capital therefore proved crucial to the development of railroads to western Massachusetts, while the "Lowell model," criticized by Weil as an exception to regional development, was adopted in Springfield for integrated production and water power. "Local dynamism" served a limited purpose and then quickly faded, 1348–54. Weil's focus on Springfield misses better examples of sustained "local dynamism" in Fall River, New Bedford, and Rhode Island, where pre–Civil War developments remained out of the grasp of Boston investors. Boston did not become, as Weil argues, "the undisputed regional center of industrial investment" (1354), even before the Civil War.

23. Smith speculates on the reason the Boston Associates did not invest in Fall River and points to the local monopoly of water power as the probable explanation for their lack of interest, *Fall River Industry,* 38. For a general history of this period of growth in American textile production, see Jeremy, *Transatlantic,* chapters 4–7.

24. Chandler, *Visible Hand,* 59. On Chandler see, chapter 5, below.

25. Lamb points out that initially the New Bedford-backed Pocassett interests might have invested in the Iron Works, but they withdrew because of "friction," 14. Smith discounts the importance of outside capital, arguing that nearly two-thirds came from local sources in the Taunton River Valley, 30–31. Dalzell acknowledges that at this time and as a matter of policy no commercial bank would even consider loaning money to manufacturing concerns, (53), but how much money was loaned privately to the shareholders of the Iron Works by their connections in Providence is not known. Lamb found the financial records of the Iron Works so complicated as to "defy analysis," and the borrowing of funds from undistributed profits among the shareholders endemic, 6–7.

26. As Dalzell notes, these investors were already rich men, 26, 48.

27. The Annawan was sometimes spelled *Anawan.*

28. On the Wilkensons' embarrassment, see Naomi R. Lamoreaux, *Insider Lending: Banks, Personal Connections, and Economic Development in Industrial New England* (Cambridge: Cambridge University Press, 1994), 14–15.

29. Jefferson Borden obituary, *News,* Aug. 23, 1887. Philip D. Borden, Jefferson's nephew, replaced Major Durfee as agent in 1843.

30. On Providence, see Hedges, *The Browns,* 249–50. On banking in general, see Lamoreaux, *Insider Lending,* chapters 1 and 2; on Providence banks' ties to the Goddard interests in Lonsdale and to the Sprague family of Cranston, see 24, 87. Lamoreaux demonstrates that kinship and friendship on boards of directors diverted bank assets to those with close personal connections and mutual economic interests.

31. John K. Walton, *Lancashire: A Social History, 1558–1939* (Manchester, U.K.: University of Manchester Press, 1987), 130–31.

32. Lamb, chap. 6, 17.

33. Lamoreaux, *Insider Lending,* 15–16.

34. Lamb, chap. 6, "The Town Matures, 1820–1830," 1–45. On the marketing of nails by the Iron Works and early spinning operations, see Brayton, *Stream,* v. 1, 40–51.

35. Ware argues that the cotton mills in Troy were sustained by the early development of calico-printing, *New England Cotton Manufacture,* 156.

36. Earl, *Centennial History,* 29–30.

37. For the history of this diffusion of calico-printing machine technology, see Jeremy, *Transatlantic,* chapter 6.

38. See Jeremy, *Transatlantic,* 110–16. The Fall River Print Works was the smallest. Jeremy examined the records of the Taunton works, 1823–1844, at the Baker Library business archives at Harvard University. The Taunton Manufacturing Company did not survive the Civil War years. Taunton's manufacturing base shifted to the Reed and Barton Silver Company and the Mason Machine Works, and the company was not a key competitor in the post–Civil War print cloth market; see Hurd, *History of Bristol County,* 823–29.

39. Jefferson's job at the company store then went to Matthew C. Durfee, a cousin of Major Bradford Durfee.

40. Earl, *Centennial History,* 35.

41. In 1785 Valentine married Elizabeth Borden of Freetown. She was a sister of Thomas and the aunt of Jefferson, Phoebe, and Richard, *FRHerald,* Mar. 23, 1901.

42. This linking of "capitalist families" through marriage or "dynastic industrialism," was also a practice in early Philadelphia proprietary manufacture, see Philip Scranton, *Proprietary Capitalism: The Textile Manufacture at Philadelphia, 1800–1885* (Philadelphia: Temple University Press, 1983), 61.

43. See Ware, *New England Cotton Manufacture,* chapter 7, "Marketing," which is based on the early business records of Almy and Brown, the Fall River Manufactory, the Pocasset Company, and the Troy Company.

44. Lamb, chap. 7, 3.

45. Brayton, *Stream,* v. 1, 19.

46. Lamb, chap. 11, 6.

47. Using Rhode Island bankruptcy files, B. Michael Zuckerman in "The Political Economy of Industrial Rhode Island, 1790–1860" (Ph.D. dissertation, Brown University, 1981), estimated that the closing of hundreds of mills between 1815 and 1860 created "a world of fundamental insecurity," 38–39.

48. Earl, *Centennial History,* 25, 32.

49. Lamb, chap. 7, 5. Hedges emphasized the cautious and conservative nature of Brown and Ives operations, *The Browns,* 257.

50. Lamb, chap. 11, 9–10.

51. Ibid., chap. 7, 2–3.

52. He may indeed have died of consumption, listed as the cause of death, but this diagnosis was often applied to any fatal condition in the nineteenth century. My guess is that Borden's incessant smoking and physical and emotional stress led to tuberculosis or cancer.

53. *FRHerald,* Mar. 23, 1901.

54. Lamb never located Holder Borden's will in the Bristol County Probate Court because Borden never made one. Lamb regards the dispersal of his Iron Works shares into the hands of Major Durfee and his three sons-in-law as a mistake, placing family interest above keeping the Iron Works shares centralized; see chapter 7, 12 and chapter 11, 1–2. Brayton, in *Stream,* 67–68, tells a dubious story about Holder Borden's fortune being kept intact and reinvested in Fall River firms by Major Durfee's second wife, Mary Brayton Durfee. Lamb observes that the "private banking practices of the Iron Works families and their companies defy analysis," but he found many notes of debt, revealing the continued policy of lending money to each other and to their companies among the Borden-Durfee Group; see chapter 11, 6–7 and below, chapter 5.

55. Lamb, chap. 7, 11.

56. *FRHerald,* Mar. 23, 1901. Hurd dubbed him "that young master business-spirit of the times," 371; Van Slyke, "a man of remarkable boldness and energy," 114; Earl, a rare combination of "bold energy, untiring industry, and unbending integrity," as quoted in *Our County and Its People: Descriptive and Biographical Record of Bristol County, Massachusetts* (Boston, 1899), 462–63.

57. From Lamb's title for chapter 12, "The Iron Works Waxes Fat."

58. Earl, *Centennial History,* 37.

59. In *The Browns,* Hedges' only reference to the Brown and Ives connection with "Holden" Borden at the Massasoit was brief, 184. Although Massachusetts dominated the early development of cotton textile manufacturing, Rhode Island was second. Its early industries were concentrated in Providence and towns just north along the Blackstone River, Peter J. Coleman, *The Transformation of Rhode Island, 1790–1860* (Providence: Brown University Press, 1969), 92, 121–23. However, Coleman did not pursue Providence investments outside the political borders of Rhode Island, thus obscuring the industrial and financial significance of *regional* development. The Blackstone River flows through both Rhode Island and Massachusetts, and Providence investments also contributed to the development of eastern Connecticut.

60. *Diary of Samuel Rodman,* 45.

61. Ware, *New England Cotton Manufacture,* 107. Ware claims that the New Bedford mill owners were men "wholly without experience in cotton manufacture." Her examination of company records indicated that their model was the Hope Mill in Rhode Island, 107. Thomas Bennett Jr. had been employed in a small Southern mill owned by one of the Wamsutta's backers, Dwight Perry of Fairhaven, Massachusetts, Stone, *History of Massachusetts Industries,* v. 1, 192. Also see, Hough, *Wamsutta.*

62. Dalzell, *Enterprising Elite,* 47.

63. James Montgomery, *The Cotton Manufacture of the United States* (Glasgow, 1840) 196–97, 157.

64. Hurd, *Bristol County,* 374–77.

65. Ibid., 374–77.

66. Philip D. Borden, "Fall River's First Railroad," unpublished paper read at the Fall River Historical Society, October 1926.

67. Andrew Robeson was president of the company, Ibid., 9, 15–16. When the Old Colony projected railroad lines into southeastern Massachusetts and Rhode Island, it required both state legislatures to grant corporate charters.

68. Lamb, chap. 12, 15. The Bordens became active politically as the town grew, see Chapters 2 and 4.

69. Hurd, *Bristol County,* 412.

70. Earl, *Centennial History,* 56; obituary, *News,* April 8, 1876.

71. Hurd, *Bristol County,* 376; obituary, *News,* Feb. 25, 1874.

72. Arthur Sherman Phillips, *The Phillips History of Fall River* in three Fascicles [volumes] (Dover Press: Fall River, 1946), v. 2, 14–15.

73. Colonel Richard and Abby Durfee Board's son Thomas J. served in the Fall River Light Infantry, but the other sons, Richard Baxter and M. C. D., do not appear to have been in the war, obituary, *FRHerald,* Nov. 22, 1902.

74. *News,* Feb. 25, 1874.

75. Obituary, *New York Times,* [*NYTimes*] Sept. 5, 1879.

76. Earl, *Centennial History,* 43.

77. *News,* obituary, Aug. 23, 1887.

78. These restrictions were lifted in 1843 by Parliament. Walton, *Lancashire,* 207.

79. Lamb could find no record of this in the Annawan or Iron Works papers and based his account on William Bagnall, *Textile Industries of the United States, 1639–1810,* v. 1 (1815) and Bagnall's notes for v. 2; see Lamb, chapter 12, 6.

80. Lamb, chap. 6, 11–13.

81. Stone, *Massachusetts Industries,* 168.

82. Earl, *Centennial History,* 39–40.

83. Lamb, chap. 12, 34. On marketing pre–Civil War textiles, see Ware, *New England Cotton Manufacture,* chapter 7; Glenn Porter and Harold C. Livesay, *Merchants and Manufacturers: Studies in the Changing Structure of Marketing* (Chicago: Ivan R. Dee, 1989), 22–28; and Chandler, *Visible Hand,* 21–27.

84. Earl, *Centennial History,* 215–17.

85. *News,* Mar. 6, 1862.

86. *Phillips History* cited a population of 593, nine square miles, but agreed with Henry Earl on the two million dollars of taxable property, v. 3, 17–20.

87. *NYTimes,* Feb. 2, 1861. The decision was not printed in the *United States Supreme Court Reporter.*

88. Earl, *Centennial History,* 217–18.

89. Ibid., 43.

90. Smith's study of the locational factors in the success of Fall River's industry cited steam power as one of the most significant, *Fall River Industry,* 40–47.

91. Smith cites 56 percent of all New England mills as water-powered in 1880 as compared with 44 percent steam-powered, Ibid., 40–41.

92. Lamb, chap. 12, 28.

93. Norman Ware, in *The Industrial Worker, 1840–1860* (Chicago: Quadrangle Press, 1964), 76–77, cites this comment from Massachusetts Senate Document no. 21 (1868) for its "callous indifference" but found Lowell's paternalism little better. In contrast, Paul F. McGouldrick in *New England Textiles in the Nineteenth Century: Profits and Investments* (Cambridge: Harvard University Press, 1968) regards the same statement as "a picturesque example" of the rise of "modernity" among treasurers and agents, indicating a "capacity for abstraction, rationality in relating means to ends, impersonality, unending search for production efficiency, and the separation of business and other goals in the course of operations" (206).

94. Lamb, chap. 12, 1–2.

95. See Sellers, *The Market Revolution* and Dalzell, chapter 1 for speculations about the different motives of the Boston Associates.

96. Lamb, chap. 12, 35–37.

97. Ibid., 48.

98. Although Lamoreaux does not explore the personalities involved in the kinship groups in New England, she argues (*Insider Lending,* 130) that Fall River banks in general, and the First National Bank in particular, followed insider lending practices at least until 1895, when most other New England banks had professionalized their management and required collateral rather than endorsed IOUs for loans. The financial power of kinship enormously expanded textile capacity.

99. Later in 1879, the Brayton interests came to control numerous mills and formed an alliance with M. C. D. Borden, Lamb, "The Entrepreneur and the Community" 105.

100. *History of the Ladies' Benevolent Society of the First Congregational Church* (Fall River, 1904), 5–14.

101. Lamb, chap. 11, 23. Lamb describes these relationships as "a self-contained economy," chap. 12, 2. Although Dalzell argues that both family relationships and business partnerships were represented in the Boston Associates

(29), he does not discuss marriages, families, or even the role of women in their philanthropic activities. Mary Ryan in *Cradle of the Middle Class: The Family in Oneida County, New York, 1790–1860* (New York, 1981), and Leonora Davidoff and Catherine Hall, in *Family Fortunes: Men and Women of the English Middle Class, 1780–1850* (University of Chicago Press, 1987) argue that the role of women in the making of middle-class families and their fortunes was active and central. Even the limited evidence on Fall River women suggests that they played a similar role.

102. Obituary, *Fall River Globe* (*FRGlobe*), Mar. 23, 1891.

103. Brayton, *Stream*, v. 1, 67–70.

104. Apparently Mary B. Durfee did not entirely cut off Borden's nieces and nephews, but whatever share they received is not known.

105. Stone, *Massachusetts Industries*, v.1, 171. William W. Crapo, "Memoir of John S. Brayton," *Proceedings of the Massachusetts Historical Society* (1906), 5.

106. Brayton, *Stream*, v. 1, 70.

107. A. Forbes and J. W. Greene, *The Rich Men of Massachusetts* (Boston, 1851), 184–86.

108. Obituary of Mary B. Young, *FRGlobe*, Mar. 23, 1891. Because of his youth and ill-health, the Yale administration sought to secure Durfee's generosity by obtaining his mother's endorsement of his notes; see correspondence between Thomas Thacher of Yale and Mrs. Young, John S. Brayton Papers, Fall River Historical Society.

109. B. M. C. Durfee to Mr. Brayton, July 26, 1865, John S. Brayton Papers.

110. Obituary, *ProvidenceJ*, Sept. 14, 1872.

111. Obituaries, *News*, Sept. 14, 1872; *FRHerald* and *FRGlobe*, Mar. 23, 1891. Also see *Representative Men and Old Families of Southeastern Massachusetts* vol. 1, 121–22. For the Newport story, *ProvidenceJ*, Aug. 26, 1868. The cause of death was also described in his obituaries and the Fall River vital records as a "passive congestion of the brain" and "an apoplectic fit."

112. Among her charities in the 1870s were the Ladies' Benevolent Society and a Woman's Union to assist self-supporting workingwomen. After S. Angier Chace ended up in state prison in 1878, she bought the lavish Chace mansion and allowed her relation, Mary Durfee Chace, to remain there for life. *Boston Herald*, [*BHerald*], Oct. 18, 1878. When Mary B. Young died in 1891, her estate was estimated at eight to ten million dollars. *FRHerald*, Mar. 23, 1891.

113. Weil makes a similar point about "matrimonial relations" operating in Springfield. "Capitalism and Industrialization," 1345–47.

114. Lamb, chap. 11, 6–7. This legacy of local domination, however, stands in contrast to Slater's moves into the southern Massachusetts towns of Oxford and Dudley where his factories intruded on community life and politics and forced him to form his mill town of Webster. See Prude, *The Coming of Industrial Order.*

2. GENDER POLITICS AND LABOR REFORM
IN THE PROTEST HERITAGES

1. Hannah was the daughter of Richard and Patty Bowen Borden and a niece of Thomas M. Borden.

2. Memoirs of Hannah Borden Cook, *FRGlobe*, Feb. 27, 1889. In 1822 David Anthony married Thomas M. Borden's sister, Mary, thus becoming Hannah's

uncle. On the early development of cotton manufactories, see Philip Thomas Silvia Jr., "The Spindle City: Labor, Politics and Religion in Fall River, Massachusetts, 1870–1905" (Ph.D. dissertation: Fordham University, 1973) part 1, 12–16.

3. Ware, *New England Cotton Manufacture*, 246.

4. *FRGlobe*, Feb. 27, 1889.

5. Norman Ware, *The Industrial Worker 1840–1860* (Chicago: Quadrangle Books, 1964). For an admirable synthesis with a national grasp of research and writing since Ware, see Bruce Laurie, *Artisans Into Workers: Labor in Nineteenth-Century America* (New York: The Noonday Press, 1989). Laurie argues that varieties of radicalism constitute the persistent theme in the nineteenth century. He insists that several worker cultures with distinctive politics and changing ideologies operated simultaneously to create nineteenth-century labor activism. Although Laurie ignores gender analysis in labor history and privileges white male artisans, his analysis, especially on the use of the state by industrial capitalists, captures the general nature of the politics of industrial life in southeastern New England.

6. Ware, *Industrial Worker*, ix–xi.

7. Ware acknowledges a good deal of contradictory evidence to this dichotomy in his last two chapters.

8. Lamb, "Entrepreneurship," chap. 6, 42; Earl, *Centennial History*, 28; Brayton, *Stream*, v. 1, 53–57.

9. *Fall River Monitor*, Feb. 17, 1827, as quoted in Lamb, "Entrepreneurship," chap. 9, 2.

10. Lamb, "Entrepreneurship," chap. 9, 4.

11. Ibid., 10.

12. Bolton, Lancashire, had mills with 100,000 spindles in 1832, compared with an average 6,000 spindles in Lowell mills. Ibid., 6–9.

13. Ibid., 36, 42, 43.

14. Benjamin Wood Pearce, *Recollections of a Long and Busy Life, 1819–1890* (Newport, 1890), 26–41.

15. Ibid., 39–41.

16. Ibid., 64–65.

17. These experiences and others were related in a letter from "P.," *Mechanic*, Dec. 7, 1844.

18. Teresa Anne Murphy, *Ten Hours' Labor: Religion, Reform, and Gender in Early New England* (Ithaca: Cornell University Press, 1992), 38–39.

19. *Monitor*, May 30, 1840.

20. The conversion to machine printing in 1846 took Benjamin Wilbur's job, and displaced 300 other workmen. See "Life of Benjamin Wilbur," typescript, 5 pages, Fall River Historical Society.

21. Obituary, *FRHerald*, *FRGlobe*, Mar. 14, 1881.

22. Pearce, *Recollections*, 42–43.

23. David Kasserman, *Fall River Outrage: Life, Murder, and Justice in Early Industrial New England* (Philadelphia: University of Pennsylvania Press, 1986). Murphy (*Ten Hours' Labor*, 99–100) treats the episode persuasively as an attack on evangelical religion and its disturbing potential to undermine order among the industrial workforce.

24. Kasserman does not address this question.

25. Engraving from the *Brief and Impartial Narrative of the Life of Sarah Maria*

Cornell (New York, 1833) as reproduced in *Catherine Williams, Fall River: An Authentic Narrative,* ed. Patricia Caldwell (New York: Oxford University Press, 1993), 66.

26. Catherine Williams, *Fall River, An Authentic Narrative* (Providence, 1833).

27. Ibid., 195–98. The poetic lines are found in Caldwell's 1993 edition, 141.

28. Williams, *Fall River* (1833), 150.

29. On Pawtucket, see Kulik, "Pawtucket Village and the Strike of 1824," 5–38. Michael Brewster Folsom, former director of the Charles River Museum of Industry in Waltham, Massachusetts, found evidence of an earlier turnout there in 1821; see Mary H. Blewett, "Machines, Workers, and Capitalists: The Interpretation of Textile Industrialization in New England Museums," in *History Museums in the United States: A Critical Assessment,* ed. Warren Leon and Roy Rosenzweig, (Urbana: University of Illinois Press, 1989), 265.

30. On the role of religion in the early labor movement in Fall River, see Jama Lazerow, "Spokesmen for the Working Class: Protestant Clergy and the Labor Movement in Antebellum New England," *Journal of the Early Republic* 13 (Fall 1993): 323–54 and *Religion and the Working Class in Antebellum America* (Washington, D.C.: Smithsonian Press, 1995), 74–79. On the failed Boston Trades' Union, see John R. Commons, *History of Labour in the United States,* v. 1 (1913; reprint, New York: Augustus M. Kelley, 1969), 379–80.

31. The classic essay on Luther is Louis Hartz, "Seth Luther: The Story of a Working-Class Rebel," *New England Quarterly* 13 (1940) 401–18.

32. Kulik, "Dams, Fish, and Farmers," 199–202.

33. Kulik, "Pawtucket Village and the Strike of 1824," 5–37.

34. Hartz, "Seth Luther," 401. Also on Luther's early years as a radical, Carl Gersuny, "Seth Luther—the Road from Chepachet," *Rhode Island History,* 33 (May 1974): 47–49.

35. Hartz, "Seth Luther," 403.

36. Seth Luther, *An Address to the Workingmen of New England* (Boston, 1832). Luther also published, *An Address on the Origin and Progress of Avarice* (Boston, 1834).

37. Title page, *An Address to the Workingmen.*

38. Hartz, "Seth Luther," 415.

39. Luther, *An Address to the Workingmen,* 27–28; Hartz, "Seth Luther," 413. Luther's religious beliefs and use of religious arguments supports the recent contentions of labor historians Teresa Murphy, Jama Lazerow, and William T. Sutton that religion has been neglected as a legitimizing force in labor politics, although none used Luther as a focus for their research.

40. Hartz describes his struggles in Boston and New York City to build unions for artisans in "Seth Luther," 406. For his activities as a Dorrite, see Coleman, *Transformation of Rhode Island,* 235, 239, 259, 271. Also see Edward Pessen, *Most Uncommon Jacksonians: The Radical Leaders of the Early Labor Movement* (Albany: State University of New York Press, 1967), 87–90, 160–61. Pessen notes (88) the disparity between Hartz's views on the importance of Luther's vision in the 1832 address and historian Arthur M. Schlesinger Jr.'s dismissal of Luther's program as routine, harmless, and of little interest.

41. On the family connections and antislavery politics in the region, see Lillie Chace Wyman, *Elizabeth Buffum Chace 1806–1899: Her Life and Its Environment* (Boston, 1914) and Elizabeth Buffem Chace, *Antislavery Reminiscences* (1891).

42. Elizabeth Buffum Chace, "My Antislavery Reminiscences," in *Two Quaker Sisters,* ed. Lucy Buffum Lovell and Malcom Reed Lovell (New York: Leverwright, 1937), 125.

43. On the Chace family as mill owners in post-Civil War Valley Falls, see chapter 7.

44. See Ronald Formisano, *The Transformation of Political Culture: Massachusetts Parties, 1790s–1840s* (New York: Oxford University Press, 1983), chapter 9 on "Antimasons and Masons."

45. Obituary of Nathaniel B. Borden, *Fall River News [News],* April 11, 1865, and *Representative Men of Southeastern Massachusetts,* v. 1, 84–87. Bruce Laurie, "The 'Fair Field' of the 'Middle Ground': Abolitionism, Labor Reform, and the Making of an Antislavery Bloc in Antebellum Massachusetts," in *Labor Histories,* 45–70.

46. *Monitor,* Sept. 11, 1830.

47. For an overview of Massachusetts politics during early industrialization, see Formisano, *Transformation.* Formisano comments briefly on Bristol County party politics, but his statewide focus does not permit him to analyze political dynamics on the local level.

48. "To The Employers of Fall River," Oct. 11, 1841, Fall River Historical Society.

49. In an appendix buried on the last page of his *Address to the Working-Men,* (39), Luther similarly called on the Congress to limit foreign workers and foreign wool to benefit American workers and farmers just as it had provided tariff protection to capitalists. But from someone like Luther, whose vision and sympathies were internationalist, this was a call for equal treatment by the Congress, not the "xenophobia" as David Zonderman called it in "Foreign Pioneers: Immigrants and the Mechanized Factory System in Antebellum New England," in *Work, Recreation, and Culture: Essays in American Labor History,* ed. Martin Blatt and Martha Norkunas, (New York: Garland Press, 1996), 178–79. Zonderman's earlier book, *Aspirations and Anxieties: New England Workers and the Mechanized Factory System, 1815–1850* (Oxford: Oxford University Press, 1992) focuses on the intellectual and emotional reactions of workers to mechanization in centralized, integrated production. This approach excludes many activist artisans, mechanics, and outworkers and their connections with factory workers. Organized by topics such as ideology, politics, and religion, Zonderman's book treats different elements of workers' lives rather than capturing their whole experience, beset with complexities and ambiguities. His work does not explore the behavior and choices made by workers in specific places and situations. Nonetheless, Zonderman's is the first intellectual history of New England factory workers.

50. *Monitor,* Jan. 1, 1842.

51. *Monitor,* Mar. 26, April 2, May 21, Aug. 20, 1842. Copies of the local Democratic paper, *The Argus,* have been lost.

52. *Monitor,* Nov. 12, 1842.

53. Ibid., Jan. 28, 1843. The legislature remained Whig and blocked many of Morton's reform proposals.

54. See Marvin E. Gettleman, *The Dorr Rebellion: A Study in American Radicalism, 1833–1849* (New York: Random House, 1975) and Coleman, *Transformation of Rhode Island.*

55. *Monitor,* April 16, 1842.

56. *Monitor,* May 21, 1842.

57. Letter from "Law and Order," *Monitor,* June 4, 1842.

58. *Mechanic,* Aug. 24, 1844.

59. See Robert J. Cottrol, *The Afro-Yankees: Providence's Black Community in the Antebellum Era* (Westport, Conn.: Greenwood Press, 1982), 68–77.

60. In *An Address on the Right of Free Suffrage* (Providence, 1833), Luther defined slavery as the "taking of a man's property, time, and services, without his consent, to apply [to] public or private uses," 6. He probably meant disenfranchised Rhode Island white men who paid taxes and performed militia and fire duty without being able to cast a ballot, but black men in Rhode Island also paid taxes and could not vote.

61. Hartz, "Seth Luther," 406–407. Hartz describes Luther's position as "equal manhood suffrage." Cottrol argues that Luther relied on vague appeals to democratic ideals, but that was insufficient for Providence blacks. They themselves had to make the case in the Suffrage Association of Rhode Island for "acceptability" and failed. The leaders of Providence's black community were often property-holders, but no blacks worked in textile mills, 106.

62. Luther, *Address on Suffrage,* 21.

63. Coleman, *Transformation of Rhode Island,* 271, 288.

64. "The People's Constitution," Article II, "Of Electors and the Right of Suffrage," in Gettleman, *Dorr Rebellion,* 209–11.

65. Cottrol, *Afro-Yankees,* 75.

66. The property qualification of one hundred thirty-four dollars in real estate remained in effect until 1888. Even the native-born had to pay a poll tax, (Gilkeson, *Middle-Class Providence,* 110). For tensions in the early 1840s between working-class Irish immigrants, native-born Rhode Islanders, and the growing interests of textile capitalism, see Charles Hoffmann and Tess Hoffmann, *Brotherly Love: Murder and the Politics of Prejudice in Nineteenth-Century Rhode Island* (Amherst: University of Massachusetts Press, 1993). Also see Noel Ignatiev, *How the Irish Became White* (New York: Routledge, 1995), 81–84. For racism as a central theme in the self-definition of nineteenth-century American workers, see David R. Roediger, *The Wages of Whiteness: Race and the Making of the American Working Class* (London: Verso Press, 1991). On the use of the term white slavery by native-born, female textile operators and shoeworkers, see Thomas Dublin, *Women at Work: The Transformation of Work and Community in Lowell, Massachusetts, 1826–1860* (New York: Columbia University Press, 1979), 106, and Mary Blewett, *Men, Women, and Work: Class, Gender, and Protest in the New England Shoe Industry, 1780–1910* (Urbana: University of Illinois Press, 1988), 128.

67. Cottrol, *Afro-Yankees,* 77–78. The black community in Providence continued to struggle for integrated education, not obtained until 1866, (90–101).

68. *Mechanic,* April 27, 1844, May 4, 1844. Born in Tiverton, Rhode Island in 1819, Almy left the family farm to be apprenticed at the *Bristol [Rhode Island] Phoenix.* He then worked as a compositor for the *Providence Journal.* See Hurd, *History of Bristol County,* 382–83; Earl *Centennial History,* 382–84; obituary, *News* May 7, 1882.

69. According to Silvia (*Spindle City,* 27–30), by 1841, there were one thousand Irish in Fall River, working largely as manual laborers and kept out of the cotton mills. That year, they formed an organization to send relief funds to their

starving relatives back home. In 1837 their first chapel had been partially destroyed by a mob.

70. *Mechanic,* May 4, 18, 1844. In contrast to the conditions in the Philadelphia region, where religious conflict was the greatest threat to class unity, Fall River's emphasis on freeborn manhood, mechanical skills, and Yankee patriotism meant that gender, race, and nativity appear more fundamentally divisive than religion. See David Montgomery, "The Shuttle and the Cross: Weavers and Artisans in the Kensington Riots of 1844," in Peter N. Stearns and Daniel J. Walkowitz, *Workers in the Industrial Revolution: Recent Studies of Labor in the United States and Europe,* (New Brunswick, NJ: Transaction Books, 1974).

71. See Pearce, *Recollections,* 16–17.

72. *Mechanic,* May 4, 1844.

73. Ibid., April 27, 1844.

74. Almy contented himself with a series of lampoons on the Bordens and Durfees which appeared throughout the summer of 1844. *Mechanic,* June 5, 22, 29; July 20, 27; Aug. 10, 17, 24, 31.

75. See Alan Dawley, *Class and Community: The Industrial Revolution in Lynn* (Cambridge: Harvard University Press, 1976); Paul Faler, *Mechanics and Manufacturers in the Early Industrial Revolution: Lynn, Massachusetts, 1780–1860* (Albany: State University of New York Press, 1981), and Blewett, *Men, Women, and Work.*

76. For an examination of the female labor protest traditions among New England shoeworkers, see Mary H. Blewett, *We Will Rise In Our Might: Workingwomen's Voices from Nineteenth-Century New England* (Ithaca: Cornell University Press, 1991). The quotations are from 39, 42.

77. Dublin, Women at Work, chapters 6, 7.

78. See Helena Wright, "Sarah Bagley: A Biographical Note," *Labor History* 20 (Summer 1979): 398–413.

79. *Monitor,* April 13, 1844. Nathaniel Borden was a Unitarian; Jefferson Borden and family were Baptists; Colonel Richard Borden, his sons, and Dr. Nathan Durfee organized and attended the Central Congregational Church.

80. *Monitor,* April 27, 1844.

81. Ibid., June 15, 1844.

82. Ibid., June 8, 1844. Unitarian minister, John F. W. Ware, disliked "the appearance of passion [expressed by male writers] in much that is written and spoken," the "saying hard things of others," the "excited state of mind," the "taunts" and "threats," see his letter to the *Mechanic,* June 15, 1844. For a different view, see Lazerow, *Religion and the Working Class,* 138–47.

83. Bronson accepted a ministry in Albany. Another outspoken ten-hour clergyman, H. P. Guilford, moved to Haverhill, Massachusetts. See *Mechanic,* May 18, 1844, June 1, 1844; Sep. 28, 1844, Oct. 5, 1844.

84. Lazerow, *Religion and the Working Class,* William R. Sutton, "Tied to the Whipping Post: New Labor History and Evangelical Artisans in the Early Republic," *Labor History* 36 (Spring 1995): 251–81.

85. Besides studying Fall River, Lazerow looked at Fitchburg and Boston, Wilmington, Delaware, and Rochester, New York. For my review of his argument, see *Journal of Social History* (Fall 1996): 301–3.

86. *Mechanic,* April 27, May 4, 11, 18, 1844.

87. Ibid., May 25, 1844.

88. Letter from "A Mechanic," *Mechanic*, May 25, 1844.

89. *Mechanic*, June 1, 1844.

90. On ten hours in Massachusetts as an unresolved issue, see Commons, *History of Labour*, v. 1, 536–48.

91. *Mechanic*, June 29, 1844; July 20, 1844.

92. *Monitor*, July 20, 1844. The Shove family corroborated this letter on July 27, 1844.

93. Ibid., July 20, 1844.

94. *Mechanic*, June 22, 1844.

95. Ibid., July 20, 1844.

96. Ibid., Aug. 3, 1844.

97. Reprinted in the *Mechanic*, July 27, 1844; Aug. 3, 1844.

98. Ibid., Aug. 3, 1844.

99. Quoted in the *Mechanic*, Aug. 10, 24, 1844.

100. *Mechanic*, July 20, 27, 1844; Aug. 3, 1844.

101. Ibid., Sept. 21, Oct. 26, Nov. 16, Dec. 21, 28, 1844. Charles Fourier was a French philosopher who advocated collective ownership and living arrangements to escape the inroads of capitalist values into family and society. Brook Farm in West Roxbury, Massachusetts, reflected his ideas.

102. *Mechanic*, Aug. 31, 1844.

103. Quoted in the *Mechanic*, Sept. 21, 28, 1844.

104. *Mechanic*, Sept. 14, 1844.

105. Ibid., Sept. 28, 1844.

106. *Boston Laborer*, as quoted in the *Mechanic*, Sept. 28, 1844.

107. *Mechanic*, Oct. 26, 1844, Nov. 2, 1844, Nov. 9, 1844. In *The Industrial Worker*, Norman Ware claims that this first convention was the most united and representative and was dominated by no faction or ideology. Ware, however, did not have access to copies of the Fall River *Mechanic*.

108. *Mechanic*, Oct. 26, 1844.

109. Ibid., Sept. 7, 14, 1844.

110. Ibid., Nov. 9, 1844.

111. *Mechanic*, Nov. 16, 1844. Almy must have meant Chicopee, as Chicopee Falls had no textile mills, but the incident does not appear in Vera Shlakman, *Economic History of A Factory Town: Chicopee, Massachusetts* (New York: Octagon Books, 1969).

112. *Mechanic*, Nov. 2, 9, 16, 30, 1844.

113. *Home and Work: Housework, Wages, and the Ideology of Labor in the Early Republic* (New York: Oxford University Press, 1991).

114. *Mechanic*, Nov. 2, 1844.

115. See letters of objection from "P" and "A Laborer" from Saco, Maine, in the *Mechanic*, Dec. 7, 1844.

116. "N. N.," *Mechanic*, Dec. 14, 21, 28, 1844.

117. "Howard," *Mechanic*, Jan. 18, 25, 1845; Feb. 1, 8, 15, 22, 1845; Mar. 1, 1845.

118. *Mechanic*, Nov. 9, 1844.

119. Ibid., Nov. 16, 1844. Chace stayed with Almy until the end.

120. See Charles E. Persons, "The Early History of Factory Legislation in Mas-

sachusetts," in *Labor Laws and their Enforcement,* ed. Susan M. Kingbury, (1911; reprint, New York: Arno Press, 1971), 24.

121. *Mechanic,* Dec. 21, 1844.

122. Ibid., Jan. 18, 1845.

123. Ibid., Dec. 21, 1844.

124. Ibid., Feb. 8, 1845.

125. See the letter of Benjamin Phelon (*Mechanic,* Feb. 15, 1845) condemning lapsed ten-hour mechanics "richly meriting the bondage under which they groaned." One ten-hour man admitted his construction company violated the limits on hours, *Mechanic,* Feb. 15, 1845.

126. Ibid., Feb. 22, 1845.

127. Ibid., Mar. 1, 1845.

128. Ibid., April 1, 1845.

129. *The Voice of Industry,* Sept. 18, 1845, reported the event, although her actual words are unrecorded.

130. See Ware, *The Industrial Worker,* 208–22, for a narrative of this dismal outcome.

131. See Murphy, *Ten Hours' Labor,* 203–12.

132. Only some scattered issues of the *Monitor* exist. The *News* became a daily paper in 1859, and as a Republican paper, Almy "identified himself with the manufacturing interests in Fall River." See Van Slyke, *Representatives of New England,* v. 1, 382–84.

133. On the Massachusetts political turmoil in New Bedford and Fall River, see *News,* Mar. 20, 27, April 10, 17, May 1, 1851. Walter C. Durfee, the son of Dr. Nathan Durfee, led the unsuccessful Cotton Whig opposition.

134. Anna Clark's *Struggle for the Breeches* examines a similar political situation involving male artisans and radicals in early nineteenth-century London whose misogynistic, homo-social male culture rejected cooperation with female activists in labor reform and confined women to strictly subordinated roles.

135. Ware, *The Industrial Worker,* 240.

136. See below, chapter 3.

137. On the shoe industry and the 1860 shoe strike, see Ware, *The Industrial Worker,* 47, but for the strike's complexities, see Blewett, *Men, Women, and Work,* chapter 5.

3. BRITISH IMMIGRANT TEXTILE WORKERS

1. For two years, Luther wandered aimlessly in frontier regions. See Gersuny, "The Road from Chepachet," 47–55.

2. On Cluer's background and controversies, see Ware, *Industrial Worker,* 139–41. Ware argues (10) that any immigrant leadership, English or German, that was offered to the American worker proved unsuccessful. On Cluer's combination of the temperance cause with ten-hour reform, see Murphy, *Ten Hours Labor,* 184–87. Also on Cluer's activities in the 1850s as an itinerant evangelical and an "ex-Methodist minister," see Lazerow, *Religion and the Working Class,* 67, 133, 219.

3. Hartz, "Seth Luther," 410. Gersuny described Luther's incarcerations in insane asylums until his death in 1863 in "Road From Chepachet."

4. On pre–Civil War immigration, see Roland T. Berthoff, *British Immigrants*

in Industrial America, 1790–1950 (Cambridge: Harvard University Press, 1953), 30–31.

5. On Martland by his shopmate, see *News,* Jan. 7, 1869. On the importance of English and Scottish machinists, mule spinners, dyers, and other skilled occupations in early New England textile mills, see Ware, *New England Cotton Manufacture,* 203–9. For similar information about Philadelphia, see Scranton, *Proprietary Capitalism,* 93–95. On the importance of British skills in American industry, especially in the 1820s and 1830s, and the reluctance of the British to share their knowledge, see Zonderman, "Foreign Pioneer Immigrants," 163–81.

6. This conclusion contradicts both David Jeremy and Charlotte Erickson who argued in *Transatlantic* and *Invisible Immigrants* that most British immigrants were technically obsolete powerloom weavers. Jeremy does give great credit both to skilled English immigrants who arrived even before Slater (see 15–18) and to the diffusion of calico-printing technology crucial to the initial development of this American industry (see chapter 6). But Jeremy insists that most English immigrants from Lancashire did not fit well into American-style mills with different kinds of work organization and, even worse, that they brought unsuitable political ideas with them including trade unionism (169–75).

7. See Cynthia Shelton, *The Mills of Manayunk: Industrialization and Social Conflict in the Philadelphia Region, 1787–1837* (Baltimore: Johns Hopkins University Press, 1986). Even "Sweet, Quiet Rockdale" in Pennsylvania felt the influence of British and Irish immigrants during a violent mule spinners and weavers' strike in 1836 when strikebreakers were called "nobs," clearly the Bristish word for "knobstick." See Anthony Wallace, *Rockdale: The Growth of an American Village in the Early Industrial Revolution* (New York: W. W. Norton, 1980), 356–59. Another severe cut in wages in 1842 produced an even more serious strike led by "a young foreign-born weaver," later identified as English, and joined by other men and women. These restless mule spinners and weavers with connections in Philadelphia and in New Jersey dunked strikebreakers in the millpond and paraded through the streets. Later the leaders were tried and convicted for conspiracy. Wallace dismisses the strikes as "ad hoc," "conservative," and unlike those conducted by more serious trade or craft unions in their inclusiveness of all skills, 359–74. In the end, according to Wallace, textile workers were deskilled and depoliticized, while the successful became managers, 380–94. As a cultural anthropologist, Wallace's lack of interest in the background of these immigrant workers is surprising.

8. As quoted in Chandler, *Visible Hand,* 69.

9. Hough's evidence in *Wamsutta* on the workforce is scanty, but he describes an early and persistent connection between Lancashire immigrants and the development of the textile industry in New Bedford, 42, 49. On British immigration to the Northeast, see Cohen, *American Management,* chapter 5.

10. Berthoff, *British Immigrants,* 31, 45. Not until the Lawrence mills began to manufacture worsted rather than woolen goods during the 1860s did Yorkshire immigrants from Bradford, England, emigrate there in large numbers, 38. American manufacturers of carpets and hosiery tried to use machinery to avoid paying the costs of expensive English workers, but in Philadelphia, skilled hand work remained important through the 1880s, 39–41. Also see Scranton, *Proprietary Capitalism,* 142.

11. Erickson, *Invisible Immigrants* (1972, reprint, Ithaca: Cornell University

Press, 1990), 236, 240, 261. She accepts the categorization of Chartists by their relatives as "irrational fanatics," 274–75, 230, 233–35. Her conclusion that English immigrants did not develop a sense of difference or superiority as a national group contradicts Richard Stott, "British Immigrants and the American Work Ethic in the Mid-Nineteenth Century," *Labor History* 26 (1985): 86–102.

12. Erickson, *Leaving England* (Ithaca: Cornell University Press, 1994), 32. Erickson's protégé, William Van Vugt, in *Britain to America: Mid-Nineteenth-Century Immigrants to the United States* (Urbana: University of Illinois Press, 1999), 63–66, focuses on British immigration in 1851 and discovers little on textile workers.

13. Berthoff in *British Immigrants* argues that needed skills plus a common language and culture determined the ease with which British emigrants blended into American society as political conservatives. If his arguments overlook the radical politics of many, his footnotes are a goldmine. Erickson's study, *Invisible Immigrants* underscores Berthoff's views. Only Erickson's early work, "The Encouragement of Emigration by British Trade Unions, 1850–1900," *Population Studies* 3 (1949): 248–73 concentrates on factory workers.

14. For an fine, inclusive overview of early political and strike activity in Lancashire, see John K. Walton, *Lancashire: A Social History, 1558–1939* (Manchester, U.K.: Manchester University Press, 1987), especially chapter 8, "Radicals and Trade Unions: Popular Protest and Working-Class Organization from the Jacobins to the Chartists." Also see Dorothy Thompson, *The Chartists: Popular Politics in the Industrial Revolution* (New York: Pantheon, 1984). For the first important wave of regional textile protest, see Robert G. Hall, "Tyranny, Work and Politics: The 1818 Strike Wave in the English Cotton District," *International Review of Social History* 34 (1989): 433–70.

15. The classic work on class formation during early industrialization is E. P. Thompson, *The Making of the English Working Class* (New York: Vintage Books, 1968). The publication of Thompson's study inspired numerous historians in Britain, the United States, and elsewhere to investigate the culture and consciousness of working-class life during economic and political upheavals. For the stunning revision of Thompson's work, see Anna Clark, *Struggle for the Breeches*. For a study of industrializing Yorkshire, see Theodore Koditschek, *Class Formation and Urban Industrial Society: Bradford, 1750–1850* (Cambridge: Cambridge University Press, 1990). On Scotland, see Anna Clark's book and Eleanor Gordon, *Women and the Labour Movement in Scotland, 1850–1914* (Oxford: Clarendon Press, 1991).

16. See Deborah Valenze, *The First Industrial Woman* (New York: Oxford University Press, 1995), 72–74, 79–80. Similar attitudes and activities among preindustrial Massachusetts shoeworkers were called "cabbaging", see Blewett, *Men, Women, and Work,* 74, 104. No American historian of textile industrialization found evidence of resistance, as Valenze did in England, from New England household workers to the introduction of water-powered spinning.

17. See James A. Epstein, *Radical Expression: Political Language, Ritual, and Symbol in England, 1789–1850* (Oxford: Oxford University Press, 1994), figure 1 (84) and chapter 3.

18. Epstein, *Radical Expression,* 89–90. He does not analyze the flaunted sexuality of the radical women but concentrates on the dwarfed children and the man in skirts.

19. For a reproduction of "Death or Liberty," see Epstein, *Radical Expression,*

93. According to Epstein (chapter 3), prior to the French Revolution, the cap of liberty was a political symbol often included in traditional and conservative depictions of Britannia, and not until the Revolution of 1789 was it redefined as specifically French or necessarily radical. He does not analyze the Cruikshank image in terms of contested gender power or as evidence of sexualized antagonism. Epstein analyzes "gender politics," 72, commenting only on the cultural tensions resulting from women participants in the political realm. Dressed in virtuous white or politicized colors, the activity of numerous moral females emerged in formal political rituals, including the presentation of a cap of liberty at the Peterloo meeting, 86–92.

20. "The Tale of Samuel and Jemima: Gender and Working-class Culture in Nineteenth-century England," in *E. P. Thompson*, ed. Kay and McClelland, 78–102.

21. Ibid., 80. The injuries of one hundred women and the deaths of two others at Peterloo may have been for female activists as well as men a decisive moment indicating a shift in political consciousness.

22. Clark, *Struggle for the Breeches*, see chapters 12 and 13. Also on the limited role of women in the Chartist movement see, Thompson, *The Chartists*. Clark ends her analysis in 1850, at the beginning of a general period of moderation in Lancashire labor politics which undercut women's activism.

23. *The Crisis of the Aristocracy, 1558–1641* (London: Oxford University Press, 1967), 20–21.

24. Walton, *Lancashire*, 125.

25. See *Class Formation and Urban Industrial Society*, especially chapters 2 and 16.

26. E. P. Thompson, *Customs in Common: Studies in Traditional Popular Culture* (New York: The New Press, 1991), chapters 4 and 5.

27. For a discussion of the impact of political reform in 1832 and the role of Chartism in Lancashire, see Walton, *Lancashire*, 156–65.

28. Many became active in New York City and elsewhere. See Ray Boston, *British Chartists in America, 1839–1900* (Totowa, NJ: Rowman and Littlefield, 1971), Appendix A, 88–97.

29. Technological changes in mule spinning, trade depression, and blacklisting in England also encouraged emigration. Cohen, *American Management*, 90–103.

30. English radicals invoked the "Constitution" in defense of their rights, meaning essentially the most liberal legal traditions, not the practices of English law. Epstein, *Radical Expression*, 75–76.

31. On the supervisory role of mule spinners, see William Lazonick, "Industrial Relations and Technical Change: The Case of the Self-Acting Mule," *Cambridge Journal of Economics* 3 (1979): 231–62, and H. A. Turner, *Trade Union Growth*. Mary Freifeld argues that women hand spinners developed a genuine craft tradition from which they were dislodged by men and machines. See "Technological Change and the 'Self-acting' Mule. A Study of Skill and the Sexual Division of Labor," *Social History* 11 (1986): 319–43. When spinning had been a cottage industry and women prepared the raw cotton or operated hand jennies, male and female spinners, unlike artisans in workshops, possessed a sense of common work and life. See Clark, *Struggle for the Breeches*, 18–22, 126–40. See Mariana Valverde, "'Giving the Female a Domestic Turn': The Social, Legal and Moral Regulation

of Women's Work in British Cotton Mills, 1820–1850," *Journal of Social History* 21 (Spring, 1988): 619–34. For changing gender definitions during the Civil War period cotton famine, see Clare Evans, "Unemployment and the Making of the Feminine during the Lancashire Cotton Famine," in *Women's Work and the Family Economy in Historical Perspective,* ed. Pat Hudson and W. R. Lee (Manchester: University of Manchester Press, 1990), 248–70. For an attempt to provide a statistical confirmation of the early nineteenth-century uncontested acceptance of the concept of the breadwinner, see Sara Hornell and Jane Humphries, "Women's labour force participation and the transition to the male breadwinner family, 1790–1865," *Economic History Review* 48 (1995): 89–117. The idea of a breadwinner's wage in England continued to be as hotly contested in the nineteenth century as was its equivalent, the family wage in America. Robert Grey's study of the factory system as a cultural construct includes discussions of gender and class relations in reform rhetoric and protective legislation that reflected primarily the interests of skilled male workers. See *The Factory Question and Industrial England, 1830–1860* (Cambridge: Cambridge University Press, 1996), 217–19.

32. See Valenze in *First Industrial Woman,* 105. A daughter's contribution to a spinner's family sustains Anna Clark's argument in *Struggle for the Breaches* about the more familial and potentially inclusive nature of the Lancashire textile trades in comparison with London's artisan crafts.

33. Lazonick, "Industrial Relations and Technical Change" and Valverde. "Domestic Turn."

34. See P. Joyce, *Work, Society, and Politics* (1980). For historian Peter Bailey's contention that respectability [like deference] represented a social role that could be used instrumentally and with calculation, see, "'Will the Real Bill Banks Please Stand Up?' Towards a Role Analysis of Mid-Victorian Working-Class Respectability," *Journal of Social History* 12 (1979): 336–53. On the alleged prevalence of the male breadwinner image among nineteenth-century skilled English artisans, but *not* textile operatives, see Keith McClelland, "Masculinity and the 'Representative Artisan' in Britain, 1850–80," in *Manful Assertions,* 74–91. Valenze, in *First Industrial Woman,* chapter 5, discusses the male breadwinner norm as part of a middle-class discourse, defending English industrialization and focusing on the woman worker as a central problem.

35. H. A. Turner, *Trade Union Growth, Structure, and Policy,* (Toronto: University of Toronto Press, 1962) and Neville Kirk, *The Growth of Working Class Reformism in Mid-Victorian England* (Urbana: University of Illinois Press, 1985). Also see Walton, *Lancashire,* 240–52. Walton's study is a general synthesis of economic development, political history, working-class life, labor protest, and cultural, ethnic and religious conflicts. See also Valenze, *First Industrial Woman,* 86; and H. I. Dutton and J. E. King, *Ten Per Cent and No Surrender: The Preston Strike, 1853–54* (Cambridge: Cambridge University Press, 1981).

36. As Valenze argues, the expense of large machines and capital outlay in general encouraged early textile developers to find the cheapest labor possible. Some male workers actually feared that machinery would soon force *all* adults out of the mills to be replaced by an entirely juvenile workforce, *First Industrial Woman,* 94.

37. Sonya Rose argues that despite the equal piece rates, equal wages for men and women weavers did not exist in the context of preferences given to male

workers in the weaving sheds. See *Limited Livelihoods: Gender and Class in Nineteenth-Century England* (Berkeley: University of California Press, 1992), 158–59.

38. Koditschek, *Class Formation and Urban Industrial Society,* 481–82 and chapter 17.

39. Boston, *Chartists in America,* 90.

40. In *Factory Girls,* Philip Foner underestimates Cluer's significance because of charges made against him of lying, bigamy, and extortion (Urbana: University of Illinois Press, 1977), 155 n. 7. Still, Cluer was invited to address the Lowell Female Labor Reform Association and remained a popular speaker on behalf of ten hours. See "A Working Woman," *Daily Evening Voice,* Feb. 23, 1867, quoted in *Factory Girls,* 343. On Walsh, see Sean Wilentz, *Chants Democratic: New York City and the Rise of the American Working Class, 1788–1850* (Oxford: Oxford University Press, 1984), 326–35. On Cluer, see Zonderman, *Aspirations,* 227, 236. For a defense of Cluer, see *Lowell Advertiser,* Dec. 13, 1845. "My Experiences as a Factory Operative," by Working Woman, *Daily Evening Voice,* Feb. 23, 1867. This class-conscious operative worked as a carder and weaver and helped gather names in Lowell for the 1840s ten-hour petitions to the legislature.

41. For an apt appreciation of Cluer, see Zonderman, *Aspirations,* 247–8.

42. A search of the index to the population census of Fall River in 1850 yielded very little information on any of the leaders of the 1848 or 1850–51 strike. Among the very few identified, there was one English immigrant. For information about 1848 textile strike in Pittsburgh over the enforcement of the ten-hour day in which women workers were actively involved, see Monte A. Calvert, "The Alleghany City Cotton Mill Riot of 1848," The *Western Pennsylvania Historical Magazine* 46, 2 (April 1963): 97–133. Convicted of "riot," women workers, some English immigrants, fled incarceration. The ten hour-law was repealed, and Pittsburgh declined as a textile center.

43. *News,* Feb. 10–Mar 30, 1848, printed editorials and a complete transcript of the grand jury inquiry, including the testimony of witnesses and the cross-examinations. The *News,* however, provided only a summary of the trial testimony, but printed the complete text of the defense and prosecution's summations and the judge's charge to the jury on March 30. The *Voice of Industry* on April 7, 1848, published a letter from the convicted John Norris, who had not testified, explaining the events from his perspective. Issues of the *Monitor* for February and March, 1848, have been lost.

44. *News,* Mar. 2, 1848.

45. Letter from John Norris to the *Voice of Industry,* April 7, 1848.

46. *News,* Feb. 24, 1848.

47. *Voice of Industry,* April 7, 1848. Later this general anxiety among native-born workers would intensify with postwar emigration; see letter from a female weaver, "Lowell Loom," to the *American Workman,* June 26, 1869.

48. *Voice of Industry,* April 7, 1848.

49. Ibid.

50. Isaac Cohen, using the 1850 and 1860 federal manuscript census returns, found 68 mule spinners in an estimated workforce of one thousand five hundred in 1850 and one hundred sixty-four mule spinners (94 percent British and Irish) in 1860, *American Management,* 94–95. Later census enumerators did not record

the jobs of Fall River cotton mill operatives. Many Irish-born immigrants had emigrated from Scotland and Lancashire, 95–96.

51. *News*, Mar. 2, 1848.

52. References to "green" in British slang ca. 1850 had the connotation of eagerly sexual women, Eric Partridge, *The Routledge Dictionary of Historical Slang* (London: Routledge Press, 1973): 400–401.

53. Testimony of David Robertson, weaver, and Braddock Davol, dress tender, both at the Troy mill, *News*, Feb. 24, 1848.

54. Other probably Yankee epithets, in origins, used for strikebreakers were "quaker's daughters," perhaps a sneering reference to anti–ten-hour Quaker minister Jacob Viney, who had brought strikebreakers to Fall River in 1844, and "crooked shanks" (crippled legs), perhaps a general insult. Neither of these terms was found in British or American dictionaries of slang.

55. *News*, Feb. 24, 1848.

56. Testimony of Mary Ann Donoly, *News*, Mar. 2, 1848. Many of these activities may have represented the classic New England "turn-out" for native-born female operatives: "demonstrations, unorganized outbursts led by a few inflammatory spirits who had little idea what they were to achieve, . . . raised the girls to a state of great excitement . . . but gained no direct results," according to Ware, *New England Cotton Manufacture*, 275–76.

57. *News*, Feb. 24, 1848.

58. Ibid.

59. Ibid.

60. Ibid., Mar. 2, 1848. Robert Grey dismissed a similar expression in 1846 by one English woman weaver about her interest in wages as "rare (and possibly unique)", *The Factory Question*, 30.

61. *News*, Mar. 30, 1848.

62. Ibid.

63. Ibid.

64. Ibid. According to the index to the federal population census of 1850 for Massachusetts, most of those who testified for and against Norris and Clark left Fall River. Among them, five male workers and ten female workers were absent from the 1850 census although the women might have married. Most were probably blacklisted.

65. *News*, Feb. 10, 1848.

66. Ibid.

67. Ibid.

68. *Voice*, April 7, 1848.

69. Wright, "Sarah G. Bagley," 389–413.

70. *ProvidenceJ*, Nov. 25, 1850.

71. *New York Tribune*, Feb. 3, 1851.

72. The Robeson operation was reorganized by the Robeson sons after bankruptcy and renamed the Fall River Print Works in 1848.

73. *News*, Dec. 5, 1850. Both Lazerow in *Religion and the Working Class* and Murphy in *Ten Hours' Labor* argue that using Sabbath breaking to criticize capitalists was an effective use of religion to criticize those employers who often proclaimed their own Christian righteousness.

74. Anthony Howe's study of English textile industrialists is called *The Cotton Masters, 1830–1860* (Oxford, Clarendon Press, 1984).

75. My thanks to David Zonderman. On English antislavery rhetoric and factory reform agitation, see Grey, *The Factory Question*, 37–47. On race and the nineteenth-century American working class, see Roediger, *The Wages of Whiteness*, especially part 2.

76. "The Ties That Bind Master and Servant in Massachusetts, 1800–1850," *Labor History* 30 (Spring 1989) 193–227. For cases concerning textile workers, see 221–25. Tomlins argues that English law so defined nineteenth-century employment but does not cite the political uses in the 1850s of master/servant discourse in Lancashire.

77. See *Oxford English Dictionary* v. 6, 1063, which refers to *hand* (entry 11) as the capacity for "doing something with the hand, and hence of doing generally; skill, ability, knack; whereas *help*, v. 7, 127–28, suggests "aid, assistance . . . to render help . . . , a domestic servant." On the meanings of *masters, servants,* and *help* among American workers, see Roediger, 47–50, 54. New England mill agents never used the term *hand* and insisted on the word *help*. Immigrant operatives continued to call themselves hands.

78. Quoted by Robert Howard in his early account of the Mule Spinners' Amalgamated Union in New England, "Progress in the Textile Trades," in *The Labor Movement: The Problem of Today*, ed. George E. McNeill (Boston, 1887), 215. Howard may have heard the story about Borden repeated by older union members after his arrival from England in 1873.

79. *News*, Dec. 5, 1850.

80. Ibid., Feb. 20, 1851.

81. Isaac Cohen's absorption in analyzing the role of mule spinners in New England textile industry led him to view the 1850–51 strike as "isolated." He regarded all spinners' strikes, as in 1850–51 as contests over craft control but overlooked their potent ideological debates over justice, tyranny, and manhood, *American Management*, 115. For a further discussion, see below, chapter 8.

82. Berthoff, *British Immigrants*, 34. In Lancashire, mule spinners retained their piecers and minders or assistants. See Cohen, *American Management*, 105–6.

83. See the account of the crushed fingers of Katy McCann, *News*, Nov. 19, 1874. For a discussion of the tensions between boys and adult males in American industry, see Ava Baron, "An 'Other' Side of Gender Antagonism At Work: Men, Boys, and the Remasculinization of Printers' Work, 1830–1920," in *Work Engendered*, 47–69.

84. On the differences between the reaction of British and American managers to the self-acting mule, see Cohen, *American Management*, 106–13.

85. *News*, Feb. 20, 1851.

86. Among those centers were the Boott and Hamilton Mills of Lowell, unspecified mills in Lawrence (probably the Pacific) and three mills at Great Falls, New Hampshire, as well as eleven mill villages in Rhode Island including, Slaterville, Woonsocket, Blackstone, and the Providence Steam Mill. The mule spinners cited cost figures for 29 ½ yarn spun at three Fall River mills (the Metacomet, Pocasset, and the Massasoit Steam Mill) and compared them with costs for the above mills, also taking into account costs of boarding, fuel, and rent. Their intent

was to prove that everywhere else in New England and also in England, spinners were paid more wages for the same work.

87. *News*, Jan. 30, 1851.

88. On Cohen's argument, see chapter 8, below.

89. "Quotity," *News*, Jan. 9, 1851.

90. *News*, Jan. 30, 1851.

91. "An Operative," *News*, Feb. 20, 1851.

92. *News*, Jan. 31, 1851. In McNeill's, *The Labor Movement*, Howard's history of New England textile workers left out any mention of weavers or carders, "Progress in the Textile Trades," 214–40.

93. Her name was not recorded, *News*, Feb. 20, 1851.

94. Similar tactics were used by Lowell mill operatives in 1848, Zonderman, *Aspirations and Anxieties*, 229–32.

95. Letter from P. S., *News*, Feb. 27, 1851.

96. *News*, Jan. 30, 1851.

97. However, for a more submissive expression of sentiments by a Yankee operative, see "The Hymn of the Fall River Turnouters," in *News*, Feb. 27, 1851.

98. All copies of this paper, which ran from March 1851 until 1852, have been lost. Webb left the mills to become a saloon-keeper, though he remained a ten-hour activist. See obituary, *FRHerald*, Nov. 24, 1884.

99. *Monitor*, April 26, 1851.

100. *News*, July 3, 1851. Silvia says that many experienced mule spinners, were recruited by the Pepperell Company of Saco, Maine (*Spindle City*, part 1, 51).

101. On this strike which challenged the mid-Victorian compromise between employers and operatives in Lancashire, see Dutton and King, *Ten Per Cent and No Surrender*. For the donation, 67.

102. The *Monitor* supported the Know-Nothing movement and the *News* opposed it, but the *News* linked the spreading disease to foreigners, *News*, Aug. 24, 1854.

103. *News*, Aug. 3, 10, 1854; Sept. 14, 1854. On the New York epidemic, see, *New York Times* article reprinted in *News*, Aug. 17, 1854.

104. *News*, Aug. 31, 1854; Sept. 7, 1854.

105. Ibid., Nov. 16, 23, 1854.

106. Ibid., Nov. 16, 1854.

107. Formisano, *Transformation of Political Culture*, 336–43.

108. *News*, Oct. 6, 20, 27, 1853; Nov. 3, 1853.

109. See David Montgomery, *Beyond Equality: Labor and the Radical Republicans, 1862–1872* (Urbana: University of Illinois Press, 1981), 119–20. Also see below, chapter 4.

110. A coalition of Whigs and Free Soilers sent the Reverend Orin Fowler of Fall River's First Congregational Church to Congress in 1848 and 1850. He died in 1852. His district was divided in half, and a Whig from Taunton and a Democrat from Marshfield replaced him. See obituary, *News*, Sept. 8, 1852; Dec. 16, 1852. Ten-hour supporter Rev. Asa Bronson tried to run for the state legislature representing a coalition of Democrats and Free Soilers, but he was defeated, *News*, Nov. 11, 1853. On the results in 1855, see the *News*, Nov. 8, 1855.

111. *News*, Nov. 4, 1858.

112. *News,* Nov. 10, 1859; Nov. 8, 1860.

113. See Berthoff, *British Immigrants,* 96; Howard, "Textile Trades," 216–19.

114. The pre–Civil War movement of Irish immigrant manual workers into textile mills was very slow; see Dublin, *Women At Work,* chapter 9. The majority of Irish immigrants came from a nonindustrialized agricultural economy; see for example, Kirby Miller, "Class, Culture, and Immigrant Group Identity in the United States: The Case of Irish-American Ethnicity," in Virginia Yans-McLaughlin, *Immigration Reconsidered,* 96–129. Historians of Irish emigration to America should include those who spent some time with their family members in English textile centers, where they absorbed a different political legacy than the one brought by most of the Irish immigrants to nineteenth-century America. But they also faced discrimination and bigotry in Lancashire and Yorkshire. See Kirk, *Working Class Reformism,* chapter 7, "Class, Ethnicity and Popular Toryism"; and Koditschek, *Class Formation and Urban Industrial Society,* 450–51.

115. Howard, "Progress in the Textile Trades," 216. This labor activity of the late 1850s counters Montgomery's pessimism about ethnic division, *Beyond Equality,* 119–21.

116. The citizens of Fall River gave twenty dollars a month to each volunteer on top of their army pay, *News,* April 25, 1861. The city government quickly scaled down this amount and later paid only a bounty of fifteen dollars to each volunteer. On the foreign-born volunteers, see *News,* April 25, 1861. Also see Earl, *Centennial History,* 206, and *Phillips History,* v. 3, 135.

117. On the building of the Andrew's Republican Party as a vehicle for Radical Republicans and labor reformers, see Montgomery, *Beyond Equality,* 120–21.

118. *News,* June 27, 1861; July 4, 11, 18, 25, 1861.

119. Earl Francis Mulderink, "'We Want a Country': African American and Irish American Community Life in New Bedford, Massachusetts, During the Civil War Era." Ph.D. dissertation: University of Wisconsin Madison, 1995, 158–60.

120. *News,* July 23, 1863.

121. See Maris A. Vinovskis, "Have Social Historians Lost the Civil War? Some Preliminary Demographic Speculations," in *Toward a Social History of the American Civil War: Exploratory Essays,* ed. Maris A. Vinovskis (Cambridge: Cambridge University Press, 1990), 20–21.

122. Howard, "Textile Trades," 216–7.

123. *News,* Sept. 25, 1865. As a war widow, Mrs. Burke was entitled to a pension, however long that took to be awarded. On the experience in Essex County, Massachusetts, see Amy E. Holmes, "'Such Is the Price We Pay': American Widows and the Civil War Pension System," in Vinovskis, *Toward a Social History,* 171–95. On the experiences with war pensions of New Bedford's Irish and African communities, see Mulderink, "'We Want A Country'," chapters 5, 6.

124. *News,* Feb. 25, 1864. The *News* did not report the results.

125. Ibid., Sept. 26, 27, 1865.

126. Ibid., Sept. 1, Oct. 31, 1865.

4. Wait, Agitate, Work, and Wait

1. See David Zonderman, "The Enduring Vision of Antebellum Labor Reform in Boston, 1848–1865," paper read at the American Studies Association,

Boston, 1993. Formisano argues that in 1852 Massachusetts textile factories and machine shops cut their hours to eleven to head off ten-hour reform, *Transformation of Political Culture*, 338–9. Fall River and many other textile centers proposed a cut back to eleven hours in October 1853, but the advocates of ten hours refused to support the change, *News*, Oct. 20, 1853.

2. In 1869 Cowley became the attorney for the Knights of St. Crispin, whose application for a state charter was defeated along with a ten-hour bill. Cowley successfully argued the case for chartering trade unions before the State Supreme Judicial Court in 1870. See obituary, *Lowell Courier*, Feb. 6, 1908, and his "History of the Ten Hour Movement," in *Lowell: A City of Spindles* (Trades and Labor Council, 1900); for quote, 257, 260; On the survival of labor reform in Boston and the establishment of the Massachusetts Bureau of Labor Statistics in 1869, see David Zonderman, "The Politics of Labor Reform in Nineteenth-Century America: The Case of Massachusetts in the 1860s," paper read at the Social Science History Association, Atlanta, Ga., 1994.

3. David Montgomery, *Beyond Equality* (New York: Alfred Knopf, 1967). In the 1970s and 1980s, Montgomery, his colleagues, and their graduate students shifted traditional labor history into studies of the dynamics of working-class culture, often as community studies. For example, see the essays in Gutman and Bell, *The New England Working Class and the New Labor History*, and *Labor Histories, Class, Politics, and the Working-Class Experience*, eds. Eric Arnesen, Julie Greene, and Bruce Laurie (Urbana: University of Illinois Press, 1998).

4. Montgomery, *Beyond Equality*, 4–13.

5. Aggregate data in 1870 indicated that light industry in Massachusetts was "sluggish," (*Beyond Equality*, 5). Boots and shoes, granite quarrying, and paper-making provide additional examples of regional economic development.

6. On worker divisions, see *Beyond Equality*, 30–44, on the New Bedford strike, see 282–92.

7. In his preface (x), Montgomery lays out a vision of "great strides" made by wage earners between 1862 and 1875, but he ends his book in 1872. He also mentions but does not explore the militancy of Fall River's English immigrant workers (277–78, 295).

8. Ibid., 445.

9. Ibid., 124–25. Montgomery argues that this committee's report supporting the eight-hour day and establishing a commission to hold hearings was of "immense" ideological significance, 125. Also see *News*, Nov. 3, 1865.

10. *Lawrence Journal and Citizen*, [*LawJCit*] Sept. 12, 1874. Through document conservation, the brittle issues of Bower's newspaper are now available on microfilm to historians. My thanks to Richard Fyffe, formerly of the Essex Institute, Salem, Massachusetts, for help in restoring this crucial piece of the Massachusetts labor press. The *News*, Aug. 22, 1865, reported on contact between Lawrence and Fall River. A speech given by Bower and printed in *LawJCit*, May 30, 1874, discussed the short term committees.

11. *News*, Oct. 28, 1865. The *News* provided a summation of each day's testimony, sometimes reprinted from the *Boston Advertiser* and the *Providence Journal*.

12. Both state laws on child education, passed in 1857, and on prohibiting the employment of children under twelve from working in textile factories, passed in 1861, were ignored in Fall River, *Phillips History*, v. 2, 77–78.

13. *News,* Oct. 28, 1865.

14. Ibid., Nov. 3, 1865.

15. Ibid., Oct. 31, 1865.

16. *News,* Nov. 2, 1865.

17. *News,* Nov. 20, 1865.

18. From the *Boston Advertiser* in the *News,* Nov. 20, 1865.

19. For the activities of the American Emigrant Company of New York in Lancashire in 1864 and 1865, see Charlotte Erickson, *American Industry and the European Immigrant, 1860–1885* (New York: Russell & Russell, 1957), 17–18, 21. New England cotton manufacturers found it hard to recruit skilled workers through these agencies as late as 1876, but depressions and strikes in England such as in 1869 and 1878 were helpful in persuading workers to emigrate, 34–35.

20. *Daily Evening Voice* (*Voice*), Dec. 4, 1864; Mar. 9, 1865; July 27, 1865.

21. Ibid., Aug. 28, 1865.

22. Ibid., Nov. 13, 14, Dec. 12, 1865; Jan. 26, 1866.

23. Ibid., April 29, 1865.

24. According to the *Voice,* June 29, 1865, the choice of commission members seemed "judicious" if not representative of working mechanics. Besides Griffin it included Joseph White, the secretary of the Massachusetts Board of Education; Frank Sanborn, secretary of the Massachusetts Board of Charities; Dr. H. I. Bowditch, a specialist in sanitation; Charles Russell, a supposedly pro-labor attorney; and Rev. William Tilden, once a ship's carpenter, head of the New South Congregational Church of Boston.

25. Griffin's warning appeared in the *Voice,* April 29, 1865. He is identified as the report's writer in the May 30, 1865 edition.

26. *Voice,* Nov. 8, 1865. On Beacon Hill after the election, only three of forty senators and twenty-three of two hundred forty representatives supported labor reform.

27. Ibid., November 10, 1865.

28. On Steward, See Montgomery, *Beyond Equality,* 249–60 and Zonderman, "Enduring Vision."

29. *Voice,* August 4, 1865. Most labor reformers thought supply and demand forces would work efficiently if freed from capitalist control, Ibid, February 11, 213, 14, 1865, Aug. 4, 16, 1865. One was Ezra Heywood, see Martin Blatt, *Free Love and Anarchism.* For the interest in ten hour activity among Rhode Island textile operatives, see *Voice,* Aug. 12, Sep. 19, 21, 23; Oct. 10, 1865.

30. *Voice,* Mar. 2, 3, 5, 6, 1866.

31. Ibid., April 21, 1866.

32. See Persons, "Protective Legislation," 19–20, 97.

33. *Voice,* Mar. 2, 1866.

34. "Lowell Loom" [a female operative], *American Workman,* June 26, 1869.

35. *News,* Feb. 15, 1867.

36. Ibid., July 18, 1868.

37. Howard erroneously dated the Biddeford conference as 1868 in "Textile Trades," 217.

38. In *Beyond Equality,* 268, Montgomery saw the passage of this law as a sop to labor reform and an insult to supporters of the eight-hour day.

39. *News,* Oct. 1, 1866.

40. Ibid., Oct. 8, 9, 16, 20, 1866. For Fall River's deficient factory schools for mill children, see Henry K. Oliver, *Report to the Massachusetts Senate*, no. 21 (1868).

41. *News*, Nov. 2, 1866.

42. Ibid., Nov. 2, 3, 1866.

43. This contradicts an assertion by David Montgomery in *Beyond Equality* (145–46) that mule spinners in 1867 acted alone to get ten hours. This may have been the case in the cities that Montgomery cited: Manchester, New Hampshire, and Lowell and Lawrence, Massachusetts, but the mule spinners in Fall River and New Bedford cooperated with other operatives. Montgomery conceded this later, 277.

44. *News*, Nov. 3, 1866.

45. Montgomery argues (Beyond Equality, 278), that all this had been accomplished in Fall River by militant English immigrant workers without the active help of Boston's labor reformers, an indication of the weak links between the reform leadership and community labor politics. But Montgomery's reliance on the work of German Marxist Frederick Sorge, the Boston *Voice*, and the 1870 *First Annual Report* of the MBLS as sources on Fall River, rather than the local press, led to some misinterpretations. For a critique of a translation of Sorge, see the Assessment of Primary Sources.

46. Howard dramatically named the 1868 strike the "winter of their discontent," in "Textile Trades," 218. As usual in his writing on textile workers, Howard mentions only the mule spinners as active in the strike.

47. In his autobiography, Frederick Douglass describes the racism he confronted in New Bedford when he tried to apply for a ship calkers's job. See *Narrative of the Life of Frederick Douglass: An American Slave* (1845; reprint, New York: Signet Books, 1968) 113–19.

48. Obituaries on Bennett, *New Bedford Evening Standard, (NBSt)*, *New Bedford Mercury, (NBMercury)*, April 18, 1898.

49. See Hough, *Wamsutta of New Bedford*, 9–41. Earl Mulderink's social analysis of New Bedford during the Civil War era, "We Want A Country," mentioned English immigrants, but lacked a contextual economic analysis of local industry for the period and remained uninterested in ten-hour activity or strikes.

50. *NBSt*, Mar. 8, 1868.

51. *NBMercury*, Mar. 4, 1868.

52. Letter from "OBED," *Voice*, Feb. 28, 1867.

53. *NBSt*, Feb. 16, 1868; *NBMercury*, Feb. 19, 1868.

54. These included skilled male warp dressers, skilled female web drawers and cloth trimmers, and "miscellaneous," probably bobbin girls and boys, *NBSt.*, Feb. 19, 1868.

55. "V.X.," Ibid., Mar. 6, 1868.

56. *NBMercury*, Mar. 4, 1868; *NBSt*, Mar. 1, 4, 1868.

57. *NBSt*, Mar. 5, 1868.

58. Ibid., Feb. 21, 1868.

59. Ibid., Feb. 19, 1868. Knowlton cautiously signed his letter, "K."

60. *NBMercury*, Feb. 19, 1868.

61. *NBSt*, Feb. 21, 27, Mar. 5, 1868.

62. "Unsigned," Ibid., Feb. 26, 1868.

63. Ibid., Mar. 2, 1868.

64. Ibid., Mar. 4, 1868.

65. Ibid., Feb. 21, 22, 1868.

66. Ibid., Mar. 5, 1868.

67. Ibid., Mar. 8, 1868.

68. Ibid., Mar. 14, 1868.

69. *Voice*, Feb. 13, 1867.

70. On Connecticut politics, see Montgomery, *Beyond Equality*, 296–302. In Rhode Island, ten hour activity rose and was stifled in 1865. On Rhode Island labor politics, see below, chapter 7.

71. *Voice*, Dec. 17, 1866; Feb. 6, 15, Mar. 7, 28, April 2, 8, 1867.

72. Ibid., Feb. 13, 1867.

73. Ibid., Jan. 12, 28, 1867.

74. Ibid., Jan. 12, 15, 1867.

75. Lowell Operative letter, Ibid., Feb. 27, 1867.

76. Ibid., Feb. 27, 1867.

77. Kershaw wove in the carpet mill, Burdock was a cotton weaver at the Lawrence mill, and Whitcher, along with several other English Canadian women, was a Lowell weaver. Among her friends, only she remained; the others returned home after their health broke down. Ibid., Feb. 17, 1867.

78. Ibid., Mar. 22, 1867.

79. The exception was Miss Caroline A. Frost, president of the Lowell Ladies' Short-Time Committee, whose words appeared in the *Voice*, Mar. 1, 1867. Nothing else is known about her activities or opinions. Even the speech by Mrs. Ira Steward to women workers in Manchester went unreported, Ibid., Feb. 26, 1867.

80. Ibid., Feb. 13, 1867. For a similar observation on the connections between race and nationality in the nineteenth-century, see Henry F. Bedford, *Their Lives and Numbers. The Condition of Working People in Massachusetts 1870–1900* (Ithaca: Cornell University Press, 1995), chapter 4.

81. *Voice*, Feb. 13, 1867.

82. Ibid., Feb. 19, 25, 1867.

83. Ibid., Feb. 25, 1867.

84. Massachusetts State Archives, O. P. Acts, 1870, as quoted in Renee D. Toback, "Protective Labor Legislation for Women: The Massachusetts Ten Hour Law" (Ph.D. dissertation, University of Massachusetts; 1985), 280–81.

85. *Voice*, April 3, 9, 1867. On the legislature, Mar. 7, 9, 18, 29, 1867.

86. Ibid., April 9, 1867.

87. For the very bitter reaction of "Workman," Ibid., June 11, 1867.

88. Ibid., April 13, 1867.

89. Ibid., Mar. 18, 29, April 11, 12, 23, 26, 1867, May 16, 28, 31, 1867.

90. Ibid., April 23, 26, May 16, 28, 31, 1867. On Lowell politics, July 30, Aug. 12, 13, Sept. 12, 1867.

91. Ibid., Oct. 16, 1867.

92. The mills in Manchester, New Hampshire, followed a similar plan to capture the market for delaine, light woolen muslin dress good that required fine yarns spun by experienced mule spinners.

93. *Voice* article, reprinted in *News*, Feb. 4, 1867.

94. *News*, April 26, 1867. Also see obituary, *FRHerald*, Mar. 14, 1881. No cop-

ies of the *Border City Herald,* 1873–1875, later the *Fall River Herald* have survived. On Lapham's run for Congress, see *News,* Nov. 4, 1874.

95. *News,* Jan. 21, 1869. According to the *News,* Jan. 13, 1869, Henry K. Oliver's report on his inspection tour of the Fall River factory school had pronounced it successful. In contrast, Yves Roby's *Les Franco-Américains De las Nouvelle-Angleterre, 1776–1930* (Sillery: Quebec Septentrion, 1990) which relies primarily on Silvia's work on Fall River, regards French Canadian immigrants to New England as politically inert communities. On French Canadians in southeastern New England, see below, chapters 6, 7, 8, and 10.

96. Ibid., Mar. 17, 1869, Nov. 12, 1869.

97. *LawJCit,* Aug. 1, 1874. The store had first opened in 1866. *News,* Feb. 3, 9, 1869; Mar. 11, 1869.

98. Ibid., Mar. 15, Dec. 27, 1869.

99. Ibid., Sept. 3, 1869.

100. *ProvidenceJ,* Mar. 31, 1869.

101. Ten Hour Association of Fall River, "To the Operatives and Working Classes of Massachusetts," May 8, 1869, Rare Book Collection, Boston Public Library.

102. *LawJ,* Aug. 2, 1873.

103. *News,* May 13, 1869.

104. Ibid., June 10, 1869.

105. Collins also supported in 1869 the formation of the Daughters of St. Crispin, an organization of female shoe workers. See Blewett, *Men, Women, and Work,* 169–71.

106. *News,* June 26, 1869; Aug. 21, 1869, Sep. 3, 1869. On anti-Chinese movements in the nineteenth century as equal to "blackness" for various ethnic groups, see Roediger, *The Wages of Whiteness,* 179–80.

107. *News,* Sept. 3, 30, Oct. 9, 23, 29, Nov. 2, 1869.

108. Ibid., Nov. 30, Dec. 1, 2, 4, 6, 1869.

109. This strategy represented a continuation of pre–Civil War anti–ten-hour tactics. Formisano, *The Transformation of Political Culture,* 336–40.

110. See Cowley, "Ten Hour Movement," 259–60 and Blewett, *Men, Women, and Work,* chapter 6.

111. On Oliver, see obituary, *Salem News,* Aug. 13, 1885; on Wright, see *LawJCit,* July 19, Aug. 2, 1873.

112. Bower served his terms as a Labor Reformer and Democratic, although he regarded himself as a Republican. In 1874 he had a patronage job at the Boston Customs House. *LawJCit,* Sept. 12, 1874.

113. Many of the poems in *Rhymes Among the Spindles* (Lawrence, Mass.: R. Bower, 1872) are collected verse, published previously in newspapers. One copy was given to the Concord Public Library, Concord, Massachusetts, in June 1873, by E. C. Damon, a local ten-hour advocate. My thanks to the rare book collection at the library. The book was dedicated to Richard Hinchcliffe's brother, John Hinchcliffe of Illinois. On John Hinchcliffe, see Montgomery, *Beyond Equality,* 217–18.

114. *LawJCit,* Dec. 12, 1874, Jan. 2, 1875, Feb. 13, 1875; April 11, 1875.

115. Ibid., May 15, 1875.

116. Obituary, *FRHerald,* Nov. 24, 1884.

117. Obituary, *Labor Standard* (*LaborSt*) (Fall River), June 4, 1881. Only two copies survived.

118. No copies of Stephenson's paper have survived.

119. *LawJCit*, Aug. 29, 1874, Sept. 19, 1874.

120. See Yearley, *Britons in American Labor,* 148–49, and Silvia, "The Spindle City," v. 1, 104–5. Also see below, chapters 8 and 9.

121. Information on Gunton comes from Judge Cowley of Lowell, *LaborSt,* Aug. 20, 1881 and the *Gunton Institute Bulletin* (Feb. 4, 1899): 431–33.

122. *Boston Herald, [BHerald]* Feb. 24, 1875. In the mid-1870s, the Fall River workforce was one-quarter American natives; one-third English immigrants (most from Lancashire); one-fifth Irish immigrants (some of whom had either been born in or worked in Lancashire); and just less than one-fifth French Canadian immigrants, some from the textile mills of Montreal. The figures are from 1878, cited in Massachusetts Bureau of Labor Statistics, *Thirteenth Annual Report* (1882): 204–5.

123. *LawJ,* Aug. 9, 1873 and *Boston Globe, [BGlobe],* Nov. 5, 6, 1873.

124. Speech by Ira Steward, *LawJ,* July 19, 1873.

125. *BGlobe,* Nov. 7, 1873.

126. Editorial, *News,* Nov. 1, 6, 1871.

127. *LawJCit,* April 4, 1874.

128. *Boston Daily Advertiser,* April 3, 1874; *BHerald,* April 3, 1874; also see *Lawrence American* April 4, 1874. On the use of "rough music" in burlesques of militia duty and injustices, see Susan G. Davies, *Parades and Power: Street Theatre in Nineteenth-Century Philadelphia* (Berkeley: University of California Press, 1986), 96–103, 160–61.

129. *News,* April 3, 1874. The editors of the *Lawrence Journal and Citizen* understood the symbols, tactics, and defiant spirit but cautioned peace and quiet on April 11, 1874. In the same issue, Richard Hinchcliffe, writing from his new home in Dover, New Hampshire, defended these political activities.

130. *BGlobe,* April 18, 1874. With their choice of Washburn, many Republicans believed they had thwarted the ambitions of the highly controversial Benjamin Butler, a Republican ten-hour man.

131. Marion Cotter Cahill, *Shorter Hours: A Study of the Movement Since the Civil War* (1932, reprint, New York: AMS Press, 1968), 108–9. For an analysis of the wording of the 1874 law, see Toback, "Protective Labor Legislation," 360.

132. *LawJCit,* June 27, 1874.

133. Ibid., May 9, June 11, 1874.

134. Until Lapham's race for mayor in 1874, only Yankee Republicans ran against each other for mayor in intraparty contests. In 1872 Robert T. Davis, a one-term mayor had run unopposed, while in 1873 John S. Brayton lost to Davenport by 525 votes. See Henry A. Fenner, *History of Fall River* (New York, 1906), 144–45.

135. *LawJCit,* May 9, 1874.

136. Dillon gave an exclusive interview to a reporter from the *NYHerald,* Sept. 21, 1874.

137. *NYHerald,* Sept. 20, 1874.

138. *NYHerald,* Sept. 20, 21, 1874. The editor termed the fire, "The Murder of Innocents," Sept. 21, 1874. For a memory of the tragedy by a nine-year-old

Irish immigrant, see David S. Lawlor, *The Life and Struggles of an Irish Boy in America* (Newton, MA: Carroll, 1936), 31–32.

139. *Labor Journal,* Sept. 26, Oct. 3, 1874. These are the only surviving copies of the paper, Fall River Historical Society. Also see Commonwealth of Massachusetts, Massachusetts Bureau of Labor Statistics [MBLS], *Fifth Annual Report* (1875), 142–77.

140. The *News* carried reports on the inquest from Sept. 22 to Oct. 3, 1874, and announced the verdict on October 5. The insurance coverage of the mill had been reported on September 19. The unsuccessful civil suit of an injured seventeen-year-old, the following year, Keith v. Granite Mill Co., was covered from July 12 to 17, 1875. The *New York Herald* [*NYHerald*] carried on-the-scene coverage hostile to the mills, Sept. 20 and 21, 1874.

141. My thanks to Jeffrey A. Northrup of the University of Massachusetts Lowell for translating the microfilm copy of *L'Echo du Canada,* 1873–76, and researching Beaugrand's life. *L'Echo,* April 25, 1874; May 16, 1874.

142. *L'Echo,* April 18, 25, May 30, June 6, July 4, 25, Aug. 22, Sept. 5, 18, 26, Oct. 3, 10, 17, Nov. 7, 28, 1874.

143. When the 1874 ten-hour law was challenged in the Middlesex district court in Commonwealth vs. the Hamilton Manufacturing Company, the judges in 1876 upheld the constitutionality of the law under the police powers of the state to protect wards of the state in a dangerous industry. For a critical view of this decision see, S. N. D. North, *Factory Legislation in New England. Its Tendencies and Effects, Its Legal and Economic Effects,* (Boston: Arkwright Club reprint, 1895), 44–46.

144. Supply and demand, as professional economists agree, operates best under conditions of perfect competition. Many nineteenth-century working people in Massachusetts, including textile and boot and shoe workers, regarded these natural laws early on as self-interested constructions by capitalists. For a plea to economists to historicize the concept of the market, see William Lazonick, *Business Organization and the Myth of the Market Economy* (Cambridge: Cambridge University Press, 1991).

5. To Dominate the National Market

1. *News,* Dec. 16, 1867. In May 1868, another Borden and Durfee-owned mill burned (*Providence J,* May 15, 1868,) but it was insured for most of its value.

2. Other competitors were the Hamilton mills in Lowell and the Harmony Mills in Cohoes, New York. The vast Sprague holdings in textiles and metalworking in Rhode Island and Connecticut and their banking interests in Providence collapsed in 1873; see the sprightly essay by Zachariah Chafee Jr., "Weathering the Panic of '73: An Episode in Rhode Island Business History," *Proceedings of the Massachusetts Historical Society* 66 (Oct. 1936–May 1941): 270–93.

3. *Woonsocket Patriot and Rhode Island State Register,* [*WoonsocketP*], Mar. 24, 1865; June 1, Dec. 28, 1866.

4. *News,* Dec. 17, 1867.

5. Hurd, *Bristol County,* 411–12, Van Slyck, *New England Manufacturers,* 117–18. The American Printing Company had acquired the Globe Print Works in 1854, Smith, *Fall River Industry,* 52.

6. Alfred Chandler, *The Visible Hand*, 1–12.

7. Ibid., 8.

8. Laurence F. Gross in *The Course of Industrial Decline: The Boott Cotton Mills of Lowell, Massachusetts, 1835–1955* (Baltimore: Johns Hopkins University Press, 1993) addresses Chandler's charge by studying a specific textile firm, including the class dynamics of the workplace.

9. Chandler, *Visible Hand*, 21–27. Chandler makes their utility clear: they advanced credit, paid for insurance and transportation, and coordinated the operations of the system. Brown and Almy of Providence marketed the product of Slater's mill in this fashion (58).

10. Chandler, *Visible Hand*, 67–71.

11. Ibid., 209–14.

12. *ProvidenceJ*, Nov. 17, 1868.

13. Earl, *Centennial History*, 162–68; Capt. Thos. E. Lynch, *History of the Fire Department of Fall River, Mass.* (Fall River, 1900).

14. *ProvidenceJ*, Aug. 29, 1870. The board of directors included S. Angier Chace, Jefferson Borden, Borden's son-in-law Walter Paine III, Thomas J. Borden, Philip D. Borden, David A. Brayton, and a number of new investors in mills.

15. *ProvidenceJ*, July 2, 1868; Mar. 30, 1869.

16. Editorial, *News*, Sept. 1, 1865.

17. *News*, Oct. 23, 1865.

18. Ibid., Nov. 7, 1866. For the immense difficulties of reorganizing cotton agriculture, the resistance of freedpeople to work under conditions reminiscent of slavery, and the general upheavals of the Reconstruction South, see Jacqueline Jones, *Labor of Love, Labor of Sorrow* (New York: Basic Books, 1985), chapters 2, 3 and Eric Foner, *Reconstruction: America's Unfinished Revolution, 1863–1877* (New York: Harper and Row: 1988).

19. *ProvidenceJ*, May 1, 1868.

20. In *Cotton and Cotton Manufactures in the United States* (Boston: Franklin Press, 1880), Edward Atkinson wrote (26) that wartime print cloth prices reached as high as thirty-three cents a yard in comparison with four cents in September 1879. He also recalled that a bale of cotton might bring over $900 during the severe war shortages. Also see, Smith, *Fall River Industry*, 48–9.

21. *Washington Tribune*, Aug. 16, 1875; reprinted in *ProvidenceS*, Aug. 21, 1875.

22. Smith, *Fall River Industry*, 49–51. In 1887 ("Progress in the Textile Trade," 217), Robert Howard compared print cloth prices in 1866 at 19 ½ cents per yard to those paid in 1887, 3 ¼ cents per yard. The high cost of scarce raw cotton explains much of the contrast.

23. Robert Williams McAdam, *Floating Palaces: New England to New York on the Old Fall River Line* (Providence: Mowbray, 1972), 24–25. After Fisk was murdered in 1871, Gould sold the Line to the Old Colony Railroad, Hurd, *Bristol County*, 336.

24. In calling himself Commodore, Fisk was tweaking the ego of Cornelius Vanderbilt, who, as the "Commodore," owned the New York Central Railroad, the chief competitor with the Fisk and Gould-owned Erie Railroad. See W. A. Swanberg, *Jim Fisk: The Career of an Improbable Rascal* (New York: Charles Scribner's Sons, 1959), 108–11, and Maury Klein, *The Life and Legend of Jay Gould* (Baltimore: Johns Hopkins Press: 1986), 80.

25. See the classic 1886 expose, Charles Francis Adams, Jr. and Henry Adams, *Chapters of Erie* (reprint, Ithaca: Cornell University Press, 1956).

26. Swanberg, *Jim Fisk,* 112–13.

27. Ibid., 116.

27. McAdam, *Floating Palaces,* 26.

28. *News,* June 7, 1869.

29. In his 1968 study, *New England Textiles in the Nineteenth Century,* McGouldrick called Fall River's growth "explosive," an "hyper-expansion," 203–4. For comparative figures for mills located "north of Boston," see table 4, below.

30. Earl, *Centennial History,* 68. In *Fall River Industry* (50–64) Smith argues that geographical and climate advantages permitted Fall River and New Bedford to gain advantage over the northern New England mills, calling the expansion a "natural" process. He overlooks, however, the factors of massive ambition and deliberate empire building. For the somewhat envious Providence perspective on Fall River's growth, see *ProvidenceJ,* Aug. 16, 1870.

31. Smith, *Fall River Industry,* 52–53.

32. *News,* May 10, 1871; July 25, 1872.

33. Stone, *Massachusetts Manufacturers,* 170.

34. Peck and Earl, *Fall River and Its Industries,* 69.

35. *ProvidenceJ,* Aug. 16, 1870.

36. Smith, *Fall River Industry,* 64–66. Apparently Smith included New Hampshire and Maine in mills north of Boston. MBLS, *Thirteenth Annual Report* (1882), 229–30.

37. Ibid.

38. Edward Chase Kirkland, *Dream and Thought in the Business Community, 1860–1900* (1956; reprint Chicago: Ivan R. Dee, 1990), 29–49, especially 39.

39. *FRHerald,* June 4, 1902.

40. *News,* Feb. 25, 1874.

41. The estate was described by a reporter for the *New York Sun,* article reprinted in the *FRHerald,* Sept. 2, 1879.

42. Kimmel, *Manhood in America,* 103–5.

43. *New York Sun,* Sept. 2, 1879.

44. In contrast, see Kirkland on the general avoidance of local and state politics by businessmen, *Dream and Thought,* 127–28.

45. Pro-mill Republicans easily controlled the local party, men uninterested in, or hostile to, the struggle of the Radical Republicans to influence state policy; see Montgomery, *Beyond Equality,* 265–77.

46. *News,* Oct. 27, 1868.

47. Ibid., Nov. 10, 1868.

48. Ibid., Nov. 2, 1868; Dec. 3, 1868.

49. Ibid., Dec. 5, 1868.

50. Paula Baker, *The Moral Frameworks of Public Life: Gender, Politics, and the State in Rural New York, 1870–1930* (New York: Oxford University Press, 1991), xv–xviii.

51. *News,* Dec. 5, 1868.

52. Hurd's *Bristol County* discusses the careers of Oliver Chace (378–79) and Crawford Lindsey (394–95).

53. Lynch, *Fall River Fire Department,* 9–10.

54. Ibid., 128–29.

55. Ibid., 75–76.

56. Lynch, *Fall River Fire Department*, 130–32, for part of the song, 132. The song's real title and the refrain, 'root Hog or Die," meant roughly go out, work hard, or suffer the consequences (*A Dictionary of Americanisms*, ed. Mitford M. Mathews [Chicago: University of Chicago Press, 1951], 1417).

57. Lynch, *Fall River Fire Department*, 142–44.

58. Ibid., 77–78.

59. *Phillips History*, v. 3, 111–14; *Fall River: City of Opportunity* (Fall River, 1910), for quote, 60.

60. *English Dialect Dictionary*, ed. Joseph R. Wright (London, 1903), v. 4, 188.

61. *News*, Mar. 1, 1873.

62. In the lists of the 1878 muster's participants (*FRHerald*, Sept. 19, 1878), Irish names appear in both companies targeted for the purge: the Annawam and the Niagara.

63. *FRHerald*, Sept. 20, 23, 1878.

64. *FRHerald*, Sept. 19, 1878.

65. *Phillips History* v. 3, 89–93.

66. *FRHerald*, June 15, 1887.

67. According to the Deed of Gift (John S. Brayton Papers), the committee initially included Mary B. Young's brother, John S. Brayton; attorney James M. Morton; Leontine Lincoln of the school committee; and the Brayton siblings, Hezekiah and Sarah. *Phillips History*, v. 2, 81–84. The splendid building is now used as a state courthouse.

68. *News*, April 24, 1851; May 2, 1861.

69. *Phillips History*, v. 3, 67; v. 2, 90–92.

70. Ibid., v. 3, 65–67.

71. Ibid., v. 3, 70–80. In 1914, the city shouldered the burden of oiling the unpaved streets. Not until the automobile became popular in the 1920s did the city provide paved roads. Cinders for sidewalks were used until 1925, when the depressed state of the textile industry dried up the source.

72. Hurd, *Bristol County*, 325.

73. *Phillips History* v. 3, 80. Kerosene lamps remained on the city's streets until 1931.

74. Board of Trade, *New Bedford, Massachusetts* (1889), 78, 302; Leonard Bolles Ellis, *History of New Bedford, 1602–1892* (1892), 721–22; Zephaniah W. Pease, *History of New Bedford* (New York: Lewis Historical Publishing Co., 1918) v. 1, 177, 187, 191, 203, 206, 308; Marsha McCabe and Joseph D. Thomas, *Not Just Anywhere* (New Bedford, Mass.: Spinner Publications, 1995), see pictures on 12, 63, 65, 67–68 for historic street restorations.

75. *Phillips History*, v. 3, 80–86, and Theodore Steinberg, *Nature Incorporated: Industrialization and the Waters of New England* (Amherst: University of Massachusetts Press, 1994).

76. The *News* became the principle outlet for these concerns. Doubtless the Democratic *Border City Herald* (later the *Fall River Herald*) was another source of complaints, but its issues between 1872 and 1876 have been lost. Other centers of industrial growth in Massachusetts also had middle-class jitters about explosive growth; see Blewett, *Men, Women, and Work*, chapter 6.

77. *News,* April 8, 1872.

78. Ibid.

79. Ibid., July 8, 1872.

80. Ibid., July 18, 1872; July 7, 1873.

81. Ibid., July 8, 1872.

82. Ibid., Feb. 10, 1873.

83. Ibid., Feb. 12, 1873. It is possible that the lost issues of the *Border City Herald* picked up the story. At the time, everyone in the city probably guessed who "Tall Oaks" was.

84. *News,* Oct. 21, 1873.

85. Ibid., Nov. 19, 28, Oct. 25, 1873.

86. *FRHerald,* April 12, 1878.

87. This was not revealed until November 1878, when the clerk was running for alderman, and was defeated in the municipal elections (*FRHerald,* Nov. 23, 25, 1878; Dec. 2, 4, 1878).

88. *FRHerald,* April 15, 1878.

89. Ibid., Sept. 13, 1878.

90. The editor was musing over the new term "kleptomania" as a diagnosis for stealing by upper class females, *FRHerald,* Oct. 31, 1878. On kleptomania as a cultural construct, see Elaine S. Abelson, *When Ladies Go A-Thieving: Middle-Class Shoplifters in the Victorian Department Store* (New York: Oxford University Press, 1989).

91. *FRHerald,* June 7, 1878.

92. In his confession, *BHerald,* Oct. 15, 1878, Hathaway exposed Dr. Durfee's and Holder B. Durfee's knowledge of Chace's activities.

93. *FRHerald,* June 17, 1878.

94. Editorial, *FRHerald,* April 22, 1878.

95. *NYHerald,* April 23, 1878.

96. *BHerald,* Oct. 18, 1878.

97. *Boston Advertiser,* May 9, 1878.

98. This document is located in the Papers of John S. Brayton.

99. *FRHerald,* Sept. 11, 1878.

100. *FRHerald,* Jan. 18, 1884.

101. Obituary, *FRHerald,* June 4, 1905.

102. *BHerald,* Oct. 15, 1878.

103. Ibid., Oct. 19, 1878.

104. Nathan Durfee's "notorious" activities as treasurer of the Massasoit Steam mills had made Boston banks suspicious of all Fall River credit. His son, Holder Borden Durfee, replaced him in December 1874 (Lamb, chap. 13, 26).

105. *FRHerald,* July 28, 1879 also printed the views of the *New York Sun, BHerald,* and the *News.*

106. "Justice," *FRHerald,* July 29, 1879.

107. Ibid., Aug. 1, 1879.

108. Ibid., Aug. 14, 15, 16, 18, 20, 21, 1879.

109. Ibid., Aug. 16, 20, 1879.

110. Another late nineteenth-century entrepreneur, Andrew Carnegie, refused to allow sentiment, loyalty, long-time personal friendship, or even gratitude

to persuade him to endorse the notes of his mentor Thomas Scott of the Pennsylvania Railroad (Harold Livesay, *Andrew Carnegie and the Rise of Big Business* [New York: Harper Collins Publishers, 1975] 95).

111. For reactions to the losses, see *FRHerald*, Aug. 21, 23, 25, 26, 27, 28, 1879. George H. Eddy, son of the respected banker Jesse Eddy and treasurer of the Flint mills, resigned over losses from futures' speculation, not for himself but on behalf of the mill, that cost $15,000. John D. Flint, the President, became treasurer (*FRHerald*, Aug. 22, 30, 1879).

112. *Taunton Gazette* in the *FRHerald*, Sept. 9, 1879.

113. *FRHerald*, Sept. 6, 1879.

114. Ibid., Oct. 15, 1879.

115. *NYTimes* in *FRHerald*, Sept. 5, 1879.

116. *BGlobe* in *FRHerald*, Sept. 4, 1879.

117. *BGlobe* in *FRHerald*, Oct. 6, 8, 1879.

118. *ProvidenceSt* in *FRHerald*, Aug. 29, 1879.

119. *English Dialect Dictionary*, v. 4 (London, 1903), 115, 135.

6. They Have Brought Their Horns With Them

1. A lapstick was used to carry a compressed sheet of cotton, called a lap, from the picking operation to the carding room. Lasalle would have easily found one lying around. My thanks to Larry Gross, former machinery curator at the Museum of American Textile History. This episode is a reconstruction of the events based on testimony given at the coroner's inquest, *News*, November 24, 1874.

2. Ibid., Nov. 27, 1874.

3. Ibid., Nov. 28, 1874.

4. "Lowell Loom," *American Workman*, June 26, 1869.

5. Oliver, *Report* (1868), 80.

6. Ibid., 69.

7. Ibid., 80–82.

8. Anonymous, "Needle and Garden," *Atlantic Monthly* 15 (May 1865), 613–21.

9. Neville Kirk, *Labour and Society in Britain and the USA* (Aldershot, Scolar Press, 1994), 2–3. For a critique of Kirk, see Philip Scranton, *American Historical Review* (Feb. 1996): 153–4.

10. See Kirk's second volume, *Challenge and Accommodation, 1850–1939.*

11. Berthoff, *British Immigrants;* Clifton K. Yearley Jr., *Britons in American Labor: A History of the Influence of United Kingdom Immigrants on American Labor, 1820–1914* (Baltimore: Johns Hopkins University Press, 1957). Yearley cites as evidence of English influence A. J. Mundella's ideas on arbitration and George Holyoake's on cooperatives. He also asserts but did not demonstrate how English law helped shape the Massachusetts ten-hour law. Like Berthoff, Yearley studied no one industry or center of production in depth. Kirk does not cite Cynthia Shelton's *The Mills of Manayunk,* an important 1986 work that specifically explores the impact of British immigration on the textile industry of early nineteenth-century Philadelphia. Nor does he refer to Richard Stott's comparison of the attitudes of British and American workers in New York City.

12. Yearley, *Britons,* 19, 90–91, 304–10.

13. Cohen, *American Management,* John Cumbler, *Working-Class Community in Industrial America. Work, Leisure, and Struggle in Two Industrial Cities, 1880–1930* (Westport; Conn.: Greenwood Press, 1979).

14. Yearley, *Britons,* 308–10.

15. Kirk, *Labour and Society,* v. 1, 4.

16. *News,* Oct. 17, 1866.

17. Ibid., Jan. 1, 1868.

18. Ibid., Feb. 1, 1868.

19. My argument emphasizes the instrumentality of deference, as does Kirk's critique of Patrick Joyce's *Work, Politics, and Society* in the *Bulletin of the Society for the Study of Labour History* 42 (Spring 1981): 41–43.

20. The strike was covered by the *News* from Mar. 1–Mar. 16, 1868.

21. *London Times,* May 5, 1869 as quoted in *ProvidenceJ,* May 14, 1869, and MBLS, *Eleventh Annual Report* (1879), 60.

22. On the 1870 strike, see MBLS, *First Annual Report* (1871), 47–93; *News,* July 21–September 16, 1870; *Boston Herald* [*BHerald*], Aug. 26–Aug. 30, 1870. Quote, *First Annual Report,* 78; *News,* July 21, 1870.

23. MBLS, *First Annual Report* (1871), 51, 55.

24. MBLS, *First Annual Report* (1871), 50. Yearley turned Sanderson into a naive innocent in *Britons,* 170. In contrast, Robert Howard, an 1873 emigrant, provided a report of the 1870 strike based on hearsay that, in his opinion, "Nearly caused a riot," and commended the strikers when "reason triumphed over passion," in "Progress in the Textile Trades," 219.

25. How many spinners' wives might have been weavers or carders is impossible to know; federal population census manuscripts in 1870 and 1880 identify all textile operatives simply as "works in a cotton mill," and the 1875 state census manuscripts are lost.

26. MBLS, *First Annual Report* (1871), 476–81.

27. MBLS, *First Annual Report* (1871), 55.

28. *News,* Aug. 8, 18, 20, 1870.

29. Lawlor, *Life and Struggles,* 24, 29–31.

30. MBLS, *First Annual Report* (1871), 482; Lillian Chace Wyman, "Studies of Factory Life: Black-Listing at Fall River," *Atlantic Monthly* (November 1888), 611, *News,* July 29, 1870, (on departing mill spinners) Aug. 8, 1870, MBLS, *Thirteenth Annual Report* (1882), 348–54.

31. This ideological argument was made in various articles in the *News* from July 23 to Aug. 20, 1870.

32. MBLS, *First Annual Report* (1871), 49.

33. MBLS, *First Annual Report* (1871), 52.

34. Ibid., 52–53. In the report Oliver footnoted Brayton's use of the fire alarm as "very questionable." For an overview of the emotional landscape of the New England textile industry with a focus on Fall River, see "Passionate Voices and Cool Calculations: The Emotional Landscape of the Nineteenth-Century New England Textile Industry," in *An Emotional History of the United States,* ed. Peter N. Stearns and Jan Lewis, (New York: New York University Press, 1998), 109–125.

35. *ProvidenceJ,* Sept. 22, 1870.

36. *News,* Sept. 9, 1870; MBLS, *First Annual Report* (1871), 90.

37. "A Workingman," *History of the Fall River Strike, Being a Full and Complete Account of the Labor Troubles from 1873 to April 5, 1875*, (Fall River, 1875), 6.

38. Kirby Miller's "Class, Culture, and Immigrant Group Identity in the United States. The Case of Irish-American Ethnicity," in *Immigration Reconsidered. History, Sociology, and Politics*, ed. Virginia Yans-McLaughlin (Oxford: Oxford University Press, 1990), 96–129, treats most nineteenth-century Irish immigrants as politically passive peasants. Other writers, however, have written compellingly about Irish immigrant radicals. See David Brundage, "Irish Land and American Workers' Class and Ethnicity in Denver, Colorado," in *"Struggle A Hard Battle." Essays on Working-Class Immigrants*, ed. Dirk Hoerder (DeKalb: Northern Illinois University Press, 1996), 62–63; Eric Foner, "Class, Ethnicity, and Radicalism in the Gilded Age. The Land League and Irish-America," *Marxist Perspectives* 1 (Summer 1978) 6–55; and Cumbler, *Working-Class Community*, 108–9. For an effort to understand the conflicting emotions of immigrants in nineteenth-century America over pride, loyalty, guilt, shame, and resistance, see Hasia R. Diner, "Ethnicity and Emotions in America: Dimensions of the Unexplored," in Stearns and Lewis, *Emotional History*, 197–217.

39. *News*, Mar. 6, 1875.

40. This conclusion, based on data from Ward 1, Fall River, 1870, suggests that like the Sicilian migrants studied by Donna Gabbaccia (*Migrants and Militants: Rural Sicilians Become American Workers* [(New Brunswick: Rutgers University Press, 1988)] 169–71) Lancashire migrants (who were also often deeply divided) were driven by occupational needs rather than kinship ties. See Michael Anderson, *Family Structure in Nineteenth Century Lancashire* (Cambridge: Cambridge University Press, 1971) for a description of these kinship networks. By 1879, however, when striking mule spinners' relatives were fired by the mills to cut off any support for the strikers, the various aunts, uncles, nieces and nephews who were affected probably represented kinship networks that had developed through marriage in America rather than by immigration. Anthony Coelho, "A Row of Nationalities: The Irish, English, and French Canadians of Fall River, Massachusetts, 1850–1890," (Ph.D. diss., Brown University, 1980) examines the federal population census of 1850, 1860, and 1870 and a sample of the 1880 census, to record all immigrant families in Fall River, 1–8. He concludes (272–73) that in contrast to kin networks in Lancashire, English immigrants in Fall River lived in nuclear families in larger numbers than in Paterson, New Jersey, or Cohoes, New York. Coelho does not include as a category Irish-born immigrants who might have passed through Lancashire.

41. See Kirk, *The Growth of Working Class Reformism*.

42. *Providence Sun, [ProvidenceS]* Feb. 27, 1875; *BHerald*, Feb. 24, 1875.

43. *LawJCit*, Feb. 21, 28, 1874.

44. Ibid., Nov. 21, 1874.

45. *LawJCit*, Feb. 14, Aug. 15, 22, 1874; *ProvidenceS*, Mar. 27, 1875; Lawlor, *The Life and Struggles of an Irish Boy in America*, 26. Also see William Lazonick, "Competition, Specialization, and Industrial Decline," *Journal of Economic History* 41 (March 1981) 31–38.

46. Interview with Jennings, *News*, Oct. 22, 1875.

47. *NYHerald*, Sept. 26, 1875.

48. MBLS, *Second Annual Report* (1871), 49, 469–70, 476–86; MBLS, *Sixth An-*

nual Report (1875), 284–90, News, Mar. 6, 1875; MBLS, Thirteenth Annual Report (1882), 209, 219, 254–60.

49. For recent work on the family wage, see Benenson, "The 'Family Wage,' " and Seccombe, "Patriarchy Stabilized: The Construction of the Male Breadwinner Norm in Nineteenth-Century Britain." For a provocative discussion of the literature on middle-class consumption and gender politics, see Mary Louise Roberts, "Gender, Consumption, and Commodity Culture: Review Essay," American Historical Review, 103 (June 1998): 817–44.

50. New York Times [NYTimes], Jan. 23, Mar. 15, 1875. See Blewett, Men, Women, and Work, 148, on the rejection of brogans.

51. News, Dec. 31, 1874, LawJCit, Jan. 2, 1875.

52. News, Jan. 4, 7, 11, 1875. On January 7, the editor of the News quoted Sevey's Labor Journal as against a strike. At the January 10 meeting, a Mr. L'Amour translated for the French weavers.

53. BGlobe, Feb. 23, 1875.

54. ProvidenceS, Jan. 30, 1875.

55. In 1875 there were approximately 8,000 weavers, 1,500 carders, and 2,000 mule spinners in the Fall River workforce or 11,500 of a total workforce of 14,216. Women represented about one-third of the 3,215 striking weavers, and about half of the weaving workforce (Fall River Strike, 12).

56. News, Jan. 14, 1875.

57. News, Jan. 18, 1875. Also see letter from Thomas Stephenson, BGlobe, Feb. 22, 1875, and letter from "Justice," BGlobe, Feb. 23, 1875, defending the women's actions and their right to do what they had done.

58. News, Jan. 18, 1875.

59. Ibid., Mar. 17, 1875.

60. BGlobe, Jan. 18, 1875.

61. News, Jan. 25, 1875.

62. Ibid., Jan. 25, 28, 1875.

63. LawJCit, Jan. 2, 1875. The strike was covered by the LawJCit between Jan. 16, and Mar. 20, 1875.

64. Ibid., Feb. 20, 1875.

65. Ibid., Mar. 13, 1875.

66. Ibid., April 16, 1875.

67. MBLS, Thirteenth Annual Report (1882), 204–5. These figures are from 1878. The Massachusetts Population Census for 1875 lists only figures for residents, not for the workforce in the textile mills, but does have comparative data for percentages of foreign-born workers in leading manufacturing towns (see tables 6 and 7). Fall River had the highest percent of foreign-born workers in the state, with Holyoke as the next highest with 51.97 percent. Lowell is listed with 35.78 percent foreign-born, Lawrence with 44.52 percent; and New Bedford with 22.97 percent (Massachusetts State Census, 1875 [Boston, 1877], 49).

68. Massachusetts State Census, 1875, v. 3, 422. Fall River figures were 11.64 percent; Lowell, 4.37 percent; Lawrence, 3.28 percent (see table 7).

69. LawJCit, Mar. 13, 1875.

70. Lowell Courier, April 21, 26, 1875. The anti-strike Courier insisted that women spinners from Salem were already at work on small mules at the Boott and the Merrimack mills, supporting a claim the Fall River mills had made in 1870.

71. Ibid., April 26, 1875.

72. *BHerald*, Feb. 1, April 25, 1875; *News*, Feb. 15, 22, Mar. 1, 17, April 5, 1875. As the technology quickly developed, ring spinning in Fall River replaced some mule spinning operations in coarse cotton warp by 1879.

73. Lincoln, *The Factory*, 95. Dorothy Thompson, *The Chartists*, 120-51.

74. *News*, Feb. 15, 1875. Mrs. Ashworth's privations during the strike suggested that she may have been a widow or female head of a family.

75. The reference to "help" suggests that the Davol weaver was native-born. Ibid., Feb. 15, 1875.

76. Ibid., Feb. 6, 1875.

77. H. Beaugrand enthusiastically estimated four thousand French Canadians in the 1874 textile workforce from a total of six thousand residents based on investigations of the city directory in "Rapport sur la population Canadienne Francaise de Fall River Mass. (1874), 2-3. Beaugrand also stated that some were overseers in the mills, a dubious claim. French Canadian immigrants represented less than 20 percent of the workforce, according to 1878 figures, or about two thousand in 1875. The classic study of this period is Ralph Vicero, "Immigration of French Canadians to New England, 1840-1900: A Geographical Analysis," (Ph.D. thesis, University of Wisconsin, 1968). Vicero's study concentrates on geographical mobility and the location of settlement. Neither Vicero nor Yves Roby's *Les Franco-Américains de la Nouvelle-Angleterre* (Sillery, Quebec: Septentrion, 1990) examines the local *or* labor press, concentrating solely on Franco-American newspapers in New England, but Roby ignores Beaugrand's *L'Echo du Canada* in Fall River.

78. *ProvidenceS*, Mar. 6, 1875. This ability to organize support probably had roots in earlier community associations or in active participation in parish affairs in Quebec. On militancy among the cotton "girls" of Quebec, mostly weavers, see Jacques Ferland, "'In Search of the 'Unbound Promethia': A Comparative View of Women's Activism in Two Quebec Industries, 1869-1900," *Labour/Le Travail* 24 (Spring 1989): 11-44.

79. Richard Sorrell, "The *survivance* of French Canadians in New England (1865-1930): History, Geography and Demography as Destiny," *Ethnic and Racial Studies* 4 (Jan. 1981) 91-109; quotation, 99. Sorrell's primary research was conducted in Woonsocket, Rhode Island.

80. Ibid., 103-4. Much of the writing on promotion of *la survivance* has focused on community leaders, except for census probes of family structure in the research of Frances Early and the wider interests of Gerald J. Brault, *The French-Canadian Heritage in New England* (Hanover: University Press of New England, 1986), 7-8, 65-67. The work of promoting *survivance* continued, Sorrell argues, with the American-born second generation of Francos, 97. Jacques Ducharme's impressionistic *The Shadows of the Trees: The Story of French-Canadians in New England* (New York: Harper and Brothers, 1943) suggests that *la survivance* reflected the commitment of the French clergy to establish and maintain parish schools, 92-3. Yves Roby examines the 1860-1900 period but seems to dismiss the ideology of *la survivance* as old-fashioned, arguing for a new social history approach that combines an interconnected analysis of the political, economic, social and religious in a "synthese les grandes tendances, les lignes maitresses . . . ." "Presentation," in *Les Franco-Américains*, 7-9. His acceptance of working-class life in chapter 2 as centered around family, community, and church nonetheless means *survivance*. See

also Gary Gerstle, *Working-Class Americanism: The Politics of Labor in a Textile City, 1914–1960* (Cambridge: Cambridge University Press, 1989), 19–31; and Ronald A. Petrin, *French Canadians in Massachusetts Politics, 1885–1915: Ethnicity and Political Pragmatism* (London: Associated University Presses, 1990), chapter 2. For critiques of the paradigm, see Andre E. LeBlanc, "French Canada's Diaspora and Labour History," *Labour/Le Travail* 20 (Fall 1987): 213–20. LeBlanc endorses the work of Philip Silvia, John Cumbler, Tamara Hareven, and Daniel Walkowitz. For an attempt to analyze *la survivance* as an historical construction, see Darren Phanuef, "Reconsidering *La Survivance:* Ethnic Tensions and the Politics of Class Among Northern New York's French Canadians, 1860–1888," unpublished paper, cited with permission of the author. For an analysis of *la survivance* as a self-interested response of Franco-American small entrepreneurs or "les elites francophones," see Pierre Antcil, "Brokers of Ethnic Identity: The Franco-American Petty Bourgeoisie of Woonsocket, Rhode Island (1865–1945)," *Quebec Studies* 12 (1991): 33–48. My thanks to Paul Dauphinais of the Canadian–American Center, University of Maine, Orono.

81. See Claire Quintal, introduction to *The Little Canadas of New England,* ed. Claire Quintal (Worcester: French Institute/Assumption College, 1983), v–x; and Philip T. Silvia Jr., "Neighbors From the North: French-Canadian Immigrants vs. Trade Unionism in Fall River, Massachusetts," 44–65.

82. Petrin (*French Canadians in Massachusetts Politics*) also made this point in his ethnocultural analysis of political participation of *Canadiens* in Massachusetts politics, 1895–1915, based on patterns of voting behavior in selected cities and towns.

83. On French Canadian workingwomen in shoe factories in eastern Massachusetts and their role in late nineteenth-century labor protest, see Blewett, *Men, Women, and Work,* 271, 274, 282, 292, 295–96.

84. Although defending immigrant textile workers against descriptions as "marionettes" or "d'eternelles victimes," Roby in *Les Franco-Américains* suggests, 9, 81–89, that the family and church together provided collective resistance to industrial mistreatment, based primarily on Tamara Hareven's analysis of early twentieth-century Manchester, New Hampshire in *Family Time and Industrial Time: The Relationship between the Family and Work in a New England Industrial Community* (Cambridge: Cambridge University Press, 1982). In the face of an organizing drive by AFL-linked textile unions after 1900 (see below, chapter 10), paternalism in Manchester mills may have been a wise defense. For a study of the depressed conditions of the Montreal economy and the impact on the working class during this period, see Bettina Bradbury, *Working Families: Age, Gender and Daily Survival in Industrializing Montreal* (Toronto: McClelland & Stewart: 1993). Although a portion of the two working-class wards in Montreal that Bradbury studied probably consisted of rural migrants, she does not use the term *survivance* and is more interested in the urban family as an intersecting ground of class and gender relations.

85. Sorrell, "The *survivance* of French Canadians," 99–100. Joy Parr finds serious resistance to gender analysis among Canadian historians, "Gender History and Historical Practice," *The Canadian Historical Review* 76 (Sept., 1995): 354–76, but calls for the acknowledgment of diversity and instability in gender meanings.

86. Petrin, *French Canadians in Massachusetts Politics,* 16–19. Although relying

on Sorrell's interpretation of *la survivance,* Petrin regards the initial period of "retreat," as "an elusive quest" (18). His argument focuses on the differences among French Canadian involvement in partisan politics in the industrial cities of Fall River, Worcester, and Holyoke and also a comparison of the towns of Spencer and Southbridge (see chapters 5 and 6). Conflicts in Fall River seemed uniquely embittered, but Petrin relies heavily on Silvia's treatment of the tensions between the Irish mule spinners and the Quebec immigrants over class issues and religion. Although the majority of French Canadian immigrants worked as weavers and carders, the labor politics of these groups is not examined. Interested in voting patterns, Petrin ignores gender analysis and focuses on male voters, ascribing differences among Little Canadas in Massachusetts to varying local economic structure.

87. For one example, Lucie Cordeau, a Lowell textile worker born in Quebec, remembered her deeply religious mother dying of a "cold" at forty-nine after seventeen pregnancies (Blewett, *The Last Generation,* 73–75). The phrase, "revenge of the cradle," is used by Sorell in "The *Survivance* of French Canadians," 100.

88. *ProvidenceS,* Mar. 6, 1875; *News,* Mar. 1, May 12, 1875; *LaborJ,* reprinted in the *News,* May 1, 1875.

89. Matthew Roth, *Connecticut: An Inventory of Historic Engineering and Industrial Sites* (Society for Industrial Archeology, 1981), 194; "The Strike At Taftville," State of Connecticut, Bureau of Labor Statistics, *Second Annual Report,* May 1875, (Hartford 1875), 127–131. The bureau was then abolished in 1875.

90. *NBSt,* June 7, 1875; *Springfield Republican,* May 26, 1875; *News,* May 12, 1875; Also see Rene L. Dugas Sr., *The French-Canadians in New England, 1871–1930: Taftville, Ct. (The Early Years)* (privately published, 1995), 18–19, 37–59, 179, 200. Led by the local Knights of Labor in the 1880s, strikers, using the word "mobstick" and painting the houses of strikebreakers with bluing, indicated some continued labor protest.

91. *Springfield Republican,* Mar. 23, 30, April 3, 11, 1875.

92. Philip Silvia, "Neighbors from the North," 48, 44–49. Silvia's views reflect those of Robert Howard.

93. *L'Echo,* Mar. 28, April 18, 25, 1874; May 16, 1874; Mar. 27, 1875.

94. He criticized these publications in *L'Echo,* April 10, 1875.

95. Beaugraud defended Quebec culture, history, and traditions of local self-government in "The Attitude of the French Canadians," *Forum* 7 (July 1899) 521–30.

96. "Heart of Iron," *L'Echo,* May 16, 1874, trans. Jeffrey Northrup.

97. Beaugrand estimated that only fifty French Canadians had the vote in a resident population of six thousand (*L'Echo,* May 2, 30, 1874). While in Canada, Beaugrand had advocated the union of Quebec and the United States. In later years he wrote many novels and stories about Canada, the most politically important a 1878 novel, partly set in Fall River, *Jeanne, la fileuse,* the first Franco-American novel. Brault (*French-Canadian Heritage,* 56–58) regards it as having "exceptional" documentary value. My thanks to Pamela Richardson for her translation. On Beaugrand, see André Sénécal, "The Economic and Political Ideas of Honoré Beaugrand in *Jeanne la Fileuse,*" *Quebec Studies* 1 (Spring 1983): 200–207.

98. On French Canadians in Albion and Manville, Rhode Island, beginning in 1880, see Peter L. Moreau, "The Preservation of Ethnic Identity in the Franco-American Villages of Lincoln, Rhode Island," in Quintal, *Little Canadas,* 84–101.

99. *LaborSt,* Oct. 15, 1881. In *Franco-Américains,* Roby asks the question: were "Des ouvriers satisfaits?", 81. Stressing the unfamiliarity of the first poverty-stricken generation of Quebec immigrants with urban industrial life, Roby argues that French Canadian textile workers avoided strikes and sought accommodation with mill management using "d'une culture ouvriere", 85–89. Even the second and third generations moved "tres lentement" toward labor activism, 89. Roby relies on evidence from late nineteenth-century Cohoes, New York, and Worcester, Massachusetts (not a large center of textile production), on early twentieth-century Manchester, and (although Beaugrand's *L'Echo du Canada* is not included) on Silvia's study centered on Fall River mule spinners and their relations with French Canadian immigrants.

100. For a discussion of French Canadian immigrants as strikebreakers in 1879 and an attempt by the state to define them as the "Chinese of the Eastern States," see chapter 8. As a testimony to the persistence of this cultural and political paradigm, see Anita Rafael, *La Survivance: A Companion to the Exhibit at the Museum of Work & Culture, Woonsocket, Rhode Island* (Providence: Rhode Island Historical Society, 1997).

101. *News,* Feb. 15, 1875.

102. Ibid., Feb. 18, 1875.

103. Ibid.

104. Ibid., Feb. 19, 1875.

105. *BGlobe,* Feb. 22, 1875.

106. Ibid. "Welter" is defined in the *Oxford English Dictionary.* v. 12, 311, as "a state of confusion, upheaval or turmoil," a usage that dates from around 1870.

107. *News,* Mar. 3, 1875.

108. Ibid., Feb. 22, 1875.

109. Ibid., March 1, 1875.

110. Ibid., Feb. 9, 10, 15, 1875.

111. Ibid., Feb. 23, 24, 1875; Mar. 6, 1875.

112. Ibid., Mar. 13, 1875.

113. Ibid.

114. MBLS, *Eleventh Annual Report* (1880), p. 38.

115. *News,* April 16, 1875.

116. *News,* April 5, 1875. Also see *ProvidenceS,* Aug. 21, 1875.

117. *LawJCit,* May 8, 15, 29, June 19, 1875.

118. *News,* May 22, 1875.

119. Ibid.

120. *News,* Feb. 22, Mar. 1, 1875.

121. Ibid., July 23–Aug. 20, 1870.

122. Ibid., Feb. 19, 1875; MBLS, *Thirteenth Annual Report* (1882), 300.

123. *NYHerald,* Oct. 19, 1875. For a comparison between attitudes of English and American workers in nineteenth-century New York City, see Richard Stott, "British Immigrants and the American 'Work Ethnic' in the Mid-Nineteenth Century," *Labor History* 26 (1985) 86–102.

124. Unfortunately, impressionistic accounts from newspapers cannot be verified in the absence of the manuscripts of the 1875 Massachusetts population census. The published report gives information on marital status of textile operatives in 1875 but no information on occupation or nationality linked with marital status.

125. *NYHerald,* Oct. 13, 1875; MBLS (1882), 338, 224.

126. See Michael E. Rose, "Rochdale Man and the Stalybridge Riot: The Relief and Control of the Unemployed during the Lancashire Cotton Famine," in *Social Control in Nineteenth Century Britain,* ed. A. P. Donajgradzki (Totowa, NJ: Rowman and Littlefield, 1977), 185–206.

127. In Edwin Waugh, *Home-Life of the Lancashire Factory Folk During the Cotton Famine* (Manchester, 1867), 269–71. Shurat was the often dirty, rotten, short-staple Indian cotton that made the weaver's work so exhausting and low paid. There were many other similar songs.

128. The publication contains a short history of events, Boston newspapers' reaction, all favorable, and an accounting of all relief money received.

129. *Fall River Strike,* 7. No records of the Fall River Board of Trade have survived.

130. Ibid., 8, 18–19.

131. The weavers' history ignored both Sevey's report in the *News* and Stephenson's complaints to the *BGlobe.*

132. *Fall River Strike,* 31–33.

133. *ProvidenceS,* Jan. 30, 1875.

134. *Fall River Strike,* 26.

135. Ibid., 26, 29, 30.

136. Ibid., 39–40.

137. *ProvidenceS,* Aug. 21, 1875. Because the *LawJCit* did not cover these events, this Democratic newspaper in Providence is the key source, in addition to the *News,* of information on Fall River, Rhode Island, and eastern Connecticut activities. The *Border City Herald* and the *Labor Journal* for 1875 have been lost, although some articles were quoted or reprinted in the available papers.

138. *Commercial Bulletin,* Aug. 28, 1875.

139. *ProvidenceS,* Aug. 7, 1875. A reporter interviewed many Fall River agents and treasurers on their attitudes toward the operatives.

140. *Commercial Bulletin,* Aug. 28, 1875. See also Oct. 2, 1875.

141. *News,* July 19–July 30, 1875; *LawJCit,* July 24, 1875.

142. Edward P. Thompson, "The Moral Economy of the English Crowd in the Eighteenth Century," *Past and Present,* no. 50 (Feb. 1971). 76–136. I agree with William Reddy that ". . . not learning the rules of the game . . . refusing to accept them [is] the true meaning of Thompson's notion of a 'moral economy.' " "The Textile Trade and the Language of the Crowd at Rouen, 1752–1871," *Past and Present,* no. 74 (Feb. 1977), 88.

143. Smith, who Morgan replaced, resigned over criticism of his handling of the union's treasury (*News,* Aug. 10, 1875).

144. *ProvidenceS,* June 12, Aug. 28, 1875.

145. *LawJCit,* July 24, Aug. 21, Bower did not comment on the Fall River vacation or lockout until late September.

146. *News,* Aug. 2, 1875. The editor of the *ProvidenceS* on Aug. 7, 1875, suggested that the weavers were applying Luddite lessons in an attempt to limit output.

147. "Culturally Speaking: Finding a Commons Between Post-Structuralism and the Thompson Perspective," *Social History* 21 (May 1996) 204–6.

148. "Letter from Tomahawk," *LaborSt,* Oct. 9, 1880; *ProvidenceS,* Aug. 14, 1875.

149. *ProvidenceS,* Aug. 14, 21, 1875; *Commercial Bulletin,* Aug. 28, 1875.

150. See Carl Gersuny, "A Unionless General Strike": The Rhode Island Ten-Hour Movement of 1873," *Rhode Island History* 54 (Feb. 1996): 21–32.

151. *ProvidenceS,* Aug. 21, 1875.

152. Ibid., Aug. 21, 1875. The vice presidents included men from the towns or villages of Woonsocket, Lonsdale, Warren, Providence, Pawtucket, River Point, Olneyville, Rhode Island, and from Taftville, Norwich, Greenville, and Wauregan, Connecticut.

153. Ibid., Aug. 7, 1875.

154. *News,* Aug. 14, 1875. *L'Echo* (Aug. 21, 1875), reported the final tally at 1,287 to return and 2,520 to stay out.

155. *L'Echo,* May 29, June 5, 12, 19, July 10, 1875.

156. The last issue was a combined *Ouvrier Canadien* and *L'Echo du Canada.* Benoit's negative views on the vacation were expressed weekly throughout August, September, and as the beginning of October, 1875. In the 1880s Beaugrand served two terms as the mayor of Montreal.

157. *News,* Sept. 3, 1875.

158. Mrs. Ashworth and Cassie O'Neill continued to take a leading part in the debates, *Ibid.,* Sept. 13, 16, 25, 1875.

159. *NYHerald,* Sept. 29, 1875; *News,* Oct. 22, 1875.

160. *Commercial Bulletin,* Oct. 2, 1875.

161. Ibid.

162. *NYHerald,* Sept. 26, 27, 1875. The first speaker, fifty-year-old William Stamson, had emigrated from Preston, Lancashire, in 1857. He had two children working in the mills.

163. *Commercial Bulletin,* Oct. 2, 1875.

164. On the importance of memories about the triumph of the customary over the market, see Andrew Charlesworth and Adrian J. Randall, "Morals, Markets and the English Crowd in 1766," *Past and Present,* no. 114 (1987) 200–213.

165. *NYHerald,* Sept. 25, 27, 1875.

166. *News,* Sept. 28, 1875, *NYHerald,* Sept. 28, 1875. Also see John Bohstedt, *Riots and Community Politics in England and Wales, 1790–1810* (Cambridge: Harvard University Press, 1983), 7.

167. *News,* Sept. 25, 27, 29, Oct. 2, 1875; *NYTimes,* Sept. 28, 29, 1875; *NYHerald,* Sept. 25, 26, 27, 28, 29, 1875; *ProvidenceJ,* Sept. 29, 1875.

168. For the distinctive role of British women as instigators of food riots, see Malcolm I. Thomis and Jennifer Grimmet, *Women in Protest, 1800–1850* (New York: St. Martin's Press, 1982), chapter 2. For a contrary view of the food riot as a preindustrial, mixed-sex event, see John Bohstedt, "Gender, Household and Community Politics: Women in English Riots, 1790–1810," *Past and Present,* no. 120 (August 1988): 88–122. For a critical review by E. P. Thompson of the concept of moral economy as used by historians, see *Customs In Common,* 259–351. I agree with Bohstedt's call for an examination of the ways food riots acted as responses to changing economic and political contexts, "The Moral Economy and the Discipline of Historical Context," *Journal of Social History* 26 (Winter 1992): 265–84.

169. *ProvidenceJ,* Sept. 29, 1875; *Commercial Bulletin,* Oct. 2, 1875; *BGlobe,* Oct. 4, 1875.

170. *Commercial Bulletin,* Oct. 2, 1875; *NYHerald,* Sept. 28, 1875; *News,* Sept.

27, 1875; *L'Echo and Ouvrier,* Oct. 2, 1875. For another translation from the French, see Sylvia Lintner, "A Social History of Fall River, 1859–1879," (Ph.D. dissertation, Radcliffe College, 1945).

171. On the persistent stigma of working-class violence, see Eugene Leach, "Chaining the Tiger. The Mob Stigma and the Working Class, 1863–1894," *Labor History* 35 (1994): 187–215.

172. These reports, which came from police, reporters, and members of militia units appeared in *News,* Sept. 29, 1875; *NYTimes* Sept. 29, 1875; *BGlobe,* Sept. 29, 1875.

173. Morgan was attacked in the *News* on Sept. 11 and Sept. 16, 1875. The *ProvidenceS,* Sept. 18, 1875, printed a defense of Morgan.

174. MBLS, *Thirteenth Annual Report* (1882), 341. In the mid-nineteenth century, Irish immigrants also faced denigration as "savages," both in America and in Lancashire; see Miller, "Class, Culture, and Immigrant Group Identity," 108–9 and Kirk, *Working Class Reformism,* chapter 7.

175. *News,* Aug. 17, 1875. The anti-union contracts were similar to those signed after the 1870 strike but included additional crippling stipulations.

176. Philip Foner in *Women and the American Labor Movement* I (New York: Free Press, 1979), 171, claims that "for many years thereafter, September 27 [the day of the bread riot] was marked in Fall River by mass meetings . . . ," events that I have been unable to verify. Foner may have come across the resolution backed by New York workingmen who advised Fall River workers to hold "in perpetual remembrance, the collisions of capital and labor on the 13th of January [1874 in Tompkins Square] and the 27th of September" (*LawJCit,* Sept. 25, 1875).

177. Howard, "Progress in the Textile Trades," 223.

178. On Fall River Irish in the Land League, see Foner, "Class, Ethnicity, and Radicalism," 23, 26–27.

179. *The Bee-Hive* (London), Nov. 20, 1875, reported that the "English element" had been blamed for all the troubles in Fall River and then forced to sign a document that rendered workingmen's freedom a "farce."

180. For a similar conclusion about Lancashire working women, see Hal Benenson, "The 'Family Wage' and Working Women's Consciousness in Britain, 1880–1914," *Politics and Society* 19 (1991): 71–118. There exist, however, important differences between the gender and class dynamics of immigrant weavers and mule spinners from Lancashire in Fall River in 1875 and what Sonya Rose discovered in Lancashire during the general Blackburn strike of 1878, see chapter 7 in *Limited Livelihoods.* Rose found the complete marginalization of women workers. The chief reason for their silence in 1878 compared to the noisy contestations in 1875 Fall River was the already established (during some earlier contest?) power of men—weavers and mule spinners—in Lancashire textile unions, their access to the press, and their domination of strike meetings.

181. "Thompson, Social History and Political Culture," 26.

7. A New Lancashire for the Northeast

1. This story is a reconstruction from an interview in the *FRHerald,* Jan. 21, 1884. All quotations are from that source.

2. Cumbler, *Working-Class Community in Industrial America* (Westport, Conn.: Greenwood Press, 1979).

3. *ProvidenceJ,* April 16, 1870; here he was referring specifically to Lonsdale.

4. *ProvidenceS,* Mar. 6, 1875. For the *Sun's* coverage of events in Fall River in 1875 and simultaneous expressions of labor protest in Rhode Island and eastern Connecticut, see the weekly issues between Jan. 23 and Dec. 4, 1875.

5. *ProvidenceS,* Jan. 30, 1875, Feb. 6, 27, 1875. *Providence Star,* [*ProvidenceSt*], Jan. 13, 1875. *In Middle-Class Providence,* John Gilkeson argues (109–10) that until the mid-1880s Providence escaped the labor unrest that convulsed other industrial centers, but he based this conclusion only the *Providence Journal.*

6. *ProvidenceSt,* Jan. 15, 1875.

7. *ProvidenceS,* Feb. 20, Mar. 6, 1875; *ProvidenceSt,* Aug. 13, 1874; Dec. 11, 1874.

8. *ProvidenceS,* Feb. 27, Mar. 6, 1875.

9. Ibid., Feb. 27, Mar. 6, 20, 1875. The *Sun* editor revealed the economic interests behind the Providence press (Mar. 20, 1875): Brown and Ives and the Republican Party backed the *Providence Journal,* while its evening edition, the *Bulletin,* belonged to one of the senators from Rhode Island and his lawyer partner. Textile manufacturer James Y. Smith and machinery manufacturer George Corliss ran both the *Providence Evening Press* and its morning edition, *The Providence Star.*

10. *ProvidenceS,* Mar. 6, 20, 1875.

11. Ibid., Mar. 27, 1875.

12. My thanks to Carl Gersuny for information about Morgan and other leaders of the 1873 strike from the *Providence Morning Herald,* May 13, 1873. The newspaper identified Corkhill as about thirty-five years old and English-born, while Biltcliffe was erroneously identified as a seventy-one-year-old immigrant from Yorkshire, not Lancashire, who had lived in the United States since 1865 with his large family. See Gersuny, "A Unionless General Strike," 21–32.

13. The standing committee for agitation included Corkhill, Ira Steward, and Henry Sevey; for Rhode Island, George F. Rhodes from Providence and William Grundy of Lonsdale; and for Connecticut William Hartley of Norwich, and Peter Brenall of Greenville, (*ProvidenceS,* Aug. 21, 1875).

14. *ProvidenceS,* Aug. 7, 1875. The *Border City Herald's* story appeared in this issue.

15. Ibid.

16. *ProvidenceS,* Sept. 18, 25, 1875.

17. Ibid., Sept. 25, Oct. 2, 1875.

18. Ibid., Sept. 25, Oct. 9, 1875.

19. Ibid., Oct. 30, 1875.

20. Ibid., Oct. 30, Nov. 6, 20, 1875. On the Chaces of Valley Falls, see above, chapter 2. See also Elizabeth C. Stevens, "'Was She Clothed with the Rents Paid for These Wretched Rooms?': Elizabeth Buffum Chace, Lillie Chace Wyman, and Upper Class Advocacy for Women Factory Operatives in Gilded Age Rhode Island," *Rhode Island History* (Nov. 1994): 107–33. Stevens also provides an analysis (118–25) of Wyman's collection of short stories on factory village life, workingwomen, and ethnic intermarriage, *Poverty Grass* (Boston: Houghton Mifflin, 1886).

21. Ibid., Nov. 6, 1875.

22. *ProvidenceJ,* April 16, 1870; Nov. 22, 1869. *ProvidenceSt,* May 7, 9, 1870. Earlier in Olneyville, the village from where Jonathan Biltcliffe spread the word about English-style cooperatives, about seventy-five spinners and weavers also struck together in 1870 over a similar wage cut (*ProvidenceSt,* Dec. 6, 1869; Jan. 7, 10, 1870). None of these strikes was successful. My thanks to Scott Molloy for his generosity in sharing his unique newspaper clippings scrapbook. All researchers in Rhode Island Labor History should consult the *Guide to the Historical Study of Rhode Island Working People,* ed. Scott Molloy, Eric Barden, and Tim McMahon (Kingston, RI: Rhode Island Historical Society, 1996).

23. *ProvidenceS,* Jan. 15, 1876.

24. Ibid.

25. *ProvidenceSt,* Jan. 14, 1876.

26. Ibid., Jan. 28, 1876, *ProvidenceS,* Jan. 15, 1876. Nabobism, according to the *Oxford English Dictionary,* referred to wealthy, pretentious persons, especially those who returned from service for the British empire in India with great fortunes. Doyle had defeated the candidate of the Sprague textile interests in 1870 (*ProvidenceSt,* May 11–12, 1870).

27. *Providence Evening Bulletin,* Jan. 1, 1874.

28. *ProvidenceS,* Jan. 14, 15, 1876.

29. *ProvidenceSt,* Jan. 22, 1876.

30. *ProvidenceS,* Jan. 19, 1876.

31. The *Hartford Courant,* December 24, 1875, provided very brief coverage. Otherwise, the strike at the Rock Woolen Mill in Rockville, near Hartford, is difficult to reconstruct because of missing issues of the *Tolland County Journal* (Rockville) at the State Library of Connecticut, Hartford, and in Rockville. The Dec. 24, and 31, 1875, issues opposed the strike and quoted the New Haven, Hartford, and Norwich newspapers, some sympathetic and some opposed. Also see, *Hartford Courant,* Dec. 24, 1875 for very brief coverage. The workers in Rockville were still on strike in January, 1876, according to *Tolland County Journal,* Jan. 14, 1876, but the surrounding issues are also missing and the state bureau of labor statistics had been abolished by that date.

32. *ProvidenceS,* Jan. 19, 1876.

33. *ProvidenceJ,* Jan. 18, 1876.

34. *ProvidenceS,* Jan. 19, 1876.

35. *ProvidenceSt,* Jan. 27, 1876.

36. *ProvidenceS,* Jan. 19, 29, 1876.

37. *ProvidenceSt,* Jan. 25, 1876.

38. *ProvidenceS,* Jan. 29, 1876.

39. *ProvidenceSt,* Jan. 28, 1876.

40. Ibid.

41. Lucius F. C. Garvin, M. D., "Sanitary Requirements in Factories . . . ," paper read at the American Public Health Association annual meeting, Boston, October 5, 1876, *Public Health Papers and Reports* v. 3, (1875–1876): 68–78. A Rhode Island ten-hour law passed in May 1885. Carl Gersuny, "Uphill Battle: Lucius F. C. Garvin's Crusade for Political Reform," *Rhode Island History* 39 (May 1980): 56–75.

42. The debate appeared in the *ProvidenceS,* Jan. 29, 1876; Feb. 5, 1876; Mar. 4, 11, 1876.

43. See three letters in the *ProvidenceS,* April 1, 1876.

44. Ibid., Feb. 19, Mar. 18, 1876.

45. Ibid., April 1, 1876.

46. Ibid., Mar. 11, 1876. For doosed, meaning deuced or damned, see *Oxford English Dictionary* v. 4, 558.

47. The family came from Walpole, New Hampshire, according to Hurd, *Bristol County,* 395–97 and obituary of Edward Kilburn, *NBSt,* Aug. 1, 1906. My thanks to Joan Barney at the Buttonwood Community Library, New Bedford, for this information.

48. *News,* Feb. 16, 1877.

49. Different settings on the rollers in the drafting machines determined the strength of the yarn. See letter from "MacIntosh," probably a shareholder, *NBSt,* Mar. 11, 1877.

50. Ibid., Jan. 22, 1877.

51. Ibid., Jan. 26, 1877.

52. Ibid.

53. Ibid., Jan. 31, 1877. For information about Ricketson also see his obituary, *NBMercury,* July 18, 1898, and *Daniel Ricketson and His Friends,* ed. Anna and Walton Ricketson (Boston: Houghton Mifflin, 1902).

54. *NBSt,* Jan. 31, 1877.

55. *NBSt,* Feb. 5, 1877. Also see the coverage of this meeting in the *NYHerald,* Feb. 5, 1877.

56. *NBSt,* Feb. 5, 1877. A tiger according to the *Oxford English Dictionary* v. 18, 78, was a "yell supplementary to three cheers," indicating a final burst of enthusiasm.

57. *NBSt,* Feb. 14, 1877.

58. Ibid., Feb. 8, 12, Mar. 30, 1877.

59. *News,* Feb. 9, 1877; Feb. 17, 1877; *NY Herald,* Feb. 23, 1877.

60. *NBSt,* Feb. 17–20, 23, 1877.

61. Ibid., Feb. 21, 24, 1877.

62. Ibid., Feb. 26, 1877.

63. *FRHerald,* Mar. 25, April 10, 1877.

64. Ibid., Feb. 26, April 25, 27, May 10, 1877. In addition to reprinting reports from the *Standard* and the *Mercury,* the editor also included hostile coverage from conservative newspapers in Boston. On changes at the *Herald,* see Henry M. Fenner, *History of Fall River* (New York, 1906), 109.

65. *FRHerald,* May 10, 15, 1877.

66. *NBSt,* April 9, 25, 1877.

67. Ibid., April 10, 13, 1877.

68. *News,* April 24, 1877.

69. *NBSt,* April 25, 1877.

70. Ibid., April 30, 1877. The "nobbstick" may have been a Yankee variant of *knobstick* or a misspelling. The meaning of the hanged black doll is unclear, but suggests a racist comment on scabs.

71. Ibid.

72. *News,* April 30, 1877; *NBSt,* May 3, 1877.

73. *FRHerald,* May 15, 1877.

74. Obituary, *NBSt,* Aug. 1, 1906.

75. *News,* Jan. 18, 1876.

76. Ibid., Feb. 29, 1876. Also see a speech by Edward T. Atkinson to the New England Manufacturing Association in Boston, providing statistical support for the export trade, May 1, 1876.

77. Ibid., Sept. 5, 7, 1876.

78. *NYHerald,* Jan. 22, 1877.

79. *News,* Feb. 19, 1877.

80. *ProvidenceS,* Sept. 25, 1875.

81. *FRHerald,* April 5, 1878.

82. "Letter from Trevor," *ProvidenceS,* Jan. 29, 1876.

83. *ProvidenceS,* Mar. 4, 1876.

84. *News,* Jan. 20, 1878.

85. Montgomery, *Beyond Equality,* 250–51. Gunton had believed that the market was too depressed to respond to the withholding of labor and that a failed strike would endanger the ten-hour movement and its coalition with Massachusetts labor reformers, "Letter from Tomahawk," *LaborSt,* Oct. 9, 1880.

86. *FRHerald,* May 7, 1879.

87. *ProvidenceS,* Oct. 16, 1875.

88. See Kenneth Fones-Wolf, "Boston Eight Hour Men, New York Marxists and the Emergence of the International Labor Union: Prelude to the AFL," *Historical Journal of Massachusetts* 9 (June 1981): 47–59.

89. See "An Open Letter to William A. Simmons, [Ex-Collector of the Port of Boston]" *LaborSt* Sept. 17, 1881. Editor J. P. McDonnell of the *Labor Standard* welcomed Gunton as a correspondent and later as a coeditor, describing him as "a natural born labor organizer" (New York *LaborSt,* Aug. 26, 1877). Gunton used the pen name "Middleton" in the *LaborSt* and probably wrote under "Bowenville" for the Lancashire *Preston Herald.* Some of the mule spinners joined the ILU, probably supporters of James Langford.

90. *LaborSt,* April 17, 1880; June 4, 1881.

91. *LaborSt,* Dec. 8, 1877. Within six months, the offices were removed from New York City to Boston because of financial difficulties and the deepening commitment of McDonnell to the workers of Paterson, New Jersey, *LaborSt,* Aug. 25, Sept. 7, 14, Oct. 26, 1878. The executive committee of the ILU stayed in New York. By February 1879 only the Fall River and Paterson editions remained until the dissolution of Gunton's edition in late December, 1881. McDonnell continued the Paterson *Labor Standard* until 1908.

92. The vote was 119 to 79, reprinted from the *BHerald* in *FRHerald,* April 15, 1878.

93. *FRHerald,* Mar. 26, 1878. On George McNeill's labor politics and his relations with Gunton, see Robert R. Montgomery, " 'To Fight This Thing Till I Die': The Career of George Edwin McNeill," in *Culture, Gender, Race, and U.S. Labor History,* ed. Robert C. Kent, Sara Markham, David R. Roediger, and Herbert Shapiro (Westport, Conn.: Greenwood Press, 1993): 4–23. Robert Montgomery, however, misinterprets many of the events of 1878 and 1879 (16–17).

94. Ibid., Mar. 29, 30, April 1, 1878. Sylvester Campbell was the president of the mule spinners' association, but Langford, the treasurer, appeared at mass meetings representing the spinners. Robert Howard, the secretary, rarely appeared at public meetings.

95. *FRHerald,* April 5, 1878.

96. Ibid., April 6, 1878.

97. Ibid., April 5, 1878.

98. *BGlobe* provided a detailed report as did the *FRHerald,* both on May 6, 1878.

99. Brian D. Palmer, "Discordant Music: Charivaris and Whitecapping in Nineteenth-Century North America," *Labour/Le Travailleur* 3 (1978): 56.

100. *LaborSt,* May 19, 1878; *BGlobe,* May 6, 1878; *NYHerald,* May 16, 1878; *BGlobe,* May 6, 1878.

101. *FRHerald,* May 6, 1878; *BGlobe,* May 6, 1878. A shoe manufacturer in 1869 had tried Chinese labor in a factory in North Adams, Massachusetts, a situation that was indelibly imprinted on the minds of New England workers. Palmer's discussion of North American customs of humiliation ("Discordant Music," 29–30), acknowledges the existence of racism in these expressions of working-class culture.

102. *FRHerald,* May 6, 1878, and *BGlobe,* May 6, 1878.

103. Jonathan Baxter Harrison, *Certain Dangerous Tendencies in American Life, and Other Papers* (Boston, 1880), 164, 165. The reference to "taking care of themselves," suggests repelling unwanted advances, but according to the short stories of Rhode Island resident and Yorkshire immigrant Hedley Smith, the phrase was often used to describe young women who also knew how to "have their fun" and prevent or terminate pregnancies by using the herb pennyroyal. See "Squire Widdop's Wooing" in *The Yankee Yorkshireman* (Detroit: Harlow Press, 1970), 31–53.

104. Harrison, *Certain Dangerous Tendencies,* 165.

105. Ibid., 178–81, 185.

106. Alexander Saxon, *The Rise and Fall of the White Republic: Class Politics and Mass Culture in Nineteenth-Century America* (New York: Verso, 1990), chapter 7.

107. See Mary H. Blewett, "George Gunton and the Amalgamated Weavers of New England and Paterson, New Jersey" paper presented at the Conference on Paterson in the State and the Nation, Paterson 1992.

108. See Herbert G. Gutman, "A Brief Postscript to Class, Status, and the Gilded Age Radical," *Work, Culture and Society in Industrializing America* (New York: Vintage, 1977), 260–92. On Gutman, see Prologue.

109. The contrasting metaphors are from the well-known work of ethnic historians Oscar Handlin and John Bodnar.

110. On Paterson's weavers, see David Goldberg, *A Tale of Three Cities* (New Brunswick, N.J.: Rutgers University Press, 1989), 19–20, 27. On other nineteenth-century militant immigrant groups to the U.S., see Donna Gabbaccia, *Migrants and Militants* and Dirk Hoerder, ed., *"Struggle A Hard Battle."* On the persistence of radicalism and the importance of repression in shaping the nineteenth-century American labor movement, see the introduction to Bruce Laurie, *Artisans Into Workers.*

111. *LaborSt,* July 21, 1878.

112. Ibid., Aug. 4, 11, 18, 1878.

113. Ibid., Sept. 14, 1878. The business community in Paterson, which supported the strike, objected to the mottoes denigrating local manufacturers (Oct. 5, 1878).

114. Ibid., July 21, Aug. 18, Sept. 7, 14, 1878.

115. Ibid., Oct. 5, 1878.

116. Ibid., Oct. 12, 1878.

117. Gunton seemed ambivalent about its future and the competition, but wished it well (*LaborSt*, Oct. 12, 1878).

118. *FRHerald*, Dec. 28, 1878. Copies of the Fall River *Labor Standard* between Dec. 14, 1878 and February 22, 1879 have been lost. The textile unions in Britain, however, were just emerging from a devastating defeat in 1878.

119. Fenner, *Fall River*, 144–45.

120. *LaborSt*, Oct. 4, 1879.

121. *FRHerald*, Oct. 17, 1878.

122. Ibid., Oct. 19, 1878.

123. Ibid., Nov. 4, 1878.

124. Ibid., Nov. 7, 1878.

125. Ibid., Oct. 18, 19, 1878. On the 1878 Lancashire strike, see Rose, *Limited Livelihoods*, chapter 7.

8. STRUGGLING OVER AMALGAMATIONS OR TRADE UNIONS

1. Wyman, "Studies of Factory Life," 605–12. On Wyman's growing interest in factory reform, see Stevens, "Was She Clothed," 107–33. Mr. W's family reportedly had seventeen children, certainly possible but unusual given the size of families among mule spinners' reported by Howard to the press. Perhaps this was an error; nothing more was said about the children.

2. Ibid.

3. Ibid.

4. See Charlotte Erickson, *American Industry and the European Immigrant, 1860–1885* (New York: Russell and Russell, 1967), 60.

5. See Cumbler *Working-Class Community*, 173–94; David Montgomery, *Fall of the House of Labor* (Cambridge: Cambridge University Press, 1987), 158–59, 163–65; Silvia, "Robert Howard, Labor Leader," *Spinner: People and Culture in Southeastern Massachusetts* 3 (1984): 142–45.

6. Montgomery, *Fall of the House of Labor*, 157, 164.

7. *Worker City, Company Town* (Urbana: University of Illinois Press, 1978).

8. William Lazonick also compares mule spinning in nineteenth-century Lancashire and New England in *Competitive Advantage on the Shop Floor* (Cambridge: Harvard University Press, 1990). His fine detailed research on Lancashire, however, is not comparable to that on Fall River, which is based on secondary, sometimes dubious, sources on mule spinning. For example, New England mule spinners are represented as geographically mobile, physically capable skilled men (no reference to the sick spinners' list) who resolved their grievances by "individual exit, not collective voice" (116).

8. For example, Carole Turbin's investigation of female collar workers in Troy acknowledges the connections with, and support of, the ironworkers, but identifies the female leaders of the collar workers' union, such as Kate Mullaney, as single women, some of whom provided for families of dependents. See Carole Turbin, *Working Women of Collar City: Gender, Class, and Community in Troy, 1864–86* (Urbana: University of Illinois Press, 1992).

9. For the Quebec rebellions as "an integral part of a chain of resistance,

authoritarianism, and bourgeois democracy," see Brian Young and John A. Dickinson, *A Short History of Quebec: A Socio-Economic Perspective* (Toronto: Copp, Clark Pitman Ltd., 1988), 143–52, especially 151.

10. *American Management*, 117–34.

11. Cohen argues that the utter failure of the mule spinners to retrieve their craft status encouraged the mill agents to move as quickly as technically possible to adopt the process of ring spinning. If the mule spinners had been thoroughly beaten by 1879, why would American managers spend money on less flexible and productive, technically primitive machinery with an untried workforce of women and children? Perhaps one reason was the decision of the mule spinners' union not to organize ring spinners.

12. Cohen might also have followed the mule spinners into the AFL, rather than compare them with the even harsher experiences of British immigrant coal miners and steel workers in American industry, see his concluding chapter 8.

13. *BGlobe*, Aug. 18, 1879.

14. *FRHerald*, Feb. 15, 1879, Feb. 21, 22, 1879.

15. Ibid., April 9, 1879.

16. Ibid., April 24, 1879.

17. *New York Herald*, July 19, 1879, quoted in *FRHerald*, June 21, 1879.

18. *FRHerald*, April 30, 1879.

19. Ibid., May 5, 6, 8, 1879. The *Herald* printed reactions from the Providence, Boston, and New York press throughout the conflict.

20. Ibid., May 8, 1879.

21. Ibid., May 12, 13, 1879.

22. Gunton may have responded, but issues of the *Labor Standard* are missing between Feb. 22 and Aug. 9, 1879.

23. *FRHerald*, May 16, 1879.

24. Ibid.

25. Ibid., May 26, 1879.

26. Ibid., June 18, 1879.

27. Ibid., May 9, June 4, 12, 1879. The technology of ring spinning in 1879 was limited to producing warp yarn in small quantities. This was a managerial bluff.

28. Ibid., June 9, 1879.

29. From the May 25 *New York Sun*, reprinted in the *FRHerald*, May 31, 1879. For a similar account in the *Boston Herald*, see *FRHerald*, June 16, 1879.

30. Quoted in *FRHerald*, June 16, 1879.

31. Ibid.

32. Ibid.

33. Ibid., June 24, 1879.

34. *FRHerald*, June 28, 1879; *LaborSt*, Aug. 9, 1879.

35. *FRHerald*, July 1, 1879.

36. Ibid., July 2, 1879.

37. Ibid., June 17, 18, 1879.

38. *BHerald* as quoted in *FRHerald*, June 23, 1879. See letter from Dennis Sullivan, a non-union spinner, to John S. Martin, *FRHerald*, June 20, 1879. Sullivan claimed that only 22 of the 39 spinners at the Durfee Mill # 2 gave notice.

39. From the June 19, 1879, *NYHerald*, reprinted in *FRHerald*, June 21, 1879.

40. *FRHerald,* June 26, 27, 1879.

41. Spencer Borden's words were remembered later by Gunton, *LaborSt,* May 8, 1880.

42. *FRHerald,* June 27, 1879.

43. Ibid., June 26, 27, 1879.

44. Jack spinning on smaller frames was more commonly used in woolen operations, and similar threats made in 1870 were never realized. In 1879 two women jack spinners arrived in Fall River but hastily left (*FRHerald,* Aug. 4, 1879).

45. Ibid., July 1, 2, 1879.

46. Ibid., July 7, 21, 1879.

47. *LaborSt,* Mar. 13, 1880; *FRHerald,* July 22, 23, 1879.

48. *BHerald,* as quoted in *FRHerald,* July 25, 1879; see also July 24, 1879.

49. *FRHerald,* July 28, 1879.

50. Ibid., July 28, 29, 31, Aug. 2, 16, 1879.

51. Ibid., Aug. 1, 25, 30, 1879.

52. MBLS *Eleventh Annual Report* (1880), 53–68.

53. See reports in *FRHerald* between Aug. 18, 1879 and Sept. 5, 1879.

54. Ibid., Sept. 13, 1879.

55. *News,* Sept. 8, 1879.

56. *FRHerald,* Sept. 15, 1879.

57. *News* and *FRHerald,* Sept. 18, 1879.

58. See Silvia, "Neighbors from the North," 49–50. Silvia explains in *Spindle City* that Bedard worked in a rural parish in Quebec, rapidly losing its population, and came to Fall River to make sure that French religion and culture were preserved. He became quite aggressive against competitive priests, secular-minded professionals or strikers within the French community, Part 1, 353–55, 369–80.

59. *FRHerald,* Mar. 3, 1879.

60. Silvia's analysis of these tensions with the Fall River Irish centers on religion and work that sometimes but not always drove the French Canadian voter into the Republican Party, see Philip Silvia, "The 'Flint Affair': French-Canadian Struggle for *Survivance,*" *Catholic Historical Review* 54: 414–35. Also see Ronald A. Petrin "Ethnicity and Urban Politics: French-Canadians in Worcester, 1895–1915," in *Massachusetts Politics: Selected Historical Essays,* ed. Jack Tager, Martin Kaufman, and Michael F. Konig, (Westfield: Westfield State College, 1998): 104–20, and William F. Hartford's discussion of how Irish American trade unionists in Holyoke blocked Franco-Americans from union leadership in *Working People of Holyoke: Class and Ethnicity in a Massachusetts Mill Town, 1850–1960* (New Brunswick: Rutgers University Press, 1990).

61. Some indirect evidence concerning the death in 1872 of a French Canadian boy whose head was crushed by a mule frame in the Granite mill (*News,* June 6, 1872) might indicate the presence of French mule spinners at that time. It is hard to believe that the other nationalities would have trained the boy. According to a local census in March 1872, there were 3,642 French Canadian immigrants in Fall River (*News,* April 6, 1872).

62. *Boston Pilot* of the Boston Catholic archdiocese, reprinted in *FRHerald,* Aug. 9, 1879.

63. *FRHerald,* Aug. 18, 1879.

64. Ibid., Aug. 18, Sept. 9, 18, 1879. See also Howard on passion and reason in 1870 and 1875 in McNeill's 1887 book.

65. *FRHerald,* Sept. 25, 1879.
66. Ibid., June 23, Aug. 4, 6, 7, 20, Sept. 4, Oct. 3, 1879.
67. Ibid., Sept. 20, 1879; *LaborSt,* Sept. 27, 1879.
68. *FRHerald,* Oct. 28, 1879.
69. Ibid., Oct. 30, 1879.
70. *LaborSt,* Oct. 25, Nov. 15, 1879; *News,* Nov. 5, 1879.
71. *LaborSt,* Nov. 8, 1879.
72. FRHerald, Dec. 8, 1879.
73. *FRHerald,* Oct. 7, 1879.
74. *LaborSt,* Nov. 29, 1879.
75. *FRHerald,* Jan. 14, 16, 1879; *LaborSt,* Dec. 13, 20, Nov. 8, 1879.
76. Ibid., Mar. 6, 13, 1880.
77. *LaborSt,* Mar. 6, 27, 1880; May 1, 1880. See Walkowitz, *Worker City,* 219–29. The second strike in 1882 was lost, but the operatives joined the Knights of Labor.
78. *LaborSt,* Mar. 27, 1880.
79. See the *LaborSt* issues between Jan. 3 and Mar. 27, 1880.
80. Ibid., Feb. 7, 1880.
81. Ibid., Mar. 6, 1880. McDonnell, editor of the Paterson *Labor Standard* also supported this kind of organization but distrusted Gunton.
82. *LaborSt,* Feb. 14, 1880.
83. Ibid., Feb. 21, 1880. The former editor of the *Labor Journal,* Henry Sevey, the Fall River correspondent for the conservative *Providence Journal,* wrote negative reports about the 1879 spinners' strike. To Gunton's deep grief, he died in a horrible accident in April 1880 (*LaborSt,* April 17, 1880). In tribute and to ease his loss, Gunton began to think of the *Labor Standard* as a continuation of Sevey's *Labor Journal.*
84. *LaborSt,* May 1, 8, 15, 22, 1880. McNeill used the Paterson *Labor Standard* to assert that he, not Steward, was the president of the New England Ten Hour Association, thus denying the existence of Gunton's organization (*LaborSt,* June 12, 1880).
85. *LaborSt,* July 3, 10, Aug. 28, Sept. 11, 1880.
86. *LaborSt,* April 10, May 22, 29, June 12, 1880.
87. Ibid., April 28, Sept. 11, 1880.
88. Ibid., June 5, July 17, Aug. 14, Sept. 18, 1880.
89. Later Parsons became a major labor figure and was martyred in the Haymarket riots (Ibid., July 24, 31, Aug. 7, 14, 21, Sept. 11, 18, 1880).
90. As quoted in *Labor St,* Sept. 11, 1880. On Gunton's campaign, see issues of Aug. 14 and Sept. 4, 1880.
91. Ibid., Oct. 2, 9, 16, 1880.
92. Ibid., Oct. 30, 1880; as quoted in the editorial, *LaborSt,* Aug. 21, 1880.
93. As quoted in *LaborSt,* Oct. 2, 1880; see also Oct. 9, 1880.
94. Ibid., Oct. 9, 1880.
95. Ibid., Oct. 23, 30, 1880.
96. Ibid., Nov. 8, 13, 1880.
97. Ibid., Nov. 3, 1880.
98. Ibid., Nov. 20, 1880.
99. Ibid., Jan. 8, 1881. Howard never revealed why he chose to emigrate in 1873. As the popular president of the Stockport Spinners' Union, his work and life seemed settled in England. He never claimed to have been blacklisted. Given

his hostile statements and attitudes toward workingwomen, I wonder if he fled an embarrassing paternity situation. Howard remained a bachelor.

100. *LaborSt,* Jan. 1, 1880; *FRHerald,* Jan. 11, Nov. 9, 1881. The state representatives elected were all three Republicans. The *Herald* remained silent on Howard's situation.

101. *LaborSt,* April 30, 1881. Gunton was working as the local correspondent for the *Providence Star.* The editor of the *Fall River Herald,* pointing out that Harrison was more than twice the size of Gunton and that the attack came without warning, strongly defended Gunton and labeled Harrison a unmanly coward. The *Fall River Sun* printed Harrison's letter, but the copy was lost. For Gunton's reaction and the defense of his libel suit by the *Fall River Herald,* see *LaborSt,* Nov. 19, 26, 1881.

102. On the testimony, see the *FRHerald* between Dec. 12 and Dec. 31, 1881, and Jan. 5, 1882. The Guntons were later divorced.

103. In 1885 Gunton moved to New York City and married a wealthy widow. He was married for the third time in 1904 to the wealthy president of the American Federation of Women, and died in 1919 (*Dictionary of American Biography,* 55–56).

104. Larry Glickman, "Workers of the World, Consume: Ira Steward and the Origins of Labor Consumerism," *ILWCH* 52 (Fall 1997): 72–86. Gompers in the 1890s (perhaps urged by George Gunton) credited Steward with advancing the union label and the AFL's support for a family wage for workingmen (80, n. 11).

105. Overreliance on Howard's "Progress in the Textile Trades" in McNeill's 1887 book led the editors of *The Encyclopedia of the American Left* (New York: Garland, 1990) Mari Jo Buhle, Paul Buhle, and Dan Georgakas to omit any reference to George Gunton, assign central importance in New England labor politics to McNeill and the ILU "founded on a spinners' union," and list J. P. McDonnell as the editor of the Fall River *Labor Standard,* 772–3.

106. *ProvidenceSt,* Mar. 12, 1881; *News,* reprinted in *ProvidenceSt,* Oct. 25, 1881; *LaborSt,* Oct. 29, Nov. 5, 1881.

107. Martin Shefter, "Trade Unions and Political Machines: The Organization and Disorganization of the American Working Class in the Late Nineteenth Century," in *Working-Class Formation: Nineteenth-Century Patterns in Western Europe and the United States,* Ira Katznelson and Aristide Zolberg ed. (Princeton: Princeton University Press, 1986), 197–276.

108. *LaborSt,* Feb. 19, 1881.

109. Ibid., Mar. 26, 1881. See also Feb. 5, 26, Mar. 12, 19, 26, April 2, 9, 1881. Julie Greene in *Pure and Simple Politics: The American Federation of Labor and Political Activism, 1881–1917* (Cambridge: Cambridge University Press: 1998) points out that the Federation was modeled "explicitly on the British Trades Union Congress," 33.

110. Stuart Bruce Kaufman in *Samuel Gompers and the Origins of the American Federation of Labor* (Westport, Conn.: Greenwood Press, 1973) 113–21, mentions George Gunton's activities and the *Labor Standard,* but there is no reference to Robert Howard. For excerpts from the hearings and a judgment on their failure, see John A. Garraty, ed., *Labor and Capital in the Gilded Age* (Boston: Little, Brown and Co., 1968), 177–78. Also see *FRHerald,* Nov. 7, 1881; Aug. 27, 1883; *Labor Leader,* Jan. 15, 1887.

111. *LaborSt,* Aug. 20, 1881.

112. *FRHerald,* Nov. 30, 1881, *LaborSt,* Dec. 3, 1881.

113. *LaborSt,* Mar. 19, 1881.

114. *BHerald,* reprinted in *LaborSt,* Oct. 23, 1880.

115. *LaborSt,* Feb. 26, 1881.

116. MBLS, *Thirteenth Annual Report,* (1882), 337–38, 351–53. For a critique of the biased structure in this report, see Assessment of Primary Sources.

117. Ibid., 201–7, 218–22, 272–75, 254–55.

118. Ibid., 316–29, 331, 340–47.

119. See Cameron, *Radicals of the Worst Sort,* 48–62. Not inclined to analyze the regional connections, Cameron argues persuasively about the gendering of labor politics, including the opposition of the mule spinners to the strike. The refusal of the national mule spinners' association to organize the ring spinners in any New England textile center and their promotion of a family wage excluded working women.

120. Alexander Saxon, *The Indispensable Enemy: Labor and the Anti-Chinese Movement in California* (Berkeley: University of California Press, 1971). On Chinese immigrants in the New England, see Ronald Takaki, "Gam Saan Haak," in *Strangers from a Different Shore: A History of Asian Americans* (Boston: Little, Brown, 1989) 95–99.

121. *LaborSt,* May 29, 1880; Jan. 15, 1881. Led by French Canadian Joseph Kaye, arrested by local police, Suncook operatives struck over a wage cut, debt bondage to company stores, and for ten hours.

122. Part III, "Uniform Hours of Labor," *Twelfth Annual Report* MBLS (1881), 321–475, especially 469–70. Although Silvia examined the French Canadian immigrant community in depth, he does not analyze this racist reference to the French, "Spindle City," Part 1, 352. Roby treats this event as unfortunate but a reflection of economic hard times in 1880–82, *Les Franco-Américaines,* 185–9. He cites a "certain F. K. Foster," a state Senator [and close ally of Robert Howard], who expressed a preference for the California Chinese to immigrants from Quebec, 187.

123. Ibid., 461–70.

124. Gerald Brault, in *French-Canadian Heritage,* argues that this controversy helped create the term "Franco-American," 68.

125. *Labor St,* June 25, 1881.

126. Unlike the new immigrants discussed by James R. Barrett and David Roediger in "Inbetween Peoples: Race, Nationality, and the 'New Immigrants,' " *Journal of American Ethnic History* 16 (Spring 1997) 3–35, French Canadians in New England did not escape association with Asians.

127. *LaborSt,* Oct. 8, 1881. Later, as the brother-in-law of Democratic mayor, John W. Coughlin, Dubuque helped the Democrats woo the Franco vote. For these political issues in Fall River, see Silvia, "Spindle City," Part 2, 755–69.

128. "The Canadian French in New England," MBLS, *Thirteenth Annual Report,* (1882), 1–92, especially 16–17, 19.

129. Gagnon pointed out the five year waiting period for naturalization, the Rhode Island requirement of property for the foreign-born to vote, and New Hampshire's prohibition of Catholics holding elected offices, MBLS, *Thirteenth Annual Report* (1882), 20–21.

130. MBLS (1882), 6. *News*, Oct. 26, 1881. Fall River's Edward J. I. Herault and Father Bedard, also testified among many others about French Canadian communities in Lowell, Lawrence, Spencer, Worcester, Marlboro, Massachusetts; Great Falls, Suncook, and Rochester, and Nashua, New Hampshire; Lewiston, Maine; and Glen's Falls, Plattsburgh, Champlain, and Whitehall, and Cohoes, New York. Also see, *FRHerald*, Oct. 26, 1881.

131. See Noel Ignatiev, *How The Irish Became White* (New York: Routledge, 1995) especially the Introduction. Ignatiev does not address the disabilities of Catholicism for the Irish in a Protestant-dominated society. David Roediger's attempts to include race and the concepts of whiteness and gender as central to labor history might also address religion as a cultural and political category of some importance to nineteenth-century labor politics, "The Crisis in Labor History: Race, Gender and the Replotting of the Working Class Past in the United States," in *Towards the Abolition of Whiteness* (London: Verso, 1994) 69–81.

132. First the Rhode Island mills cut wages 10 percent, followed by Lewiston, Maine; Lowell; the Atlantic mill in Lawrence; and the Cocheco mill in Dover, New Hampshire, *FRHerald*, Jan. 5, 10, 21, 22, 24, 1884.

133. Ibid., Jan. 23, 1884.

134. Ibid., Jan. 31, 1884. See Simeon B. Chase's letter of Feb. 4, 1884, to the *FRHerald*, explaining the board's logic (*FRHerald*, February 9, 1884).

135. Ibid., Feb. 4, 1884. Later when the issue of providing filling became vital, two other mills owned by the Sagamore and the Wampanoag were also struck (Silvia, "Spindle City," part 1, 280–81).

136. *BGlobe*, reprinted in *FRHerald*, Jan. 28, 1884.

137. Several other union spinners were also convicted and fined, victims of a police "sting" operation (*FRHerald*, Jan. 9, 1884).

138. In contrast, Cumbler in *Working-Class Community* argued that the 1884 strike demonstrated class unity and progress in union organization of textile operatives in Fall River, 177–84.

139. *FRHerald*, Feb. 6, 1884.

140. *FRHerald*, Jan. 28, Feb. 1, 6, 1884. In March another Lancashire immigrant weaver committed suicide. Forty-year-old Henry Brooks arrived in the United States in January 1884 and failed to find work in either Lowell or Fall River. His family of five had remained in England (*FRHerald*, Mar. 13, 1884).

141. As quoted in *FRHerald*, Feb. 8, 1884. See also Mar. 5, 1884.

142. Ibid., Mar. 19, 1884. Weavers at the Crescent, the Barnaby, the Davol, the Mt. Hope, and the King Philip later joined.

143. Ibid., Feb. 5, 6, 8, 9, 11, 12, 14, 1884.

144. *FRHerald*, Feb. 4–7, 13, 16, 23, 1884.

145. *FRHerald*, April 28, 1884.

146. Ibid., March 7, 19, 1884. Also see Felix Albert, *Immigrant Odyssey: A French-Canadian Habitat in New England* (Orono, Maine: University of Maine Press, 1991).

147. Ibid., April 4, 5, 7, 1884, June 14, 1884.

148. Only a few operatives remained in the mill. They escaped, but a young Portuguese boy burned his face and hands, trying to use a fire escape ladder. See Ibid., April 24, 25, 28, 1884.

149. Philip Silvia, "Position of Workers in a Textile Community," 230–48.

150. See Laurie, *Artisans into Workers*, chapter 6.

151. Boris, *Home to Work*, 38. Boris argues (33–45) that Gompers and Adolph Strasser of the Cigar Makers' International Union adopted a policy of exclusivity for "skilled northern European white men," even after a general strike in 1877, during which unorganized Bohemian men and women working in tenements joined with factory workers (including single working females), thus demonstrating the possibilities of organizing all sites of production and both sexes.

9. PIECING UP THE FALL RIVER SYSTEM

1. See Victoria Lincoln's ingenious reconstruction in 1968 of the Borden case in *A Private Disgrace: Lizzie Borden By Daylight*, 81, 120, 154, 183. For a recent but unconvincing critique of Lincoln, see "Lizzie Cold, Lizzie Hot, Lizzie Warmed Over," in *Spinner: People and Culture in Southeastern Massachusetts* v. 2 (1982), 81–95. In 1897, Lizzie Borden was arrested for shoplifting, behaving in a way similar to her bouts of epilepsy in 1892 as described by Lincoln, 305–6.

2. Lincoln, *A Private Disgrace*, 35, 81, 127–28, 138, 201; *Phillips History*, v. 3, 99. According to the 1897 *Fall River City Directory*, 49, 53, 54. Andrew J. Borden was a director in the Brayton-controlled B. M. C. Durfee Safe Deposit and Trust Company and the Troy Cotton and Woolen Manufactory and president of the small Union Savings Bank.

3. Lincoln, *A Private Disgrace*, 170, 229. Lincoln argued that Jennings knew she was guilty, but his records of the case were still under family protection in 1968 when *A Private Disgrace* was published. After the acquittal, Jennings never spoke to Lizzie Borden or of the case to anyone, (22–23). She died in 1927. For an analysis of the jury's decision as influenced by social prescriptions about the nature of upper-class womanhood, see Kathryn Allamong Jacob, "She Couldn't Have Done It, Even If She Did," in Randy Roberts and James S. Olson, *American Experiences: Readings in American History*, 2d. v. (Glenview, Ill.: Scott, Foresman/ Little, Brown Education, 1990): 48–58.

4. See "Lizzie Cold . . .", 88–89.

5. Philip Scranton, *Figured Tapestry: Production, Markets, and Power in Philadelphia Textiles, 1885–1941* (Cambridge: Cambridge University Press, 1989); and *Endless Novelty: Speciality Production and American Industrialization, 1865–1925* (Princeton: Princeton University Press, 1997).

6. On this shift, see Blewett, *Men, Women, and Work*, chapter 9.

7. Gross' *The Course of Industrial Decline* focuses on one textile mill in Lowell during the period, 1871 to 1904, but the Boott mill is examined in the context of regional competition in Rhode Island and Philadelphia. The Boott mill adopted many Fall River practices.

8. Scranton's *Endless Novelty* describes the ways in which the practices of the large corporations that dominated the Second Industrial Revolution (1865 to 1925) are characterized by "technical ingenuity, organizational refinement, marketing savvy, and the power derived from pursuing efficiency and economies of scale" (6), in contrast with the irrationalities of the Fall River system.

9. Louis Galambos, *Competition and Cooperation: The Emergence of a National Trade Association* (Baltimore: John Hopkins Press, 1966), 13.

10. Focusing on structural mergers in the steel and paper industries, Na-

omi R. Lamoreaux in *The Great Merger Movement in American Business, 1895–1904*. (Cambridge: Cambridge University Press, 1985) provides a context for M. C. D. Borden's response to severe price competition in the cloth market during the same period. The corporate mergers that took place, Lamoreaux argues, were not historically inevitable or necessarily more efficient. Borden's operations are a good example of that point and reflect her alternative model of slowly growing industries that instead of merging formed stable oligopolistic relations to cut the costs of production, (189).

11. Celebrating historical complexity and contingency, Scranton offers a vigorous critique of arguments that privilege large corporations and mass production as dominant during the Second Industrial Revolution (*Endless Novelty*, 4–9).

12. *Figured Tapestry*, 174. Scranton concludes only that "Fall River represents the extreme of staple rigidity" (179).

13. *FRHerald*, Oct. 29, 1901. Montgomery in *Fall of the House of Labor* views the sliding scale of wages negotiated by Howard as a "triumph" (163), but he did not examine the workings of the system.

14. Montgomery assesses Howard's work as leader of the mule spinners' association and the head of the Knights of Labor District very positively based on the work of Philip Silvia and the published praise of Frank Foster, Howard's associate, *Fall of the House of Labor*, 163–68.

15. Mule spinner Thomas O'Donnell of Fall River, who became treasurer of the mule spinner's union in 1894, provided detailed testimony about conditions in the mills at the 1833 Senate hearings, see Garraty, *Labor and Capital in the Gilded Age*, 33–36. The *FRHerald* of July 7, 12, 1888, and Sept. 7, 12, 1888, reported on Howard's handling of grievances.

16. Greene in *Pure and Simple Politics* analyzes the development of Gompers' attitudes toward partisan politics in the late nineteenth century as a step by step process through which "inclusive strategies gradually disappeared" (47).

17. *FRHerald*, Oct. 2, 1888; for an assessment of his political career, see November 2, 1892.

18. Leon Fink, "Class Conflict American-Style," *In Search of the Working Class: Essays in American Labor History and Political Culture* (Urbana: University of Illinois Press, 1994), 15–32.

19. Paul Buhle, "Knights of Labor in Rhode Island," *Radical History Review* 17 (Spring, 1978): 39–73, esp. 46–51. By 1886, there were twelve thousand Knights in Rhode Island, including many women textile operatives. Skilled workingwomen joined the union organization at the Wanshuck worsted mills in Providence with English, Irish, and German members of the Knights. Similar activism occurred in Olneyville, Lonsdale, and Ashton where English immigrant workers predominated, (52–54). The male Knights in Rhode Island supported women's issues including childcare, woman suffrage, and the inclusion of females into the organization (58–59). With the shift in 1886 of the Rhode Island Knights away from labor issues to political reform and opposition to strikes and the establishment of the Slater Club, an organization of textile industrialists that successfully countered the Knights in politics, the Rhode Island organization "faltered." Nonetheless, according to Buhle, the Knights left a rich legacy of factory legislation and the organization of a labor vote in the reactionary Republican state, (61–67). Ardis

Cameron was more critical of the treatment of women textile workers in the Lawrence, Massachusetts, local of the Knights, organized by Mary Halley. Cameron criticized Robert Howard's advocacy in Lawrence of the family wage and the elimination of all married women from textile work, thus allegedly opening two and a-half million jobs for men, as detrimental to women's interests, *Radicals of the Worst Sort*, 61, 65. See also, Montgomery, *House of Labor*, 159. On Howard's role in the Knights and his disillusionment, see Silvia, "Spindle City," Part 2, 452–5; and on shoeworkers, see Blewett, *Men, Women, and Work*, chapter 8.

20. *FRHerald*, Feb. 7, 1894. Also see, Ileen A. DeVault, "'To Sit Among Men': Skill, Gender, and Craft Unionism in the Early American Federation of Labor," in *Labor Histories*, 259–83.

21. On Evans, *FRHerald*, Feb. 9, April 3, 11, July 28, Dec. 27, 1888; Feb. 5, Mar. 26, 1889. On the formation of the union, Mar. 11, 1889.

22. Ibid., Jan. 30, Feb. 15, 20, 27, 1889.

23. Ibid., Mar. 9, 11, 12, 14, 18, 1889.

24. Ibid., Mar. 11–16, 18, 22, 1889.

25. Ibid., Mar. 20–23, 1889.

26. Ibid., Mar. 22, 1889.

27. Ibid., Feb. 9, 1888; Mar. 11, 13, 14, 20, 1889. On the historic gendering of wages paid to women workers, Alice Kessler-Harris, *A Woman's Wage: Historical Meanings and Social Consequences* (Lexington: University Press of Kentucky, 1990).

28. *FRHerald*, Mar. 25, 27, 28, 1889.

29. Ibid., Mar. 27, 28, 1889.

30. Ibid., Mar. 28, 1889. None of this material cited in 1889 about the 1875 strike appeared in Howard's chapter in the 1887 O'Neill book.

31. *FRHerald*, Aug. 10, 14, 1889. Similar stories appeared in the *Fall River Globe* [*FRGlobe*] in Aug. 1889. When the editors of the *News* purchased controlling interest in the *Herald*, the *Globe* began publication in 1885 as a Democratic, pro-labor newspaper.

32. *FRHerald*, Aug. 15, 19, 1889.

33. From the *New York World* and *BGlobe*, as reported in the *FRHerald*, Mar. 12, 14, 1889.

34. In 1911 the refusal of the Lawrence mills to maintain piece rates while weekly hours fell to fifty-four led to the great Bread and Roses strike of 1912.

35. Later Randall would switch parties and become an "independent" Republican in 1898; see below, chapter 10. See also *FRGlobe*, Oct. 31, Nov. 1, 2, 4, 6, 8, 9, 1892.

36. A five-month long weavers' strike at the King Phillip mill beginning in February 1894 had drained the new union's treasury (*FRGlobe*, Aug. 7, 14, 20, 1894).

37. Maldwyn A. Jones, "The Background to Emigration from Great Britain in the Nineteenth Century," in *Perspectives in American History*, ed. Donald Fleming and Bernard Bailyn, v. 3, *Dislocations and Emigration: The Social Background of American Immigration*, (Cambridge: Charles Warren Center, Harvard University, 1974), 3–94, especially 53–4, 90–91. Also see below table 10.

38. Notice of the National Cotton Mule Spinners' Association of America, *FRGlobe*, Aug. 31, 1894.

39. *FRHerald*, Aug. 7, 1894. *FRGlobe*, Aug. 8, 1894.

40. *FRHerald*, Aug. 7, 8, 9, 10, 1894. On this legislation, see Sarah Scovill Whittelsey, *Massachusetts Labor Legislation: An Historical and Critical Study*, (Annals of the American Academy of Political Science supplement, May 1901) chapter 1.

41. *FRHerald*, Aug. 11, 14, 18, 20, 1894. Secretary Whitehead, a recent immigrant from Lancashire and its moderate labor politics, considered Evans "a crank."

42. *FRHerald*, Aug. 8, 11, 14, 1894.

43. *FRGlobe*, Aug. 16, 1894.

44. From the *Providence]* in the *FRHerald*, Aug. 8, 14, 1894. See also *FRGlobe*, Aug. 25, 30, 1894.

45. *FRGlobe*, Aug. 14, 16, 18, 1894.

46. *FRHerald*, Aug. 18, 1894.

47. Ibid., Oct. 26, 1894.

48. *FRGlobe*, Aug. 9, 23, 1894; *FRHerald*, Aug. 23, 1894.

49. *FRGlobe*, Aug. 21, 1894.

50. *FRHerald*, Aug. 21, 22, 1894. On Howland's opposition to the dominance of Wamsutta influence in New Bedford and his suicide after his financial collapse in 1897, see Thomas A. McMullin, "Lost Alternative: The Urban Industrial Utopia of William D. Howland," *New England Quarterly* 55 (1982): 25–38. For a brief overview of late nineteenth-century labor politics in New Bedford, Thomas A. McMullin, "The Immigrant Response to Industrialism in New Bedford, 1865–1900," *Massachusetts in the Gilded Age: Selected Essays*, ed. Jack Tager and John W. Ifkovic, (Amherst: University of Massachusetts Press, 1985), 101–21.

51. Wamsutta Directors' Minutes, December 18, 1884, January 13, 1885.

52. *FRGlobe*, Aug. 17, 23, 28, 1894.

53. *FRGlobe*, Aug. 21, 22, 23, Sept. 1, 1894.

54. Ibid., Sept. 7, 1894; *FRHerald*, Oct. 11, 1894.

55. As did the *Cotton and Wool Reporter* and many other newspapers, the editor of the *Fall River Globe* mercilessly attacked the judgment and values of the mill managers as cowardly, contemptible, and unbusinesslike, Aug. 8, 9, 16, Sept. 17, Oct. 1, 1894.

56. *FRGlobe*, Aug. 31, 1894.

57. Ibid., Aug. 27, 1894.

58. Ibid., Sept. 9, 1894.

59. Ibid., Sept. 12, 13, 14, 15, 1894.

60. Ibid., Aug. 29, 1894.

61. John K. Walton, *Fish and Chips and the British Working Class, 1870–1940* (Leicester: Leicester University Press, 1992).

62. *FRHerald*, Sept. 18, 1894.

63. *FRHerald*, Sept. 19, 22, 1894; *FRGlobe*, Sept. 22, 1894.

64. *FRHerald*, Sept. 29, 1894.

65. His closest allies on the executive committee, who backed his harsh dealings with the operatives, were the agent at the Cornell mills and the treasurer at the Chace mills. All three were relatively newcomers in Fall River.

66. *FRGlobe*, Sept. 18, 21, 1894.

67. *FRHerald*, Oct. 8, 11, 1894; *FRGlobe*, Sept. 21, 22, 25, 26, 28, 29, Oct. 1, 3, 4, 5, 8, 9, 10, 11, 1894.

68. *FRGlobe,* Oct. 12, 1894.

69. Ibid.

70. Ibid., Oct. 13, 1894.

71. Ibid., Oct. 15, 1894.

72. Reed hooks and steel combs are used during the weaving process.

73. *FRGlobe,* Oct. 12–29, 1894.

74. Ibid., Oct. 25, 1894.

75. Ibid., Oct. 20, 1894.

76. Ibid., Oct. 24, 1894.

77. Ibid., Oct. 22, 1894.

78. William F. Hartford, in *Where Is Our Responsibility? Unions and Economic Change in the New England Textile Industry, 1870–1960* (Amherst: University of Massachusetts Press, 1996), accepts uncritically the work of Silvia and Cumbler to explain the formation and persistence of "the Fall River system of trade unionism" as a regional model.

79. Robert N. Burnett, "Matthew Chaloner Durfee Borden," *The Cosmopolitan,* 36 (Nov. 1903): 62–4; obituaries, *FRHerald,* May 27, 1912; *NYTimes,* May 28, 1912.

80. *FRGlobe,* Mar. 12, 1898.

81. *Fall River City Directory,* 1892, 36, 41.

82. *FRHerald,* Aug. 15, 1888.

83. *FRGlobe,* Aug. 13, 1889.

84. Burnett, "Matthew Chaloner Durfee Borden," 62–4.

85. *FRGlobe,* Oct. 23, 1894. Only an inventory of Borden's library remains from his personal effects. Glenn Porter and Harold C. Livesay in *Merchants and Manufacturers: Studies in the Changing Structure of Nineteenth-Century Marketing* (Baltimore: Johns Hopkins University Press, 1971) confine their discussion of the Iron Works marketing activities to the period before the takeover, but Matt Borden's press reports and trade journals give an overall picture of his secret decisions.

86. *Endless Novelty,* 3.

87. Jno. Gilmore Speed, *A Fall River Incident or A Little Visit to a Big Mill* (New York City, 1895), 11–25.

88. George Otis Draper, "The Present Development of the Northrop Loom," *Proceedings of the New England Cotton Manufacturers' Association,* v. 83, 88–110. Draper used his contacts in the New England Association, devoted to mechanical and technical developments, to push his inventions. Also see Frank P. Bennett's memoir in typescript (editor of the *American Textile Journal*), formerly the *American Cotton and Wool Reporter*), 98–106. Bennett contemptuously blamed both "hidebound" agents and the resistance of weavers and the loom fixers' union for the refusal to adopt the Northrop loom, 100–106. My thanks to Claire Sheridan, Librarian, American Textile History Museum for granting access to Bennett's typescript prepared by Paul Hudon. See also Scranton, *Figured Tapestry,* 175. On Cumnock, Gross, *Course of Industrial Decline,* 59–60. For the development and strategy of the Draper family firm, see William Mass, "Mechanical and Organizational Innovation: The Drapers and the Automatic Loom, *Business History Review* 63 (Winter 1989): 876–929.

89. Speed memorialized the 1895 events in a small, beautifully embossed book, *A Fall River Incident or A Little Visit to a Big Mill,* illustrated by W. Louis Sontag,

Jr., privately printed in 1895 by Borden in New York City and issued as a souvenir. Speed described the guest list as "many of the most distinguished and influential men in New York and Philadelphia," 12, 35–6. For the Borden quote, 92.

90. The city government decided to use the money to build a Boys' Club.

91. FRHerald, Feb. 2–18, 1897.

92. FRHerald, Feb. 9, 1897. In "The Entrepreneur and the Community," in *Men in Business,* William Miller, ed., (New York: Harper and Row, 1962), Robert K. Lamb discusses (105) the career of M. C. D. Borden only as a product of kinship relations in the community of Fall River, which became first an industrial subsidiary to Providence, then "a satellite of New York." For Lamb, the key regional influence remained the textile mills of Lowell financed with Boston capital (106–17), but he never finished his study of Fall River in the post–Civil War period.

93. *FRGlobe,* Feb. 24, 1898. Robert T. Davis, a Fall River investor, expressed this opinion during a hearing of the Massachusetts House Committee on Labor.

10. THE ASCENDANCY OF TRADE UNIONS AND COMBINATIONS

1. On the 1898 strike, see the Scrapbook of Clippings Concerning the 1898 Textile Strike at New Bedford, 4 vols., collected and compiled by the former editor of the *New Bedford Evening Standard,* Widener Library, Harvard University. Hereafter *NBScrapbooks.*

2. Whittelsey, *Massachusetts Labor Legislation,* 32–33.

3. *Boston Post,* Jan. 16, 1898, in v. 1–2, NBScrapbooks. The vast majority of weavers in New Bedford were Lancashire immigrants, Irish, and French Canadians with smaller numbers of Portuguese, Germans, and Poles. According to the *Census of Massachusetts,* 1895, v. 1 (Boston, 1896), "Population and Social Statistics," 598–99, German immigrants represented three percent of New Bedford's residents in 1895. Many Germans in New Bedford were socialists.

4. *Boston Post,* Jan. 16, 1898, in v. 1–2, NBScrapbooks.

5. Arthur M'Ewen, "The Meaning of the Cotton-Mill Strike," *Journal,* January 18, 1898. For an example of the *Journal's* picturesque articles on suffering and poverty, see Eva McDonald Valesh, in v. 1–2, NBScrapbooks, Jan. 19, 1898.

6. *Competition and Cooperation* also considers the New England Cotton Manufacturers' Association, devoted to improvements in technology, and the Southern Cotton Spinners' Association, concerned with high freight rates and excessive commission charges for the emerging southern textile mills.

7. Galambos, *Competition and Cooperation,* 23–36. In an opening gambit, the Arkwright Club reprinted in 1895 an attack by S. N. D. North from the *Bulletin of the National Association of Wool Manufacturers* on state regulation as a dangerous violation of the economic laws of competition and the constitutional privilege in the fourteenth amendment of freedom of contract. Active in testimony during 1894 and 1895 for the repeal of the 1892 fifty-eight hour law were Dalton of Lowell and Boston banker, T. Jefferson Coolidge, probably the leaders of the club in the late 1890s.

8. The Arkwright Club left no manuscript collection.

9. For testimony by Boston banker, T. Jefferson Coolidge, in 1895 using southern competition in an effort to repeal the fifty-eight hour law, see Whittelsey, *Factory Legislation,* 60–61. In 1880, the Arkwright Club had issued a short report on

southern competition, "Report of the Committee on Southern Competition," (Boston, 1880).

10. Galambos, *Competition and Cooperation*, 13, 24.

11. Atkinson may have based his judgment in 1881 on the eight page Arkwright report of 1880 on southern competition. See Harold Francis Williamson, *Edward Atkinson: The Biography of An American Liberal* (Boston: Old Corner Book Store, 1934), 133, 147, 166–76; Broadus Mitchell, *The Rise of Cotton Mills in the South* (Baltimore: The Johns Hopkins Press, 1921); and Gavin Wright, *The Political Economy of the Cotton South* (New York: Norton, 1978).

12. For the entire report, see *FRGlobe*, Dec. 16, 1879.

13. *FRGlobe*, Dec. 9, 1897. A special committee empowered to set the Fall River wage cut consisted of many of the "ultras" from the 1894 strike.

14. The Goddard Brothers and the B. B. & R. Knight firm had brought Rhode Island into the wage reduction scheme. See *FRGlobe*, Dec. 31, 1897, and Jan. 1, 7, 1898. Also see Dec. 22, 24, 1897.

15. *FRGlobe*, Dec. 18, 1897.

16. On organizational activities prior to 1901, see Herbert J. Lahne, *The Cotton Mill Worker* (New York: Farrar & Rinehart, Inc., 1944), chapter 13. Lahne relied heavily on secondary sources for the late nineteenth century and on Senate hearings in 1885 and 1910 and regarded new immigrants from southern and eastern Europe as a key source of strikebreakers who undermined wage standards. He also accepted the characterization by employers and mule spinners of French Canadian workers as generally docile and conservative and greatly exaggerated their numbers in New England mills by 1880, 71–75.

17. *FRGlobe*, Dec. 21, 1897.

18. Ibid., Dec. 28, 1897.

19. Lahne, *Cotton Mill Worker*, 184–185.

20. *FRGlobe*, Jan. 8, 1898.

21. Ibid., Dec. 22, 24, 1897.

22. Ibid., Dec. 29 to 31, 1897; Jan. 1, 2, 1898.

23. Ibid., Jan. 4, 5, 6, 7, 1898.

24. On Howard, *FRGlobe*, Dec. 29, 1897.

25. Ibid., Dec. 17, 29, 1897.

26. For an incomparable look at the first generation of southern textile workers in the Piedmont region, see Jacquelyn Dowd Hall et. al., *Like A Family: The Making of a Southern Cotton Mill World* (Chapel Hill: University of North Carolina Press, 1987).

27. *FRGlobe*, Dec. 29, 1897.

28. Ibid., Dec. 27, 1897.

29. Robert Howard spent a month in Atlanta during the 1897 strike as a representative of the American Federation of Labor, (Ibid., Dec. 22, 23, 27, 1897). On working-class racism during the Atlanta strike, see Tara W. Hunter, *To 'Joy My Freedom: Southern Black Women's Lives and Labors after the Civil War* (Cambridge: Harvard University Press, 1997), 114–20. On the efforts of the Knights of Labor and the National Union of Textile Workers, see Melton Alonza McLaurin, *Paternalism and Protest: Southern Cotton Mill Workers and Organized Labor, 1875–1905* (Westport, Conn.: Greenwood Press, 1971).

30. *FRGlobe*, Dec. 29, 1897.

31. On the New Journalism, 1883–1900, see *American Journalism History: An Annotated Bibliography*, William David Sloan, comp. (Westport, Conn.: Greenwood Press, 1989), 151–65. On Valesh, see Rhoda R. Gilman, "Eva McDonald Valesh: Minnesota Populist" in *Women of Minnesota: Selected Biographical Essays*, ed. Barbara Stuhler and Gretchen Kreuter (St. Paul: Minnesota Historical Society Press, 1977): 55–76; and Foner, *Women and the American Labor Movement*, v. 1, 222, 249.

32. *Journal*, Jan. 18, 19, 20, 1898, and *World*, Jan. 22, 1898, in v. 1–2, NBScrapbooks; Whittelsey, *Massachusetts Labor Legislation*, 33.

33. *NBSt*, May 23, 1898, in v. 4, NBScrapbooks.

34. *Journal*, Jan. 10, 20, 1898, in v. 1–2, NBScrapbooks.

35. *World*, Jan. 22–25, 1898, in v. 1–2, NBScrapbooks. "The New Slavery of the North," *World*, (n. d.) in v. 3, NBScrapbooks. On the role of women workers in the organization of the United Garments Workers, see Foner, *Women and the Labor Movement*, v. 1, 224–26.

36. *Journal*, Jan. 21, 25, 1898; *World*, Jan. 19, 22, 23, 1898; *FRGlobe*, Jan. 20, 1898; *Boston Post*, Jan. 21, 1898, in v. 1–2, NBScrapbooks.

37. *Journal*, Jan. 19, 24–28, 1898; *Boston Post*, Jan. 25, 1898, in v. 1–2, NBScrapbooks.

38. *World*, Jan. 21, 1898; *FRGlobe*, Jan. 21, 1898, in v. 1–2, NBScrapbooks.

39. On Gallagher, see *Journal*, Jan. 22, 24–26, 1898, in v. 1–2, NBScrapbooks.

40. *Journal*, Jan. 22–26, 1898, in v. 1–2, NBScrapbooks.

41. *FRGlobe*, Jan. 19, 1898.

42. Quoted by Elizabeth L. Baker in *World*, Jan. 22, 1898; *Boston Post*, Jan. 25, 1898, in v. 1–2, NBScrapbooks.

43. *Boston Traveler* [*BTraveler*], Jan. 26, 29, 1898; Feb. 3, 4, 1898, in v. 1–2, NBScrapbooks.

44. *Journal*, Jan. 27, 28, 1898, in v. 1–2, NBScrapbooks; *Journal*, 29, 1898, in v. 3, NBScrapbooks.

45. *BTraveler*, Jan. 29, 1898; Feb. 10–12, 1898; *FRHerald*, Feb. 5, 1898; *World*, Jan. 28, 30, 1898; *Journal* Jan. 29, 1898, in v. 3, NBScrapbooks.

46. *BTraveler*, Jan. 26, 1898, in v. 1–2, NBScrapbooks.

47. *World*, Jan. 29, 1898, in v. 1–2, NBScrapbooks. Also see McMullin, "Immigrant Response to Industrialism," 115–16. Fall River's primitive Methodist church, attended by English operatives, published a monthly journal (location unknown), edited by a minister from New Bedford, the Reverend Acornley (*BTraveler*, Feb. 3, 1898, in v. 3, NBScrapbooks).

48. *World*, Jan. 29, 1898; *Journal*, Jan. 31, 1898, in v. 1–2, NBScrapbooks.

49. *FRGlobe*, Jan. 21, 1898, in v. 1–2, NBScrapbooks.

50. *FRGlobe*, Jan. 6, 1898, and *Boston Post*, Jan. 26, 1898 in v. 1–2, NBScrapbooks. *PJournal*, Feb. 1, 1898, in v. 3, NBScrapbooks.

51. *FRGlobe*, Feb. 9, 1898. Gallagher's lawyer was John W. Cummings of Fall River, presumably being paid by the New York *Journal*.

52. Roberts, "Gender, Consumption, and Commodity Culture," 843–44.

53. For example, *FRGlobe*, Feb. 9, 10, 12, 1989.

54. *NBMercury*, Feb. 16, 1898, in v. 4, NBScrapbooks.

55. Ibid.

56. *NBSt*, Feb. (n. d.), 1898, in v. 3, NBScrapbooks.

57. *FRGlobe*, Feb. 16, 1898.

58. Quoted in *FRGlobe*, (n. d.), v. 3, NBScrapbooks.

59. See letters from "Order" and "Duty," *NBSt,* Mar. 7, 26, 1898, in v. 4, NBScrapbooks. Also see, *NBSt,* Mar. 10, 12, 15, 18, 1898, in v. 4, NBScrapbooks.

60. *NBSt,* c. Feb. 9, 1898, in v. 3, NBScrapbooks; and Lahne, *Cotton Mill Worker,* 184–85.

61. The speech, "What Means This Strike?" was reported in the *Fall River Herald* and the *New Bedford Standard,* Feb. 13, 1898, and was republished in full in Daniel DeLeon, *Socialist Landmarks: Four Addresses* (Palo Alto, Calif.: New York Labor News: 1952), 83–120. According to L. Glen Seretan in *Daniel DeLeon: The Odyssey of an American Marxist* (Cambridge: Harvard University Press, 1979), the New Bedford speech sought to advance the cause of the ST and LA, as an alternative to trade unions and failed strikes, 156–65.

62. *NBSt,* Feb. 11, 1898, in v. 3, NBScrapbooks.

63. *San Francisco Call,* Feb. 13, 1898, in v. 3, NBScrapbooks; *NBMercury,* c. Feb. 13, 1898, in v. 4, NBScrapbooks.

64. *FRGlobe,* Mar. 5, 1898; *NBMercury,* Mar. 5, 1898, in v. 4, NBScrapbooks.

65. Ibid.

66. *New York Sun,* c. Mar. 6, 1898, in v. 4, NBScrapbooks. Montgomery argues in *Fall of the House of Labor* (168) that the SLP seemed to appeal more to union leaders in textiles than to the rank and file operatives, but an examination of electoral returns in southeastern New England in the elections of 1898 and 1900 reveals rank and file support.

67. *NBSt,* Mar. 12, 1898. Nick Salvatore's *Eugene V. Debs: Citizen and Socialist* (Urbana: University of Illinois Press, 1982) explores Debs' conception of manhood in the 1880s and 1890s, as personal honor, industry, and individual responsibility to duty (46–47, 61–63, 171–72) and his attitudes toward women as homebound, morally superior care-givers, but useful members of the Social Democracy (215–17).

68. *NBSt,* Mar. 12, 1898. In 1898 DePew was the president of the New York Central Railroad and Sage a major investor in Western Union, both enemies of Debs' American Railway Union in 1894.

69. *NBSt,* Mar. 5, 1898, in v. 4, NBScrapbooks.

70. *FRGlobe,* Mar. 5, 8, 1898.

71. Ibid., April 7, 1898. Paul Buhle suggests that the legacy of the Knights encouraged many AFL members in Rhode Island to become Christian Socialists, ("Knights of Labor in Rhode Island," 64–65).

72. In 1898 Skahan did poorly in Fall River but beat the Democratic candidate in six towns on Cape Cod (*FRGlobe,* June 1, 1898.) See also *FRGlobe,* Nov. 7, 1900. McMullin ("Immigrant Response to Industrialism," 113–14) suggests that the socialist debates and activities in New Bedford were divisive and weakening for organized labor. The fourth candidate was former congressional representative Charles S. Randall, who ran as an Independent Republican and carried New Bedford. Still, Henry F. Bedford, in *Socialism and the Workers in Massachusetts, 1886–1912* (Amherst: University of Massachusetts Press, 1966) argues that a reformist socialism appealed more to native-born, skilled, and well-organized workers, such as the boot and shoe workers of Haverhill and Brockton in eastern Massachusetts, than to immigrant workers in textile centers.

73. For Moran's reporting for the *Atlanta Constitution,* reprinted in the Boston press, Feb. 11–15, 1898, see v. 4, NBScrapbooks.

74. The *New Bedford Standard* employed a special correspondent in Oldham,

Lancashire, who interviewed both mill owners and labor leaders, some with relatives in New England, during the strike. The *Standard* also reprinted articles from
the *Cotton Factory Times*. See *NBSt*, Feb. 8, 11, 14, 22, 1898, in v. 1–2, NBScrapbooks; Jan. 21, 1898, in v. 3, NBScrapbooks; Mar. 8, 23, 29, 1898, in v. 4, NBScrapbooks.

75. See Kirk, *Labour and Society*, v. 2, 239–44.

76. *NBSt*, Feb. 11, 1898, in v. 1–2, NBScrapbooks; Mar. 30, 1898, in v. 4,
NBScrapbooks.

77. *NBSt*, Mar. 19, 1898, in v. 4, NBScrapbooks.

78. *ProvidenceJ*, Mar. 5, 1898, in v. 4, NBScrapbooks.

79. *FRGlobe*, Feb. 17, 18, 1898.

80. Ibid., Jan. 18, 1898.

81. For a detailed description of the process of textile production in the early
twentieth century, see Blewett, *The Last Generation*, 9–20.

82. *FRGlobe*, Jan. 20, 1898.

83. Al Priddy [Frederic Kenyon Brown], *Through the Mill: The Life of A Mill Boy*
(Boston: Pilgrim Press, 1911), 257–64.

84. *FRGlobe*, Jan. 23, 1898.

85. Ibid., Jan. 24, 1898.

86. *NBSt*, April 16, 1898, in v. 4, NBScrapbooks.

87. *FRGlobe*, Mar. 2, 3, 5, 1898.

88. Ibid.

89. *FRGlobe*, April 6, 8, 1898. In *Fall of the House of Labor*, Montgomery assumes
that the changed name of the national spinners' organization meant that they
actually organized the ring spinners (157). I agree with Silvia's conclusion ("Spindle City," part 2, 546–48) that this did not happen.

90. *BTraveler*, Mar. 18, 1898; and *NBSt*, c. April 2, 1898, in v. 4, NBScrapbooks.
The reasons for these attitudes expressed by French priests are unclear. They acknowledged that most French Canadian workers were not union members, and
their efforts were confined to their own community.

91. *NBSt*, April 4, 1898, in v. 4, NBScrapbooks.

92. Lahne dismissed this period of New England labor organization, prior
to the formation of the UTW-AFL as "a tortuous maze of struggle," *Cotton Mill
Workers*, 175.

93. *NBSt*, March 19, April 2, 4, 12, 14, 15, 16, 21, 22, 25, May 10, 21, 23,
1898, in v. 4, NBScrapbooks.

94. *FRGlobe*, April 23, 1898.

95. Hoganson cites gender as a coalition-building ground for imperialism
(*Fighting for American Manhood: How Gender Politics Provoked the Spanish-American and
Philippine-American Wars* [New Haven: Yale University Press, 1998], 1–14, espe-
cially 8).

96. Gail Bederman, *Manliness and Civilization: A Cultural History of Gender and
Race in the United States, 1880–1917* (Chicago: University of Chicago Press, 1995).
Bederman pointedly rejected essentialism and demonstrated the changing social
construction of masculinity in the late nineteenth century. I never discovered the
word *masculinity* as an early or mid-nineteenth-century usage.

97. On John Golden's conservatism, see Mary Mulligan, "Epilogue to Lawrence: The 1912 Strike in Lowell, Massachusetts," in *Surviving Hard Times: The
Working People of Lowell*, ed. Mary H. Blewett (Lowell Museum, 1982), 43–62, 79–

104; Melvyn Dubofsky, *We Shall Be All: A History of the Industrial Workers of the World* (Chicago: Quadrangle Books, 1969); Cumbler, *Working-Class Community,* 198–211; Cameron, *Radicals of the Worst Sort,* 121, 127.

98. *FRGlobe,* April 20, 30, May 3, 18, 1898.

99. Ibid., Mar. 15, 1898.

100. Lahne, *Cotton Mill Workers,* 72. Silvia argues in "The Position of 'New' Immigrants in the Fall River Textile Industry," *International Migration Review* 10 (1976) that by 1910 workers of French Canadian background out-numbered the nineteenth-century English and Irish immigrants (223). Charles B. Spahr wrote a pro-corporation survey of New Bedford in 1899. He believed the reports of clergy rather than weavers and described "clean dust," "clean odors," and mill noise as a soothing sedative, *Outlook* (Feb. 4, 1899): 285–94. See also *NBSt,* Feb. 6, 1899, in v. 4, NBScrapbooks.

101. See Blewett, *Last Generation,* 151–53, 180–92.

102. *Boston Transcript,* Feb. 8, 1899, in v. 4, NBScrapbooks.

103. *BGlobe,* Dec. 30, 1900, in v. 4, NBScrapbooks.

104. *Boston Post,* Dec. 20, 1903, in v. 4, NBScrapbooks. For the growing conviction by the textile workers of Lowell, Massachusetts, between 1910 and 1960, to keep their children out of the textile mills, see, Blewett, *The Last Generation.*

105. Lahne generally regarded workingwomen as obstacles to unionization, but admitted that between 1901 and 1915, the UTW-AFL did little better in New England than previous unions, *Cotton Mill Workers,* 194.

106. Mari Jo Buhle's *Women and American Socialism, 1870–1920* (Urbana: University of Illinois Press, 1981) focused on native-born socialist-feminists and radical immigrant women, primarily of German background. Socialists established the first *Frauenbund* outside of New York in New Bedford, (33), but Buhle did not examine women socialists from Lancashire, such as Harriet Pickering, among textile workers in Rhode Island and Massachusetts.

107. William E. Forbath, *Law and the Shaping of the American Labor Movement* (Cambridge: Harvard University Press, 1991), x. Forbath dismisses historians who reject the "constitutive" rather than the "reflective" aspects of the law as scholars caught up in "collective denial" (x).

108. For these events see *FRHerald,* Sept. 2–20, 1899, and Sept. 18, 1900.

109. See Galambos, *Competition and Cooperation,* 33–36; *FRGlobe,* Aug. 24–Oct. 4, 1900; *American Wool and Cotton Reporter,* Aug. 9, 16, 1899.

110. *ProvidenceJ,* quoted in *FRGlobe,* Sept. 6, 1900. See also *FRGlobe,* Aug. 24, 31, Sept. 5, 1900; *American Cotton and Wool Reporter,* Aug. 9, 16, Sept. 20, 27, Oct. 4, 1900.

111. *FRGlobe,* Aug. 24, 29, 31, Sept. 1, 5, 6, 10, 13, 14, 1900.

112. *FRHerald,* Nov. 7, 1901. The struggle was covered in the *FRHerald* between Oct. 14 and Dec. 24, 1901.

113. *FRHerald,* Oct. 14, 1901.

114. Quoted in Burnett, "M. C. D. Borden," 63.

115. *FRHerald,* Oct. 25, 1901.

116. Ibid., Oct. 28-Nov. 9, 1901.

117. See Lahne, *Cotton Mill Workers,* 194–95. On the conservative role of the AFL union in a 1903 Lowell strike, see Shirley Zebroski, "The 1903 Strike in the Lowell Cotton Mills," in Blewett, *Surviving Hard Times,* 43–62.

118. *FRGlobe,* Oct. 29, Nov. 19, 1901.

119. *FRGlobe,* Dec. 24, 1901.

120. T. M. Young, *The American Cotton Industry: A Study of Work and Workers* (New York: Charles Scribner's Sons, 1903), 2, 4, 10–13, 129–30.

121. Ibid., 138–39. Young regarded the American eagerness for new technology as "the most valuable lesson" for Lancashire manufacturers.

122. Lahne (*Cotton Mill Workers,* 73, 193) states that immigrants from southern and eastern Europe replaced thirteen thousand strikers as a result of mass "discrimination," by which he probably means blacklisting. On the 1904–1905 strike that involved large numbers of women weavers and demonstrated the conservative unionism of O'Donnell, Tansey, and Golden, see Cumbler, *Working-Class Community,* 198–211.

123. Lahne, *Cotton Mill Workers,* 194–96.

EPILOGUE

1. *Wade's Fibre and Fabric,* June 1, 1912, July 9, 1910.

2. Al Priddy [Frederic Kenyon Brown], *Through the Mill; The Life of a Mill Boy* (Boston: Pilgrim Press, 1911).

3. Priddy, *Through the Mill,* 280.

4. Ibid., 278–79.

5. Ibid., 281.

6. Ibid., 284.

7. Ibid., 288. Brown published his five articles for *The Outlook* in 1911 as an undergraduate at Dartmouth College. Later he became a Congregational minister and a supporter of the Christian Endeavor movement to uplift promising young boys from their lives of poverty and drudgery and give them a sense of respectable Christian manhood.

8. *NYTimes,* May 28, July 24, 1912.

9. See Stone, *History of Massachusetts Industries,* v. 1, 178–88. Out of 251 industrial firms in 1930, only 41, or 16 percent, made "strictly cotton" goods.

10. *Fall River: City of Opportunity* (Fall River, 1910), 103–4.

11. My deep thanks to Brian Hall of Burnley, Lancashire, for newspaper accounts, searches for sources, and published letters from Burnley immigrants to New England.

12. *Burnley Express,* May 15, 1912; *FRHerald,* April 29, 1912, reprinted and "extensively reported" in the Burnley press, correspondence of Brian Hall to author, Sept. 3, 1991.

13. On the activities of the IWW in 1905 and 1912, see Lahne, *Cotton Mill Worker,* 195–6. On the revival of Lancashire militancy, see Joseph L. White, *The Limits of Trade Union Militancy: The Lancashire Textile Workers, 1910–1914* (Westport, Conn.: Greenwood Press, 1978).

14. For another example of the erasure of historical memory about nineteenth-century Fall River, see the memoirs of James Chace, *What We Had: A Memoir* (New York: Summit Press, 1990).

ACKNOWLEDGMENTS

The making of a big book, preceded by lengthy periods of research and revision, gathers many debts. The interested expertise of university and archival librarians proved crucial to my endeavors. Deborah Friedman, Marion Drouin, Ron Karr, and Paul Coppens at University of Massachusetts Lowell; Jamelle Tanous Lyons, Michael Martins, Marie-Clair Lajoie, and Florence C. Brigham at the Fall River Historical Society; Richard Fyffe at the Essex Institute; and Claire Sheridan at the Museum of American Textile History were among the most outstanding in skill, energy, patience, and cheerful support for a harried scholar. Ben Franckowiak, Director of Libraries at the University of Massachusetts Lowell, and his staff looked the other way while I made copies from microfilm in numbers beyond belief. The Essex Institute, the Boston Public Library, the Rhode Island Historical Society, the Old Dartmouth Historical Society, the Concord Massachusetts Public Library, the Harvard University Archives and the Pusey, Baker, and Widener Libraries, the Firestone Library at Princeton University, the University of Massachusetts Dartmouth Library, the Connecticut State Library, and the Slater Mill Historic Site provided access to important primary sources. Louise Kittredge of Newton, Massachusetts, graciously invited me into her home to read, copy, and discuss her family's personal papers concerning her grandfather, Jonathan Thayer Lincoln. Graduate students at the University of Massachusetts Amherst, where I was privileged to teach for a few years, became lively critics and friends. From among them, Jean Sherlock and Marion Mollin did duty as research assistants. Brandon Johnson and Darren Phaneuf continue to provide support as they pursue their careers. For special favors, many thanks to Dick Butsch, Philip Silvia, Brian Hall of Burnley, Lancashire, Pam Richardson, Jeffrey Northrup, Pat Malone, Scott Molloy, and Charles Montalbano.

The revision process was greatly helped by generous reactions to papers, chapters, and draft articles from Ava Baron, Dean Bergeron, Ira Berlin, Hal Benenson, John Cumbler, Bella Bianco Feldman, Ron Formisano, Dana Frank, Donna Gabbacia, Carl Gersuny, Larry Gross, Helmet Gruber, Susan Hartmann, Dick Kirkendall, Angel Kwolek-Folland, Bruce Levine, Walter Licht, Tessie Liu, Carol Morgan, Bruno Ramirez, Sonja Rose, Christine Skwiot, Elizabeth Stevens, Joel Trotter, Car-

491

ole Turbin, and David Zonderman. My thanks to the editors and readers at *ILWCH* and *Gender & History,* and to Peter Stearns and Jan Lewis, editors of *An Emotional History of the United States* (New York: New York University Press, 1998); to Ava Baron, editor of *Work Engendered: Toward a New History of Men, Women, and Work* (Ithaca: Cornell University Press, 1991); and to Mark Carnes and Clyde Griffen, editors of *Meanings for Manhood: Constructions of Masculinity in Victorian America* (Chicago University of Chicago Press, 1990), all of whom provided space for my ideas. To the audiences, copresenters, chairs, and commentators at conferences of the International Labor and Working-Class History organization, the 1992 conference on Paterson in the State and the Nation, the American Studies Association, the Social Science History Association, the Organization of American Historians, and the American Historical Association, many thanks for bearing with me.

I am deeply grateful to Deborah Valenze and Jonathan Prude for their heroic reads of a bulky manuscript and their many supportive, critical comments. Bruce Wilcox, a prince among university press directors, lent me unfailing support and encouragement. Clark Dougan, senior editor at the University of Massachusetts Press, patiently waited out the taming of the monster. Copyeditor Ella Kusnetz added zealous dedication to the final shaping of the book.

Peter Blewett helped me through the recurrent periods of intensity, bordering on the obsessional, the elations of discovery and progress, and the moments of distress and exhaustion. His unfailing support and love sustained me in ways that remain fundamental to our lives together.

INDEX